DIRTY
WORK

The CIA in Western Europe

DIRTY
WORK

The CIA in

Western Europe

Edited by **Philip Agee**
and **Louis Wolf**

LYLE STUART INC.

SECAUCUS, N. J.

First edition
Copyright © 1978 by C. I. Publications, Inc.
All rights reserved, including the right to reproduce
this book or any portion thereof in any form.
Published by Lyle Stuart Inc.
120 Enterprise Ave., Secaucus, N. J. 07094
Published simultaneously in Canada by George J. McLeod Limited
73 Bathurst St., Toronto, Ont.
Manufactured in the United States of America

Library of Congress Cataloging in Publication Data

Dirty Work.

   1. United States. Central Intelligence Agency—Addresses, essays,
lectures. 2. Europe—Politics and government—1945–   —Addresses, essays, lectures.
I. Agee, Philip.   II. Wolf, Louis.
JK468.I6D57   327'.12'06173   78-19176
ISBN 0-8184-0268-7

Credits and Permissions

Contents

What They Do: How and Why

What They Do: Western Europe

Conclusion

Appendix

Editors' Preface

Defectors are the scourge of any intelligence agency, and for years Central Intelligence Agency "case officers" and their counterparts in other countries have made a deadly game of wooing each other to defect and to bring their secrets with them. But ever since the late 1960s and the Vietnam War, the CIA—indeed, the entire American government—has faced an even more dangerous threat. Several of the brightest agents have quit in disgust and, instead of defecting to the Soviets (which is the way the game is supposed to be played), they have told their secrets to the world, and especially to the American people.

Daniel Ellsberg, a former U.S. Defense Department official, openly published *The Pentagon Papers*. Victor Marchetti, a top aide to the CIA's Deputy Director, joined with former State Department intelligence officer John Marks, to write *The CIA and the Cult of Intelligence*. Philip Agee wrote his *Inside the Company: A CIA Diary*. John Stockwell sent his open letter to Stansfield Turner and authored a book, *In Search of Enemies*;

Frank Snepp has exposed the last days of U.S. rule in Saigon; and several other intelligence veterans have testified before Congress or given their stories to eager journalists. We can undoubtedly expect more revelations from some of the 800-odd Agency personnel who are being fired by the new Director of the CIA.

Even worse, many of the new "defectors" are continuing to use their skills to help the CIA's victims, as individual investigators and through various publications. Even recent books by pro-CIA spokesmen, now retired from the Agency, provide valuable additional information on how and through whom secret intervention abroad works.

And that is what really bothers the Agency.

Take, for example, the case of an earlier *Who's Who in the CIA*—a little red book published in 1968 in East Germany by Dr. Julius Mader. At the time, most people generally suspected that the book came from East German intelligence, if not directly from the Soviets, and the CIA could easily write the whole business off as an enemy operation. Besides, the book made too many mistakes. Several of those named turned out to be straight diplomats, and worse, Dr. Mader included the names of several prominent politicians—such as the late Hubert Humphrey and Eugene McCarthy—who, whatever their faults, had only passing contacts with the CIA.

The new effort to unmask CIA people, inspired by the new American counterspies, presents the Agency with an entirely different kettle of fish. Instead of a little red book published somewhere in Eastern Europe, we have an avalanche of articles in a wide array of generally commercial newspapers and magazines, written by an even more varied assortment of independent journalists and documented by official U.S. government publications. A massive international conspiracy? No, just the result of a simple method that allows anyone in the world to see for themselves Who's Who in the CIA.

No wonder the CIA is worried.

The present volume attempts to trace the impact of the new counterspies from the 1974 article showing "How to Spot a Spook" to a summary of what has since appeared in the European press on the CIA in Western Europe.

But the effort to unmask the CIA's personnel and their operations is continuing and expanding beyond the scope of this volume. Researchers in Paris, London, and Washington have already amassed some 40,000 pages of documentation from State Department publications, U.S. Embassy personnel lists, diplomatic lists of foreign ministries abroad, and other perfectly "overt" sources. They are now assembling these documents in a global index of CIA operations personnel that will be available to every interested scholar, historian, journalist, and political activist who seeks to oppose secret intervention by the CIA.

The researchers also plan a continuing program to distribute regular bulletins worldwide which will report personnel transfers and new assignments. This effort will also include exposure of the CIA's attempts to carry out secret activities through its cooperating foreign intelligence services around the world, and the similar operations of multinational corporations.

The field is wide open and begging for organization. Collection of names and organizations for indexing, storage, and retrieval on the CIA's penetrations of trade unions, political parties, media, churches, student groups, and all the plethora of past and present covert action operations is now under way and expanding. An international "CIA Watch" is really possible. No one who wants a say in his or her political, social, or economic situation need be intimidated through fear of secret agencies. Demystification of the CIA and its allied agencies comes through exposure, and the past several years have given us confidence, knowhow, and great optimism.

We hope this volume is a worthy continuation of the struggle, and an opening to an even more effective effort.

PHILIP AGEE
LOUIS WOLF

August, 1978

Introduction:
Where Myths
Lead to Murder

by Philip Agee

Today the whole world knows, as never before, how the U.S. government and U.S. corporations have been secretly intervening in country after country to corrupt politicians and to promote political repression. The avalanche of revelations in the mid-1970s, especially those concerning the CIA, shows a policy of secret intervention that is highly refined and consistently applied.

Former President Ford and leading government spokesmen countered by stressing constantly the need for the CIA to retain, and to use when necessary, the capability for executing the kinds of operations that brought to power the military regime in Chile. Ford even said in public that he believed events in Chile had been "in the best interests of the Chilean people."[1] And even with President Carter's human rights campaign there has

[This article was written in London and Amsterdam, late 1977, for this book. It has not previously appeared in print.]

been no indication that the CIA has reduced or stopped its support of repressive dictatorships in Iran, Indonesia, South Korea, Brazil, and other bastions of "the free world."

The relevations, though, have not only exposed the operations of the CIA, but also the individual identities—the names, addresses, and secret histories—of many of the people who actually do the CIA's work. This book brings together the recent exposures of those named as CIA employees, and we hope it will contribute to the growing opposition to what the CIA is and what it does.

Yet, with all the newly available information, many people still seem to believe the myths used to justify this secret political police force. Some of the myths are, of course, actively spread by my former CIA colleagues; others come from their liberal critics. But whatever the source, until we lay the myths to rest, they will continue to confuse people and permit the CIA—literally—to get away with murder.

Myth Number One: The CIA is primarily engaged in gathering intelligence information against the Soviet Union.

This is perhaps the CIA's longest-playing myth, going back to the creation of the Agency in 1947 and the choice of the name "Central *Intelligence* Agency." As the Agency's backers explained the idea to the American Congress, afraid even in those early days of getting dragged into unwanted foreign adventures, the CIA was needed to find out what a possible enemy was planning in order to protect the United States from a surprise attack. Americans at the time still shared a vivid memory of the unexpected Japanese attack at Pearl Harbor, and with the likelihood that the new enemy—the Soviet Union—would soon have atomic bombs, no one could really doubt the need to know if and when an attack might come.

The real success in watching the Soviets, however, came from technological breakthroughs like the U-2 spy plane and spy-in-the-sky satellites, and the job of strategic intelligence fell increasingly to the technically sophisticated U.S. National Security Agency. The CIA played a part, of course, and it also provided centralized processing of information and data storage. But in its operations the CIA tended to put its emphasis on covert action—financing friendly politicians, murdering suspected foes, and staging *coups d' état.*

This deeply involved the Agency in the internal politics of countries throughout Western Europe, Asia, Africa, the Middle East, and Latin America, as well as in the Soviet bloc. And even where CIA officers and agents did act as spies, gathering intelligence information, they consistently used that information to further their programs of action.

The CIA's operatives will argue that the ultimate goal of discovering Soviet and other governments' intentions requires live spies at work in places like the Kremlin—that the Agency exists to recruit these spies and to keep them alive and working. A Penkovsky or two should be on the payroll at all times to keep America safe from Russian adventures. This argument may influence some people, because, theoretically, spy satellites and other forms of monitoring only give a few minutes' warning whereas a person in the right place can report on decisions as soon as they are made, giving perhaps days or weeks of warning. Such a spy might also be of great value for the normal conduct of relations—whether in negotiations, cooperation, or confrontation.

Nevertheless, the vast CIA effort to recruit officials of importance in the Soviet Foreign Ministry, Defense Ministry, KGB, and GRU has never had significant success. There have indeed been defections, but these, I was told in the CIA, had nothing to do with the elaborate traps and snares laid out by the CIA around the world. They resulted from varying motivations and psychological pressures operating on the official who defected. In this respect, the CIA's strengthening of repressive foreign security services, necessary for laying out the snares (telephone tapping, travel control, observation posts, surveillance teams, etc.), can scarcely be justified by the nil recruitment record.

Today, notwithstanding recent "reforms," the CIA remains primarily an action agency—doing and not just snooping. Theirs is the grey area of interventionist action between striped-pants diplomacy and invasion by the Marines, and their targets in most countries remain largely the same: governments, political parties, the military, police, secret services, trade unions, youth and student organizations, cultural and professional societies, and the public information media. In each of these, the CIA continues to prop up its friends and beat down its enemies, while its goal remains the furthering of U.S. hegemony so that American multinational companies can intensify their exploitation of the natural resources and labor of foreign lands.

Of course this has little to do with strategic intelligence or preventing another Pearl Harbor, while it has a lot to do with the power of certain privileged groups within the United States and their friends abroad. The CIA spreads the myth of "intelligence gathering" in order to obscure the meaning of what the Agency is really doing.

Myth Number Two: The major problem is lack of control; that is, the CIA is a "rogue elephant."

This myth comes not from the CIA, but from its liberal critics, many of whom seem to believe that all would be well if only Congress or the President would exercise tighter control. Yet, for all the recent horror stories, one finds little evidence that a majority in Congress want the responsibility for control, while the executive branch continues to insist—rightly—that the Agency's covert action operations have, with very few exceptions, followed the orders of successive presidents and their National Security Councils. As former Secretary of State Kissinger told Representative Otis Pike's Intelligence Investigating Committee, "Every operation is personally approved by the President."[2]

For its part the Pike committee concluded in its official report, first published in "leaked" form by the *Village Voice,* that "all evidence in hand suggests that the CIA, far from being out of control has been utterly responsive to the instructions of the President and the Assistant to the President for National Security Affairs."[3]

So the problem is said to be with the presidents—Democratic and Republican—who, over the past 30 years, have given the green light to so many covert operations. But why were the operations necessary? And why secret? The operations had to be secret, whether they involved political bribes, funding of anti-Communist journals, or fielding of small armies, because in every case they implied either government control of supposedly non-governmental institutions or violation of treaties and other agreements. In other words, hypocrisy and corruption. If the government was going to subvert free, democratic, and liberal institutions, it would have to do so secretly.

There is, however, a more basic reason for the secrecy—and for the CIA. Successive administrations—together with American-based multinational corporations—have continually demanded the freest possible access to foreign markets, labor, agricultural products, and raw materials. To give muscle to this demand for the "open door," recent presidents have taken increasingly to using the CIA to strengthen those foreign groups who cooperate—and to destroy those who do not. This has been especially clear in countries such as Chile under Allende, or Iran 20 years earlier under Mossadegh, where strong nationalist movements have insisted on some form of socialism to ensure national control of economic resources.

The CIA's covert action operations abroad are not *sui generis.* They happen because they respond to internal U.S. requirements. We cannot wish them away through fantasies of some enlightened President or Congress who would end American subversion of foreign peoples and institutions by the wave of a wand. Not surprisingly, the U.S. Senate rejected by a very wide margin a legislative initiative that would have prohibited covert action programs by the CIA.

Only prior radical change within the U.S., change that will eliminate the process of accumulating the value of foreign labor and resources, will finally allow an end to secret intervention abroad. Until then, we should expect more intervention by the CIA and multinational corporations—not less. Increasingly important will be the repressive capabilities of the Agency's "sister" services abroad.

Myth Number Three: Weakening the CIA opens wider the door for Soviet expansion and eventual world domination.

This myth is peddled especially hard at times when liberation movements make serious gains. Former President Ford and Dr. Kissinger used it frequently during the CIA's ill-fated intervention in Angola, and we continue to hear it again as liberation movements seek Soviet and Cuban help in their struggles against the apartheid policies of the white Rhodesians and South Africans.

The problem for America, however, is not "Soviet expansionism," despite all the anticommunism with which we are indoctrinated practically from the cradle. The problem, rather, is that the American government, preeminently the CIA, continues to intervene on the side of "friends" whose property and privilege rest on the remnants of archaic social systems long since discredited. The political repression required to preserve the old order depends on American and other Western support which quite naturally is turning more and more people against the United States—more effectively, for sure, than anything the KGB could ever concoct.

As Senator Frank Church explained in an interview on British television, "I'm apt to think that the Russians are going to choose [sides] better than we will choose nine times out of ten. After all we're two hundred years away from our revolution; we're a very conservative country."[4]

When searching for people contributing to Soviet expansionism and to the eventual isolation of the United States, the finger must point at the CIA and at those who make the policy executed by the CIA.

Myth Number Four: Those who attack the CIA, especially those who have worked in the intelligence community, are traitors, turncoats, or agents of the KGB.

This has been the Agency's chief attack on me personally, and I'm certain that the fear of being tarred with the same brush is keeping many CIA veterans from voicing their own opposition. But as with earlier efforts to find the "foreign hand" in the American antiwar movement, the CIA has failed to produce a shred of evidence that any of its major American (or European) critics are in the service of any foreign power. The reader will also see that the articles and authors appearing in this book are far too diverse and spontaneous to have been "orchestrated," either by the KGB or by some other person or institution. The KGB no doubt appreciates the Agency's indirect compliments, but revulsion alone toward what the CIA is and does has been a quite sufficient stimulus.

Would-be "reformers" of the CIA have also discovered how the Agency reacts to criticism. According to Representative Pike, the CIA's Special Counsel threatened to destroy Pike's political career. In a conversation with Pike's chief investigative staffperson, the Special Counsel was quoted thus: "Pike will pay for this [directing the vote to approve the committee report on the CIA]—you wait and see. I'm serious. There will be political retaliation. Any political ambitions in New York that Pike had are through. We will destroy him for this."[5]

CIA veterans must not be intimidated by the Agency's false and unattributed slander. We have a special responsibility for weakening this organization. If put at the service of those we once oppressed, our knowledge of how the CIA really works could keep the CIA from ever really working again. And though the CIA will brand us as "traitors," people all over the world, including in the United States, will respond, as they have already, with enthusiastic and effective support.

Myth Number Five: Naming individual CIA officers does little to change the Agency, and is done only to expose innocent individuals to the threat of assassination.

Nothing in the anti-CIA effort has stirred up more anger than the publishing of the names and addresses of CIA officials in foreign countries, especially since the killing of the CIA Station Chief in Athens, Richard Welch. CIA spokesmen—and journals such as the *Washington Post*—were quick to accuse me and *CounterSpy* magazine of having "fingered" Welch for the "hit," charging that in publishing his name, we were issuing "an open invitation to kill him."[6] The Agency also managed to exploit Welch's death to discredit and weaken those liberals in Congress who wanted only to curtail some of the Agency's more obvious abuses. The second section of this book makes abundantly clear that *CounterSpy* had nothing to do with the Welch killing.

The result of the Agency's manipulations isn't hard to predict. The CIA, for all its sins, came out of the recent investigations *strengthened* by the Ford "reforms," while the Congress may attempt to pass an official secrets act that will make it a crime for any present or former government official ever again to blow the whistle by making public classified information. No more *Pentagon Papers*. No more Watergate revelations. No more *CIA Diaries*.

Nonetheless, the naming goes on. More and more CIA people can now be held personally accountable for what they and the Agency as an institution do—for the real harm they cause to real people. Their military coups, torture chambers, and terrorism cause untold pain, and their backing of multinational corporations and local elites helps push millions to the edge of starvation, and often beyond. They are the Gestapo and SS of our time, and as in the Nuremberg Trials and the war in Vietnam, they cannot shed their individual responsibility simply because they were following a superior's orders.

But apart from the question of personal responsibility, the

CIA remains a secret political police, and the exposure of its secret operations—and secret operatives—remains the most effective way to reduce the suffering they cause. Already a handful of journalists and former intelligence officers have managed to reveal the names and addresses of hundreds of CIA people, and even the *Washington Post*—which condemns us for doing it —has admitted that our efforts added greatly to the CIA's growing demoralization. We also noticed from our own investigations that the Agency was forced to step up its security precautions and to transfer many of those named to other posts. All of this disrupts and destabilizes the CIA, and makes it harder for them to inflict harm on others.

Of course, this book will again raise the cry that we are "trying to get someone killed." But, as it happens, violence is not really needed. By removing the mask of anonymity from CIA officers, we make it difficult for them to remain at overseas posts. We hope that the CIA will have the good sense to shift these people to the increasingly smaller number of safe posts, preferably to a desk inside the CIA headquarters at Langley, Virginia. In this way the CIA will protect the operatives named —and also the lives of their potential victims.

From the old song and dance of the "intelligence gathering" to the claim that "those who expose are the murderers," these five myths won't simply vanish. The CIA—and its allies—will continue to propagate them, and the CIA's critics will have to respond. We must increasingly expose these myths and the crimes they cover up.

But besides debating, there is much more that we can do— especially in furthering the exposure of the Agency and its secret operatives. The CIA probably has no more than 5,000 officers experienced in running clandestine operations and, as this book suggests, it should be possible to identify almost all of those who have worked under diplomatic cover at any time in their careers. While this volume lists mainly those named as CIA operatives in Europe, we hope additional volumes can be published on the CIA's people in other areas. All that is required is a continuing effort—and a novel form of international cooperation. Here's how:

> 1. In each country a team of interested people,
> including journalists, should obtain a list of all the
> Americans working in the official U.S. Mission:

the Embassy, consulates, AID offices, and other U.S. installations. This list can be acquired through a friend in the host Foreign Ministry, in the American Embassy—or by other means.

2. The team should then get past editions of the necessary public documents—*U.S. Foreign Service Lists* and *Biographic Registers* (both published by the Department of State) from a local library, and the *Diplomatic List* and *Consular List* published regularly by every Foreign Ministry. The *Diplomatic and Consular Lists* will contain the name and addresses of the higher ranking members of the official mission, including some of the CIA people.

3. Check the names as suggested in the various articles in this book, especially John Marks' "How to Spot a Spook." Watch carefully for persons carried on the Foreign Ministry's *Diplomatic and Consular Lists,* but who are missing from the recent *Biographic Registers* and *Foreign Service Lists.* Most of these will be CIA people purposely left off the State Department lists.

4. After narrowing down the list of likely suspects, check them with us c/o C. I. Publications, Inc., P.O. Box 50053, F Street Station, Washington, D.C., 20004, and with other similarly oriented groups.

5. Once the list is fully checked, publish it. Then organize public demonstrations against those named—both at the American Embassy and at their homes—and, where possible, bring pressure on the government to throw them out. Peaceful protest will do the job. And when it doesn't, those whom the CIA has most oppressed will find other ways of fighting back.

Naturally, as new CIA people replace the old, it will be necessary to repeat the process, perhaps every few months. And as the campaign spreads, and the CIA learns to correct the earlier and more obvious flaws in its use of State Department cover, we will have to develop new ways to spot them. Already the Agency has gotten the State Department to restrict circulation of the all-important *Biographic Register,* and it is likely that the Administration will in future place more of its people under cover of the Department of Defense (for example, in military bases, and in Military Assistance Groups), the Drug Enforcement Agency, and the multinational corporations.

In rare cases, the CIA may even attempt changing the identities of certain operatives. Nonetheless, the CIA will always need a secure base in embassies and consulates to keep its files and communications facilities, and there are many ways to identify the CIA people in these missions without relying on public documents.

Within the United States, people can help this campaign by supporting the groups struggling to stop covert intervention abroad. There is also the need for continuing research into current CIA operations, and new programs to identify and keep track of all the FBI special agents and informers, military intelligence personnel, and the Red Squads and SWAT groups of local and state police departments.

Together, people of many nationalities and varying political beliefs can cooperate to weaken the CIA and its surrogate intelligence services, striking a blow at political repression and economic injustice. The CIA can be defeated. The proof can be seen from Vietnam to Angola, and in all the other countries where liberation movements are rapidly gaining strength.

It is hoped that this book will aid this struggle, together with the struggle for socialism in the United States itself.

Notes

1. News conference, September 16, 1974, reported in the *International Herald Tribune,* September 18, 1974.

2. Testimony by Kissinger to House Select Committee on Intelligence, October 31, 1975, as reported in the *International Herald Tribune,* November 1–2, 1975.

3. Report of the House Select Committee on Intelligence, as reported in the *Village Voice,* February 16, 1976, p. 84.

4. "Newsday," BBC-2 television, February 18, 1975.

5. Hon. Otis Pike, speech on floor of U.S. House of Representatives on March 9, 1976, as reported in the *International Herald Tribune,* March 11, 1976.

6. Editorial, *Washington Post,* as published in the *International Herald Tribune,* December 30, 1975.

In the
Beginning

Introduction

Where did the effort to unmask the CIA begin?

The CIA would like to throw the blame on some coordinated campaign by Philip Agee or *CounterSpy* magazine, and in their less modest moments, perhaps, Agee or *CounterSpy* might appreciate the compliment, since they did make a major contribution. But, in fact, one of the most important beginnings came when former State Department intelligence officer John Marks wrote his now-celebrated "How to Spot a Spook," for the November 1974 *Washington Monthly*, the first article in this section. Many journalists and former intelligence officers already knew the rather simple methodology Marks spelled out, and, strange as it seems, at the time Agee and others felt that Marks might have made a mistake in making the method public. So much for coordination.

But, both the moral imperative to name names, of which Agee speaks, and the inherent newsworthiness of the operations, won out. Agee soon brought out his *CIA Diary,* in which he revealed the names of many of his former colleagues. He also published a commentary on "Exposing the CIA" in *CounterSpy*. which is presented here, and in the same issue, *CounterSpy* presented a detailed listing of over 100 CIA Chiefs of Station. (This was the list which included the name of Richard Welch, then in Peru, but soon to move on to Greece.)

For all its initial effort, however, the "campaign" lacked momentum; unlike the CIA, with its paid journalists and subsidized news services, neither Marks nor Agee nor *CounterSpy* had the organization to orchestrate a major international campaign.

However, journalists and political activists alike began to see the value of the method, and the important exposés which were possible. Godfrey Hodgson's piece on "Cord Meyer: Super-spook," which ran in the *Sunday Times* of London, demonstrated that such items could reach the journalistic establishment. And Philip Agee showed with his letters to the Portuguese people that the campaign was not simply an academic exercise. The battle was on.

How to
Spot a Spook

by John Marks

Both the Soviet and American intelligence establishments seem to share the obsession that the other side is always trying to bug them. Since the other side is, in fact, usually trying, our technicians and their technicians are constantly sweeping military installations and embassies to make sure no enemy, real or imagined, has succeeded. One night about ten years ago, a State Department security officer, prowling through the American embassy in Santiago, Chile, in search of Communist microphones, found a listening device carefully hidden in the office of a senior "political officer." The security man, along with everyone else in the embassy, knew that this particular "political officer" was actually the Central Intelligence Agency's "Station Chief," or principal operative in Chile. Bugging his office would have indeed been a major coup for the opposition. Triumphantly, the

[This article first appeared in the November 1974 issue of *Washington Monthly*, Washington, D.C.]

security man ripped the microphone out of the wall—only to discover later that it had been installed by the CIA station chief himself.

The reason the CIA office was located in the embassy—as it is in most of the other countries in the world—is that by presidential order the State Department is responsible for hiding and housing the CIA. Like the intelligence services of most other countries, the CIA has been unwilling to set up foreign offices under its own name, so American embassies—and, less frequently, military bases—provide the needed cover. State confers respectability on the Agency's operatives, dressing them up with the same titles and calling cards that give legitimate diplomats entree into foreign government circles. Protected by diplomatic immunity, the operatives recruit local officals as CIA agents to supply secret intelligence and, especially in the Third World, to help in the Agency's manipulation of a country's internal affairs.

The CIA moves its men off the diplomatic lists only in Germany, Japan, and other countries where large numbers of American soldiers are stationed. In those countries, the CIA's command post is still in the U.S. Embassy, but most of the CIA personnel are under military cover. With nearly 500,000 U.S. troops scattered around the world, the CIA "units" buried among them do not attract undue attention.

In contrast, it is difficult for the CIA to dwell inconspicuously within the American diplomatic corps, since more than a quarter of the 5,435 employees who purportedly work for State overseas are actually with the CIA. In places such as Argentina, Bolivia, Burma, and Guyana, where the Agency has special interests and projects, there are about as many CIA operatives under cover of substantive embassy jobs as there are legitimate State employees. The CIA also places smaller contingents in the ranks of other U.S. government agencies which operate overseas, particularly AID's police training program in Latin America. [EDITORS' NOTE: After much public outcry about U.S. exportation of repression via massive supplying of police equipment and training foreign police in methods of interrogation and torture since 1961, AID's Office of Public Safety was closed down by Congress in July 1975.]

What is surprising is that the CIA even bothers to camouflage its agents, since they are still easily identifiable. Let us see why the embassy cover is so transparent:

● The CIA usually has a separate set of offices in the Embassy, often with an exotic-looking cipher lock on the outside door. In Madrid, for example, a State Department source reports that the Agency occupied the whole sixth floor of the Embassy. About 30 people worked there; half were disguised as "Air Force personnel" and half as State "political officers." The source says that all the local Spanish employees knew who worked on what floor of the Embassy and that visitors could figure out the same thing.

● CIA personnel usually stick together. When they go to lunch or to a cocktail party or meet a plane from Washington, they are much more likely to go with each other than with legitimate diplomats. Once you have identified one, you can quickly figure out the rest.

● The CIA has a different health insurance plan from the State Department. The premium records, which are unclassified and usually available to local employees, are a dead giveaway.

● The Agency operative is taught early in training that loud background sounds interfere with bugging. You can be pretty sure the CIA man in the Embassy is the one who leaves his radio on all the time.

● Ironically, despite the State Department's total refusal to comment on anything concerning the CIA, the Department regularly publishes two documents, the *Foreign Service List* and the *Biographic Register,* which, when cross-checked, yield the names of most CIA operatives under embassy cover. Here is how it works:

America's real diplomats have insisted on one thing in dealing with the CIA: that the corps of Foreign Service Officers (FSO) remain pure. Although there are rumors of exceptions, CIA personnel abroad are always given the cover rank of Foreign Service Reserve (FSR) or Staff (FSS) officers—not FSO. Of course, there are some legitimate officials from the State Department, AID, and USIA who hold FSR and FSS ratings, so care must be taken to avoid confusing these people with the spooks.

To winnow out the spooks, you start by looking up in the *Foreign Service List* under the country in question—for example, China. The letters in the third column from the left signify the man or woman's personnel status and the number denotes his or her rank. On the China list, David Bruce is an "R-1," or Reserve Officer of class 1, the highest rank. John Holdridge is a regular Foreign Service Officer (FSO) of the same grade, and secretary Barbara Brooks is a Staff Officer, class 4.

PEKING (U.S. LIAISON OFFICE) (LO)

Bruce David KE	chief USLO	R-1	5-73
Holdridge John H	dep chief USLO	O-1	5-73
Jenkins Alfred Les	dep chief USLO	R-1	
Brooks Barbara A	sec	S-4	5-73
McKinley Brunson............	spec asst	O-6	5-73
Zaelit Lucille	sec	S-5	5-73
Anderson Donald M	pol off	O-4	6-73
Hunt Janice E	sec	S-8	12-73
Lilley James R	pol off	R-3	
Pascoe B Lynn	pol off	O-5	7-73
Horowitz Herbert Eugene ..	econ/cml off	O-3	6-73
Morin Annabelle C............	sec	S-7	7-73
Rope William Frederick	econ/cml off	O-4	4-73
Blackburn Robert R Jr	adm off	O-3	4-73
Herrera Delia L	sec	S-6	5-73
Lambert William F............	coms/rec off	R-6	2-74
Lucas Robert T	coms/rec off	S-2	7-73
Morin Emile F..................	gen ser off	O-5	3-72
Peterson Robert D	coms/rec off	R-6	7-73
Riley Albert D..................	coms/rec off	S-5	5-73

Now Holdridge almost certainly can be ruled out as an operative, simply because he is an FSO. Not much can be told one way or the other about FSS Brooks because, as is the case with most secretaries, the State Department does not publish much information about her. David Bruce might be suspect because of his "R" status, but a quick glance at the *Biographic Register,* which gives a brief curriculum vitae of all State Department personnel, shows him to be one of the high-level political appointees who have "R" status because they are not members of the regular Foreign Service. Similarly, the *Register* report on FSR Jenkins shows that he had a long career as an FSO before taking on the State Department's special assignment in Peking as an FSR:

> **Bruce, David KE**—b Md 2/21/98, m (Evangeline Bell). Princeton U AB 19. Mem Md bar. US Army 17-19, 42-45 col overseas. PRIV EXPER priv law practice 21-26, mem State legis 24-26, 39-42, with bank-priv bus

28-40, chief rep Am Red Cross (England) 40-41, GOVT EXPER with Off Strategic Sers 41-45, asst sec of Com 47-48. ECA Paris R-1 chief of mission 5/48. STATE AEP to France 5/49. Dept under sec of state 2/52, consult to sec of state 1/53. Paris R-1 pol off-US observer to Interim Comm of EDC, also US rep to European Coal-Steel Community (Luxembourg) 2/53. Dept consult to sec of state 1/55. Bonn AEP to Germany 3/57-11/59. London AEP to Great Britain 2/61-3/69. Dept R-1 pers rep of Pres with pers rank amb to hd US del at Paris meetings on Viet-Nam 7/70-4/71. Peking chief liaison off 3/73.

Jenkins, Alfred leSesne—b Ga 9/14/16, m. Emory U AB 38, Duke U MA 46. US Army 42-46 1st lt. PRIV EXPER prin-supt pub schs 40-42. STATE Dept FSO unclass 6/46. Peiping Chin lang-area trainee 9/46, O-6 11/46. Tientsin pol off 7/48, O-5 4/49. Hong Kong chief pol sect 7/49. Taipei pol off 7/50, O-4 6/51. Dept 3/52. O-3 9/54. Jidda couns, dep chief mission 2/55. Dept det Nat War Coll 8/57, O-2 2/58, dep dir Off of SE Asian Aff 6/58, reg plan ad Bu of Far E aff 8/59. Stockholm couns, dep chief mission 10/61, cons gen 3/62, O-1 3/63. Dept FS insp 8/65, det Nat Security Counc 7/66, FS insp 1/69, dir Off of Asian Communist Aff 7/70, superior honor award 71, dir for People's Rep of China, Mongolia, Hong Kong–Macao aff 2/73. Peking dep chief liaison off 4/73. Lang Ger. (w—Martha Lippiatt).

Note that there are no gaping holes in their career records, nor did either of these men serve long tours with nameless Pentagon agencies, nor did they regularly change their status from "R" to "S" to "GS" (civil service).

Now, for purposes of comparison, examine the record of the CIA's man in Peking, a "political officer" named James R. Lilley:

Lilley, James R—b China Am parents 1/15/28, m. Yale U BA 51. US Army 46-47. GOVT EXPER anal Dept of Army 51-58. STATE Manila R-6 7/58. Dept 10/60. Phnom Penh 9/61, R-5 3/63. Bangkok 4/63. Dept 8/64. Vientiane pol off 6/65. R-4 5/66. S-2 4/68. Hong Kong 5/68, R-4 5/69. Dept 7/70, GS-15 fgn aff off 4/71, R-4 det lang trng FSI 7/72-4/73. Lang Fr, Rom. (w—Sally Booth).

The *Foreign Service List* provides another clue, in the form of diplomats' official assignments. Of all the jobs real State Department representatives perform, political reporting is generally considered to be the most important. Although *genuine* FSRs frequently hold administrative and consular slots, they are almost never given the important political jobs. So where an FSR *does* appear in the listing with a political job, it is most likely that the CIA is using the position for cover. There is an exception to this rule: A comparatively few minority-group members who have been brought into the Foreign Service as Reserve Officers under a special program. They are found exclusively in the junior ranks, and their biographic data is complete in the way the CIA people's is not.

Finally there is another almost certain tipoff. If an agent is listed in the *Biographic Register* as having been an "analyst" for the Department of the Army (or Navy or Air Force), you can bet that he or she is really working for the CIA. A search of hundreds of names found no legitimate State Department personnel listed as ever having held such a job.

In an embassy like the one in Santo Domingo, the spooks in the political section outnumber the real FSOs by at least seven to three:

Political Section

Beyer Joel H	pol off	R-5	7-72
Brugger Frederick A	pol off	R-7	9-72
Bumpus James N	pol off	O-4	7-72
Chafin Gary E	pol off	O-6	8-73
Clayton Thomas A	pol off	R-3	5-71
Dwiggins Joan H	pol off	R-7	3-72
Fambrini Robert L	pol off	S-2	6-73
Greig David N Jr	pol off	R-5	8-71
Guell Janet E	sec	S-8	12-73
Markoff Stephanie M	sec	S-8	6-73
Merriam Geraldine C	clk-typist	S-9	2-73
Mooney Robert C	pol off	R-6	8-72
Morris Margaret A	clk-typist	S-10	12-73
Pascoe Dorothy L	sec	S-7	2-74
Ryan Donald G	pol off	R-8	8-73
Williams Albert N	pol off	O-3	7-73

While Donald Ryan is an "R" in the political section, there is not sufficient data published about him to verify his status.

It was by studying these documents that I learned that the CIA has sent an operative to Peking. For confirmation, I called the State Department's ranking China expert, Acting Assistant Secretary of State Arthur Hummel. After I identified myself as a reporter working on a magazine article and explained where I had gotten my information, Hummel shouted, "I know what you're up to and I don't want to contribute. Thank you very much!" and slammed down the phone.

Another State official confirmed that the decision to send an operative to Peking was made in early 1973, but declared that making public the operative's existence could "jeopardize" Chinese-American relations. Neither this official nor any of his colleagues seemed willing to consider the notion that the U.S. government was under no obligation to assign a CIA man there —or anywhere else, for that matter. The first American mission to China since 1949 certainly could have been staffed exclusively with real diplomats if concern about damaging relations were so high. To have excluded the Agency from Peking, however, would have gone against a basic axiom of the post–World War II foreign policy establishment: the CIA follows the flag into American embassies.

The Chinese government is presumably clever enough to identify the operative by sifting through the public documents available. In fact, his arrival may well have been cleared with the Chinese, who probably wanted reciprocal privileges for their secret service in Washington. Such are the arrangements the world's spooks are so fond of working out with each other—the Soviet KGB and the CIA even exchange names of intelligence analysts assigned to the other's capital.

Sacrificing "State"

Much to the alarm of a few high State Department officials, the proportion of CIA to State personnel abroad has been steadily rising in recent years. The precise figures are zealously guarded, but several State sources confirm the trend. They cite as the main reason for this tilt toward the CIA a series of government-wide cutbacks that have hit State proportionately harder than the CIA. What troubles State is not, as one career diplomat put it, "the principle" that State should provide the CIA with cover. That is unquestioned, he says. Rather, most legitimate diplomats do not like being a minority within their own profession or having the rest of the world confuse them with the CIA's dirty tricksters. They generally regard themselves as working at a higher calling.

While the State Department has been comparatively honest in accepting the personnel cuts ordered by the Johnson and Nixon administrations, two sources familiar with the CIA budget report that the Agency has done everything possible to escape the reductions. Traditionally, when outsiders—even Presidents— have tried to meddle with the Agency's personnel allotment, the CIA has resisted on "national security" grounds. And when that argument failed, the CIA resorted to bureaucratic ruses: cutting out a job and then replacing the person eliminated with a "contract" or "local" employee, who would not show up on the personnel roster; or sending home a clandestine support officer —a specialist in things like renting "safe houses," "laundering" money, and installing phone taps—and then having the same work done by experts sent out from Washington on "temporary duty."

Not only does the State Department provide the CIA with cover, but the Senate—and especially its Foreign Relations Committee—encourages the current practice of sending over 25% of our "diplomatic" corps abroad under false pretenses. Every year the Foreign Relations Committee routinely approves and sends to the full Senate for its advice and consent lists of "Foreign Service Reserve Officers to be consular officers and secretaries in the Diplomatic Service of the United States of America." In 1973, of the 121 names submitted by the State Department, more than 70 were CIA operatives. According to a knowledgeable source, the committee is informally told the number of CIA people on the lists, but "not who they are." No Senator in memory has publicly objected to being an accomplice to this cover-building for the CIA.

Just this spring [1974], the State Department took official, if secret, notice of its declining presence overseas compared to the CIA when Secretary Henry Kissinger authorized a high-level study of State-CIA staffing. The Department's top administrator, L. Dean Brown, who had urged the study be made in the first place, gave the job to Malcolm Toon, a career diplomat serving as U.S. Ambassador to Yugoslavia. Toon returned to Washington to compile the top-secret report.

Asking not to be named and refusing to provide the specific figures, a source close to Kissinger says that Toon's report calls for a substantial reduction in the number of CIA operatives abroad under State cover. The source adds that Kissinger has not made up his mind on the issue.

Kissinger has always acted very carefully where the CIA is concerned. One of his former aides notes that the Secretary has regularly treated the Agency with great deference at government meetings, although he has often been privately scornful of it afterward. In any case, Kissinger is unquestionably a believer in the need for the CIA to intervene covertly in other countries' internal affairs—he was the prime mover behind the Agency's work against Salvador Allende in Chile. The question of how much cover State should provide the CIA, however, is chiefly a bureaucratic one, and is not basic to Kissinger's foreign policy. The Secretary therefore will probably not take a definite position until he sees how much opposition the CIA will be able to stir up in the White House and in the congressional subcommittees that supposedly oversee the Agency.

The CIA has lost no time in launching its counteroffensive. At a July 19 off-the-record session with key Democratic congressional aides, Carl Duckett, the CIA's Deputy Director for Intelligence, complained about the reductions recommended by the Toon report. According to a source who was present, Duckett said that, even without further embassy cuts, the CIA now doesn't have enough people overseas.

CIA officials must be especially concerned about Toon's recommendations, since in countries where there are no U.S. military bases, the only alternative to embassy cover is "deep," or nonofficial, cover. American corporations operating overseas have long cooperated in making jobs available to the CIA and would probably continue to do so. Also, the Agency would probably have to make more use of smaller firms where fewer people would know of the clandestine connection. Two examples of this type are:

● Robert Mullen and Company, the Washington-based public relations concern for which E. Howard Hunt worked after he left the CIA and before the break-in at Democratic National Headquarters. Mullen provided CIA operatives with cover in Stockholm, Mexico City, and Singapore, and in 1971 set up a subsidiary in cooperation with the CIA called Interprogres, Ltd. According to a secret Agency document released with the

House Judiciary Committee's impeachment evidence, "At least
two [CIA] overseas assets have tangential tasks of promoting
the acceptance of this company as a Mullen subsidiary."

   ● Psychological Assessment Associates, Inc., a Washington psychological consulting firm specializing in behavioral
research and analysis. By the admission of its president John
Gittinger, most of the company's business since it was founded
in 1957 by three ex-CIA psychologists has come from Agency
contracts. The firm had two "representatives" in Hong Kong, at
least until June of this year [1974].

   Unless their cover is blown, companies of this sort and operatives who work for them cannot be linked to the U.S. government. But the Agency has learned over the years that it is much
more difficult and expensive to set up an operative as a businessman (or as a missionary or newsman) than to put him in an
embassy. As a "private" citizen, the operative is not automatically exposed to the host country's key officials and to foreign
diplomats, nor does he have direct access to the CIA communications and support facilities which are normally housed in embassies. Moreover, as an ex-CIA official explains, "The deep
cover guy has no mobility. He doesn't have the right passport.
He is subject to local laws and has to pay local taxes. If you try
to put him in an influential business job, you've got to go through
all the arrangements with the Company."

Who Needs Gumshoes?

   Everything argues for having the intelligence agent in the embassy—everything, that is, except the need to keep his existence
secret. The question then becomes whether it is really that important to keep his existence secret—which, in turn, depends on
how important his clandestine activities are.

   Could any rational person, after surveying the history of the
last 20 years, from Guatemala to Cuba to Vietnam—and now
Chile—contend that the CIA's clandestine activities have
yielded anything but a steady stream of disaster? The time has
come to abolish them. Most of the military and economic intelligence we need we can get from our satellites and sensors (which
already provide nearly all our information about Russia's nuclear weaponry) and from reading the newspapers and the super-
abundant files of open reports. As for political intelligence—
which is actually an assessment of the intentions of foreign lead-

ers—we don't really need this kind of information from Third World countries unless we intend to muck about in their internal affairs. With the Soviet Union or China—countries powerful enough to really threaten our national security—timely political intelligence could be a great help. But for the past 25 years we have relied on open sources and machine-collected intelligence because our agents have proven incapable of penetrating these closed societies. There is not enough practical benefit gained from the CIA's espionage activities to compensate for our nation's moral and legal liability in maintaining thousands of highly trained bribers, subverters, and burglars overseas as "representatives" of our government. The problem of getting good, accurate, reliable information from abroad is a complicated one, beyond the scope of this article, but, to paraphrase Mae West, covert has nothing to do with it.

Exposing
the CIA

by Philip Agee

During the 1960s, when I worked as a CIA operations officer in
Latin America, I often reflected on the exceptional number and
variety of operations that I took over from other officers or
initiated myself. At times, more experienced men observed that
I was fortunate to be gaining experience in "across-the-board"
operations: from political action operations with government
ministers to Communist Party penetration operations, to surveillance teams, telephone tapping, and trade union operations.

One of the keys to my capacity to work on many operations at
once, thereby to contribute in a proportionately greater way to
CIA goals, was the lack of any opposition of significance. In
most of Latin America, indeed in much of the Third World, the
local security forces were penetrated and manipulated by the
CIA—in some cases they were the very creatures of the Agency

[This article first appeared in the Winter 1974/1975 issue of
CounterSpy magazine, published in early 1975 in Washington, D.C.]

—in such a manner that they practically never were allowed to interfere with or jeopardize the (CIA) station's "unilateral" (i.e., unknown to the local service) operations. Similarly, while my name appeared from time to time in the local left-wing press as a CIA officer, no one ever demonstrated hostility to me, picketed my home, threatened me if I didn't leave the country, or made me feel uncomfortable in some other way. I was allowed to achieve all the mischief I could, always with impunity, and restrained only by internal CIA procedures and practices. Officers experienced in European countries, however, where greater security precautions and procedures were required, were able to handle only a fraction of the operations that we "Third World Officers" could take on.

I used to think that if left-wing Ecuadoreans, Uruguayans, or Mexicans ever found out what I was really up to, they would make it impossible for me to remain in their country. Even bourgeois nationalists would have made life impossible for me. I wondered if my "friends" on the right and in the "center" would have been able to protect me. But no one ever bothered me because no one knew, really, the scope of my work, and of the overall station's operational programs wherever I was working.

But times are different now. As each new spate of revelations of CIA operations occurs, the pattern emerges more clearly. The 1967 revelations, the CIA's support to the Watergate coverup, the revelations of "destabilization" operations against the Allende government, *CIA And The Cult Of Intelligence* by John Marks and Victor Marchetti, my book, and others yet to appear —all these revelations help to reveal a pattern of CIA support to minority Third World regimes that inflict terrible repression on their own people in order to retain power and privilege—countries that welcome exploitation of their natural resources and workers by transnational companies. These minority regimes, in fact, have no other role than to serve their own interests by serving the interests of foreign, particularly U.S., corporations.

No longer can ignorance of the CIA's operations and of the purpose and effect of those operations be allowed to delay positive action to defeat them. Now more than ever, concerned Americans, together with the Third World peoples victimized by the CIA and the economic and social injustices that the CIA enforces, can discover what the CIA is all about.

What can be done to defeat this sinister secret police force?

One effort could be directed toward elaborating a set of indicators which would be based on known types of CIA operations that have visible effects—the construction of a composite model, in other words. Such a model might also include non-CIA factors such as impressions conveyed in U.S. government statements, levels of military and economic aid, levels of credits from international institutions such as the World Bank, the IMF (International Monetary Fund), regional development banks, as well as private financial institutions. Once the model is constructed, a search for appropriate indicators in the country of interest, e.g., Portugal, could proceed. What one might have at any given moment would be a greater or lesser certainty that destabilization programs against a country's left-wing and/or nationalist forces are increasing or decreasing. But in the absence of access to documents or to a participating CIA employee who wants to talk, such an effort must remain highly speculative.

Other efforts might well be directed toward lobbying against the CIA and raising public consciousness in the U.S. against this organization. But given the overwhelming defeat in October 1974 of Senator Abourezk's amendment to prohibit *illegal* CIA activity, one cannot be sanguine about effective congressional restraints on the Agency—the Congress, after all, created the CIA and gave it autonomy to commit all kinds of crimes in the name of the American people. Someday, perhaps, the Congress may include enough fair-minded people to curtail the CIA and other interventionist agencies, but action should be taken now by those who are concerned.

The most effective and important systematic efforts to combat the CIA that can be undertaken right now are, I think, the identification and exposure of its people working abroad. Working through careful analysis of the U.S. government employees country by country abroad, the CIA people can be identified and exposed through periodic bulletins disseminated to subscribers, particularly individuals and organizations in the foreign country in question. Photographs and home addresses in the foreign capital or cities having consulates should be included. Having this information, the peoples victimized by the CIA and the economic exploitation that the CIA enforces can bring pressure on their so-often compromised governments to expel the CIA people. And, in the absence of such expulsions, which will not be uncommon, the people themselves will have to decide what they must do to rid themselves of the CIA.

Some may object that, in the face of such a campaign, the CIA will simply change its cover mechanisms and make identification more difficult. This will indeed occur, but so many CIA people can be identified from personal knowledge and past covers already a part of the public records, that more effective cover will be difficult and very slow to develop. Meanwhile, important steps can be taken to weaken the Agency and its support of injustice.

In October 1974 I announced the names and addresses in Mexico City of 35 official cover (Embassy) CIA people and two nonofficial cover people. Probably about ten more nonofficial cover people were working in Mexico City posing as students, businessmen, tourists or retired people. Within a few days, both the Chief of Station, Richard Sampson, and the Deputy Chief of Station, Jonathan Hanke, were withdrawn from Mexico. Perhaps others on the list will be withdrawn soon, or expelled, or forced to leave by the Mexican people. As a former operations officer, I can assure you that such precipitate withdrawals are very disruptive and reduce the effectiveness of the whole station program. Those who remain will have to beware of action by the Mexican people and will have to install greater security devices in their operations—thus reducing their capacities.

Similar revelations are going to follow, but I believe this campaign should be organized in a systematic way by concerned Americans in the U.S., perhaps in the way that certain of the earlier efforts against the Vietnam War were undertaken. Surely if one opposed intervention against the Vietnamese people, one would also have to oppose the lower-level and usually quieter intervention by the CIA.

This campaign could remove the key to CIA effectiveness in destabilizing progressive and revolutionary forces seeking social justice and national dignity in the Third World. That key is secrecy, and when it is peeled away, there, standing naked and exposed for all to see, is the CIA secret policeman, who only hours before was lurking in the darkness to bribe a military officer, a student leader, a journalist, a politician, or a trade unionist. Take away secrecy and the CIA officer becomes impotent.

We know enough of what the CIA does to resolve to oppose it. What we should do now is to identify and expose each of the people who instrument and execute the CIA's programs. People failed to campaign effectively against the CIA in the past because the CIA programs and people were unknown. Now that impediment is being removed.

Chiefs of Station

from CounterSpy *magazine*

In the wake of revelations about covert operations abroad, and intelligence operations at home, the Central Intelligence Agency stands in the middle of a storm of controversy. Members of Congress and editorial writers are calling for the abolition of covert operations by the CIA. A handful of congressional committees and a Presidential Blue Ribbon Panel have promised to investigate the situation. And the Agency itself is purging the leftover cold-warriors in its midst. When the ardent breezes from Capitol Hill wane, knowledgeable insiders claim that government will have responded to public sentiment with stern promises that future CIA activities will be strictly controlled.

> [This article, without byline, first appeared in the Winter 1974/1975 issue of *CounterSpy* magazine, published in early 1975 in Washington, D.C. Several additional Chiefs of Station were listed in the subsequent issues of *CounterSpy*, December 1975 and Spring 1976. These names are included in the list.]

The President and the Director of Central Intelligence, William Colby, oppose those forces that would have covert operations abolished. Colby admits that abolition would not seriously impair the national security of the United States. But, they argue, covert operations give the President a foreign policy option somewhere between diplomatic posturing and open intervention.

In fact, covert operations are more than just an option. Since Congress left a tiny loophole in the National Security Act of 1947, covert operations, and the clandestine network required to support them, have been used on a literally daily basis to enforce foreign policy. Covert operations and their support are big business, utilizing $550 million of CIA's $750 million annual budget, and 80% of that agency's employees. And these figures do not include $50 to $100 million set aside for use by the CIA director in emergencies, and thousands of "contract employees."

Colby maintains that the current era of detente has brought a much lower level of covert operations than in past years. Other sources, primarily foreign newspapers and governments, however, indicate that covert operations are continuing on a level comparable to past eras. In recent months allegations have been made that operations have occurred or are occurring in: *Vietnam, Thailand, Laos, Cambodia, Portugal, Spain, Greece, Cyprus, Dhofar, Rhodesia, South Africa, Italy, Argentina, Peru, Venezuela, Ethiopia, and Great Britain.* For the present, of course, all indications of covert activity remain allegations that are not yet supported by documentation. As in the past, the Central Intelligence Agency will not comment on covert operations alleged to be in progress.

Covert operations do not occur in a void. The Central Intelligence Agency maintains a world-wide clandestine apparatus of Agency employees posing under a variety of "covers," local informers, proprietary organizations, and technical facilities. As technological development has made it possible for almost all intelligence to be collected without using agents, it is clear that this clandestine infrastructure has only one purpose: covert activities.

Most of these covert activities have taken place within the emerging nations of the Third World. The initial rationale for targeting these countries arose out of a belief that the Third World was to be the battleground of the Cold War. In recent years a new rationale has developed as Third World countries have exhibited an increasing tendency to exercise their sovereignty over raw materials and overseas investments integral to the present economy of the United States. The CIA presence within socialist countries is usually much more oriented toward intelligence collection and analysis.

Bureaucratically speaking, this clandestine network and the covert operations it spawns, operates under the *Directorate of Operations*—better known as Clandestine Services—section of the Central Intelligence Agency. Two of the Agency's other three Directorates, *Management and Services, and Science and Technology,* are largely used by Clandestine Services. Management of this clandestine infrastructure begins with ten CIA officers appointed by Colby to coordinate both intelligence gathering and operational functions. (This is one of the widely trumpeted reforms instituted by Colby.) Moving down the line, analytical and managerial functions are performed by various staffs that are divided along geopolitical lines. These divisions maintain liaison personnel within their particular area. Until the recent shift in the internal situation in Ethiopia, for example, CIA's Africa liaison officer was stationed at a secret National Security Agency/CIA base within that country.

The key figures, at least in an operational sense, within the CIA infrastructure are known as Chiefs of Station (COS). Usually located within the U.S. Embassy compound, Chiefs of Station are charged with maintaining, creating, and exploiting the infrastructure within a given country. CIA influence within political parties, civic associations, student groups, labor unions, media, the military, and other governmental agencies can accurately be described as a web with the Chief of Station at its center.

The Department of State usually provides the COS and other CIA personnel with cover stories, hiding them among real Foreign Service Officers, and providing them with diplomatic immunity. In many countries, CIA personnel are found in the U.S. Embassy's "political" section.

In nations where U.S. presence is extensive, additional managerial personnel known as Chiefs of Base (COB) may be located within U.S. consulates and/or military facilities. In India, for instance, the CIA maintains four known facilities at New Delhi, Bombay, Calcutta, and Madras. All these facilities are under diplomatic guise. In Germany, on the other hand, CIA activity is mixed between military and diplomatic facilities. In many areas where the CIA uses military bases for cover, these bases house large technical support facilities that cannot be housed in embassies and consulates.

Those CIA personnel living under diplomatic cover are relatively easy to spot. Other intelligence services, host governments, regular visitors, and even local nationals employed by the Embassy have little or no trouble spotting CIA personnel. Dead giveaways for the casually interested person include exotic locks on office doors, a health insurance plan different from that of State Department employees (with readily available premium records), and cryptic references in the State Department's *Biographic Register* to periods of time assigned to one of the military services as an "analyst" or "political affairs officer."

The fact that other intelligence services and host governments are usually aware of the CIA's presence has never really troubled the Agency. The United States and the Soviet Union, for instance, regularly swap names of intelligence personnel assigned to each other's countries for "area familiarization" purposes. And while the CIA isn't about to open overseas branch offices, à la Chase Manhattan Bank, there are certain advantages to letting your presence be known. Disgruntled individuals have little trouble locating the Agency, and Third World security forces often look to the CIA for technical assistance.

In some countries, particularly when a potentially explosive political situation may be brewing, a CIA officer may be installed as Ambassador. Richard Helms, former Director of Central Intelligence, was assigned to mercurial Iran after the Watergate crisis forced him to leave his post. And political parties in Venezuela have reacted to the nomination of Harry W. Shlaudeman as U.S. Ambassador by charging that he is a CIA operative being sent in to subdue the increasingly nationalist policies of that country.

U.S. foreign policy, both overt and covert, is administered through what is known as the "country team" concept. This "country team," nominally headed by the Ambassador, is composed of the highest ranking Foreign Service Officers within a given country, including the COS. Its job is to concretize the often vague platitudes issued by Washington. The CIA's role in all this, of course, is the implementation of clandestine aspects of foreign policy, a role that has been unquestioned until lately.

An example of this clandestine policy and implementation can be seen with tensions that existed between the U.S. and Cuba during the early 1960s. The goal of U.S. foreign policy was to isolate Cuba from the rest of the non-Communist world. In Latin America, governments were pressured to break diplomatic relations. Those governments that opposed U.S. policy toward Cuba soon began experiencing internal strife and economic chaos, directed, of course, by the CIA. Governments in Ecuador and Argentina, among others, were overthrown as the result of CIA activities.

The range of covert actions available to the CIA is limitless where a strong infrastructure exists, and can even include such "simple" exercises as spray painting right-wing slogans on walls. Most actions are approved by staff within the Directorate of Operations, with only the larger and more expensive ones going to the National Security Council or the Forty Committee for approval.

Two categories of covert action exist: Psychological Warfare and Paramilitary. Psychological Warfare actions, as defined by former CIA agent Philip Agee, include "propaganda (also known simply as media), work in youth and student organizations, work in labor organizations (trade unions, etc.), work in professional and cultural groups, and in political parties." He goes on to define paramilitary actions as "infiltration into denied areas, sabotage, economic warfare, personal harassment, air and maritime support, weaponry, training and support for small armies."

The Chief of Station is charged with overseeing the use of these techniques and the network of contacts that makes them possible. The world-wide infrastructure maintained by the CIA intervenes in the affairs of other nations on a daily basis, not "from time to time as the National Security Council may direct."

Despite the national debate currently in progress, the American public is still being asked to leave evaluation of this nation's security forces to dubiously qualified experts. The record of such experts in overseeing the activities of the Central Intelligence Agency is clear: power continues to be abused, nations and peoples are being denied the right of self-determination, and the clandestine infrastructure that makes covert action possible continues to remain unchecked.

Since foreign intelligence services, host countries, and other interested parties have an awareness of the CIA's world-wide clandestine presence, the American people have a right to know as much as those outside the United States do. The time has come for the cloak of secrecy surrounding the activities of the CIA to be examined and cut down to size, a size that reflects the people's right to know.

In keeping with the belief of the Fifth Estate that the people have a right to know about the nature of their security forces, and Philip Agee's statement following is a list of the CIA's Chiefs of Station and Chiefs of Base from around the world. The list is accurate as of June 1974, and contains as many personnel working under diplomatic cover as we were able to locate. Due to transfers and other causes, there may be a few inaccuracies.

For purposes of this list, CAS means "Controlled American Source," a name used to route information to intelligence offices. COS means "Chief of Station" and COB means "Chief of Base."

CAS—Kabul
U.S. Embassy
Kabul, Afghanistan
COS—Samuel H. Rickard III

CAS—Algeria
Embassy of Switzerland
U.S. Interests Section
Algiers, Algeria
COS—Edward R.M. Kane

CAS—Vienna
U.S. Embassy
Vienna, Austria
COS—Charles Trofford Malton Jr.

CAS—Dacca
U.S. Embassy
Dacca, Bangladesh
COS—George T. Walsh

CAS—Brussels
U.S. Embassy
Brussels, Belgium
COS—Michael S. Thompson

CAS—Antwerp
U.S. Consulate General
Antwerp, Belgium
COB—Rowland E. Roberts Jr.

CAS—La Paz
U.S. Embassy
La Paz, Bolivia
COS—Frederick W. Latrash

CAS—Brasília
U.S. Embassy
Brasília, Brazil
COS—Wilfred D. Koplowitz

CAS—Recife
U.S. Consulate General
Recife, Brazil
COB—Thomas J. Barrett Jr.

CAS—Rio de Janeiro
U.S. Consulate General
Rio de Janeiro, Brazil
COB—Stephen F. Creane

CAS—Rangoon
U.S. Embassy
Rangoon, Burma
COS—Clyde R. McAvoy

CAS—Bujumbura
U.S. Embassy
Bujumbura, Burundi
COS—John C. Beam

CAS—Phnom Penh
U.S. Embassy
Phnom Penh, Cambodia
COS—John F. McCarthy III

CAS—Yaoundé
U.S. Embassy
Yaoundé, Cameroon
COS—Jeff Corydon III

CAS—Ottawa
U.S. Embassy
Ottawa, Canada
COS—Cleveland C. Cram

CAS—Bangui
U.S. Embassy
Bangui, Central African Empire
COS—William L. Mosebey Jr.

CAS—Santiago
U.S. Embassy
Santiago, Chile
COS—Stewart D. Burton

CAS—Bogotá
U.S. Embassy
Bogotá, Colombia
COS—Nestor D. Sanchez

CAS—San José
U.S. Embassy
San José, Costa Rica
COS—Comer W. Gilstrap Jr.

CAS—Prague
U.S. Embassy
Prague, Czechoslovakia
COS—Richard A. Kahane

CAS—Santo Domingo
U.S. Embassy
Santo Domingo, Dominican
Republic
COS—Thomas A. Clayton

CAS—Quito
U.S. Embassy
Quito, Ecuador
COS—Paul V. Harwood

CAS—Guayaquil
U.S. Consulate General
Guayaquil, Ecuador
COB—Norman M. Descoteaux

CAS—Cairo
U.S. Embassy
Cairo, Egypt
COS—Arthur M. Niner Jr.

CAS—San Salvador
U.S. Embassy
San Salvador, El Salvador
COS—Kenneth R. Goodman

CAS—Addis Ababa
U.S. Embassy
Addis Ababa, Ethiopia
COS—Eugene L. Jeffers Jr.

CAS—Helsinki
U.S. Embassy
Helsinki, Finland
COS—William C. Simenson

CAS—Paris
U.S. Embassy
Paris, France
COS—Eugen F. Burgstaller

CAS—Berlin
U.S. Mission
West Berlin
COS—George Weisz

CAS—Accra
U.S. Embassy
Accra, Ghana
COS—Joel D. Ticknor

CAS—Athens
U.S. Embassy
Athens, Greece
COS—Stacy B. Hulse Jr.

CAS—Guatemala City
U.S. Embassy
Guatemala City, Guatemala
COS—Edwin M. Terrell

CAS—Conakry
U.S. Embassy
Conakry, Guinea
COS—Peter V. Raudenbush

CAS—Georgetown
U.S. Embassy
Georgetown, Guyana
COS—Robert H. Riefe

CAS—Port-au-Prince
U.S. Embassy
Port-au-Prince, Haiti
COS—James D. Montgomery

CAS—Tegucigalpa
U.S. Embassy
Tegucigalpa, Honduras
COS—Glenn O. Brown

CAS—New Delhi
U.S. Embassy
New Delhi, India
COS—William C. Grimsley Jr.

CAS—Bombay
U.S. Consulate General
Bombay, India
COB—Edward J. Gotchef

CAS—Calcutta
U.S. Consulate General
Calcutta, India
COB—E. Norbert Garrett III

CAS—Madras
U.S. Consulate General
Madras, India
COB—Jack S. Ogino

CAS—Jakarta
U.S. Embassy
Jakarta, Indonesia
COS—Clifton R. Strathern

CAS—Medan
U.S. Consulate
Medan, Indonesia
COB—Thomas L. Norwood Jr.

CAS—Surabaya
U.S. Consulate
Surabaya, Indonesia
COB—Robert H. Mills

CAS—Tehran
U.S. Embassy
Tehran, Iran
COS—George W. Cave

CAS—Rome
U.S. Embassy
Rome, Italy
COS—Howard E. Stone

CAS—Abidjan
U.S. Embassy
Abidjan, Ivory Coast
COS—Martin J. Bergin Jr.

CAS—Kingston
U.S. Embassy
Kingston, Jamaica
COS—Thomas J. Keenan

CAS—Amman
U.S. Embassy
Amman, Jordan
COS—Frederic H. Sabin III

CAS—Nairobi
U.S. Embassy
Nairobi, Kenya
COS—Howard T. Bane

CAS—Kuwait
U.S. Embassy
Kuwait, Kuwait
COS—Robert C. Ames

CAS—Beirut
U.S. Embassy
Beirut, Lebanon
COS—John J. Seidel Jr.

CAS—Luxembourg
U.S. Embassy
Luxembourg, Luxembourg
COS—Felton M. Wyatt

CAS—Bamako
U.S. Embassy
Bamako, Mali
COS—Raymond F. Denicourt

CAS—Valletta
U.S. Embassy
Valletta, Malta
COS—George A. Chritton

CAS—Port Louis
U.S. Embassy
Port Louis, Mauritius
COS—Vasia C. Gmirkin

CAS—Rabat
U.S. Embassy
Rabat, Morocco
COS—Charles G. Cogan

CAS—Casablanca
U.S. Consulate General
Casablanca, Morocco
COB—Mark T. Colby

CAS—Kathmandu
U.S. Embassy
Kathmandu, Nepal
COS—Joseph A. Murray Jr.

CAS—Managua
U.S. Embassy
Managua, Nicaragua
COS—Joseph Piccolo Jr.

CAS—Kaduna
U.S. Consulate
Kaduna, Nigeria
COB—Robert W. Ince

CAS—Muscat
U.S. Embassy
Muscat, Oman
COS—Robert L. Headley Jr.

CAS—Islamabad
U.S. Embassy
Islamabad, Pakistan
COS—Donald F. Vogel

CAS—Karachi
U.S. Consulate General
Karachi, Pakistan
COB—Edward R. Brown

CAS—Panama City
U.S. Embassy
Panama City, Panama
COS—Joseph Y. Kiyonaga

CAS—Lima
U.S. Embassy
Lima, Peru
COS—Richard S. Welch

CAS—Manila
U.S. Embassy
Manila, Philippines
COS—George T. Kalaris

CAS—Warsaw
U.S. Embassy
Warsaw, Poland
COS—Carl E. Gebhardt

CAS—Bucharest
U.S. Embassy
Bucharest, Romania
COS—Jay K. Gruner

CAS—Jidda
U.S. Embassy
Jidda, Saudi Arabia
COS—Raymond H. Close

CAS—Dakar
U.S. Embassy
Dakar, Senegal
COS—Charles L. Randolph

CAS—Singapore
U.S. Embassy
Singapore, Singapore
COS—David T. Samson

CAS—Mogadiscio
U.S. Embassy
Mogadiscio, Somalia
COS—David P. Hunt

CAS—Pretoria
U.S. Embassy
Pretoria, South Africa
COS—Jarrel H. Richardson

CAS—Colombo
U.S. Embassy
Colombo, Sri Lanka
COS—James A. Higham

CAS—Khartoum
U.S. Embassy
Khartoum, Sudan
COS—Murat Natirboff

CAS—Dar es Salaam
U.S. Embassy
Dar es Salaam, Tanzania
COS—Harry S. Slifer Jr.

CAS—Ankara
U.S. Embassy
Ankara, Turkey
COS—John H. Hoskins

CAS—Istanbul
U.S. Consulate General
Istanbul, Turkey
COB—Robert B. Goodwin

CAS—Abu Dhabi
U.S. Embassy
Abu Dhabi,
    United Arab Emirates
COS—James M. Fernald

CAS—London
U.S. Embassy
London, United Kingdom
COS—Cord Meyer Jr.

CAS—Hong Kong
U.S. Consulate General
Hong Kong, United Kingdom
COS—Joseph J. Simon

CAS—Montevideo
U.S. Embassy
Montevideo, Uruguay
COS—Martin C. Hawkins

CAS—Caracas
U.S. Embassy
Caracas, Venezuela
COS—Wade E. Thomas

CAS—Saigon
U.S. Embassy
Saigon, Vietnam
COS—Thomas Polgar

CAS—Danang
U.S. Consulate General
Danang, Vietnam
COB—James M. Howley

CAS—Bien Hoa
U.S. Consulate General
Bien Hoa, Vietnam
COB—Thomas W. Lamb

CAS—Belgrade
U.S. Embassy
Belgrade, Yugoslavia
COS—Richard F. Stolz Jr.

CAS—Zagreb
U.S. Consulate General
Zagreb, Yugoslavia
COB—Paul J. Redmond

CAS—Kinshasa
U.S. Embassy
Kinshasa, Zaire
COS—James Kim, Stuart E.
Methven

CAS—New York
U.S. Mission to the United
Nations
New York, New York
COS—Rudulph E. Carter

CAS—Geneva
U.S. Mission to the European
Office of the United Nations
Geneva, Switzerland
COB—Leo Sandel, Throop M.
Wilder Jr.

CAS—Paris
Office of Permanent U.S.
Representative to UNESCO
Paris, France
COB—John H. Kenney

[EDITORS' NOTE: Further investigation has revealed that a few of those named by *CounterSpy* were not, in fact, Chiefs of Station. *CounterSpy*'s mistake—and it is a common one—was to give as the Station Chief the highest ranking CIA person shown on the *Foreign Service List*. The FSLs, however, frequently fail to show the names of the very top CIA people in certain countries, especially in Europe.

For example, in the case of Austria, the FSL for June 1974 showed a political officer (FSR-3) named Charles T. Malton, Jr. Malton's career history in the 1974 *Biographic Register* clearly marked him as a long-time CIA officer, and since the FSL showed no other CIA officer with a higher grade or greater seniority, *CounterSpy* named him as Chief of Station. Other available sources, however, showed a higher ranking CIA official above Malton in the U.S. Embassy in Vienna—a CIA official whose name was carefully dropped from recent FSLs and *Biographic Registers*. This vanishing spook, the real Chief of Station in Vienna in 1974, was Hugh Montgomery, who was later identified holding down the top spot in Rome. (See "Hello Hugh Montgomery" by Steve Weissman, in this volume.)

The same mistake appeared in the case of South Africa, where Francis J. Jeton was actually higher ranking than the man named, Jarrel Richardson; and in the case of the United Kingdom, *CounterSpy* correctly named station chief Cord Meyer, Jr., even though his name was also absent from the FSLs. For the most part, though, the *CounterSpy* list seemed to be correct, and where the individuals named were not Chiefs of Station, they appeared to be high-ranking CIA officials in any event.]

Cord Meyer:
Superspook

by Godfrey Hodgson

A little before eight o'clock each morning, an unobtrusive ritual
is enacted on the corner of South Eaton Place and Chester Row
in Belgravia.

The tall house on the southwest corner has two entrances.
First, out of the main porch in South Eaton Place, a houseboy in
a white jacket emerges and scans both streets. The pavements
are empty. It will be an hour before the au pair girls drag the
little boys in blazers to school, and almost two hours before the
City men puff off to Sloane Square Underground. Satisfied, the
houseboy steps inside, presumably to telephone for the car.

A few minutes later, it slides up, a long black American sedan,
left-hand drive. The driver gets out. He is a burly, stone-bald
man with dark glasses. A Kojak fan. He, too, scans the pavements, theatrically, puts his chauffeur's cap on, and gets back
into the car.

[This article first appeared in the *Sunday Times Magazine* of
June 15, 1975, in London.]

Then, abruptly, a grey man with a grey suit and grey hair hurries out of another entrance at the other side of the house. He's tallish, fiftyish, fit: a tennis player. He gets into the passenger seat and the big car slides away.

Punctually and early, like the bureaucrat he is, but also with the circumspection of his profession, and with just a residual hint of adolescent pleasure in playing cloak-and-dagger games, Cord Meyer, Junior, head of the London station of the CIA, is off to the office.

There have been reports that Meyer is due to be replaced this summer, and other reports that, no, he's here to stay. [He was replaced by Edward W. Proctor in late 1976.]

There are, again, those in Washington who maintain that Meyer was sent to London in 1973 to take charge of the entire CIA operation in Western Europe. What with the oil crisis, and Portugal, and Italy, and the British miners' strike, the theory was that the stirring days of the late 1940s, when the CIA reckons it saved Europe from Communist subversion, were here again. Washington decided—on this interpretation—that the London job, with a supervisory function for Western Europe as a whole, needed a senior man, and the fact that Meyer had experience of clandestine operations—which he does—was a bonus.

But then there are other people in Washington who lift their eyes to the heavens and say: "Listen, what with Watergate, and a presidential commission *and* the Congress, not to mention the Press, investigating the agency, the last thing anyone needs is any more Chile-style publicity. Meyer has been put out to grass in London."

But these are after all only theories, because, whatever anyone may try to tell you, even the world's leakiest secret intelligence agency doesn't discuss its personnel policy in public.

What is not in doubt is that Cord Meyer, Jr., is no ordinary head of the CIA's London station.

His family, on both sides, were wealthy, and his father, after making a supplemental fortune in real estate development to add to the family sugar interests, became an American diplomat. Cord and his twin brother grew up in the world of John P. Marquand's novels and John O'Hara's stories. They went to St. Paul's, in New Hampshire, one of the two or three best-known and most expensive American private boarding schools. At

Yale, Cord graduated *summa cum laude,* six months early, because this was December 1942, and he and other young men in
his class were in a hurry to get into uniform. He became a
Marine lieutenant.

In July 1944, during the landing on Guam, a Japanese grenade
rolled into his foxhole. He lost the sight of one eye and for a few
agonizing moments he thought that he was totally blind. Then,
as he described the experience in a short story later, he thought
he could see a single star in the sky.

"Fearing that he might have created it out of the intensity of
his wish," he wrote, "he let the lid close and then forced it open
again. The star lay still in the now soft and friendly dark. It
flooded his being like the summer sun. He saw it as the window
of Hope."

In the seven months he spent in hospital, Meyer made up his
mind to spend his life working to prevent war. "If possible," he
wrote from hospital to his parents, "I should like to make a life's
work of doing what little I can in the problems of international
cooperation."

In a sense, he has made those problems his life's work. But
not quite, perhaps, in the sense he meant then.

He started out as a radical. "I wish," he wrote in the story I
have already quoted, "that all those in power, countrymen and
enemies alike, who decided for war, all those who profit by it,
lay dead with their wealth and their honors."

In 1945 he went to the conference which drew up the United
Nations Charter in San Francisco. He became one of the leaders
of the American Veterans' Committee, a liberal servicemen's
organization expressly intended to challenge the conservative
American Legion. Two years later he became one of the moving
spirits of the United World Federalists. Their goal was world
government. For four years Meyer traveled tens of thousands of
miles, he talked, he lectured, and he wrote a highly persuasive
book, *Peace or Anarchy,* all drumming home the message that
world government was the only alternative to nuclear catastrophe. He was so persuasive that in 1947 he was chosen as one of
the 10 outstanding young men in America. (One of the others
was a young congressman from California called Richard M.
Nixon.)

Then, in 1951, at the personal invitation of the director, Allen
Dulles, he joined the CIA.

His career has been made, not in intelligence, in the strict sense of the word, but in the departments which come under the authority of the Deputy Director for Plans, which is a euphemism for clandestine operations, and is not unjustly known in Washington as the "department of dirty tricks."

He began by working for Tom Braden, who later resigned and became a fashionable liberal columnist. Braden has admitted that he was responsible for pouring CIA money into the trade union movement, both in America and in Europe. Later, Meyer worked for the legendary Thomas Karamessines: it was widely believed that he would succeed "the Greek" as Deputy Director for Plans—"Washington's closest equivalent," according to the late Stewart Alsop, a considerable authority on these matters, "to James Bond's boss, 'M.'!"

Meyer, in other words, worked for that part of the agency which organized the penetration of trade unions in Europe and Latin America; which mounted the Bay of Pigs fiasco; and which certainly helped to overthrow governments secretly in Iran, Guatemala, Guyana, Brazil, Greece, and Chile.

In 1972 the *Washington Post*'s Lawrence Stern revealed that the CIA's intervention on behalf of the Christian Democrat, Eduardo Frei, cost $20 million and dwarfed even the later effort against the Allende government. "One of the key figures in the 1964 intervention," Stern reported, "was Cord Meyer, Jr. He directed the CIA's covert programs to neutralize Communist influence on important opinion-making sectors such as trade unions, farmer and peasant organizations, student activities and the media." That was what "international cooperation" had come to mean for Meyer.

Late in 1966, a disgruntled member of the staff of the National Student Association—roughly the equivalent of the NUS—blew the whistle. The CIA, he said, had been secretly subsidizing the foreign activities of the NSA for years.

Then it gradually emerged that the subsidies to the NSA were only a fraction of the CIA's secret support for voluntary organizations. Through an ingenious structure of front organizations, conduits, "pass throughs," and other devices, the CIA was pouring millions of dollars a year into trade unions, cultural activities, and educational institutions all over the world—including some activities in the United States, where it was specifically forbidden to operate by the National Security Act of 1947, its charter. (In recent weeks it has emerged that the Agency has also been using business firms, including the publishers of the

Fodor guide books, and the J. Walter Thompson advertising agency, as cover.)

"The 'spook' in charge of covertly subsidizing the overseas activities of the National Student Association and other youth groups, labor and professional organizations," the *New York Times* reported on May 30, 1967, was Cord Meyer, Jr.

Perhaps in the long run the most influential investment the CIA made was in trade unions. Without it, for example, the successful right-wing *coup d'état* in Brazil in 1964 would probably have been impossible. But many intellectuals, both in the U.S. and in Europe, were more shocked to learn that the Congress for Cultural Freedom had been secretly on the American government's payroll for years. The Congress held high-powered conferences to which European intellectuals were glad enough to be invited in the 1950s. It also published serious monthlies like *Encounter* in London, which provided a forum for long political and literary articles by British and European intellectuals who had few comparable outlets elsewhere, and also for the exposition of the "end of ideology" dogma—which meant the end of all ideologies except that of American liberalism. No other single incident, perhaps, has done more to discredit the CIA with American intellectuals than the NSA affair. President Johnson was constrained to issue an order ending all secret CIA financing of voluntary organizations.

On the face of it, you might think that to be "blown" in this way ought to have proved fatal to Meyer's career. That supposition rests on a misunderstanding, however. The CIA is not a rogue agency. What it does is done in obedience to presidential orders. As the official inquiry into the NSA and consequent revelations noted, "such assistance was given pursuant to National Security Council policies beginning in October 1951."

Five years later, he was briefly in the public eye again. In the summer of 1972, he turned up in the office of his old friend and former fellow World Federalist, the Kennedy entourage's favorite publisher, Cass Canfield of Harper and Row, to ask if the agency could see galley proofs of a book which alleged that it had been involved in the heroin trade in South-East Asia. The book was by a Yale graduate student called Alfred McCoy. Fashions in idealism had changed at Yale in 30 years.

Harper did submit the galleys. The CIA responded with suggested corrections which a Harper editor described as "laughably pathetic." The book was published uncorrected. The only effect of Cord Meyer's attempt to apply his *imprimatur* was a little welcome prepublication publicity.

I met Cord Meyer socially several times in Washington in the early 1960s. I remember two occasions in particular with painful clarity. The second was at a party given by the book review department of the *Washington Post*. Meyer there picked a violent quarrel with the *Post*'s foreign editor on the grounds that he had printed some news which Meyer felt ought not to have been printed.

The first occasion was the very first dinner party I was invited to in Georgetown, the elegant eighteenth-century and mock eighteenth-century district where Meyer and many other senior officials with private means live. Georgetown was always fashionable. The Kennedys made it known as fashionable to every magazine reader in the country, and the Meyers were very much a part of the Camelot scene. Cord Meyer's first wife was a friend of Jacqueline Kennedy Onassis, and her sister was then married to Kennedy's friend Ben Bradlee, now editor of the *Washington Post*.

Meyer spent about an hour bullying an elderly Canadian diplomat about why Canadians should be so perverse as to wish to remain independent of the United States. It was a subject on which no Canadian diplomat could possibly have engaged in argument with an American official. The diplomat, who had a serious heart ailment, was visibly distressed, but Meyer ploughed on, without wit, taste, or mercy. On both occasions his fervor and unreasonableness were disturbing.

It has been a sad trajectory, from the young idealist to the angry intellectual gendarme in the department of dirty tricks.

Personal tragedies, as well as public experiences, shaped the man. (Meyer's twin brother was killed on Okinawa in 1945. His nine-year-old son was killed by a car in 1959, and his first marriage ended in divorce shortly afterward. Five years later, his former wife was murdered while going for a walk along the towpath in Washington.) But the transformation of Cord Meyer is a story of broader relevance than any banal American tragedy or private grief, frustrated ambition or embittered idealism. It is the tragedy of an entire generation of the American ruling class. Cord Meyer, Yale '43, the man with a golden future behind him, epitomizes a class and a generation who seemed to have the whole world as the raw material for their ambitions and their ideals. They have ended up, as he has, powerful, comfortable, angry, frustrated, and above all puzzled that their superiority is so little appreciated.

For Cord Meyer and for his generation, the crucial experience was that of McCarthyism. He was not a witch-hunter, as those with an oversimplified view of the CIA might suppose. He was a victim. Or rather he had a narrow escape. At a certain price . . .

Many people, no doubt, think of the CIA as being automatically on the side of reaction. It has, indeed, all too often taken the side of reaction all over the world. But, in American political terms, the CIA has always had a split ideological personality.

It has, of course, found room for many "conservatives": an industrialist like John McCone as Director, a military man like General Vernon Walters as Deputy Director, and assorted anti-Communist bigots right down the bureaucratic ladder to the former FBI men, the Ukrainian émigrés, and the Cuban refugees who do the dirty work.

Yet the CIA's position within the U.S. government has by no means usually been the hard right-wing position. On Vietnam, the *Pentagon Papers* show how often it took a more "liberal" position than other agencies. In terms of personality, the dominant group in the CIA has been made up of men who, at least until the crisis of the Vietnam war, called themselves liberals: men like Richard Helms, Richard Bissell, Frank Wisner, James Angleton, William Putnam Bundy, William Colby. . . and Cord Meyer.

One should not make the mistake of supposing that they were ever very far to the left. Some of the clever young men from Ivy League universities who were recruited into the agency in its early years really did have strongly progressive views. Rev. William Sloane Coffin, who ended up on trial alongside Dr. Benjamin Spock, was one of them, and perhaps for a while Cord Meyer was another.

But when people spoke of Bissell or Wisner or Bundy as "liberals," they didn't really mean that they had left-wing views. They meant two other things which were associated with that elastic adjective, "liberal." They meant that they were "internationalists," in the sense of advocating American intervention around the world. And they meant that they were what used to be called "gentlemen": educated men from the upper middle class.

For both reasons, they were natural targets for McCarthy. While on the surface McCarthy, Nixon, and the other witch-hunters of the early 1950s were in pursuit of the agents of foreign communism, in fact they were after their own domestic enemies. One aspect of McCarthyism was that it was the revenge of the isolationist Middle West, and of the isolationist ethnic groups, Irish- and German-Americans, on that "internationalist," pro-British elite which had demanded intervention. Secondly, it was a movement fired with populist resentment against the elite, the Establishment. That was why McCarthy went after Acheson with such venom. The charge that Acheson, the architect of the Truman Doctrine, was soft on communism, was never convincing. The charge that he was the kind of man who bought his suits in Savile Row was persuasive, and McCarthy knew it.

In conjunction with his assault on the State Department, therefore, it was inevitable that McCarthy should have fired a few salvos at the new agency which was no less committed to "internationalism," and if anything even fuller of just the breed of rich, clever, idealistic, and superior young men that McCarthy and his yahoos could least abide. Meyer was an obvious target, on all four grounds.

The charges did not need to be specific. The FBI obligingly reported that Meyer was "an admitted World Federalist" and that he had "knowingly associated with Communists." Given the fact that he had spent two years fighting the Communists round a table on the American Veterans' Committee, and then rather more than two years traveling round the country proclaiming his allegiance to World Federalism, the charges might have been comic, if they hadn't been so dangerous.

Many men in his position gave up and resigned. Meyer fought. He was allowed three months' leave to prepare his defense, and with his lawyer he produced several hundred pages of rebuttal. In November 1953, Allen Dulles called him in to tell him he was cleared. He had satisfied the inquisitors of his ideological orthodoxy. He was free to become an inquisitor himself.

Friends say that he was irremediably scarred by the experience. He himself has said that during those months he read Kafka's *Trial,* and with a new understanding. Meyer had always been anti-Communist. Now he seems to have decided that never again would he leave room for the slightest doubt about the totality of his commitment to the hardest of hard anti-Communist lines.

Traumatic and decisive as the McCarthy episode was, it was after all only a special case of a general proposition. American society is not appreciative of elites. In the America in which Cord Meyer's generation grew up, life was genuinely hard for most Americans. While he was at St. Paul's and Yale, something approaching a quarter of the working population was out of a job. The farmer, the unemployed worker, the immigrant's son, had to learn to be tough in that America. Those who grew up in sheltered homes and private schools seem to have acquired a special compulsion to prove how tough they were, too. And this syndrome in individual psychology—it is, after all, the Hemingway syndrome—had its political equivalent. The "liberals"— the foreign policy elite to which Cord Meyer and his friends in Georgetown and the CIA belonged—had to prove that they were as red-blooded in their Americanism as anyone else. As much as anything else, this auction in political masculinity was the cause of the war which they have just lost. Yet there was also a fatal survival of the old New England moralism. Meyer's generation and class never, in Cromwell's phrase, bethought themselves in the bowels of Christ that they might be mistaken.

The story remains a tragedy. As Daniel Patrick Moynihan has said of the elite to which Meyer belongs: "Life is tragic for those who are impelled by conscience to pursue objectives which can be attained only through means which conscience finds abhorrent."

The CIA in
Portugal

by Philip Agee

The revolutionary process in Portugal is being attacked by the guardians of capitalist countries' interests, of which the U.S. Central Intelligence Agency is the most notorious and powerful. I see the signs daily. These counterrevolutionary activities are similar to what I did in the CIA for more than ten years during the 1950s and 60s. I send this letter as part of a continuing effort by many Americans to end imperialist intervention and support to repression by the U.S. government.

In the Azores as well as in mainland Portugal, in the Catholic Church, in political parties, and even within the armed forces, the CIA and its allies are working to create enough chaos to justify an attempt by the so-called moderates to take over the Revolutionary Government.

Since the fall of fascism in Portugal, I have tried to follow developments and have twice visited your country. While my

[This article was written in London in August 1975, and was then circulated as "A Letter to the Portuguese People."]

study of the visible signs of CIA intervention is still incomplete, there is good reason to alert you to what I have seen. Last week a U.S. Senator announced that the Communist Party of Portugal is receiving $10 million per month from the Soviet Union, a figure he attributed to the CIA. Two days later Deputy CIA Director General Vernon Walters (who visited Lisbon to survey the political situation in August of 1974) confirmed the Senator's claim. Secretary of State Kissinger, for his part, publicly warned the Soviet Union recently that assistance by them to the Portuguese revolutionary process was endangering detente. These statements suggest that the American people are being prepared for another secret foreign adventure by the CIA.

I will describe below what I believe are CIA operations, along with a list of the names and residences in Portugal of as many of the CIA functionaries as I can identify.

The size of the overall U.S. government mission in Portugal is shocking, especially its heavy dominance by military personnel. The mission totals 280 persons, of whom about 160 are Americans, with the rest being Portuguese employees. Of the Americans, 105 are military personnel assigned mainly to the Military Assistance Advisory Group, the office of the Defense Attache and the COMIBERLANT command of NATO.

Of the approximately 50 American civilians in the mission about 10, I believe, are employees of the CIA. No less than 10 additional CIA functionaries are probably working in Lisbon and other cities, having been assigned ostensibly for temporary duties so that their presence is not included on Embassy personnel lists, nor reported to the Portuguese Foreign Ministry.

One must also assume that additional CIA operations officers have been placed under cover in American military units in Portugal, where their experience in political operations—far superior to that of their military colleagues—will be most effective. While efforts to divert the revolution through General Spinola have failed, new efforts are being made daily in the struggles to stop the revolution.

Without doubt, the CIA officers in other U.S. embassies, most likely in Madrid, Paris, and London, have personnel assigned to Portuguese operations that are undertaken in these countries rather than in Portugal proper. The most sensitive operations of the CIA probably are occurring in other European cities rather than in Lisbon.

Who specifically are responsible for operations against Portugal? The CIA is only one of the various U.S. agencies working against the revolution, under the guidance of Ambassador Carlucci. Although Carlucci is not a CIA man, he must carefully direct and coordinate all U.S. counterrevolutionary operations, including those of the military services. His top-level team includes: Herbert Okun, his Minister Counselor and Deputy Chief of Mission; John Morgan, the Chief of the CIA; Admiral Frank Corley, Chief of the Military Assistance Advisory Group; Colonel Peter Blackley, Chief of the Defense Attache Office; Charles Thomas, Counselor for Political Affairs; and Navy Captain James Lacey, senior U.S. military representative of the COMIBERLANT NATO Command. Each of the U.S. military units, along with the CIA and State Department personnel, are responsible for one or more of the specific counterrevolutionary programs.

In order to preserve imperialist interests in Portugal, the revolution must be diverted from its current directions, and the U.S. government is not alone in its efforts. I strongly suspect that Kissinger many months ago urged the leaders of Western European governments to intervene themselves directly to reverse the Portuguese revolutionary process, arguing that the problem is essentially European and that the CIA has been limited in its capabilities by recent revelations.

In 1948, when the Communist Party of Italy was about to win the elections, the U.S. government alone threatened to halt aid for reconstruction, and even to launch a military invasion. In recent days, the EEC presidents themselves have threatened to withhold financial assistance from Portugal unless their style of democracy is established. Other similarities between post-fascist Portugal and post–World War II Europe are striking. In Greece, France, and Italy, the U.S. government established governments submissive to American economic interests while simultaneously providing alternatives to left-wing governments led by the same political forces that provided the backbone of the Resistance in World War II.

The chosen solution in that era was predominantly Christian Democracy or Social Democracy and the trade union movements corresponding to each. The promotion of these same forces in Portugal since April 1974 suggests to me that the CIA, probably in coordination with other Western European intelligence services, is attempting the same solutions that were successful in other countries following World War II.

What specifically is the CIA doing in Portugal? The first priority is to penetrate the Armed Forces Movement in order to collect information on its plans, its weaknesses, and its internal struggles; to identify the so-called moderates and others who would be favorable to western strategic interests. The CIA would use information collected from within the MFA for propaganda inside and outside Portugal designed to divide and weaken the MFA.

Other CIA tasks include: false documents and rumor campaigns, fomenting of strife, encouraging conflict and jealousy. Moderates are being assisted where possible in their efforts to restrain the pace of revolutionary development toward socialism. The final goal is for the so-called moderates to take control of the MFA and all Portuguese military institutions.

U.S. military schools have trained over 3,000 Portuguese military personnel since 1950. Detailed files have been accumulated on every one of them—their personalities, politics, likes and dislikes, strengths, weaknesses, and vulnerabilities. Many of these will have already been selected as contacts to be developed within the Portuguese military establishment, with emphasis on developing close relations with as many MFA members as possible.

Significant efforts have already been made—and these, too, have failed—to date—to strengthen Social Democratic and Christian Democratic political parties. The CIA's normal procedure is to maintain friendly relations (and often to give financial support) with leaders of "moderate" opposition political parties who are forced to live in exile. The purpose is to reap large benefits when such politicians return home. Often paid agents are infiltrated into these exile groups in order to obtain additional information.

The CIA may have intervened in the recent electoral campaign to ensure that the results would "prove" that the majority of Portuguese favor a more "moderate" pace for the revolution. James Lawler, the CIA Deputy Chief of Station in Lisbon, engaged in just such operations in Brazil (in 1962) and in Chile (in 1964) where many millions of dollars were spent by the CIA to promote the election of the U.S.-approved "moderates."

In trade unions, the CIA has also been unsuccessful so far, but obvious efforts continue. As in Italy and in France after World War II, the CIA is probably trying to split the trade union movement by helping to establish an affiliate of the International

Confederation of Free Trade Unions, and by promoting ties between Portuguese industrial unions and the International Trade Secretariats. Michael Boggs and Irving Brown, both officials of the AFL-CIO with notorious ties to the CIA, visited Portugal last year. Although the capitalist-controlled trade union institutions failed to establish footholds when the trade union law was approved in January, the ICFTU is still trying, through its representative in Portugal, Manuel Simon.

The CIA is also using the Roman Catholic Church for its ends. Recently a reliable source in Washington told me that large amounts of money are going from the United States to the Catholic Church for combating the revolution in Portugal. The Church's opposition to the workers' control of Radio Renascença should alert us to the identity of interests between the Portuguese hierarchy and American economic concerns.

Propaganda campaigns are central for all important CIA political operations. These campaigns prepare public opinion by creating fear, uncertainty, resentment, hostility, division, and weakness. Newspapers, radio, television, wall painting, postering, fly sheets, and falsified documents of all kinds—the CIA uses many different techniques. In Portugal, these have had little success so far, mainly because workers have taken control of the public information media. But the CIA must continue to aid —in every possible way—the efforts of "moderate" political forces to establish and maintain media outlets that the CIA can use for placing its materials.

Outside Portugal the campaign to discredit the revolution is having success. In Europe and America we see the themes clearly: "The MFA has failed to follow the will of most Portuguese as reflected in the April elections. . . . The Portuguese people have sadly 'lost' their freedom with the diminishing in importance of the elected assembly. . . . The press has 'lost' its freedom. . . . Portugal needs 'stability' to solve its social and economic problems. . . . The revolutionary leadership is inept and unable to stop the economic downturn.'' These propaganda themes are preparing the U.S. and western public opinion for acceptance of intervention and a strong right-wing military government if the "moderate" solutions fail. These themes present the usual false dilemma: Portugal will have either capitalist democracy or cruel heartless Communist dictatorship with attendant dull, austere living conditions. There has, of course, been little comparison of Portugal today with the cruelty and hardships of capitalist economics under the former fascist political system.

As in the campaign against Chile, economic warfare is the key for cutting away public support from the revolutionary leadership. By withholding credits and other assistance from bilateral and multilateral lending institutions, great hardships will befall the middle and working classes. Private investment credits can be frozen, trading contracts delayed and cancelled, and unemployment increased, while imperialist propaganda will place the blame on workers' demands and the government's weakness rather than on lending institutions and their deliberate policies of credit retention. The effects of these programs in Chile during the Allende administration are known to all.

Propaganda exploitation of economic hardship will thus prepare at least a limited public acceptance of a strong military government that suddenly appears to "restore national dignity, discipline, and purpose." If there is a Portuguese Pinochet, he ought to be identified now.

In coming months we will probably see intensification of the CIA's operations to create fear, uncertainty, economic disruption, political division, and the appearances of chaos. Political assassinations must be expected, along with bombings that can be "attributed" to the revolutionary left. Mr. Morgan, the head of the CIA in Lisbon, learned these kinds of operations when he served in Venezuela (1966–1968) and in Brazil (1970–1973). The "death squads" that were established in those countries during the last decade must be anticipated and stopped before they flourish in Portugal.

Greater militancy by reactionary elements in the Catholic Church must also be expected in their effort to undermine the revolution. As "moderate" electoral solutions become more and more remote, the CIA and its "sister" services will increasingly promote Chile-style "stability" as the only remaining way to "save" Portugal.

The separatist movement in the Azores, already gaining momentum among U.S. residents of Azores origin, may be promoted by the CIA as a last resort for preserving U.S. military bases there. In Angola, the CIA is not standing idly by, where exceptional resources must be kept in capitalist hands. The FNLA is likely being supported by the CIA through Zaire in order to divide the country and prevent MPLA hegemony.

What can be done to defeat this intervention? Clearly the

revolutionary process itself and the people's support and participation through organs of popular power is the strongest defense.
Nevertheless, imperialist agents ought to be identified and exposed using many of the CIA's own methods against them.
Careful control must be maintained of all entries and exits of
Portugal by U.S. citizens, both through immigration control and
through the issuance of visas for diplomatic and official passports by Portuguese embassies and consulates.

In the CIA, I worked to install in Uruguay a system whereby
all visitors' visas from socialist countries would require approval
of the Uruguayan Director of Immigration, with whom I worked
closely, giving recommendations on each visa request. Background investigations of the employment histories of U.S. government officials usually reveal which ones are CIA officers posing as diplomats. Moreover, all "private" U.S. citizens must be
monitored for possible CIA connections: businessmen, tourists,
professors, students, and retired people. Once these people
have been exposed, the Portuguese people themselves must be
prepared to take the action needed to force the CIA people out
of Portugal. The slogan "CIA OUT" must become a reality.

The shocking U.S. military presence in Portugal could well be
ended altogether. The only "advice" and "assistance" that a
U.S. military group can now give in Portugal is how to make a
counterrevolution.

I list here below the CIA people known to me, and those
whom I believe to be CIA personnel. Some might have left
Portugal recently, but I believe that most of them are still there:

> **John S. Morgan,** (Chief of Station), Av. Suíça 3,
> Estoril
> **James N. Lawler,** (Deputy Chief of Station), Av. de
> Brasil 28, Cascais
> **Philip W. Snell,** Rua da Beira 6, Carcavelos
> **Leslie F. Hughes,** Praceta da Rua A 3 Lote 3N, Quinta
> da Lagoa, Carcavelos
> **Frank Lowell,** Praça das Aguas Livres 80, esq. Lisboa
> 2
> **Gerald D. Zapoli,** Address unknown
> **Donna J. Caldwell,** Praça das Aguas Livres 60D, esq.

Changes in the CIA in Portugal

by Philip Agee

Since public exposure in August 1975 of CIA personnel assigned under diplomatic cover of the U.S. Embassy in Lisbon, a number of changes have been made including the assignment of a new Chief of Station, one new operations officer, and two new communications officers.

The new CIA Chief is David D. Whipple, 53, a veteran of over 25 years' service in the CIA. After military duty in World War II, Whipple attended the University of Southampton in England and Dartmouth College and the School of Advanced International Studies in the U.S. His first CIA assignment was under State Department cover to Saigon and Hanoi from 1950 to 1953. During 1953–1956 Whipple served in Rangoon, again under diplomatic cover, and from 1958 to 1961 in Bangkok where he was a CIA police advisor under cover of the International Cooperation

[This article was written in London in July 1976, and was then circulated as "Changes in CIA Personnel between August 1975 and July 1976."]

Administration, predecessor of the Agency for International Development.

Whipple was transferred to the U.S. Consulate in Elizabethville, Congo (now Lubumbashi, Zaire) arriving in February 1961 just days after the CIA's efforts to assassinate Patrice Lumumba finally produced the Congolese leader's death. Judging from Whipple's State Department cover rank, he probably became the Chief of the CIA's office in the Elizabethville Consulate. He would have replaced the unidentified CIA officer mentioned in the Senate assassinations report as having sent a secret cable to Washington in mid-January 1961 rejoicing over Lumumba's delivery to certain death in Elizabethville.

After two years in the Congo, Whipple went on to assignments in London (1967–1970) and Helsinki (1971–1974) before replacing John Morgan as Lisbon Station Chief sometime during late 1975. Whipple's diplomatic cover title is Embassy Attache and his home address is Avenida Portugal 7, Estoril, telephone number 26-11-68.

The CIA's new operations officer is Joseph J. Marques, 35, who also appears to have arrived in late 1975. Marques is using the cover title of Third Secretary in the U.S. Embassy and he has had previous assignments in Rio de Janeiro (1972–1974) and Brasilia (1974–1975). The recently arrived communications officers are Donald Riebhoff and Tony Van Twisk, both of whom arrived in mid-1975.

CIA personnel who have remained in Lisbon despite exposure in 1975 include the Deputy Chief of Station, James Lawler, who, like Whipple, uses Embassy Attache cover. Lawler lives at Avenida de Brasil 28, Cascais, telephone 286-5300, and he has served previously in Brazil, Chile, and Venezuela. Another communications officer who appears to have remained in Lisbon is Leslie Hughes who lives at Praceta da Rua A, Lote 3N, Quinta da Lagoa, Carcavelos, telephone 247-0833.

Whether or not public exposure was responsible for the personnel changes cannot be determined, although Morgan only served for about two years in Lisbon—a short tenure for a CIA Station Chief. Similarly Philip Snell, who apparently was replaced by Marques, served only about a year in Lisbon. Certainly from the way developments in Portugal since August 1975 have served to favor American government interests, the transfers would not likely have resulted because these officers failed in their duties.

As Portugal enters, in July 1976, a new phase of its post-fascist era by installation of its first elected government, the question of how much foreign influence has been involved, particularly CIA influence, can still neither be avoided nor definitively answered. However, there can now be little doubt that intervention by Western European governments, by Social Democratic and Christian Democratic political parties, and by conservative political forces has been considerable and encouraged by the American government.

U.S. policy on Portugal after the April 1974 coup against fascism was clarified in an interview with Secretary of State Kissinger published in *Time* on October 27, 1975. Kissinger seemed not to have varied far from his normal activist-interventionist stance: "My position has been that without a systematic effort to encourage the pluralistic forces in Portugal, they would be defeated." After mentioning disagreement between him and Western European political leaders, who apparently believed pluralistic forms could develop under the earlier, leftist Goncalves regime, Kissinger added that "during the summer [of 1975] the West Europeans came to the same conclusions we had earlier reached: namely, that pluralism had to be actively encouraged."

The Europeans' systematic and active encouragement of pluralism in Portugal was in part to condition collective economic aid from EEC countries on establishment of a government that would include participation by Mario Soares' Socialist Party and the "moderates" within the Armed Forces Movement known as the Group of Nine and headed by Melo Antunes. Undoubtedly Kissinger was referring to the meeting in July 1975 of the chiefs of government of the nine EEC countries in Brussels where they announced that the $840 million economic aid program then under consideration for Portugal would depend on the achievement of "pluralistic democracy" in that country.

For the West Europeans, as for Kissinger, pluralism meant a government freed from control by the radical elements of the AFM and by the Communist Party of Portugal. That government was soon established in September 1975 following the violence, crises, and instability of the previous months—not unlikely promoted by the CIA and other Western intelligence services.

Meanwhile West European political parties like the Social Democrats were also active. On August 2, just as the Portuguese crisis was building to a climax, the Social Democratic leaders established in Stockholm a Committee for Friendship and Solidarity with Democracy and Socialism in Portugal.

Participating in the meeting, which followed the Helsinki Summit Conference, were Harold Wilson, British Prime Minister; Helmut Schmidt, West German Chancellor; Willy Brandt, Chairman of the German Social Democratic Party; Olof Palme, Swedish Prime Minister; Bruno Kreisky, Austrian Chancellor; Francois Mitterand, leader of the French Socialist Party; and, of course, Mario Soares. At a followup meeting in London during early September, just as the acceptable pluralistic government was taking power in Portugal, the European Social Democrats pledged financial and moral support for the Portuguese Socialist Party. By this time, according to a report by the *New York Times'* Robert Semple, the Brandt party had already quietly given the Soares party several million dollars worth of office supplies, newsprint, typewriters, and cash.

Although European Social Democrats presumably would have funds of their own for intervention in Portugal, they also appear to have served as conduits for getting CIA money into that country. Indeed, one possibility is that Kissinger's encouragement of intervention by the Europeans was meant to pave the way for more substantial CIA intervention—using the Europeans as cover.

According to a report by the *New York Times'* Leslie Gelb published on September 25, 1975, the CIA had transferred to the Portuguese Socialist Party and other Portuguese political organizations several million dollars in each of the last several months. The report, attributed to four official sources in Washington, added that Western European trade unions were also being used as conduits for CIA money for Portugal. These unions might well be some of those that belong to the International Confederation of Free Trade Unions headquartered in Brussels—generally regarded as the European trade union structure of the Social Democratic parties—and probably some of the European-based International Trade Secretariats.

By October 7, 1975, the foreign ministers of the EEC countries meeting in Luxembourg agreed to a first-aid package for Portugal equivalent to $180 million at low interest over the next two years. By late October the Ford Administration had requested Congressional approval of $85 million for Portugal, and other financial assistance has included a $100 million loan from the European Free Trade Association, with Sweden and Switzerland making the biggest contributions. More aid will likely follow installation of the new government.

Even after the right wing of the Portuguese military services were able to seize the pretext of a supposed "Communist plot" in late November 1975 and to disarm and dismantle the radical military units, the European Social Democratic parties continued their support for the Portuguese Socialist Party. Meeting in Oporto on March 13–14, 1976, right in the middle of the electoral campaign for the new Portuguese parliament, Brandt, Palme, Kreisky, and the others reiterated their solidarity with the Portuguese Socialist Party and without doubt contributed to the victory of the Soares party in the elections on April 25. Also participating in the March conference was Otto Kersten, long-time leader of the International Confederation of Free Trade Unions.

With the Portuguese Socialist Party now embarking on minority parliamentary government in the midst of grave economic crisis and the difficulties of absorbing the half-million immigrants and returnees from Angola, and even with the strong, Gaullist-style presidency safely occupied by the military leader of the rightist victory in November, stability in Portugal of the type favorable to Western interests would still appear to be a serious concern for the CIA and the American government.

Already there are signs that the forces adversely affected by the radical economic programs adopted during the 18 months following the coup against fascism are regaining their strength. Whether they succeed or not in forcing a return to private capitalism where it was eliminated is uncertain. Their success will depend in part on whether the more advanced provisions of the new Constitution are enforced. The conservative decree of the final "provisional" cabinet in July 1976, limiting workers' control of industry against the spirit if not the letter of the Constitution, is one ominous indicator.

Almost certainly the struggle will intensify for establishment of a social democratic trade union movement, controlled by the Socialist Party and affiliated with the ICFTU, as a rival for the Communist Party–dominated Intersindical, which since January 1975 has been the only recognized national labor confederation. Political warfare will also continue in other institutions such as youth and student organizations, professional and cultural societies, and the public information media.

Plenty of work remains for the CIA and its Western European

allies in their efforts to prevent in Portugal the continuing left-ward trend along the Mediterranean. The first task of disarming the radical military units and preventing the spread of workers' control and institutions of popular power seems to have been achieved. The Communist Party of Portugal has had only limited success in elections, and union among left-wing parties has also been limited. For the time being NATO and Western European capitalist solidarity has been preserved in Portugal, at least partially thanks to intervention and "systematic, active encouragement" from the Western Europeans and the CIA.

Of very high priority in the immediate future for the CIA and its allies will be the prevention of a working coalition between the Socialist Party and the Communist Party of Portugal on the order of the Italian or French varieties. Should the current animosity prevailing between these two parties begin to diminish, or should a common enemy such as Spinola's Portuguese Liberation Army based in Spain become a real threat and thereby unite the two parties, intensified political intervention will be needed again. Continuing efforts to discredit and divide the forces supporting the presidential campaign of Otelo Saraiva de Carvalho should also be expected.

With earlier efforts now bearing fruit, but with a critical period ahead, Whipple, Lawler, Marques, and their colleagues may well find themselves with even more important and subtle requirements for secret intervention.

The Turning Point: The Richard Welch Affair

Introduction

When three masked gunmen drove into the wealthy Athens suburb of Psychico in December 1975 and coolly assassinated the CIA Chief of Station Richard S. Welch, they sent chills down the spines of many thousands of operatives around the world. But even in the immediate panic, the CIA brass in Langley set out on one of their most clever media campaigns. Although Welch had been named in the *Athens News,* an English-language newspaper, as the local Chief of Station one month before his death, the Agency knew he had also been named by *CounterSpy* magazine as the Chief of Station in Peru, nearly a year earlier.

The CIA quickly disseminated the *CounterSpy* "connection" and in a short-term victory managed to turn Welch into a martyr, using his death to frighten many of its would-be reformers in Congress and the press. The killing gave Congress an excuse to back down and the press—at least in the United States—a pretext to lose interest.

Immediately after the assassination, a CIA spokesman announced to the Associated Press that "we've had an American gunned down by other Americans fingering him," and a White House representative stated that the death was at least in part a result of the publication of the name.

Only later did the truth come out. Well before the *Athens News* published the letter naming Welch, the underground organization that killed him had been watching his residence, which for years had been known in Athens as the home of the CIA's Chief of Station in Greece. In fact, the CIA had even warned Welch at the outset of his tour in Athens that his house was marked, and he replied that he preferred to remain living there.

Moreover, David Phillips, the head of the Association of Former Intelligence Officers and arch-foe of *CounterSpy,* was reported in the papers shortly after Welch's death to have received a letter from him only four days previously, inviting him to "come visit us in our home, which is very pleasant, if somewhat notorious." Moreover, *Diplomatic Lists* published by the Greek Foreign Ministry confirm the fact that the house was indeed well known. As early as November 1959, the Chief of Station, Laughlin Austin Campbell, lived two doors away, and in December 1968, Chief of Station James M. Potts moved to the house which Welch later occupied.

The articles which follow detail the drama, including the communique of the group which staged the assassination. Paul Jacobs' article demonstrates where the moral outrage should lie. Morton H. Halperin's research exposed the media manipulation by the CIA. But it took more than a year for the full truth to come out.

The Letter to the *Athens News*

by The Committee of Greeks and Greek Americans to Prevent Their Country, Their Fatherland From Being Perverted to the Uses of the CIA

Dear Reader:

The destructive activities of the CIA toward the Greek people and the wrecking of our democratic freedoms by this same organization in the past has been written about in detail in the press this past year. Much of this information is now out of date. The CIA continues its evil work here and in this first letter to you we intend to expose some of it to the light of public infamy. We have contacts in other countries who have helped us collect this material, but we have been able to gather most of the facts here. We have concentrated on observing this enemy.

We have listened at the American Club in Kifissia, really a hangout for spies, at certain cocktail circuits where the CIA

[This Letter to the Reader was published in the English-language *Athens News* of November 25, 1975, under the heading "Greek Committee Reveals the CIA Menace in Athens."]

agents who stick together do not imagine we can deduce what they are saying, and to a small extent, when needed, have we had to shadow their coming and going from their buildings. First we intend to expose the native American agents who have been sent against us and save the Greek Americans for a later time.

Richard Welch

The CIA agents have been talking for months about the new head of their group who has been here since the summer. He followed Mr. Stacy Hulse, Jr. whose job was to keep General Ioannidis in control, but he failed at this. For punishment he has now been sent off to the small CIA group which they call a station in Canada. The Athens group or station is now under the head of Mr. Richard S. Welch. He is from Connecticut, where he was born in 1929. Soon after he graduated from Harvard University in 1951, he came to Athens where he worked using JUSMAGG, the military aid organization, as a cover. It is for the contacts that he made at that time and also because he speaks Greek that he has been sent back here again. His job is to see that the Karamanlis government does not get out of control. He also served in Cyprus from 1960 to 1964. He then passed a number of years in Latin America where he helped to control the countries there on behalf of American imperialist interests. Just before he came to Greece, he was in Peru. There was a bloody revolt against the government of that country during which many people lost their lives. It was charged that CIA was behind this revolt. It was time for Mr. Welch to leave Latin America even if Mr. Hulse had not failed in Greece.

Mr. Welch now uses American Embassy cover for his activities. He is listed as a First Secretary there. He lives in the usual CIA house where all CIA Station Leaders have lived at No. 5 Queen Frederika in Psychico. The reader can telephone him for his comments on these accusations at 671-2055.

Ronald Estes

Another change in the CIA organization is signified by the arrival of Mr. Ronald E. Estes. He also worked in this country several years back, usually in the north of Greece. He used the JUSMAGG cover. He then served in Cyprus with Mr. Welch. After that he joined the State Department for cover reasons and in 1966 and 1967 he was in Prague under the cover of an economic officer. After a few years in America at the CIA center he served in Beirut as an economic and commercial officer in the American Embassy before coming to Athens. He is again under the cover of JUSMAGG. Mr. Estes is known in CIA circuits as an expert in Russian intelligence matters. In Athens he first worked for a short period with Mr. Hulse, helping that station leader with the impossible job of controlling General Ioannidis. He is now working with Mr. Welch on the Greek matters. Mr. Estes also lives in the well known CIA house on No. 12 Queen Frederika in Psychico. The reader can telephone him for his defense against these accusations at No. 671-4654.

William Lofgren

Another new CIA agent to arrive in Athens is Mr. William S. Lofgren. This agent was completely exposed in the Greek newspapers almost as soon as he arrived here. His previous service in India and Lebanon was also exposed as was the fact that he was expected to work on the Chinese, the Arabs, and the Greeks. For the cover for his activities he uses the American Embassy political office. He lives at No. 5 Kalvou in Psychico. His comments can be obtained through telephone No. 671-3980.

When the last agent who was second in command of the CIA station in Athens, Mr. James Baldwin, left the country after many years, he was succeeded by Mr. Robert Larson who only remained a short time. Mr. Larson was then succeeded by Mr. James MacWilliams. He is a junior officer, but he has served already in India.

He is an expert in Russian and Greek matters at the same time. He lives in another CIA house at No. 13 Karsoli Dimitriou in Philothei. He uses the cover of the Embassy political office too. His comments can be obtained from his telephone No. 39-23-90.

A check of the JUSMAGG telephone book confirms that many of the CIA agents exposed in the past—particularly the experts in Russian matters as Mr. John Palavich, Mr. Stephen Winsky, and Mr. William Bright—are still in Athens and at work against us and friendly countries.

We have in mind next however to expose particularly Americans of Greek origin. We believe that there remain a few new agents of native American origin who we are checking on and if we can establish that they are CIA agents in truth, we will include information on them along with that on the Greek Americans.

With a firm plea for your support,
Committee of Greeks and Greek-Americans to Prevent Their Country, Their Fatherland, From Being Perverted to the Uses of the CIA.

News Stories:
Athens

From the Athens News

U.S. EMBASSY AIDE ASSASSINATED
(December 24, 1975)

A SPECIAL ASSISTANT TO THE UNITED STATES AM-
BASSADOR IN ATHENS, MR. RICHARD WELCH, WAS
ASSASSINATED OUTSIDE HIS HOME IN THE ATH-
ENS SUBURB OF PSYCHICO LATE YESTERDAY AF-
TERNOON BY ONE OF THREE UNIDENTIFIED,
MASKED GUNMEN, WHO WERE SEEN SPEEDING
AWAY IN WHAT WAS DESCRIBED AS A "BLACK"
CAR AFTERWARDS

The motive for the killing is not immediately known and police,
aided by U.S. Embassy security staff, have begun an investiga-

[These articles appeared in the *Athens News* on the dates
given, and typify stories around the world, including the
mention of *CounterSpy* from the beginning.]

tion into the killing. The immediate vicinity of the shooting has been cordoned off by order of the Athens Suburbs Chief of Police and the Athens Suburbs Security Police.

Police sources say that the gunmen fired three times, at point-blank range. One of the bullets apparently penetrated the victim's brain. *Athens News* received confirmation from the Athens Emergency Hospital that Mr. Welch was dead on arrival at the hospital.

Mr. Welch was born in Connecticut and graduated from Harvard University. He spoke fluent Greek and originally came to Athens with the JUSMAGG military aid program. He has also served in Latin America prior to his present posting in Greece.

Mr. Welch was returning home after attending a reception at the residence of the American Ambassador. He had just left his car when the gunmen drew up and opened fire.

GROUP CLAIMS CREDIT FOR ASSASSINATION
(December 24, 1975)

An organization called the "Union of Officers for the National Ideal," has claimed credit for the attack on the American diplomat Richard Welch. The group made the claim in an anonymous telephone call Wednesday morning to an Athens evening newspaper.

On the other hand, a [Greek] government communique published Wednesday morning declared that "the cowardly assassins of the American diplomat Richard Welch are, at least from the point of view of their mentality, foreigners to the Greek people, to honor, and the national interests, which they have tried to injure."

RICHARD WELCH WAS THE CIA CHIEF IN GREECE
(December 25, 1975)

Richard Welch, the "special assistant to the U.S. Ambassador" in Athens who was assassinated in the Greek capital Tuesday by three unknown assailants, was actually an official of the CIA, according to the Intelligence Documentation Center, a private group in Washington which was founded three years ago by critics of American intervention in Vietnam, and which specializes in revealing the activities of the American intelligence services.

CounterSpy, a publication of the group, identified Mr. Welch as the CIA chief in Peru from 1972 to the beginning of this year.

Last February 8, while Mr. Welch was still in the American Embassy in Lima, a spokesman for the Peruvian Ministry of Foreign Affairs intimated to a Washington press conference that the CIA had been implicated in the rioting that took place in Peru at the time.

The spokesman, Mr. Oscar Faura, charged that the disorders had been orchestrated with a view to provoking tension with Chile.

Until now the Department of State has refused to specify Mr. Welch's exact duties in the Embassy in Athens. The CIA has equally held back from any comment.

GOVERNMENT VOWS TO DISCOVER THE KILLERS
(December 27, 1975)

The bullets of the unknown assassins of Richard Welch, have caused great concern in government circles.

From the moment Premier Karamanlis was informed of the event, he kept continual telephone contact with Foreign Minister Bitsios and Press Undersecretary Lambrias. According to authoritative sources, the Premier has decided to discontinue his Christmas vacation and return to Athens as soon as possible.

Tuesday night the Greek government issued a statement deploring the crime and assuring that the Greek authorities would do all in their power to discover the assassins.

Describing the assassins as cowards, the statement stressed that they could not possibly belong to the Greek people, whose honor and national interests they have deliberately tried to harm.

The statement added that the Greek government and appropriate authorities will do all in their power to discover the hideous criminals.

The Ministers of Coordination and National Defense, P. Papaligouras and E. Averof, acting on instructions of the Prime Minister late Tuesday night, called on the U.S. Ambassador in Athens, Jack Kubisch, and expressed deep sympathy at Welch's assassination.

A. Vakalopoulos, diplomatic counselor to the President of the Republic, also called on the U.S. Ambassador and expressed Mr. Tsatsos' grief.

Public Order Minister Solon Ghikas announced yesterday that action has been taken from the very first moment for the apprehension of the assassins. Measures have also been taken to prevent them from escaping abroad.

Meanwhile, a meeting was held yesterday morning at the Public Order Ministry. The participants in the meeting included police and gendarmerie officials and members of the National Security Service (YPEA).

During the meeting it is believed that existing evidence was closely examined and measures of further action considered.

The murder has also resulted in extra police protection for all U.S. diplomats in Athens.

Police sources said that extra protection is also being provided for 10 Russians whose names were distributed in a report handed out by a group called "The Committee to keep Greece Greek." The Russians were accused of using their diplomatic cover here for spying activities.

Welch's assassination is reportedly thought to have some connection with the recent kidnapping of ministers of OPEC countries.

Meanwhile, the American Embassy issued the following communique yesterday morning:

"The U.S. Embassy confirms that R. S. Welch, an envoy of the American Embassy, was shot and killed right in front of his home by unknown assailants.

"The Embassy is keeping contact with the authorities who are searching for the culprits. The Embassy will not disclose further details until the outcome of the search is made known and until close relatives are informed."

REWARD OFFERED FOR WELCH'S KILLER
(December 30, 1975)

The Greek government today put a price on the heads of three unidentified men who shot dead American CIA agent Richard Welch in an Athens suburb last Tuesday.

The Ministry of Public Order said a decree in the official *Gazette* offered five million drachmas (about £75,000 sterling) for information leading to the arrest of the three men.

One to two million drachmas (about £15,000 to 30,000 sterling) would be paid for any information which might help police in their investigation.

The three men killed Welch as he returned home from a Christmas party. They fled in a car and six days after the murder police are still seeking them.

Mr. Welch, 46, held the post of Special Assistant to U.S. Ambassador Jack Kubisch but the White House has acknowledged he was a Central Intelligence Agency man.

A secret political group claimed responsibility yesterday for the assassination. The group said in a statement sent to foreign news agencies that the "execution" was to demonstrate that the Greek government and Army were under the control of U.S. imperialism.

The group called itself "Organization of 17 November," after the date of a 1973 student revolt against the military regime of former president George Papadopoulos.

WELCH'S BROTHER PUTS BLAME ON *COUNTERSPY*
(January 1, 1976)

The family of slain Central Intelligence Agency official Richard S. Welch knew of his work but never thought much about the potential danger of the job, his brother said.

"I heard about his death after finishing Christmas shopping in downtown Providence," George P. Welch, a 47-year-old salesman, said Tuesday. "It came as a tremendous shock."

"He never said he had any feeling about danger although in retrospect he must have known there was some. He just thought the job he did was very important. He was a very patriotic fellow."

Richard Welch, 46, was shot down by three masked men in Athens last week. His body was returned to the United States Tuesday for burial at Arlington national cemetery.

In an interview, George Welch said he believed his brother joined the Agency shortly after his graduation from Harvard University in 1951. He said his brother told him he was joining the Agency but never discussed details of his work.

Richard Welch, born in Hartford, Connecticut, grew up in nearby Providence and attended classical high school, getting honor grades. "He was a hard worker," George Welch said. "He studied Greek in school. He loved Greece."

Welch said he considered it wrong for *CounterSpy*, a Washington publication, to publish the names of agents, including that of his brother. The magazine had disclosed Welch's role before he was slain and a similar description was printed in the English-language *Athens News*.

"For a foreign paper like *Athens News*, there's not much you can do," he said. "But for an American publication to put another American in jeopardy is reprehensible," said George Welch.

The Fifth Estate
Responds

by *The Organizing Committee for a Fifth Estate*

The attempts of CIA officials, both current and retired, and their supporters to cast the Fifth Estate with even partial responsibility for the death of the CIA Station Chief in Athens, Greece, is an attack on all Americans who have had the courage to voice opposition to this secret police force and the anti-democratic corporate empire it serves. In an hysterical campaign, similar to classical CIA propaganda operations abroad, the CIA is attempting to shift the onerous history of 30 years of villainous rampage against the people of the world to those who have exposed the truth of CIA murders and lies.

Reactionary elements of the Press have been stampeded into thoughtless commentary in contradiction to the facts known to their own journalists. Right-wing thugs have threatened to kill members of the Fifth Estate, Congress, and a Presidential candidate. Even the President has lent his support to this campaign.

[This press release was issued by the publishers of *Counter-Spy* magazine on December 28, 1975, in Washington, D.C.]

But the Press overreacting to confusing events is nothing new or unmanageable. The ravings of rightist cowards rarely initiate political change. And we doubt if this is the first or last time Jerry Ford will be deceived by the CIA.

We are not intimidated and this campaign will ultimately fail.

We are grieved that Mrs. Welch is now a widow and her family is without a father. We do not condone or support this shooting. But we do understand why Mr. Welch was killed. This CIA Station Chief died as a direct result of world-wide hostility which the CIA has helped generate against the United States. As a CIA operative, Welch knew that his role in coordinating covert operations to secure the exploitive investment climate for multinational corporations could, someday, lead to his death.

Throughout the world people are demonstrating that the age of economic exploitation and political repression brought by CIA assassination, *coups d'état*, secret wars, massive illegal domestic spying, lies, and deception must now come to a close. The possibility of violent retribution for this exploitation and repression must now be a fact of life with CIA agents.

For many Greeks, the name of the CIA brings back horrid memories of U.S.-supported torture, brutal imprisonment, and death from a CIA-installed military dictatorship. These memories are freshened by Greek anger at CIA intervention recently in Cyprus. Such emotions based on political fact are felt by many throughout the world. In Greece, these emotions led to months of demonstrations and official denouncements before this shooting.

However, if anyone is to blame for Mr. Welch's death, it is the CIA that sent him to Greece to spy and intervene in the affairs of the Greek people and to rendezvous with a death symbolic of the horrible essence of the CIA. When the *Athens News* publicly identified him, there was no excuse for the CIA to keep him there. The blood of Mr. Welch is on the hands of the CIA and its supporters and not on the pages of *CounterSpy*.

CounterSpy, the quarterly journal of the Fifth Estate, has a policy of publishing names of CIA operatives in its feature "CIA Around the World: We Thought You'd Like to Know." Any names of CIA officials published by the foreign or American press will be reprinted in *CounterSpy*. We reprint the names to demonstrate to the American people the pervasiveness of CIA activities. Reprinting names reinforces political fact and demystifies the power of the CIA. The Station Chief in most countries is well known to both the governments, political parties, foreign press as well as those opposed to the CIA presence in their countries. Only those who live in the United States are denied this information. We believe Americans have a right to know what acts are being committed in our name and who are the perpetrators of these acts. Reprinting these names is one way for us to protest the existence of the CIA and the covert actions it implements without sanction from the American people.

Richard Welch was identified first in 1967 in a German book, *Who's Who in the CIA,* which has been widely distributed throughout the world. More recently his name appeared in Spanish language newspapers in Peru. Maryknoll priests while in Peru jotted his and other CIA operatives' names down and during a visit to Washington, D.C., asked us for confirmation that Welch was indeed with the CIA. By using documents published by the Department of State and freely available to the public, we made this confirmation and reprinted his name in *CounterSpy.* But his move to Greece was unknown to us and we have had no contact with the Greek newspaper that identified him. It is a fragile coincidence that links *CounterSpy* to these events.

If the CIA believes it can continue this charade of focusing blame on its opposition, it is foolish. The questions which will be asked once the hysteria has dissipated are: Why was Richard Welch recently transferred to Greece? What has the CIA planned for the people in that region of the world? What is the CIA doing there now? What was Richard Welch, and what are those who have replaced him, doing in Peru?

If the CIA continues to intervene in the affairs of all countries, including Greece and Peru, or to suppress national patriotic liberation movements and the popular opposition to the CIA and its corporate masters, similar events will undoubtedly occur. The movement against the CIA is not responsible for these occurrences. The CIA, with its murderers and torturers, has now added the blood of one of its own to the long list of victims it has denied life.

Communique

by The November 17
Revolutionary Organization

[EDITORS' NOTE: As the communique notes, the day of the assassination of Richard Welch, this group sent its first communique to the Athens media. Although it was referred to in the *Athens News,* it was never published, in Greece or elsewhere. Several weeks later the group apparently mailed this lengthy communique to numerous media, including *Liberation.* For many months the editors of *Liberation* debated the genuineness of the communique. Nearly a year later, a police officer of the deposed *junta,* noted for his brutality, was murdered with, according to Greek authorities, the same weapon. *Liberation* decided the communique was authentic, and published large parts of it. While the communique appears genuine, many Greek leftists do not believe that this organization was part of their movement. The entire communique is published here for the first time; the portions which did not appear in *Liberation* are in brackets.]

> [This communique was issued in early 1976, with copies mailed to various newspapers and magazines. On December 24, 1976, large portions of it were published, in French, in *Liberation,* in Paris, France.]

[The Truth about the Execution of Richard Welch (Chief of the CIA Station in Greece) and the Manipulation of Public Opinion in Greece and Abroad]

[On December 23, 1975, Richard Welch, First Secretary at the American Embassy—but in fact Chief of the CIA Station in Greece—was returning home with his wife and driver after a reception given by the U.S. Ambassador. At the moment he was entering his house, a commando unit of three members of the Greek Revolutionary Organization "November 17" executed him, immobilizing his wife and driver. A mystery has intentionally been created around this action. Through a broad and stupefying operation, the Greek government, with the collaboration of the press, has been able to bolster, in an odd way, the line inside the CIA: Welch had some enemies inside the CIA, who shot him, or he was killed by the KGB. Even today, two months after the execution, few people in Greece or abroad know the truth.]

[Facing this mystery and confusion, we find ourselves obligated to appeal to the foreign press to reestablish the truth. For the first time, we are going to explain exactly how we carried out this action. We are going to explain why the mystery and confusion exist. And we are going to prove through the details we reveal for the first time that the letter in the *Athens News* had no link whatsoever with our operation. It is merely a coincidence that this exposé appeared a month before our operation. Our decision, as well as our investigation of Welch, came well before, as the explanations below will prove, and which can be verified by the Americans and the Greek Criminal Investigation Department.]

[The day after the action, the newspapers discussed the event on the front page, and could not hide the real activities of Welch, because of the revelations in the *Athens News*. They began to attack the criminal activities of the CIA in this country in mystery-style articles. They wrote that Welch was the instigator of events in Cyprus in 1964; that he was a specialist in the "destabilization" and overthrow of governments, that he was working closely with Ambassador Kubisch, who was Kissinger's advisor for Chilean affairs during the Allende regime, etc.]

[So these articles on the CIA and its criminal activities in Greece led more and more people to justify and to approve of the execution, even within the Karamanlis party. Since the action had these important repercussions, and was generating approval and even enthusiasm among the masses, the government decided to act quickly. The first measure was to forbid the publication of all information on Welch. This measure was respected in part by the newspapers, which nevertheless continued to discuss the CIA over the next several weeks. At the same time, the government has interrogated, searched, and followed approximately 2,000 left activists; put up a reward for us of the fabulous (for Greece) sum of five million drachma; and undertaken a most important operation of confusion and manipulation. They passed "information" to Greek journalists, to "prove" this action was an internal CIA affair, or the consequence of a struggle with the KGB.]

[The government did everything possible to spread confusion, to create mystery, and to hide the truth: that simple activists with relatively simple means could have "hit" the CIA Chief of Station in Greece.]

[So the unfolding of the operation has been described a dozen times in the newspapers in mystery-style articles with details which give the reader the impression that something is fishy. The newspapers invented theories: the fact that three bullets were shot proves that we were professionals from the secret services, who are the only people who act this way. They asked: How did we know the driver was not armed, and that he was not going to shoot back? Just another proof that we were CIA agents. How did we know the time that Welch was supposed to return? We were waiting for him at the very second he got back. So, we had an informant in the Ambassador's house. This action was too well organized, too scientific to be done by Greek activists, who are not capable of such precision. A "liberal" newspaper considered it suspect that Mrs. Welch and the driver were not also executed. Professionals do not leave any witnesses unless they are sure they will not talk. All of this crap finally created confusion and doubt in the masses.]

[Yet all the newspapers knew the truth from the very first day! The very evening of the operation, we sent to all of them some political texts where we explained the reasons for this operation. The same evening we called three newspapers claiming credit for the action and telling them where to go to get the texts that we left for them in different parts of Athens. Finally, that same evening, we distributed tracts in other areas of Athens.]

[Three days later, the 26th of December, faced with the attitude of the press, we sent a letter to the newspapers denouncing all the lies which were appearing. The press did not mention any of this, and on the contrary continued their romance. Some journalists, even from left-wing newspapers, claimed that they were holding information from absolutely reliable sources, proving it was the CIA, and challenging anyone to contradict them. They were issuing challenges, but they were carefully hiding the truth.]

[In these texts, we explained that we had decided to execute Richard Welch as an example, because as CIA Chief of Station in Athens he was responsible, as well as the other professional agents, for all the crimes committed by American Imperialism, and particularly by the CIA against our people. Among them, the most important: setting up and supporting the Fascist Dictatorship for seven years; and the coup in Cyprus in July 1975, with thousands dead and two million refugees. Welch, as a Station Chief, had a direct responsibility. He was not a minor official, a simple executive.]

[The main problem in Greece is its dependence on American Imperialism. The Karamanlis government has never done anything about this, and finds itself tied to the Americans. Getting out of NATO remains only words. The American bases and the ships of the Sixth Fleet are still here. Even more, Americans, considering Greece as a safe country, are in the process, according to the Greek newspapers, of moving the General Staff of the CIA for the Middle East and the offices of the multinationals from Beirut to Athens. The graffiti "exo i Americani" ("out with the Americans"), which was the main cry during the popular insurrection of November 1973 and which was still dominant after the fall of the dictatorship, has been seen by millions of demonstrators going past the American Embassy this last November 17. The Americans are still the masters here; the government cannot do anything; all that is left for us is to go on with the struggle against them, using simultaneously both pacific and legal means of struggle, and other means of struggle.]

On the other hand, neither Welch's wife nor his driver had any direct responsibility for the crimes committed by the CIA against our people. That is why he, and only he, was executed. And these are the unique reasons we chose the method we did. We wanted to exclude any possibility of harming others, even by accident. We wanted to carry out the action correctly and efficiently. And that is why we had to take more risks in stopping our car and getting out of it, instead of choosing an easier way, such as throwing a bomb or a grenade, or using a machine gun from our car. In such a case we might have hit someone besides Welch.

[The Investigation and the Operation]

The former Station Chief, Stacy Hulse, left Athens on May 30, 1975. He was living in the same house, 5 Vassilis Frederikis, in Psychico. Welch arrived in Athens around the 15th of June. He lived for three weeks in the villa of the Deputy Chief of the CIA, Ronald Estes, number 12 of the same street. For a month or so, the villa was closed. Welch moved in to number 5 on Wednesday, July 9. His driver was also different; he was not the same one Hulse used to have, contrary to what the newspapers wrote. We learned the name of Welch and his function through a very easy means, which we will not reveal for the moment.

Welch left with his driver every morning around 8:30 A.M., and returned between 6:30 and 7:30 P.M. His driver would park his own car, an AMI-6, orange, registered as BE-9339, along the sidewalk, near the villa. He would get the black Ford, registered as CD3-131, out of the garden, and drive Welch to the Embassy. Welch went out at night very seldom, contrary to the Deputy, who went out nearly every night. Welch was always home before 11:00 P.M. On weekends, he would go out during the day, using, since the end of September, a second car, a white Mustang registered as CD3-181, which he kept in the garage.

[What struck us was that these professional killers considered Greece so safe that they never took any security measures. We thought they must have had some bodyguards, but nothing. They felt safe, like at home. Only after the November 17 demonstration did they become scared, and barricade themselves at home. Welch did not go out for the next two weeks, even on weekends, and did not park his car along the sidewalk, outside the villa, as he used to do fairly often before.]

[On July 27, Sunday, Welch ate lunch at 1:30 P.M. with his father at the Theoxenis de Kifissia Restaurant. He drove his car. He never took any security measures, except that he always looked intently at the people who passed him. He wore grey pants and a blue summer shirt. As he had parked the car a bit away, and his father was tired, he walked about 50 meters to the car and backed it down to his father.]

Welch went to the movies on Tuesday, November 11, at 6:30 P.M. (to the Astron Theater in the Ambelokipi area), with his wife and another woman, to see *Godfather II.* That night he was driving his white Mustang, which he parked along the sidewalk, near the theater, leaving his key on the dashboard. They sat in the balcony and left about 10:00 P.M. That night, the black Ford was parked along the sidewalk in front of the main entrance to the villa, and when they arrived home around 10:30, the conditions for the operation were ideal. While Welch was parking the Mustang in the garage, the two women went into the house; then he came out through the garage door, walked 15 meters in the darkness toward the black Ford to park it in the garden. We passed by him while he was walking, and it would have been very easy for us to shoot him. There was nobody around.

We give these details to show that we had decided on the operation and begun the investigation of Welch as soon as he arrived in Athens, that is to say, far before the publication of the *Athens News* letter of November 23.

The Operation

The operation itself happened as follows. The car we used was neither a Mercedes nor a Fiat, as described in the press. It was a light green Simca that we had "expropriated" on December 12, in the Pagrati area. The night of December 23, we realized that Welch had gone out. The black Ford was not in the garden as it was every day after 7:30 P.M., and the driver's car was parked by the sidewalk. We deduced that Welch had gone to some reception with the driver. We did not know if there were two, three, or four in the car, but our action plan covered these possibilities. We parked the car around 9:00 P.M. on the left side of Mazaraki Street, approximately halfway down the street, and we waited. We knew he would pass by this place, as he always did, and we would wait till 11:00 P.M. at the latest. At 10:23, we saw the black Ford, and we let it pass by. When it got to the intersection of Vassileos Pavlou and Mazaraki streets, we started the car and followed them slowly. We let them go down further a little and they parked in front of the garden door, perpendicular to the sidewalk in order to go into the garden. The driver got out of the car, opened the left rear door, and Mrs. Welch got out; then he turned to open the gate of the garden. At that precise moment, we turned left, and we parked slowly, right behind the Ford, on the left side of the street. The three of us got out of the car immediately, with our faces covered. As they saw us, the driver turned, and said, like it was a joke, "What's happening?" The comrade who was supposed to fire, ordered, "Hands up!" and went over to the right door, where he saw Welch, who had just gotten out of the car. The second comrade threatened Mrs. Welch and the driver with his machine gun. The third of us came around on the right to cut off any flight by Welch to the main door of the villa. The comrade who was to shoot, came closer to Welch and ordered again, "Hands up!" Welch, who spoke good Greek, answered in English, "What?" At this point the comrade fired three shots in rapid succession with his pistol, a Colt .45. With the first shot, Welch fell down. The driver, as soon as he heard the first shot, hid behind the Ford. Mrs. Welch remained still, near us, looking at us. She did not say anything and did not move. Immediately, we went back into the car, and left as follows: we turned left on Tsakona Street and left again into Narkissou Street. Straight ahead till Amarylidos where we went left and then right onto Yakinton Street, where we abandoned the car, near the corner of Papadiamanti Street. From there, we drove away in another car, taking all our belongings.

As incredible as it seems, the Simca that we used was not found by the police for more than a week after the action, even though it was less than one kilometer from the scene of the action, and did not have a license plate. In passing along Kifissia Avenue, which is a main street, it could still be seen. A week later, December 30, we decided to call the newspapers, giving its description. [And we did this so the owner could have it back. We had placed ten cassettes, which were in the car, under the front seat, and we told the newspapers this, because we thought the police might take them and say we stole them. Tuesday, we called *Ta Nea* and *Eleftherotypia*.] The next day, the car was still there, so Thursday evening, we called the English journalist Tonge, and the next day the police took the car.

[The police hid their inability, and did not want to confess that in looking for Fiats and Mercedes, they had failed to discover our car. Two or three days after our phone calls to the newspapers, they announced that they had discovered this Simca, but they said they were not sure it was used in the operation. They even said they left it as a trap, to see who would steal it! They never revealed our phone calls establishing that we were the ones who had carried out the operation.]

We have described the operation in such detail only to show that there is no mystery at all. To show that everything was organized and done in a very simple way. To show that it was us who carried out this operation.

The government, the press, and the political parties dare not say the truth—and this is the significance and the impact of the action on the population. They have preferred talking about "instigators" of the Junta, because they realized that their supporters and the common people approved of our action, even asking themselves why it had not been done earlier, in view of the enormous crimes committed by the CIA against the Greek people. And this was the logical and simple thing which people had begun to think, before the newspapers began to "doubt."

Who Is
Richard Welch?

by Paul Jacobs*

On January 17, 1969, the FBI helped murder Black Panther
member John Huggins in a dining hall at UCLA.

Oh, an FBI agent did not actually pull the trigger—that was
done by a member of US, a black nationalist group. But, mor-
ally, the FBI must share responsibility in his death, for the Bureau now admits that it fomented dissension and fierce fights
between US and the Black Panthers.

I was particularly angered by this latest revelation of wrongdoing by a federal agency, because John Huggins was my friend.
A gentle, thoughtful young man, he was on his way to achieving
a position of leadership in the Black Panthers. If he had lived,

[This article appeared in the Winter 1976 issue of *Counter-
Spy* magazine which appeared in February 1976.]

*Paul Jacobs died while this book was in preparation. He
was a valiant fighter for justice, and he and his work will be
long remembered and appreciated.

Huggins would have helped make the organization into an unusually effective voice. With his murder, the Panthers lost, the black community lost—the whole country lost.

Paradoxically, the words that I have used to describe Huggins have the same eulogistic ring as those widely used to characterize Richard Welch, the CIA Station Chief in Athens who was murdered on his doorstep in mid-December shortly after his name was made public by radical periodicals here and abroad. Now portrayed as a victim of a cabal that would betray our national-security apparatus, Welch has been virtually canonized as a national hero.

Not so with John Huggins, victim of truly sinister government activity, who goes unhonored. And what of the FBI? Its complicity in his murder rates just an asterisk in its laundry list of dirty tricks.

Meanwhile, the people who published the fact that Richard Welch was a CIA agent are pilloried savagely, much as were those of us who, a few years ago, charged that U.S. agencies were stirring up trouble in New Left and militant racial organizations. Back then, they called us "paranoid."

Not many people believed what we said about the FBI, despite the hard evidence we assembled. Nor did many believe us when we insisted the CIA was engaged in continuous efforts to assassinate foreign leaders and overthrow certain governments.

Most distressing, however, is the fact that, even after top FBI and CIA officials have admitted past misdeeds, most Americans have yet to understand that such activities are directly related to our government's policies, foreign and domestic.

Instead, it is generally assumed that provocation, assassination and intervention are ugly but necessary tasks carried out by patriotic citizens acting on orders from superiors. Endowed with the federal government's dignity and institutionalized in an agency like the CIA, murder and assassination (known in the trade as "termination with prejudice") have become, in the name of patriotism, ethically acceptable.

As a result, each time the names of CIA agents are made public (it happened again last week), the media and government officials have fulminated. Over and over we have been told that Welch was a gentle man, motivated by the highest of ideals, fluent in many languages, a man on his way up in the CIA hierarchy, a man, who, almost blind in one eye, never fired a weapon himself.

This flood of posthumous praise only diverts the public from the crucial questions, which have to do not with the man's personal attributes but with his political activities.

How does the CIA Station Chief in Greece—or any other Station Chief anywhere in the world, for that matter—spend his days? And nights? And weekends? Did Richard Welch simply sit in his office and translate Greek newspaper stories into English? Is it not possible that this gentle CIA official, who may never have fired a gun himself, issued orders that required other agents, perhaps family men themselves, to fire guns and kill Greeks or Cypriots or South Americans? And if he did this, why should anyone be surprised that he might be killed on his own doorstep?

These are cruel questions, but they need to be answered—along with other, equally significant, questions. For example, the CIA has admitted it tried, on a number of occasions, to kill Fidel Castro. Secret agents failed in that effort, but how many ordinary Cubans who supported Castro did the CIA manage to have murdered? Cuban officials insist such killings took place, and if they are correct, what justification can the CIA offer for those actions?

Even when committed under the banner of patriotism, these are foul deeds. It is those who blow the whistle on the CIA who deserve our praise, not the agents who commit or commission murder in faraway lands.

The FBI is no less sensitive than the CIA about the operations of its *agents provocateur* in domestic politics. I discovered this several years ago when I wrote and narrated a segment of the Great American Dream Machine, a magazine-like TV program that ran on public television. In that report, three paid informers discussed on camera how they had been instructed by FBI agents (whom they named) to provoke violence, blow up bridges, and if necessary kill—all to bring disrepute to the left.

I attempted to get statements from the agents themselves and from the Bureau, but all efforts failed. Then, a couple of days before the telecast date, J. Edgar Hoover joined the agents in threatening libel suits. Hoover even said he was preparing to turn the case over to the Justice Department (which, of course, is exactly what the CIA is now attempting to do with those who published Welch's name).

One hour before the program was to be aired, top management of the Public Broadcasting Service canceled the FBI segment. It was broadcast later by Channel 13 in New York as part of a different kind of program concentrating on the cancellation itself rather than on the propriety of FBI actions.

This change of focus is, of course, what is happening today in the Welch matter: attention is being shifted to the wrong concern. The current furor is over the naming of names, not over the propriety of illicit political activity by federal agencies.

Many people have been hurt by the actions of the CIA and FBI, directly or indirectly. Some have been killed, and not always for very good reasons—my friend John Huggins among them.

For Huggins, I feel deep grief. So, too, for Richard Welch, the human being. But for Richard Welch, the CIA agent, I cannot mourn. After all, no one *has* to work for the CIA or FBI. It's a matter of free choice; if agents don't like their work, they can quit, as some have done.

To me, it seems inevitable that the CIA's political murders should be followed by reprisals against its agents. Perhaps murders and countermurders should not take place in a civilized world, but it should come as no real surprise—nor cause grief— when a CIA agent gets killed in the line of "duty."

When you work for the CIA, as Richard Welch did, you make enemies. And when you make enemies you may get killed—it is as simple as that.

CIA News
Management

by Morton H. Halperin

When Richard Welch arrived in Athens in June 1975, to become
the CIA Station Chief, his superiors at the Agency's Langley,
Virginia, headquarters were concerned about his safety. Their
anxiety did not stem from the fact that some months earlier an
American publication called *CounterSpy* had identified him as
former Station Chief in Peru. Rather, the concern was based on
Welch's choice of residence.

The house in an Athens suburb had been the residence of a
succession of station chiefs over many years and was widely
known in the Greek capital as such. The officials at CIA headquarters, aware of these facts, also knew that anti-Americanism
was at a fever pitch in Greece, with much of the antagonism
directed at the CIA.

It was decided to warn Welch. In keeping with the deference

[This article first appeared in the *Washington Post* on January 23, 1977.]

traditionally accorded a field representative by CIA headquarters, Welch was given no clear, unequivocal order not to move into the old residence. However, sources who have seen the pertinent CIA cable—it has never been released but was referred to briefly in the Senate Intelligence Committee report— say it all but instructed Welch to find another home.

The combined judgment of the people at headquarters, the cable said, was that it would be wisest for him to live elsewhere. Welch was advised in the strongest possible terms that there would be concern for his safety should he move into the traditional residence. Reportedly, there was specific reference to the danger of assassination.

Welch was unpersuaded. Back to Langley went a cable saying that, for administrative convenience and other reasons, Welch would take the chance.

All of this was well known at CIA headquarters when news arrived that Welch had been shot to death as he and his wife returned home late at night from a Christmas party at the American Ambassador's home. But none of this pertinent information was made public at the time. Instead, the CIA swung into action with a classic "disinformation" campaign directed not at some hostile intelligence agency or enemy nation but at the American public.

The CIA's then-press spokesman, Angus Thuermer, began calling the reporters who normally cover the intelligence agencies. Thuermer, as was his habit, spoke on deep background; the newsmen could use the information but not attribute it to any source.

What Thuermer said was that Welch had been identified as a CIA agent in *CounterSpy,* the magazine published by an anti-CIA group called the Fifth Estate. He did not tell the reporters that the CIA had warned Welch not to live in the house in front of which he was killed or that the house was known in Athens as the home of the CIA Station Chief.

Accepted Line

The point here is not whether the assassins learned of Welch's identity because of the *CounterSpy* article or his choice of residence—it is well known that in most capitals, particularly in Western countries, anyone who really wants to learn the CIA chief's name can do so. The point is rather that the CIA engaged in news management immediately after his death to make a political point.

The disinformation campaign was a success. The stories filed out of Washington on Welch's death that night all noted that he had been listed in *CounterSpy.* None mentioned the CIA warnings to Welch as to his place of residence.

The message was underlined when a CIA official, permitting himself to be identified as a "U.S. intelligence source," told the Associated Press that "we've had an American gunned down by other Americans fingering him—right or wrong—as a CIA agent." A few days later the White House press spokesman said Welch's death had come at least in part as a result of publication of his name. The *Washington Post* reflected typical journalistic acceptance of the CIA line when it said editorially that Welch's murder "was the entirely predictable result of the disclosure tactics chosen by certain American critics of the Agency."

Thus, the Welch murder has become part of CIA mythology. The assassination was, of course, tragic and inexcusable, but the aftermath points to the dangers of permitting an intelligence agency to use the flow of information to distort public debate on vital issues.

What They Do:
How and Why

Introduction

Naming names is only part of the effort. Understanding some of
the motivations and mechanics of the Agency is extremely important. The data collection goals of intelligence work, and the
use of vehicles outside the Agency's normal diplomatic or military covers are often overlooked. The following two selections
give some idea of the scope of the intelligence inquiry, quite
apart from direct involvement in the internal affairs of other
nations, and of some of the intricate methods whereby the
Agency operates outside the embassies and the consulates.

KIQs—Key Intelligence Questions—are just that, the fundamental economic, political, and social information the government seeks from its operatives in order to plan policy. In 1976
Philip Agee received through the mail from "an admirer" a copy
of a confidential memorandum by Henry Kissinger outlining
eight KIQs issued by the Director of Central Intelligence. The
memo, which has been authenticated, and an analysis by Agee,
follow this introduction.

The use of businesses owned in whole or in part by the Agency—"proprietaries"—is widespread. John Marks' "The CIA's Corporate Shell Game" gives some idea of the scope and the intricacies of this facet of the espionage routine.

What Uncle Sam Wants to Know About You: The KIQs

by Philip Agee and Henry Kissinger

So often in the business of spying the most important activities —far from being the most exciting—tend to be the most boring and tedious. This is especially so with respect to the critical process of deciding how to allocate the limited number of spies and technical collection devices. Somehow, intelligence collection priorities must be decided on all levels from the individual operations officer managing several different operations to the Director of Central Intelligence and his staff in the CIA Headquarters. For, without the conscious and painfully deliberate "targeting" of intelligence collection "assets," the information the President and other top policy makers need is likely to be incomplete.

> [This document, with Agee's introduction, was first published by the Agee-Hosenball Defence Committee in mid-1977 in London. The authenticity of the document was confirmed by the American Embassy in London to the *Sunday Times* in late 1976.]

One of the main reasons for the establishment of the Central Intelligence Agency in the wake of World War II was to *centralize* the national intelligence effort so as to avoid gaps and overlaps as much as possible. As the President's chief intelligence officer, the Director of Central Intelligence was supposed to coordinate the collection and production of all the intelligence agencies in Washington from the Department of Agriculture's information service to his own CIA. So much for the theory. In practice, no DCI was ever able to coordinate the activities of the entire intelligence community.

According to the final report of the Senate Intelligence Investigating Committee under Frank Church, each of the Directors of Central Intelligence failed to coordinate and effectively to direct the overall intelligence collection and production efforts because they all lacked sufficient statutory or executive authority to overcome the special provincial interests of the military and others who controlled intelligence agencies other than the CIA. The result was, in fact, a system of gaps and overlapping that was both costly and, at times, dangerous.

When William Colby became DCI in 1973, he installed several innovations that he hoped would improve his ability to manage the intelligence community as a whole. For the production of National Estimates, considered to be the highest level and most refined of intelligence reports in that they seek to predict both short- and long-range developments in other countries, Colby established a system of eleven National Intelligence Officers (NIOs), each of whom was responsible to the DCI for intelligence collection and production in his geographical or functional specialty. Colby assigned the NIOs to coordinate the drafting of National Intelligence Estimates among the various agencies of the intelligence community. The NIOs also played an important role in the functioning of another of Colby's innovations, the system known as Key Intelligence Questions (KIQs).

Director Colby's new intelligence management system consisted of a limited number of Key Intelligence Questions that, in theory, would fulfill the most important intelligence needs of national policy makers. Acting for the DCI, who issued the KIQs, the National Intelligence Officers were assigned to coordinate the allocating of resources toward answering the KIQs with representatives from the various collection and production agencies outside the CIA.

For fiscal year 1975 there were a total of 69 KIQs, approximately one-third of which dealt with Soviet foreign policy motivations and military technology. Others dealt with international terrorism and negotiating positions of the different sides in the Arab-Israeli conflict.

Although the report of the Senate Intelligence Investigating Committee revealed that the KIQ system was not notably more successful in achieving reallocation of resources toward priority issues, the questions in themselves are important because they deal with major information needs.

In June 1976 I received from an anonymous sender a State Department document dated 3 December 1974 which contained the CIA's Key Intelligence Questions on economic, financial, and commercial reporting requirements for fiscal year 1975, together with a substantial discussion of each. According to the document, these KIQs had been ratified by the National Security Council Intelligence Committee, chaired by Secretary of State Kissinger. In all, eight economic topics are covered by these KIQs which consist of KIQs No. 56 through 63 of the total of 69 for fiscal year 1975.

On my first reading of the document I was convinced of its authenticity because of the format (I had read hundreds of such Department of State Airgrams while I was in the CIA) and because of the government jargon contained in the text. I wanted to be extremely cautious, however, in order to avoid falling for an embarrassing provocation (in case the document were apocryphal and had been sent to me by the CIA), so I took no action to publish the document until, quite surprisingly, the U.S. Embassy in London confirmed the authenticity of the document I had received anonymously. During the first week of November 1976, my friend and journalist colleague, Mr. Steve Weissman, called at the American Embassy to ask for an interview with the new CIA Chief of Station, Dr. Edward Proctor, whose presence in Britain Mr. Weissman had just discovered. He told the embassy press officer that he wanted to speak to Mr. Proctor about, among other things, the CIA's economic, financial, and commercial intelligence reporting requirements contained in the State Department KIQ document, a copy of which I had given to Mr. Weissman, who was writing an article for the *Sunday Times.*

In an apparent attempt to discredit Mr. Weissman, an officer of the Embassy telephoned the *Sunday Times,* warned that a fake document on the KIQs had been circulating in Europe, and finally agreed to allow a *Sunday Times* reporter to review both

CONFIDENTIAL

the faked document and the original. Mr. Derek Humphry, the *Sunday Times* reporter, read both documents in the Embassy and took notes from the sections of the faked document that had been added by the forger to emphasize that the KIQs were designed to support subversion and economic warfare by the United States against friends. In fact, there was no need to make the original true document any worse. Mr. Humphry confirmed that the text of the document I had received anonymously was the same as the text of the original true document signed by Secretary of State Kissinger and shown to Mr. Humphry in the U.S. Embassy along with the forgery.

On reviewing these intelligence collection requirements, one must keep in mind that although officers of the Department of State are ordered in this document to seek answers to the questions through their normal open sources, diplomatic conversations, and other overt means, the CIA is required to fulfill the very same information needs through spies and other means of espionage. The National Security Agency has the same reporting requirements which it attempts to satisfy through operations to monitor and analyze both government and private communications all over the world.

While not the most gripping document in the world to read, the KIQs clearly show the role of the American intelligence community in support of American companies. Two of the KIQs ask specifically for information on the economic performance of the major non-Communist industrial nations (naming the United Kingdom and others by name), and on the positions these countries are likely to take in coming international trade and financial negotiations. Concerning financial negotiations with the International Monetary Fund, the KIQs ask for information on the objectives of "priority countries" (West Germany, Japan, France, the United Kingdom, and others), and timely reporting on "prepared negotiation strategies including initial proposals and fall-back positions." Information on foreign competition for American companies' exports is, as would be expected, of special interest. Two other KIQs request information on the foreign assets like bank and investment accounts of the major oil exporting countries, particularly the Arabs, on the vulnerabilities of these countries to competitive energy resources, and on the prospects for converting their oil exports into imports of military hardware.

Other KIQs relate to production of raw materials and various primary products, other countries' stockpiling and marketing

CONFIDENTIAL

policies, and to trade balances and political stability in the major LDCs (Less Developed Countries like Brazil, Mexico, and India). Still another KIQ asks for information on production and demand for food and other commodities such as cotton, while in another KIQ the requirements are for data that will help American companies compete more effectively for foreign contracts to build nuclear power plants and pipelines and to sell aircraft.

The following note accompanied the document:

> Dear Sir:
> With this letter I am sending you a document that will be of interest to you. You will understand that the sensitivity of this matter makes it impossible for me to meet you for the time being. Please use this material in any way you wish. I hope I will be able to send you more before too long. The work that you and others like you are doing is very inspiring. I wish you success.
>
> An admirer

AIRGRAM

Classification:
CONFIDENTIAL

Message reference
A-8450
TO: ALL AMERICAN DIPLOMATIC AND CONSULAR POSTS AND USOECD PARIS, USEC BRUSSELS, USNATO BRUSSELS, US MISSION GENEVA, USIAEA VIENNA, USUNIDO VIENNA
FROM: Department of State   Date: 3 December 1974
GDS
ECRP XX
FY 1975 Coordinated Statement of Priority Economic, Financial, and Commercial Intelligence Requirements Worldwide of the Washington Economic Community
Department of State Airgram A-2251, 14 March 1973

The referenced Airgram, the first in this series, commenced with a statement that remains valid:

> The Executive Branch's priority needs for economic intelligence on foreign countries are determined by important US interests and the strategies adopted to pro-

tect or advance them. These interests and strategies
have a new importance resulting from the changed
place of the US economy in the world. US economic
intelligence needs center around the motivations and
assessments of other countries in the economic field.
In particular, reporting is requested on how host-coun-
try domestic and international economic policies and
programs are likely to support or conflict significantly
with US policies and programs. The past is of interest
to the extent that it illuminates these essential ingredi-
ents of US economic policy formulation.

In the intervening period, since March 1973, detailed guidance
has been supplied triannually to eight regions of the world by the
Economic Alert Lists (EALs). (The annual Economic Reporting
Guides, after a poll of representative embassies, have been abolished.) The EALs are prepared by the US Intelligence Board's
Economic Intelligence Committee and include inputs from the
entire Department as executive agent of the Combined Economic Reporting Program (CERP). The current update of the
over-all statement (now on a fiscal year basis) places in context
specific guidance provided subsequently by the Economic Alert
Lists and is intended for all officers charged with responsibility
bearing directly or indirectly on the broad economic/financial/
commercial area.

The general priority subjects set forth below are to a varying
degree applicable to all diplomatic and consular posts. They are
the eight economic topics contained in the Key Intelligence
Questions (KIQs) for FY 1975, issued by the Director of Central
Intelligence, and are designed to be responsive to and to support
the following objective for the intelligence community:
"Provide reliable, timely, and comprehensive information and
assessments relevant to US international economic policy decisions and negotiations."

These questions were formulated, it will be noted, in consulta-
tion with senior policy officers of the principal departments and
entities concerned with international economic relations. Subsequently, they were ratified by the National Security Council
Intelligence Committee which is chaired by Secretary Kissinger.
The KIQs are identified by number for reference purposes: the
order of their listing should not be regarded as implying any
internal priority. By definition, all *Key* Intelligence Questions
are of *major* importance.

CONFIDENTIAL

Washington continues to welcome suggestions as to how, to what extent, and in what manner the US Government efforts at the post or elsewhere can influence attitudes and positions in a manner beneficial to US economic objectives.

> *56. What are the changes in the measures of current performance and leading indicators of future perform-ance of the economies of the major non-communist industrial nations, especially Italy, Japan, Germany, France, the UK, Canada, Norway and Sweden?*

Include these governments' domestic and foreign economic policy responses to those changes, and the likely effect of these responses on the future performance of these economies and the US economy.

The assessment of the current and likely future performance of the major economies and the effect of foreign economic events on the US economy is a task that is routinely performed by the economic intelligence community. The singling out of this task as a Key Intelligence Question for FY 1975 reflects the uncertainties inherent in the world-wide adjustment to the change in the price of oil. The simultaneous pressures of rapid inflation, low or negative rates of growth of output, and wors-ened balances of trade that now impinge on the governments of most of the major industrial nations could conceivably produce a series of mutually inconsistent and self-destructive policy de-cisions that would greatly accelerate existing recessionary forces and threaten to reverse the trend of world economic inte-gration and political cooperation.

The types of information on which continuous and timely re-porting is required, particularly for the priority countries, are:

> 1. Detailed current measures of economic per-formance including statistics on the structure and distribution of national income, international trade and finance, wages and prices, the govern-ment-sector budget, tax receipts, domestic mone-tary and financial variables, employment and un-employment, excess productive capacity, and leading indicators of future performance such as advance export orders, planned capital construc-tion, and surveys of consumer expectations.

2. Official and unofficial forecasts of national income and product, the balance of trade and payments, wages and prices, and unemployment.

3. The likely content and timing of projected domestic and foreign economic-policy decisions by government or actions by major economic groups such as unions or producer associations, and the sources of uncertainty as to timing or content.

4. Estimates of the effect of current or projected policy decisions or events on the level, structure, and distribution of national income, the balance of trade and payments, wages and prices, and unemployment.

5. The nature of the economic policymaking process in government including:

    a. The perceptions and objectives of individual economic policymakers and the institutional interest of bureaucratic elements that play a principal role in economic policymaking.

    b. The current and projected division of authority or influence over the major areas of economic policymaking.

    c. The determinants of the distribution of influence over economic policymaking by individuals, bureaucratic elements, or outside groups.

    d. Shifts in demands of economic pressure groups such as labor unions and opposition political parties.

57. What are the principal objectives of the major economic powers (especially France, West Germany, Japan, the UK, Italy, Canada and Brazil) in forthcoming multi-lateral trade (GATT) and financial negotiations (IMF)?

Include their possible negotiating tradeoffs and the electoral and intragovernmental factors that affect these objectives and tradeoffs. With respect to multilateral trade negotiations, appraise the consequences of alternative trade agreements to the US foreign trade balances.

Report on potential issues in the trade negotiations that may affect the availability to the United States of imported supplies of key commodities; government strategies for developing those industries, including agriculture, in which the United States has an export interest, particularly high-technology areas and those that could make heavy inroads into US domestic markets, such as shoes and textiles.

Report on indications of intended foreign actions relating to such international monetary questions as alternative exchange-rate regimes and margins of fluctuation, the numeraire of the monetary system, and the roles of Special Drawing Rights, gold, and reserve currencies; consolidation of reserve currency holdings; balance-of-payments adjustment mechanism, including criteria for adjustment; uses of capital and other balance-of-payments controls.

Report on efforts by private industry to influence governmental negotiating positions. Include also efforts to establish new non-tariff barriers, such as unreasonable product standards or safety specifications, made by private industry or trade associations.

For the priority countries especially, but to some extent for all countries, timely reporting is required on:

1. Prepared negotiation strategies including initial proposals and fallback positions.

2. Pre-negotiation perceptions of and reactions to US negotiating strategy.

3. Perceptions of the progress of negotiations and changes in objectives and bargaining strategies during the course of negotiations.

4. The determining factors in the policymaking process including:

a. The perceptions and objectives of individuals and the institutional interests of bureaucratic elements that play a major role in policymaking.

b. The division of authority or influence over policymaking between individuals and bureaucratic elements.

c. The content and relative influence of major pressure groups such as trade unions and opposition political parties.

58. What are the changes in composition and location of the foreign assets of the major oil exporting countries, and what are their policies with respect to channeling funds on longer terms than heretofore through multilateral institutions, the Eurodollar market, US financial markets and direct loans or grants to the LDCs?

Continual, recurrent reporting for the OPEC countries (in particular, Saudi Arabia, Kuwait, Iran, Iraq, Abu Dhabi, Libya, Venezuela, Nigeria and Indonesia) is needed on:

1. Accrued earnings from exports.

2. Payments received for exports or from foreign investments and the structure of time lags between accruals of earnings and receipt of payments for oil exports.

3. Current imports of goods and services and information relevant to estimation of future import levels.

4. Payments for imports and changes in the lags between time of import and time of import payment.

5. The composition of direct investments made by these countries.

6. Loan or grant commitments to foreign governments or multilateral institutions and the timing of disbursement against these loans or grants.

7. The composition by location, denominated currency, and maturity of financial asset portfolios held by official or quasi-official institutions and current changes in the composition of these portfolios.

8. Policies governing choice of location, denominated currency, and maturity of future purchases of financial assets by official or quasi-official institutions.

9. Policies with respect to further direct loans or grants to governments or multilateral organizations.

10. Indications of intentions to make large abrupt changes in the composition of financial portfolios (in particular, shifts to or from assets denominated in dollars).

59. What are the policies, negotiating positions and vulnerabilities of the major petroleum exporters with respect to the production and marketing of oil, and how are these policies affected by the prospects for development of non-OPEC energy sources?

Continuous and detailed reporting is needed on:

1. Current and forecasted production, export, and productive capacity of primary energy by type (oil, gas, coal, and elements of the nuclear fuel cycle) in both the OPEC countries and those non-OPEC countries that are major producers of primary energy.

2. Current and estimated future consumption of primary energy by type for those countries that are major consumers of energy.

3. The policies, plans, and negotiating strategies concerning production, price, and export of oil and gas of individual governments and associated institutions such as OPEC and OAPEC.

4. Policies of the major energy-consuming countries that affect their levels of imports and consumption of energy.

5. Bilateral arrangements between the OPEC countries and major energy-consuming countries concerning the supply and financing of exports of oil and gas.

6. Information relevant to estimates of the future reserve and balance-of-payments position (in particular, plans concerning major investment projects and imports of military items) of each OPEC country and those countries such as Canada, Mexico, and Norway that might have potential to increase world energy supplies.

7. Perceptions of key policymakers and significant political and bureaucratic elements of each OPEC nation concerning:

> a. The oil marketing policies of their own nations and other OPEC nations.
>
> b. The reaction of the US and other governments of major oil-consuming nations to these policies.
>
> c. The vulnerability of these policies to actions by the oil-consuming nations and other OPEC nations.

8. The production, marketing, and investment policies of the major US and foreign oil companies and the status of negotiations between the companies and host governments.

60. What changes in production, control and pricing policies are the major producers of important raw materials or primary products, including Canada and Australia, considering either individually or in concert?

CONFIDENTIAL

Report on steps being considered or taken by either government or the private sector in other countries to limit or regulate the quantity, price or state of processing of raw materials normally exported—particularly steps affecting US access to such materials, government attitudes toward and strategies for multilateral cooperation among exporters or between producers, exporters and importers in efforts to stabilize the market either when such commodities are in globally short supply or when they are trending toward oversupply.

In particular, detailed and timely collection and reporting is needed on:

1. Current statistics on and forecasts of productions, exports, inventories, productive capacity, prices, and consumption of important raw materials and primary products for most countries.

2. Inventory and stockpiling policies of producing and consuming nations and international price support organizations.

3. Plans of producing governments to play a larger role in controlling or influencing production and price by unilateral or, especially, collective action.

4. Actual or planned shifts, whether or not stimulated by government policies, of emphasis varying from exporting basic raw materials to processing domestic raw materials and exporting them in a processed or further refined or fabricated form.

61. How have changes in the relative prices of imports and exports (petroleum, fertilizer and grain in particular) affected the food supply, foreign trade and prospects for economic growth and political stability of the major LDCs (especially India, Pakistan, Brazil, Egypt, Mexico, South Korea, Argentina, Uruguay and Chile)?

Report on attempts of the LDCs to attract foreign capital to ease balance-of-payments problems; government attitudes toward use of grants, loans, or concessionary purchase arrange-

CONFIDENTIAL

ments to lessen the pressure of high import prices on their economies; measures taken or contemplated to reduce consumption of high cost imports or to develop export industries and new export markets.

In particular, detailed and timely reporting is needed on:

1. Current economic performance and population growth.

2. Estimated production and consumption of food-stuffs; estimated production and utilization of agricultural inputs.

3. The sources and potential magnitude of error in current official economic statistics.

4. Projected foreign-exchange earnings on current account.

5. Projected availability of net capital imports (concessional and commercial).

6. The composition of imports for alternative import levels; estimates of the effect of changes in the level of imports on growth prospects.

7. Estimates of the effect of government policy decisions on the net availability of foreign exchange, food import requirements, distribution of income, productivity of investment, and future population growth.

62. What is the likely demand (especially by the USSR, China, India, Japan, Indonesia, Bangladesh) for imports of wheat, soybeans, rice, corn, and cotton, and what are the capabilities of countries other than the U.S. (especially Canada, Argentina, Australia, Brazil and Thailand) for supplying these commodities to the world market?

Report on changes in government policies that affect agricultural productivity; investments in the agricultural sector or in the infrastructure serving agriculture; changes in reserve stocks requirements; problems encountered in planting, harvesting, or transporting agricultural products; developments in foreign demand for or supply of raw materials or foodstuffs, especially grain, that may indicate possible world shortages such that external demand for US products could lead to shortages in the United States.

Also, detailed and timely reporting is needed on:

1. Current information on crop prospects in each of the main importing and exporting nations (including the EC as a group).

2. Current information on importer and exporter stock levels (and, for the USSR, the condition of stocks), and importer and exporter views of their consumption and stock requirements.

3. Current information on trade and expected trade in these commodities.

4. Information on future production plans to include changes in cropping patterns and investment.

5. Prospects for the modernization of agricultural production techniques ('The Green Revolution').

63. What actions are being taken or planned by foreign governments or private groups that could so substantially affect the ability of American business to compete for foreign sales as to involve the US interest in an important way?

Examples are sales of aircraft, nuclear power plants, enriched uranium and major construction programs such as the Suez pipeline.

Report on government anti-inflation or anti-recession actions that serve to stimulate exports or protect home industries, including the setting of export prices that do not fully reflect the domestic price level, preferential credit arrangements, tax incentives, export development programs, adjustments assistance programs, administrative barriers to imports, regulations influencing the import or export of industrial technology, trade agreements involving trade restraints or safeguards, and attempts to negotiate large contracts.

Also report on government measures affecting operations of

CONFIDENTIAL

US subsidiaries abroad or restricting US equity ownership or sectors of operations; intentions of governments to nationalize or expropriate US-owned property; changes in general economic, tax, tariff, and subsidy policies that impede or stimulate foreign direct investment; official and private attitudes toward US investments; and requirements for US subsidiaries overseas to reinvest profits within the foreign country.

KISSINGER

CLEARANCES:
TARIFF: G. ECKLUND
INT: B. BURNS
AID: J. HOATH
TREAS: L. ELSBERND
COMM: M. RENNERT
CIEP: J. DUNN
STR: G. FEKETEKUTY
EXIM: S. POLLACK
LAB: B. WHITE
AGRI: W. GASSER
DOT: P. BRONEZ
OMB: A. DONAHUE
CEA: J. KVASNICKA
ARMY: LT. C. K. MONTGOMERY
NAVY: CAPT. G. WALKER
AF: J. D. PAFENBERG
DIA: H. FORBES
NSA: S. BURN
AEC: M. EISENSTEIN
OPIC: P. DICKERSON
ACDA: R. PAJAK
FRB: R. BRYANT
STATE: G. GOLDSTEIN
(INR)

The CIA's
Corporate Shell Game

by John Marks

Jeffrey A. Manley has his name on the door at Burwell, Hansen and Manley, but he is not allowed to use his own firm's Xerox machine. The problem, according to Manley, is that he doesn't have a government security clearance and the copier is located in a room full of classified documents. Manley, a mustachioed young Harvard law graduate, observes that a closed-circuit television system scans the law firm's reception room in downtown Washington and that the monitor is located in a part of the office he has never entered.

These extraordinary precautions at Burwell, Hansen and Manley exist because the firm shares office space with Southern Capital and Management Corporation and Southern Capital is what is known in the intelligence trade as a "proprietary." It is, in other words, a wholly owned and operated subsidiary of the CIA.

[This article first appeared in the *Washington Post* on July 11, 1976.]

So far as is known, Southern Capital is the CIA's largest remaining proprietary. Its work in managing the CIA's $30 million investment portfolio is so secret that the Agency persuaded the Senate Intelligence Committee not to press for the company's actual name, instead calling it "The Insurance Complex."

For more than two decades, the CIA has made extensive use of proprietaries like Southern Capital to hide operations under the mantle of private enterprise. In order to incorporate and run this "business" empire, the Agency has relied on lawyers. Washington is a city of lawyers. Therefore, it is hardly surprising that the local bar brims with lawyers who perform secret services for the agency's overlapping, interlocking network of front companies. The trail of lawyers leads from Southern Capital to more than 15 recently discovered proprietaries in the Washington area alone. Some have been disbanded; others, like Southern Capital, are still active.

"Insurance Complex"

Southern Capital, our starting point, takes the CIA straight to Wall Street. It is the investment arm of an assortment of proprietary financial companies, located mainly in foreign tax havens such as the Bahamas, Bermuda, the Cayman Islands, and Panama. Southern Capital was created in 1962 as a front insurance company to provide coverage for agents and equipment involved in covert operations—particularly those connected to CIA-owned airlines. "The Insurance Complex" then branched out into other entrepreneurial ventures. It received money from CIA insurance premiums, from deductions taken from secret agents' pay and—at least once in the past 10 years, according to a CIA budget specialist—from funds left over from the Agency's congressional appropriation.

By the late 1960s, Southern Capital had on hand between $25 and $30 million, which it invested in a mix of stocks, bonds, and other securities—both foreign and domestic. During the early years, according to a former employee, investment decisions were made largely by the brokerage firm of Scudder, Stevens and Clark. (There is no evidence that the brokerage firm knew of the CIA tie.) But in either 1969 or 1970, an internal CIA study concluded that the Agency would receive higher profits if CIA experts decided what to buy and sell. A special CIA board of directors chaired by then General Counsel Lawrence Houston took over the selection of securities for Southern Capital.

On this committee—which was called the MH MUTUAL group—sat the CIA's chief of budgeting, the director of finance, and the head of the office of economic research. This last member was particularly important, according to an inside CIA source, because he enabled Southern Capital to "draw on the advice of the (CIA's) economic research people. Any stockbroker would like 300 trained experts giving advice. If it was not a conflict of interest, it at least should have been offered to the public."

The proprietary's best earner was Eurodollar deposits made through the Morgan Guaranty Bank's Brussels office with a return of 13% at one point, a former employee recalls. After the MUTUAL committee took over, Southern Capital branched out from its normal blue-chip purchases to more speculative fields, including short-term buys of Swiss francs and several hundred thousand dollars in Mexican pesos. Another source reports that during the early 1970s, when the CIA was working secretly with ITT to keep Salvador Allende from power in Chile, Southern Capital owned some ITT stock. MUTUAL Chairman Houston told the Senate committee: "Well, a couple of times our investment advisor recommended a stock which I knew we had big contracts with, and I told the board no, this involves a conflict of interest. We won't touch it."

The net profit on Southern Capital's portfolio in 1974 was more than $1.5 million, according to the Senate report. Most of that money never found its way onto Southern's balance sheets, however, because it legally belonged to proprietary insurance and financial companies in overseas tax havens. Southern Capital, as a Delaware corporation doing business in the District of Columbia, did submit U.S. tax returns but was under no obligation to list the money it made for its sister proprietaries. The company kept three or four lawyers busy full time, a former Southern employee recalls. "Mr. Evans was a stickler on legality," he says.

"Mr. Evans" is Marvin L. Evans, who ran Southern Capital for the CIA until his retirement in 1973. Evans extends the proprietary trail to Africa, among other places, and his stewardship illustrates how difficult it becomes to sort out the private interests of the proprietary managers from the "official" interests of the CIA. According to a former associate of Burwell, Hansen and Manley, Evans not only managed the CIA's portfolio but also ran an in-house investment club for people working in the office.

One of Evans' private law clients, a Miami man named Thomas R. Green, runs a string of air companies in Florida, Africa, and the Caribbean. Africair, Green's holding company, is apparently not an outright proprietary, but it has done considerable business for the CIA. Marvin Evans now owns 15% of Green's Africair; Green served on the board of directors of Southern Capital.

One of Africair's largest subsidiaries is Pan African Airlines, based in Lagos, Nigeria. According to CAB records, this company makes 80% of its revenues from a single U.S. government contract for air service to remote outposts in West Africa. The CIA is a major participant in that contract, according to a State Department official who puts its value for the year at $575,000. Informed CIA sources report that Pan African was set up in 1962 in close cooperation with the Agency and is considered inside the CIA to be a covert "asset."

In 1975, Africair sought CAB approval to merge with Southeast Airlines, which flies in Florida and the Caribbean. In that filing, Africair noted its companies were making profits from their African operations at rates "more than adequate to cover" the losses it expected from Southeast. Africair received CAB approval, and thus profits received in large part from unpublicized CIA business were used to subsidize air service in Florida.

Neither Green nor Evans would return a reporter's repeated phone calls requesting information about the various intertwined relationships. Evans' phone was disconnected the day after the first attempt was made to contact him. Even a direct appeal to Africair's Washington lawyer, James Bastian (also the long-time attorney for the CIA's best known proprietary, Air America), asking him to seek a response from Evans and Green produced no reply.

Airline Connection

The Pan African Airlines setup is not isolated. The CIA has used its proprietaries to establish influence over many of the world's airlines, especially in the Third World. To see how this is done, it is necessary only to follow men connected to Southern Capital. Two of its directors have also served on the board of a related proprietary known as United Business Associates. During the mid-1960s, UBA had offices at 818 18th Street N.W. —with at least two other CIA fronts on the same floor.

A former UBA officer recalls that one of the company's biggest operations was a deal to finance a national airline for Libya, then a kingdom. "Our interest was to lend money for the purpose of controlling the airline," he says. "It was to offset the Communists from moving in."

The money—reportedly several million dollars—was to come from other CIA proprietaries, according to the ex-officer, and UBA had a plan to win over the Libyan government. "The way we set it up was like this: We had to offer them control over 20% of the stock of the corporation and we would lend them the money. Then we would have to put one of their natives alongside every American in a similar position. Talking about kickbacks, that's the name of the trade over there. That's how we covered the men of the cabinet . . . And if we ever called that note, they would have taken the franchise away."

UBA did not win the franchise, but neither did TWA which was in at least indirect competition with the Agency's UBA, having prepared a feasibility study.

Why this great intelligence interest in airlines? Orvis Nelson, an aviation veteran who worked with the CIA to set up Iran Air in the early 1950s, explains: "If I were sitting in a position where I was curious about what was going on in troubled areas, there are two things I would be damned well interested in. The first is information. The second is transportation to get in and out, to get any information and, perhaps, to do some other air activities. You have mobility. You know who and what are going in and out. You know who people's associates are. You are in a position to move your people about."

Orvis Nelson, now 69 and still going strong, has set up 16 airlines in his time and has run his own supplemental carrier. Sometimes he has cooperated with the CIA—but he vehemently states he has never been under the Agency's control. He won't state which of his airline deals involved the CIA. He does say, however, that U.S. government involvement in foreign airlines is as great as ever.

Some of America's commercial airlines have worked closely with the CIA in the past. A retired CIA operative with 20 years of field experience recalls, "When we wanted something from Pan Am, we went right to Juan Trippe" (the corporation's ex-chief). In Panama, the former operative says, the Agency had a deal with Pan Am in the mid-1950s under which CIA men could rummage through baggage during transit stops. The airline even provided them with mechanics' overalls.

United Business Associates had other ways of getting information from foreign countries and planting agents in key places. An ex-employee remembers: "We were running companies all over the world as a management concern. We would hire and place a manager into a company, and he would then report back to us as far as the financial records were concerned. In turn, we would report back to the investor." The investor was the CIA.

Similarly, in recent years the CIA has set up management consultant firms in the international energy field. An executive at one of Wall Street's most important investment banks confirms that certain consultant firms with ties to U.S. intelligence win governmental and private contracts in the Middle East as management experts and use these positions to gather secret economic intelligence. The investment banker reports that this data is then passed on, at least in part, to American companies in a position to profit from it.

From the CIA's point of view, of course, the principal value of the proprietaries' penetration of international business comes from the knowledge and consequent leverage flowing back to the Agency. It has gathered voluminous information on both Americans and foreigners—information which is preserved in orange cardboard folders, known as "201 files." According to a source familiar with the CIA's economic records, the 201 file on international stock manipulator Robert Vesco alone is more than six inches thick.

Embarrassing Moves

The managers and employees of CIA proprietaries are an extremely mobile group of people, moving frequently among companies and government agencies. Their activities must be accomplished secretly, without revealing CIA connections, and this requirement sometimes puts other government agencies in compromised positions.

For example, in 1973 a Thai national named Puttaporn Khramkhruan was arrested on charges of smuggling some 59 pounds of opium into the United States. The U.S. attorney's office in Chicago was forced to drop the case because the Thai was a CIA agent and the Agency was unwilling to supply data in court about his background and activities. Former CIA Director William Colby told an inquiring congressional committee last year: "It was quite easy to see that his activity for us would be revealed in the course of the trial. We requested the Justice

Department not to try him for this reason. They agreed.''

One matter that would have presumably been revealed at a trial was that Puttaporn was carrying out his supposedly anti-drug intelligence work under the cover of a handicraft business set up for him by Joseph Z. Taylor and Associates. That firm was another CIA proprietary, whose corporate secretary once worked for United Business Associates.

The Taylor firm's work as a CIA front compromised another government entity, the Agency for International Development. Then-AID Director John Hannah had announced in 1970 that AID provided no cover to the CIA anywhere in the world outside of Laos. In fact, with the apparent knowledge of Hannah, the CIA's Taylor and Associates was then in the midst of a seven-year, million-dollar effort to train Thailand's border police, under the cover of an AID contract. In 1974, Joseph Taylor himself received a high State Department appointment from President Nixon.

The CIA's protective arrangements for its proprietaries extend far beyond the Justice Department or AID to other federal agencies. The CIA has stopped audits—or started them—at the IRS. It has interceded successfully at the highest levels of Treasury, Commerce, the CAB, the FAA, and even the Park Police. It has also been able to influence Air Force issuance of lucrative Military Air Transport contracts.

Lawyers who have had ties with CIA proprietaries have also represented well-known figures in politically charged cases. Before Jeffrey Manley's arrival, the covering Burwell firm was known as Burwell, Hansen and McCandless. Robert McCandless resigned as a partner in 1973 in order to serve as co-counsel to John Dean in the Watergate proceedings. Jeb Magruder, another key witness against Nixon aides in Watergate trials, had a lawyer, James Bierbower, who had served as vice president of Southern Air Transport, one of the CIA's largest air proprietaries. To complete the circle, Bierbower worked out of the same office in the mid-1960s as Southern Capital's Marvin Evans, and Evans later shared space with McCandless' firm.

(McCandless, when queried by a reporter, claimed he had not known of the CIA involvement with his firm. Bierbower refused comment, saying he could not talk about clients.)

"The lawyers lend an aura of legitimacy and protection in the proprietary world," an ex-CIA staff attorney notes. And it follows that the most prestigious lawyers afford the most legitimacy. The CIA has obtained the services of top-flight lawyers, as the path from Southern Capital shows. Two of the firm's officers have been lawyers in the Washington law firm of Purcell and Nelson. Four lawyers in Purcell and Nelson have served as directors or officers of CIA companies in at least seven instances.

Three lawyers at another prestigious Washington firm, Leboeuf, Lamb and Leiby, were officers during the sixties of another proprietary, Foreign Air Transport Development, which was organized, according to D.C. corporate records, for "investing in foreign air carriers." Two lawyers at another downtown law firm, John Mason and Gerald Malia, served as lawyers and officers for several CIA companies. The list goes on.

The Agency apparently wanted proprietary boards that read like membership lists in the American establishment. The boards of CIA proprietaries, such as Radio Free Europe, included in the sixties well-known names from the worlds of commerce, finance, and the media, among them: Richard Mellon Scaife of the Pittsburgh banking family, General Motors chairman James Roche, publisher John Hay Whitney, ex-United Fruit president Thomas D. Cabot, CBS president Frank Stanton, and socialite Winston Guest. There were retired generals such as Lucius Clay and officers of such companies as American Airlines, Intercontinental Hotels, Bell Helicopters, and Virginia Gentleman distilleries. Southern Capital's two presidents have been the late Henry Koch, who was director of financing for the World Bank's International Finance Corporation, and Leigh Cramer, a retired vice president of the First National City Bank.

"You're dealing with your conservative element in the higher price bracket, for the most part," a retired CIA man noted. "Even so, you've got to run Agency security checks on them to make sure they're not supporting every radical cause on the street."

On occasion, these security investigations, which are carried out without the knowledge of the person concerned, can have unexpected consequences. An attorney whose firm set up proprietaries for the CIA during the 1960s recalls that Agency sleuths turned up information that the firm's receptionist was a madam running a string of call girls. "The fact that our receptionist had a lot of phone calls was not unusual," the lawyer says, "but we were told she was a weak link and we ought to get rid of her."

Taciturn Crew

Most of the roughly 40 lawyers and outside directors contacted for this article did not want to talk about their involvement with the CIA—or about anything else for that matter. One lied about his CIA connection, but later admitted it. The lawyers tended to cite the attorney-client privilege as reason for their silence, even when they also had served as corporate officers. A few of the lawyers made impassioned pleas for anonymity, arguing that revelations of CIA work would do damage to their careers.

In view of this vulnerability, why did so many lawyers flock to the CIA's service? One former CIA official says the lawyers are drawn to proprietary work because they enjoy "a sense of intrigue that a lawyer doesn't get drafting a will." A knowledgeable lawyer cites a more practical reason that might have applied to some. "Working for the CIA can be important in the way you impress clients. It allows you to say, 'I'm in here tight on important national security matters.'"

The late Howard Hughes, whose companies held huge CIA contracts, apparently believed that CIA ties helped business. According to testimony of his former lieutenant, Robert Maheu, Hughes felt that "if he ever became involved in any problem with the government, it would be beneficial for him to be in a position of being a front."

Money is a practical motivation for those lawyers who are paid according to their normal fees schedule. The most often cited reason for cooperation with the CIA, however, was patriotism. Arlington lawyer L. Lee Bean explains his own involvement thus: "I had polio and I happened to be 4-F. I tried to get into the war in a crazy way. Then I was told by a dear friend of mine that, if I would work with the Agency, it was a way to help my country. It was the patriotic thing to do, I thought. I still do. . . . Regardless of what's happened to the CIA, on the whole it's done a good job."

The CIA has never had trouble getting the "front people" it wants. Retired General Counsel Lawrence Houston told a reporter that he had approached hundreds and hundreds of lawyers over the years and only met one who turned him down—and that man refused because the CIA wouldn't pay him enough. According to CIA sources, there is still no scarcity of eminent new recruits.

Willing Recruits

None of this means that there was a huge conspiracy at the heart of the U.S. government or that lawyers or prominent establishment figures knew about illegal CIA activities—just that hundreds, if not thousands, of prominent outsiders were willing to work with the CIA. Within this context, the CIA was able to assemble a farflung commercial empire that feeds off its own earnings as well as government funds. Proprietary revenues from outside the CIA averaged over $30 million per year, according to the Senate report. That is money earned independently of Congress and not reflected in the CIA budget—which is secret anyhow.

Now, according to the Senate committee report, the large CIA airlines have been sold off, and Southern Capital is the last sizable profitable front. The Senate report does not state, however, that the CIA has unloaded the air proprietaries to companies and individuals with which it has long been closely connected and that the Agency will almost certainly be able to make continued use of these world-wide assets.

Moreover, there is room for doubt about whether the Senate committee got even a close approximation of Southern Capital's operations or intertwined connections. According to two sources familiar with the committee's work, the staff conducted virtually no independent investigation, relying almost exclusively on records volunteered by the Agency. As one of the sources states with real bitterness, "Listen, the proprietary section of the report was done in the last month or two, and it was based on whatever the CIA told them. . . . The Agency wouldn't let them see, for example, the basic files on the air proprietaries."

As for Southern Capital, the Senate committee did find that "serious questions remain as to the propriety of using such a mechanism to provide insurance and retirement benefits for Agency employees." Nevertheless, the committee recommended that the company's investment programs be permitted to continue with some restrictions—which the CIA had already imposed on itself. Southern Capital will no longer buy stock in American companies, and it reportedly will not be used in support of operational activities.

The CIA refused, however, to answer a reporter's written questions on why the money currently invested by the CIA front cannot be put into non-controversial government bonds or why its payments cannot be made through regular Agency channels instead of through corporate cover.

The CIA has clearly not given up on Southern Capital. As the Senate report notes, the Agency has plans to establish within the Southern Capital complex several new corporate "shells" which can be "adapted to various new CIA missions."

The Washington Lawyers

Plush Washington law offices may seem far removed from the grisly and often illegal world of covert operations, but the CIA's proprietary companies can provide a connection. Take the experience of an Arlington law firm.

In the early 1960s, its senior partner, L. Lee Bean, was contacted by an old friend from his University of Virginia days named Robert G. Harper. Harper worked out of offices on 17th Street NW shared by the firm of Purcell and Nelson, and he secured the aid of Bean's firm in setting up two CIA proprietaries.

One was called Zenith Technical Enterprises, and until 1966 it provided cover to the CIA's entire Miami station, which was the Agency's biggest installation anywhere outside of Washington. Zenith Technical was one of over 50 proprietaries the CIA maintained in Florida alone for Cuban operations. From behind Zenith's cover, the CIA waged a secret war against Castro, featuring sabotage, crop destruction, and numerous assassination attempts.

The other proprietary set up by Bean's firm became Anderson Security Consultants, Inc., located first in Arlington and then in a low modern building in Springfield. Anderson's ostensible function was to provide security services to private industry, banks, and schools, but in fact its main job was to serve as the hidden operational arm in the Washington area of the CIA's Office of Security. The Senate Intelligence Committee deals with Anderson Security in its report, but calls it only "the Security Project."

Starting in 1967, Anderson Security tried to gather information and infiltrate Washington-area peace and civil rights groups —in order, the Agency later claimed, to provide advance warning of demonstrations that might threaten CIA buildings. Within the Agency, this domestic surveillance program was code-named "MERRIMAC." A few months after it began, CIA agents operating under it were instructed to collect information on who was contributing money to the targeted groups—a far cry from protecting buildings.

The Rockefeller Commission found that these MERRIMAC activities "exceeded the CIA's statutory authority."

Another Arlington lawyer, who helped Bean set up both Anderson Security and Zenith Technical, explains his current feelings: "As I look at it now, I see the potential evils, but where do you draw the line? How do you deal with Communists? You have to look at the framework of what things were like then."

Asked if he felt misused after creating companies involved in attempted assassination and illegal domestic spying, the lawyer replied, "Yes, very definitely. They traded on my patriotism. My loyalty to my country has been used improperly—all under the guise of 'we can't tell you anything because of the secrecy, but believe us, it's all for the good. We're the good guys; we're trying to help and you can help us.' I fell for it. I never dreamed that our little tiny action would end up this way . . . We do this as lawyers every day, never knowing what will be done with the legal entities we set up."

What They Do:
Western Europe

Introduction

Although the Welch killing and the Agency's manipulation of it slowed Congress' "determination" to investigate Agency abuses and the American media's efforts to expose them, the backlash had little effect in Europe. Most European analysts and journalists were unhindered by any myths about the sanctity or the decency of the American intelligence community. Indeed, commercial media openly competed among themselves and with the left-wing papers to see who could name the most CIA people.

The articles which follow demonstrate the breadth of the investigations in nearly every country in Western Europe. This selection is by no means complete. Rest assured that the campaign is in full swing.

The CIA in Post-Franco Spain

by Cambio 16 *(Research team: Eduardo Chamorro, Galo Freixet, Consuelo Alvarez de Toledo, Nicole Szulc, and Steve Weissman)*

From the top floors of the American Embassy in Madrid, behind the tightly locked doors of the so-called Office of Political Liaison, the CIA chief in Madrid, Robert Gahagen, and his clandestine action team closely watch the dynamic of Spanish political life in the era begun with the death of Francisco Franco. What are they saying about the conflicting demands of the left, the right, and the center? And what are their plans for a country that is not their own?

After the failure in Southeast Asia and the ongoing storm in the Middle East, the panorama that Gahagen sees and analyzes holds a crucial importance for the Americans, who see recent events in Spain as part of a sequence that, from Turkey to Portugal, could pose a serious threat to their interests.

Faced with this panorama, Gahagen has his problems. At the moment American diplomats and politicians—especially in Con-

[This article first appeared as "La CIA, Aqui, Ahora," in the January 12, 1976, issue of *Cambio 16*, in Madrid, Spain.]

gress—are feeling particularly tired of their old activism in foreign affairs. Vietnam and Watergate have dampened their eagerness to intervene, and as one veteran of the diplomatic wars put it to *Cambio 16:* "You get tired of prescribing for all the world's ills, especially when you realize that the medicine you've prescribed doesn't always work."

Nonetheless, Spain isn't Tibet or even Laos—countries where the CIA found themselves forced to retreat—and when it comes to defending their bases, businesses, ideology, and influence, the Americans are not prepared to step back and run the risk of the country slipping through their hands. Not where the country —Spain—has been for many years an objective of the highest order.

So, the Americans are far from giving up their old interventionist approach, even when it could lead to a new stage in the Cold War. This was the meaning of Kissinger's public warning to the Soviets over the lack of cooperation shown by the Portuguese Communists or Angolan MPLA—a warning even more caustic in the statements of the leaders of the Democratic Party, who seem even more determined to block any gain by the left in Western Europe.

As they put it in their own statements on the future of Spain, the United States favors only "Spain's closer links with the European groupings." Or, in other words, the American perspective sees Spain's entry into NATO and the Common Market, as well as—given Europe's attitude toward the Spanish monarchy—a major opening toward democracy. And so the United States would be prepared to support King Juan Carlos I, as they had been doing before the death of Franco.

In this context of weariness, international frustration, a real necessity to intervene, and restrained support, Gahagen weighs the range of his decisions. In a non-public, though not secret, fashion, his team—along with the State Department diplomats— maintains systematic contacts with a wide range of Spanish politicians, from the Franco diehards in "the bunker" to leaders of the Socialist and Christian Democratic opposition. Many of these people regularly visit the American Embassy in Madrid— though some prefer to meet elsewhere—and during recent years these contacts have led to a stream of invitations to well-placed politicians, independent journalists, and leaders of the moderate opposition to visit the United States as participants in the International Visitors Program. And although the invitations all come from the Ambassador, Gahagen and his men take part in maintaining the contacts and selecting the visitors, some of whom even belong to the *Junta Democraticá.*

Do these contacts with the opposition go beyond a friendly smile and a trip to the U.S.A.? Most likely they do. Knowingly or not, the majority of the leaders of the Spanish opposition have for many years gravitated around groups financed by the CIA—groups such as the Congress for Cultural Freedom and the International Commission of Jurists.

At present, according to the *New York Times,* the CIA has channeled millions of dollars to Portuguese Socialist and Christian Democratic groups which have close contacts in Spain. And, as has become known, part of this passing of funds took place through channels that the CIA established in the Socialist parties of Western Europe.

On the same plane, but without any proof, some observers even speculate on the possibility that the Americans are maintaining official contacts with Santiago Carrillo and his Communist Party. A recent article in the influential *Foreign Affairs,* which often reflects the foreign policy of the American government, suggested that Carrillo wouldn't be so bad, and observed that "Europe and the U.S., if they are to deal with Spain at all, will presumably have to adjust to the presence of communists near the center of power . . ."

Equally, widely believed rumors from Washington indicate that, in return for stability, the CIA is seriously considering the possibility of taking a new attitude toward the existence of Europe's more "moderate" Communist parties. If that were the case, Gahagen and his Liaison Office would be holding secret meetings with the Spanish CP, hiding from the Spanish "bunker" and the right wing of the American Congress one of the more important facets of their *liaisons dangereuses.*

Reality, however, contrasts sharply with such suppositions. The Department of State recently vetoed the issuance of a visitor's visa to a well-known leader of the Italian Communist Party, while the American Embassy in Spain has apparently forbidden the establishment of contacts with the Spanish Communist Party (PCE). So American anticommunism clearly continues. And, paradoxically, while the Americans artificially exaggerate the Communist threat, they appear to underestimate the PCE's actual strength and potential influence. In fact, the Americans almost seem to believe that a moderately civilized transition government would bring with it the disappearance of the left as a problem. "The United States continues to see no advantage in dealing with the Communists anywhere in Western Europe," a well-placed source told *Cambio 16.* "The policy continues to be one of keeping Santiago Carrillo as ostracized as possible and hoping that he remains there permanently."

But what if ostracism doesn't work? What if the *aperturistas* and moderate opposition can't contain the political ferment? What if there were a massive strike wave and the Communists ended up in some kind of coalition government? What, in the end, if the worst fears of the "bunker" prove real? The answer, as everyone knows, would be the intervention of one military group or another. The military attaches at the American Embassy already appear to have close contacts with Spain's military and security services, and the attaches themselves are all officials of the Defense Intelligence Agency (DIA), the Pentagon's intelligence arm, which competes against—and collaborates with—the CIA.

In addition, the United States has ample programs of military training and cooperation and, according to a well-informed source, the Americans try to use these programs to get influential contacts among the Spanish military, and, where possible, to help these contacts move up the ladder to posts of even greater influence. At present, however, neither DIA nor CIA seems to be using their contacts to favor a military solution to Spain's political problems. Covert action rarely strays too far from overt policy, and—so far, at least—the policy is to back the moderate civilians.

Still, should the moderate civilians fail or the *apertura* go too far, the Americans know where to look within the military. And should their military contacts feel little inclined to intervene, the Americans—and especially the CIA—know exactly how to spur them on with a good dose of chaos. In Chile, the CIA helped do it all, from creating a shortage of toilet paper to backing strikes, terrorism, and provocation. In Spain, they might try something else. But whatever the "dirty tricks," it's still what Kissinger calls "destabilization," and on the top floors of the American Embassy in Madrid, that's still the specialty of the house.

According to some sources, the CIA now view events in Spain much as the Americans viewed events in postwar Europe. In this perspective, they would channel aid to Socialist and Christian Democratic groups as a means of solidifying and strengthening them against the Communist Party, which is supposed to have organizational superiority. Such a program would certainly fit with the State Department forecasts on the future of Spain in the 1970s, made prior to the death of Franco. Of the three political groups considered—Socialists (PSOE), Christian Democrats, and Communists—the State Department saw the PCE (with an estimated membership of 30,000) as the major focus of the problem, as much for its ability to organize as for its relations with the Catholics and the more moderate left.

In this scheme, the PSOE appeared as the country's most important sector—and the PCE's principal adversary on the left. But, according to officials in Washington, this confrontation could be dampened by the attitude of PSOE's younger members, for whom the PCE seemed a natural ally. These nuances, of course, would shape the work of the American intelligence services, given prospects for a future Socialist Congress.

As for the Christian Democrats, Washington considers them incapable of filling the role that their older brother in Italy played during the postwar years. For the American intelligence agencies, the Spanish Christian Democrats lack organization and are too ideologically diversified—disqualifying them for the role of containing the Communists. As may be inferred from the statements of sources close to these agencies, this role would be filled with greater chances of success by other groups such as the *Organización Revolucionaria de Trabajadores* and the *Unión General de Trabajadores* in Madrid and the north of Spain, by the *Unión Sindical Obrera* in the Basque country, and by the *Oposición Sindical Obrera* in Madrid and Valencia.

Naturally, the fate of each group analyzed by the CIA and State Department implies the possibility of "covert aid" and its subsequent utilization. And here the ground becomes slippery, since in the majority of cases the recipients don't know—and the American intelligence services don't want them to know—that they are being supported.

The American intelligence services know their own servants and they also know the advantages of passing unnoticed: to appear clearly linked with any of the organizations they actually help would prove fatal. So, the protests of innocence on the part of the recipients are often as legitimate as the covert aid of which they are accused is real.

Still, the American interests in Spain are such that the view doesn't seem to be blocked by so dense a cloud. In fact, the

American secret services could be said to have thrown off their hats, their trench coats, and their dark glasses, and emerged to dance under the lights, as seems already to have happened in Madrid where perhaps the fundamental point is not to play, but to win. As may be understood from the statements of Kissinger, the most important thing for American interests in Spain is not to stop a Communist *coup*—which would not be tolerated by certain domestic groups—but to avoid a shift to neutralism in Spanish foreign policy. This is the real danger for the U.S.A.

Washington's new strategic planning passes right through Spain, since the Iberian Peninsula is an extension of the African-Atlantic shelf. The Sahara, Angola, the independence movements in the Azores and Canaries, the Paris-Madrid-Rabat axis all form part of the same story. And it is no longer a matter of facing up to the Soviets, but of keeping alive the superpower muscle, creating *focos* of activism to block the process of normalization in international relations.

All of which explains the direct American participation in the question of the Sahara and American support to the "Marcha Verde," which the Department of State carried out in a fashion that was as discreet as it was efficient. With the handover of the Sahara to Morocco, the officers of the American intelligence services gained the isolation of Algeria, the division of the Third World, and the security of the monitoring units on Ceuta and Melilla and the base on Tenerife—which some people talk about as if they don't exist, but which the countries of the Third World already take as fully functioning.

The outcome of the Sahara problem represents the return of American vigilance to a vital area ignored during the escalation in Vietnam. Already the Americans have secured the oil route that passes through Las Palmas and along the coast of Angola and the monitoring of the Soviet Mediterranean fleet from the south, thus reinforcing NATO's most vulnerable zone. And all of this would be put at risk if Spain were to become truly neutral.

The democratization of Spain can become as genuine as the neutralism that comes with it—in which case, the American bases would be evacuated, producing fundamental geopolitical changes in the area. Faced with this possibility—and in spite of what might be most convenient for the government in Madrid— the United States would not be prepared to tolerate a Mediterranean Switzerland.

To stop this neutralism seems to be the most evident objective of the clandestine activism of the American intelligence services in Spain, whose work—whatever some theorist of the "bunker" might think—would not be governed by the hypothetical danger of a Communist takeover.

CIA Operations in Greece

by *Yiannis Roubatis and Karen Wynn*

Background of the CIA in Greece

Since the end of the Second World War, Greece has been one of the most important operations centers of the Central Intelligence Agency. During the decade of the 1960s the Central Intelligence Agency used Greece as its base for extensive operations directed against countries in the Mediterranean. During the same period, the American intelligence operations in Greece were among the most extensive in countries of comparable size, and were considered by the CIA among the most important in all of the European continent. During the same decade, the CIA station chief in Athens presided over the activities of more than 200 CIA officers and other employees. The CIA conducted its operations in Greece from at least five specific sites. They were: 1) the American Embassy in Athens; 2) the Metohikon Tamion Stratou Building on Panepistimiou Street; 3) the Nea Makri communica-

[This article first appeared in the Athens daily *Ta Nea* of February 22, 23, and 24, 1978.]

tions base; 4) the Tatoi communications facilities, and 5) the American Consulate building in Thessaloniki. The facilities used by the American intelligence agency for the support of its operations in the sixties, are today among those covered by the Defense Cooperation Agreement between the Greek and American governments. (The DCA was signed in the summer of 1977 in Athens by representatives of the Karamanlis and Carter administrations, but has yet to be put in force.)

Interviews with former employees of the CIA and with other individuals who have followed the activities of American intelligence agencies in the Mediterranean area reveal today that Greece was the center for intelligence-related operations in such countries as: Libya, Ethiopia, Iran, Iraq, Jordan, Saudi Arabia, Lebanon, Turkey, Cyprus and Syria. There are no indications that, as of this writing, these operations and activities are not still going on.

As far as can be determined from the interviews, these activities of the Central Intelligence Agency began as early as 1960, and were probably going on before. On October 1, 1977, the CIA's senior officer in Athens from 1962 to 1968, John M. Maury, lecturing at American University in Washington, D.C., publicly confirmed that Greece was used as a base of operations by the Central Intelligence Agency. Maury stated that, ". . . Greece was a convenient and friendly home base for activities going on in neighboring areas. . . ." Maury, however, attempted to convey the impression that it was toward the socialist countries to the north of Greece that most of the operations originating in Greece were directed. This statement is misleading because during the period of his tenure, Greece was a base for activities mostly into Mediterranean rather than eastern bloc countries.

The CIA station in Athens was established in the late 1940's by the Greek–American CIA officer Thomas Karamessines, who later on became the Deputy Director for Plans, the number three position in the CIA—head of the branch that coordinates all clandestine services. The unusually extensive staff maintained by the CIA in Athens coordinated the support groups and the communications centers servicing the intelligence operations efforts of the United States in the countries mentioned above, called "NE" (Near East) Division. Elements of the support groups belonged to the Technical Services Division or TSD, one of the five "operations" departments of the CIA station in

Greece. The communications centers were part of the Communications Department or MENCA, a semi-autonomous group administered through CIA headquarters in Langley, Virginia.

Until 1967, the TSD offices were located on the fifth floor of the Metohikon Tamion Stratou Building. Later on, the offices were moved to larger quarters on the sixth floor. The Technical Services Division officers provided specialized back-up for CIA operations. TSD assistance to other branches of the CIA included electronic monitoring devices, various gadgets for surveillance, special weapons for clandestine operations, drugs for use in such operations, forged documents and other similar material. Most of the TSD officers had experience in radio and electronics; a few were engineers.

Traveling was an important aspect of the life of the TSD staff in Greece. As the major support group for covert operations in countries outside of Greece, the TSD officers were kept very busy. When one of the CIA case officers in one of the countries mentioned above determined that the operations he supervised required some form of special device, he would ask the CIA station in Athens for assistance. The chief of operations in the Athens station would then dispatch to the CIA station or base requesting assistance one or more of the TSD experts. (A "Station" is equivalent to an "Embassy"; Thessaloniki is a "Base," which is equivalent to a "Consulate.") Such a specialist would fly to the area where his services were needed, perform the necessary work, and then return to Greece. According to a former CIA employee, the TSD people did not use State Department diplomatic passports when they traveled because of hostile State Department policies. Civilian and military passports were used. Another of our sources remembered that the TSD staff "very often would make their own passports. They were capable of that kind of thing. They could forge documents, so making fake passports presented no particular problems to them."

The TSD activities involved aggressive operations originating in Greece and directed against an area, a country, or an individual outside of Greece. It is unclear if the various Greek governments of the 1960s were aware of the TSD activities and the diplomatic risks involved in permitting the CIA to use Greece as a base for these offensive operations in other countries.

It would be misleading to suggest that the TSD specialists worked only outside of Greece. On many occasions the expertise of the TSD staff was utilized within the country. For example, when in 1966 the CIA Deputy Chief of Station in Greece, Harris Greene, considered a plan to discredit Andreas Papandreou, it was the TSD specialists who made him aware that they had the capacity to deliver LSD into Greece and to get it into Mr. Papandreou's drinking water on some public occasion. According to people who are in a position to know, the whole effort was abandoned only when medical specialists advised Greene that there was no way to assure that once ingested by Mr. Papandreou, the LSD would have the intended results. Other activities of the TSD within Greece included the installation of electronic listening equipment, the bugging of telephone lines, and routine breaking-and-entering into homes and offices.

Dr. Sidney Gottlieb, who recently figured in hearings in the American Senate as one of the main actors in the covert CIA testing of mind-bending drugs on U.S. citizens, was the overall director of TSD during the period under discussion. He developed, among other things, highly poisonous substances such as shell-fish toxin, which was held in secret by lower level CIA officials in defiance of the U.S.–Soviet ban on biological warfare materials. Dr. Gottlieb made several trips to Athens during the 1960s.

In addition to the TSD, the Communications division, or MENCA, was also part of the activities of the CIA in Greece. With its main headquarters in the basement of the American Embassy in Athens, MENCA was the largest operation of the CIA in Greece in terms of personnel. There were—and still are today—two relay stations. Site A relay station is in Tatoi, Site B in Nea Makri. MENCA personnel were mainly occupied with reception and transmission of information from both the CIA and the Department of State throughout the Middle East. For example, when a CIA officer in Syria wanted to send a message to the CIA headquarters in the United States, that message would be received in the basement of the American Embassy in Athens. From the Embassy, with the use of one of the two relay stations, that message would then be transmitted to the United States. The Nea Makri relay station was shared by the CIA and the U.S. Navy, while the Tatoi relay station was an exclusive CIA facility.

Organization of the CIA

Thomas Karamessines established the first CIA Station in Athens some time in the late 1940s. From the very beginning, the Athens station was considered one of the most important CIA stations in all of Europe because of the strategic importance of Greece in the Mediterranean. With the passage of time, the station grew to become not only one of the most important but also one of the largest, serving as a staging base for operations in the Near East. By the middle of the 1960s, no fewer than two hundred salaried CIA officers and employees worked for the American intelligence agency on a career basis, not including those individuals—Greek or non-Greek—who worked for the Agency on a contract basis.

The CIA Chief of Station at the time (1962-1968), John M. Maury, had offices in the American Embassy as well as in the Tamion Building. (A station chief is, as a rule, a seasoned spymaster who runs operations in the field. To become a station chief is to reach the top rung of a professional spy's ladder abroad.) Maury's assistant, the Deputy Chief of Station, also had offices in both buildings. James M. Potts held that office from November 21, 1960, to May 24, 1964. Potts was replaced by Harris C. Greene, who arrived in Athens on May 27, 1964, and left in early 1969 when he was reassigned to Bern, Switzerland. (Potts returned to Athens to become the station chief from the middle of 1968 to August of 1972.) Both the Chief of Station and his deputy had diplomatic covers. Maury appeared as "First Secretary, Political Officer, Special Assistant to the Ambassador," while his deputy had the cover of "Attache, Political Officer."

The majority of the CIA case officers had offices in the Tamion Building, near Constitution Square.

The CIA operation in Greece was divided into two parts: the administrative or "support" personnel and the "operations" personnel. There were about forty support employees, performing housekeeping and clerical duties. In a sense, they formed the CIA bureaucracy in Greece. The rest of the CIA people belonged to the operations component, including 125 assigned to MENCA.

Steve Milton was the Chief of Operations during the period under discussion, and was replaced at the end of the decade by Peter Koromilas. Milton was a Greek-American recruited into the CIA sometime during the end of the 1940s. He was in the habit of telling people that he was "America's foremost expert on Greece." There has been some speculation in Washington that Milton was reassigned to positions outside of Greece after 1970 because of his mistaken evaluation of dictator George Papadopoulos. According to this account, Milton had been the most important booster of Papadopoulos among the operations people in the CIA. When Papadopoulos did not perform as expected, Milton was sent to Saigon and Tehran. Saigon assignments were a demotion for Europe-based operations officers with no previous Southeast Asian experience at that time.

Milton was in charge of four divisions, each with a specific operational task. Each of these divisions was headed by a division chief responsible to Milton for the activities under his control. Milton in turn was responsible to the Deputy Chief of Station, Harris C. Greene. During the latter part of the decade, Milton was bypassed by the division chiefs, who would go over him to the Deputy Chief. In the words of one case officer, "Milton became somewhat of a joke at this time." (Milton was once enraged when the guard at the fifth-floor offices in the Tamion Building did not recognize him and refused him entry. Milton replaced the guard with a combination lock.)

The four operations divisions under Milton's control were: the Greek desk, the Soviet Bloc or SB desk, the Technical Services or TSD, and the Paramilitary branch. The Communications division, MENCA, was administered separately but provided operations support to the other four. TSD and MENCA were engaged in activities that included support of CIA operations in countries other than Greece, called collectively NE Division (Near East). The Greek desk and the Paramilitary branch were engaged in operations within the country. SB carried on operations within Greece against Russian and Eastern Bloc country targets.

MENCA was the largest CIA operation in Greece with some 125 employees. TSD had about 15 officers, the Soviet Bloc desk 7 case officers, the Greek desk 12, and the Paramilitary group 1 to 2 case officers. (A "case officer" is a CIA employee trained to recruit and "handle" people in a position to know information useful to American intelligence. Such people might include cabinet ministers, prominent businessmen, diplomats, chauffeurs, government employees, people who work closely with suspected Soviet agents, travel agents, reporters, maids or bartenders. In Greece during the 1960s, most agents and contacts were

Greek, but foreigners were also used. A case officer is responsible for anywhere from one to twenty or more "assets," depending on his energy and ambition. Assets are either agents or contacts, plus any purely technical operation a case officer "runs" —supervises—such as telephone taps and microphones.)

The case officers used the expertise of the TSD officers for the collection of information through electronic devices. However, according to individuals who are in a position to know, in the period between 1965 and 1969, the CIA had arrived at some agreement with "people in OTE" (the Greek Telephone organization), so that when a case officer wanted a telephone bug installed, he would "call a contact number in OTE and the job would be done." It cannot be confirmed that similar arrangements between the CIA and OTE employees exist today.

CIA case officers routinely assumed that when OTE installed such a device, KYP (*Kentriki Ypiresia Pliroforion* or Central Information Bureau—Greece's equivalent to the FBI and CIA put together) would be informed. There are indications that KYP and the CIA had some sort of "gentlemen's agreement" to share information collected in Greece. However, the CIA station chief was convinced that KYP was infiltrated by "Russian" agents. As a result, when the CIA in Greece wanted to eliminate what was called "the security problems of KYP," the TSD people would install such devices as were needed without informing KYP. TSD specialists during this period installed electronic monitoring devices capable of listening in on most of the telephone sets that belonged to higher diplomats and military attaches of Eastern Bloc countries. In installing these telephone bugs, TSD technicians used, when necessary, vehicles painted to look like OTE trucks.

Most of the CIA officers were assigned to Greece for four years. As a rule, only the Greek, Paramilitary, and Soviet Bloc desk case officers spoke fluent Greek. Station Chief John Maury spoke no Greek at all. Most of them learned Greek at the Foreign Service Institute in Washington, D.C. FSI, as the institute is usually called, is a training facility maintained by the U.S. Department of State, where diplomats, military and CIA officers take language training and courses introducing them to the history and politics of the countries to which they are assigned. CIA assignments usually begin and end in July or August, so that the children of the CIA officers can attend school without interruptions.

John Maury, during his speech at American University, in
addition to suggesting that the station's interests pointed only
north to the socialist countries, asserted that during the 1960s,
the interest of the Agency in the political developments within
Greece was minimal. He tried to leave the impression that the
CIA in Greece was mostly a support operation for activities
outside of Greece. But the CIA was very much involved in
activities within Greece. There were more case officers assigned
to the Greek and Paramilitary desks than to the Soviet Bloc
desk. In addition, CIA officers who worked with him in Athens
were very much surprised to learn that Maury described himself
in his speech as a "Soviet Bloc expert." While in Athens, Maury
had shown very little interest in Soviet Bloc operations but was
more than involved in the work of the Greek desk case officers.
At CIA parties and social events, his deep interest and involvement in Greek politics would surface, usually in the form of
anecdotal put-downs like the one the week after the military
takeover of the country. In a conversation with Maury, American Ambassador Phillips Talbot remarked that the *coup* was "a
rape of democracy." Maury answered with the following question: "How can you rape a whore?"

The Paramilitary Group

Hidden away among the more than 200 Clandestine Services
people of the CIA in Greece was a curiously low-key operation
called the Paramilitary Group. Perhaps no activity of the CIA
could be as clearly linked to the possibility of internal subversion as this group. The existence of such a group was not unique
to Greece. Similar paramilitary groups, directed by CIA officers,
operated in the Sixties throughout Europe. As a rule, CIA officers avoided as much as they could becoming case officers in
this group: the exposure of an officer to foreign nationals meant
the end of any possibility for advancement within the CIA, and
shunning even by fellow CIA officers.

In Greece, the Paramilitary Group came into existence sometime in the early 1950s. From 1963 to 1967, a Greek–American
CIA agent with considerable prior military service in the United
States Army was the person who directed the operations of the
group. In 1967, this officer was transferred to Vietnam and a
junior officer took over. The Greek–American CIA officer recruited several groups of Greek citizens for what the CIA called,

"a nucleus for rallying a citizen army against the threat of a leftist *coup*." Each of the several groups was trained and equipped to act as an autonomous guerrilla unit, capable of mobilizing and carrying on guerrilla warfare with minimal or no outside direction.

The members of each such group were trained by the CIA in military procedures. As far as can be determined, most of the paramilitary groups trained in two camps: one near Volos, and the second on Mount Olympos. After the initial training sessions, the groups would drill in isolated areas in Pindos and the mountains near Florina. These guerrilla groups were armed with automatic weapons, as well as small mountain mortars.

The weapons were stored in several places. Most of the military supplies were cached in the ground and in caves. Each member of these paramilitary groups knew where such cached weaponry was hidden, in order to be able to mobilize himself to a designated spot, without orders. Constant problems developed with keeping the project secret. One CIA officer described it as "a nightmare." "No sooner would a cache be put into the ground than one of the recruited Greeks would get drunk in a bar and start blabbing about the weapons," he said, requiring him to relocate the cache and find a replacement for the offender. In addition to arms, food and medical supplies would also be cached.

During the period between 1963 and 1969, the paramilitary branch of the CIA in Greece was a completely separate operation. There seems to have been no contact, official or otherwise, with the Joint United States Military Assistance Group in Greece (JUSMAGG). At this time, it is not known if there existed any contact between these paramilitary groups and elements of the Greek Armed Forces that took part in the 1967 *coup d'état*.

According to a former Clandestine Services source still under the CIA's secrecy oath, the new head of the paramilitary branch who took over in 1967 had no military experience and had not previously engaged in paramilitary operations. Soon after, he approached a CIA supply officer with an unusual request. Neatly typed out, using U.S. Army catalogue numbers and descriptions, was an order for a full field hospital, including sophisticated equipment for surgical procedures not undertaken in guerrilla war situations, to be requisitioned from the U.S. Army through CIA channels. The hospital supplies included drugs with fairly short expiration dates of effectiveness, such as penicillin. Operating tables and other bulky items too large to cache in the ground were also requested.

The CIA supply officer, a former military man, trained in logistics, questioned the paramilitary officer on the appropriateness of the order for his task. Rather than contest the evaluation of the supply officer, the paramilitary branch head indicated that "he would check the matter out," and never returned. What makes the whole affair even more peculiar is the timing of the request. Constantine, the ex-king, had just returned from a visit to the United States, where he had several meetings with high American officials including President Johnson. It is conceivable, though no proof can be found at this time, that the CIA officer wanted the field hospital for use in the king's *coup*, which took place, unsuccessfully, later the same year.

The Paramilitary Group, as far as can be determined, was never disbanded. In the eyes of senior CIA officials, the groups under the direction of the paramilitary branch are seen as a long-term "insurance" for the interests of the United States in Greece, to be used to assist or to direct the possible overthrow of an "unsympathetic" Greek government. "Unsympathetic" of course to American manipulation.

The American Factor in Greece: Old and New

by Philip Agee

[AUTHOR'S NOTE: The following article on the CIA's presence in Greece was commissioned by the Athens newspaper *Ta Nea* in March 1976, just a few months after the killing of Richard Welch. The article included the names and addresses of approximately 100 of the CIA's staff employees in Athens, gleaned from a U.S. Mission list of 1974. Shortly after the article was commissioned, however, the editor of *Ta Nea* received a death threat if he proceeded with publication. The editor reconsidered his offer. Eventually, the article, with the names, was published in the Greek political monthly, *Anti,* in May 1977. *Anti's* editor, Christos Papoutsakis, was imprisoned and tortured under the CIA-supported "Colonels" regime (1967–1974), and his brother died in one of the regime's torture chambers. When the article and names were published, the Greek government tried unsuccessfully to buy every copy of that edition of *Anti.*]

[This article first appeared in the May 1977 issue of *Anti,* in Athens.]

The Greek people today offer enormous hope to many millions of the "free" world's population forced to suffer the relentless repression and increasing injustices inflicted by right-wing dictatorships.

Indonesians, Brazilians, Koreans, Africans, Chileans, Uruguayans, Iranians—people the world over see in Greece the proof that their own regimes, in most cases installed or sustained with substantial clandestine intervention by the American CIA, can also be defeated some day.

Thirty years of intervention by successive American administrations are finally ending in a stunning series of defeats that underline the transitory nature of U.S. efforts to prevent peoples from achieving national liberation and from installing some variety of socialism. These efforts began in Greece, and here since 1947 practically every conceivable method of "counterinsurgency" has been used from military aid and intervention to more refined psychological campaigns to promote anti-left hysteria, to escalation of repression by security services, to fabrications, provocations, and rigged elections, to a military *coup* justified by a "Communist plot," to political assassination and mass torture of political prisoners.

Increasing numbers of Americans, sensitized by the ghastliness of Vietnam and by domestic political scandals, are comprehending how the U.S. government, in its foreign policy as well as in its domestic programs, serves privileged, minority interests —the interests of owners and managers of multinational companies, of professionals and politicians who serve them, of the military establishment and defense contractors. These millions of alienated Americans are not simply dropouts, apolitical since withdrawal from Vietnam. Many are continuing to take positive action to defeat intervention in other parts of the world, and where intervention is secret (as in most countries) defeat can be inflicted, at least in part, by exposure. Perhaps nowhere is it more important than in Greece for Americans to help expose and defeat the apparatus for clandestine intervention by the U.S. government.

The CIA's clandestine methodology has been well exposed during the past two years through several books by former CIA officers, by official investigations and reports, and by investigative journalism and leaks to the press. Those in Greece who study these methods will be better able to identify certain events as probable results of intervention by the CIA, and perhaps even to anticipate such intervention. But in addition to exposing *what* the CIA does, it is equally important to expose *who* does it, that is, who the CIA people operating in Greece are, and who their local collaborators and agents are. Helping to expose the CIA personnel working in Greece must be a top priority of the "new American factor," for if the Greek people wish to expel the CIA, they must know who they are.

There remain, of course, those Americans whose interests demand intensification of clandestine intervention in Greece. For these, the "old American factor" must be preserved, strengthened, and applied more effectively than ever. For these, the Americans who work to expose the CIA's operations and personnel are antipatriotic—even those concerned only with "abuses" and "failures." Indeed the killing of one exposed CIA operative provided just the issue needed by the Ford Administration to ward off any meaningful congressional reforms to limit a President's capability for clandestine wheeling and dealing. Nevertheless, so much has been revealed that few people can now deny that subversion of "free" institutions by the CIA and its promotion of hypocrisy, corruption and political repression are in fact the real antipatriotic and antihuman actions by Americans in the international order.

We have made an analysis of the personnel assigned to the U.S. Mission in Greece in order to discover which offices in the Mission provide cover for the CIA. Although the list of personnel was from 1974, and many of those we have identified as CIA employees will by now have been transferred to other countries, the analysis is useful because it will assist in discovering the CIA personnel currently assigned in Greece and also the general size and scope of the CIA's main offices there. Moreover, by exposing the CIA people working in Greece during the period of the military dictatorship, their return to Greece later or their continued presence now will be difficult. The following analysis probably has current validity, given the custom in the CIA to use the same cover structures year after year.

No Greek will be surprised to learn that the CIA has a very large contingent in the huge American diplomatic and military mission. As many as 130 U.S.-citizen, staff employees of the CIA appear to be working in the mission which altogether totals more than 800 people (not including several of the large military bases such as those in Crete). These CIA employees are under thin cover in the Embassy (Office of the Special Assistant, Political Section, and Administrative Section) and in the Joint U.S. Military Advisory Group in Greece (JUSMAGG) in the Tamion Building.

The Special Assistant to the Ambassador and another officer, John J. Shea, together with two secretary-typists, comprise the Office of the Special Assistant located on the third floor of the Embassy next to the Ambassador's office. Shea, who is 51, appears to have been a bona fide State Department officer from 1950 until 1957 during which he served in Rome and Baghdad and was given Arabic language training. In late 1957, however, Shea was assigned to the CIA office in the Political Section of the U.S. Embassy in Rome where he worked until reassignment to Washington in 1965. He again served in Europe (Paris, 1968–1970 and Rome, 1970–1972) but returned to Washington to the Foreign Service Institute during 1972–1973, probably to study Greek. He arrived in Athens in June 1973.

The Embassy Political Section, also next to the Ambassador's office, provides cover for two CIA operations officers. In 1974 these were James D. Baldwin and Daniel K. Webster. Baldwin, however, was replaced in June 1974 by Robert H. Larson who in turn was transferred in April 1975 to the CIA office in the Political Section of the U.S. Embassy in Nicosia, where he continues according to available records. Larson's replacement in Athens appears to have been William S. Lofgren who arrived from Nicosia in January 1975, and he is also assigned to the Political Section of the Athens Embassy. In fact Larson and Lofgren appear to have swapped jobs. Webster also left Athens and was replaced by James W. McWilliams who arrived in June 1975.

Both Lofgren, 39, and McWilliams have had previous assignments of interest. Lofgren served in U.S. Embassies in New Delhi (1969–1971) and Beirut (1971–1973) before assignment to Cyprus in 1973. McWilliams served in the U.S. consulates in Bombay (1969–1972) and Calcutta (1972–1974) before coming to Athens. These two officers undoubtedly are instructed to use their cover in the Embassy Political Section in order to meet Greek political figures and officials of the other diplomatic missions in Athens—always, of course, for the purpose of assessing them for recruitment as spies for the CIA.

The rest of the CIA personnel in the Embassy are assigned to five communications offices, all nominally part of the Embassy Administrative Section, Area Telecommunications Office, on the second floor, except for one communications office next to the Office of the Special Assistant (the CIA Chief). This office, room 320 of the Embassy, is staffed by five telecommunications officers and is probably the office in charge of ordinary communications of the CIA's Athens Station. The other four communications offices, however, appear to be a radio relay station for communications between CIA offices in the Near and Middle East and the CIA's main headquarters communications facility at Warrenton, Virginia, not far from Washington.

The largest of the offices of the relay station, designated Regional Relay Facility (RRF), has 49 telecommunications officers assigned to operate the radios and cryptographic machines used for sending and receiving the large volume of CIA messages between Headquarters and the other stations to the east. There is also a logistics section with six persons assigned, and another office with the embassy designation T/I (meaning unknown) which has nine people working in it. The 64 people working in this relay facility are, of course, vital for maintaining the CIA's communications with other countries and probably have only a marginal importance to the CIA's Greek operations.

The fifth CIA communications office in the Embassy is also called an Area Telecommunications Office and it occupies rooms 239 and 253 with 15 people assigned. The chief of the entire CIA communications operation, who was Florend Kindell in 1974, is in this office which probably also includes the CIA's main file room and administrative section (finance, logistics, etc.). Frank Guldseth appears to be the Chief of Administration for the CIA Station but he departed in mid-1975. His replacement is probably Alfred C. Moran who arrived in May 1975.

The transmitters and receivers for at least part of this communications operation are probably in the Embassy where they can be adequately protected. However, the Area Telecommunications Office also has a transmission and receiving site in New Kifissia which is manned by nine technicians, all of whom appear to be Greek employees who may think they work for the U.S. Embassy rather than for the CIA. Still another ATO Greek employee works in Marathon. Altogether then, the CIA has some 84 employees under Embassy cover in communications offices with an additional group of ten Greek employees working at communications facilities outside the Embassy.

The main operational office of the CIA in Athens is in the Tamion Building under cover of the military assistance mission known as JUSMAGG. Altogether, JUSMAGG personnel number about 110 and these are divided bureaucratically into a Headquarters section and Army, Navy, and Air Force sections. Within the Headquarters section about 40 CIA employees are working. All are civilians, ostensibly working for the Department of Defense. However, the CIA office is physically separate from the bona fide military assistance mission, having its own entrance and elevator.

A number of the CIA officers working under JUSMAGG cover have had interesting previous assignments under cover of the Department of State and the Agency for International Development. Ronald Estes, for example, served under State Department cover in the U.S. embassies in Nicosia (1962–1964), Prague (1965–1967), and Beirut (1970–1973). He was given Czech language training before his Prague assignment, and he probably learned Greek for his previous assignment in Nicosia.

Jerry Ferentinos served under cover as a political officer in the U.S. Consulate General in Hong Kong (1961–1964) and as an "executive assistant" in the Embassy in Vientiane (1966–1968). His service in Laos was during the period of the CIA's "secret war," using tens of thousands of Meo tribesmen in their doomed efforts to defeat the national liberation forces.

Thomas Foster was a telecommunications assistant in New Delhi (1966–1969) while Norman Goldman worked under cover as an economic and commercial officer in the Consulate General in Lahore, Pakistan (1968–1971). Ronald Nordeen used the cover of a "political assistant" in the Embassy in New Delhi (1962–1964) and became a Vice-Consul when transferred to the Consulate in Madras (1964–1968).

John Palevich had cover as a "research analyst" for the Department of the Army (1958–1961), as a Vice-Consul in Berlin (1961–1963), Third Secretary in Warsaw (1963-1966), and as an "economic officer" in Vientiane (1966–1967). Robert Rayle appeared to have been under rather deeper cover during 1961–1965 when he worked first as a "marketing consultant" and later as a "researcher." Discovery of Rayle's ostensible employers during those years would probably reveal another "private" organization providing cover for CIA employees. Rayle went on to work in the U.S. Embassy in New Delhi (1965–1968) under cover as a "political-economic" officer. Still another of the JUSMAGG cover officers is Stephen Winsky who served in Helsinki (1961–1966) as a Second Secretary and Vice-Consul. Winsky speaks Greek.

Probably the most dangerous of the JUSMAGG employees

who appear to be CIA officers is William Evans. He worked under cover as a civilian employee of the Department of the Army during the 1950s, but in 1959 he went to Jakarta with the Agency for International Development in the notorious Public Safety Program of assistance to foreign police and security services. Evans was transferred from Jakarta to Saigon in 1962, to Hue during the same year, and back to Saigon in 1965. He was a "public safety advisor" throughout these assignments within the deadly "pacification" campaigns in Vietnam. Evans, although formally assigned to JUSMAGG, has his office in the Embassy with the same number as the Deputy Chief of Mission (336). This would place him almost next to the Office of the Special Assistant. He might well be the CIA's Deputy Chief of Station.

Two other CIA officers under JUSMAGG cover have offices in the Embassy as well as in the Tamion Building. They are George Kublik and Louis Pagano, whose embassy office (326) places them next to the CIA communications office (320) and the CIA Chief's office (Office of the Special Assistant, room 329). Kublik and Pagano may be in charge of the flow of secret documents between the CIA offices in the Embassy and the Tamion Building.

For many years the CIA has had a base in Thessaloniki which is subordinate to the main station in Athens. The CIA people there appear to be a civilian in the Thessaloniki office of the JUSMAGG organization and an officer under State Department cover in the Consulate General since January 1975.

Besides the offices already named, which are used for cover by the CIA, there is another office in the U.S. Mission that attracts attention. This is called USAFE (for United States Air Force, Europe) Detachment 6. This office employs 17 persons, all but two of whom are men, but in spite of being a military office all of its personnel are civilians. The U.S. Embassy directory provides telephone numbers for a "commander" and a "staff duty officer" but without names. This office is also in the Tamion Building, and while it may be still another CIA cover office, a strong possibility exists that this is a communications monitoring unit of the super-secret National Security Agency.

The NSA has the job of monitoring commercial and governmental communications all over the world, partly for military purposes and partly for economic reasons to assist American multinational companies against their foreign competitors. According to a former NSA analyst who was assigned to the huge monitoring facility at Istanbul during the late 1960s, the NSA monitoring operation in Greece is under CIA control. Greek government and military communications are monitored not only to collect information against Greeks, but also to monitor the military communications security of Greek forces. According to the ex-analyst, the Greek systems for secret communications are provided by the NSA and thus are easily monitored and decrypted. Communications of other embassies in Athens are, of course, also targeted by the NSA unit.

Couldn't the Greek government know that so many CIA people are masquerading as Department of State and Pentagon employees? Wouldn't the CIA still have close relations with KYP and other Greek services? Certain government cooperation with the CIA may well exist in spite of the CIA's flagrant support of the former military dictatorship. Only a few weeks ago a person with very good connections in Greece told me that on two occasions during 1975, the American Embassy was given 500 blank carnets by the Greek Foreign Ministry, and that no record existed in the Foreign Ministry to indicate to whom the carnets, which reflect the diplomatic status of the bearer, were issued. This report may not be true, but there can be no doubt that the CIA will try to conceal most of its employees from the local government in every foreign country.

The CIA people in Greece right now must surely be continuing the interventionist policy adopted in the U.S. in 1947 and followed without exception ever since. Intelligence information collection has no purpose except to be used for action, and covert action in all its varieties is the end of the cycle. As the Greek people continue to move toward their liberation, the need for retrogressive influence and action will correspondingly increase.

People like Shea, Lofgren, McWilliams, Estes, Ferentinos, and the rest are planning at this very moment the Aspida plots of tomorrow, the Pericles and Prometheus Plans of next year, and the revitalization of Organization X and IDEA for the long run. They are planning the next round of antileft hysteria, forging the documents to "prove" intervention by "foreign ideologies," i.e., anti-imperialist, and preparing new special emergency measures to facilitate repression. People the world over are watching to see if the CIA will somehow win the next round or whether Greeks will at last defeat this secret political police and its local collaborators.

Hello
Hugh Montgomery

by *Steve Weissman*

When the new CIA chief for Italy—Mr. Hugh Montgomery—
took up his post in the Eternal City in November 1975, he must
have counted himself a lucky man. Rome, for all its crises,
remains one of the plushest posts for Uncle Sam's secret agents,
and the 52-year-old Montgomery could look forward to chalking
up new *coups* in his long and distinguished CIA career.

But last week the Roman holiday of Mr. Montgomery came to
a screeching halt when critics of the CIA in the American Congress made headlines by leaking to the press one of the world's
least secret secrets—that the Americans were once again giving
covert funds to anti-Communist politicos in Italy. Then, just as
the CIA's lame-duck director William Colby was publicly deny-
ing the payoffs, the supposedly undercover Montgomery received an unexpected telephone call at his private residence on
the Aventine Hill.

[This article first appeared as "Ecco La CIA in Italia," in the
January 15, 1976, issue of *La Repubblica*, in Rome.]

Would Dr. Montgomery be willing to grant an interview? asked the caller.

"No!" exploded the CIA chief as he slammed down the receiver. "No, I certainly would not!"

Montgomery's anger at being so quickly exposed reflects the personal dilemma of America's top crypto-diplomats. After Vietnam and Watergate, neither Congress nor the press is prepared to permit the CIA to go on operating in the dark. And with so many people shining light on their activities, the Agency can no longer protect their covert operations—or even their own operatives, as was shown by the recent killing of Montgomery's counterpart in Athens, Mr. Richard Welch.

"The shoe is really on the other foot now," commented former CIA operations officer Philip Agee. "For years the CIA has secretly terrorized people all over the world. But now that CIA people are becoming publicly known, they are the ones who will have to look both ways every time they cross the street. And the more time they spend having to worry and watch their step, the less time they will have to pay off politicians, help the local police, or run clandestine operations."

Montgomery, as chief, runs his supposedly secret empire—and recruits his Italian agents and allies—from rooms 257–262 in the new wing of the American Embassy. Official American and Italian records list Montgomery and most of the other occupants of these rooms as "attaches" and "political officers." But given the carelessness of the CIA in creating fictitious posts to give their people cover over the years, it has been possible to identify most of them as CIA simply by knowing how to use publicly available biographic records from the U.S. State Department, along with confidential information from within the Embassy itself.

The list of these CIA "political officers" includes William Acon, Mario Cioci, Robert Devereux, and Michael E. Kostiw. In response to repeated telephone calls, Mr. Montgomery's secretary has also confirmed that Montgomery is in fact the successor to the previous CIA chief in Rome, Howard E. Stone, who had earlier been exposed by the American magazine *Counter-Spy*.

Apart from these phoney diplomats, the new wing of the American Embassy also gives cover to a larger, more secret CIA unit—the so-called United States Army Southern European Projects Unit. In recent years this unit has numbered as many as 14

—all CIA civilians despite the military name, and the group has included at least one police advisor with experience in Laos and Vietnam. According to one of its members—CIA veteran Charles Gale, Jr.—the chief of the project is Michael C. Sednaoui.

Other CIA officials have been identified in the Embassy's telecommunications office, among the consular staff in Milan and Rome, and on the Embassy's economic staff. Mr. Christopher Costanzo, an economic officer whom Philip Agee remembers personally from the CIA, has denied knowing Agee or working for the CIA. "Frankly, I'm shocked that there are people trying to dig into other people's lives," he said.

In all, the CIA is believed to have over 40 people inside the Embassy, with several others working here under cover of various military installations and multinational corporations.

Mr. Montgomery, who oversees the entire operation, has served an earlier tour of duty in Rome from 1965 to 1969, and has also served in Athens, Moscow, and Paris. On coming to Rome, his automobile carried diplomatic plates from Vienna. A Ph.D. from Harvard, Montgomery was at the university at the same time as the recently slain Richard Welch and Secretary of State Henry Kissinger.

The CIA in Italy:
An Interview with
Victor Marchetti

by *Victor Marchetti and*
Panorama

Q: It has been said that the CIA secretly financed some Italian organizations. What can you say about this?

A: For a certain period of time, i.e., the 1950s, the CIA spent from $20 to $30 million a year, or maybe more, to finance its programs in Italy. It supported cultural and youth organizations; newspapers; labor unions, of *proven* anti-Communist leanings, linked with the American AFL-CIO; Catholic groups . . .

Q: Which groups?

A: The only thing I know is that in the 1950s and 60s the CIA gave economic support to many activities promoted by the Catholic Church, from orphanages to the missions. Millions of dollars each year.

[This article first appeared as "Le mani sull'Italia," in the May 2, 1974, issue of *Panorama*, in Milan.]

Q: Do you remember to whom the money went?

A: To a great number of bishops and monsignors. One of them was Cardinal Giovanni Battista Montini. It is possible that Cardinal Montini did not know where the money was coming from. He may have thought that it came from friends in the United States or from the American government.

Q: Why did Cardinal Montini receive that money?

A: Because he was promoting orphanages. The thinking was that if such institutions were adequately supported, many young people would be able to live well there and so would not one day fall into Communist hands.

Q: Did the CIA also finance political parties? Which ones?

A: CIA policy has always been to finance all parties opposed to communism and first of all the Christian Democratic Party.

Q: Did CIA assistance to anti-Communist organizations and political parties continue through recent years?

A: In the 1960s, CIA expenditures in Italy went down to about $10 million a year. According to the plans, they should have gradually come to an end with the finish of that decade. The Cold War was over and the Communist threat in Italy seemed to have diminished. But in 1969 Graham Martin, the American Ambassador in Rome [he was assigned to Rome from 1969 to 1972; he was the last American ambassador to South Vietnam], wanted it to start all over again.

Q: What do you mean?

A: Martin wanted to recommence secret assistance, first of all to the Christian Democrats, but also to some other political groups.

Q: Is Martin a CIA man?

A: As far as I know, Martin is not a CIA man. But in all countries CIA activities are supervised by the U.S. Ambassador. Some ambassadors work in close contact with the CIA; others dislike the CIA and try to keep away from it.

Q: How many men are on the CIA payroll in Italy?

A: I do not know exactly. CIA employees, in the strict sense of the term, must number from 40 to 50. They operate around the U.S. Embassy and other small bases in the country. Then there is the network of agents and informants.

Q: So Martin was the type of ambassador who supported CIA programs?

A: Yes. Martin is a very aggressive and harsh man who uses all means, including the CIA, to attain his goals. He is one of those ambassadors who reflect Nixon's tough line of action.

Q: According to the *New York Times,* there were secret meetings between Martin and Amintore Fanfani [a high-ranking CD official, Secretary-General of the Party since June 1973 and for a time Premier of Italy] in 1970. During these meetings it is alleged that there was discussion of possible CIA financing for Fanfani supporters, about $1 million, in order to contain the drive from the left in Italian political life. Can you tell us whether this story is true?

A: I think so. As far as I know, the *New York Times* article is very good. It has a lot of valuable information in it.

Q: It has been said that in your book you mention Fanfani, and that such passages have been censored. Is this true?

A: My book is primarily historical. But the CIA does not want to me to talk even about the past. In fact, I cannot talk. I did not mention Fanfani by name. I talked about political parties. . . . In short, if I tell what has been censored in my book, I disobey an order from a federal court. And if an article would then be published on it, the CIA would come down here the next day and bring me to court.

Q: Can you deny that Fanfani is mentioned in your book?

A: As I said before, I do not remember having mentioned names. At least I can't remember it right now. Even if I would remember it, I would not say so, because there is an injunction against me. . . . It is possible that I mentioned him, If so, it would be in the context of financial help to Italians and the

Christian Democrats. Graham Martin wanted to resume such aid. At that time, he wanted to support Fanfani. He was concerned about Fanfani's ability to maintain his position. . . . It must have been something like that. . . . I do not mean that Fanfani is a CIA agent. Martin only wanted to help him stem the tide and prevent undesirable elements, such as Communists or left-wing Socialists, from taking over too much power or influence.

Q: How would the CIA react today if Italy went too far to the left?

A: The CIA has its emergency plans. . .

Q: Is a *coup d'état* similar to the one that brought the colonels to power in Greece, with the help of the CIA, as it is said, possible in Italy?

A: Certainly. If Communists and Socialists were to extend their influence—which I don't think is probable—we can well imagine that support to Italian colonels would not be lacking.

Q: What can you say about relationships between the CIA and the Italian secret service and armed forces?

A: There is considerable collaboration in many spheres between Italy and the United States. For example, Italian secret service officers are being trained in the U.S.A. Of this I am sure.

Q: What kind of training?

A: The CIA gives Italian officers—and officers from many other countries—basic training in espionage and police activities. They are trained, for example, to confront disorders and student demonstrations, to prepare dossiers, to make the best possible use of bank data and tax returns of individual citizens, etc. In other words, to watch over the population of their country with the means offered by technology. This is what I call technofascism and it is already operative in the United States. . . . This type of activity is a far cry from the legitimate work of a secret service, namely the gathering of political, economic, and military information on one or another foreign nation.

Q: Do you think there is some connection between CIA emergency plans and the training of allied and Italian officers in the U.S.A.?

A: Yes, but a remote one. . . .

Q: Which does the CIA trust more: the Italian army or the *carabinieri* [the national police force]?

A: I think the *carabinieri*.

Q: You said that if Italian Communists were to . . .

A: I said that if it were thought that Italy might turn communist, if a new Luigi Longo [famous leader of the Italian Communist Party after World War II] managed to gather, let us say, 50% of the votes and would thus be in a position to form a government—a government that would announce its intention to nationalize industries and turn over the Naples naval base to the Soviets—you may be sure that the CIA and the U.S. government would do everything to cause a delay. More than that: in such an event, if the only way to avoid Communist control of Italy would be to support neofascist forces, there would be no hesitation in having recourse to the neofascists. That's what happened in Chile. All means were used to combat Salvador Allende, from espionage to economic pressure. The military stepped in for the *coup de grâce*. William Colby, CIA Director, says that after all it was not so bad: civil war was averted.

Q: Is there any evidence that General Augusto Pinochet, head of the Chilean military junta, had direct connections with the CIA?

A: I don't know. I have the impression that the CIA knew what Pinochet was planning, and that it supported and encouraged him. . . .

Q: Many in the U.S.A. and elsewhere believe that CIA activities are meant to shore up democracy where it seems to be threatened. . . .

A: With that motivation we went to the extent of supporting corrupt dictatorial regimes, such as those in South Vietnam and South Korea, to mention only two examples. Yes, we wanted to export democracy. We exported fascism instead. Democracy is like religion: it cannot be imposed. It can be spread only if those who preach it practice it. One day I finally understood these things. That was why I decided to leave the secret service.

What the CIA
Is Looking for
in France

by Rene Backmann, Franz-Olivier Giesbert, and Olivier Todd

Forty-four CIA agents named in a Parisian daily. A new blow to America's intelligence services. But it won't stop the maneuvering in France between spies of the East and West.

Liberation—the staff-run and privately-printed daily of the new extreme left—has become famous from Wissembach (Vosges) to Washington, D.C. "We usually sell around 20,000 copies," explained editor Serge July. "On Tuesday, January 13, we sold more than 30,000." At the newsstands in the embassy districts, certain of the more discreet customers even carried off their copy of *Libe* under wraps.

The names of 44 CIA agents in Paris, plus the private addresses of 9 of them, shouted *Liberation* in issues number 629 and 630. It was, undeniably, a scoop.

Libe's facts are, for the most part, correct. Named for the first time in France by *Le Canard Enchaîné,* Eugen Burgstaller is

[This article first appeared in the January 1976 issue of *Le Nouvel Observateur*, in Paris.]

indeed the CIA Station Chief in our country. At least in the "developed countries," it is almost an American tradition to let it be known who the CIA chief is.

Nonetheless, the *Liberation* pieces do have their faults. Like an Embassy employee listed as a telecommunications expert, who—in fact—only stamps passports. Or another, listed as the CIA's second-in-command, who actually left several months ago, along with many of his colleagues. For all its precautions, *Liberation* also, in some cases, mixes together the chiefs and the underlings, the penpushers and the analysts.

The Welch Case

The daily writes: "It is easier to spot the chiefs of the CIA than the 'honorable correspondents' of the Soviet Union. And that is undoubtedly to the credit of the United States." The newspaper also claims that it would reveal the names of the KGB men "if the American Embassy would be kind enough to furnish them." All a bit naive, since all of Parisian intelligence— from the big embassies to the small—knows very well that the Soviets have two "masters of the hunt" now in the capital. For the KGB, the "resident" is Ivan Petrovitch Kisliak. And, every bit as important, for the GRU—the intelligence service of the Soviet Army's high command—Nicolai Evdokimov. In the official yearbooks, the two men are listed as "embassy counselors," of the third and sixth rank respectively. But complete Soviet yearbooks are as hard to find in Paris as in Moscow.

The *Liberation* affair is troubling for the Americans. It is part, according to them, of some sort of grand international conspiracy, which is—though surely not in the case of *Liberation*—run all the way from Moscow.

The first list of CIA agents stationed abroad appeared in Mexico in 1974, giving the names—real or imagined—of agents based there. In May 1975, some British journalists published a similar list for their country in *Time Out*, and on Thursday, January 15, 1976, they added three names to the list, stirring up a quarrel between *The Times* and the *Washington Post* and embarrassing Harold Wilson in the House of Commons.

At the outset, a liberal American magazine, *CounterSpy*, had published a list of the CIA station chiefs in some one hundred countries—but without giving their private addresses. The journalists of *Liberation* made use of *CounterSpy's* methods—cross-checking diplomatic yearbooks, foreign service codes and classifications, and the special insurance policies held by CIA agents. It was quite a job.

In Washington, of course, they are thinking above all about the publication in the *Athens News* on November 25, 1975, of the name and private address of Richard Welch, the CIA chief in Greece. Welch was killed on December 23, and it seems a case of cause and effect.

Elsewhere, on January 13, 1976, the Spanish magazine *Cambio 16* confined itself to the names of "nine members of the CIA stationed in Madrid," and other documents of this kind are going to appear in Italy, and undoubtedly in West Germany and the Netherlands.

If the anti-CIA operation continues at this rate, says Henry Kissinger, "the United States will end up without a secret service." Equally moved, the State Department spokesman Robert Funseth declared that all of this could "incite madmen and fanatics to attack diplomats." And it is true that the published lists do not distinguish activists from analysts, or professional killers from specialists like the one played by Robert Redford in *Three Days of the Condor,* who takes apart the texts of speeches, expense accounts, newspaper articles, and letters—which is the case with 99% of the CIA agents who work in France.

Victor Marchetti, a former CIA man who was among the first to write a book denouncing the crimes and blunders of "the Company," thinks that the CIA is again interested "in Portugal, Germany, Great Britain, Italy, and France." In France, the CIA specialists are interested in everything—from civilian industry to military production, from foreign policy to domestic problems. They frequent all the key *milieux.* They watch all the political parties. At Parisian dinners, people from most of the parties can be found at their tables. The CIA gleans intelligence at all levels.

The Balance of Terror

In France, the CIA is certainly not looking to "destabilize" the regime, and in any case, no one in Paris seems unduly worried. At the meeting of the Council of Ministers on Wednesday the 14th, the delicate subject of the list published by *Liberation* was not even raised. Neither Michel Poniatowski, the minister in charge of the *Direction de la Surveillance du Territoire (DST)*, nor Yvon Bourges, who oversees the activities of the *Service de Documentation Exterieure et de Contre-Espionage (SDECE)*, even mentioned it. "Ponia" fled from journalists; his press secretary was ill—how convenient—and contented himself with issuing a statement: "The French secret services have no part in this information. . . . It is clearly established that it originates from abroad."

With that in mind, in Paris and the provinces the protection of certain Americans has been assured or reinforced. At the request of Washington? For the French police, it was only a few more men and women to protect.

Public opinion and the press are divided, and the division is not simply between right and left. Some magazines see *Liberation*'s campaign of denunciation as an invitation to murder. For *Le Monde*, there is nothing dishonorable in working for a secret service, which must by definition remain secret. *L'Humanité* waffles around on the issue, and certainly does not side with the *gauchistes*. Even on the left, aside from those who applaud *Liberation*'s initiative, others have questions. Is this a fight against imperialism? Well, since there are two imperialisms, we must fight them both at the same time. On the other hand, the revelations may expose the unmasked agents to the risk of being slaughtered, like Richard Welch in Greece, and is that really revolutionary? And, finally, doesn't the balance of espionage contribute to the balance of nuclear terror? And if that's the case, isn't it dangerous to compromise one side or the other?

The Socialist Party wants the National Assembly to hold a closed meeting to hear from the government on the relationship between SDECE and CIA. In effect, they are asking that we Americanize our ways a bit: no other of the world's secret services has been looked at as closely by the legislature as has the CIA, especially in Senator Frank Church's report, which was published on November 20, 1975. This report reveals that the CIA's "clandestine services" arranged to get rid of Fidel Castro in Cuba, Rafael Trujillo in the Dominican Republic, Ngo Dinh Diem in South Vietnam, and General Rene Schneider in Chile.

But the report concludes that, in the final analysis, the United States was not directly implicated except in the case of Trujillo. The Church report, though very critical of CIA interventions in many Third World countries, still insists on the need for an intelligence service, above all to monitor the international arms race, nuclear and other.

The Risks of the Trade

Men of good faith, such as Serge July, figure that secret service agents, no matter who, must take on the risks of their trade. And Serge July clearly defines his aim: "It's psychological, a matter of shaking the resolve of CIA agents troubled by the personal repercussions of their action. For the agent himself, there is no other solution than to ask a change of assignment."

July thinks a lot about the Third World. "France remains a land of refuge," he argues. "There are Latin American refugees, Palestinians, and African revolutionaries. The CIA watches them, looking to set them up. . . .There are some strange SDECE-SAC-CIA encounters." For SAC, *Liberation* is getting ahead, and perhaps a bit too quickly, though that remains to be seen.

SDECE and the CIA are another matter. France and the United States are part of the Atlantic Alliance. In the permanent struggle against the other alliance, the Warsaw Pact, the CIA and SDECE work together quite naturally, spontaneously, organically. In espionage and counter-espionage, intelligence and counter-intelligence, as in other fields, it is sad but true that the two camps are still confronting one another, and France remains one of the fields of battle.

In our country, almost all of the men in charge of the CIA have diplomatic cover. This is not the case with certain of the top people of the KGB and GRU. In France, the Americans and the Soviets have roughly the same number of diplomats. For SDECE, every Soviet diplomat is a potential agent, but they do not assume the same about the Americans. The French services also pay infinitely more attention to the rare Russian terrorists and students than to the many Americans—apart from Jane Fonda. They very closely watch, for example, the flying and non-flying personnel of Aeroflot.

SDECE and the CIA trade all their useful tips on the arrival and departure of suspects. Some of this information passes through the DST. As a general rule, though, all of the embassies —be they Israeli or Arab—are warned "if there's something in the wind." Diplomacy, as well as national defense, demands this courtesy.

And then there's the painful problem of the diplomat-agents who go too far. Many of their departures go unannounced. Many agents of the Eastern Countries leave at the first frown to avoid the scandal of expulsion. They are not expelled officially and with all the distress that would then be so visible. Like when a Soviet air attache put a gyroscope and an element from a Thompson laser into his coat pocket at an aeronautics exhibition in 1973—not every Soviet agent is a Kim Philby. Or like when some Cubans were evidently too clearly implicated in the saga of Carlos, who killed two French police officers in 1975. That's beyond the rules of the game. The DST spot and keep a close eye on the French who work for the KGB and CIA. In principle, the DST does not work with the CIA, and at a certain point it should work against them. But in the world of intelligence agencies, there's a lot of swapping around. Unlike their CIA counterparts, however, DST officials don't have the means to drop in for a drink at the Crillon bar.

Suspicious Contacts

The vast majority of espionage crimes and offenses come out of the blue. For the little peccadilloes, then, the golden rule is that it's better to keep an eye on a known agent than to have to build up a dossier on his totally unknown replacement. Certain French generals, retired or not, might think and say that our national defense ought to be all-encompassing—as much against the West as against the East. This surely isn't the view of the secret services. Nontheless, during the summer of 1975, 11 CIA agents were—not expelled, *Alliance oblige*—but invited by the French government to leave. It seems that these gentlemen had involved themselves in the affairs of a third country.

Despite a few smudges of this kind, the relationship between SDECE and the CIA seems more flexible and harmonious under Valery Giscard d'Estaing than under Charles de Gaulle. The General, doubting the loyalty and effectiveness of the official services in the struggle against the OAS [Secret Army Organization], asked Roger Frey, Jacques Foccart, and other old faithfuls from the Resistance network to recruit some "dependables." This implied, among other things, men who would keep their distance from the Americans.

In 1960, some of the key station chiefs of French intelligence were summoned to Paris, where they were informed of the new diplomatic orientation—no more allegiance to the United States, though on the small everyday matters some rapport would be maintained. In this period, surveillance against agents from the Socialist countries was reduced. The European and American "stations" were reinforced, both in size and in quality. And there wasn't even any hesitation in asking a SDECE "plumber" to install a microphone in the hotel room of Under-Secretary of State George Ball, who was engaged in friendly negotiations with the French government.

In Paris, the DST—that is to say, counter-espionage—installed wiretaps on the telephones of the American Embassy in order to detect suspicious contacts (which would have included those of the CIA), and to monitor two diplomats—Larry Gourlay and Charles Lester, who were in charge of the CIA's liaison with the DST and SDECE. According to Victor Marchetti, the relationship was so bad during this period that the CIA nearly broke relations with SDECE.

There were also some rather big waves: the SDECE station chief in Washington since 1951, Philippe Thyraud de Vosjoli, was ordered to obey the new rules and give information on the United States. He refused, and in 1963 handed his resignation directly to President de Gaulle. It was said at the time in the Elyseé, that "Vosjoli has been turned by the CIA." And they never forgave him, among other things, for spreading a rumor of high treason—that a close collaborator of the chief of state had been a Soviet agent. This was the time of the angry boulevard Mortier, the headquarters of SDECE.

Prime Minister Georges Pompidou took a lot less interest in intelligence matters than had his predecessor, Michel Debré, and ideologically, he moved away more easily from the strict Gaullist orthodoxy. Still, the relationship between SDECE and the CIA became strained again on October 29, 1965, when Mehdi Ben Barka was kidnapped from right in front of the *drugstore* on Saint-Germain. It was said, but never proved, that the CIA was involved, and de Gaulle wanted as little talk about it as possible from SDECE.

"Dynamic Filing"

When Colonel Count Alexandre de Marenches became chief of SDECE, relations with the CIA got better. Good-natured but energetic, and as much in favor under Valery Giscard d'Estaing as under Georges Pompidou, Alexandre de Marenches took some drastic steps. He chopped 800 agents from SDECE, nearly half its strength. This included those considered too pro-Israeli; those who were sympathetic to Thyraud de Vosjoli and did not accept the political shift; and also those used up or compromised in shady affairs, or unfit for "recycling." On one axis, it was purged for morality; on the other, for politics.

Marenches figured that it was necessary to modernize "the fish pond." They weren't going to take lessons from the British, with whom SDECE never had a good understanding, especially in Africa. There was also no question of seeking advice from the other side of the Rhine, where, for one thing, they took *their* lessons from Washington. Might as well go directly, then, since the Americans—less numerous than the Soviets, but at the time more effective—wanted nothing more than to make us welcome. The fashion was computers, a weak point of the Soviets—and therefore of the KGB and GRU. The grand opening—SDECE hired an elephantine UNIVAC 9400 computer, and went as far as recruiting operators from among the service's soldiers. It was just as in the United States.

How do the Americans find their brains? They send their headhunters to the universities. In France, the hunt began in the elite schools. In the United States, many universities had worked for the CIA, at times without knowing. In France, contracts were even made with various scientific research groups.

The American secret services also taught the French how to do "content analysis." Today, for example, the Americans and the French study the differences between the speeches of Khrushchev and Brezhnev with respect to their complaints against different countries. The Americans in Paris, besides the personal contacts they might have, also study "frequencies"— how many times are the words "workers," "dictatorship of the proletariat," and "workers' control" (*autogestión*) repeated in speeches of left-wing leaders. And so links with the CIA were progressively tightened, especially after M. Sauvagnargues, in Ottawa in June 1974, showed himself to be infinitely more polite and understanding than M. Jobert. Intelligence, it seems, follows politics.

Shortly after the Ottawa meeting, some SDECE technicians went for training to the CIA's home base in Langley, Virginia, where they were introduced to the "dynamic filing" of intelligence records. In the autumn, two SDECE representatives,

General Lacaze and Colonel Lionnet, accompanied by the then-assistant director of DST, Guy Xoual, went to the Hotel Westbury in Brussels to take part in a seminar on Eastern Europe organized by the Danish Colonel Erik Fournais, chief of NATO's intelligence, and with the CIA represented by James Angleton. Then, last summer, Alexandre de Marenches made a study tour of the United States, visited the CIA, and brought home a reform project for SDECE that was in part inspired by the American organization.

According to Victor Marchetti, these renewed ties between the CIA and SDECE "remain surprisingly good today." This is shown in their close collaboration in southern Africa, where the French and American services stand shoulder to shoulder, taking turns delivering arms and instructors to the FNLA and UNITA in Angola, while the GRU do the same for the MPLA. At airports in Zaire and South Africa, American C-130s and French Transalls unload their cargoes of ammunition and light armored cars side by side. In Paris, DST agents protect General Spinola when he visits Eugen Burgstaller at his home. It is generally the official travel service which assures the safety of foreign personalities.

Who's Who in the KGB

Given this climate of international cooperation, just what is the CIA now looking for in France? "To start with, they want to stop the left from coming to power, and wants even more to stop Communist participation in the government," says Philip Agee, a former CIA agent who, like Marchetti, has written a journal of his years in the CIA. "For the CIA this is evidently the priority of priorities, as it is in all the countries of the Atlantic alliance. Then, Paris is a sort of a crossroads for the Third World. You have many Arabs and Africans here—in the embassies, the universities, and the international organizations. These are just the people the CIA is looking to recruit to become agents when they return to their own countries. At the beginning of the '60s, one of my friends, Anthony Smith, was sent to one of your universities to establish relations in this way. Finally, you have a lot of exiles here—Chileans, Spaniards, Moroccans, and Iranians. The CIA tries to penetrate their *milieux*. I remember that in Montevideo we had our feelers out among the Brazilian exiles."

The CIA has ties to all the secret services of the Western world. They recruit agents among them, and it isn't rare for western intelligence agents to put the interests of the CIA before those of their own national agencies.

"As for industrial espionage, the CIA doesn't hold back," Philip Agee goes on. "I believe that in France the CIA is very interested in French industry's technical innovations as regards the metro." Interviewed the day after *Liberation* published its list, Agee figured that it was "at least 95% correct."

For certain diplomats and military experts in the West, "there is a kind of trial of strength between the KGB and the CIA. In France, as elsewhere, the Soviets are looking to dismantle the American intelligence networks in order to hasten the breakdown of capitalism. American liberals and French *gauchistes*, scandalized by certain of the CIA's crimes and interventions, are voluntarily or involuntarily collaborating in this struggle." But surely no one is going as far as to claim that magazines like *CounterSpy* or newspapers like *Liberation* are in the pay of the KGB.

Faced with publication of lists of their members—real or imagined—the CIA is not responding by publishing an international "Who's Who" of the KGB or GRU—no doubt to keep the game from becoming even more complicated. And it doesn't seem that Henry Kissinger will raise the subject in the course of his coming trip to Moscow; between the SALT talks and Angola, the agenda is sufficiently charged. But, who knows?

West Germany:
An Interview
with Philip Agee

by Philip Agee and
Informations Dienst

Philip Agee was a CIA agent in various countries for 12 years. As it became clear to him what this work really meant, he left the secret service and published his experiences, in order to give a picture of the work and methods of the CIA to those who are affected by them. In the last issue of *ID* we published some of his experiences in Latin America, typical activities of the CIA. In *ID* 93 we published his warning about CIA counterrevolutionary activities in Portugal. To go with our publication of names of CIA agents in West Germany, we interviewed him about the specific situation in Germany.

ID: Philip, where exactly does the CIA operate in Germany?
PA: First I shall warn you that my knowledge in this area is limited to informal conversations over the years, since I never worked directly on German affairs. But, given the enormous

[This article first appeared in the January 31, 1976, issue of *Informations Dienst*, in Frankfurt, Federal Republic of Germany.]

presence of the United States in Germany, the CIA has a number of different covers to work behind. A large proportion of the officers are under cover as Embassy staff in Bonn. Very many, probably the majority, work under military cover. The biggest CIA base in West Germany may be one of the Army bases in and around Frankfurt. There are also CIA units in Berlin and Munich.

ID: What exactly do these units do?

PA: Those units which work under military cover will be doing investigative work all over the country. They are highly qualified technicians who tap telephones, open mail, keep people under surveillance, and encode and decode intelligence transmissions. Usually they work very closely together with the local security organizations. Other units are charged with special responsibilities for making contact with organizations and people within the political establishment. All information collected is used to infiltrate and manipulate these organizations. In Bonn, in particular, the CIA will try to get at the Chinese, Cuban, and East European embassies, to check on their mail and visitors, and if possible to recruit their staff.

ID: The U.S.A. and the CIA have been active in Germany for many years. What would you estimate have been the political consequences of CIA activities here?

PA: Since World War II, the aim of U.S. foreign policy has been to guarantee the coherence of the western world under the leadership of the U.S.A. CIA activities are directed toward achieving this goal. They first had to establish or revive various anti-Communist, pro-American institutions. Left opposition movements had to be discredited and destroyed. Activity on all levels was directed to this end. For example, the anti-Communist trade unions were used, and they received massive CIA support. National and international organizations with Communists in their membership were isolated; or attempts were made to exclude opposition elements. Where this did not succeed, they founded new, strictly anti-Communist organizations in the same fields. The International Confederation of Free Trade Unions, for example, took on this function in the 1950s. In such cases, only a small circle of people are informed of such CIA infiltration because if it were widely known, this would destroy the desired image of genuine, nongovernmental, liberal institutions, which the CIA's front organizations must always appear to be.

ID: What are the specific aspects of the CIA's work in West

Germany at the moment? In particular, who has been and who will be supported?

PA: After World War II, West Germany was a crucial area. In order to secure U.S. interests there, the CIA supported not only the CDU (Christian Democratic Union), but also the SPD (Social Democratic Party) and the trade unions. The CIA wanted the influence of the two major political parties to be strong enough to shut out and hold down any left opposition. Postwar Germany was one of the most important operational areas for far-reaching CIA programs, designed to create an internal structure for the Federal Republic which would be pro-American and anti-Communist, and to secure commercial interests. And, further, the CIA always wants to be in a position to find out what the Soviet Union is doing.

ID: Is it the case that today the CIA tries to act against the New Left?

PA: Oh, there isn't any doubt about that. In particular, it will be worried about opposition groups among soldiers in the West German Army, and it will try to work against them.

ID: What form does cooperation between the CIA and the West German secret service take?

PA: As I mentioned before, as regards phone-tapping, mail opening, and surveillance of people, the CIA works very closely with the local security authorities. As a rule, cooperation between the CIA and the security authorities of another country includes operations carried out by the local service itself, on the suggestion of the CIA. And often they protect CIA activities from any legal consequences. But, particularly in Germany, there are difficulties. The CIA does not trust the German secret services very much because there are a lot of East German and Soviet agents in them. And that is not the least reason for the high number of CIA agents in Germany, because they also have to keep an eye on the German secret services.

ID: It is now known that the CIA used the English news agency Reuters to push specific propaganda stories into well-known newspapers. How does this system work?

PA: Most CIA stations pay journalists to publish the CIA's propaganda as if it were the journalist's own work. They pass on faked and true news as authentic news to agencies and important newspapers. This works in the following way. A CIA unit gives a fictitious or suitably dressed-up report by cable to the local CIA officer who is responsible for propaganda. He writes a story from it, and gives it to the CIA's contact journalist. The journalist places the story in his paper. Once the story is published somewhere, other CIA propaganda agents pick it up and, citing the newspaper as a source, and as authority for the story, try to get it published in other papers all over the world. At the time of the Allende government in Chile, in particular, thousands of slanderous and distorted stories were published inside and outside Chile. When I was working in Montevideo as a CIA case officer, we had a highly-placed journalist who gave CIA stories to other journalists. They all had contacts with him, and they were responsible for getting the stories published. Since I published my experiences in the CIA, I have been a target myself for such false stories. About every six weeks, there appears somewhere or other a curious report which is intended to discredit me. A *Los Angeles Times* correspondent recently filed a report in which he asserted that I had given the name of a Polish Army officer who was a western spy to the KGB. The story is complete fiction, but its function is clear.

ID: Have the numerous details published recently about the CIA changed anything?

PA: As long as U.S. policy itself does not change, we can only hinder its application by fighting against the instruments of that policy. That's why it is important to publish the names and addresses of CIA agents—once they are known, they have to leave. And thus the power and the ability of the CIA to install a new Pinochet is limited. And that is exactly the reason for doing it—certainly not in order to get anybody shot.

How CIA Money
Took the Teeth Out
of British Socialism

by Richard Fletcher

Since World War II the American government and its espionage branch, the Central Intelligence Agency, have worked systematically to ensure that the Socialist parties of the free world toe a line compatible with American interests. CIA money can be traced flowing through the Congress for Cultural Freedom to such magazines as *Encounter* which have given Labour politicians like Anthony Crosland, Denis Healey, and the late Hugh Gaitskell a platform for their campaigns to move the Labour Party away from nationalization and CND-style pacifism. Flows of personnel link this Labour Party pressure group with the unlikely figure of Prince Bernhard of the Netherlands, who has for 20 years sponsored the mysterious activities of the anti-Communist Bilderberg group launched with covert American funds. There is no suggestion that these prominent Labour politicians have not acted in all innocence and with complete propriety. But it could be asked how such perspicacious men could

[This article originally appeared in London, in 1975.]

fail to inquire about the source of the funds that have financed the organizations and magazines which have been so helpful to them for so long. Nevertheless, they are certainly proud of the critical influence their activities had in the years following 1959 when they swung the British Labour Party away from its pledge to nationalization, enshrined in the celebrated Clause IV, and back toward the commitment to NATO from which the Campaign for Nuclear Disarmament had deflected it. CIA operators take the credit for helping them in this decisive intervention which changed the course of modern British history. The cloak-and-danger operations of America's Central Intelligence Agency are only a small part of its total activities. Most of its $2,000 million budget and 80,000 personnel are devoted to the systematic collection of information—minute personal details about tens of thousands of politicians and political organizations in every country in the world, including Britain. And this data, stored in the world's largest filing system at the CIA headquarters in Langley, Virginia, is used not only to aid Washington's policy machine, but in active political intervention overseas—shaping the policies of political parties, making and unmaking their leaders, boosting one internal faction against another, and often establishing rival breakaway parties when other tactics fail.

In fact the CIA carries out, at a more sophisticated level, exactly the same sort of organized subversion as Stalin's Comintern in its heyday. One of its targets in the years since World War II has been the British Labour Party.

The Labour Party emerged from the war with immense prestige. As the sole mass working-class party in Britain, it had the support of a united trades union movement whose power had been greatly enhanced by the war, and it had just achieved an unprecedented electoral victory. The established social democratic parties of Europe had been destroyed by the dictators, while in America all that remained of the socialist movement was a handful of sects whose members were numbered in hundreds. Labour was undisputed head of Europe's social democratic family.

But as the euphoria wore off, old differences began to emerge with prolonged postwar austerity. The left wanted more socialism and an accommodation with the Russians, while the right wanted the battle against Communism to take precedence over further reforms at home. And those who took this latter view organized themselves around the journal *Socialist Commentary*, formerly the organ of anti-Marxist Socialists who had fled to Britain from Hitler's Germany. The magazine was reorganized in the autumn of 1947 with Anthony Crosland, Allan Flanders, and Rita Hinden who had worked closely with the émigrés as leading contributors. And *Socialist Commentary* became the mouthpiece of the right wing of the Labour Party, campaigning against left-wingers like Aneurin Bevan, whom they denounced as dangerous extremists. Crosland, who ended the war as a captain in the Parachute Regiment, had been President of the Oxford Union, and a year later, in 1947, became Fellow and lecturer in economics at Trinity College, Oxford. Flanders was a former TUC official who became an academic specialist in industrial relations and later joined the Prices and Incomes Board set up by the Wilson government. Rita Hinden, a University of London academic from South Africa, was secretary of the Fabian Colonial Bureau—an autonomous section of the Fabian Society which she had set up and directed since the early forties. In this position she exercised considerable influence with Labour ministers and officials in the Colonial Office, maintaining close links with many overseas politicians.

The new *Socialist Commentary* immediately set out to alert the British Labour movement to the growing dangers of international communism, notably in a piece entitled "Cominformity," written by Flanders during a period spent in the United States studying the American trade union movement. The journal's American connections were further extended by its U.S. correspondent, William C. Gausmann, who was soon to enter the American Government Service, where he rose to take charge of U.S. propaganda in North Vietnam, while support for the moderate stand taken by Crosland, Flanders, and Hinden came from David C. Williams, the London Correspondent of the *New Leader*, an obscure New York weekly specializing in anti-communism. Williams made it his business to join the British Labour Party and to take an active part in the Fabian Society.

This close American interest in socialism on the other side of the Atlantic was nothing new. During the war the American trade unions had raised large sums to rescue European labor leaders from the Nazis, and this had brought them closely in touch with American military intelligence and, in particular, with the Office of Strategic Services (OSS), whose chief in

Switzerland and Germany from 1942 to 1945 was Allen W. Dulles, later, of course, to become famous as head of the CIA in its heyday.

The principal union official in these secret commando operations had been Jay Lovestone, a remarkable operator who had switched from being the leader of the American Communist Party to working secretly for the U.S. government. And as the Allied armies advanced, Lovestone's men followed the soldiers as political commissars, trying to make sure that the liberated workers were provided with trade union and political leaders acceptable to Washington—many of these leaders being the émigrés of the *Socialist Commentary* group. In France, Germany, Italy, and Austria, the commissars provided lavish financial and material support for moderate Socialists who would draw the sting from left-wing political movements, and the beneficiaries from this assistance survive in European politics to this day—though that is another story.

In America the *New Leader* came to provide one focus for these activities, organizing a weekly meeting of minds for professional anti-Communists in the unions, universities, and government service, both at home and abroad. It had a relatively large paid staff and a world-wide network of overseas and roving correspondents. Its guiding spirit as Executive Editor and business manager was Sol Levitas, a Russian émigré who had worked with Trotsky and Bukharin during the Russian Revolution of 1917 and had fled from Stalin's prisons to the U.S. in 1923, bringing with him a lifelong hatred of Bolshevism. Amongst Levitas' "boys," as he liked to call them, were Melvin J. Lasky, an ex-Trotskyist from New York's City College who joined the staff in 1941; Daniel Bell, a former Managing Editor of the *New Leader* who is now a professor at Columbia University; and Irving Brown, Lovestone's hatchet man in the European trade unions.

The *New Leader* claimed to be independent, but in 1949 it carried a piece by Allen Dulles advocating a "commission of internal security," to examine subversive influences in the U.S. and to "use the institutions of democracy to destroy them" which, in the light of Dulles' work helping the White House reorganize OSS as the Central Intelligence Agency, was rather like the head of MI5 writing for the *New Statesman*. And at this time too, although the *New Leader* was issuing frantic appeals for funds to pay off its $40,000 worth of debts, it started appearing in April 1950 as a new *New Leader* with an expensive *Time*-like magazine format.

The importance of this dramatically reborn publication for British and European Labour parties was that it now began openly to advocate the infiltration of foreign socialist parties, echoing the arguments of James Burnham who, in his book *The Coming Defeat of Communism*, proposed that "the Western World, led by the United States, should go over to the offensive by using the same sort of methods—open and covert—that the Kremlin has so massively employed." Allan Flanders contributed an article to the revamped magazine on the British Labour Movement, and in 1954 Denis Healey, who had entered Parliament as a Labour MP in 1952, became the *New Leader*'s London correspondent.

American Cold War strategy, as Burnham and the *New Leader* had proposed, now moved into the financing of world-wide front organizations, and in June 1950 the free world's top men of letters were duly assembled in the Titania Palace Theater in the U.S. zone of Berlin, before an audience of 4,000, to launch the Congress for Cultural Freedom, a body whose purpose was to "defend freedom and democracy against the new tyranny sweeping the world." It was no coincidence that the main organizer and chairman of the congress was Melvin Lasky, who in 1948 had been "lent" by the *New Leader* to the U.S. High Commission in Berlin, where he had set up a successful literary magazine, *Der Monat,* with the encouragement of General Lucius D. Clay, head of the military government. Nor that the man chosen to head the permanent secretariat of the congress was an official of the American military government, Michael Josselson, who administered and arranged the financing of the vast organization.

The congress seemed to have unlimited funds which were said to come from Jay Lovestone's union in America, and CCF, as it came to be known, was soon organizing political seminars and student exchanges, and publishing literature on a world-wide basis in support of the new youth organizations which suddenly emerged to fight the Communists—notably the International Student Conference at Leiden in the Netherlands.

In 1953 the Congress for Cultural Freedom launched *Encounter,* an English language monthly which was an immediate success under the editorship of Irving Kristol, another of Levitas'

New Leader protégés and an ex-Lovestoneite, and soon a bewildering range of publications in several languages had joined the CCF stable, with *Encounter* becoming one of the most influential journals of liberal opinion in the West.

As the CCF network grew it embraced many prominent figures in the British Labour Party—among them Anthony Crosland, who began attending CCF seminars, where he met Daniel Bell, who was at this period moving away from journalistic red-baiting in the *New Leader* toward academic respectability. Bell's thinking was later summarized in his book *The End of Ideology*, and it formed the basis of the new political thesis set out in the major work that Crosland was now writing and which was published in 1956 under the title *The Future of Socialism*. The book had also been influenced by the arguments put forward at the conference of the Congress for Cultural Freedom held in the previous year in Milan, where principal participants had included Hugh Gaitskell, Denis Healey, and Rita Hinden as well as Daniel Bell and a bevy of American and European politicians and academics.

Put at its simplest, Bell and his colleagues argued that growing affluence had radically transformed the working class in Europe —and Britain—which was now virtually indistinguishable from the middle class, and thus Marx's theory of class struggle was no longer relevant. Future political progress, they thought, would involve the gradual reform of capitalism and the spread of equality and social welfare as a consequence of continued economic growth.

Crosland's book, though not original in content, was a major achievement. In over 500 pages it clothed the long-held faith of Labour's new leader Hugh Gaitskell in the academic respectability of American political science and was immediately adopted as the gospel of the party leadership. Labour's rank and file, however, still clung to their grassroots socialism, and Gaitskell's obvious preferences for the small coterie of cultured intellectuals and visiting foreigners who met at his house in Frognal Gardens, Hampstead, alienated the party faithful, and gave added bitterness to the internecine quarrels that were to follow Labour's defeat in the 1959 election.

In 1957 Melvin Lasky had taken over the editorship of *Encounter* which had, by then, cornered the West's intelligentsia through its prestige and the high fees it was able to pay. Lasky was a trusted member of Gaitskell's inner circle and was often to

be seen at his parties in Hampstead, while Gaitskell became at
the same time a regular contributor to the *New Leader*. Sol
Levitas would drop in at his house on his periodic tours to see
world leaders and visit the CCF in Paris.

It was during the fifties, furthermore, that Anthony Crosland,
Rita Hinden, and the other members of the *Socialist Commentary* group adopted the argument put forcibly in the *New Leader*
that a strong united Europe was essential to protect the Atlantic
Alliance from Russian attack, and European and Atlantic unity
came to be synonymous in official thinking as Gaitskell and his
friends moved into the party leadership. They received transat-
lantic encouragement, furthermore, from a New York-based
group called the American Committee on United Eruope, whose
leadership was openly advertised in the *New York Times* as
including General Donovan, wartime head of OSS, George Mar-
shall, the U.S. Secretary of State, General Lucius D. Clay, and
Allen Dulles of the CIA.

This high-powered and lavishly funded pressure group—
whose thesis was essentially that a United Europe would defend
America's interest against Russia—financed in Europe the so-
called "European Movement," whose inspiration was a friend
of Hugh Gaitskell's, Joseph Retinger, an elderly Polish James
Bond, who, after a professional career as an *éminence grise,* had
come to rest at the Dutch court under the patronage of Prince
Bernhard.

Retinger had, furthermore, secretly persuaded Shepard Stone
of the U.S. High Commission in Germany to finance his European Movement out of so-called "counter-part funds"—Mar-
shall Aid repayments which the Americans banked in Europe.
Later he promoted select gatherings of European and American
politicians, businessmen, aristocrats, top civil servants, and military leaders to propagate the ideals of Atlantic and European
unity. Invitations to these Bilderberg Group meetings—named
after the Dutch hotel where the first gathering was held in 1954—
were issued personally by Prince Bernhard on Retinger's recommendation. Few of those who received the card of invitation
embossed with the Royal Netherlands coat of arms declined to
spend three or four days in civilized discourse with the world's
leaders in luxurious surroundings—certainly not Hugh Gaitskell
and Denis Healey, who were founder members of the group
along with such diverse personalities as the president of Uni-
lever and Sir Robert Boothby.

Healey, an ex-Communist, had been head of the International Department at Transport House before entering Parliament in 1951. He was a convinced supporter of Atlantic Union and spread the message through *Socialist Commentary* and the *New Leader,* for whom he wrote nearly 80 articles before joining the Labour government as Defense Minister in 1964.

While top people were relaxing with Prince Bernhard, the Congress for Cultural Freedom was establishing solid ties with the coming man of the British Labour Party, Anthony Crosland, who was by now acknowledged as the party's chief theoretician. He had lost his seat at Westminster in the 1955 election, but in the following years was traveling regularly to Paris to plan the international seminars of the CCF with Melvin Lasky and Michael Josselson under the directorship of Daniel Bell. Michael Josselson, who in 1967 admitted that he had for 17 years been channeling CIA money into the CCF, has described to us Crosland's role at this period. Crosland's contribution, he says, was "encouraging sympathetic people" to participate in the seminars sponsored by the congress all over the world. Hugh Gaitskell traveled in these years to congress functions in Milan 1955, New Delhi 1957, the island of Rhodes 1958, and Berlin 1962. Crosland himself traveled to Vienna in 1958, to Berlin in 1960, and to Australia and Japan in 1964 on a congress-sponsored tour.

He was at this date a member of the International Council of the CCF after nearly a decade working to remodel European socialism in the image of the American Democratic Party, a cause for the sake of which the CCF had financed a systematic campaign of congresses, seminars, and private gatherings for leading Socialists throughout Europe. This had been backed up by the fullest publicity in *Encounter, Preuves, Der Monat,* and the other CCF journals—whose influence was further extended by discreet arrangements with *Socialist Commentary* for publishing each other's pamphlets and articles.

Rita Hinden was by now the editor of *Socialist Commentary* and playing a similar role to Crosland in picking African participants for congress seminars. Michael Josselson describes her as "a good friend of ours. We relied entirely on her advice for our African operations." She also visited India and Japan on a CCF-sponsored trip after the Suez crisis, speaking on the theme that traditional socialism was irrelevant in a modern capitalist society where there was full employment.

This was the nub of the matter. Many of Europe's Socialist

parties still had old-fashioned Marxist notions written into their rulebooks, which had become an embarrassment to their leaders. A glaring example was the British Labour Party whose Clause IV—"common ownership of the means of production, distribution and exchange" and so on—sounded to some like a passage from the *Communist Manifesto*. The proof of its irrelevance seemed provided by the 1959 General Election in which Anthony Crosland regained his seat at Westminster, but which represented a catastrophic defeat for the Labour Party. The day after Labour's defeat, Roy Jenkins, Anthony Crosland, and Douglas Jay were among a small group who met with Gaitskell at his home. They decided that the time had come for Labour to drop its old commitments and get rid of its cloth cap image which had become an electoral liability.

Douglas Jay immediately wrote the now celebrated article which appeared in *Forward* the following week, calling for the abandonment of Clause IV and a change in the Labour Party's name. And early in 1960, *Socialist Commentary* commissioned Mark Abram's firm, Research Services Ltd., to carry out an attitude survey on "Why Labour Lost." The results were published in the journal's May to August number, and they confirmed the Gaitskell thesis that nationalization was a liability. This Abrams survey had been turned down by the Labour Party Executive before the 1959 election as being too costly. But now *Socialist Commentary* found the money to pay for it and in February 1960 William Rodgers, General Secretary of the Fabian Society since 1953, organized a letter of support to Gaitskell signed by 15 young parliamentary candidates. Shortly afterward, a steering committee was set up with Rodgers as chairman, and including some of the signatories of the Gaitskell letter together with Crosland, Roy Jenkins, Patrick Gordon Walker, Jay, other party members from Oxford, and some sympathetic journalists. This group started work on a manifesto to be released in the event of Gaitskell's defeat in the defense debate at the party conference. This duly occurred in the autumn of 1960, when the Campaign for Nuclear Disarmament triumphed in its campaign to win the Labour Party to a neutralist program.

So in October 1960 Rodgers and his friends released their manifesto in 25,000 copies with widespread press coverage. Calling for "Victory for Sanity"—a dig at their old enemies, the "Victory for Socialism" group—they appealed to party members to rally behind Gaitskell and his conference call to "fight and fight and fight again." They also issued an appeal for funds with which to continue the campaign, and in mid-November Rodgers reported to the steering committee that many small donations had been received, together with a large sum from a source which wished to remain anonymous.

Rodgers' windfall enabled the group to take a permanent office and appoint paid staff. The title "Campaign for Democratic Socialism" was chosen and a six-man Executive Committee set up with Rodgers as full-time paid Chairman. The Committee was told that available funds were sufficient for a year's activities, and CDS thus had a start on its opponents who, in spite of their widespread support in Labour constituencies and trade-unions, were unable to raise more than a few hundred pounds over the following year and had to rely entirely on volunteer workers. At CDS's disposal were fieldworkers in the constituencies and unions, whom it supported with traveling expenses, literature, and organizational backup, tens of thousands of copies of the manifesto, pamphlets and other publications, plus a regular bulletin, *Campaign,* circulated free of charge to a large mailing list within the movement. And all this was produced without a single subscription-paying member.

CDS achieved its objectives. The unions cracked under the pressure and the Labour Party returned to the Atlantic fold at the party conference in 1961 after a campaign by the most effective pressure group the party had ever seen. Rodgers was its driving force. With financial backing assured, he created an organization whose influence was out of all proportion to its original support among party members. Whoever put up the money could justly claim to have changed the course of the history of the Labour Party and Britain in the 1960s.

Nor did the importance of CDS vanish totally after it had restored the Labour Party to commitment to NATO, for its adherents felt bitterly betrayed when Hugh Gaitskell later qualified his support for Common Market entry at the Brighton Conference in 1962. Standing at the back of the hall Rodgers turned to the party press officer, John Harris—later Roy Jenkins' PR man —and said "I'm through with that man, John." Anthony Crosland, furthermore, supported Gaitskell's compromise and so also lost the backing of the ardent marketeers, who henceforward rallied around Roy Jenkins.

The main significance of all these divisions was that they

helped Harold Wilson to capture the leadership on Gaitskell's death. Finding the parliamentary party molded in the Gaitskell image, its policies firmly rooted in Crosland's *Future of Socialism,* Wilson made no attempt to alter the package which became the program of the next Labour Government.

Throughout this postwar period the party apparatus remained firmly in orthodox hands, particularly the International Department of which Denis Healey had been head until he entered Parliament in 1951. Then in 1965 his old post was taken over by J. Gwyn Morgan, one of the rising generation of party and union officials whose careers began in the National Union of Students, to whose presidency he had been elected in 1960 on an anti-Communist ticket. As President he took charge of international affairs, representing the Union in the International Student Conference at Leiden, and on leaving the NUS in 1962 he became Assistant General Secretary of ISC in charge of finance. In this capacity he negotiated with the American foundations which supplied the bulk of ISC funds and supervised expenditure of the several million dollars devoted to world-wide propaganda and organization. In 1964 he became Secretary General of ISC.

In his five years' association with the organization he visited over 80 different countries and got to know personally many heads of government and leaders of the world's principal social democratic parties. An ardent pro-European and active supporter of Roy Jenkins, he was an obvious choice to fill the vacant slot as head of Labour's Overseas Department at the beginning of 1965. Two years later Morgan was promoted to the newly created post of Assistant General Secretary of the Labour Party, with the expectation that he would fill the top job on Harry Nicholas' retirement.

But early in 1967 the U.S. journal *Ramparts* revealed that since the early Fifties the National Student Association of America had, with the active connivance of its elected officers, received massive subventions from the CIA through dummy foundations and that one of these was the Fund for Youth and Student Affairs which supplied most of the budget of ISC. The International Student Conference, it appeared, had been set up by British and American intelligence in 1950 to counteract the Communist peace offensive, and the CIA had supplied over 90% of its finance. The Congress for Cultural Freedom was similarly compromised. Michael Josselson admitted that he had been channeling CIA money into the organization ever since its foundation—lately at the rate of about a million dollars a year—to support some 20 journals and a world-wide program of political and cultural activities. Writing of Sol Levitas at the time of his death in 1961, the editor of the *New Leader,* William Bohm, said, "The most amazing part of the journalistic miracle was the man's gift for garnering the funds which were necessary to keep our paper solvent from week to week and year to year. I cannot pretend to explain how this miracle was achieved . . . we always worked in an atmosphere of carefree security. We knew that the necessary money would come from somewhere and that our cheques would be forthcoming."

The "Miracle" was resolved by the *New York Times:* the American Labour Conference for International Affairs which ran the *New Leader* had for many years been receiving regular subventions from the J. M. Kaplan Fund, a CIA conduit.

The CIA had taken the lessons taught back in the early Fifties by Burnham and the *New Leader* to heart. With its army of ex-Communists and willing Socialists it had for a while beaten the Communists at their own game—but unfortunately it had not known when to stop and now the whole structure was threatened with collapse. Rallying to the Agency's support, Thomas Braden, the official responsible for its move into private organizations, and Executive Director of the American Committee on United Europe, explained that Irving Brown and Lovestone had done a fine job in cleaning up the unions in postwar Europe. When they ran out of money, he said, he had persuaded Dulles to back them, and from this beginning the world-wide operation mushroomed.

Another ex-CIA official, Richard Bissell, who organized the Bay of Pigs invasion, explained the Agency's attitude to foreign politicians: "Only by knowing the principal players well do you have a chance of careful prediction. There is real scope for action in this area: the technique is essentially that of 'penetration' . . . Many of the 'penetrations' don't take the form of 'hiring' but of establishing friendly relationships which may or may not be furthered by the provision of money from time to time. In some countries the CIA representative has served as a close counsellor . . . of the chief of state."

After these disclosures the CCF changed its name to the International Association for Cultural Freedom. Michael Josselson resigned—but was retained as a consultant—and the Ford Foundation agreed to pick up the bills. And the Director of the new

Association is none other than Shepard Stone, the Bilderberg organizer who channeled U.S. government money to Joseph Retinger in the early Fifties to build the European Movement and then became International Director of the Ford Foundation.

When Rita Hinden died at the end of last year after 20 years as editor of *Socialist Commentary*, George Thomson—a pillar of CDS who resigned recently from Labour's front bench with Roy Jenkins—paid tribute to her key role in transforming the Labour Party. In the Fifties, he said, her "ideas were greeted with outraged cries of 'Revisionism.' But by the mid-Sixties the revisionism of *Socialist Commentary* had become the orthodoxy of the Labour Movement." And Denis Healey's comment was equally revealing. "Only Sol Levitas of the American *New Leader,*" he said, "had a comparable capacity for exercising a wide political influence with negligible material resources." He obviously hadn't paid a visit to Companies House whose Register shows that in recent years *Socialist Commentary* has been drawing on a capital reserve of over £75,000.

Through its network of front organizations, magazines, and subsidies, the CIA in the late Fifties and early Sixties had a decisive effect on socialism throughout Western Europe, and in Britain in particular, but the Gaitskellism that it backed is now on the retreat. For those Labour leaders who, in all innocence, built their careers in the seminars of the Congress for Cultural Freedom and the columns of *Encounter* or the *New Leader,* rather than in the trade union branch or on the conference floor, are now feeling the lack of a mass base within the party.

Attacked by Gaitskell at the Labour Party Conference in 1960 as a fellow traveler, Michael Foot retorted "but, who are *they* traveling with?" and the question is one that other members of the party echo. For the chairmen of the world's largest capitalist organizations, monarchists, ex-Nazis, commanders of the American and German forces, the Crown Princes of Europe, and CIA agents do indeed make strange traveling companions for Socialists.

The CIA
Backs the
Common Market

by Steve Weissman, Phil Kelly, and Mark Hosenball

Cord Meyer Jr.'s main task as head of the U.S. Central Intelligence Agency's operation here may be to ensure Britain's entry into the Common Market. New evidence developed by investigators in Britain and America shows that Meyer and his predecessor as head of the CIA's International Organization Division, Tom Braden, engaged in a major operation in the 1950s and 60s to secretly build up the groups which are now pushing Britain into Europe.

The European Movement, the elite international pressure group which takes much of the credit for the founding of the Common Market, took secret U.S. funding. Its British Council is currently leading the "Keep Britain In" Campaign. The European Youth Campaign, which was the European Movement's most active component in the Fifties, was almost totally funded by the American government. Members of organizations affiliated to the campaign are still active in pro-Europe circles.

[This article first appeared as "Uncle Sam Goes to Market" in the May 23, 1975, issue of *Time Out*, in London.]

The chief vehicle in the covert funding of pro-Europe groups was the CIA-created American Committee on a United Europe. Founded in 1949 by Major General William J. Donovan, head of American wartime intelligence, the committee kicked off its pro-Europe campaign by inviting leading Europeans over to speak in America, among them Sir Winston Churchill, Lord Layton, EEC founders Paul Henri-Spaak and Robert Schuman. More formally organized in 1950, the Committee coopted long-time CIA director Allen Dulles to be its Vice Chairman, and employed Tom Braden as its Executive Director. Braden at the time was head of a division of the CIA's "department of Dirty Tricks" which, he later revealed, ran an entire network of political "front" organizations which served CIA purposes. In 1967, it was revealed that the Paris-based Congress for Cultural Freedom and its London magazine, *Encounter,* were part of this network. But until recently little was known about the secret work of the American Committee on a United Europe.

The Committee made no secret of its Cold War views. To its delight, the nascent European Movement wanted a supranational Western bloc, a United States of Europe. More important, the European Movement backed the rearmament of Germany, which the U.S. government saw as key to winning the Cold War with Russia and to economic expansion of the West. The U.S. was particularly interested in incorporating the European states into a European Defense Community which would make such rearmament politically acceptable.

To do this, it backed the European Movement financially. Movement activists like Duncan Sandys came to the U.S. to speak at fund-raising dinners sponsored by the American Committee. The response was gratifying, but not sufficient. So the American Committee, with its direct links to the CIA's clandestine operators, became a conduit for secret U.S. government subsidies to the Europeans.

During the period 1947–1953 about £380,000 of U.S. government money passed secretly from the CIA-controlled American Committee to the European Movement. The subsidies comprised almost half of the European Movement's total budget. (The committee's secret funding role became known through the discovery of an obscure Oxford doctoral thesis written by one F. Rebattet, the son of a former secretary-general of the European Movement, who had access to the Movement's secret archives.)

The largest secret contribution to Europe was sparked off by the success of a massive Communist Youth Rally in 1951 in East Berlin. When John J. McCloy, U.S. High Commissioner for Germany, saw intelligence films of the rally, he instructed his staff to organize a response. An aide, Shepard Stone, was sent to see top officials of the European Movement. He asked them whether they were willing to stage an anti-communist counter rally. At first, the Europeans agreed. But, to the annoyance of the Americans, they later decided instead to conduct an ongoing propaganda campaign to win European youth to the idea of European unity.

Thus was born the European Youth Campaign. It lasted from 1951 to 1959, and was by far the most active component of the European Movement during that period. In one year alone (1952), the Campaign organized 1899 sessions and conferences, 900 cinema shows, distributed 1.8 million brochures, staged 21 exhibitions, and managed to secure 2,400 minutes of radio time for the cause of European unity. Secretary of the British section of the European Youth Campaign was Maurice Foley, later a Labour MP and Minister. Virtually every penny he, and the Campaign's other organizers spent, came from the U.S. government.

In eight years £1.34 million of secret money was passed on to the Youth Campaign by the CIA's American Committee on a United Europe. During this period, in 1954, an enthusiastic pro-European named Cord Meyer Jr. took over the funding administration. He is now CIA chief in London.

The CIA funding of pro-Europe student groups through "conduit" foundations was exposed by *Ramparts Magazine* in 1967. Records now in the possession of a U.S. Congress sub-committee suggest such funding may have amounted to hundreds of thousands of pounds.

If secret CIA financing of European groups has continued since 1967, it's been well camouflaged. When we contacted Ernest Wistrich, current director of the European Movement in Britain, he denied that his particular organization, which was first incorporated in 1954, had ever received CIA money, and claimed that when he joined it in 1967, it was nearly broke and he had to "build it up from almost nothing."

Mike Fallon, secretary-general of the British Youth European Federalists and Youth Organizer of the current Britain in Europe campaign, conceded last week that the CIA did provide funds in the past for European Youth activities. "It did in the '50s," he said. "I only wish it did now!"

The CIA
Makes the News

by Steve Weissman

When the American Central Intelligence Agency recently let slip that they had made extensive use of certain unnamed journalists, both for spying and for propaganda, newshounds the world over began trotting out long lists of likely suspects. One story that actually appeared in print told of the then CIA Director, William Colby, openly admitting the Agency's manipulation of the British-owned wire service, Reuters. Another story recalled earlier CIA media operations, from Radio Free Europe to the Rome *Daily American,* and everywhere eager young reporters tried desperately to uncover the names of those 11—or was it 12?—full-time CIA staffers supposedly doing their dirty tricks under journalistic cover.

It was all great fun while it lasted—newsmen chasing their own tail—and thanks to some very wary editors, few new faces ever came to light. But one name that did still haunts the CIA

[This article first appeared as "CIA, Students of Conflict" in the August 1976 issue of *Embassy Magazine*, in London.]

and the world's press—a highly urbane journalist named Brian Crozier.

As far as anyone knew before the fur went flying, Crozier was just another of London's well-placed wordsmiths. An Australian by birth, he had made his mark as editor of the *Economist's* confidential *Foreign Report*, author of an admiring biography of the Spanish dictator Francisco Franco, and chief of an international news service called Forum World Features and a think-tank on problems of terrorism and guerrilla warfare, the widely quoted Institute for the Study of Conflict.

This at least was how Crozier looked *before* he fell victim to the American penchant for slugging things out in public. The *after* view was a bit seamier, as several of those famous Washington leaks—and a few from London as well—revealed that the CIA secretly owned Crozier's Forum World Features and that they had also put up the money to start his Institute for the Study of Conflict. And so Crozier became the man in the middle —one of the CIA journalists who got caught making the news.

Crozier, of course, isn't the only one to be acutely embarrassed by the CIA scandals. But his story touches on what might become one of the more intriguing questions of the entire affair. For even as the Congress was investigating some of Crozier's covert propaganda activities in Latin America, he and his colleagues were helping to set up a new Institute for the Study of Conflict right in the heart of Washington, D.C. And among the Americans involved with him in this highly suspect intervention into the American political scene are two of the most likely candidates to serve as the next Secretary of State.

The first inkling that Crozier was standing in the line of fire came in April 1975, when a team of British journalists from the TV series "World in Action" descended on Washington to do a story on the CIA. The team talked to the usual assortment of insiders and soon uncovered a fascinating memo which purported to have come from inside CIA headquarters. The memo appeared to have been written in May 1968; it was addressed to the Director of Central Intelligence (at the time Richard Helms) and it gave "an operational summary" of a CIA propaganda outfit located in London and called Forum World Features (FWF).

"In its first two years," the memo explained, "FWF has provided the United States with a significant means to counter Communist propaganda, and has become a respected feature service well on the way to a position of prestige in the journalism world."

The memo also mentioned in a handwritten note that Forum was "run with the knowledge and cooperation of British Intelligence."

Further checking confirmed that the memo was authentic and that the CIA had originally created a Forum news service as part of an earlier operation, the heavily funded Congress for Cultural Freedom. Then in 1965, as the Cultural Freedom group and its lead magazine, *Encounter,* came under growing suspicion, the CIA renamed the news service Forum World Features, and shifted it to the cover of a Delaware corporation called Kern House Enterprises—a CIA "proprietary" headed by the millionaire businessman John Hay Whitney, a former U.S. Ambassador to the Court of St. James's and publisher of the *International Herald Tribune.*

The Agency turned to Crozier to oversee operations in London, and as far as anyone knew, Forum World Features was a small commercial news service, selling weekly packets of feature stories to as many as 50 newspapers all over the world.

Why did the CIA go to all this trouble? Chiefly to make propaganda. Among the well-written and generally innocuous articles that Forum sent out each week, the CIA could easily slip in straight American propaganda, especially when it came to the war in Vietnam, or the campaign against the Allende government in Chile.

The Agency could also use Forum to send almost anyone anywhere as "a journalist," and to give research and other backup to good friends such as Sir Robert Thompson, the former British security chief in Malaya, and a key advisor to the Americans on Vietnam. Control, of course, remained with the Americans, who had at least one "case officer" in the Forum office—a career CIA man named Robert Gene Gately, who was last seen as a member of the CIA Station in the American Embassy in Bangkok, Thailand.

This, in brief, was the story as it came together in the spring of 1975, and when the editor of "World in Action" decided that it was too hot to handle on TV, it filtered down to the London news and entertainment weekly *Time Out,* and from there to the pages of the *Guardian,* the *Irish Times,* the *Washington Post,* and even John Hay Whitney's own *International Herald Tribune.*

Later, as the congressional investigations heated up, a CIA spokesman quietly admitted to the *Washington Post* that the story was true and that the CIA did own Forum. But by the time anyone could get to the scene of the crime, Crozier had completely shut down the entire Forum operation. As it was explained by the sympathetic London *Sunday Times,* costs were going up, and Forum simply ran out of money.

And so the story—like Forum itself—would have died right there if Crozier had only followed the first rule of covert operations: When your cover is blown, keep quiet. But Crozier did just the opposite. Instead of quietly nursing his wounds, he feigned innocence and angrily yelled "Rape!"

It was all a "smear campaign," he charged. And he would not talk to the *Time Out* journalists because they were all part of "the conspiracy."

Now to most journalists—in fact, to most people—those are fighting words, and evidently someone took offense. Within days of Crozier's first blast, a weary postman trundled up to *Time Out* with several bundles of documents which appeared to have come from the internal files of Crozier's other operation, the Institute for the Study of Conflict.

Who had sent them? And more important, were they real? *Time Out*'s staff were wary, and as one of the journalists on the story, I can report that we all had visions of our favorite intelligence agency doctoring up phony documents just to entrap us in criminal libel. But again Crozier saved the story. Hearing that *Time Out* had the documents, he charged that someone had stolen them from the Institute, and within hours two highly embarrassed police detectives—"We don't like to get involved in these journalistic disputes," they explained—were calling at my flat. The documents, it seemed, were very real indeed.

As the story later appeared in *Time Out,* the documents showed in intimate detail how the Institute had grown directly out of the small library and research staff that the CIA's Kern House Enterprises had financed within Forum World Features. By 1968, Crozier was calling this his Current Affairs Research Services Center, and in January 1970 he wrote to Sir Peter Wilkinson (later Coordinator of Intelligence and Security in the British Cabinet Office) and asked his help in transforming the Forum research unit into a full-fledged Institute for the Study of Conflict.

Was the Institute, like Forum, intended as a covert operation?

The evidence suggests that it was, though not necessarily an American operation. In fact, in a letter to the *International Herald Tribune,* the well-known foreign correspondent Bernard Nossiter claimed that he had been told by a senior official in British intelligence that Crozier's Institute was actually run by the British. Perhaps. But, as the internal documents show, the Institute worked hand in glove with Forum and the CIA.

Crozier continued to run both Forum and the Institute. The two operations shared writers, and even certain staff. And as with Forum, the money to start the Institute and its monthly "Conflict Studies" came from the CIA's Kern House Enterprises. Many of Forum's internal records ended up in the Institute's files which were delivered to *Time Out.*

As with many of their front organizations, the Agency evidently wanted the Institute to stand on its own feet. But as late as 1972, where the presently available records stop, Kern House was still providing a small subsidy, which the Institute's annual budget called essential to financial viability. Present records also suggest the possibility, as yet unconfirmed, of more recent CIA funding.

From the start, the CIA's interest in the Institute appears to have been less in research than in propaganda. Few, if any, of the Institute's widely quoted publications have broken any new ground intellectually. But they have given academic respectability to old anti-Communist clichés, whether on Vietnam or Angola. And they have pushed a revival of Cold War thinking in the face of detente, and a stiffening of preemptive police and military measures to combat "subversion" and industrial unrest.

The trick, of course, is in the magic word "Institute." Where the CIA used Forum to reach newspaper readers, and the earlier Congress for Cultural Freedom to woo intellectuals, Crozier's Institute offered professional and authoritative-sounding analyses, both for the general public and for more specialized audiences of academics, policy makers, police officials, and military commanders.

In 1972, for example, the Institute joined with the Confederation of British Industries to launch a private campaign against "subversive elements." The Institute then published a special report on "Sources of Conflict in British Industry," and in early 1974, just as the striking miners forced Prime Minister Edward Heath to call elections, the London *Observer* ran a section of the report blaming left-wing militants for Britain's industrial unrest.

It now appears from the Institute's own correspondence that most of the "evidence" for the red-baiting allegations came from the files of well-known and widely disregarded right-wing organizations.

Even closer to the bone, the Institute prepared a special manual on counterinsurgency for the British police and regularly participates in training programs at the National Defence College and the Police College. The Institute's "line" appears to encourage preemptive surveillance and other measures against a broad range of "subversives," a term which could easily include law-abiding trade union militants and anti-establishment intellectuals.

The theory, as one staff member put it, seemed to be that the police have to deal with subversion because it might lead to terrorism. Or, alternatively, one might draw a more sinister interpretation from a recent magazine article in which Crozier looked to the armed forces to step in following the breakdown of Western democracy. As Crozier sees it, the breakdown—and the subsequent military intervention—seem to be inevitable.

Like Forum, of course, the Institute's impact has extended far beyond its base in Britain. In France, a small group around former prime minister Antoine Pinay helped pay for an Institute study on "European Security and the Soviet Problem." The study took a predictably Cold War turn, and according to internal records, the aging Pinay and his friends were so delighted that they personally showed it to Nixon, Pompidou, Kissinger, and the Pope.

Similarly, in the Netherlands, Crozier and his colleagues work closely with the East-West Institute and its International Documentation and Information Centre, which has gained fame for its who's-who and what's-what listings of left-wing activities in Europe.

The Institute's records also show close contacts with top police officials in Rhodesia and South Africa, as well as with other leaders around the world. But Crozier's biggest impact could come in the United States, despite a supposed ban on any CIA-backed propaganda within the country. Crozier himself has appeared before the Senate Subcommittee on Internal Security to testify on what he called "transnational terrorism," while the Institute has consistently worked with American counterparts on joint conferences and publications. This cooperation has expanded over the years, and finally in March 1975, the Washington Institute for the Study of Conflict held its first meeting in Washington.

For all the success, however, Crozier appears to be losing his credibility. Despite his denials, too many people now know of the CIA's role in both Forum World Features and the Institute for the Study of Conflict, and every time the story is told, Crozier allows himself to show more and more of his anger in public. And no wonder. Like so many of the CIA's covert propagandists, he had a good thing going, and he's now in danger of losing it all.

The CIA in Switzerland

by Philip Agee

The American Central Intelligence Agency has a sizable presence in Switzerland with offices in the U.S. Embassy in Bern, in the Consulate in Zurich, and in the U.S. Mission to the European Office of the United Nations and Other International Organizations in Geneva. An analysis of available documents on the American missions in these cities has revealed at least one CIA officer in Zurich, about nine in Bern, and about 20 in Geneva.

(Until recently) the CIA Station in the Bern Embassy (was) is headed by Frank W. Jones Jr., 55, who came to Bern in August 1973. Jones is a graduate of the U.S. Military Academy at West Point and has spent almost 20 years in the CIA. His overseas assignments prior to Bern were in Munich (1958–1959), Warsaw (1959–1962), Nicosia (1962–1965), Oslo (1968–1970), and Geneva (1970–1973). In all of his assignments Jones has worked under

[This article was written in July 1976, in London. It has not previously been published.]

cover as a Department of State official in the U.S. Mission where he was assigned.

Other CIA officers in the Bern Embassy would include Terrell W. Hutchison, an Attache; and Paul Van Marx, another Attache. Recently assigned in Bern as CIA communications officers are Bruce Chaney, James Mitchell, and Joseph White.

The only officer in the Bern group that I knew personally is Paul Van Marx, 50, whom I first met while at Headquarters briefly in 1964. After having worked in the CIA's Western European Division and having served under cover in the U.S. Consulate in Zurich (1958–1963), Van Marx was reassigned to the Agency's Western Hemisphere Division. In 1964 he was the officer in charge of the Uruguayan Desk, and in 1965 he was assigned to the U.S. Embassy in Bogotá, Colombia, under cover as a political officer.

The only CIA officer so far identified as working in the Zurich Consulate is Harvey Ginsburg, 54, who has apparently been in Zurich since 1968. Ginsburg's previous assignments were in The Hague (1955–1960) and London (1964-1968) after having attended Yale and Oxford universities in the late 1940s and early 1950s.

The largest CIA office in Switzerland is in the Geneva Mission. While in the CIA, I learned that this office is responsible for the Agency's efforts to penetrate the UN and other international organizations in Geneva, particularly the ILO and the international trade unions that have their headquarters in Geneva. Of special importance for the CIA in Geneva, as in other European cities such as Paris, London, and Brussels, is the recruitment of people from Third World countries who may be working in the UN or in the other international organizations, or in Third World official missions in Geneva. From relative safety, operations to recruit these people are made, with the expectation that after working for the CIA in Geneva, the people will continue when they return to their countries of origin.

The main CIA office in the Geneva Mission is called the Office of the Special Assistant, and it occupies the fifth floor of the Mission building. About 16 people work on this floor, all of whom appear to be CIA employees except Robert Pfeiffer who is a State Department officer responsible for labor affairs. Perhaps his office is close to the CIA because of the CIA's need to coordinate constantly their Geneva-based labor operations with the State Department labor affairs officer which is normal procedure. Indeed Pfeiffer may well be working under CIA direction in trade union matters.

In Geneva, a senior CIA officer in this section is Clarence Barbier, 54, whose previous assignments under State Department cover were to Saigon (1958–1962), Singapore (1962–1964), and Jakarta (1966–1969). Barbier probably was the Chief of Station in Jakarta, assisting the Indonesian military government, which the CIA helped bring to power, in its repressive operations following the 1965 *coup.*

Other CIA officers in the Special Assistant's office include:
> *Throop Wilder,* cover title: First Secretary in UN Specialized Agencies affairs, e.g., ILO.

> *Kevin Maloy,* Second Secretary in UN Specialized Agencies affairs.

> *Nancy Ford,* Attache in UN Specialized Agencies affairs.

> *Dennis Bleam,* Attache.

CIA officers under cover in other sections of the mission are Ronald Cerra in the Political Section as a Second Secretary and Leo Sandel in the International Economic Affairs section as a First Secretary.

Additionally, the CIA's Geneva office includes about four clerical secretaries and two communications officers: Alan Lourie and John Rose.

Besides the CIA's work against the UN specialized agencies in Geneva, and the other international organizations headquartered in Switzerland, the three offices would also have a number of other targets. The Bern Station no doubt is responsible for operations to penetrate the Swiss government, seeking "agents of influence" and for liaison operations with the Swiss security services. This Station also would be responsible for operations against the Soviet Embassy in Bern as well as the embassies of all the other socialist countries. Some of these operations would be effected jointly with the Swiss services and others would be undertaken without the knowledge of Swiss services. Penetration of the Swiss services through recruitments of Swiss security officials is of course one of the important purposes in engaging in liaison and joint operations with the Swiss.

One final area of CIA operations in Switzerland concerns third countries such as France and Italy. In January 1976 it was revealed in Washington that during the previous month President Ford had approved the CIA's spending of six million dollars between then and the next Italian elections—then thought to occur most probably in 1977. Because of the sensitivity of political intervention in a sister NATO country, these operations may well be staged from a neighboring country such as Switzerland, particularly the meetings with agents and the passing of money. Such operations no doubt would involve close supervision by Ambassador Davis in Switzerland as well as by the Ambassador in the target country. The CIA's support for Italian neofascists, as revealed in the report of the House of Representatives Select Committee on Intelligence (the Pike committee), would probably also require meetings and passage of money outside of Italy, most probably in Switzerland.

Goodbye
Bruce Hutchins

by Jan Guillou and
Roger Wallis

The American espionage agency, the CIA, has been permitted to work freely in Sweden for almost 20 years. Never in that time has an American CIA man been taken to court or deported. The CIA has worked under the protection of the Swedish Secret Service (SÄPO) and the Intelligence Service (IB).

Sweden remains a key area for CIA work. A large percentage of the American Embassy staff are employed by the CIA. They infiltrate the Foreign Ministry and the mass media. They spy on Swedish as well as on foreign interests in Sweden. They continuously break Swedish law and act as nonchalantly as if they were in their own backyard.

Eleven months ago, however, the CIA cornered the wrong man— a free-lance journalist named Arthur Opot. And that is where the present story begins.

[This article first appeared as "CIA i Sverige" in the March 4-17, 1976, issue of *Folket i Bild–Kulturfront*, in Stockholm, Sweden.]

Arthur Opot has a serve that lands far outside the tennis court or else sneaks over the net like a boiled potato. His backhand is even worse. He is, in short, a novice on the court. Still, it gives him exercise, and so Arthur and his acquaintances among the African diplomats in Stockholm used to play tennis every Saturday in Solna in the outskirts of town.

It was after one of these amateurish matches in April 1975, and Arthur was sitting alone drinking orange juice in the clubhouse. Two Americans stood near his table. One of them excused himself, saying that he had just gotten a telephone call and had to return to work. The other American, named Bruce, turned to Arthur and suggested a game, as he had suddenly lost his partner. . . .

Afterwards, as they drank orange juice and talked politics, generally Bruce joked around lightheartedly. He told Arthur that he was an American diplomat in the Embassy's "political section." Then he looked at his watch, excused himself, and left.

The CIA had established the first contact. Everything had been thought out in detail, and the plans for recruiting Arthur had already been described in an initial file, together with facts about Arthur that the CIA had already collected through other contacts. Preliminary analysis had shown that it would be worth the effort for one of the CIA station's own officers to try to recruit him directly. What's more, the CIA thought that they had a hold on Arthur. So the rest of the recruiting operation promised to be pure routine.

As if by accident, Bruce and some of his friends happened to be playing tennis the following Saturday at the same time as Arthur. They needed a fourth for doubles, and after the match Bruce and Arthur talked. Bruce offered Arthur lunch, saying that the conversation had been so interesting that they really must continue.

And so the recruiting went on according to plan. The next stop was lunch at the Gondolen Restaurant on May 5. Bruce talked mostly about China and how "the Company" (CIA men always call it "the Company") was about to investigate a potential defector at the Chinese Embassy in Stockholm. And now that they had gotten into the subject, if an independent person—like, for example, Arthur—would help out in the operation, he would be very well paid. Not in Sweden, of course, where all the money would go for taxes. But with discretion and without taxes to a bank account in Switzerland.

Bruce ordered another whiskey. He lifted the glass and allowed the yellow liquid to swirl around. "Arthur, let me put it this way," he said. "If you scratch my back, I'll scratch yours."

The recruiting had reached the crucial point, but Bruce showed nothing of the nervousness he must have felt. Even in Sweden, people sometimes stand up at this point, finish their whiskey, leave the table, and ask never to be contacted again.

But Arthur stayed. The whole thing seemed almost unbelievable, so much so that Arthur thought the bit about "scratching his back" might be a homosexual advance. Still, Bruce was clearly telling him that he worked for the CIA and that he offered money to people willing to cooperate. It was all too unreal, and by the end of the long lunch Bruce was talking of other things.

Following this explicit recruiting attempt by the CIA, Arthur went directly to two of his colleagues at Radio Sweden's Foreign Department, Roger Wallis and Kim Loughran. To their surprise, he told them that the CIA had just tried to recruit him. The three of them discussed what had happened, and soon they came to an agreement. If Arthur's story held up, this was a chance that every journalist dreams about—to hook the CIA without any effort. It could be risky, of course, like fishing for cod and suddenly hooking a two-meter-long shark. So they decided to wait until the possibility of writing an article became clearer.

Some days later, Bruce telephoned Arthur and invited him for another lunch—at the Djurgårdsbrunns Vårdshus. This time, Bruce was with two colleagues, one of them the CIA Station Chief in Stockholm, Paul Garbler. The conversation touched on various topics, like what it was like being a foreigner in Stockholm, American policy, and political developments in Africa.

By now, the recruitment had moved to a level where the "case officer"—Bruce Hutchins—was using the help of colleagues to assess his victim. Every intelligence agency tries carefully to evaluate a potential agent's personality, and above all, the means they might use to buy or threaten him into service. What is the victim's attitude toward liquor? Is money more important than ambition? If so, how much will it cost? What are his preferences in food and wine? How to assess his general political outlook? His attitude toward communism?

During the following weeks, Bruce Hutchins thought he was slowly turning the screw. From the beginning, it must have seemed as if Arthur was curious (which he was) and, later, as if he was slowly but surely sliding into something that implied acceptance. Then Hutchins played his trump card. And all of a sudden it was no longer a half-joking piece of journalism into which Arthur had been drawn. In a surprising twist, it became dead serious.

Nearly everyone has a crucial weakness. It might be something in his personality; it might be discontent over failure in his career. When the espionage service finds what that weakness is, they can often turn it into a trump in recruiting. But someone's weak point might be one of his relatives. And this was the sort of trump card that Bruce Hutchins sprang on Arthur at the Bellmansro Restaurant in the middle of May 1975. As Hutchins began to make the decisive move, Arthur felt a cold chill creeping up his spine.

Calmly and in great detail, Hutchins told Arthur how much "the Company" already knew about him. This included a great deal about his personal finances and family background, and many of the details were so exact that Arthur himself could hardly have given a more complete description. When Arthur asked how the hell Bruce had gotten to know so much about him, Bruce answered that in the Company they knew their jobs, knew when they were looking at the right man, and left nothing to chance. Even this was an elementary psychological trick, used by nearly every espionage service. Then, after a while, Bruce got to the point.

He spoke of Arthur's relatives in Africa, and about those the Company had located. And suddenly, as if in passing, he told Arthur how the authorities of an East African country had arrested his cousin "C" only days before. At the moment the cousin was being tortured, Bruce added, and, with pretended nonchalance, "Well, you know yourself how things happen down there.

"And so you see, Arthur, here's an example of how I can scratch your back. If you join with the Company and cooperate with me, we'll see to it that this fellow down there is immediately freed. Okay?"

Arthur felt that he was about to be trapped. What had started as a playful idea for an article about which Arthur had often joked with Kim and Roger—"What the hell do they think, that I'm going to become a traitor just for some whiskey?"—had become serious business. There he is, knowing that one of his close relatives is being tortured while he sits at a restaurant in a foreign country, and across the table someone asks if he would like the torture stopped.

Arthur agreed to join the Company. Certainly he intended to play the game as long as his cousin was under arrest, and he definitely intended to write the article. But even if Hutchins had any idea of Arthur's intentions—to play along only as long as his cousin was being tortured—it would hardly have mattered. Once involved in working for an espionage service, leaving is never that easy.

Once Arthur had definitely agreed to cooperate, Hutchins gave him the first basic lesson. From his briefcase, he produced a set of photos—black-and-white portraits taken with a tele-photo lens. They showed the most important officers on the staff of the Russian Embassy in Stockholm, all members of the Soviet intelligence service, the KGB. Bruce pointed to the photos and gave the names one by one: Georgij Motchalov, embassy coun-selor and the KGB chief in Sweden; Anatolij Semenov, second secretary; Nicolai Kozotkikh, second secretary; Rudolf Bak-ushev, second secretary; and third secretary Sergei Chobni-akov.

For a newly recruited CIA agent, the lesson—going through the local KGB gallery—might seem a little strange. But Bruce explained. From now on Arthur would be spending a lot of time with the diplomats in Stockholm, and as a result, he would come across people from the KGB. And as they too were skilled re-cruiters . . .

"You see, we don't want any kind of ping-pong between us and them," Bruce warned, "so stay away from these people from now on."

And so, the recruiting phase of this routine CIA operation was finished. Bruce had been through it dozens of times before, and without any failures. A shark, he had swum about in Helsinki and Stockholm for several years, never failing with his victims. But this time he had Arthur Opot in his jaws. And that was the beginning of the biggest blunder the CIA had ever committed in Sweden, a disastrous "flap," as the CIA euphemistically calls it when something goes completely haywire.

But who is Arthur Opot? And what had made him such an excellent target for CIA recruiting in Sweden? The answer is surprisingly simple. Arthur was perfect for one of the CIA's permanent operations in Sweden—infiltrating the African em-bassies and recruiting agents among the African residents.

Arthur Opot is 27 years old, a citizen of Kenya, and a free-lance journalist in the foreign broadcasting service of Radio Sweden. Journalism, as a rule, is one of the best "covers" for an agent. Journalists can show up anywhere and continually ask questions about almost everything—all without causing suspicion. More specifically, though, the African colony in Stockholm is rather small and hard to penetrate. There are only 50 Africans working in the embassies in Stockholm, and for the most part they tend to stick together. Arthur Opot, however, often spent time with the diplomats, as did other Africans in Stockholm. According to the CIA's preliminary assessment, this made Arthur an excellent access agent—a middle link for more important recruiting operations among the diplomats. With further investigation, the CIA also learned that Arthur is married to a Swedish woman who is a member of both the Swedish-Tanzanian Friendship Association and a small leftish company called "Trade-Front," which specializes in importing consumer goods from China, Vietnam, Tanzania, and North Korea. So Arthur's cover must have seemed nearly perfect. The CIA then investigated Arthur's finances and drinking habits, and later, when Bruce boasted of how much the Company knew about Arthur, it became clear that they had carried their investigation rather far even before the first contact with him. Where their information came from is impossible to prove. But Arthur, as well as his wife Bibi, seem convinced that a lot of personal information had come from an African diplomat who has now left Stockholm, but who had clearly cooperated intimately with Bruce Hutchins.

For Bruce, everything seemed to have turned out as expected. Arthur appeared recruited. All that remained now was to make sure that the tortured cousin was released, and gradually Arthur's objections would be swept away with money and with the fact that he was already working for the Company. But, for once, Bruce and the other CIA officers at the station in Stockholm had made a blunder. A massive blunder. Arthur had no intention of becoming a servant of the CIA.

The question—as interesting as it is hard to answer— is how the CIA people in Stockholm could make such a disastrous misjudgment. A possible answer, one that has occurred to us several times while working on this report, is a point made by a KGB defector this January on a TV-2 program about the KGB. As he saw it, the KGB generally believed that the CIA suffers from a much too simplified, one-dimensional view of people. When the CIA makes a personal investigation, they concentrate primarily on the victim's drinking and sexual habits, and also on his financial needs and his attitude toward world communism.

Anyone who is anti-communist, who likes whiskey and beautiful women, and who also lacks money would—in this simplified view—almost certainly accept CIA recruitment. According to the Russian defector, the KGB would make a greater effort to find out about the victim's psychology and subjective feelings about himself. What never occurred to Bruce Hutchins was that Arthur Opot found it completely inconceivable to become a traitor, to sell his own people to the American espionage agency. One needn't be a "Communist" to come to such a simple standpoint. But this apparently never occurred to Hutchins.

After the decisive meeting in May at the Bellmansro Restaurant, when Bruce had threatened Arthur with the continued torture of his cousin in Africa, forcing Arthur to agree to work for the Company, Arthur Opot went directly back to his friends at Radio Sweden and told them just how serious the game had become.

The three discussed the situation and soon came to the same conclusion as would any journalist under the same circumstances. They would write the article and they would really expose the CIA. Arthur would pretend to join the CIA and see what happened. He would not, however, give any significant information to Bruce. On the contrary, they agreed that Arthur would give false answers to Bruce's questions. And so they would see how long their masquerade could last.

Once this was decided, things moved ahead rapidly. Bruce now acted as if the recruiting was over; the only thing to do was to define Arthur's work and goals, and to arrange certain very poor security measures. For future meetings, they chose four places: in order of preference, "The Tree" at the railway station in Stocksund; "The Restaurant" at number 50 Strindbergsgatan in the Gärdet section of Stockholm; "The Hotel" at the Esplanade cinema; and "The Farm," Bruce Hutchins' home at number 37 Riddarvâgen in Lidingö. ("The Farm" is CIA slang for the Camp Peary training base in Virginia—code name ISOLATION.) Arthur's code name would be LASSE, and if he wanted to initiate an unscheduled meeting he was to call Bruce at the Embassy (telephone 63-05-20, extension 244; or, directly, 63-05-21), introduce himself as LASSE, and mention a time, which would be for a meeting at "The Restaurant." Bruce never suggested any further security measures, except to warn Arthur never to mention to anyone, not even to Bibi, his wife, that Bruce and he worked together.

It was already June 1975, and the work Bruce started to spell out almost exclusively focused on African diplomats and the Chinese diplomat whom the CIA thought a potential defector—the second secretary Cheng Yueh, who works on cultural affairs. (According to the CIA, Cheng also does other, more important work.) If Arthur could help the present operation to get Cheng to defect, he would be paid hundreds of thousands of kronor (tens of thousands of dollars).

To improve his contacts with the Chinese Embassy, Arthur was to use his existing contacts at the Tanzanian Embassy. This would bring invitations to the kinds of parties the Chinese diplomats attend. Another key task was to try to get confirmation from the Somalian diplomats in Stockholm on whether or not the Soviet Union had established a naval base in Somalia—a question widely discussed at the time. In addition, Bruce wanted personal information on most of the African diplomats in Stockholm. Arthur started to deliver falsified information, and plenty of it. His main, and very simple, rule: Tell Bruce exactly the opposite of what was really true.

Soon Bruce tells Arthur that his cousin "C" has been released. Arthur makes some rather expensive telephone calls to Africa to confirm that "C" had been arrested for unknown reasons, that he had been badly tortured,. and that, for reasons unknown, he had now been released. Bruce points out that the Company can easily arrange for "C," or any other of Arthur's relatives, to get the same treatment again, if Arthur refuses to continue cooperating. "This is not meant to be a threat, but just to let you know," Bruce explains.

It was now summer. Arthur and his two colleagues, Roger and Kim, decided that it was time to bring a newspaper into the project before it went any further. They discussed the question and then approached the big daily newspaper *Dagens Nyheter.* But the editors weren't interested in exposing the CIA. The next choice was *Folket i Bild,* and the present collaboration began.

Arthur continued to give Bruce false information. But now Arthur had a whole team of reporters with whom he could discuss his assignments. For the most part, Bruce's questions still concerned personal information on various African diplomats.

To help Arthur establish contact with the potential defector at the Chinese Embassy, Bruce suggested that Arthur arrange for some Chinese recordings to be played on the foreign broadcasts. Later that autumn, Arthur also got a document said to come from the Angolan liberation movement FNLA, but probably falsified by the CIA. Bruce instructed Arthur to take the document to the Chinese Embassy, pretending that he had gotten it from a foreign journalist and had thought it might be of interest. In this way he was to try to promote discussion on the FNLA and see if he could discover any signs of change in the Chinese attitude toward the MPLA-FNLA conflict in Angola. Generally, he was to try to improve his personal relations with the Chinese.

On one occasion, Bruce took Arthur to his home ("The Farm") and lectured him on the Company and its work. For the most part, Bruce talked about democracy and how to defend it. "We in the Company fight against ideologies," he explained. The Company was going to save the world from communism, and would have succeeded already if they didn't have to deal with incompetent politicians—senators and congressmen—who were always throwing monkey wrenches into the works. Politicians didn't have the complete information that the Company had, and as a result, they often made deeply undemocratic decisions—that is, decisions harmful to democracy. Thus it was a real honor to fight alongside the Company, and the Company compensated those who helped very well indeed.

On the other hand, Arthur should never try to fool around with the Company. That could result in death. Besides, he would soon be taking a polygraph test, a routine for every agent, even the career CIA officers. (Polygraph, an advanced lie detector the CIA uses, is a machine which simultaneously measures blood pressure, heartbeat, and sweat on the palms.)

The rest of the conversation was devoted to the potential Chinese defector and the situation in Africa. Bruce told Arthur that a *coup d'état* would soon take place in Nigeria (a *coup* that later did take place), and also that the Company was preparing a *coup* in Somalia (where, to our knowledge, no *coup* attempt has happened so far). Arthur was to try to get further personal information on the Somalian diplomats in Stockholm.

On Wednesday, September 3, Bruce picked Arthur up in front of Radio Sweden and instructed Arthur to arrange some parties for African diplomats that fall. Bruce had a list of those to be invited—some 30 people connected with various African embassies in Stockholm, mostly from Zaire, Zambia, and Tanzania. The guests all had some link with the political sections of the embassies—or with the coding departments. (Every embassy has a department that works on coding secret political messages to the home country.)

Bruce would also be invited to the party, along with some ten others—it made no difference whom—to create a politically less homogeneous gathering. The chief purpose of the project seems to have been to give Bruce a chance to make personal contact with those diplomats in Sweden who were the CIA's target group. Of course, Bruce picked up the tab for food and whiskey.

Months later, on November 22, a similar event was arranged, and after both parties Bruce and Arthur met for several days to assess those who had attended.

On September 19, Bruce first raised the possibility that the CIA would send Arthur to Angola. According to the initial plan, Arthur would go as a journalist to FNLA-controlled areas to collect material for newspaper articles which could be worked on and "improved" by the CIA office when he returned to Stockholm. Then, with the help of CIA contacts, the prepared articles would be published in convenient Swedish newspapers. The aim of the operation was to show the Soviet-supported liberation movement, the MPLA, in as bad a light as possible.

As it turned out the actual trip took place under completely different circumstances. This was because of what Hutchins called "the catastrophe," namely, the decision of the American Congress not to allocate to their government the needed resources for full-scale intervention in the ongoing Angolan war. Bruce called this a catastrophe since the decision, made as usual by dumb politicians, left Angola "wide open" for a Soviet-Communist takeover.

With the changed situation, Arthur was now to go to MPLA-controlled areas, primarily Luanda, to collect political and military intelligence on the MPLA government. If one studies the list of questions given to Arthur (see page 234), it is possible to see almost exactly how the CIA assessed the Angolan situation at the time, both politically and militarily. Moreover, the questions are so demanding that no one, no matter how skilled, could have compiled complete answers in a single trip to Luanda. In fact, the questions the CIA wanted answered would require the simultaneous efforts of several different agents.

It might seem surprising that the CIA would send an agent like Arthur Opot on such an exacting and dangerous mission (where discovery would mean death). But apparently, in contrast to several other agents, Arthur had a perfect cover. He was a journalist from Radio Sweden. Besides, at the time Angola was clearly the CIA's top priority; they were sending abroad all their available agents. The CIA's purpose was, presumably, to collect as much information as rapidly as possible to prove that Angola was about to become a Soviet colony (unless the "free world" intervened in time).

As Arthur's team of reporters now saw the situation, it was all becoming a bit sticky. Clearly, the "report" Arthur would deliver when he returned to Stockholm would not make any CIA chief very happy, and this coming fiasco would make it impossible to continue the comedy. So, after discussing the problem, we decided to break off the masquerade as soon as we could and to publish what we had. This gave us a splendid chance to check on the CIA's relationship with the Swedish Secret Service (SÄPO).

Arthur and Bruce met again on December 30, and Arthur received some 12,000 kronor ($3,000) and a form with the questions to be answered. He was previously required to fill out a routine form before receiving any major mission, the PRQ (Personal Record Questionnaire). No one can be used for any CIA operational assignment until one is approved by the Operational Approval Branch of the CIA's Counter-Intelligence Staff in the United States. Arthur appears to have passed the security check without any problem. He could now be sent on his first mission to Luanda, Angola. The comedy had really gone too far.

We thought it would be a simple thing to get Arthur sacked from the CIA. We knew that his Angola "report" would contain falsified information and a load of distorted, albeit plausible, rubbish, which we would concoct. In addition, we arranged a telephone call that we thought would surely get Arthur sacked in a second.

Arthur's wife Bibi, who had known about the project all along, simply called Bruce Hutchins a few days after Arthur's departure. She made the call to the American Embassy and said that she wanted to speak with Bruce Hutchins. She told him her name and said that Arthur had lost his money in Angola. And, she insisted, since he was in Angola on a CIA mission, the CIA had to find a way to get him more money. Bruce first told Bibi that it wasn't possible. Then, later on, he called her back and asked for a meeting.

Note the following details: The wife of an agent telephones directly to the Embassy. She gives her name. She asks to talk to a named person. She gives the name of a CIA agent who's somewhere in the world on a mission. She points out that the CIA had paid for the mission. She demands more money.

Bruce doesn't deny any of it. He simply says that it's impossible and then asks for a meeting.

Every embassy telephone is tapped by the Swedish Intelligence Service. A single call to Georgij Motchalov or one of his colleagues on the KGB staff at the Soviet Embassy would bring immediate and drastic consequences. Within 24 hours, the KGB officer would have left Sweden and all further contacts with the agent or his wife would immediately be terminated.

Where the CIA is concerned, however, things don't work that way. Instead, Bruce went out, telephoned Bibi Opot, and arranged to see her the following evening, January 8, in the bar of Stockholm's Grand Hotel. Bruce orders some whiskey and proceeds to threaten Bibi with death. He tells her how extremely dangerous it would be if someone learned what he or Arthur were doing. In particular, he wanted her to know that Bruce Hutchins is living a life where any day he could return from work to find a murderer hiding in his house. And now Bibi Opot could end up in the same situation. . . .

That is, unless they were able to work the whole thing out in a better way. Namely, Bibi would also start working for the Company. To the Company, $10,000 was worth no more than a nickel, especially when it concerned operations among the Chinese in Stockholm. A Chinese defector, or valuable information from inside the Chinese Embassy, would be well compensated. Since Bibi was working at the "Trade-Front," she could easily establish good relations with the Chinese. All in all, there were superb possibilities for future cooperation.

Bruce then gave Bibi 1,300 kronor (about $350), the money Arthur would need to support himself during his stay in Luanda. Bruce also began to talk about politics, and as usual his tongue loosened in direct relation to the quantity of alcohol he consumed. He talked a lot about the "Cuban crisis," which led him to the subject of Kennedy. He himself was a Kennedy man, he said, and pointed out to Bibi that Kennedy had fought for democracy, justice, and human rights.

A few days later, Arthur returned after completely failing in Angola. Bruce rented room 561 at the Sheraton Hotel; using a false name, and for two days (January 12–13) questioned Arthur, who only gave him false or distorted information.

By this time, Arthur must have appeared to be the most useless agent the CIA had ever had. Extraordinarily, however, Bruce continued to demand more information. They had already met about 20 times since spring, and throughout the time Arthur had done nothing but arrange two parties and dish out several confused personal descriptions. And now the trip to Angola, which turned out to be a double failure. First, it proved Arthur had mentioned his activities to an uninvolved outsider, who had, on top of that, eventually telephoned the Embassy and allowed the Swedish Intelligence Service to tape-record everything. Second, Arthur failed to carry out a single task in Angola.

But, for all of this, Bruce gave Arthur another delicate mission—to return to Angola and to fail once again. We discussed this on the reporting team, and it seemed most unlikely that the trip was some kind of trap. If Bruce really was suspicious, he certainly wouldn't have given Arthur the document which defined the tasks for the second trip. The document exposed Bruce too heavily. It even asked for information about two Swedish journalists in Angola, making Bruce guilty of espionage—something far more serious than his earlier offense of unauthorized intelligence activity.

Arthur made up his mind to go to Angola a second time. The advantage was that we could now find out if it was possible to be sacked by the CIA for incompetence. It would also give us more time to work on the article without making Bruce Hutchins suspicious.

Bruce Hutchins is protected from the law because of his diplomatic immunity. If he had been a so-called deep-cover agent—a CIA officer working under a non-diplomatic cover, as for example an airline representative—he would have been taken to court in Sweden. The offenses would have been blackmail (a maximum of 6 years in prison); unauthorized intelligence activity (attempts to collect information about other foreign diplomats, a maximum of 2 years); and possibly illegal threat (a maximum of 2 years) and espionage (a maximum of 6 years). If Bruce Hutchins is still in Sweden when this article is published, he will be deemed "persona non grata" by the Swedish Foreign Office. And, if that happens, Bruce Hutchins will become the first American diplomat ever to be deported from Sweden.

Bruce Hutchins is one of about ten CIA officers in the American Embassy in Stockholm. He's in his forties and has probably never had any other job. This means that he was recruited in the most common way, directly from an American university. It also means that he must have done quite well at the university. No doubt history and political science were among Bruce Hutchins' areas of specialization.

It's hard to get an exact picture of the qualities that make a young American student join the CIA. The long testing program is so hard that almost 99% of the applicants are sifted out. The CIA security check takes about six months (no "Communist" relatives, no close relatives in Eastern Europe, no sensational sexual perversions, etc.).

Generally, it can be assumed that those accepted into CIA service have a far above average intellectual capacity, a remarkable interest in politics, good physical fitness, a strong desire to hold on to their own positions, and a desire to participate in creating politics. The training takes several years and includes technical aspects (radio operation, bugging, codes, photography, letter-opening, etc.) as well as special military training and political education, where the courses concentrate on the structure and organization of Communist parties and/or intensive political studies of the country where the applicant will first be posted. Bruce Hutchins has previously been stationed in Moscow, where the working conditions certainly are radically different from those in Sweden. Before coming to Sweden in 1972, he also had spent several years in Helsinki, working primarily on infiltrating and trying to influence every political force with any connection to the Soviet Union, which in Finland is a big job.

In Stockholm, Hutchins' main work is to infiltrate the diplomatic missions of the Third World and also to gather information on the Swedish government's relationship with Third World countries.

Like those of other intelligence agencies, the CIA's activities are strictly "compartmentalized." This means that each employee has to maintain his special work and place on the team, just like a disciplined football player. Only the head of the CIA station should have an overview of all of the operations in a particular place. The purpose of this compartmentalization is obviously to minimize the damage in the event of what the CIA calls a "flap," such as this article will cause for Bruce Hutchins and the CIA. A single defector or exposed CIA officer should never be able to expose the entire local CIA operation.

Bruce Hutchins' methods of work in Stockholm show several surprising features. He and the other CIA officers can often be seen in Stockholm's bars and restaurants, and their favorite spot is the English Tudor Arms pub on Grevgatan in Stockholm. Ironically, the Tudor Arms also used to be the favorite of agents of the Swedish Intelligence Service's Information Bureau. The CIA also has permanently rented rooms at the American Sheraton Hotel, which they chiefly use to meet with agents.

Most remarkably, Hutchins and some of his colleagues act rather openly as members of the CIA. When playing darts, they carry on their conversation in internal CIA slang, which any security officer or foreign intelligence agent would immediately recognize.

Hutchins is well known at the Tudor Arms as a bad loser at darts. But if he wins, he suddenly buys a round. His consumption of alcohol is enormously high. His favorite drink is a "Rob Roy" (whiskey and red vermouth).

On Wednesday, January 7, one of the members of the reporting team from *FIB-Kulturfront* went to the Tudor Arms to wait for Hutchins. Only hours before, he had gotten the dramatic telephone call from Bibi Opot telling him that his agent in Angola was about to turn into a "flap," and we were interested in how he was reacting.

Hutchins got to the Tudor Arms about 6:00 P.M. and immediately started a four-hour-long game of darts, constantly drinking Rob Roys. When he won a game, he bought drinks for everyone around. When he lost, he swore and threw the darts on the floor. After four hours of loud-mouthed buffoonery, Hutchins invited several people—including the *FIB-Kulturfront* reporter!—to the Ostermalmskallaren Restaurant, where the doorman refused to let him in because he was too drunk. However, the *FIB* reporter managed to get them by the doorman by showing his press card. And so the drinking went on, all on the CIA's expense account. The night ended at 2:00 A.M. with Hutchins staggering to his car, which was parked outside the Alexandra night club. By that time he'd been drinking at bars and restaurants for nine hours. Standing by the car were two uniformed policemen, who asked in surprise if Hutchins really intended to take the car.

"Don't you worry, this is my car," slurped the CIA man.

Hutchins continued to argue with the policemen for some time, but they couldn't arrest him since he had identified himself as a diplomat. Hutchins tried to provoke the policemen into taking his car keys by force. Finally, the incident ended with Hutchins voluntarily giving them the keys, taking a taxi to his home in Lidingö, returning to the scene of the crime, and—still drunk—driving his car home. Hutchins regularly drives while drunk.

The huge consumption of liquor is inevitably part of CIA work. (A CIA man hardly pays for such expenses out of his own pocket; in Hutchins' case the expenses probably reached some 5,000 kronor [about $1,200] a month.) Contacts are made in restaurants and every intelligence agency lives off its contacts. Besides, money and his standard of living play a big part in measuring success for a CIA man. For example, when Bruce and his wife.Lou Ann go out for the evening, the children—aged six and four—are supposed to look after one another. And they get paid for it: the older child gets 3 kronor ($1) an hour, the younger $1^1/_2$ (50¢).

The importance of such behavior is not on the level of personal morality, of course. An intelligence officer should be trained to take minimal risks when he's at work. So, at the very least, it's remarkable that a CIA man in Stockholm can behave as Hutchins does. Even a small automobile accident when he's intoxicated could lead to a flap. A diplomat would then risk being removed from the country, and if he's a CIA officer, he would leave a lot of agents and informants without their "case officer." In addition, letting it be known publicly that he works for an intelligence agency would be against all rules and regulations. So the self-assured nonchalance that Hutchins shows, as when he threatened Arthur Opot's wife with death the day after his night out on the town, might seem a bit confusing.

The explanation of this extreme nonchalance and breaking of every kind of security regulation must be the favorable "operational climate" in Sweden.

The Swedish Secret Service have never bothered to pursue a CIA man. SÄPO chases only Eastern European diplomats and the organized Swedish left. From a CIA point of view, SÄPO is an ally that would never get in the way of any CIA operation. The CIA can behave as if Stockholm were its own backyard, and as if there weren't any risks at all. The Soviet KGB are probably green with envy.

The entire top floor of the American Embassy in Stockholm is the CIA's "operations center" in Sweden. From here, the CIA runs the hundreds of informers and agents who operate in Swedish society. The CIA's most important so-called operational targets in Sweden are the Foreign Office and mass media, Swedish foreign aid policy, Third World embassies, and Eastern European agents.

The CIA is the world's second largest intelligence agency, after the Soviet intelligence and security service, the KGB, which is more than ten times as big. (When making comparisons, it should be pointed out that the major part of KGB resources are spent on the control of citizens within the Soviet Union.)

Information differs on the total budget of the CIA, but the most recent figure reaches some 50 billion Swedish kronor (about $10 billion), a sum corresponding to five times the total Swedish defense budget! The CIA has at least 15,000 employees, plus hundreds of thousands of informers and so-called agents all over the world.

Through the flood of memoirs written by ex-CIA employees and the various investigations made over the past few years by the American Congress, a great deal is now known of CIA operations in international politics, primarily in Indochina.

However, almost nothing has been published about CIA operations in Sweden. We can assume, nonetheless, that CIA activities here are far more extensive than in most other countries of the world. In most American embassies, CIA employees do not make up more than 20% of the total staff. In Sweden, as many as one third of the embassy staff are employed by the CIA.

Pure military espionage gets a very low priority at the CIA station in Stockholm. This is because the Swedish armed forces are so intimately linked with the American arms industry that the American intelligence service automatically gets a huge amount of information without any kind of effort. In addition, the Swedish Intelligence Service has for years been one of the CIA's allies, and will remain so in the future, as was demonstrated by the "Intelligence Investigation Report." This report proposed that the enlarged Swedish Intelligence Service have its staff trained by foreign intelligence agencies, and as there is no likely alternative to the CIA, our future IB officials will be even more intimately linked to the CIA than at present. Moreover, since the CIA continually tries to recruit agents from among officials of foreign intelligence agencies, it is plausible to assume that a certain part of the future Swedish intelligence staff will be found on the CIA payroll.

The head of the Swedish Secret Service, Hans Holmer, has publicly admitted that his agency also cooperates with the CIA, which gives a fairly clear picture of the operational climate in Sweden. This operational climate is an assessment of the possibilities of activity in a particular country and is the basis of all CIA work. The CIA's first question: What is the attitude of the local security service toward us? The second: What is the attitude of the local intelligence agency toward us? And only then, in the third question, does the CIA even begin to ask about the attitude of the local *government*. From a CIA point of view, the working conditions in Sweden are just as good as those in, for example, West Germany. The Swedish security service has never bothered the CIA. Nor has the press posed any problem.

The CIA's espionage activities in Sweden are concentrated almost exclusively on political and economic information. There are, however, two totally separated target areas. One is foreign embassies and intelligence agencies, the other is Swedish life.

As in any other country, the CIA in Sweden naturally directs operations against the Soviet Union and its allies, and also against China. But in Stockholm, the CIA's attitude toward the Soviet KGB is characterized by a curious ambiguity. In part, this is because Stockholm acts as an international way station for espionage. Stockholm is neutral ground, a place where intelligence officials meet to exchange agents and the like. Examples of this are often quite comical. The head of the Swedish CIA station, Paul Garbler, meets at his home (Elfviksvagen 44, Lidingö) with all sorts of Swedish people and international delegations. One night it might be a group from a ministry or a trade union, the next a group of West German intelligence officers. But, occasionally, he also has visitors from the KGB. And there is only one visible difference between the KGB visits and those of other groups. After every KGB visit, technical experts from the American Embassy search the house with special instruments to ferret out possible hidden microphones.

About six months ago, the CIA's James Skove happened to attend the same class in Swedish as a KGB officer named Vladimir. They both found the coincidence amusing and often went to the Tudor Arms to drink beer together after class.

Of course, the other side of the relationship between the CIA and KGB and the KGB's allies (mainly the Czech and East German organizations) is much more conventional. As everywhere else in the world, both sides work at recruiting each other's agents and infiltrating each other's embassies.

Undoubtedly, CIA espionage against Third World embassies in Stockholm is of the highest priority. In terms of international politics, Sweden is a key country, and the CIA continuously gathers information on coming Swedish political initiatives in relation to the Third World. Among others at the CIA station in Stockholm, George D. Swerdlin gathers information and plans disruption of Sweden's program of development aid. From diplomatic sources whom we have promised not to reveal, we have obtained thorough descriptions of how Swerdlin has tried to find proof that Sweden links its development aid to political demands. This has surprised African diplomats, since Swerdlin appears to believe that Sweden uses its development aid in the same manner as would a superpower—that is, as a means of political pressure.

But Swerdlin also plans disruptive actions against Swedish development aid. He does this by preparing a base for American or American-influenced "countercontributions" and for political resistance in Sweden against certain targets for Swedish aid, such as Vietnam and Cuba.

In dealing with Sweden and the Third World, operational activities at the CIA station fall into several different target areas. The Foreign Office is one of the most important Swedish targets, and there is no doubt that the CIA can get hold of secret information from the FO. The latest example was the CIA's proven knowledge of the Palestine Liberation Organization's plans to establish an information office in Stockholm. The CIA was aware of these plans long before they became public, and the American Ambassador in Stockholm was able to express his discontent with the Swedish government.

As it happens, the CIA's Bruce Hutchins dealt precisely with this matter. One of the top officials to deal with Arab questions in the Swedish Foreign Office is married to a woman who has enjoyed a long and intimate relationship with Hutchins. The woman and Hutchins meet regularly in Stockholm, though theirs is not a personal relationship.

Besides the Foreign Office, another key operational target for CIA infiltration is Radio Sweden. And, since the initial plan for Arthur Opot's trip to Angola involved publishing propaganda with the help of a network of CIA contacts, it's clear that the CIA has on its payroll Swedish journalists of some influence. This is hardly surprising, since an ongoing mission of every CIA station is to establish such contacts. The system of contacts has a double purpose. On the one hand, journalists work in a milieu where the flow of information is intense and therefore they can become superb informers. On the other hand, journalists employed by the CIA can easily create the desired propaganda.

Our description of what the CIA does in Sweden is necessarily fragmentary and incomplete. Obviously, we have had sources of information other than Arthur Opot's masquerade. And the need to keep these sources anonymous—a precondition for getting information from diplomatic sources—has made our description less precise than we would have liked.

Finally, it's important to emphasize the obvious. There are 10 to 15 CIA men at the Embassy in Stockholm. If we assume that each of them handles at least 10 local "agents," we get an approximate measure of the extent of CIA activities in Sweden. In other words, for all its detail, this article has probably not described more than 1% of CIA activity in Sweden.

The Documents Given to Arthur Opot

(Reproduced exactly as they were typed)
[*First Document*]
1. Regarding the OAU meetings: What are the MPLA/ Soviet/Cuban behind-the-scenes efforts to persuade delegates to recognize the MPLA government in Angola? What specifically is the MPLA doing to put forth charges of South African intervention in Angola and to minimize counter-charges of Soviet and Cuban support to MPLA? Of particular interest are MPLA action plans for OAU meetings. What sort of contingency plans does MPLA have should efforts at the OAU fail (in other words, what would be the MPLA reaction if the OAU decides to send a peace-keeping force into Angola?)? How would MPLA deal with international pressure to permit FNLA and UNITA participation in an independent Angolan government?

2. There is a pressing need for confirmation and details on the reported arrival in Congo (Brazzaville) and/or Angola of MIG-21 aircraft. According to some reports, MIGs were delivered to Brazzaville in early November, and press reports of 14 November quote East European sources in Luanda as saying about 400 Soviets have arrived in Luanda for the purpose of manning tanks and MIG-21s in support of MPLA.

3. Information is needed on the control mechanisms the MPLA government has instituted in Luanda (people's vigilante groups, block committees, "poder popular" elements) that are used to keep vigilance over the population and to control them—the same as in Soviet bloc and Cuba and wherever and whenever communist parties take control.

4. How many Soviet technical and military advisors are there in Angola and Cabinda? What are their specialties and military ranks and where are they de-

ployed? We would appreciate the names and ranks of any high-level Soviet or bloc military officers.

5. What are the current MPLA military units, their sizes, leaders and deployment? How large and how well-armed is the MPLA force advancing on FNLA headquarters in Ambriz? Latest information indicates that this force is 80 kilometers south of Ambriz. How many Soviets and Cubans are with this force? The same information is needed on MPLA deployments in the south and the east, particularly in Henrique de Carvalho.

6. What is MPLA short-range political planning for the post–civil war period? If MPLA should win Angola, how do they plan to deal with or relate to the pro-FNLA Bakongo and the pro-UNITA Ovimbundu tribals? In this regard, are there any Bakongo or Ovimbundu tribals in the MPLA? If so, how many?

7. What are the MPLA's foreign policy plans? Does it envision or wish to establish relations with known or presumed supporters of FNLA and UNITA, including Zaire, China and the U.S.? Would it reopen the Benguela railroad to Zaire? What are its intentions toward South Africa and support to liberation groups in Namibia and Rhodesia? What about relations with Portugal?

8. There are indications of developing factionalism within the MPLA (mulatto versus black) (moderate versus radical) (Neto versus anti-Neto). How extensive and significant is this factionalism? Identify those in each faction—the strength of their following, their points of view, their political orientation. There is particular interest in information about those who express a willingness to negotiate a peaceful reconciliation and the formation of a multiparty government. There is also interest in any MPLA disenchantment with the Soviets and Cubans and vice versa.

9. Since October, Cuban troops and advisors reportedly have been transiting Pointe Noire, Congo, en route to Angola and Cabinda. We need to know how many Cubans are now in Angola proper, how many are in Cabinda, how many more are coming and how

long they will all stay? How did or how do they travel (plane? ship? direct from Cuba?)? What percentage of the Cuban personnel are military and what branches do they represent (army, navy, air)? What are their specialties? Are any of them pilots and, if so, how many and what will they fly? Provide details on the amounts and types of military equipment they are providing. Who proposed direct Cuban involvement (the Cubans, Congolese, Soviets or MPLA)? Provide the names of Cuban officers in Angola and Cabinda.

[*Second Document*]
A. Any further information on the presence of MIG-17 aircraft, such as when were they sent to Luanda and how were they transported to Luanda? It would be helpful if you can manage to see one of the MPLA aircraft, to see for yourself what model it is. The MIG-17 is a swept-wing aircraft and carries two external fuel tanks, one under each wing. The MIG-21, on the other hand, is a delta-wing jet fighter with a stream-lined fuel tank carried under the central portion of the aircraft. The MIG-21 also has a nosecone which ex-tends forward through the round opening in the front of the fuselage.

B. In addition to those questions given you earlier:
    1. At the battle fronts: information on the presence and activities of Cuban and Soviet advisors and/or troops as well as the type and quantity of weapons available at each front visited. Also need the MPLA long-range battle plans.

    2. What are the MPLA intentions toward the upcoming February OAU Council of Minis-ters meeting in Addis Ababa? Especially, how would MPLA use this meeting to further their campaign for OAU recognition, particularly now that so many OAU countries have recog-nized the MPLA?

    3. All possible information is needed on Coto Cabral (bio data, date of birth, education, etc.). What specifically is his position (title & authority) in MPLA? What specifically is his

position as spokesman for the mulattos? As
the MPLA hierarchy is largely mulatto, it is
not clear how Cabral fits in as their
spokesman.

4. Gather background information on Leif
Biureborgh. Who employs him? Is he a businessman or paid by the MPLA or by the
Swedish government/Social Democratic party? Assessment of him is needed.

5. Who is the SR representative already
there, who is too conservative to be permitted
to visit the fronts? All info on his: bio,
assessment.

C. Details are needed on any support (money, materiel, troops) to MPLA from African countries and possibly from Latin American countries. On December
29, the head of a three-man delegation travelling to
African and Latin American countries, Carvalho Dos
Santos, said during a press conference in Guyana that
countries which have promised military aid to the
MPLA are Nigeria, Guinea, Guinea-Bissau and the
Congo. According to Dos Santos, the aid would consist of troops, equipment and guns.

D. We need evidence and details of any Soviet pressure on MPLA to accept a compromise solution with
the FNLA and UNITA, that is, a government of national unity with the MPLA taking the major power
role.

E. There is a recently-constructed Soviet radar system in Luanda airport, about 200 meters south of the
airport control tower, mounted on the roof of a small
building. We are interested in the specific purpose of
the system, its effective range, the radio frequency/
frequencies on which it operates, the circumference/
diameter/depth (at the center) of the dish, a description of any attachments or projections from the dish
(length and width) and the Soviet name or designation
of the system.

F. A Soviet Kotlin Class guided missile destroyer, the

NAKHODCHIFYY, was observed northwest of Pointe Noire, Congo, on 6 January, possibly en route to Angola to join the landing ship transport which is located off the Pointe Noire coast. We are interested in Soviet plans for the *NAKHODCHIFYY*: Was it en route to Pointe Noire and if so what was its mission? Is the landing ship transport (1st) being actively used to deliver Soviet Weapons to Pointe Noire for the MPLA? If so, what weapons and in what quantities? What deliveries are expected in the future and when?

G. What is the total cost of the Soviet Weapons sent to Angola, including the cost of shipping and the cost of transporting and maintaining Cuban troops and materiel in Angola. (If you get anything on this, please indicate the period covered by your figures.)

What the Documents Tell Us

As far as we know, documents of this kind have never before been published. One has only to look briefly at the questions to realize that one of the central myths of modern espionage is completely false. Satellites and other technical gadgetry have not been able to replace the human agent out in the field. Satellites can photograph large objects, but not political ideas.

The CIA's questions show precisely what modern espionage really looks like. They show the gathering of both political and military intelligence. To help create a base for the activities of the American-backed wing of the OAU, it was important to have information on what the MPLA would do at the OAU conference in Addis Ababa. In the event of an MPLA victory on the battlefield, it was vital to have information on the internal situation within the MPLA. In making plans for the future in Angola, it was important to know about the possible internal tendencies in the MPLA that would back appeasement and a coalition government.

At times, it's difficult to demarcate which is political information and which is military. The CIA's urgent need to know whether MIG-21s or MIG-17s had been stationed in Angola relates to planning for a continuing war. The MIG-21 is a fighter plane. If MIG-21s were in Angola, the MPLA and the Soviet Union would be expecting a coming air war against hostile aircraft. The MIG-17 is a tactical strike aircraft. If MIG-17s were there, they were probably intended for use against hostile armored columns on the ground.

Asking whether Cuban or Russian pilots were going to fly the planes was important politically—in determining the degree of direct Russian intervention.

The dispassionate tone of the questions comes from the fact that this is a secret document and has nothing to do with public propaganda. The questions also give a rather exact picture of what the CIA really knew and did not know at the time. (In the hands of the Russian intelligence agencies, the documents would have been very valuable at the time. By now they are already useless.)

Those who are interested in knowing how the CIA gradually got answers to these questions should look through *Newsweek* magazine during the month of January (1976). In the magazine, it's possible to follow how one piece of the puzzle after another fell into place. It's no secret that the information and analyses on Angola published in *Newsweek* were those of the CIA.

Arthur Opot, the *FIB-Kulturfront* reporter inside the CIA, had "failed" completely in giving sensible answers to any of these questions. He also lost all his money and had to return to Sweden without fulfilling his mission.

Finally, we should emphasize that the questions posed in the documents are far too detailed and demanding for a single agent to cover completely in a report. Agents are not supermen. On the other hand, Arthur Opot was not the CIA's only envoy in Angola. If we assume that 15 to 30 agents worked on the questions at the same time in Luanda in January, we get a picture of how espionage really works. "The spy is looking for pieces to a jigsaw puzzle," said the wartime slogan on Swedish matchboxes. Or, rather, the spymaster and his computer fit the pieces together.

The decision at CIA headquarters to send the totally inexperienced Arthur Opot to Angola suggests that the question of Angola was of highest priority and that the CIA was using all available resources.

This conclusion is strengthened by the fact that Arthur, despite his terrible "failure," was immediately sent back to Angola. For two days, on January 12 and 13, the CIA's Bruce Hutchins questioned Arthur Opot in a rented hotel room (room 561, Sheraton Hotel) before giving up. After a severe dressing down and withdrawal of a previous payment commitment,

Bruce Hutchins and his superior decided nevertheless to send Arthur back to Angola! This certainly gives the impression that the CIA regarded virtually any chance to obtain information from Angola as extremely important.

The second spy mission to Angola was dramatically different from the first. The CIA now appeared by some unknown means to have obtained reports on Swedes who were in Angola. Our man was therefore instructed to check on and to gather biographical, political, and economic information on them. And so the CIA gave proof that they also practice espionage directly against Swedish interests.

By this point, however, it had become impossible to carry on the comedy any further. We were now racing against time: Would we be able to publish this article before the CIA realized that they had been taken?

Comparing the questions from the two missions, it's possible to draw some immediate conclusions. By the second mission, the level of difficulty has been decreased. This shouldn't be surprising, since LASSE had "failed" completely on the first mission. Moreover, some of the CIA's questions look like an attempt to monitor what might have been negotiations between the U.S. and the Soviet Union. Question "D" asks for proof of Soviet pressure on the MPLA toward a compromise solution over the heads of the Angolan people. This kind of monitoring is typical of modern intelligence activity in the era of peaceful coexistence. It is absolutely essential to know if the other side is observing the rules that have been secretly negotiated, and only the intelligence agencies can answer questions like that.

Of the military questions, "E" has particular interest. Satellites and spy planes can certainly photograph a radar system, but the photographs can't tell what kind of radar it is. If, for example, the radar were connected to an air-defense missile system, the consequence would be far different than in the case of ordinary search radar.

Questions "B-4" and "B-5" have a very special character. They suggest that the CIA had obtained information from other sources on the two people in question. The Radio Sweden man in Africa ("B-5") is Ingemar Odlander, who earlier held a managerial post on the news program "Report." The questions on Odlander seem quite normal. Every espionage organization regards journalists as "hot prospects," since journalists gather information (often much more effectively than do "agents") and also create an arena for political propaganda through their news reports. Almost every foreign correspondent has at least once come across an "agent."

Sometime after these questions were asked, Ingemar Odlander ran into some inexplicable difficulties with his work permit in Kenya, which might have something to do with the CIA's investigation of him. If so, Odlander could proudly prove that the CIA was unhappy with him. Whether or not they are, however, is a question on which *Folket i Bild* can offer no definite opinion.

The CIA's interest in Leif Biureborgh is quite a different matter. Biureborgh holds down several different jobs in Angola. Sometimes he pretends to "represent" the Swedish Social Democratic Party. He is also a journalist (he has signed several "heroic" articles during the last year) for the Social Democratic press and at the same time runs some slightly unclear business interests. Obviously, through their intelligence activity, the CIA has gotten some preliminary knowledge about all of this. And this has made Biureborgh a person worth investigating. Hundreds of such routine investigations are made every year, on possible Swedish agents, though without any concrete results.

Since Bruce Hutchins is protected by his diplomatic immunity, the judicial aspects of the CIA's investigation about Swedish citizens in Angola is only of theoretical interest. In general, however, questions such as those in the second document implicate the CIA in the crime of direct espionage against Swedish interests. (From a security point of view, for example, even Radio Sweden is a classified institution.)

Since Arthur Opot "failed" as an agent even on his second mission, the relationship between him and his "case officer" Bruce Hutchins began to get worse, to say the least. Arthur returned to Sweden in February, and since the comedy with the useless agent could hardly be carried any further, the reporting team immediately started to finish the article. Up to the stage of printing and publishing, Arthur prolonged his relationship with Bruce Hutchins as far as possible. The question—still unanswered—was whether the CIA station in Stockholm would finally realize that there was something fishy about their "useless agent." So, we don't know at present whether Bruce will still be in Sweden when the article comes out. But if he is, there will probably be something of a race between the CIA and the Swedish Foreign Office. And then the question will be whether the CIA will have time to recall Bruce Hutchins from Sweden before he gets thrown out.

Postscript

Just a few days before the article was finally published, the CIA actually fired the "useless agent," Arthur Opot. Hutchins gave Arthur a piece of paper on which to sign a promise that he would never expose anything about his relationship with the American government. Then he gave Arthur 1,700 kronor (about $400) and a last warning that went something like this: "Remember one thing, Arthur. If anything comes out about our relationship, it's your ass that's gonna fry, not mine."

Well, the article came out in early March, and it was Hutchins' ass that fried, not Arthur's. The day after publication, Bruce suddenly left Sweden, and the U.S. Embassy officially notified the Swedish Foreign Office that he was gone, which was taken as confirmation of Arthur Opot's story. It was also learned that Hutchins' colleague, James Skove, had left the country a couple of weeks earlier, and George Swerdlin was expected to leave as well.

The Swedish Secret Service investigated the entire situation, in part to see if they could bring any charges against Arthur and the *FIB-Kulturfront* reporting team. Then, after three weeks, the public prosecutor announced that he would bring no charges against either the journalists or the diplomats, and the following day, the Foreign Office formally notified the U.S. Embassy that the Swedish government "strongly disapproved" of Hutchins' activities in Stockholm—the strongest diplomatic protest that Sweden had ever made in its relations with the United States.

On a more personal level, it also seems that Bruce Hutchins might have pocketed for himself some of the money meant for Arthur. No intelligence service would find it worthwhile to sign a final contract with an agent and then give him the paltry sum of $400 to terminate the relationship. Such a situation would demand a sum at least ten times as big.

Mr. Hutchins will certainly have quite a lot to explain to his superiors back in the United States.

Conclusion

Introduction

What does it all mean? For the first time since the Bay of Pigs fiasco, the Central Intelligence Agency has been put on the defensive. Morale has plummeted. From the exposure of operations in the wake of the bloody *coup* in Chile to the widespread revelations of case officers' identities described in this book, the CIA has taken a beating.

But the Company is no ordinary organization. It commands mind-boggling resources. It is constantly reorganizing and regrouping to stave off the curtailing of its powers. As we go to press, the CIA is in a turmoil. Every day a new development is in the works. The machinations of the current Director, Admiral Stansfield Turner, are assailed from all directions, and President Carter and Zbigniew Brzezinski's other colleagues from the Trilateral Commission and NATO hover in the wings.

Through it all, Phil Agee has continued the struggle, being buffeted from country to country: deported from England, deported from France, deported from Germany, finally deported from the Netherlands. And every deportation is coupled simultaneously with sanctimonious but unbelievable denials from the U.S. government of its lack of complicity. By now it seems the government should realize that the counterattack against the crimes of the CIA is not a one-man battle. The methods are public knowledge; the means are simple; and the fight has just begun.

In this section, Michael Getler's piece from the *Washington Post* gives a flavor of the effect of exposures on the Agency; Phil Agee's lengthy Bicentennial contribution suggests long-range plans; Phil Kelly describes the machinations behind Agee's many deportations; and the *CovertAction Information Bulletin* examines some of the many faces of the new Turner regime.

CIA Morale Plummets

by Michael Getler

The publication of names of CIA employees overseas has brought about a marked decline in the already low morale of Agency personnel overseas.

Western intelligence officials in several overseas locations, most of whom were still trying to ignore the CIA's tainted public-image problems just a few months ago, now privately acknowledge that there has been a sharp and dramatic drop in morale in recent weeks. They say that it is affecting not only the Agency's ability to gather intelligence but also that it is causing severe personal strain as well.

"It's like Berlin right after the war," a veteran official said. "You suddenly start driving with one eye on the rear-view mirror; the nervous tension slips back into your life and you bring all that home with you to the family at night."

[This article first appeared in the January 16, 1976, issue of the *Washington Post;* it appeared the next day in the *International Herald Tribune,* in Paris.]

In recent weeks, interviews with a number of officials close to the U.S. intelligence service disclosed that the year-long exposé of CIA wrongdoing in Congress and the press created serious problems, not just in the office, but at home for an increasing number of Agency workers.

The concerns most often mentioned were about teenage children who now questioned how their fathers made a living and why, even if they were not spies, they worked for the CIA.

That kind of problem, rarely discussed openly, has now been heightened for many families with the publication of many names of CIA employees, most of whom do not work as spies, but who now feel somewhat threatened that an assassin or terrorist will strike haphazardly at their families.

Under different circumstances, the publication of employee names, and in some cases addresses, would be viewed with concern but not alarm, sources say. It has, in fact, happened before in some countries.

But the murder of CIA Station Chief Richard Welch in Athens on Christmas Eve "has given rather dramatic proportions to this thing. Publishing names is a very, very bad thing to be doing now, it's becoming fashionable and it's going to generate another murder," a senior official said.

The prediction that murders will follow is widely shared by other intelligence officers.

"Nobody's panicked," said another veteran officer, "but the thing is gnawing away at us. The impact is beginning to show. The Congressional review, the whole hoopla for more than a year now, was having a wearing-down effect. Now, rightly or wrongly, there is the new element of danger due to Welch and the publishing of names. There has been a quantum increase in depression and concern and nobody seems able to help or to stop what is undoubtedly ruining our ability to gather intelligence."

"It certainly is unsettling, these names appearing in print, coming after a long, hard struggle," another source said. "It's like they are using the [congressional] assassination report almost as a backdrop to the attempts against us."

"The Agency has really been shattered," he adds. "We are going to need a lot of forthright executive support to recover."

Where the CIA's most recent troubles will lead in terms of its ability to operate overseas, is in doubt. Some officers feel that the widespread disclosure of employee identities will almost certainly serve to drive the Agency underground. "One can only stop it by doing a better job of hiding CIA personnel," says an officer. "But it is an enormous problem."

For one thing, the job of both providing and keeping up a good cover, or hidden identity, takes an enormous amount of time, several sources say, all of which takes away from the time an agent can spend gathering intelligence. It will, in general, weaken CIA abilities, they say.

Many of the veteran CIA employees are already known to their counterparts around the world. In fact, officials acknowledge that "Who's Who in the CIA" published in 1968 in East Germany and compiled by Communist intelligence, identified many of the old-timers well before the current rash of disclosures.

But the chances are that new officers coming into the field will be given much better cover, which will not allow them to be picked so easily out of State Department registers or embassy telephone books. Still, because of the vast size of the CIA and the technical apparatus it uses, it is virtually impossible for them not to operate out of the relative security of the U.S. embassies.

The Final Straw

Though many of the individual disclosures over the last year of domestic surveillance by the CIA and consideration of assassination plots have been more startling, the impact of the Welch murder and publication of hundreds of names, primarily by leftist publications around the world, seems to be the final straw that is breaking the back of CIA morale in the field.

In France and England, where more than 70 CIA names have recently been disclosed in each country, there is little danger perceived by CIA men.

The problem is much more serious in countries such as Greece, Portugal, Spain, Italy or in Africa where there is serious anti-U.S. feeling and where politically motivated assassination is viewed as possible.

A similar fear exists here in West Germany, where no alleged CIA names have been published yet, but there is still a troublesome but small band of terrorists operating.

"We're living in a world of armed lunatics who attack facilities as a form of political expression," an agent said. "Whether they are professional terrorists or just punks, they will be inclined to go for the CIA guy if this kind of singling out goes on.''

Informants acknowledge that most of the names being disclosed are in fact CIA employees, though a number of inaccuracies are said to have appeared on published lists, especially among the 44 names of alleged CIA agents in France published thus far by the leftist newspaper *Liberation.*

Some Americans are reportedly being moved to new addresses for security after some addresses also were published.

There is concern in several U.S. embassies that the rush to publish is also spilling over into wrongly identifying legitimate diplomatic corps employees and widespread frustration at what is viewed as a public failure to understand that only a relatively small percentage of CIA employees are engaged in what could be called spying, while the bulk serve as analysts or liaison men with their counterparts in allied intelligence services.

The current situation, combined with what is perceived as an unending flow of negative news about the United States and the CIA, is also playing a major part in the surfacing of some serious pessimism about the future, among at least some veterans.

"The intelligence community represents people of a certain stripe," a senior officer said. "There is obviously some cold warrior in us because most of us still believe that the objective of the Soviet Union has not changed in 30 years and that objective is to get the United States out of Europe.

"Right now," he said, "they are getting some help."

Intelligence officials, including non-Americans, are wary of the idea that what is happening now, in the disclosure of names, is part of a civic-minded attempt to curb Agency activities that undermine U.S. democracy and self-esteem and the governments of other countries.

Most officials see it as the work of leftists and their sympathizers among disgruntled former CIA and Foreign Service employees.

The principal figure is ex-CIA man Philip Agee, who lives in Britain, where his book, *Inside the Company: CIA Diary,* was published last year.

However, according to Phil Kelly, one of the journalists on the British magazine *Time Out,* which has published 65 alleged CIA names in the last year, Mr. Agee's assistance was only incidental in their case.

Based on Techniques

Mr. Kelly said *Time Out*'s identification of people in England is based mostly on techniques published by former Foreign Service officer John Marks in a November 1974 article in the *Washington Monthly* called "How to Spot a Spook."

Mr. Kelly said that Mr. Agee helped the *Time Out* reporters "refine their methods."

In Paris, *Liberation* claimed that it came up with its list of names in France through use of the embassy directory, various identification codes, and the help of other journalists in London and Washington who were "fed up with the clandestine activities of their government around the world."

The reference to other journalists was widely assumed to mean the "Fifth Estate" group in Washington that publishes the magazine *CounterSpy.*

Revelations in Rome

ROME—A U.S. author writing in a 3-day-old Italian leftist newspaper today published the names of seven alleged CIA agents operating in Rome.

Steve Weissman, a former editor of the U.S. liberal magazine *Ramparts,* published the names in the third issue of *La Repubblica,* a non-Communist leftist tabloid. He wrote that he believed total CIA strength in Rome exceeded 40 persons, operating from cover jobs in the U.S. Embassy, military units, and multinational companies.

A U.S. Embassy spokesman declined comment on the story.

Unlike newspapers which published similar lists in France and Greece, *La Repubblica* did not print the alleged agents' street addresses or telephone numbers.

14 Named in Greece

ATHENS—The weekly magazine *Politika Themata* in this week's edition printed the names of 14 Greek-Americans allegedly working for the CIA.

The magazine is owned by Yannis Horn, the publisher of the *Athens News,* the English-language daily which revealed Mr. Welch to be CIA chief in Greece.

The magazine said it had taken the names from the book published in East Berlin in 1968 and brought up to date with new information covering last year.

Where Do We
Go From Here?

by Philip Agee

The feeling is one of being completely overwhelmed, like drowning in controversy, issues, sensational revelations, myriad opinions from everywhere on what to do.

It's not just the energy required for absorbing well over 2,000 pages of official reports from the Rockefeller Commission, the Senate and House investigating committees, the Murphy Commission, and the Ford reforms—there's also two years' accumulation of continuous media output. Heavy enough for an average observer, an interested journalist, or even a political activist. Heavier still for someone who has been a part of the controversies for two years after having spent four years researching and

[The original version of this article was first published by Jean-Paul Sartre in the September 1976 issue of *Les Temps Modernes,* in Paris, in a special issue dedicated to alternative views of the American Bicentennial. A revised version was published in mid-1977 in London, by the Agee-Hosenball Defence Committee. It was further updated by the author for this book.]

writing an account of the preceding 12 years' work inside the CIA.

I've read all those reports and hundreds of newspaper cuttings because I want to get perspective on what's happened with the CIA, FBI, and other intelligence and security services. I want to be able to judge whether anything has changed. Or whether business will go on as usual inside the political police forces once the sensations subside.

Not many people worked on both sides. Lots were victims and others were victimizing—my distinction, I suppose, was to have done both. But that makes evaluation harder, not easier. And, of course, I can be no "impartial" observer.

So many people have asked, often not so delicately, how in hell I've survived and why the CIA didn't make me disappear and don't I think I'm in danger. I used to laugh. But not now. Now I too am beginning to wonder.

Studying the results of the different investigations produced a kind of psychological disorientation, now a little schizophrenic, now a little paranoid. I'd go along reading intensely about the nature of counterintelligence or about problems of coordination among agencies or about the functions of the Director of Central Intelligence with the same kind of uncritical, receptive mind frame I'd had studying the very same things in the CIA's training classrooms back in 1957. Suddenly I would realize where I am now, having done the unthinkable in resolving to take positive action against the CIA by revealing its operations and naming all those names. Like alternating between two personalities—like the way I vacillated for a time over whether to name any names at all. Perhaps a partial throwback to the Jesuit-imbued attitude of being *in* the world but not *of* it.

Just as often, I'd get the feeling that some disaster was imminent, that there's simply no way to survive the immense and vast apparatus for repression that I was reading about. Sure, I was reading about the past, but every morning I was also reading of people disappearing in Buenos Aires, assassinations of Uruguayans I might have known, "suicides" in jail. Then a friend would telephone and ask me what that odd clicking sound was, and I'd say "they" probably just don't want me to forget "they're" there. Then back to reading and to straining my imagination to comprehend the CIA's plot to give Fidel Castro a diving suit dusted inside with enough fungus to give him a chronic case of "madura foot" skin disease, with the suit's breathing apparatus also contaminated with tuberculosis bacilli.

Attitudes, feelings, emotions—they add up to a sense of vulnerability to retaliation, maybe once the dust stirred up by revelations and investigations begins to settle. But no thought of withdrawal into some secure isolation—even if that were possible. That's what I did for a while after leaving the Agency. Now is the time to sum up, evaluate what's been accomplished, and look ahead to the next round.

Conventional Europeans often express dismay over our American propensity for self-destruction. They see us as a society bent on some kind of superexplosion and then, perhaps, collapsing into a black hole. More often than not, I suspect, what these people really fear is that America will cease being the main prop for their own failing economic and social systems. Cold War rhetoric revives as new efforts appear to create a psychological climate of fear and tension with respect to "national survival." We see this in America as well.

Those of us who see the CIA and other security services as impediments to achieving a higher form of democracy must answer the charge that we are encouraging world domination by the Soviet Union; that we are paving the way for imposition of a Soviet-style system in the United States; that we are increasing the possibility of nuclear war by encouraging the development of global imbalance. If the past few years are any indicator, maybe before this century ends the U.S. and some few allies, like South Africa and Israel, could end up isolated and armed to the teeth in an increasingly hostile world with nuclear war becoming acceptable as "the only way out."

We can argue that Soviet intent to rule the world is neither demonstrable nor realistic—that domination of its immediate border areas is quite distinct from the rest of the world as evidenced by the Yugoslav experience as well as by Italian, French, Spanish, and other Communist parties' rejection of the Soviet version of internationalism.

But we shouldn't be only defensive. We should show the significance of the best of American traditions for the future of socialism, particularly our deep-rooted belief that people must have strong protections against oppression by government bureaucracy. Herein lies the optimistic interpretation, the one we should emphasize, of the past two years' CIA revelations, indeed of the 15 years from the civil rights movement through the Vietnam War and Watergate. Here we can see genuine popular traditions that must be preserved and cultivated while casting off the institutions of the past that serve only a small elite.

We must also defend against the false dilemma that either we move forward within traditional institutions or we destroy the nation. Neither the Russian nor Chinese nor any other "nation" was destroyed in their socialist revolutions, although certain privileged groups did disappear as groups. Quite the contrary, in spite of the human cost that in any case would compare favorably with the early generations of ordinary people under colonialism and industrial capitalism. National survival, in fact, isn't the question: it's whether the old dominance by capitalists will drag all of us down to dangerous and bitter isolation, or whether the United States under socialist leadership can effectively transfer its wealth of technology, capital, and other resources for the benefit of all. Our opponents will always try to confuse their class survival by equating it with "national survival."

When we read of "national security" and "survival" in the various reports on the CIA and the FBI, we're reading about *their* security and survival, not ours. Those are *their* security services, not ours. It's their *class* security that they equate with the "nation's survival." Probably not even Marx himself could have imagined the kind of public debate within the ruling class over security services that would demonstrate so clearly the nature of class struggle. Here we've read of cobra venom, poison dart guns, electronic eavesdropping, provocation of violence—all done by security services for a class that now rebukes those services for having acted "illegally." The rebuke is mild— 20 years of crimes and not one indictment—but significant nonetheless. All in all, these investigations have been a ruling class affair.

In analyzing the positive side of the past 15 years, however, we ought not to credit spasms of conscience among decision makers. Spontaneous, popular pressure forced their decisions to retreat first here and then there—not overlooking, of course, the determination and heroism demonstrated by the national liberation movements in Vietnam, Cuba, Angola, and so many other places. But, aside from ideology, we have learned an immense amount of specific information that will serve for future defense and protection when repression is intensified and the old methods are applied once again.

Psychological distractions aside, the various reports make extremely fascinating reading despite frequent repetitions, and they must be valued as the result of the first significant investigation of American intelligence and the last for many years to come. Taken altogether, they constitute a treasure of information on institutionalized counterrevolution and should be read and studied by every political activist. We ought to assume that what is said in these reports is probably true, although from what is not said we also have much to learn.

First, the cost in people and money. None of the reports reveals how many people are employed in the U.S. intelligence effort, although the Department of Defense had over 100,000 people working in intelligence at the end of FY 1975 with the trend markedly downward.[1] Adding personnel of the FBI's counterintelligence efforts, the CIA, National Security Agency, intelligence components of the Department of State, the Department of the Treasury, and the Drug Enforcement Administration, the total might pass 150,000—although the Senate committee report mentions "hundreds of thousands of people."[2]

None of the reports mentions explicitly the overall total of money spent on American intelligence activities, nor do they reveal how much the CIA or the NSA, for example, spend. These omissions reflect a considerable victory for President Ford, inasmuch as all the investigating commissions in varying degrees recommended giving the public some idea of what intelligence costs the country. Ford fought against disclosure of even the grand total for all intelligence on the ludicrous argument put forth by the CIA that extrapolations could lead the KGB to discovery of the CIA's capabilities.

The House of Representatives committee under Congressman Otis Pike found that the total intelligence budget is "more than $10 billion,"[3] which is "3 to 4 times more costly than the Congress has been told,"[4] and possibly five times more.

We get a hint, however, of the overall intelligence cost in the Senate committee's report. In each place where the amounts spent on intelligence, and their percentage as a part of the federal budget, were mentioned, the figures were deleted. Except once where, apparently by clerical oversight, the overall national (strategic) intelligence cost is said to represent about 3% of the total federal budget for FY 1976.[5] In dollars this would amount to about $11.2 billion and would include the total approved budgets of the CIA, DIA, NSA, and National Reconnaissance Office. However, according to the Senate committee, adding tactical intelligence and indirect support costs would double the amount spent on intelligence to $22.4 billion.

As to what proportion of the intelligence budget is spent by the CIA alone, the Senate committee's report also gives some clues. Item: "The DCI (Director of Central Intelligence) controls less than 10% of the combined national and tactical intelligence efforts."[6] Item: "Real executive authority over at least four-fifths of the total resources spent on intelligence activities has resided with the Secretary of Defense."[7] Item: The Department of Defense "controls nearly 90 percent of the nation's spending on intelligence programs."[8] Thus the CIA would be spending between $1 and $2 billion depending on whether one takes the combined national, tactical, and indirect support costs as the total, or simply the national program ($11.2 billion) as the total.

According to the Senate committee's report, the buying power of the intelligence budget has been steadily decreasing since the mid-1960s even though the budget itself, due to inflation, has been increasing in numbers of dollars spent. In 1976, according to the report, the buying power in real terms is about equal to the intelligence budgets of the late 1950s.[9]

How is the money divided among the target countries? "Nearly two-thirds of the (FY 1975) resources consumed, 65 cents of each dollar, were directed toward the Soviet Union and U.S. commitments to NATO; 25 cents of each dollar were spent to support U.S. interests in Asia, with most of this targeted against China; the Arab-Israeli confrontation in the Middle East claimed seven cents; Latin America, less than two cents; and the rest of the world, about a penny."[10]

Predominance of technical intelligence programs is evident. The commission investigating government organization for foreign affairs, established in 1972 under the veteran State Department "trouble-shooter" Robert D. Murphy, stated in its final report in mid-1975: "Today the bulk of information comes from open sources, overhead reconnaissance, and electronic signals and communications, with only a small but possibly critical component derived from clandestine sources."[11]

The Senate committee's report is more specific: "Approximately 87 percent of the resources devoted to collection is spent on technical sensors compared to only 13 percent for HUMINT" (traditional undercover agents and overt human sources).[12] The committee concludes, however, that in intelligence as elsewhere, machines cannot completely replace men: "The United States cannot forego clandestine human collection and expect to maintain the same quality of intelligence on matters of the highest importance to our national security."[13] This statement accurately reflects the CIA's traditional concern that too often only humans can report on secret intentions.

As an aid to the CIA's critical HUMINT program, it seems, the tradition of plying people with booze is still as strong as ever. The House committee reported that one typical, medium-sized CIA Station "spent $86,000 in liquor and cigarettes during the past five years. The majority of these purchases were designated 'operational gifts'—gifts to friendly agents or officials in return for information or assistance."[14] At another unnamed CIA Station, the Pike committee reports, $41,000 were spent on liquor in 1971, and that Station Chief, since transferred, is now in charge of CIA operations in Angola, i.e., during the doomed CIA–South African intervention in the 1975 civil war.[15] One must hope that this officer will now be placed in charge of the CIA's operations in Namibia or Zimbabwe.

We discover, then, confirmation that the overhead reconnaissance programs and the other technical collection operations, mainly the NSA's SIGINT programs for interception and analysis of communications and electronic emissions, devour the lion's share of the national intelligence budget. Analysis and preparation of finished reports also receives appropriate emphasis, as does the CIA's counterintelligence efforts against other security services which are largely a part of the overall HUMINT program. Not overlooked, however, in the Senate, House, and Murphy Commission reports is the continuing need to rely on the most controversial of the CIA's activities: covert action.

The Murphy Commission defines covert action as "activity abroad intended not to gather information but to influence events, an activity midway between diplomacy and war. It has taken many forms, from the financial support of friendly publications to the mounting of significant paramilitary efforts."[16] Similarly the Pike committee defines covert action as "activity other than purely information-gathering, which is directed at producing a particular political, economic, or military result."[17] Senator Church's committee describes covert action as "the secret use of power and persuasion"[18] and as "clandestine activity designed to influence foreign governments, events, organizations or persons in support of U.S. foreign policy conducted in such a way that the involvement of the U.S. Government is not apparent."[19] Covert action operations, in the Senate report, include "political and propaganda programs designed to influence or support foreign political parties, groups, and specific political and military leaders; economic action programs; paramilitary operations; and some counter-insurgency programs. Human intelligence collection, or spying, and counter-espionage programs are not included under the rubric of covert action operations."[20]

Expressed still another way, covert action is the way the CIA *uses* the information it collects in order to penetrate and manipulate the institutions of power in a given country, i.e., the military services and political parties, the security services, the trade unions, youth and student organizations, cultural and professional societies, and the public information media. Covert action is the way the CIA props up and strengthens the "friendlies" and disrupts, divides, weakens, and destroys the "enemies." Covert action, then, is the American euphemism for subversion and counterrevolution.

Both the Senate and the House committees questioned the CIA's statutory authority to engage in covert action since no explicit power for such operations was granted to the Agency in pertinent legislation such as the National Security Act of 1947 and its amendment, the Central Intelligence Agency Act of 1949. Successive administrations since covert action began in 1948 have justified these operations on the vaguely worded authority in the 1947 law for the CIA to "perform such other functions and duties related to intelligence affecting the national security as the National Security Council, may, from time to time, direct."[21] Nevertheless, only when the Hughes-Ryan amendment to the Foreign Assistance Act was passed in 1974 did the Congress recognize the legitimacy of covert action. This amendment required the President to report to six congressional subcommittees "in a timely fashion" the scope and description of all covert action operations and to certify that each such operation is important to the national security of the United States. Besides extending congressional control over covert action and legitimizing it, this amendment also—not unintentionally—killed the old doctrine of "plausible denial" wherein presidents could plead ignorance of covert action, operations that become "blown."

The report of the Senate committee, Book I, contains a most useful background section on the history of the CIA and particularly on the attitudes of leading American government figures at the beginning of the Cold War. Frequent repetition of these themes highlighting the Soviet/International Communist threat, as the early justification for covert action operations, suggests their persistence in the thought patterns of those who drafted the current Senate report, as we shall see when covert action is recommended for the future.

> The Second World War saw the defeat of one brand of totalitarianism. A new totalitarian challenge quickly arose. The Soviet Union, a major ally in war, became America's principal adversary in peace. The power of fascism was in ruin but the power of communism was mobilized. Not only had the communist parties in France, Italy and Greece emerged politically strengthened by their roles in the Resistance, but the armies of the Soviet Union stretched across the center of Europe.[22]

> Following the war there was a distinct possibility of a Soviet assault on Western Europe. Communist regimes had been established in Poland, Hungary, Romania and Bulgaria. Czechoslovakia went Communist in 1948 through a *coup* supported by the Russian Army. There was the presence of the Soviet Army in Eastern Europe and the pressure on Berlin.[23]

> By late 1946 cabinet officials were preoccupied with the Soviet threat, and over the next year their fears intensified. For U.S. policymakers, international events seemed to be a sequence of Soviet incursions. [Communist gains are cited in Iran, Greece, Poland, Hungary, Romania, the Philippines, Czechoslovakia, France, and Italy.] Policymakers could, and did, look at these developments as evidence of the need for the United States to respond.[24]

The CIA's covert action operations are everywhere seen in these reports as a response to the Soviet threat, looming either directly or through national Communist parties. The first covert action arm of the CIA, the Office of Policy Coordination, was established in 1948 by a directive that also referred to the "vicious covert activities of the USSR."[25] OPC was authorized to engage in "covert political, psychological, and economic warfare. These early activities were directed against the Soviet threat. They included countering Soviet propaganda and covert Soviet support of labor unions and student groups in Western

Europe, direct U.S. support of foreign political parties, 'economic warfare,' sabotage, assistance to refugee liberation groups, and support of anti-Communist groups in occupied or threatened areas.''[26]

Still another precise description: "Psychological operations were primarily media-related activities, including unattributed publications, forgeries, and subsidization of publications; political action involved exploitation of dispossessed persons and defectors, and support to political parties; paramilitary activities included support to guerrillas and sabotage; economic activities consisted of monetary and fiscal operations.''[27]

Perhaps the best description of the attitude during the early Cold War is this Churchillian passage from the 1954 investigation of intelligence organization under the Hoover Commission:

> It is now clear that we are facing an implacable enemy whose avowed objective is world domination by whatever means and at whatever cost. There are no rules in such a game. Hitherto acceptable norms of human conduct do not apply. If the U.S. is to survive, longstanding concepts of "fair play" must be reconsidered. We must develop effective espionage and counter-espionage services. We must learn to subvert, sabotage and destroy our enemies by more clever, more sophisticated and more effective methods than those used against us. It may become necessary that the American people will be made acquainted with, understand and support this fundamentally repugnant philosophy.[28]

No attempt is made in any of the reports to evaluate, with the benefit of hindsight, the validity of U.S. fears of the Soviet Union following World War II. Neither is there any suggestion that Soviet actions may have been a response to aggressive CIA operations. We find little evaluation of the early CIA operations directed against Eastern Europe and the Soviet Union, except that some of the more provocative actions ended in the mid-1950s. Indirect admission of failure is evident in the discussion of the CIA's expansion of paramilitary operations in the Far East during the Korean War: "During this period the CIA's Office of Procurement acquired some $152 million worth of foreign weapons and ammunition for use by guerrilla forces that never came into existence.''[29]

Nevertheless, the Deputy Directorate of Plans (also known as the Clandestine Services), which was in charge of the CIA's clandestine collection and counterintelligence programs and its covert action operations, came to dominate the Agency. Covert action operations also came to dominate the Agency's operational patterns around the world, no doubt in response to National Security Council Directives such as this one which ordered the CIA to:

> Create and exploit problems for International Communism;
>
> Discredit International Communism, and reduce the strength of its parties and organization;
>
> Reduce International Communist control over any areas of the world.[30]

Covert action operations not only became the major instrument in the American foreign policy goal to "roll back the Iron Curtain." "Covert action soon became a routine program of influencing governments and covertly exercising power—involving literally hundreds of projects each year. By 1953 there were major covert operations underway in 48 countries, consisting of propaganda, paramilitary and political action projects. By the 1960s, covert action had come to mean any clandestine activity designed to influence foreign governments, events, organizations or persons in support of United States foreign policy. Several thousand individual covert action projects have been undertaken since 1961."[31] One project, the report fails to make clear, can go on for many years as long as renewals are approved.

"The Committee has found that the CIA has conducted some 900 major or sensitive covert action projects plus several thousand smaller projects since 1961."[32]

Since the revelations of CIA covert action operations sparked by *Ramparts Magazine* in 1967 these activities have decreased. "The period 1968 to the present has registered declines in every functional and geographic category of covert action—except for paramilitary operations in the Far East which did not drop until 1972. The number of individual covert action projects dropped by 50 percent from fiscal year 1964 (when they reached an all-time high) to fiscal year 1968."[33]

Nevertheless, covert action has by no means ended. "Yet, the overall reduction did not affect the fundamental assumptions, organization and incentives governing the DDO [the new name for Deputy Directorate of Operations, the Clandestine Services]. Indeed, in 1975 clandestine activities still constituted 37 percent of the Agency's total budget. The rationale remains the same, and the operational capability is intact—as the CIA activities in Chile illustrated."[34]

Thirty-seven percent of the Agency's budget provides hundreds of millions of dollars for current covert action operations. As the Senate committee's report points out: "The number of projects by itself is not an adequate measure of the scope of covert action. Projects can vary considerably in size, cost, duration, and effect. Today, for example, one-fourth of the current covert action projects are relatively high-cost (over $100,-000 annually)."[35]

Both the Church and the Pike committees' reports are replete with information on general categories of the CIA's operations and on specific operations as well. Both committees studied specific covert action projects in detail, the Church committee reviewing these operations over the past 25 years and the Pike committee reviewing all projects approved by the Forty Committee (the group chaired by the President's national security advisor with participation by the Undersecretary of State and the Deputy Secretary of Defense) during the past ten years. The Pike committee found that since 1965 the largest category of individual covert action projects requiring approval outside the CIA (32%) was for financial election support to foreign politicians and political parties. Twenty-nine percent of Forty Committee approvals during the same period were for media and propaganda projects, while 23% were for paramilitary activities (secret armies, financial support to warring factions, training and advisors, and shipment of arms and ammunition).[36] The Pike committee also found that "a plethora of foreign civic, religious, professional, and labor organizations have received CIA funding without special geographical concentration but with plenty of Third World emphasis."[37]

In the 900 "major or sensitive" covert action projects discovered by the Church committee, together with "several thousand" smaller projects undertaken since 1961, funds were provided for "a seemingly limitless range of covert action programs affecting youth groups, labor unions, universities, publishing houses, and other private institutions in the United States and abroad."[38] A former Station Chief in one country where covert action programs were heavy and persistent testified to the Senate committee that "any aspiring politician almost automatically would come to CIA to see if we could help him get elected. . . . They were the wards of the United States, and that whatever happened for good or bad was the fault of the United States."[39]

In the media field the Pike committee reported that "by far the largest single recipient has been a [unnamed] European publishing house funded since 1951."[40] For its part the Church committee revealed that prior to 1967 the CIA had "sponsored, subsidized or produced over 1,000 books, approximately 25 percent of them in English. In 1967 alone, the CIA published or subsidized over 200 books, ranging from books on African safaris and wildlife to translations of Machiavelli's *The Prince* into Swahili and works of T. S. Eliot into Russian, to a competitor to Mao's little red book, which was entitled *Quotations from Chairman Liu.*"[41] Among the books was the fabricated *Penkovsky Papers,* supposedly based on writings of the famous Russian spy.

The importance of books is recognized in the CIA, as in this passage from a memorandum written in 1961 by the Chief of the Covert Action Staff: "Books differ from other propaganda media, primarily because one single book can significantly change the reader's attitude and action to an extent unmatched by the impact of any other single medium."[42] For this reason, presumably, the CIA has continued to publish books. Although it apparently ceased publishing in the U.S. in 1967 (following the major scandal relating to the CIA's penetration of domestic institutions, especially the National Student Association), the CIA since then "has published some 250 books abroad, most of them in foreign languages."[43]

The Church committee reveals that the Agency continues to penetrate the journalistic profession. "The CIA currently maintains a network of several hundred foreign individuals . . . who provide the CIA with direct access to a large number of newspapers and periodicals, scores of press services and news agencies, radio and television stations, commercial book publishers, and other foreign media outlets."[44] Concerning U.S. journalists, "Approximately 50 of the assets are American journalists or employees of U.S. media organizations,"[45] with about half of these accredited and the rest free-lance. In early 1978, the CIA asserted its need for continued utilization of journalists on a "voluntary basis."

Orchestration of propaganda through these journalist agents is illustrated by this extract from a CIA cable, dated September 25, 1970, relating to propaganda against the Allende election: "São Paulo, Tegucigalpa, Buenos Aires, Lima, Montevideo, Bogotá, Mexico City report continued replay of Chile theme materials. Items also carried in *New York Times* and *Washington Post*. Propaganda activities continue to generate good coverage of Chile developments along our theme guidance."[46]

Religious organizations, clergy, and missionaries have long been used by the CIA both for intelligence collection and for covert action. The Senate committee reports "direct operational use of 21 individuals" in this field who were Americans,[47] and although the CIA in February 1976 renounced any "secret paid or contractual relationship" with American missionaries or members of the clergy, the Agency's use of foreigners in this field presumably will continue.

The most important general category of covert action operations about which very little is said in these reports is the trade union field. CIA programs in national and international labor unions were vast in scope during the 1950s and 1960s, and the lack of serious discussion of them in the Senate and House committees' reports is, to me, a very strong indicator that the Agency continues to be quite active promoting "moderate," "nonpolitical," docile trade unions. The only significant mention of labor operations in the Pike report is the brief statement that "one labor confederation in a developing country received an annual subsidy of $30,000 in three successive years."[48]

The Church report simply mentions that prior to the 1967 scandals the Agency had enjoyed "the cooperation of an American labor organization in selected overseas labor activities."[49] The report goes on to reveal that after the "tightening up" in the wake of the 1967 scandals, the Agency decided to continue to fund "several international trade union organizations."[50] Aside from suggesting the continuing importance of the CIA's labor operations, these scant references say quite a lot about senators' and congresspersons' deference to the electoral importance of George Meany, the President of the American Federation of Labor and from the beginning the CIA's "Mr. Big" in labor operations.

American academics get high marks from the Senate committee on their cooperation with the CIA which "is now using several hundred American academics, who in addition to providing leads and sometimes making introductions for intelligence purposes, occasionally write books and other material to be used for propaganda purposes abroad. . . . These academics are located in over 100 American colleges, universities and related institutes. . . . The Committee notes that American academics provide valuable assistance [for] obtaining leads on potential foreign intelligence sources, especially those from communist countries [who are among the] many foreign nationals in the United States."[51]

In paramilitary operations, the Church committee confirms CIA participation in the overthrow of Arbenz in Guatemala in 1954 and in attempts to overthrow Sukarno in Indonesia in 1958,[52] as well as similar operations in Korea, Vietnam, Cuba, and Laos. In a critical vein, however, the committee finds that "of the five paramilitary activities studied by the Committee, only one appears to have achieved its objectives. The goal of supporting a central government was achieved—the same government is still in power many years later. There were a few sporadic reports of the operation in the press, but it was never fully revealed or confirmed." Even so, "in no paramilitary case studied by the Committee was complete secrecy fully preserved."[53]

One's thoughts run immediately to the Congo-Zaire of the early 1960s when considering which "success" the Church committee means—especially when, a couple of paragraphs later, testimony is cited on the difficulty of withdrawing from paramilitary operations once started: "This is well-illustrated by the case of the Congo, where a decision was taken to withdraw in early 1966, and it took about a year and a half before the operation was terminated."[54]

The key figure in the CIA's successful Congo-Zaire paramilitary operations of the 1960s was, of course, Col. Joseph Mobutu, now known as President Mobutu Sese Seko. Could Mobutu also be the unnamed "Third World leader" who received $960,000 over a 14-year period, according to the Pike committee report?[55] Not many others have survived for 14 years. No matter, the Pike committee's revelation is sure to sour the CIA's relations with other Third World "leaders" whose bribes may only have totaled a few hundred thousand dollars.

Two major CIA paramilitary operations are described by the House of Representatives committee: support to the Kurdish nationalist movement in Iraq in 1972–1975[56] and support to the Holden Roberto and Jonas Savimbi factions in the 1975 civil war in Angola.[57]

In order to cause problems for Iraq, the Shah of Iran, who was engaged in a border dispute with Iraq, asked Dr. Kissinger and President Nixon for U.S. participation in his program of support to the Kurds, led by Mustafa Barzani, who were then in armed rebellion against the Iraqi central government. Eventually some $16 million was spent by the CIA on this operation, only a fraction of what the Shah spent, but valued by the Shah and Barzani both for its symbolic importance and, to Barzani, as a guarantee against any sudden cutoff of the Shah's aid. According to the committee, the U.S. aid was also undertaken "as a favor to our ally [the Shah] who had cooperated with U.S. intelligence agencies [the CIA] and had come to feel menaced by his neighbor [Iraq]."[58]

Barzani on numerous occasions expressed his distrust of the Shah's intentions, and he showed his appreciation to Kissinger by sending him three rugs and, when Kissinger married, a gold and pearl necklace. Nevertheless, the aid was not meant to provide for a final Kurdish victory and the limited autonomy that Barzani had fought for since the 1920s. "The United States personally restrained the insurgents from an all-out offensive on one occasion when such an attack might have been successful. . . ."[59]

In early 1975, as soon as the Shah got his border concessions from Iraq, he cut off aid to the Kurds, and the CIA did too. The cutoff came as a severe shock. "A CIA cable from the COS [probably in Tehran] to the [CIA Director] describes the method used by our ally [the Shah] to inform the ethnic group's [the Kurds'] leadership. On March 5, a representative of our ally's intelligence service [no doubt the dreaded SAVAK secret police] visited the Headquarters of the ethnic group and 'told (them) in bluntest imaginable terms' that the border was being closed, that assistance had ended, and that the Kurds should settle with the Iraqis on whatever terms they could get."[60] The Iraqis, knowing of the cutoff, took the offensive and eliminated Kurdish resistance.

In the aftermath, 200,000 Kurdish refugees were created, but despite pleas from Barzani the U.S. refused to extend humanitarian assistance. The Shah forcibly repatriated to Iraq over 40,000 Kurds who sought refuge in Iran, and the U.S. refused to admit even one Kurdish refugee even though they qualified for admittance as political asylees. As one "high U.S. official" told the Pike committee staff, "Covert action should not be confused with missionary work."[61]

The Angolan intervention by the CIA, though widely reported, is clarified in the Pike committee report. Support for the Holden Roberto group began in January 1975, and in midsummer support for the Savimbi forces began. The House committee concludes that the Soviet-Cuban buildup to help the MPLA (which the Soviets had supported for ten years against Portuguese colonialism) came as a reaction to the startling gains of the Roberto and Savimbi forces thanks to the $31 million worth of assistance pumped in by the CIA. As to the reasons for the U.S. getting involved, CIA Director William Colby could find scant ideological differences among the three groups, "all of whom are nationalists above all else,"[62] according to the committee. Responding to committee questions, Colby said, "They are all independents. They are all for black Africa. They are all for some fuzzy kind of social system, you know, without really much articulation, but some sort of let's not be exploited by the capitalist system."

> **Mr. Aspin** *(a committee member)*: And why are the Chinese backing the moderate group?
>
> **Mr. Colby:** Because the Soviets are backing the MPLA is the simplest answer.
>
> **Mr. Aspin:** It sounds like that is why we are doing it.
>
> **Mr. Colby:** It is.[63]

Another reason, the committee concluded, was Kissinger's desire to encourage "moderate" independence groups in southern Africa and the stability of such figures as Mobutu, who supported Roberto, and President Kaunda of Zambia who supported Savimbi. "Past [U.S.] support to Mobutu, along with his responsiveness to some of the United States' recent diplomatic needs for Third World support, make it equally likely that the paramount factor in U.S. involvement is Dr. Kissinger's desire to reward and protect African leaders in the area."[64]

The most complete account of any major CIA covert action operation is the Senate committee's separate 62-page report on operations in Chile from 1963 to 1973.[65] It is unique as an official account of the many secret methods used by three successive American administrations to prevent the Chilean people from exercising their right to choose their own political leadership. Altogether, over $13 million was spent, and this money, if calculated at its blackmarket buying power, may well have had an impact equivalent to three or four times as much.

Great detail makes this report exceedingly important not only as a clarification of what happened in Chile, but for its value in analyzing future "destabilization" operations and defeating them. It's all there: millions of dollars to the non-left political parties, mainly the Christian Democrats; huge amounts also to *El Mercurio,* the media giant; financial support to the truckers who paralyzed the economy in 1972 and 1973; financial support to the right-wing terrorist organization, *Patria y Libertad;* economic squeeze through retention of credits, both by private institutions and through U.S. dominance of the multilateral agencies; CIA weapons to a group planning the assassination of Army General Schneider in order to provoke a military *coup;* ITT's offer of $1 million to the CIA for use against the 1970 Allende campaign and its later spending, with CIA assistance and participation by other U.S. companies, of some $700,000 in the campaign; finally, the revolting but logical CIA support for the security services of the Pinochet regime.

The CIA's political intervention in Italy over the years has been more successful, in that its clients, principally the Christian Democrats (but also the neofascists), have managed to retain power, if only just, for almost 30 years. The Pike committee report describes how the CIA has spent some $75 million in Italian political campaigns since 1948, with $10 million spent in the 1972 elections alone.[66] Of more importance, perhaps, was the CIA's passage of $800,000 to General Vito Miceli, former head of Italian military intelligence and a leader of the neofascist MSI. Miceli at the time (1972) was awaiting trial (he still is) for his part in the 1970 right-wing *coup* plot known as the Borghese affair.[67] Although the CIA opposed giving Miceli the money, spending of which was uncontrolled but supposedly for "propaganda activities," American Ambassador Graham Martin insisted and prevailed in order "to demonstrate solidarity [with Miceli] for the long pull."[68] Martin went on to preside over the final collapse in South Vietnam.

Not included in the Pike committee report but certainly worth recalling is the decision by President Ford, leaked to journalists in early January 1976, approving during the previous month the spending by the CIA of some $6 million between then and the next Italian general elections. Indicative also of Ford and Kissinger thinking on the "long pull" in Italy was the visit in late

September 1975 of neofascist leader Giorgio Almirante to Washington where, among other activities, he met with staff members of the National Security Council—the body (chaired by the President) that governs the CIA.[69]

Perhaps with Italy in mind, the Church committee warned that "covert action techniques within or against a foreign society can have unintended consequences that sometimes subvert [sic] long-term goals. For instance, extended covert support to foreign political leaders, parties, labor unions, or the media has not always accomplished the intended objective of strengthening them against the communist challenge. In some cases it has both encouraged a debilitating dependence on United States covert support, and made those receiving such support vulnerable to repudiation in their own society when the covert ties are exposed."[70] As if in longing for "the good old days," the Senate committee concluded: "Some covert operations have passed retrospective public judgements, such as the support given Western European democratic parties facing strong communist opposition in the later 1940s and 1950s. Others have not. In the view of the Committee, the covert harassment of the democratically elected government of Salvador Allende in Chile did not command U.S. public approval."[71]

In a similar vein, the Senate committee laments two other grisly CIA programs: assassinations against foreign leaders ("an aberration") and the use of biological and chemical agents against people ("massive abridgements of the rights of American citizens"). The 350-page assassination report[72] contains a massive amount of data, including extracts from previously secret internal CIA communications, on the Agency's involvement in attempts to assassinate five foreign leaders:

Patrice Lumumba. In 1960 the CIA sent assassins and poison to the Congo in order to kill Lumumba, but appropriate access to the Congolese leader was never obtained. Nevertheless, the CIA had foreknowledge of Mobutu's plans to deliver Lumumba to his enemies in Katanga in January 1961, and knew that Lumumba would most probably be assassinated by those enemies. The Senate committee concludes: "There is no evidence of CIA involvement in this plan or in bringing about the death of Lumumba in Katanga."[73]

As background, the Senate report states the problem:

In the summer of 1960, there was great concern at the

> highest levels in the United States government about the role of Patrice Lumumba in the Congo. Lumumba, who served briefly as Premier of the newly independent nation, was viewed with alarm by United States policymakers because of what they perceived as his magnetic public appeal and his leanings toward the Soviet Union. . . . In mid-September, after losing a struggle for leadership of the government to Kasavubu and Joseph Mobutu, Chief of Staff of the Congolese armed forces, Lumumba sought protection from the United Nations forces in Léopoldville. . . . Early in December Mobutu's troops captured Lumumba . . . transferred Lumumba to . . . Katanga province. Several weeks later Katangan authorities announced Lumumba's death.[74]

Meanwhile, the CIA's plotting to assassinate Lumumba had proceeded following "President Eisenhower's strong expression of concern about Lumumba at a meeting of the National Security Council on August 18, 1960 [which was] taken by Allen Dulles as authority to assassinate Lumumba. . . . Indeed one NSC staff member present at the August 18 meeting believed that he witnessed a presidential order to assassinate Lumumba."[75]

The report is unclear on how much the CIA helped Mobutu to capture Lumumba during the period between his escape from UN custody on November 27, 1960, and his capture on December 3. A November 28 cable reads: "(Station) working with (Congolese government) to get roads blocked and troops alerted (to block) possible escape route."[76] Nevertheless, a CIA officer in Léopoldville at the time, Victor Hedgman, testified to the committee that he (Hedgman) was "not a major assistance" in tracking down Lumumba.[77]

The committee could find no evidence that the CIA was behind the decision to turn Lumumba over to Katangan authorities, although up to the time of the turnover on January 17, 1961, the CIA "was convinced that 'drastic steps' were necessary to prevent Lumumba's return to power."[78] At the very same time Mobutu himself was on the verge of being overthrown by a mutiny of the Léopoldville garrison which, according to a CIA cable, "will mutiny within two or three days unless drastic action taken to satisfy complaints."[79]

The UN report written in the aftermath of Lumumba's assassination mentioned others, followers of Lumumba, who had been delivered by Mobutu to Katanga and who "were killed there in horrible circumstances."[80] Knowing of these precedents, the CIA Station in Katanga (Elizabethville) could scarcely conceal its glee on learning of Lumumba's delivery by Mobutu. In a cable to Washington, the CIA chief in Katanga, paraphrasing a popular song of the time, joked: "Thanks for Patrice. If we had known he was coming we would have baked a snake."[81]

Fidel Castro. The Senate committee found "concrete evidence of at least eight plots involving the CIA to assassinate Fidel Castro from 1960 to 1965. Although some of the assassination plots did not go beyond the stage of planning and preparation, one plot, involving the use of underworld figures, reportedly twice progressed to the point of sending poison pills to Cuba and dispatching teams to commit the deed. Another plot involved furnishing weapons and other assassination devices to a Cuban dissident. The proposed assassination devices ran the gamut from high-powered rifles to poison pills, poison pens, deadly bacterial powders, and other devices."[82]

"The most ironic of these plots took place on November 22, 1963—the very day that President Kennedy was shot in Dallas—when a CIA official offered a poison pen to a Cuban for use against Castro while at the same time an emissary from President Kennedy was meeting with Castro to explore the possibility of improved relations."[83]

Other plots were designed to ruin Castro's image: to spray his broadcasting studio with a chemical that produces effects similar to LSD; to dust his shoes with a strong depilatory that would make his beard fall out (already tested on animals); to give Castro cigars impregnated with a chemical that produces temporary disorientation.

Other plots to assassinate Castro involved giving him a box of his favorite cigars contaminated with botulinum toxin "so potent that a person would die after putting one in his mouth."[84] Another would use an exotic seashell, rigged to explode in an area where Castro commonly went skin diving. Other targets of assassination in Cuba, one would have assumed, were Raul Castro and Che Guevara.

Rafael Trujillo. From the spring of 1960 until Trujillo's assassination on May 30, 1961, the CIA was in contact with political dissidents, at least some of whom effected the assassination. Although three pistols and three carbines were passed to the dissidents, the Senate committee could not find "direct evidence that the weapons which were passed were used in the assassination."[85] Although there was no doubt that the dissidents intended to assassinate Trujillo, and the weapons were given for that purpose, an attempt was made to cover up U.S. government sponsorship.

"The day before the assassination a cable, personally authorized by President Kennedy, was sent to the United States' Consul General in the Dominican Republic stating that the United States government, as a matter of general policy, could not condone political assassination, but at the same time indicating that the United States continued to support the dissidents and stood ready to recognize them in the event that they were successful in their endeavor to overthrow Trujillo."[86]

According to the Senate report, American desire to eliminate Trujillo was partly a public relations concern and partly fear of another Cuba. "He was regarded throughout much of the Caribbean and Latin America as a protege of the United States. Trujillo's rule, always harsh and dictatorial, became more arbitrary during the 1950s. As a result, the United States' image was increasingly tarnished in the eyes of many Latin Americans. Increasingly American awareness of Trujillo's brutality and fear that it would lead to a Castro-style revolution caused United States officials to consider various plans to hasten his abdication or downfall."[87] Had Trujillo survived only a few years he would have had plenty of support and company, starting with the Brazilian generals in 1964, and followed by the other harsh, right-wing regimes promoted by the CIA in Latin America later in the 1960s and 1970s.

General Rene Schneider. As a constitutionalist and Commander of the Chilean Army, General Schneider was a principal obstacle to the CIA's attempts to prevent Salvador Allende from taking office after his election. Schneider was shot resisting a kidnapping attempt on October 22, and he died three days later. The Senate committee found that "the United States government supported, and sought to instigate a military *coup* to block Allende. U.S. officials [CIA and U.S. Army Attache] supplied financial aid, machine guns, and other equipment to various military figures who opposed Allende. Although the CIA continued to support the *coup* plotters up to Schneider's shooting . . . it does not appear that any of the equipment supplied by the CIA to *coup* plotters in Chile was used in the kidnapping.''[88] In fact, the report states, ''the CIA had withdrawn active support of the group which carried out the actual kidnap attempt on October 22.''[89] Again, the Senate committee is very careful to separate the intent of the CIA and U.S. policy makers by distinguishing the policy of assassination from the act as it finally occurred.

Ngo Dinh Diem. Diem, the South Vietnamese dictator, and his brother Nhu, were assassinated during a Generals' coup on November 2, 1963. The committee found that ''although the United States supported the *coup,* there is no evidence that American officials favored the assassination. Indeed, it appears that the assassination of Diem was not part of the Generals' pre-*coup* planning but instead was a spontaneous act.''[90]

Aside from these five specific cases studied by the Senate committee, evidence was also discovered that during the early 1960s the CIA established an assassination capability (termed ''Executive Action'' in the Agency) for general purpose targeting . The Agency cryptonym was ZRRIFLE. ''In general, Project ZRRIFLE involved assessing the problems and requirements of assassination and developing a stand-by assassination capability; more specifically, it involved 'spotting' potential agents and 'researching' assassination techniques that might be used.''[91] The committee found no new plots that might have come under authority of this project, but the project was eventually merged with other efforts under way to assassinate Fidel Castro.

It is important to place the CIA assassination plots within the larger context of covert action operations and policy goals in the countries concerned. As the report points out, in all five cases of CIA involvement, the principal figures were impediments to American policy goals. That Castro survived, or that the others may not have been killed directly by the CIA, in no way detracts from the importance of these revelations and the value of the Senate report.

The Senate committee's findings are also rich in detail on the CIA's programs for testing and using chemical and biological agents (which at certain times overlapped with similar programs of the U.S. Army). Although these programs apparently started with defense against possible hostile chemical or biological attack in mind, the committee found that "soon this defensive orientation became secondary as the possibility of using these chemical and biological agents to obtain information from, or to gain control of, enemy agents, became apparent."[92]

As early as 1947 the U.S. Navy began research into the possible speech-inducing drugs such as scopolamine and mescaline (Project CHATTER).[93] The CIA followed with a variety of programs beginning with Project BLUEBIRD in 1950 (renamed Project ARTICHOKE in 1951) in which interrogations were conducted overseas using psychiatric examinations, sodium pentothal, and hypnosis.[94] MKNAOMI was a joint CIA-Army project to stockpile severely incapacitating and lethal biological and chemical materials and the means for their application.[95] This program lasted from 1952 to 1970 and included development of poison darts and dart guns, not only for killing but also for temporary incapacitation. One such gun could fire darts "coated with a chemical that would incapacitate a guard dog in order to allow CIA agents to knock out the guard dog silently, enter an installation, and return the dog to consciousness when leaving."[96] Sabotage of field crops was also a capability developed under MKNAOMI, but perhaps the most sensational occurrence was the refusal of the CIA officer in charge of the project's shellfish toxin (approximately 11 grams, about one third of the total world production and sufficient for tens of thousands of lethal darts) to destroy the poison when President Nixon so ordered in 1970. The scientist stored the toxin in a CIA laboratory where it went unnoticed for five years.[97]

The principal CIA chemical and biological program was MKULTRA. This program, which lasted from 1953 through the late 1960s, was concerned with "the research and development of chemical, biological and radiological materials capable of employment in clandestine operations to control human behavior."[98] Techniques included "radiation, electroshock, various forms of psychology, psychiatry, sociology, and anthropology, graphology, harassment substances, and paramilitary devices and materials."[99] Testing occurred under both laboratory conditions and "normal life settings"—including the administering of drugs like LSD to unwitting subjects. At the federal drug rehabilitation center in Lexington, Kentucky, the CIA tested hallucinogenic drugs on addicts and "as a reward for participation in the program the addicts were provided with the drug of their addiction."[100] The widely reported death of Dr. Frank Olson, an army scientist who committed suicide from depression eight days after being surreptitiously given LSD by the CIA, occurred under MKULTRA.[101] But in spite of Olson's death, the CIA continued to give LSD to unsuspecting victims for ten more years. Thus, in order to observe the behavior of persons after taking the drug unwittingly, "the individual [CIA officer] conducting the test might make initial contact with a prospective subject selected at random in a bar. He would then invite the person to a 'safe house' where the test drug was administered to the subject through drink or in food. CIA personnel might debrief the individual conducting the test, or observe the test by using a one-way mirror and tape recorder in an adjoining room."[102] In 1973, not surprisingly, CIA Director Richard Helms ordered that all MKULTRA documents be destroyed.

The U.S. Army also used LSD as an aid to interrogation in projects THIRD CHANCE and DERBY HAT. One such interrogation appears in the committee report as an extract from the Army report: "Stressing techniques employed included silent treatment before or after [LSD] administration, sustained conventional interrogation prior to [LSD] interrogation, deprivation of food, drink, sleep or bodily evacuation, sustained isolation prior to [LSD] administration, hot-cold switches in approach, duress 'pitches,' verbal degradation and bodily discomfort, or dramatized threats to subject's life or mental health."[103]

Another Army interrogation, this one using LSD on a suspected Asian espionage agent, is equally disturbing:

> At 1120, sweating became evident, his pulse became thready. He was placed in a supine position. He began groaning with expiration and became semicomatose.
>
> At 1148, responses to painful stimuli were slightly improved.
>
> At 1155, he was helped to a sitting position.
>
> At 1200, he became shocky again and was returned to supine position.
>
> At 1212, he was more alert and able to sit up with help
>
> At 1220, subject was assisted to the interrogation table.
>
> At 1230, he began moaning he wanted to die and

usually ignored questions. Rarely he stated "he didn't know."

At 1250, his phasic alertness persisted. He frequently refocused his eyes with eyelid assistance. He frequently threw his head back with eyes closed.

At 1330, he was slightly more alert. He was force-walked for 5 minutes. He physically would cooperate until he became shocky again (sweating, thready pulse, pale).

The interrogation continued for seventeen and one-half hours after the drug was administered.[104]

Just three years earlier a staff study prepared in the Army unit responsible for these projects discussed the moral and legal aspects of using LSD in interrogations: "It was always a tenet of Army Intelligence that the basic American principle of the dignity and welfare of the individual will not be violated. . . . In Intelligence, the stakes involved and the interests of national security may permit a more tolerant interpretation of moral-ethical values. . . . Any claim against the U.S. Government for alleged injury due to [LSD] must be legally shown to have been due to the material."[105]

The problem of hypocrisy attendant upon the double standard and violation of professed principles is consistently present in the report of the Senate committee and is alluded to in the reports of the House committee, the Murphy Commission, and the Rockefeller Commission. The Murphy Commission, for example, concluded that new measures should be taken "to insure that in both word and deed our own foreign policy reflects devotion to high ethical standards" and "to insure that due consideration is given to ethical arguments in the setting and carrying out of policy."[106] Nevertheless, adds the report, "The ethical responsibilities that man has to man and nation to nation, where neither recognized rights nor dramatic misfortunes are involved, are subtle and less certain" even though they "lie close to the heart of many current international differences [such as] arms control and disarmament, including weapons design and strategic doctrine; problems of the redistribution of wealth, including terms of trade, and transfers of capital and technology, and food and population policies."[107] Yet in discussing the need for the CIA to continue covert action operations, the Murphy Commission is "realistic." "But we live in the world we find, not the world we might wish. Our adversaries deny themselves no forms of action which might advance their interests or undercut ours."[108]

The Senate committee also found that "many covert operations appear to violate our international treaty obligations and commitments, such as the charters of the United Nations and the Organization of American States,"[109] but it could not resolve this contradiction. Indeed, according to the American Constitution, treaties once ratified become "the law of the land" and those persons who violate treaties ought to be liable to prosecution in American courts.

Despite the Constitution, the Senate and the House of Representatives have both rejected proposals by members that would require stricter practicing of principles. In September 1974 the House defeated a proposal to forbid the CIA from financing operations "for the purpose of undermining or destabilizing the government of any foreign country." A month later the Senate defeated a motion that "would have forbidden any agency of the United States Government to carry out any activity within any foreign country which violates or tends to encourage the violation of, the laws of the United States or of such countries, except for activities 'necessary' to the security of the United States and intended 'solely' to gather intelligence."[110]

Nevertheless, the various investigating committees were established because of gross violations by the CIA and other agencies of certain American laws. Each committee adopted the same frame of reference which with a few exceptions conveniently and effectively sets aside the ethical and moral considerations. They limited their concerns to compliance with American laws, not those of other countries, and to what security services should be allowed to do to American citizens, not to foreigners. Particularly in the report of the Senate committee, the ethical and moral issue tends to blend into the discussion of whether U.S. laws have been violated, not whether the U.S. government should or should not violate its treaty obligations or other countries' laws.

The contradiction is, of course, insoluble so long as "liberal" and "free" institutions need direction, control, and funding by government, i.e., by the CIA. Most of the CIA's covert action operations imply corruption of "nongovernment" institutions which cannot seem to prosper by themselves. Thus the real principle in operation is that "free" institutions, such as foreign electoral processes, must be made to work in favor of "American interests." As increasingly they do not, they must be made "unfree" by control and direction in favor of the interests represented by the U.S. government.

By concentrating on rights of Americans and compliance with American laws, the various reports interpose nationalism and the liberal concept of the state in order to obscure and conceal the national and international class interests that are the *raison d'être* for the security services and for what they do.

Even so, the revelations of domestic "abuses" are valuable as indicators of what should be anticipated when the next round of protest and pressures for change develops. Both the Senate committee and the Rockefeller Commission reports show clearly the collection of information against dissenters, peaceful as well as violence-prone, and the use of the information to disrupt, harass, and weaken the organizations and individuals who were targeted. The picture emerges of an enormous covert action program within the United States against those who would correspond to the targets of the CIA's destructive covert action programs abroad, with the addition of certain liberal and right-wing groups.

The principal agencies involved in the domestic security programs were the FBI, CIA, National Security Agency, U.S. Army intelligence, and Internal Revenue Service. Among their targets were "persons with 'anarchist or revolutionary beliefs' or who were 'espousing the line of revolutionary movements, hate organizations, rabble rousers, key activists, black nationalists, white supremacists, agitators, key black extremists.' "[111]

The sheer mass of files and investigations gives some idea of the scope of these programs. The FBI, for example, has an index of 58 million cards of names and organizations through which it retrieves information contained in over 6.5 million files. It has compiled 480,000 files from investigations of "subversives" and 33,000 files from investigations of "extremists."[112] Through the SHAMROCK program of the NSA, which lasted from 1947 to 1973, millions of telegrams were intercepted and read. Between 1940 and 1973, 12 different letter-opening operations were conducted by the FBI and the CIA, resulting in the illegal opening of hundreds of thousands of letters. From 1953 to 1973 the CIA screened more than 28 million letters, photographed the exteriors of 2.7 million, and opened about 215,000.

The Internal Revenue Service targeted over 10,000 persons for special tax examinations for political reasons. The Army, for its part, amassed files on 100,000 Americans "encompassing virtually every group seeking peaceful change in the United States."[113]

The CIA, in its CHAOS program of disruption from 1967 to 1974, created 10,000 files on Americans with the names of 300,-000 Americans indexed. (The Agency's main index file in the Directorate of Operations contains about 7.5 million names, down from 15 million a few years ago. It also has some 750,000 individual personality files.) For collection of intelligence from American domestic sources, the CIA has another index, containing about 150,000 names, and approximately 50,000 files on "active" sources. The CIA's Office of Security has some 900,-000 files, almost all of which relate to individuals, including 75 sitting members of Congress. It also has records on about half a million people who have visited CIA installations, and until 1973 it maintained "extensive computer lists of approximately 300,-000 persons who had been arrested for offenses related to homosexuality."[114]

Although the FBI had been engaged in what amounted to covert action operations against left-wing groups in the United States since the 1930s, the main buildup came as a result of the civil rights and antiwar movements of the 1960s. Pressures from Presidents Johnson and Nixon to discover the "foreign hand" behind these movements were partly the reason, but the information was also used in ways designed to weaken them. The FBI's programs to infiltrate organizations continue with over twice as much spent in 1976 on informants against "subversive" organizations than against organized crime.

Besides asking *what* the different intelligence and security services have been doing, the House and the Senate committees also asked the question *how well* have the services been performing. Success or failure, in this respect, depends on one's point of view. The Senate committee report cites the CIA's interventions in Guatemala and Iran and in Western Europe after World War II as "successful" operations, yet laments the intervention in Chile as lacking popular support of the American public. The breaking of American laws by the FBI, CIA, and other services is seen as "failure" whereas the CIA's advanced technical collection programs are considered "successful." On the other hand, the CIA is seen to have "failed" in fulfilling its original task of centralizing the intelligence collection, analysis, and production processes of the government.

The House of Representatives committee reported a number of dramatic "failures" of the CIA. Among these were the failure to anticipate adequately the Tet offensive of 1968, the Czechoslovakian invasion by the Warsaw Pact armies, the 1973 Yom Kippur offensive by the Egyptians and Syrians, the fall of the fascist regime in Portugal in April 1974, the Indian nuclear explosion, and the 1974 *coup* against the Makarios government in Cyprus.

One searches the reports in vain for meaningful evaluations of the CIA's interventions to install or strengthen the current repressive regimes in countries such as Indonesia, South Korea, Iran, the Philippines, Brazil, Uruguay, Bolivia, and Chile. Almost nothing appears to suggest that the CIA works intimately with the security services of these and other right-wing governments to support the torture, assassination, and other forms of political repression prevalent in those countries. Such support often has the effect of covert action operations because of its impact on local political stability. In a somewhat peripheral manner, the Senate committee recognizes this when it recommends that the CIA be forbidden by law from providing support "for police or other internal security forces which engage in the systematic violation of human rights."[115]

Such a recommendation, if enacted, would be a positive development, but most probably the views of Senator Goldwater will prevail. In a statement of his individual views appended to the Senate committee report, Goldwater observed, "In some instances it is necessary for U.S. intelligence services to cooperate with the internal security forces of nations where there is systematic violation of human rights. The purpose of such cooperation is to gain foreign intelligence on vital targets. In order to gain the cooperation of the internal security forces in these countries, support is sometimes a condition for cooperation. In a world where the number of authoritarian regimes far outnumbers the number of democratic governments, such a prohibition limits the flexibility of our intelligence services in defending America."[116] Senator Goldwater might as well have been speaking for the CIA, but he too failed to acknowledge that the CIA supports political repression to weaken left-wing movements as a goal in itself, quite apart from the support given as an inducement to a local service to tap the Soviet Embassy's telephones.

Without adequately discussing the CIA's support and promotion of political repression, the Senate and House committees fail altogether to give the American people a better understanding of why a Station Chief was assassinated and why indeed the CIA is so despised and brings so much scorn on the United States in foreign countries. This omission should not surprise anyone for, as with covert action operations, these activities are needed to prevent real change—or at least to delay change as much as possible.

Many recommendations for reorganization and stricter control of the security services are contained in the reports: the Rockefeller Commission made 30 recommendations; the House committee, 32; the Senate committee, 87 on foreign intelligence and covert action and 96 on domestic intelligence. The Murphy Commission made 14 recommendations directly relating to intelligence. Practically all the recommendations are designed to strengthen the intelligence agencies of the government by making them more effective and keeping their operations secret. In all of the reports, more effective congressional oversight and control is recommended through the establishment of new intelligence oversight committees to replace the current weak supervision by Congress. Recommendations would also prevent future CIA law-breaking within the United States and assassination of foreign leaders during peacetime. A number of bureaucratic changes within the intelligence community are also recommended, from changing the name of the CIA to FIA (Foreign Intelligence Agency) and giving the DFI (Director of Foreign Intelligence) an office near the White House, to abolishing the Defense Intelligence Agency. The recommendations also reflect wide agreement that the DCI's position should be strengthened so that he can effectively coordinate the whole national intelligence apparatus.

The Senate committee and the Rockefeller Commission recommended the enactment of legislation that would provide criminal penalties for unauthorized disclosure of secret government information, one of the measures designed to cloak the CIA in secrecy again. If enacted, such a law would make it a crime to leak to the press the kind of information that caused the investigations in the first place.

Just how many of the various recommendations are finally adopted will depend in part on the Congress. President Ford, in February 1976, provided by Executive Order for a number of reforms and recommended others to the Congress for legislation, including the secrets act.[117] The main feature of the Ford reforms is that they add and change names but little else. Covert action, for example, now becomes "special activities." A new Committee of Foreign Intelligence chaired by the DCI is established in the National Security Council in order to improve management and budgeting of the intelligence activities. The Forty Committee that previously was supposed to review and approve sensitive and expensive covert action projects is replaced by an Operations Advisory Group and upgraded to include the Secretaries of State and Defense rather than their deputies. The DCI receives more power and in effect may become a strong director of the entire intelligence community, with the assistance of a new Deputy Director for the Intelligence Community. A new Intelligence Oversight Board, closely aligned with the Inspectors General of the intelligence agencies, will presumably detect possible "abuses" before they get out of hand.

Political assassination is declared prohibited, but other forms of covert action continue. The CIA's domestic activities are indeed curtailed, but exceptions to new rules governing the FBI would still allow for penetration and disruption of certain domestic organizations (those composed primarily of non–United States persons) by this agency. Nevertheless, President Ford asked the Congress for new legal authority for mail intercept operations and for repeal of the requirement that he advise the six congressional subcommittees of all covert action operations. Instead, only the new intelligence oversight committees would be kept informed, and to some extent the doctrine of "plausible denial" might return.

How, then, should we view these past few years? Does the continuation of the CIA's covert action operations abroad imply a defeat of those opposed to secret American intervention and support to political repression abroad? Does continuation of the FBI's collection of intelligence on left organizations inside the country also amount to defeat?

I believe the revelations of the past few years constitute a great popular victory, even when weighed against the absence of effective reforms. In the first place, popular movements have gained a huge body of knowledge concerning the methods and specific operations of the institutions of counterrevolution. Obviously, one must know how these institutions operate in order to anticipate their moves and defeat them. Second, the revelations served to continue the alienation process, probably in fact to hasten the legitimacy crisis that everyday is separating more and more people from the government and traditional institutions. What better subject could be found to demonstrate hypocrisy, corruption, and the ways in which the government in general tends to serve privileged, minority interests? Third, the revelations, especially those relating to Chile, demonstrate more clearly than ever how the activities of the CIA are tailored to meet the security needs of American-based multinational companies. Much of the CIA's operational program in foreign countries, particularly in the Third World, can now be seen as designed to promote optimum operating conditions for these companies. Fourth, the revelations and investigations demonstrate once again what is best in the American system: separation of powers, free flow of information, checks and balances, need for protection of the individual from oppression by government bureaucracy. Fifth, the lack of meaningful reforms demonstrates the limits of the liberal reform process. Those who may have hoped for abolishment of the CIA or of covert action operations may well reconsider whether they may have been putting the cart before the horse. Only after power is taken away from the owners, managers, and their politicians can their instruments of repression be dismantled. After all, the law that established the CIA was based in large part on recommendations made by a New York investment broker.[118]

The revelations, scandals, investigations, recommendations, and reforms are also an integral part of developments in other countries: in Vietnam, Cambodia, Laos, Mozambique, Angola, Guinea-Bissau; also in Chile, Argentina, Brazil, Indonesia, Iran, and Zaire. The investigations may have been a ruling-class affair in the United States, but they are also a contribution to liberation movements everywhere because they are so instructive on the techniques and institutions of counterrevolution. Taken in the international context, these events constitute still one more important, yet partial, victory for ordinary people.

There is no reason for paranoia on the part of those who reject and resist. The siege mentality is *theirs* as they try to hold onto each piece of territory for exploitation of resources and cheap labor. Yet no one can deny that socialism is advancing from region to region and from year to year. As for the CIA, those of us who are able should continue to make every effort to expose who they are and what they are doing in order to reduce their effectiveness and to hold them up to ridicule and scorn.

In June 1976 I spoke at an alternative Bicentennial celebration in Copenhagen. Also speaking was a representative of the Cherokee people of North Carolina. He described how fatuous the celebration of 200 years of conquest and exploitation was, since his people had been in America for some 25,000 years. He also described how Native Americans were marching across the country from the Pacific to the Atlantic coast. When on July 4, 1976, the candles were lit on the two-hundredth birthday cake of the United States, the Native Americans, he said, would be there to blow them out. This attitude, the exposures of secret intervention and repression, and the continuing growth of popular movements in the United States are the real reasons for celebrating the Bicentennial.

Notes

1. Final Report, Book I, Foreign and Military Intelligence, United States Senate Select Committee to Study Governmental Operations with Respect to Intelligence Activities, U.S. Government Printing Office, Washington, D.C., April 26, 1976, p. 340.

2. *Ibid.*, p. 17.

3. Report of the House Select Committee on Intelligence, Ninety-fourth Congress, as published in *Village Voice*, New York City, February 16, 1976, p. 72.

4. *Ibid.*, p. 72.

5. Final Report, Book I, Foreign and Military Intelligence, *op. cit.*, p. 470.

6. *Ibid.*, p. 333.

7. *Ibid.*

8. *Ibid.*, 319.

9. *Ibid.*, p. 337.

10. *Ibid.*, p. 348.

11. Report of the Commission on the Organization of the Government for the Conduct of Foreign Policy [Murphy Commission], U.S. Government Printing Office, Washington, D.C., June 1975, p. 98.

12. Final Report, Book I, Foreign and Military Intelligence, *op. cit.*, p. 344.

13. *Ibid.*, p. 437.

14. Report of the House Select Committee on Intelligence, *op. cit.*, February 16, 1976, p. 74.

15. *Ibid.*, p. 74, and footnote, p. 75.

16. Report of the Commission on the Organization of the Government for the Conduct of Foreign Policy, *op. cit.*, p. 100.

17. Report of the House Select Committee on Intelligence, *op. cit.*, February 16, 1976, p. 83.

18. Final Report, Book I, Foreign and Military Intelligence, *op. cit.*, p. 141.

19. *Ibid.*, p. 131.

20. *Ibid.*, footnote, p. 45.

21. *Ibid.*, p. 131.

22. *Ibid.*, p. 19.

23. *Ibid.*, p. 22.

24. *Ibid.*, p. 105.

25. *Ibid.*, p. 144.

26. *Ibid.*

27. *Ibid.*, footnote, p. 105.

28. *Ibid.*, p. 9.

29. *Ibid.*, p. 145.

30. *Ibid.*, p. 146.

31. *Ibid.*, p. 153.

32. *Ibid.*, p. 445.

33. *Ibid.*, p. 148.

34. *Ibid.*, p. 123.

35. *Ibid.*, p. 148.

36. Report of the House Select Committee on Intelligence, *op. cit.*, February 16, 1976, p. 84.

37. *Ibid.*

38. Final Report, Book I, Foreign and Military Intelligence, *op. cit.*, p. 183.

39. *Ibid.*, p. 155.

40. Report of the House Select Committee on Intelligence, *op. cit.*, February 16, 1976, p. 84.

41. Final Report, Book I, Foreign and Military Intelligence, *op. cit.*, p. 453.

42. *Ibid.*, p. 193.

43. *Ibid.*, p. 454.

44. *Ibid.* p. 455.

45. *Ibid.*

46. *Ibid.*, p. 200.

47. *Ibid.*, p. 202.

48. Report of the House Select Committee on Intelligence, *op. cit.*, February 16, 1976, p. 84.

49. Final Report, Book I, Foreign and Military Intelligence, op. cit., p. 183.

50. *Ibid.*, p. 188.

51. *Ibid.*, p. 452.

52. *Ibid.*, p. 24.

53. *Ibid.*, p. 155.

54. *Ibid.*, p. 156.

55. Report of the House Select Committee on Intelligence, *op. cit.*, February 16, 1976, p. 84.

56. *Ibid.*, p. 85.

57. *Ibid.*

58. *Ibid.*

59. *Ibid.*

60. *Ibid.*, p. 87.

61. *Ibid.*, p. 85.

62. *Ibid.*

63. *Ibid.*, p. 88.

64. *Ibid.*, p. 85.

65. Covert Action in Chile, Staff Report of the United States Senate Select Committee to Study Governmental Operations with Respect to Intelligence Activities, U.S. Government Printing Office, Washington, D.C., April 26, 1976.

66. Report of the House Select Committee on Intelligence, *op. cit.*, February 16, 1976, pp. 84–85.

67. *Ibid.*, p. 71.

68. *Ibid.*, p. 87.

69. *International Herald Tribune*, Paris, October 6, 1975, p. 2.

70. Final Report, Book I, Foreign and Military Intelligence, *op. cit.*, p. 445.

71. *Ibid.*

72. Alleged Assassination Plots Involving Foreign Leaders, an Interim Report of the Select Committee to Study Governmental Operations with Respect to Intelligence

Activities, United States Senate, U.S. Government Printing Office, Washington, D.C., November 20, 1975.

    73. *Ibid.*, p. 49.
    74. *Ibid.*, pp. 13–14.
    75. *Ibid.*, pp. 13, 13f.
    76. *Ibid.*, p. 48.
    77. *Ibid.*, p. 49.
    78. *Ibid.*
    79. *Ibid.*
    80. *Ibid.*, p. 50.
    81. *Ibid.*, p. 51.
    82. *Ibid.*, p. 71.
    83. *Ibid.*, p. 72.
    84. *Ibid.*, p. 73.
    85. *Ibid.*, p. 191.
    86. *Ibid.*
    87. *Ibid.*
    88. *Ibid.*, p. 5.
    89. *Ibid.*
    90. *Ibid.*
    91. *Ibid.*, p. 182.
    92. Final Report, Book I, Foreign and Military Intelligence, *op. cit.*, p. 471.
    93. *Ibid.*, p. 387.
    94. *Ibid.*, pp. 387–388.
    95. *Ibid.*, p. 388.
    96. *Ibid.*, p. 361.
    97. *Ibid.*, pp. 362, 389.
    98. *Ibid.*, p. 389.
    99. *Ibid.*, p. 390.
    100. *Ibid.*, p. 391.
    101. *Ibid.*, p. 394.
    102. *Ibid.*, p. 400.
    103. *Ibid.*, p. 415.
    104. *Ibid.*, pp. 415–416.
    105. *Ibid.*, pp. 416–417.
    106. Report of the Commission on the Organization of the Government for the Conduct of Foreign Policy [Murphy Commission], *op. cit.*, p. 113.
    107. *Ibid.*, p. 114.
    108. *Ibid.*, p. 100.
    109. Final Report, Book I, Foreign and Military Intelligence, *op. cit.*, p. 142.
    110. *Ibid.*, p. 502.
    111. Final Report, Book II, Intelligence Activities and the Rights of Americans, United States Senate Select Committee, *op. cit.*, p. 166.
    112. *Ibid.*, p. 167.
    113. *Ibid.*
    114. Report to the President by the Commission on CIA Activities within the United States [Rockefeller Commission], U.S. Government Printing Office, Washington, D.C., June 1975, p. 249.
    115. Final Report, Book I, Foreign and Military Intelligence, *op. cit.*, p. 448.
    116. *Ibid.*, p. 590.
    117. Presidential Executive Order No. 11905, The White House, February 18, 1976.
    118. Final Report, Book I, Foreign and Military Intelligence, *op. cit.*, p. 21.

The Deportations of Philip Agee

by Phil Kelly

The deportations from Britain of Philip Agee and Mark Hosenball were another blot on the much bespattered reputation that Britain once held as a haven for refugees. It is a reputation which should long ago have been lost. Once, we allowed Karl Marx to live in London and work at the British Museum. But Britain's Interior Ministry—the "Home Office"—and the police kept a close watch on this German revolutionary and his friends. Marx was allowed to stay because the Government of the day reckoned he would cause more trouble for Imperial Germany than for Imperial Britain.

Strict self-interest has guided the British state when deciding on which foreigners might be graciously allowed to live here. Those unwelcome have been thrown out—deported in some

[This article was written for this book. Some of the material on the British deportation appeared in *The Leveller* in London, in mid-1977.]

cases to their deaths. In the nineteenth century, Marx was accepted. In the twentieth, Trotsky was not. Nigerian Chief Anthony Enahoro was handed back to his political opponents and executed. Two officers concerned in a plot against the autocratic King Hassan of Morocco were likewise handed over to their deaths. German student leader Rudi Dutschke was thrown out after the Special Branch discovered that he had actually spoken to some British socialists. Hundreds who fled from the Turkish invasion of Cyprus are being forced back to the island to live in over-crowded refugee camps. A former Home Office minister, Alex Lyon, has revealed that Chilean refugees applying to come to Britain were vetoed by the British security services, who checked with the CIA, who in turn asked their friends in the DINA, the Chilean secret police.

Philip Agee arrived in Britain in 1972, and was allowed in by a Conservative Government. He lived in Britain for four years before a Labour Home Secretary decided that he was a danger to national security. When he arrived, his book, *Inside the Company: CIA Diary*, was little more than a manuscript. Even when it became clear that Penguin Books was to publish it, the book was after all, only about Latin America, where there are few British business interests to protect.

With the publication, things changed. At the end of 1974, Philip Agee's name was brought to the attention of the British public. In a short time, he made it clear that he was available to help anyone who wanted to work against the CIA. By helping in naming agents, by recounting his experiences on public platforms not only in Britain but throughout Europe and further afield, he drew attention to the activities of the secret police of American imperialism.

To his homes near Truro and in Cambridge came sackfuls of correspondence and many visitors seeking advice on how the CIA had manipulated and penetrated organizations and the political life of their own countries.

Independently, Mark Hosenball and I had started working on the names of CIA officers under diplomatic cover in the London Embassy, and we naturally approached Agee. Early in 1975, I met him for the first time. Apart from one or two who had been stationed in Latin America with him, it was not he who named the names. But he was an invaluable source of help on the structure of the CIA. He had never worked on joint operations with the British security services, and so knew next to nothing about the CIA's liaison with them. It is easy, however, to ascertain that this has been and still is extensive.

While the names were published in the London weekly entertainment and politics magazine *Time Out*, the rest of the press showed a cold indifference. Other left-wing papers also published the names, but one journalist for a national daily—the liberal *Guardian*—had his story spiked in front of his eyes. "These men," said the editor, "are our friends."

This was also the attitude of the British Government. Harold Wilson, then Prime Minister, told Parliament in answer to questions on the CIA's role here that they were here "with the knowledge and consent of Her Majesty's Government." More than 70 CIA personnel work under diplomatic cover in the huge U.S. Embassy in Grosvenor Square in London's fashionable Mayfair district. Naming their names was unspectacular but essential work in tracing the influence they have on the political life of Britain.

Other work consisted of tracing forward old "front" organizations of the CIA. Time and time again we found that operations which had been exposed—particularly in the media and cultural matters—simply carried on slightly altered, even with the same personnel. Perhaps the greatest *coup* was the closure of the CIA-front "news agency," Forum World Features, which hurriedly pulled down the shutters in 1976, just as an article appeared in *Time Out*. True to form, however, its successor organization, the Institute for the Study of Conflict, continued to function. The revelations were greeted with cold fury by the right-wingers doing the CIA's work, but there was apparently little they could do.

Philip Agee confined his advice to matters within his personal experience. But from a small circle of journalists and researchers emanated stories not only about the CIA, but about the British intelligence services. It was natural that those British journalists interested in the CIA were also investigating Britain's counterpart, the Secret Intelligence Service, SIS, also known as MI6, and the the Security Service, the internal security service, also known as MI5.

On the CIA, Agee was an untiring guide and counsellor on possible avenues for research, and most importantly, on the political motives of the Agency. This was strictly limited to matters within his own competence, which did not include British agencies.

As Philip Agee's work against the CIA became more widely known, and the activities of the CIA became a part of regular news coverage, it seemed more rather than less likely that he would be allowed to stay. He clearly took no interest in British security matters, and writing about the CIA had become a respectable journalistic activity.

When the deportation orders came in November 1976, they were unexpected. And the allegations, against Agee and Mark Hosenball, claimed that they had damaged British interests. Agee was accused of maintaining regular contacts harmful to the United Kingdom with foreign intelligence officers; the Home Office further claimed that he had been and continued to be involved in disseminating information harmful to the security of the United Kingdom, and had aided and counselled others in obtaining for publication information which could be harmful to the security of the United Kingdom.

Hosenball was alleged to have sought to obtain and to have obtained, for publication, information harmful to the security of the United Kingdom, including information prejudicial to the safety of servants of the crown.

The political climate in which these allegations arose was the sharp drift to the right which had occurred after Prime Minister Harold Wilson resigned in March 1975. Wilson, who later also criticized Britain's security services, was no progressive. But his successor James Callaghan was a man of the Labour Party's traditional right. In September 1976, Home Secretary Roy Jenkins resigned to become President of the European Commission. Jenkins was also on the right of the Party, but regarded as liberal on such issues as race and immigration, and "civil liberties" matters. More liberal, that is, than his successor, Merlyn Rees. Rees is a man of no great talent or achievement, and has risen in the Labour Party because of relatively mindless devotion to its "apparat." He was, significantly enough, Northern Ireland Minister before Callaghan appointed him to the Home Office. In Ulster, close collaboration with, and reliance on, the security services was essential. This habit he appears to have carried with him into his new task. Certainly, neither Agee nor Hosenball had done anything significantly different in their work between Jenkins' resignation and Rees' decision to order their deportations.

In the next seven months, as they fought the deportations, neither man ever officially discovered any more details of what was behind them. But some details leaked out. It seems clear

that the cases, while distinct, were linked. The CIA had probably been pressuring the British to curtail Agee's activities for
some time: that much was made clear by a former senior CIA
"dirty tricks" man, James Angleton. But the British Secret Intelligence Service could not convince a minister that the CIA's
reasons were sufficient grounds for the British Government to
act.

The close relationship between SIS and the CIA is well
known. It seems that Agee, while never intending to do anything
to damage British security interests, was more or less bound to
do so in the end. It was his trip to Jamaica, in September 1976,
which trod on British toes. Agee went to Jamaica to expose the
CIA-backed campaign of destabilization against the moderate
social-democratic government of Michael Manley. Manley had
committed the cardinal sin, in American eyes, of being too
friendly with Cuba. Jamaican politics, in which the gun has always played a role, had erupted into violent confrontation.

On the invitation of several Jamaican groups, Agee went to
the island, and helped in the naming of nine CIA officers active
in the destabilization campaign. Several had experience in similar activities elsewhere in Latin America. It now seems clear
that the British intelligence services were also involved in the
actions against Manley. This is not surprising, as Jamaica is a
former British colony, and still a Commonwealth country.

The Jamaica visit seems to have been the bait with which the
security services hooked Rees: it was characterized as clear
evidence that Agee's activities were harmful to Britain's world-
wide interests as well as those of the U.S. As far as Agee, his
friends and lawyers could ever ascertain, it was MI6 which
pushed the deportation recommendation on to the Home Office,
which duly complied.

Hosenball, on the other hand, appears to have offended the
British internal security service, MI5. Five thousand strong,
MI5 was created as a counter-espionage organization before
World War I, as hysteria swept the country over a rumored
invasion of German spies. Over the last few years, it has concentrated increasingly on left-wing activity in politics and the
trade unions, all of which is entirely British in origin, and totally
legal.

MI5 officers are civilians, though the service is structured on
military lines, with military ranks. They operate in total clandes-
tinity and have no powers of arrest. When, as a result of their

surveillance and other activities, MI5 officers wish to make an arrest, they call in their "errand boys"—officers of the police Special Branch—to make arrests.

Hosenball was an indefatigable enquirer into areas which the British press ignores. In May 1976, he was co-author with journalist Duncan Campbell of an article in *Time Out,* entitled "The Eavesdroppers," which dealt with the technical ability of the U.S., Britain and their allies to intercept commercial diplomatic and military telecommunications traffic. This article attracted the attention of the authorities: one person extensively quoted in it, U.S. writer Winslow Peck, was denied entry to Britain at the end of June 1976.

The authorities took their time. They were clearly not ready to move in July, when Hosenball moved from *Time Out* to the conservative London *Evening Standard* newspaper, for the conditions of his work permit were altered to allow him to take the job.

The deportations came like a bolt from the blue. A hastily-convened "Agee-Hosenball Defence Committee" met in the offices of the National Council for Civil Liberties, and a campaign was hurriedly organized. Friends and colleagues of the two men gathered and began making plans to publicize the cases. Both men were offered by the Home Secretary the opportunity to "make representations" against the deportations before a three-person panel appointed by him. Both decided to take that opportunity.

Philip Agee, with the support of the Defence Committee, decided to make the deportation a public issue. Hosenball took a different view. He had done fewer stories about American and British espionage. The British press is hackled by the Official Secrets Act, which forbids publication of most information about the workings of government, and especially the activities of the military and secret organizations. It wears these shackles voluntarily, operating the D-notice system, under which a committee of media owners and managers liaise with civil servants and military personnel, deciding which stories to suppress. Thirteen standing instructions on types of stories which must be suppressed are in the desks of all British newspaper editors.

Hosenball had no chance to do such stories on the *Standard.* But he still maintained his interest—in the extreme right, and into South African secret service activity in Britain. Sir Harold Wilson was hinting to several people that the South Africans were active in Britain, and that a disaffected right-wing clique inside Britain's security service was also working actively against the Labour Government, and Hosenball knew of these hints. This story has broken since. One other story, about corruption allegations concerning a minister, has also broken into the open.

The cases were linked. If nothing else, it was a clear attack on journalists working in areas which the Establishment found uncomfortable. But the effort to run a united campaign was sabotaged by the management of the *Evening Standard.* Hosenball was told not to approach the Defence Committee, and to have nothing to do with its campaign. He was faced with an unpleasant choice. Virtually everyone he knew urged him to join Philip Agee in a public campaign, which would have exposed the dangerous stupidity of the deportations, and would have focused on the hidden role of the security services. The management of the *Standard* wanted no part of this, and he was told that unless he played it their way, he would have no money to finance his legal advice, and that he would lose his job. Without a job, he would have no right to stay in Britain anyway.

The two were allowed to present their appeals to a three-person panel appointed by Merlyn Rees, of which more later. It was no trial, but the lawyer chosen for Hosenball by his employers had a record of stiff opposition to political activity around a trial—"Defence Committees" and the like. Many of Hosenball's friends felt that if they were not lawyers or Members of Parliament, there was nothing they could do. Most people realized that though Hosenball's deportation was a scandal, it was against Agee that the authorities bore the major grudge.

Hosenball withdrew from contact with his old friends for almost the whole seven months. The Committee continued to use his name, because it was also against his deportation. But he— and the *Standard*'s management—campaigned separately, approaching Members of Parliament on his behalf alone, and so on. This much must have been evident to the Home Office, which was carefully monitoring the reaction to its decision.

The *Evening Standard* in fact served Mark very badly. After splashing his case for a couple of days, it then gave little prominence. It never mentioned Defence Committee activity. The proprietors of a conservative newspaper had no wish to illuminate the deep-rooted illiberality of the British system. Indeed, *Evening Standard* Chairperson Charles Wintour was made a Companion of the Most Honourable Order of the British Empire in 1977, "for services to journalism."

In fact, of the national dailies, only the liberal *Guardian* was sympathetic to the campaign against the deportations. As Defence Committee activities expanded, more and more organizations expressed their opposition to the deportations. But skilled news management by the Government kept the spectre of national security ever present. Whispers from Ministers to senior MPs were used: Liberal Party leader David Steel was told that Agee was responsible for the death of two British agents. Editors of several papers, attending a reception at Downing Street, the Prime Minister's home, were told that the deportations were no threat to press freedom, or to journalists who stuck to the traditional areas, were assured that national security really was at stake, and were asked to play down the deportations. The BBC was similarly asked to play things down. A directive went out that Agee was only to be interviewed if the interview was cleared by senior management. Right-wing newspapers appeared with all sorts of stories blaming Agee for the death of a Western agent in Poland, claiming that he was an agent of the KGB or Cuban intelligence.

The Defence Committee adopted a dual approach. Firstly, it attacked the procedure under which the two men were condescendingly allowed to "make representations" against the Rees decision. Secondly, it attacked the myth of national security— that is, that there exist interests which all sections of the nation have in common, which are above political debate and which are not to be drawn into the political arena. Secret activities, which go on under the cloak of national security, are self-justifying. Because they are secret, no one knows about them. Because no one knows about them, they cannot be discussed, and because they cannot be discussed, they remain secret. To lift the veil even to inquire, without making judgments, is already to be disloyal as a citizen, and a threat if one is an alien.

Secret activities—particularly covert action in foreign countries—are as much the task of the world's intelligence services as the gathering of information. To hammer this message home, the Defence Committee produced thousands of copies of pamphlets, and tens of thousands of leaflets from its temporary headquarters at the NCCL's office. The Home Office was picketed regularly.

Philip Agee himself played a major part in the defense campaign. In contrast to Hosenball's silence, he was constantly making statements, giving detailed press interviews, and speaking at public meetings, keeping up an impressive pace which inevitably took its toll. On November 30, the first London public meeting was held, with Judith Hart, MP, a leading Labour Party member, Ian Mikardo, MP, Alan Sapper of the film and TV technicians union, and historian E.P. Thompson. By mid-February, Agee had spoken at the National Union of Students conference in Blackpool, and in Glasgow, Newcastle, Birmingham, Brighton, Bristol, Coventry, Manchester, Cambridge, Swansea, and Cardiff, in addition to London.

Philip Agee had directed his education campaign on the CIA towards the labor movements of various countries. The labor movement had the most to gain from a campaign against covert action by intelligence agencies, action which is so often directed against labor, democratic and progressive organizations. So the Defence Committee concentrated on the trade unions and the Labour Party.

Early in the campaign, spontaneous support for Agee and Hosenball in the labor movement manifested itself in a surprising fashion. Shortly after the deportations were announced, the Labour Party, with the Trades Union Congress, held a rally and march against racism. This in itself was an unusual occurrence: the Labour Party and the TUC take to the streets with reluctance. Demonstrations are the specialty of left-wing political groups, or of trade unionists or others with a specific grievance. A handful of Agee's supporters formed the main part of the National Union of Journalists contingent on the march.

Merlyn Rees was speaking. It had been decided that the presence of the Defence Committee, and the leaflets distributed to marchers, would be sufficient. There was to be no heckling of Rees. In Trafalgar Square, Rees took his turn in the speaking order. While the other speakers had been heard in respectful silence, a few started to shout. The majority of demonstrators took up the chant—"Merlyn Rees, CIA; Agee, Hosenball must stay." Rees was drowned out: not a word was heard.

The appeal against the deportations was under a singular procedure without parallel anywhere in the Western world. Although they were told no details of the charges against them and not one jot of the evidence, Agee and Hosenball were allowed to "make representations" against their deportations. These "representations" were to be heard by a panel of three men, appointed by the Home Secretary. This procedure was invented by the then Conservative Home Secretary, Reginald Maudling, in 1971, after the deportation of the partially-invalid German student leader Rudi Dutschke. Dutschke was in Britain for medical treatment after a right-wing assassination attempt, and was alleged to have broken the conditions of his stay by meeting political activists. This hearing was embarrassingly public, and it became clear that police Special Branch evidence of his contacts was gained by telephone tapping and mail opening.

Maudling, in introducing the Conservative Party's 1971 Immigration Act, invented the panel procedure, under which those recommended for deportation "by reasons of national security" would be given only a statement of the allegations against them, but would have no chance to confront their accusers. Both Agee and Hosenball prepared long statements, but as Agee said, it was a question of looking back over every detail of four years' residence in Britain, looking for details which could have appeared suspicious, and explaining them. The accused and their lawyers were forced to become prosecutors in their own cases.

The panel of three—the "silent knights," as they were dubbed —were Sir Derek Hilton, Chairman of the Immigration Appeals Tribunal, which hears the more normal appeals under the 1971 Act; Sir Clifford Jarrett, and Sir Richard Hayward. Hilton was in the Special Operations Executive (SOE) during the war, Britain's own dirty tricks outfit, the forerunner of the OSS and the CIA. Jarrett was a career civil servant who ended up as Permanent Secretary of the Admiralty, Britain's Navy Department. Hayward was a full-time official of the Union of Postal Workers (UPW), whose union was affiliated to the PTTI, one of the "trade secretariats" heavily infiltrated by the CIA. Later, he joined the Post Office Board, and the Union deprived him of his honorary membership because of his conduct during a national postal strike in 1971. All three men could be relied on to place considerations of "national security" above respect for free enquiry.

The panel refused all requests from Agee's lawyer Larry Grant to provide more details of the charges, or to open up the tribunal proceedings. The atmosphere of secrecy was calculated to help the Government's case in the public relations battle to convince public opinion that Agee and Hosenball were indeed security risks.

Hosenball, in keeping with his low-key campaign, meekly obeyed the requirements of secrecy. Agee and his supporters, on the other hand, determined to report every aspect of the proceedings to the press and the world, and this was duly done at press conferences after each session.

Agee's witnesses included Members of Parliament Stan Newens, Judith Hart and Alex Lyon, the latter two both former government ministers; National Union of Journalists' General Secretary Ken Morgan; Neil Middleton of Agee's publisher, Penguin Books; Tom Culver, the British representative of the American Civil Liberties Union; and journalists Martin Walker, Stuart Tendler and Christopher Roper. Agee was allowed an adjournment until February and produced as further witnesses Ramsey Clark, formerly Lyndon Johnson's Attorney General; Sean MacBride, the UN High Commissioner for Namibia and Nobel Peace Prize winner; Melvin Wulf of the ACLU; Morton Halperin, formerly aide to Henry Kissinger; and Alvaro Bunster, Chilean Ambassador to Britain during the Popular Unity period.

Hosenball put together an equally impressive list of supporters, including journalist Duncan Campbell, who told the panel that he had written most of the controversial "Eavesdroppers" article, and MP Paul Rose, who explained the investigations which he and Hosenball had been involved in to expose the activities of the ultra right in Britain, and their international links.

The Defence Committee concentrated its efforts on working up a public campaign on behalf of the two men. Normally, to gear up British political parties and trade unions takes months. The Defence Committee had no idea how much time was available for campaigning, but nevertheless managed to persuade the executives or top officials of many major unions to protest against either the procedure or the deportations themselves. Much assistance came from the men's own Union, the NUJ. But the protesters included the Transport and General Workers' Union, the National Union of Railwaymen, and leaders of twenty major unions. The TUC General Council, on which "moderates" have a majority, was persuaded to send its General Secretary, Len Murray, to see Rees. But the General Council only "noted" his report of the Home Secretary's account of the problems which he faced in "national security matters."

Hundreds of local trade union branches protested, as did local

Labour and Liberal parties, and left groups. The National Executive Committee of the Labour Party protested, but the Government disregarded it; there is no formal control by the National Executive over a Labour Government in office.

In Parliament, a succession of "Early Day motions" kept the issue alive during the campaign. Early Day motions are expressions of MPs' opinions: more than 150 signed various motions condemning the treatment of Agee and Hosenball. Several delegations of MPs called on Rees.

Most of the activity came from MPs in the center and on the left of the Labour Party. The Conservatives and the Labour right would rather not concern themselves with matters which the Government of the day chooses to designate as concerning "national security." The Liberal Party was apprehensive about the procedures, but Prime Minister Callaghan used his personal friendship with Liberal leader David Steel to assure him that Agee and Hoṣenball really were risks. Steel shut up.

Rees promised Parliamentary debate after he had considered the panel's verdicts on the two. But dramatic events intervened.

In February 1977, on the day that Rees announced his decision to uphold the deportations, Special Branch officers swooped down on three supporters of the Defence Committee and arrested them.

Two of the three were journalists; Duncan Campbell who had co-authored the "Eavesdroppers" article with Mark Hosenball, and Crispin Aubrey, a staff reporter with *Time Out,* and an active member of the Defence Committee. The third man, John Berry, was a former corporal in the Royal Corps of Signals, the British Army regiment which provides the personnel for, among other things, Britain's extensive technical intelligence network. He had approached the Defence Committee because he wanted to draw attention to the extent to which Britain was involved in secret surveillance, and the extent to which Britain's surveillance organization, Government Communications Headquarters, or GCHQ, was under the control of its U.S. equivalent, the National Security Agency (NSA).

Although Special Branch detectives carried out the arrests, at John Berry's London home, they were acting, as they often do, as the errand boys for MI5. Remarks made by the police officers made it clear that they had been alerted to the meeting between the three men only a short time before it happened. It had been arranged on the telephone, after John Berry had made his initial

contact with the Defence Committee by letter. Only by listening
to telephone conversations or opening mail could MI5 have
known about the meeting. The arrests followed a number of still-
unexplained incidents of break-ins and disappearances of items
in the homes and cars of Defence Committee members.

The three men were held in a police station for 48 hours,
denied any access to a lawyer. During this time, the homes of
Duncan Campbell and Crispin Aubrey were searched, and extensive journalistic files—relating to quite different matters—
were removed. The men were charged under the Official Secrets
Act, and at first were refused bail, though this was later granted.

British newspapers are much more circumspect about cases
before the courts than the U.S. press. This is supposed to protect the defendant. But in a patently political case like the arrests
of Aubrey, Berry and Campbell—the ABC case, as it has become known—it has inhibited them from publishing the repeated
assertions of those connected with the Agee-Hosenball Defence
Committee, and the rapidly-formed ABC Defence Committee,
that this was an astute political move on the part of the security
services. It was meant to serve as a further deterrent, first to
those like John Berry who wanted, like Philip Agee, to reveal
part of the inside story of security organizations, and second to
those journalists like Mark Hosenball who were willing to write
about it.

The *sub judice* rule operates in such cases to the benefit of the
police: the impression to be gained from the media is that
"there's no smoke without fire."

There is an acceptance among a broad section of public opinion in England that the security authorities do not move without
reason, and a preparedness to trust the Government on matters
which it chooses to refer to as affecting "national security."
This distinguishes British politics sharply from post-Watergate
America. As a result of the deportations of Agee and Hosenball,
and the continuing campaign for Aubrey, Berry, and Campbell,
this trust is beginning to wear thin. But there is not the same
spirit of enquiry among the British press as the American. The
carrot of the lobby system, a most efficient news management
tool, and the stick of the Official Secrets Act with its voluntary
counterpart, the D-notice system, has fattened the British press
into a dangerous complacency.

Agee challenged the deportation decision in the Scottish
courts, and Hosenball in the English. Scotland's separate legal

system didn't save Agee: the judges ruled that as far as immigration matters were concerned, Merlyn Rees had jurisdiction in Scotland too. Hosenball had no better luck. Lord Denning, Master of the Rolls and President of the Appeal Court, told him that "in matters of national security, natural justice may have to take a back seat." In no court was it possible to question Rees' motives, or the evidence on which he reached his decision. All the judges were interested in was whether he was legally entitled to order the deportation, and it was clear that he was. Appeals to the European Court of Human Rights at Strasbourg failed also, because the court held that the right to trial and to hear the evidence against one applied only to citizens. Former U.S. Attorney-General Ramsey Clark described the panel procedure as "lawless," but the British seemed not to know who he was.

The speeches, the public meetings, the marches, went on. The final episode was the Parliamentary debate in May 1977, postponed several times because of the court appeals. Former Home Office Minister Alex Lyon demolished official arguments about the procedure adopted; Stan Newens for Agee, and Paul Rose for Hosenball paid tribute to the work the two men had done; Tory rightwinger Stephen Hastings quoted several libelous allegations about Philip Agee from an obscure right-wing publication; and Merlyn Rees summed up, claiming yet again that the decision had been his, that he had not been influenced, that the national security of the country was at stake. The Government won the vote, with a motley collection of the Labour right, Tories and Liberals against the Labour left and one Welsh nationalist, a voting pattern which is far from abnormal in Parliament these days. At the beginning of June, Hosenball and his new wife departed for the United States, and Agee left for Holland on the cross-channel car ferry.

His problems were far from over. Agee's friend Angela Seixas remained in Britain, to clear up their affairs and to try to sell their house in Cambridge. Agee visited several countries, deciding eventually that his work would be best continued in France. Having stayed there six weeks, he went to Boulogne in August to meet Ms. Seixas, arriving on the channel ferry. The Border Police, with agents of the internal security service DST, kidnapped him and pushed him over the border.

Back in Holland, Agee learned in November that the Dutch Government was not willing to let him stay. They cited a letter he had written to a British left-wing magazine *The Leveller,* and his intention to compile a list of all those people and organizations which had worked for the CIA.

Misrepresentation was piled again on smear. Early allegations from Holland's justice ministry to his lawyers claimed that Agee's activities "could" endanger Holland's relationship with other countries. As time went by, the "could" became "would."

A similar legal and political defense campaign was mounted in Holland, with the trade union movement and the social-democratic Partij van de Arbeid playing an important role. Although the Dutch Minister of Justice denied any communication between "governments" on the deportation, he conceded that there had been communication between the "secret services." Again, Agee's supporters pushed matters as far as a debate in Parliament, but it was lost.

At Christmas 1977, on his way to visit friends in Hamburg, Agee was seized by West German border guards, kept overnight in a cell, and then flung out—with an unnecessary degree of unpleasantness.

In May 1978, his application to visit Norway for two days was summarily turned down.

One man clearly cannot present such a threat to the security services of the entire Western world. The spectre which is haunting the world's security services is the discovery of the extent to which they work together on projects directed against Third World countries, and their own citizens. It will come out if a systematic analysis is made of the activities and personnel of the world's largest secret police force, the CIA. As Philip Agee himself has put it: "Is it paranoia to suggest a conspiracy when one expulsion follows another, without a single charge of illegal activity, even in the United States? Yet these actions are designed to silence, disrupt and discredit a critic of his own country's foreign policy, exercising a right explicitly protected by the acknowledged covenants on human rights, to which these countries are signatory."

Turner's "Born Again" CIA

by CovertAction Information Bulletin

Not even a Bicentennial celebration and presidential elections stopped the legacy of illegal CIA programs from hitting the front pages. Every new revelation brought forth another wave of criticism and rejection from around the world. Left waiting for the new President were incomplete Congressional investigations, a flurry of pending suits for damages, and President Ford's stale reforms which placed no new limitations on the spy agencies except to outlaw assassinations.

When Carter promised a fresh team, an open government, and an end to secret ivory-tower policy making, most Americans did not think it meant tightening the bolts of government secrecy, bringing back some of the key men who gave us Vietnam, or leaving national security questions to the top members of the Trilateral Commission, an elite foreign policy club about which most people knew nothing. But it is commonplace for every new

[This article was written in Washington in 1978, for this book.]

Commander-in-Chief, suddenly absorbed in secret briefings, real-life intrigues and other initiations, to become spy-happy. Carter's enchantment immediately dissolved any plans to cut back government secrecy.

One of his first actions was to tighten severely access to information about CIA covert operations and plug up potential leaks. He reduced from 40 to five the number of White House intimates with access. He was "shocked" to learn how many Members of Congress received CIA briefings and recommended the number be slashed to one single joint committee with limited membership (though this is not expected to win Congressional approval). He ordered an internal review of all the government intelligence-gathering units, and began bringing in the new team.

At least 15 members of the Trilateral Commission were appointed to Cabinet or other top positions, and at least six others were selected as presidential advisors—all from the 65 American Commission members carefully selected by its founder, David Rockefeller, and Director, Zbigniew Brzezinski. In a nutshell, the Commission's philosophy presupposes that, in the long run, the survival of modern capitalism will be best served by active cooperation rather than indiscriminate competition between the industrialized powers of North America, Western Europe, and Japan. The Commission was Carter's introduction to foreign policy circles which eventually became the target for the heaviest injection of Trilateral expertise. It was therefore no surprise that Carter chose Brzezinski for National Security Affairs Advisor. Secretary of State Cyrus R. Vance was also an activist in the New York-based organization, a Vietnam War policy-maker and early advisor to the Carter presidential campaign. Vice President Walter F. Mondale, United Nations Ambassador Andrew Young, Defense Secretary Harold Brown, Treasury Secretary W. Michael Blumenthal, former Budget Director Bert Lance, and Ambassador to Italy Richard Gardner, were some of the other Trilateral appointees.

After one month Carter's momentum came to an abrupt halt with the nomination of liberal Theodore Sorensen for CIA Director (and with the sudden revelation of long-standing CIA payments to King Hussein, and others, which Carter tried to prevent from being published). After conservatives led a successful campaign to force Sorensen to withdraw his name, Carter nominated four-star Admiral Stansfield Turner. A Rhodes Scholar and former Annapolis classmate of Carter, Turner passed congressional inspection without any of the scrutiny given Soren-sen. His military achievements and academic approach impressed liberals and conservatives. He had risen rapidly through the naval ranks to become commander of NATO forces in Southern Europe. Early reports showed that the Admiral's shake-em-up policies had succeeded in the Navy, so why not let him loose at Langley?

Turner moved briskly, catering to Cabinet members, listening to the Senate oversight committee, meeting regularly and privately with Carter, and became the first CIA Director to set up an office next door to the White House, in the Executive Office Building. The President told the new CIA chief: "One of the greatest surprises to me in coming to office is how effective the CIA is." What resulted from all the meetings was the most comprehensive organizational and procedural transformation since the CIA's creation 30 years ago. Turner proposed that a director of national intelligence, with centralized control over the intelligence community, be created with himself in that position. Another officer would be named to run the CIA itself. And so the plan developed.

By May 1977 Carter had abolished the Foreign Intelligence Advisory Board, an independent body created by Eisenhower in 1956 to review intelligence efforts. Its functions would be resumed by the new Intelligence Oversight Board, a Ford creation, by the new Inspector General post at the CIA and by congressional oversight committees. Opponents of this move complained that the abolition of the advisory board eliminated a necessary independent assessment by persons outside the intelligence sphere; Carter named Thomas L. Farmer, a Washington lawyer and former CIA man, to chair the Oversight Board.

Carter's internal review was completed by August and became the basis of Executive Order No. 12036, signed January 24, 1978. It set up four new special divisions, streamlined jobs to avoid overlap and generally made spying a centralized, more efficient, and allegedly legal government activity.

The first committee of planners and goal-setters is called the National Security Council (NSC) Policy Review Committee, and is chaired by Turner. It "defines and establishes priorities for intelligence consumers," says one official, adding that this body "will drive the whole process" of setting budget and analysis priorities. The dirty tricks team sits as the NSC Special Coordination Committee, a reincarnation of the "40 Committee." It is headed by Brzezinski and recommends and approves all covert operations and other sensitive jobs conducted by the government, including the FBI. It is the first such body designed to coordinate overall government counterintelligence activities. The advisory panel, called the National Foreign Intelligence Board, began functioning in November 1977 to advise Turner on production, coordination and budgets. In addition to Turner and cabinet secretaries from State, Defense and Justice, officials from the Energy Department, Defense Intelligence Agency, FBI, National Reconnaissance Office, and the National Security Agency also belong. The coordinators work at the National Intelligence Tasking Center, chaired by Turner, and are responsible for peacetime assignments to all the intelligence agencies. It is run by Lt. Gen. Frank A. Camm, a former Army Engineers officer, but the Defense Secretary can take over by presidential order in times of war or crisis. Turner established the brain trust at the National Foreign Assessment Center, run by another Trilateral Commission member, Robert Bowie, who was once a key advisor to John Foster Dulles, and more recently a professor at Harvard. The center is staffed by 1,200 intelligence analysts from the CIA and a group of high-ranking estimate specialists who provide policy makers with the major trends abroad that affect U.S. foreign and economic policies.

Membership in all these special committees varies some, but the core clique includes Brzezinski, Turner, Vance, Brown, Mondale and Blumenthal. (A key element of Brzezinski's Trilateral plan included reorganizing the NSC to include the Secretary of the Treasury, who had previously been excluded from its deliberations.)

Labeled Carter's biggest sweep was handing over the highly-centralized power and leadership to the CIA Director, who now assigns tasks, reviews results, and controls budgets over not only the CIA, but also the intelligence sections of the Army, Navy and Air Force, the National Reconnaissance Office, Treasury Department intelligence, Drug Enforcement Agency intelligence, National Security Agency, Defense Intelligence Agency, research and development divisions of the Energy Department, and even the counterintelligence branch of the FBI. Turner chairs the four decision-making bodies and acts as the intelligence community's principal spokesperson to Congress, the news media, and the public. He is also the first CIA Director to sit in on all cabinet meetings. When Turner was granted power to decide on the final budgets, he reportedly said, "He who has the budget, has the golden rule." Veto over the budget allows Turner to halt or nurture programs as he wishes, even if the money goes through the Defense Department. This job alone involves oversight and control of between seven and twelve billion dollars annually.

Operational control and hire-fire powers still remain with the heads of the relevant agencies, and each continues to maintain an independent analytical capability, to assure dissenting views and competition. Competition is still a real phenomenon and minor rifts between Defense Secretary Harold Brown and Turner, and between Turner and Secretary of State Vance, have already surfaced. To give himself some leverage, Brown appointed a retired four-star Admiral, a former CIA official who served as Deputy to CIA Director George Bush. Admiral Daniel J. Murphy, now Deputy Under Secretary of Defense for Policy is in charge of intelligence and counterintelligence, but his key task is to work with Turner, a close friend, on budgeting and Pentagon assignments. For the first time, Pentagon intelligence gathering has been coordinated under the Defense Secretary and one person is organizing the various strands of data from such offices as the Defense Intelligence Agency, the National Security Agency, the Defense Mapping Agency, the National Reconnaissance Office, as well as the Office of International Security Affairs, yet another Pentagon division that deals with strategic arms talks, NATO, and defense-related diplomatic issues. Brown was understandably seeking to exert his own power in the intelligence community after Turner successfully gained control of most functions, despite Brown's vigorous objections. Murphy is "considered a very strong leader who's able to hold his own in the bureaucracy. He's a strong type, and that's obviously why Brown needs him," said another source to a *New York Times* reporter.

Turner took charge of the CIA at a critical period in history. Public exposure of those accustomed to operating in the dark, the rapid turnover in directors (five in less than five years), half-prescribed reforms and the rumored reorganization plans had repercussions in the nervous Agency, especially in its operations arm. Robert D. (Rusty) Williams, hired by Turner from Stanford Research Institute to investigate the Directorate for Operations, agreed with the CIA's own studies; the Operations division was overstaffed and top-heavy with senior grade officers. During the summer Turner carefully prepared a plan with personnel and house psychologists to minimize the turbulence of eliminating 820 operations positions out of 4,730. He had inherited recommendations for more drastic cuts, but decided that instead of getting rid of 1,400 employees in six to eight years, 800 positions, many unfilled at the time, and many at headquarters, could be eliminated over two years. Operations personnel had already been trimmed down from 8,000 at the peak of the Vietnam War, and Schlesinger had begun the scale-down in 1973 when he eliminated 2,000 positions throughout the Agency.

Most of the victims of the "October massacre" were veteran clandestine operatives notified by a two-sentence mimeographed form letter signed by William W. Wells, head of Operations. The open resentments were apparently unexpected by Turner, and they tended to exaggerate the move to draw even more attention to the Director's "ruthless" military style. Calling those who leaked their pity to reporters "crybabies," for which he later semi-apologized, Turner only aggravated more employees, many of whom had worked for the CIA for several decades. In fact, only 45 people were fired outright, from the first batch of 212 notices. Others have been retired and the CIA personnel office was looking for government jobs for the rest. (Of course, as former Director William Colby recently said on a radio interview, "They could always write books.")

There were thirteen major overseas positions affected, including Chiefs of Station in Germany, Austria, Norway, Sweden, Luxembourg, Spain, Switzerland, Canada, Australia and Japan. Three Chiefs came home from Latin America to retire. By the end of 1978 almost 20 percent of the operations branch will reincarnate as authors, lecture-circuit pros, local police chiefs, foreign agents, lobbyists, whistle-blowers, private corporate spies, and many will join the strident Association of Former Intelligence Officers (AFIO), the club for burned-out spies.

The firings may have shaken morale, but there were several warnings. The first tipoff to the cuts occurred in July when Deputy Director E. Henry Knoche suddenly resigned after 24 years' service, over disagreement with Turner's policies. At the same time, reports that Turner was seeking early retirements for many senior operations officers were disingenuously denied: "There are no plans for forced retirement or removals of any top CIA officials, there are no plans for major changes in the CIA organization at this time," Turner stated. But word got out in August, and by October eight-page memos circulated, detailing the criteria used for selection for the list.

Two months after the dismissal notices went to the first 200 senior members, the top clandestine officers began receiving them as well. By late December, William W. Wells, the signer of the controversial notices, had himself retired. Knoche's deputy, Louis Latham, resigned under pressure; then Wells' top assistant, the legendary and elusive Cord Meyer, Jr., was ousted, as was Theodore Shackley, his other top deputy, and Campbell James, another Company legend. These removals were seen as Turner's attempt to break up remnants of the "old boy network" of senior operatives. A former aide to Turner summed up his motivations this way: "He is very uncomfortable with their [the clandestine branch] basic uncontrollability. He doesn't like their fine clothes and accents, their Cosmos and Yale and Georgetown clubs. They're simply not good sailors. He finds them sneeringly elliptical. It drives him crazy. He just can't get hold of this maddening quicksilver."

"Wild Willy" Wells and Shackley were considered two of the CIA's top clandestine operators. Wells was Station Chief in Tokyo and Hong Kong and once headed the CIA's European operations division. Shackley directed the secret war in Laos, and was actively involved in CIA operations in Vietnam, during the Cuban missile crisis, and in Berlin. Campbell James, a distant relative of Teddy Roosevelt, was also a prime operative in Laos. Cord Meyer, Jr., a much-decorated CIA officer, recently was Station Chief in London after many years coordinating, among other things, the Agency's infiltration and manipulation of the National Student Association.

Wells was replaced by John N. McMahon, who was acting deputy for intelligence. McMahon is a 26-year CIA veteran whose specialty in the past had been in the area of science and technology. Because he came up from the bottom on the scientific side of the CIA, it fueled the theory that Turner was expanding technological spying and cutting back on human intelligence gathering. In fact, McMahon does have experience in operations from the years he spent developing technological exotics for CIA covert actions. He's known as a superb manager, and according to one colleague, "He'll have the Directorate of Operations eating out of his hands in sixty days."

Turner placed John Koehler at the Directorate for Resource Management, a branch designed to supervise the budget, estimated at more than $800 million a year; Leslie Dirks is the CIA's new deputy for Science and Technology; and John F. Blake was chosen as Deputy for Administration.

Due to Turner's expanded role, the new Deputy Director now has day-to-day operational control over the CIA. He is Frank Carlucci, imported for the job from the U.S. Embassy in Portugal, a veteran civil servant who was given full status as stand-in for Turner at White House and NSC meetings and who receives intelligence evaluations formerly limited to the Admiral. Carter considered Carlucci for several other major appointments, but abandoned plans when Democrats in Congress complained of his many high positions in the Nixon administration. His foreign service career began in 1956 in Johannesburg, until 1959, the Belgian Congo until 1964, Zanzibar for a year, Brazil until 1969, and back home to Nixon's Office of Economic Opportunity. In 1971 he was assistant Director of the Office of Management and Budget. In 1972 Nixon moved him to HEW, where he remained until 1975, when he was abruptly sent off as Ambassador to Lisbon amidst the throes of the battle between communists and socialists. He won praise for opposing Henry Kissinger's proposal to withdraw American support from the Lisbon regime when it seemed for a time that communists were winning. But Democrats only routinely inquired into Carlucci's sensitive past when it came time for confirmation in Congress. They quickly voted in Committee to confirm, 10-0. Carlucci replaced Jack Blake, a career CIA officer who was acting Deputy Director since July 1977, after Knoche's resignation.

Although Carlucci, 47, is expected to smooth ruffled feathers at the CIA, there is doubt that the Agency will be able to adjust abruptly to the new procedures—if they want to. According to one victim of the layoffs, despite all the media exposure of the CIA, the organization remains essentially unchanged. No matter who rules, says Donald S. Jordan, it's run by elitists, most of whom are contemptuous of "idiots" in the unwashed general public and who are willing to lie to Congress whenever necessary. Appalled at the indifference he observed among high-level officers, Jordan said that fabricated information goes into CIA files regularly. He remembers one CIA agent justifying his imaginative report to headquarters: "OK, so some of it is made up, so what? So it really doesn't hurt. It'll increase our budget, we'll get a few more people." Jordan is a 26-year veteran in the domestic service as a public representative.

He thinks he was asked to leave because he was listed in the potential whistle-blowers file. The 57-year-old officer claims CIA "super-grades" and high-level appointees maintain one set of legitimate personnel records and another set on complainers. It's used to control, harass and oust employees who disagree or criticize their bosses, he said. Jordan was one of the first officers to comply with a new CIA regulation requiring employees to report possible wrongdoing. His grievances were ignored, he says, and the Inspector General in charge began to cover up the problems in domestic activities which he reported. His attempts to inform the Admiral met with no response. According to Jordan, most employees won't change their thinking, and their main concern with the Agency is that it was "caught" and that regulations don't mean anything.

Indeed, an administrative official at the CIA said "there's a lot of bureaucratic ass-covering that goes on when guys write long-range stuff. They don't want to be wrong, so they tend to be glib and platitudinous." According to *Newsweek,* the CIA even prepared a five-year plan in 1977 with one solution to all the scrutiny and criticism: "We are dealing with our cover impediments by creating a truly clandestine corps of operations officers," notes one section of the ambitious plan. "[This will be] an extremely delicate undertaking with many complex operations and support ramifications that will require adroit handling by our most experienced people."

Those who interpreted Turner's housecleaning to reflect the downgrading of covert actions declared it "the end of an era" of secret spies. But epitaphs are premature, as Turner himself contends: "We have not by any means abandoned covert action . . . it does continue . . . I'm dedicated to preserving the capability to turn to political action when it suits the purpose and when properly authorized." Human spying operations "will continue to be an absolutely essential arrow in our quiver." From 1961 to 1976 roughly 900 major covert operations were carried out, and several thousand smaller projects. Nothing invites tombstone inscriptions yet; in fact the traditional structure of the CIA, including the trimmed-down operations branch, has only been reconstructed. And like a born-again Christian, it will carry forward with more fervor than ever before.

The Agency is not only preserving its options on covert action; it is also struggling to keep knowledge of these activities from the State Department. In October 1977, after considerable negotiations between the Agency and State, President Carter had published an Order stating that all Ambassadors have the authority to review all message traffic involving U.S. personnel under their jurisdiction. Admiral Turner and Secretary Vance sent out identical "guidelines" to their people, indicating that Ambassadors had the right to be kept informed of Agency activity, but Turner simultaneously sent an additional directive to his Station Chiefs prohibiting communication of details of covert operations and administrative procedures. The dispute continues, and the Ambassadorial corps is reportedly quite unhappy over the present state of affairs.

New division titles, deputies, and authority lines haven't affected intelligence-gathering ratios. Approximately 50 percent of intelligence-gathering comes from open sources, such as newspapers, films and speeches. The source for another 40 percent is technological devices such as satellites, high-speed spy planes, cameras, eavesdropping devices and other gadgets. The remaining ten percent has historically been dependent on human information collectors. The human resources, which former Deputy Director Lt. Gen. Vernon Walters calls "the most vital part because it alone can reveal intentions," are still critical requirements. Intentions are precisely what's on today's agenda. Since the government knows who has how many of what, the real priority is focusing on foreign government plans for those capabilities. Of those human intelligence (HUMINT) collectors, about one-third are scattered around the world while the remainder play support roles at home. The CIA still has about 6,000 employees outside Langley and about 1,400 at headquarters. Clandestine activities do not require huge bureaucracies; in fact they can severely handicap operations. Not only do covert capabilities remain, but as Turner recently said, "We are retaining a paramilitary capability on stand-by as part of our covert action kit." According to *Newsweek*, this secret paramilitary unit has at least 50 members.

Turner's moves add more red tape, but with authorization all covert action can continue. Turner is said to have told one Western European Chief of Station that "the only difference now is that all covert operations henceforth will be conducted legally."

Other significant changes occurred in the analytical arm of the CIA, which must evaluate and synthesize the information collected by the Operations arm. Information by itself is not intelligence, and the analysts in the intelligence community must expand and improve the "product." The CIA in particular hopes to rejuvenate its relationships with American academicians by allowing more flow of information to leave the CIA. Foreign policy requirements will make more use of diplomatic weapons requiring more information on subjects such as food, population, climate, culture, and economics. More and more reports are being made public: "I'm just so proud of what we have contributed in the past nine months to the public debate on major issues," says Turner. "Look at this morning's newspapers, there's a long story on Soviet oil-extraction problems. We triggered that last April by releasing a study on Soviet oil."

The CIA's think tank "is getting more sophisticated," said Dennis Berend, assistant public affairs officer. "There are enough people here with doctorate degrees, in any field you can name, to staff a university. You need a Master's degree to get a job in some areas," he adds. Reflecting the academic disciplines that contribute to the Agency's analytical output are the offices of economic research, scientific intelligence, strategy research (arms and military preparedness), computer science and geography-cartography.

In recent years, a major shift in focus has been from military analysis to economic research in recognition of the broad impact of economic conditions on the political community. Recent titles of CIA studies include: "World Steel Market—Continued Trouble Ahead"; "China—1977 Midyear Grain Outlook"; "Communist Aid to the Less Developed Countries of the Free World, 1976"; and "International and Transnational Terrorism—Diagnosis and Prognosis." The increasing emphasis on analyses led to the establishment of the National Foreign Assessment Center, headed by Trilateral Commission member Robert Bowie, which will sift analyses from all the agencies.

Carter is said to be making heavy demands on the CIA to improve its predictions and analysis of economic and political developments. And one CIA analyst complained, "The facts aren't always exciting enough for Stan [Turner]; he orders the intelligence estimates to be jazzed up," in order to please the President.

Turner is indeed jazzing up everything at the CIA, and it has been most notable in its public relations. Turner is accepting interviews, releasing inside photos of the headquarters building, writing opinion columns in newspapers, and generally trying to leave the impression that the CIA has recuperated fast. He logically counters every criticism and smoothly glosses over rumors of low morale, lousy predictions and costly waste. Former Deputy Director Ray S. Cline has said, "The Central Intelligence Agency, with the famous acronym that has become a worldwide public relations liability, should cease to exist. . . . Realism suggests we will do better with some new name." Cline suggests something like Central Intelligence for Foreign Affairs Research (CIFAR). This step, while controversial, is expected to come to be, but Cline should know that public relations requirements are not that simple. On the one hand Turner must convince critics that the Agency has changed its methods, and on the other hand he must assure supporters that the CIA has not relinquished its covert capabilities.

The CIA must attract and recruit scholars and students while at the same time, reassure foreign intelligence agencies that it is still able to keep a secret. Its relations with the higher education community are expanding, despite public outcry over operations like MKULTRA, and the Agency statistics support its claims. They report that job inquiries are at a high level. In 1976 the CIA had 37,000 inquiries for 1,100 vacancies. CIA recruiters still vigorously tour college campuses, and one school, Bowling Green University, nominated the Agency's recruiting officer as Recruiter of the Year.

A surprising amount of media coverage has been supportive, focusing now on the importance of covert action and criticizing "hyper-suspicious investigative reporters" of trying to endanger national security. An enormous public relations effort to end the season of attack on the CIA once and for all and "let them get back to work" has left public criticism from civil liberties and other watchdog public interest forces on the back pages. The backlash is undoubtedly orchestrated by the Agency as much as possible—likely one of its most urgent covert operations ever carried out and, in direct violation of its charter, right here in America—as both major columnists and Congressional oversight spokespersons have begun spreading fears of the effects of criticism and complaints, while launching an educational campaign on the importance of secrecy. During recent hearings on CIA ties to journalists, it was revealed that the CIA had become a professional opinion molder and that such operations were vital for "the national interest." Ray Cline testified that CIA-press relations should not be eliminated; after all, said the former Deputy Director with a straight face, "the First Amendment is only an amendment."

According to the Church Committee, in February 1976 fifty American journalists were working for the CIA. Carl Bernstein wrote in *Rolling Stone* that "more than 400 American journalists . . . in the past 25 years have secretly carried out assignments for the CIA," according to CIA documents. For thirty years the CIA has been engaged in an unremitting, though largely unrecognized, effort to shape foreign opinion in support of U.S. policy abroad. American journalists were just one part of its propaganda campaign, and its efforts contributed to distortion of the news at home as well as abroad. Why are we to believe it has ended?

The CIA has at various times owned or subsidized more than 50 newspapers, news services, radio stations, periodicals and other communications entities, sometimes in the U.S. but mostly overseas. Another dozen foreign-based news organizations, not CIA-financed, were infiltrated by paid CIA agents. Nearly a dozen American publishing houses, including some of the most prominent names in the industry, have printed at least a score of the more than 250 English-language books financed or produced by the CIA since the early 1950s, in many cases without being aware of the Agency involvement. A substantial number of the bogus news stories planted abroad were published as genuine in the United States, a phenomenon the CIA calls "blowback," "replay" or "domestic fallout." And Carter's rules don't even attempt to change that game. The Agency warns diplomats and other key officials to ignore news stories the CIA has planted overseas. But how is the public to sift out the lies and dis-information? Some CIA propaganda efforts, especially during the Vietnam War, were set in motion specifically for U.S. consumption.

All these methods require secrecy and Carter's changes have only strengthened that ingredient. The President has stated in the new Executive Order that many of "the documents that implement this Order will be classified because of the sensitivity of the information and its relation to national security," but he promises they will be consistent with the Order. There is, of course, no logical reason to believe this, any more than there was to believe Richard Nixon or John Mitchell in the heyday of their promises. This is especially true because the actual implementation of the Order is the exclusive dominion of the intelligence community, a dilemma analogous to the illogic of supposing that a police department can impartially rule in cases involving charges of police brutality. Contrary to Carter's cam-

paign rhetoric, his rules for classification only perpetuate the
secrecy mania of the federal government. They do not reduce
the number of people and agencies authorized to classify information, nor shorten the period during which secrets will be kept.

Indeed, the ACLU and other groups contend that Carter's
changes are a step backward from the inadequate restrictions of
the Ford administration and in several areas make Nixon's rules
seem more lenient. New restrictions on spying operations require case-by-case approval by the Attorney General and can be
carried out if the targeted person or organization is believed to
be acting as an agent for a foreign power. Then there are the
exceptions. It's considered "legal" by the Agency to spy on
individuals who might reveal classified information, or former
spies, or potential recruits, or those who are in contact with
someone who is believed to be a foreign agent, or in contact with
someone who is the subject of a foreign intelligence or counterintelligence investigation. Use of warrantless electronic surveillance is also authorized in such cases, even though the only
Federal appeals court to rule on the subject has condemned the
practice as unconstitutional, and the Senate rejected authorizing
legislation by a resounding 95–1 vote. The term "agent of a
foreign power" is not defined in any way in the Order and count-
less other loopholes remain.

All the "prohibitions," too, can still be undertaken "legally,"
so long as they have high Executive approval, even assassination, which is the *only* activity absolutely "prohibited" by the
Executive Order. As Admiral Turner points out with bizarre
logic, "I am categorically prohibited from doing it (assassinations). If we were in some *extremis* situation where it was justified to take human life for a good cause, like a hijacking, why, at
least we could get the President to make an exception."

The Order does not prohibit intelligence agencies from making
use of reporters, teachers, students, clergy, or any other specific
group of Americans, although it suggests outright manipulation
is bad manners. The Order still permits the channeling of money
to political factions in foreign countries and the use of operatives to try to destabilize foreign governments.

Congressional legislation is expected to add restrictions on the
agencies through the charter which is due to be completed by
mid-1978. Carter's Executive Order, even after a lot of input
from the Senate Select Committee on Intelligence and the new
House Select Committee (whose staff head is a former CIA

officer), does not give Congress veto power over any plans for covert operations, and the agencies are only required to inform the committees "in timely fashion," which Congressional members can just hope means before takeoff, not after a crash landing. Oversight committee members complacently assure us their information about operations and plans of the various agencies in the intelligence community is current and adequate.

One future battle remains around the National Security Agency, which was created by presidential directive and has no legislative sanction whatsoever. A second battle looming is that the American public still has no budget or employment figures for the vast intelligence-gathering network of the U.S. government. It is estimated at $7 to $12 billion annually embracing about 200,000 employees with around 40,000 of these forming a core group.

Many Americans still don't realize the sheer size and complexity of the other agencies. For example, the CIA is estimated to spend in excess of $800 million annually, while the intelligence branch of the Treasury Department spends an estimated $926 million annually. The National Security Agency budget is believed to be much more, approximately $1.3 billion a year, and its highly technological spying apparatus on American soil and around the globe still holds the biggest secrets of all. The military branches are by far the largest without even a reliable estimated budget. It is even possible that there are other agencies we don't yet know exist.

The Central Intelligence Agency is but one branch of the U.S. intelligence community, and that community is only one very deeply-rooted tree in the enormous forest constituting the military-industrial establishment, that continuously rips away large chunks of the government budget from the social areas desperately requiring attention, including public health, welfare, unemployment, housing and education.

As Congressman Otis Pike pointed out, it's not worth it; "we're talking about a tired middle-aged bureaucracy and we should be rubbing their noses in the billions they have spent to make bad calls on major events." In addition to these billions of dollars is the cost in human lives, not only as the direct result of thousands of CIA covert actions, but as a result of the monstrosities the CIA left behind. Over one hundred foreign intelligence agencies, a vast majority of which the CIA created and/or nurtured, are gears in political machines the United States has propped up for its own economic needs. The CIA has had to initiate new operations and projects just to monitor its own left-overs, like Iran's SAVAK, the Korean CIA and the Cuban exile groups. American-made equipment has been used for many years by officers trained in the U.S. by U.S. agencies in U.S.-created torture techniques. When Turner said the work of the CIA "will be legal and consistent with American values," to which and to whose values does he refer? Does our intelligence community represent American values? Does it function in the interests of the American people?

Carter, Turner, and the Trilateral Commission indeed represent a system of values—but they are the values of corporate capitalism and a warmed-over Western hegemonism. The influence of the multinationals is primary, and the political leaders have discovered that the CIA and other intelligence forces have been years ahead of them in recognizing the preference for co-operation over competition among the industrialized non-socialist nations. We have already seen the new Trilateral cooperation in action when France intervened in the fight for the Western Sahara and helped put down the uprising in Shaba province in Zaire. We've seen cooperative action in southern Africa between Britain, Germany and Israel. But the sharing strategy is not always popular, or economical. Cooperation has been a struggle for the U.S. government which had to be pressured to purchase European military equipment as well as sell its own new lines, while the conflict over trade balances has been sharpest between the U.S. and Japan.

Another obvious example is the deportation campaign against Philip Agee. Despite protestations to the contrary by the nations involved—the United Kingdom, France, West Germany, and the Netherlands, as well as the United States—no one seriously believes that U.S. prompting was not behind the moves.

The chief surprise to date of the Carter policy is its emphasis on human rights. This messianic component has never been so purely stated since Woodrow Wilson's time. Human rights, said Mr. Carter in early 1977, would be the "backbone of our foreign policy." Restoring America's role as a "light unto nations," Carter hopes to achieve— in political terms—a Second Coming. Although U.S. military and/or economic aid was cut to Argentina and Uruguay because of human rights abuses in those nations, the same moral criterion was selectively used or simply not applicable to "strategically-placed allies" like South Korea,

Indonesia, the Philippines, Iran, Brazil, and other nations that consistently violate human rights. These same locales, where the CIA has bred its own Frankenstein police and security services, still maintain close working relationships with the CIA.

NATO is obviously a top priority for the Trilateral thinkers on the Carter team. Commander of NATO General Alexander Haig said in an interview in early January 1978, "NATO is increasingly affected by threats outside the alliance's boundaries . . . the West has to take a collective political decision." The growth of "Eurocommunism," as in Italy, France, and Spain, and to some extent Greece and Turkey, could not be ignored by the administration. Asked if covert action was ruled out in Italy, Zbigniew Brzezinski has said, "I'm not going to make any blanket promises as to what we might or might not do." And Carter himself antagonized millions of Europeans by overtly threatening the French and Italian Socialists over possible ties with the Communists.

Haig also defended the neutron bomb as "a logical modernization step in terms of military needs," despite the fact that several nations in NATO oppose the weapon. Haig added that NATO forces "must be armed with regional military capabilities which could be employed as deterrent forces to prevent the escalation of Third World dynamics into major conflicts." Indeed, those "Third World dynamics" are another priority. Despite the CIA's "victories" for U.S. policy in Guatemala, Guyana, Zaire, Indonesia, Iran, Uruguay and Chile (among others), U.S. policy makers are faced with an ever-expanding list of CIA "losses" including Cuba, Angola, Guinea-Bissau, Mozambique, Vietnam, Cambodia, Laos and Jamaica. If liberation movements continue to challenge the decaying leaderships that are backed up by the Western world, the administration will need more popular support for some sort of intervention, be it small covert operations teams or economic pressure. Thus the re-creation of the emotive and bogus external threat wrapped in the Soviet or Cuban flag or fear of terrorism.

U.S. leaders seem to have finally agreed that the heavy-handed direct military intervention of the Sixties did not contribute to America's world image and only injured the U.S. corporate world strategy, as did certain zealous CIA actions. Now they'll follow the lead of the multinational perspective. However bruised, the American corporate empire must try to keep itself afloat and it clearly cannot choose to become progressively isolated from world affairs. Its needs will always require covert action and intervention in the internal affairs of other nations. To this the people of the United States must continue to shout no. Attempts to convince the public that these intelligence activities are no longer needed or used on anything but a minimal scale cannot be accepted as sincere. Rest assured that deep in its heart, the born-again CIA still lusts after power and influence.

APPENDIX

I. The Official Biographies

by Louis Wolf

A. Introduction

The biographies that follow show the official career histories of several hundred Americans, many of whom were recently identified in the European press or *CounterSpy* magazine as employees posted abroad by the Central Intelligence Agency and the National Security Agency. We have compiled the biographies from official publications of the U.S. Department of State, including the last 30 years' editions of the *Biographic Register* and the *Foreign Service List,* as well as from the official lists of the Diplomatic Corps published by the various host governments. We have also made use of other, less public information from within several American embassies, and other sources as noted on the individual biographies.

All of those named here have been found working in American embassies, consulates and missions, either as diplomats under cover of the Department of State, or under cover as civilian employees of the Departments of Defense, Army, Navy or Air Force. In the case of State Department cover, the identifications

have been made by using the general method described by John
Marks in "How to Spot a Spook" (see page 29); by Philip Agee
in "Exposing the CIA" (see page 40); and in other similar articles. In the case of Defense Department or other military cover,
the identifications have come largely from the less-accessible
U.S. government sources.

Readers should remember that the diplomatic ranks, foreign
service ratings, and job descriptions all come from official
sources and are in many cases nothing but convenient fictions.

In every instance, we have checked and double-checked the
available information, and have eliminated any doubtful entries.
In several cases the original identification is derivative, since the
person was exposed in a publication either reprinted or referenced in this book. But all of these people as well have been
double-checked against the appropriate governmental publications and sources, and a few have been eliminated from these
biographies because of incomplete confirmation.

It should be noted that in a publication of this magnitude,
despite all precautions and the elimination of doubtful entries,
an error or two is possible. All of the factual biographic data
have been taken from official sources, and are presumed accurate, although inaccuracies in publications such as the *Biographic
Register* or *Foreign Service List* are not inconceivable. Still it is
possible, although the editors are unaware of any such instance,
that a person whose biography clearly indicates intelligence connections, and who fits the confirmed patterns, might because of
some peculiar circumstances not be directly involved in intelligence. Nevertheless we do not believe that to be the case with
any of the entries retained for publication.

It should also be remembered, as the biographies demonstrate, that many of the people listed here were not continuously
engaged in intelligence work. Some have gone back and forth
from other activities to intelligence work; some are clearly no
longer in the field; some are retired; some are deceased. When
reviewing a biographical entry, the methodology described in
the first section of this book must be kept in mind. That process,
and the notes which follow this introduction to the biographies,
will clarify when and where each person was in the intelligence
field.

The value of this list will vary from user to user, and the
editors hope that researchers may find many helpful applications
of the information. As these people move from post to post,
their past connections and activities will be known. In addition,

the historical applications of this information can be extremely helpful to everyone interested in the political struggles which involve and have involved American intervention. By relating the dates and locations of assignments to political events in the countries involved and the years in question, important interrelations can be discovered.

The remainder of this section explains how to read and use the biographies.

B. How to read the official biographies

NAME

> The biographies appear in alphabetical order according to surname, which is given first.
>
> > Garbler, Paul
> >
> > or
> >
> > Walsh, George T.

ADDRESS

> Where available, we have given the latest known home address and telephone number. In many cases these are out-of-date, but we have included them because newly-arriving CIA people often move into houses vacated by their departing colleagues.
>
> > as of 5/75:
> > 44 Elfviksvagen
> > 181 90 Lidingo
> > Sweden
> > 765-4510
>
> Note that "as of" signifies the *last* date for which we can confirm the validity of the address and telephone even when official sources confirm the person was in the country beyond that date.

DATE & PLACE OF BIRTH

> The first entry under the name and address contains information on the date of birth and the American state or foreign country in which the person was born. If neither is available, we have put "not known."
>
> > b. 1 January 1925
> >
> > or
> >
> > b. not known

CHRONOLOGY
> Each entry is preceded by the year, the years, or the month and year. Note that the dates sometimes overlap.
>> 1957-59
>> 1958
>> 4/59
>
> In some cases, we have not been able to find the exact date on which a certain posting begins and have given the date as of the *first source* in which the posting is mentioned.
>> as of 10/65

UNIVERSITY EDUCATION
> Most of those named have completed their bachelors or masters degree (BA, BS, BFS, MA, MS) or even a doctorate (PhD) before joining government service. But many of them continue their education while in government, in which case the dates will overlap.
>> 1946-49   Department of the Army
>>   political affairs analyst
>> 1947   Harvard University BA
>
> A few appear to have attended universities, often outside the United States, without getting a degree. In some of these cases, the person might have been posing as a student or instructor while carrying out some other task.

MILITARY SERVICE
> Many of the people included will have served in the armed forces before taking a civilian post in the government. In most cases, this military service will be quite separate from later work in intelligence. But in the case of many of the CIA old-timers, military service during World War II was often actually a cover for work in the Office of Strategic Services, the predecessor of the CIA.
>> 1941-44   U.S. Army overseas 1st Lieutenant
>
> In at least one case—that of Paul Garbler—we see a CIA man reassigned to military service so that he can take up the post of military attache, and then after three years unaccounted for in official sources, going back under diplomatic cover as a high-ranking political officer.
>> Assistant Naval Attache
>> Assistant Naval Attache for Air

as of 10/65-7/68	not listed in Department of State records; assignment not known
8/68	Department of State Port-of-Spain, Trinidad & Tobago (E) political officer

PRIVATE EXPERIENCE

Many of the people listed will have worked at non-governmental jobs prior to joining government service. If, however, the private experience comes after assignment to some government department, it is probably cover for intelligence activity, often as part of a CIA proprietary corporation or front organization. The best example is from the career of George T. Walsh:

1950-51	Department of Defense research analyst
1951-52	private experience unspecified cultural foundation public relations manager
1953-54	unspecified airlines public relations adviser
1954-55	George Washington University Law School
1955-57	private experience unspecified motion picture company foreign representative
1957-58	unspecified travel publications company
11/58	Department of State Colombo, Ceylon (E) Attache & political officer

DEPARTMENT OF DEFENSE

DEPARTMENT OF THE ARMY

DEPARTMENT OF THE NAVY

DEPARTMENT OF THE AIR FORCE

These are civilian departments of the government, as

distinct from the actual military services, and they are often used to give cover to CIA personnel, generally under vague job descriptions, such as "analyst" or "foreign affairs officer." We have indented the job descriptions, which sometimes change during the course of time.

1957-59   Department of the Air Force
                analyst
1959-61   plans officer

DEPARTMENT OF COMMERCE

DEPARTMENT OF THE TREASURY

DEPARTMENT OF HEALTH, EDUCATION AND WELFARE

These are also civilian departments of the government, and it is known that in some cases they are also used to give cover to CIA personnel.

Department of Commerce
industrial specialist

DEPARTMENT OF STATE

Most of the people listed in this book have at one time in their careers served under cover of the Department of State, either assigned to Washington ("Dept.") or to some overseas post.

4/67   Department of State
        Dept.
7/67   Paris, France (E)
        political officer

We have tried to give the overseas posting according to the names that the U.S. Government used at the time (e.g. Congo or Zaire, Leopoldville or Kinshasa, Egypt or U.A.R.). We have also given the diplomatic status of each post at the time. For example:

(E) = Embassy
(CG) = Consulate General
(C) = Consulate
(M) = Mission

Under each posting, we have tried to give both the diplomatic grade and the official job description, where available.

> London, U.K. (E)
>> First Secretary &
>> political officer

The diplomatic grades are normally capitalized and include:

>> Attache, Assistant Attache
>> First, Second & Third Secretary
>> Consul, Vice-Consul

The official job descriptions, or functional listings, include:

>> Special Assistant to the Ambassador
>> political officer
>> economic-commercial officer
>> economic officer
>> consular officer
>> visa officer
>> telecoms officer

In some cases, we have included the official name of the office in which the person worked. Such names are part of the CIA's cover arrangement with the Department of State.

>> Political Liaison Office
>> Office of the Special Assistant
>> Regional Reports Office
>> etc.

FOREIGN SERVICE RATINGS

In the column closest to the right-hand margin, we have given the person's official foreign service rating each time that a change in the rating takes place. The foreign service ratings of CIA personnel, though, are just cover ratings, as they all carry GS ratings, usually higher than their cover rating. The rating begins with a letter. These include:

>> O = Foreign Service Officer
>> R = Foreign Service Reserve Officer
>> RU = Foreign Service Reserve Officer Unlimited
>> S = Foreign Service Staff Officer
>> iO = Foreign Service Information Officer

CIA officers have not carried the "O" rating, at least not until the present, although the regulations might change.

This is because, as John Marks writes, the State Department has always insisted "that the corps of Foreign Service Officers (FSOs) remain pure." But please note, not all of those with "R" or "S" ratings are CIA. Also note that in a few cases a person might resign from the State Department, and an "O" rating, and join the CIA.

9/56	Department of State	
	Dept.	
9/57	resigns as foreign service officer	
10/57	Department of State	
	Rome, Italy (E)	
	political officer	R-4

The number following the "O" or "R" or "S" gives the grade. The highest "R" grade is "1" and the lowest "8" or, at an earlier period, "11." The lowest "S" grade is "10" or, at an earlier period, "22." Note that in 1956 the Foreign Service ratings scheme was amended, creating eight numbered ranks instead of 6. This caused many rating levels to become one number higher, though the job and salary remained the same.

In many of the biographies in this book, it is apparent that a person's given rating changed from R to S or vice versa, and sometimes back again, after a lapse of about ten years. In order to maintain the means of cover for its people who have been integrated into the foreign service, the CIA has had to adhere to Department of State personnel regulations that specify an R or an S rating may not be held for over ten years at a time.

GOVERNMENT SERVICE RATINGS

At various points in his or her career, a person might change from a foreign service rating to a government service rating, or "GS." Here, the higher the number, the higher the grade, starting at "1" with the highest being "18."

OTHER RATINGS

Some of those named also have carried other ratings, especially in the late 1940's, when the rating scheme was much more complex.

AGENCY FOR INTERNATIONAL DEVELOPMENT (AID)

This is the American foreign aid program, which generally works under the control of the Department of State, but with its own career patterns. In earlier incarnations, it has been called the International Cooperation Administration, the Mutual Security Administration, and the Economic Cooperation Administration, and also included the Development Loan Fund.

Department of State	
London, U.K. (E)	
economic officer	R-5
Agency for International Development	
Caracas, Venezuela (E)	
program officer	R-4
Agency	R-3

"Agency" means assignment to AID headquarters in Washington.

Where available, we have included the name of the person's husband or wife, as of the most recent available official source, to aid in further identification. We have tried to give the wife's maiden name.

In this connection, it must be said that wives (and husbands) nearly always know what agency is employing their spouse. Normally, they have an active role to play in maintaining cover, even on occasion taking part in specific operational activities. Thus, the spouse of a CIA officer is not "just a wife (or husband)."

LANGUAGE

We have listed any foreign language competencies given in the official biographies. But the official information appears to be incomplete, and it is known that several of the people speak a second and even a third language fluently, even where the information is missing from the official biographies.

SOURCES

We have given the official sources from which we have taken the information. In most cases, we have consulted many more volumes of a given publication than we have listed here. But in all cases, those we have listed should be sufficient to confirm the accuracy of each entry. Generally, the most recent confirmatory source is given first, followed by other, earlier sources which indicate changes in posting or additional information.

BR 1974

FSL 6/73, 2/71, 1/62

Stockholm Diplomatic List 5/75

Stockholm Embassy Sources

The "BR," or *Biographic Register,* is published by the Department of State, and appeared almost yearly from 1870 through 1974, when publication in a readily available form was stopped in an attempt to curtail further exposures. The "FSL," or *Foreign Service List,* is also published by the Department of State, and has appeared regularly 2-4 times a year through August 1975, after which it was terminated for the same reason. The *Diplomatic Lists* are published by the foreign ministries of each country and appear at varying intervals. In some cases, we have been able to update a particular issue by telephoning the ministry in question. "Embassy Sources" refer to periodic publications from the relevant embassy or to oral information from embassy personnel.

In those instances where a person whose biography appears in this book has not previously been identified publicly, the reader will note that the person is now serving or has recently served in a country in Western Europe.

C. List of abbreviations and special terms

AA	Associate of Arts degree
(AF)	State Department Bureau of African Affairs
Agency	Assigned to Agency for International Development, Washington, D.C.
(ARA-LA)	State Department Bureau of Inter-American Affairs, Bureau for Latin America
A/OC	Office of the Deputy Assistant Secretary for Communications, State Department Bureau of Administration
Apt.	Apartment
b.	born

BA	Bachelor of Arts degree
BBA	Bachelor of Business Administration degree
BE	Bachelor of Education degree
BEc	Bachelor of Economics degree
BFS	Bachelor of Arts in Foreign Service degree
bldg.	building
BR	*Biographic Register* (followed by date of publication)
BS	Bachelor of Science degree
BSEE	Bachelor of Science in Electrical Engineering degree
BSF	Bachelor of Science in Forestry degree
BSFS	Bachelor of Science in Foreign Service degree
(C)	Consulate
(CG)	Consulate General
cR	Foreign Service Career Reserve Officer
Dept.	Assigned to the Department of State, Washington, D.C.
(E)	Embassy
(EA)	State Department Bureau of East Asian & Pacific Affairs
(EUR)	State Department Bureau of European Affairs
FSL	*Foreign Service List* (followed by date of publication)
FSO	Foreign Service Officer
FSR	Foreign Service Reserve Officer
FSS	Foreign Service Staff Officer
GS	Government Service Officer
HICOG	Office of United States High Commissioner for Germany
HICOM	High Commissioner for Germany
iO	Foreign Service Information Officer (United States Information Agency)
IO	State Department Bureau of International Organizations
(INR)	State Department Bureau of Intelligence and Research
Jr.	junior
JUSMAGG	Joint United States Military Assistance Group for Greece.

(L)	Legation
LLB	Bachelor of Laws degree
LLM	Master of Laws degree
(M)	Mission
MA	Master of Arts degree
MIA	Master of International Affairs degree
MPA	Master of Public Administration degree
MS	Master of Science degree
MSEE	Master of Science in Electrical Engineering degree
NATO	North Atlantic Treaty Organization
(NEA)	State Department Bureau of Near Eastern & South Asian Affairs
not known	unknown, information not available
O	Foreign Service Officer
(O)	Deputy Assistant Secretary for Operations, State Department Bureau of Administration
OCA	Office of Coordinator and Advisor—Germany
(Off)	Office
OMGUS	Office of Military Government United States in Germany
(O/OC)	State Department Office of Communications
O/MA	State Department of Management
OSD/ISA	Office of Secretary of Defense/International Security Affairs—Germany
PhB	Bachelor of Philosophy degree
PhD	Doctor of Philosophy degree
R	Foreign Service Reserve Officer
RL	Foreign Service Reserve Officer Limited
RU	Foreign Service Reserve Officer Unlimited
S	Foreign Service Staff Officer
SPA	Office of the Special Assistant—Switzerland
SUSLO	Office of the Special United States Liaison Officer (National Security Agency)—United Kingdom

telecoms	telecommunications
U.K.	United Kingdom
UNESCO	United States Mission to the United Nations Economic, Social & Cultural Organization
U.S.	United States
USAREUR	United States Army Europe—Germany
USAFE	United States Air Force Europe
USASEPU	United States Army Southern European Projects Unit—Italy
USCOA	Office of the Chief of Mission and U.S. High Commissioner—Austria
U.S.S.R.	Union of Soviet Socialist Republics
USUN	United States Mission to the United Nations

D. Career Samples

We have reprinted on the following pages four entries from the Official Biographies, with each entry annotated, to give some idea how a biography, particularly a lengthy one, can be studied.

① Latest known address and telephone.

② Date and place of birth.

③ Received undergraduate degree

④ Private employment experience.

⑤ Actual military service—it is believed however that he was a member of the wartime Office of Strategic Services (predecessor of the CIA), and that at some point during the post war period he joined the CIA while remaining under military cover until age 38.

⑥ Left his military cover and comes under Department of State cover for his first posting, probably as Chief of Station.

⑦ This reasonably high Foreign Service Reserve Officer rating was assigned him upon entry because of his long military service.

⑧ Change in diplomatic rank.

⑨ Returned to Washington, in all likelihood to CIA Headquarters in Langley, Virginia for training.

⑩ Promotion in Foreign Service Reserve Officer rating level.

⑪ Reassigned to military cover as a naval attache, this time also with a promotion in military rank.

⑫ Whereabouts not ascertainable—was likely undergoing advanced training at CIA Headquarters.

⑬ Reassigned to State Department cover for a second posting with a very high Foreign Service Reserve Officer rating.

⑭ Returned to Washington or Langley.

⑮ Posted once more to Sweden under diplomatic cover, this time definitely as Chief of Station.

GARBLER, PAUL

①   as of 5/76:
44 Elfviksvägen
181 90 Lidingö
Sweden
765-45-10

②   b. 4 January 1918   New Jersey

③   1939   University of Florida BA

④   1939-41   private experience
          food equipment company
          sales engineer

⑤   1941-56   U.S. Navy overseas Lieutenant Commander

⑥   4/56   Department of State
          Stockholm, Sweden (E)
          Attache   ⑦   R-4

⑧   6/56   Second Secretary

       9/59   Dept.

⑨   3/60   ⑩   R-3

       8/61   U.S. Navy commander
          Moscow, U.S.S.R. (E)
          Assistant Naval Attache
          Assistant Naval Attache for Air

⑫ as of 10/65-7/68   not listed in Department of State records;
          assignment not known

⑬   8/68   Department of State
          Port-of-Spain, Trinidad & Tobago (E)
          political officer   R-2

⑭   11/72   Dept. (ARA-LA)

⑮   as of 11/73-   Stockholm, Sweden (E)
    at least 5/76   Attache
          (CIA Chief of Station)

     Wife: Florence Fitzsimmons

     Sources: BR 1973, 1960
          FSL 6/73, 2/73, 9/68, 6/65, 1/62,
            10/59, 7/56

① Latest known address and phone.

② Date and place of birth.

③ Military Service.

④ Attended college; apparently transferred directly to the University of Maryland.

⑤ Joined the CIA as a communications specialist.

⑥ Attended university (not known whether as a student or instructor or whether any degree was awarded), probably for additional academic training.

⑦ Attended university (not known whether as a student or instructor or whether any degree was awarded), probably for training about the country of his upcoming assignment.

⑧ First posting under Department of State cover—age 31.

⑨ Even though he was already employed for 6 years by the CIA, he was given quite a low Foreign Service Staff Officer rating level.

⑩ Returned to CIA Headquarters, probably for further training in the communications field.

⑪ Second posting under Department of State cover.

⑫ This time, he gets a healthy jump in Foreign Service Staff Officer rating level.

⑬ Returns to Washington or Langley for training or Headquarters duty.

⑭ Whereabouts not ascertainable; may have been posted to other countries under Department of State or military cover, or may have continued training or duty at CIA Headquarters.

⑮ Third posting under Department of State cover.

⑯ Switched from ''S'' to ''R'' rating.

McGEE, JOSEPH V.

①   as of 3/76:
20-A Clareville Street
London SW 7
U.K.
373-1883

②   b.   10 January 1928   New York

③   1946-53   U.S. Air Force overseas

④   1952-53   Hofstra College

⑤   1953-59   Department of the Army
     communications specialist

⑥   1954-56   University of Maryland

⑦   1956-58   George Washington University

⑧   11/59   Department of State
     Nicosia, Cyprus (E)
     communications specialist   ⑨   S-8

⑩   12/60-7/63   Department of the Army
     communications specialist

⑪   8/63   Department of State
     Accra, Ghana (E)
     communications specialist   ⑫   S-4

⑬   11/65   Dept.

     as of 1/67   (O/OC)

⑭   as of 5/68-4/74   not listed in Department of State records;
assignment not known

⑮   5/74   Department of State
     London, U.K. (E)
     telecoms officer   ⑯   R-4

     as of 12/76   Dept. (A/OC)

     Sources: BR 1974, 1967
FSL 8/75, 6/74, 1/68, 1/67, 10/60, 1/60
London Embassy Sources
Department of State Source

① Latest known address and telephone.

② Date and place of birth.

③ Attended university; not known whether any degree was awarded.

④ Period during which whereabouts are not ascertainable.

⑤ Military service.

⑥ Private employment experience.

⑦ Joined the CIA at age 31, upon or near the time of its official creation by Congress. This is a common military cover for case officers.

⑧ First posting under Department of State cover with International Cooperation Administration/ Agency for International Development.

⑨ The Foreign Service Reserve Officer rating given to him on entry to diplomatic cover. It is rather low for someone 41 years old who has already been in the CIA for 12 years, but his actual Civil Service rating (and therefore, salary) was undoubtedly higher.

⑩ Change in job title indicating a slight promotion.

⑪ Second posting under cover with AID.

⑫ Promotion in Foreign Service Reserve Officer rating level.

⑬ Third posting, this time under Direct Department of State cover, with promotion in Foreign Service Staff Officer rating level. "Political officer" is also a typical cover title.

⑭ The shift from "R" (Reserve) to "S" (Staff) is common in the careers of CIA personnel operating under diplomatic cover.

⑮ Promotion in Foreign Service Staff Officer rating level.

⑯ Fourth posting, under Department of State cover, as a consular officer.

⑰ Fifth posting, again under Department of State cover, once again as a consular officer.

⑱ Returned to Washington or to Langley, possibly for Headquarters duty or another posting overseas.

SEVIER, LEWIS V.

①   as of 12/74:
    22 Rue Marbeau
    75016 Paris
    France
    553-5406

②   b.   14 March 1918   Colorado

③   1937-39   l'Ecole Libre des Sciences Politiques

④   1940-41   not given in Department of State records;
                        not known

⑤   1942-45   U.S. Army overseas 1st Lieutenant

⑥   1945-47   private experience
                        manufacturing company salesman

⑦   1947-59   Department of the Army
                        program analysis officer

⑧   ***10/59   Agency for International Development
                        Cairo, U.A.R. (E)
                        assistant program officer   ⑨   R-5

⑩   3/60   operations officer

⑪   8/60   Karachi, Pakistan (E)
                        program analyst

⑬   4/64   ⑫   R-4

        6/66   Department of State
                        Beirut, Lebanon (E)
                        political officer   ⑭   S-2

⑮   2/69   S-1

⑯   7/72   Marseille, France (CG)
                        consular officer

⑰   8/73   Paris, France (E)
                        consular officer

⑱   as of 8/77   Dept. (EUR)

    Wife: Doris Wrigley

    Sources: BR 1974, 1963
                  FSL 8/75, 10/73, 10/72, 1/67, 1/61, 1/60
                  Paris Embassy Source
                  Department of State Sources

***Appointment began under AID's predecessor agency until 1961, the International Cooperation Administration.

① Latest known address and telephone.

② Date and place of birth.

③ Military service.

④ Attended university, apparently dropped out after two years or else transferred directly to George Washington University.

⑤ Joined one of the agencies which existed between the dissolution of the Office of Strategic Services in 1945 and the establishment of the CIA in 1947—either the Strategic Services Unit or the Central Intelligence Group.

⑥ Awarded his undergraduate degree.

⑦ Attended law school; not ascertainable whether or not for a degree.

⑧ Joined the CIA—age 26.

⑨ First posting under Department of State diplomatic cover.

⑩ Foreign Service Staff Officer rating level upon integration into the Foreign Service.

⑪ Promotion in Foreign Service Staff Officer rating level.

⑫ Reassigned to CIA Headquarters, probably for additional training.

⑬ Second posting under Department of State diplomatic cover.

⑭ Switch "S" to "R" rating—R-5 being equivalent to S-3.

⑮ Provided with diplomatic cover title in addition to his official job title.

⑯ Promotion in Foreign Service Reserve Officer rating level.

⑰ Reassigned to Washington, probably for duty at CIA Headquarters.

⑱ Third posting under Department of State diplomatic cover.

⑲ Provided with diplomatic cover title of Consul in addition to his official job title.

⑳ Fourth posting under Department of State diplomatic cover.

㉑ Promotion in Foreign Service Officer rating to a senior level.

㉒ Whereabouts not ascertainable; may have been posted to some other country under Department of State or military cover, or else may have continued duty at CIA Headquarters.

㉓ Fifth posting under Department of State Diplomatic cover.

McGHEE, WILLIAM MORROW

①	as of 9/77: 11 Chester Square London SW 1 U.K. 730-5641				
②	b. 8 July 1922	South Carolina			
③	1942-46	U.S. Army overseas			
④	1943-44	University of California			
⑤	1946	Department of the Army area specialist			
⑥	1947	George Washington University BA			
⑦	1947-48	George Washington University Law School			
⑧	1948-53	Department of the Army assistant to the chief			
⑨	1/53	Department of State Manila, Philippines (E) Attache & political officer	⑩	S-5
⑪	1/55			S-4
⑫	3/55-4/58	Department of the Army foreign affairs officer		
⑬	5/58	Department of State Addis Ababa, Ethiopia (E) economic officer	⑭	R-5
⑮	8/58	Second Secretary & economic officer		
⑯	2/61			R-4
⑰	12/61	Dept.		
⑱	8/65	Hong Kong, U.K. (CG) political officer		
⑲	10/65	Consul & political officer		
⑳	5/68	Singapore, Singapore (E) political officer		
㉑	4/70			R-3
㉒	as of 10/71	Dept. (NEA)		
㉓	as of 2/72-11/74	not listed in Department of State records; assignment not known		
㉔	as of 12/74- at least 6/78	Department of State London, U.K. (E) Attache & political liaison officer		

Wife:	Nancy Mersh
Sources:	BR 1971, 1966, 1953 FSL 10/71, 9/68, 7/62, 7/58, 4/55, 4/53 Singapore Diplomatic and Consular List 1/71 London Diplomatic Lists 6/78, 8/76, 12/74 London Embassy Sources

II. Who's Who

ACON, WILLIAM J.

as of 8/73:
5 Piazza Stefano Jacini
Bldg. A
Rome
Italy
327-3894

b. 6 April 1921	Netherlands	
1939-40	private experience foreign bank clerk	
1940-41	jewelry company	
1943	naturalized as U.S. citizen	
1943-45	U.S. Army overseas 2nd Lieutenant	

1945-46	Department of the Army
	   Office of the Military Government
	   United States (in Germany) (OMGUS)
	     investigator	

1946-47	researcher	
1947-48	research assistant	
1947-48	Georgetown University School of Foreign Service	

1950-52	Mutual Security Agency
	   Agency
	     international economist
		GS-5

1951	University of Chicago BA, MA	

12/52	Department of State
	   Rome, Italy (E)
	     Assistant Attache &
	     labor officer
		S-8

1/55		S-7
7/57		S-6
9/58	Dept. (EUR)	
6/59		R-6

2/61	Paris, France (E)
	   Attache &
	   political officer	

9/62	Dept.	
4/64		R-5
9/64· at least 3/78 4/65	Rome, Italy (E) Attache & political officer	R-4
Wife:	Rosetta Villareale-Graziano	

Sources: BR 1973, 1963, 1953
                                FSL 6/73, 1/65, 10/58, 4/53
                                Rome Diplomatic Lists 3/78, 7/73
                                Rome Embassy Source

AFRICH, ROSE F.

   as of 9/74:
   2 Via Filippo Civinini
   Apt. 5
   Rome
   Italy
   87-85-55

   b.   not known

      as of 9/74   Department of State
                                   Rome, Italy (E)
                                      political section

      Source: Rome Embassy Source

ALBRIGHT, JOY

   as of 2/76:
   Kolumbusring 7/6
   5300 Bonn-Bad Godesberg
   Germany
   37-58-70

   b.   not known

      as of 2/75 -   Department of State
      at least 2/76   Bonn, Germany (E)
                                      Office of the Coordinator and Advisor

      Source: Bonn Embassy Source

ALDRIDGE, MILTON

   as of 1/74:
   25 Areos Street
   Kifissia
   Athens
   Greece
   801-6843

   b.   17 July 1938

         5/72   Department of State
                                   Athens, Greece (E)
                                      telecoms engineer   R-5
                                      (Regional Relay Facility)

      as of 11/74-4/78   not listed in Department of State records;
                                assignment not known

      as of 5/78   Department of State
                                   Athens, Greece (E)
                                      probably telecoms

Wife:	Louise
Sources:	BR 1974
	FSL 6/74, 6/72
	Athens Embassy Source
	Department of State Sources

ALHIMOOK, DANIEL

b. 15 October 1926	Maryland	
1943-44	private experience	
	aircraft company clerk	
1944-46	U.S. Marine Corps overseas	
1950	Johns Hopkins University BA	
1950-61	Department of the Army	
	analyst, translator	
4/61	Department of State	
	The Hague, Netherlands (E)	
	Attache &	
	political officer	R-6
4/64		R-5
6/64	Tokyo, Japan (E)	
	Attache &	
	economic officer	
8/64	Second Secretary &	
	economic officer	
11/66	Dept. (EA)	
4/67		R-4
6/70	Milan, Italy (CG)	
	Consul &	
	economic-commercial officer	
8/73		S-2
as of 11/74	Dept. (EUR)	
Wife:	Irene Zawadski	
Sources:	BR 1974	
	FSL 11/74, 10/70, 1/67, 7/64, 7/61	
	Milan Consular List 3/74	
	Department of State Source	

ALLEN, THOMAS M.

as of 1/74:
24 Proteos Street
New Kifissia
Athens, Greece
802-8054

b.   not known

8/72-	Department of State	
at least 8/75	Athens, Greece (E)	
	telecoms assistant	S-9
	(Area Telecommunications Office)	
as of 10/73		S-8
as of 11/74	telecoms support officer	
as of 11/75	Dept. (A/OC)	
Sources:	FSL 8/75, 6/74, 10/73, 6/73	
	Athens Embassy Source	
	Department of State Source	

ALLNER, FREDERICK A. Jr.

as of 1/78:
28, Pourtalesstrasse
3074 Muri
Bern
Switzerland
52-35-49

b. 27 November 1924	Maryland	
1943-46	U.S. Navy overseas Ensign	
1948	Princeton University BA	
7/49	Department of State	
	Tihwa, Sinkiang, China (C)	
	clerk	S-12
2/50	resigned from Department of State	
5/50	Department of State	
	Jakarta, Indonesia (E)	
	Vice-Consul	S-11
as of 10/51-5/54	not listed in Department of State records;	
	assignment not known	
6/54	Department of State	
	Jakarta, Indonesia (E)	
	Assistant Attache &	
	political officer	S-9
***5/56	Surabaya, Indonesia (C)	
	Vice-Consul	
7/56	Dept.	
8/56		S-8
7/57		S-7
7/59		R-6
5/60	Vienna, Austria (E)	
	political officer	
4/62		R-5

4/64		R-4
10/64	Attache & political officer	
9/65	Bonn, Germany (E) Attache & political officer	
4/67		R-3
as of 1/69	Dept. (0)	
as of 5/69	(EUR)	
as of 1/70-7/75	not listed in Department of State records; assignment not known	
8/75- at least 1/78	Department of State Bern, Switzerland (E) Attache	
Sources:	BR 1969, 1966, 1955 FSL 9/69, 1/69, 1/67, 7/60, 10/56, 7/56, 10/54, 7/51, 7/50 Bern Diplomatic Lists 1/78, 7/76 (updated)	

***Also assigned to the then-Portuguese Colony of Timor

ALMY, DEAN J.

as of 11/75:
Av. Generalisimo
núm. 35
Madrid
Spain
455-60-18

b. 18 December 1926	New Jersey	
1943-46	U.S. Marine Corps overseas	
1951	George Washington University BA	
1951-55	Department of the Army political analyst	
1954	Yale University	
1954-55	Cornell University	
1/56	Department of State Medan, Indonesia (C) political officer	R-6
3/56	Vice-Consul	
7/56		R-7
6/58	Dept.	
3/59-4/60	Department of the Army foreign affairs officer	

5/60	Department of State Kuala Lumpur, Malaysia (E) political officer	R-6
8/60	Vice-Consul & political officer	
10/62	Manila, Philippines (E) Attache & political officer	
3/63		R-5
9/63	Second Secretary & political officer	
8/65	Dept. (EA)	
5/66		R-4
3/67	foreign affairs officer	GS-14
as of 9/67-8/73	not listed in Department of State records; assignment not known	
9/73- at least 5/77	Department of State Madrid, Spain (E) Attache & political liaison officer	
Wife:	Barbara A.	
Sources:	BR 1967, 1957 FSL 5/67, 7/60, 10/58, 4/56 Madrid Diplomatic Lists 5/77, 11/75, 5/74 Madrid Embassy Source	

ALTMAN, DAVID R.

    b. not known

5/74- at least 8/75	Department of State Stockholm, Sweden (E) telecoms support officer	S-6
Sources:	FSL 8/75, 6/74	

AMES, ROBERT C.

    as of 1/75:
    19, Bneid Al-Gar
    Kuwait
    Kuwait
    42-22-34

    b. 6 March 1934

6/62	Department of State Dhahran, Saudi Arabia (CG) economic assistant	S-6
8/65	Beirut, Lebanon (E) cover position not known	

5/67	Agency for International Development Taiz, Yemen (Office) assistant program officer	S-5
9/67	Department of State Aden, Southern Yemen (E) economic officer	
2/69	economic-commercial officer	S-4
as of 1/70	Dept. (NEA)	
5/70	Beirut, Lebanon (E) economic-commercial officer	R-6
7/71	Dept. (NEA)	
5/73		R-5
6/73	Tehran, Iran (E) cover position not known	
8/73- at least 8/75	Kuwait, Kuwait (E) Second Secretary & political officer	
as of 10/75	Dept. (NEA)	
Wife:	Yvonne Blakely	
Sources:	BR 1974 FSL 8/75, 10/73, 10/71, 1/70, 1/68, 9/67, 1/67, 1/63 Kuwait Diplomatic and Consular List 1/75 Department of State Source	

AMIANO, SUZANNE K.

as of 12/74:
Hotel Plaza Mirabeau
10 Avenue E. Zola
75015 Paris
France
577-7200

b. not known

as of 12/74	Department of State Paris, France (E) Regional Reports Office
Source:	Paris Embassy Source

ANDERSON, GARY I.

b. not known

4/75	Department of State Manila, Philippines (E) telecoms support officer	S-6
as of 11/77	Lisbon, Portugal (E) probably telecoms	

Wife: Barbara

Sources: FSL 8/75
                               Department of State Sources

ANDRESS, ROSEMARIE

as of 6/75:
58 Queen's Gate Terrace
London SW 7
U.K.
584-2495

b.   not known

as of 12/74   Department of State
                                   London, U.K. (E)
                                       Joint Reports & Research Unit

as of 9/75   not listed in Department of State records;
                               assignment not known

Sources: London Embassy Sources

ARNST, WILLIAM F.

as of 2/76:
Steubenring 4/5
5300 Bonn-Bad Godesberg
Germany
37-86-74

b.   not known

as of 2/75-   Department of State
at least 2/76   Bonn, Germany (E)
                                       OCA Research Unit

Wife: Jean

Source: Bonn Embassy Source

ATKINS, EDWIN FRANKLIN

as of 9/74:
113 Via Della Giustiniana
Rome
Italy
699-6107

b.   15 October 1929   New York

     1951   Harvard University BA

     1951-54   Department of Defense
                                   political analyst

     1/55   Department of State
                                   Cairo, Egypt (E)
                                       political officer

7/56		R-7
2/59		R-6
10/59	Dept.	
12/60	Foreign Service Institute Arabic language training	
6/61	Baghdad, Iraq (E) economic officer	
8/61	Second Secretary & economic officer	
4/62		R-5
12/63	Dept.	
1/65		S-3
1/66		S-2
6/68	Khartoum, Sudan (E) political officer	R-4
10/69	Dept. (EUR)	
10/70	Milan, Italy (CG) consular officer	
7/73- at least 8/75	Rome, Italy (E) consular officer	
2/76		R-3

Wife: Elaine Perry

Sources: BR 1974, 1970, 1967
            FSL 8/75, 4/75, 6/74, 2/71, 9/68, 4/64,
               10/61, 4/59, 10/56, 4/55
            Rome Diplomatic List 8/73 (updated)
            Rome Consular Lists 3/75, 3/74
            Rome Embassy Source
            Department of State Source

ATKINS, JOHN W.

b.   not known

3/63	Department of State Warsaw, Poland (E) probably telecoms	rating not known
as of 1/67-7/69	not listed in Department of State records; assignment not known	
8/69	Department of State Manila, Philippines (E) telecoms specialist	S-5
as of 10/70	telecoms officer	
as of 2/72	Dept. (EA)	

4/72	Vienna, Austria (E) telecoms officer
9/74	Quito, Ecuador (E) telecoms officer
as of 5/77	Dept. (A/OC)
Sources:	FSL 8/75, 11/74, 6/72, 9/69, 10/65 Department of State Source

BAFFA, FRANCIS R. JR.

b. not known

6/74	Department of State Athens, Greece (E) telecoms (Area Telecommunications Office) S-7
as of 12/76	Dept. (A/OC)
Source:	FSL 8/75, 11/74 Department of State Source

BAILEY, MALCOLM B.

as of 3/76:
48 Boydell Court
St. John's Wood Park
London NW 8
U.K.
722-5189

b. not known

as of 6/75- at least 3/76	Department of State London, U.K. (E) Joint Reports & Research Unit
Wife:	Bernadette
Source:	London Embassy Sources

BAIRD, DOROTHY H.

as of 12/74:
36 Rue Fondary
75015 Paris
France
734-0488

b. not known

as of 12/74	Department of State Paris, France (E) Office of the Special Assistant
Source:	Paris Embassy Source

BAKER, JESSE L.

> as of 1/74:
> 23 Rodon Street
> New Kifissia
> Athens
> Greece
> 801-3368

b. 30 December 1941	Alabama	
1960-64	U.S. Air Force	
***1966	Ohio Technical College EA	
1967-73	Department of the Air Force electronic technician	
6/73	Department of State Athens, Greece (E) telecoms technician (Area Telecommunications Office)	R-8
as of 11/76	Dept. (A/OC)	
Wife:	Rosalie Wilkerson	
Sources:	BR 1974 FSL 8/75, 10/73 Department of State Sources	

***Bachelor's Degree in Electronic Analysis

BAKER, ROBERT J.

b. 10 November 1931		
6/66	Department of State Athens, Greece (E) telecoms technician	S-6
as of 5/68		S-5
as of 5/69	not listed in Department of Stare records; assignment not known	
7/72	Department of State London, U.K. (E) telecoms technician	R-6
as of 8/75	Dept. (A/OC)	
Wife:	Jo Ann	
Sources:	BR 1974 FSL 8/75, 10/72, 5/68, 1/67 London Embassy Sources Department of State Source	

BAKKE, ALFRED C.

> as of 12/75:
> 116 Weimarer Strasse, Apt. 4

1190 Vienna
Austria
36-56-13

b.   not known

6/68	Department of State Abidjan, Ivory Coast (E) telecoms officer
12/71	Vientiane, Laos (E) telecoms officer
5/74	Vienna, Austria (E) telecoms officer
as of 7/77	Dept. (A/OC)
Wife:	Barbara
Sources:	FSL 8/75, 6/74, 2/72, 1/70 Vienna Embassy Source Department of State Sources

S-6

BAKOS, DENNIS M.

as of 1/74:
47 Arvis Street
Kifissia
Athens
Greece
801-2925

b.   not known

6/72	Department of State Athens, Greece (E) telecoms assistant (Area Telecommunications Office)
as of 11/74	telecoms support officer
as of 10/75	Dept. (A/OC)
Wife:	Dorothy
Sources:	FSL 8/75, 6/74, 6/73 Athens Embassy Source Department of State Source

S-7

BALDWIN, JAMES DONALD

as of 7/74:
13 Karaoli Dimitriou Street
Philothei
Athens
Greece
681-4562

b. 27 August 1929	New Jersey
1951	Amherst College BA

1951-54	U.S. Army overseas
1954-55	private experience unspecified airlines
1955-65	Department of the Army area analyst
1963	Georgetown University MA
8/65	Department of State Dept. Foreign Service Institute Serbo-Croat language-area training R-4
7/66	Belgrade, Yugoslavia (E) economic officer
9/68	Dept. U.S. Mission to the United Nations (USUN) political advisor
9/69	Athens, Greece (E) Second Secretary & political officer
5/72	R-3
as of 7/73	First Secretary & political officer
as of 11/74	Dept. (EUR)
as of 8/75	not listed in Department of State records; assignment not known
Wife:	Diana Ryan
Sources:	BR 1974, 1970, 1966 FSL 4/75, 11/74, 9/69, 1/67, 10/65 Athens Embassy Source Athens Diplomatic Lists 7/74, 1/71

BANE, HOWARD T.

as of 2/76:
38 Hooigracht
The Hague
Netherlands
46-77-80

b. 5 August 1927	Virginia
1944-46	U.S. Navy overseas
1949-50	Department of State Dept. clerk
1950-51	drafting officer
1951	Georgetown University BA
1951-55	Department of the Army research analyst

6/55	Department of State
	Bangkok, Thailand (E)
	    Assistant Attache &
	    political officer R-5

7/56	R-6
1/57	Second Secretary & Vice-Consul
7/58	Dept.

9/59	New Delhi, India (E)
	    Second Secretary &
	    political officer

3/60	R-5
6/62	Dept.

7/64	Accra, Ghana (E)
	    political officer R-4
	    (CIA Chief of Station)

8/67	Dept. (AF)
5/68	R-3
8/69	Nairobi, Kenya (E) political officer

as of 6/74-
at least 2/76
	The Hague, Netherlands (E)
	    Attache
	    (CIA Chief of Station)

Sources:	BR 1973, 1957 FSL 6/74, 1/70, 9/67, 10/64, 1/63, 10/59, 10/58, 7/55 The Hague Diplomatic Lists 2/76, 7/75, 6/74

BARBIER, CLARENCE E.

b. 12 January 1922	Connecticut
1942	Yale University BA
1942-46	U.S. Army overseas Lieutenant
1946-58	Department of the Army operations officer

1/58	Department of State
	Saigon, Vietnam (E)
	    Attache &
	    political officer

6/62	Dept.

7/62	Singapore, Singapore (E)
	    Consul &
	    political officer R-4

9/62	Consul

4/64		R-3
8/64	Dept.	
7/66	Jakarta, Indonesia (E) Special Assistant to the Ambassador	
8/69	Dept. (EA)	
as of 1/70-1/75	not listed in Department of State records; assignment not known	
as of 2/75- at least 1/76	Department of State Geneva, Switzerland (M) Attache & SPA	

Wife: Marietta Notary

Sources: BR 1974, 1964
                    FSL 6/73, 5/69, 1/67, 10/62
                    Geneva Consular Lists 1/76, 10/75
                    Geneva Mission Source

BARNES, EDWARD O.

b. 30 July 1914	Washington, D.C.	
1935	Catholic University BA	
1936-43	Department of the Treasury Division of Investments chief	
1939	Catholic University LLB (member Washington D.C. bar)	
1943-46	U.S. Army Captain overseas	
1946-52	Department of the Treasury Division of Investments chief	
1952-64	Department of the Army liaison officer	
5/64	Department of State Munich, Germany (CG) political officer	R-4
8/64	Consul	
3/69		R-3
as of 2/72	not listed in Department of State records; possibly retired	

Wife: Alice Blanchard

Sources: BR 1971, 1967
                    FSL 10/71, 7/64

BARRETT, JOHN W.

    b.   not known

7/75	Department of State
	Athens, Greece (E)
	    telecoms support officer
	    (Area Telecommunications Office)
		S-8

as of 11/77	Bamako, Mali (E) probably telecoms	
Source:	FSL 8/75 Department of State Source	

BARRETT, THOMAS JOSEPH Jr.

    as of 7/75:
SQS 305
Building B, Apt. 302
Brasília
Brazil
42-0446

b. 9 August 1919	Pennsylvania	
1938-42	private experience paper company market analyst	
1942	National Youth Administration budget officer	
1942-43	U.S. Army	
1943-45	Foreign Economic Administration assistant chief of section	
1945-47	private experience newspaper reporter	
1947	George Washington University BA	

1947-50	private experience
	    sewing machine company (Latin America)
	    economic reporter, superintendent	

1950-53	Mutual Security Agency research analyst	

11/53	Department of State
	Rio de Janeiro, Brazil (E)
	    Assistant Attache &
	    political officer
		S-7

10/56	Guayaquil, Ecuador (CG) Vice-Consul	S-6
12/57	Consul	

1/59	Lima, Peru (E)
	    Attache &
	    political officer
		R-5

5/60	Rio de Janeiro, Brazil (E) Attache & political officer	
8/60	Brasília, Brazil (Office) Attache & political officer	
3/63		R-4
7/63	Dept.	
5/65	Pôrto Alegre, Brazil (C) Consul, Attache & political officer	R-3
8/67	Dept. (ARA-LA)	
9/67	political officer	
1/70	foreign affairs officer	GS-14
1/72	Saigon, Vietnam (E) cover position not known	
12/73	Recife, Brazil (CG) political officer	R-3
7/74- at least 8/75	Brasília, Brazil (E) Attache & political officer	
Sources:	BR 1974, 1971, 1968 FSL 8/75, 11/74, 2/74, 1/70, 1/68, 6/65, 4/64, 10/60, 7/60, 4/59, 1/57, 4/54 Brasília Diplomatic Lists 7/75, 10/74	

BARTLEBAUGH, RICHARD T.

as of 1/74:
33 Platonos
Nea Politia
Kifissia
Athens
Greece
801-1411

b. not known

7/72	Department of State Athens, Greece (E) telecoms assistant (Regional Relay Facility)	S-8
as of 11/74	not listed in Department of State records; assignment not known	
Wife:	Gwendolyn	
Sources:	FSL 6/74, 6/73 Athens Embassy Source	

BATCH, JAMES E.

   as of 1/74:
   2 Grammou Street
   Kifissia
   Athens
   Greece
   801-7408

   b.   not known

   6/71-   Department of State
   at least 1/74   Athens, Greece (E)
                                 general services assistant   S-7
                                 (Area Telecommunications Office)

   Wife: Theresa

   Sources: FSL 10/73, 6/73
                            Athens Embassy Source

BATSON, CHARLES C.

   as of 3/76:
   2 Middlefield
   St. John's Wood
   London NW 8
   U.K.
   586-1030

   b.   not known

   9/59   Department of State
                               Addis Ababa, Ethiopia (E)
                                 communications assistant   S-9

   4/62   Nicosia, Cyprus (E)
                                 communications assistant

   as of 1/63   (Regional Relay Office)   S-6

   3/64   Athens, Greece (E)
                                 communications assistant

   10/65   Manila, Philippines (E)
                                 telecoms specialist

   as of 1/70   Dept.   S-5

   as of 10/70-4/75   not listed in Department of State records;
                            assignment not known

   5/75   R-4

   as of 7/75-   Department of State
   at least 3/76   London, U.K. (E)
                                 telecoms officer

   11/77   award for length of service

   Wife: Joyce

   Sources: FSL 8/75, 5/70, 1/70, 9/69, 1/67, 4/64, 1/63, 7/62, 1/60
                            London Embassy Source
                            Department of State Sources

BAXTER, MORRIS V.

    as of 3/76:
54 Princes Court
88 Brompton Road
London SW 3
U.K.
589-0238

    B.   not known

as of 12/74-
at least 3/76
	Department of State
	    London, U.K. (E)
	        Joint Reports & Research Unit

Wife:	Frances
Sources:	London Embassy Sources

BEAM, JOHN C.

b. 25 March 1935	Montana	
1956	Montana State University BA	
1956-59	U.S. Army overseas	
1960-65	private experience foreign trade consultant	
1965-67	Department of Commerce investment specialist	
5/67	Department of State Rabat, Morocco (E) consular officer	R-6
1/70	Dept. (AF)	
4/70		R-5
7/71	Bujumbura, Burundi (E) political officer	
4/72	political-economic officer	
4/74		R-4
7/74	Rabat, Morocco (E) economic-commercial officer	
as of 8/76	Algiers, Algeria (E) cover position not known	
5/77		RU-4
as of 1/78	First Secretary (Economic-Commercial Affairs)	
Wife:	Josephine Brosnahan	
Sources:	BR 1974 FSL 8/75, 11/74, 10/71, 5/70, 9/67 Algiers Diplomatic List 1978 Department of State Sources	

BEARMAN, SIDNEY

> as of 11/77:
> 2 Clabon Mews
> London SW1
> U.K.
> 589-9166

b. 15 August 1925	Massachusetts
1943-46	U.S. Army
1950	Brown University BA
1950-52	Columbia University
1952-56	Department of the Army political analyst

8/56	Department of State
	    Bern, Switzerland (E)
	        political officer R-7

2/59	R-6

as of 1/60-3/74	Central Intelligence Agency
	    Office of Current Intelligence
	        became chief of Far Eastern Division
	        & China Task Force

as of 4/74-
at least 6/75
	Department of State
	    London, U.K. (E)
	        Attache &
	        political liaison officer

as of 8/75-10/77	assignment not known

***as of 11/77	private experience
	    London, U.K.
	        Research Associate at International
	        Institute for Strategic Studies

Wife:	Dorothy R.
Sources:	BR 1959 FSL 10/59, 10/56 London Diplomatic Lists 6/75, 4/74 London Embassy Sources International Institute for Strategic Studies Sources

***According to sources at the International Institute for Strategic Studies, his present research deals with China's perspective of the strategic environment, with a planned duration of one year.

BECKETT, DONALD F.

b. 22 April 1925		

5/70	Department of State
	    Athens, Greece (E)
	        telecoms officer
		S-3

2/72		S-2
as of 10/73	Dept. (NEA)	

as of 2/74	not listed in Department of State records; assignment not known	
Sources:	BR 1973 FSL 10/73, 10/70	

BEGLEY, JOSEPH M.

b. not known

9/68	Department of State Monrovia, Liberia (E) telecoms assistant	S-6
as of 2/71-4/76	not listed in Department of State records; assignment not known	
5/76		R-6
as of 7/76	Department of State Athens, Greece (E) probably telecoms	
Sources:	FSL 10/70, 1/69 Athens Embassy Sources Department of State Sources	

BEHRENS, JAMES E.

as of 1/74:
9 Menexedon Street
Ekali
Athens
Greece
803-2062

b. not known

7/70	Department of State Nicosia, Cyprus (E) telecoms technician	S-5
9/72	Athens, Greece (E) telecoms technician (Area Telecommunications Office)	
as of 1/75	Dept. (A/OC)	
Wife:	Caron	
Sources:	FSL 6/74, 10/72, 10/70 Athens Embassy Source Department of State Sources	

BEMUS, HERMAN H.

b. not known

1/74	Department of State Kuwait, Kuwait (E) telecoms assistant	S-8

as of 6/74	Dept. (NEA)	
as of 10/77	Bern, Switzerland (E) probably telecoms	

Sources: FSL 8/75, 6/74, 2/74
                         Department of State Sources

BENDER, JACOB E. Jr.

as of 1/74:
3 Kritis Street
Kifissia
Athens
Greece
808-0491

b.   not known

6/72	Department of State Athens, Greece (E) telecoms assistant (Regional Relay Facility)	S-7
as of 11/74	telecoms support officer	S-6
as of 10/75	Dept. (A/OC)	

Wife: Pat

Sources: FSL 8/75, 6/73
                         Department of State Source

BENDER, PAT

as of 1/74:
3 Kritis Street
Kifissia
Athens
Greece
808-0491

b.   not known

as of 1/74	Department of State Athens, Greece (E) telecoms secretary (Area Telecommunications Office— Logistics section)

Husband: Jacob E.

Source: Athens Embassy Source

BENEDICT, GARY D.

b.   not known

10/71	Department of State New Delhi, India (E) telecoms assistant	S-8

4/74- at least 8/75	Copenhagen, Denmark (E) telecoms support officer
as of 11/74	S-7
Sources:	FSL 8/75, 6/74, 6/73

BENEDICT, JULIA L.

as of 7/75:
191 Grove End Gardens
18 Abbey Road
London NW 8
U.K.
289-3035

b. not known

as of 12/74	Department of State London, U.K. (E) Joint Reports & Research Unit
as of 8/75	not listed in Department of State records; assignment not known
Source:	London Embassy Source

BENISH, ALBERT

as of 6/75:
53 Boydell Court
St. John's Wood Park
London NW 8
U.K.
722-0036

b. not known

as of 6/75	Department of State London, U.K. (E) Joint Reports & Research Unit
as of 12/75	not listed in Department of State records; assignment not known
Wife:	Rosalie
Source	London Embassy Source

BENISH, ROSALIE

as of 6/75:
53 Boydell Court
St. John's Wood Park
London NW 8
U.K.
722-0036

b. not known

as of 6/75	Department of State 　　London, U.K. (E) 　　　　Joint Reports & Research Unit
as of 12/75	not listed in Department of State records; assignment not known
Husband:	Albert
Source:	London Embassy Source

BENNETT, WILLIAM E.

b.　22 December 1938	West Virginia
1960-61	Department of Agriculture 　　management trainee
1961-64	U.S. Army overseas
1965-72	Department of the Army 　　program analyst
1970	George Washington University BS
6/72	Department of State 　　Berlin, Germany (M) 　　　　political officer　　　　　　　　　R-6
as of 11/74	not listed in Department of State records; assignment not known
Wife:	Patricia Kaercher
Sources:	BR 1974 FSL 6/74, 10/72

BERG, JOHN W.

as of 6/75:
4 Square de l'Alboni
75016 Paris
France
520-50-54

b.　11 May 1927	Maryland
1945-46	U.S. Army
1948	Gettysburg College BA
1948	private experience 　　manufacturing firm cost clerk
1949	Columbia University MA
1949-55	Department of the Army 　　political officer
3/56	Department of State 　　Rome, Italy (E) 　　　　Attache & 　　　　political officer　　　　　　　　　R-4

7/56	Warsaw, Poland (E) Attache & political officer	R-5
6/59	Vienna, Austria (E) political officer	
10/60		R-4
10/63	Dept. (EUR)	
12/64		S-2
1/66		S-1
as of 9/69-12/73	not listed in Department of State records; assignment not known	
as of 1/74- at least 6/75	Department of State Paris, France (E) Office of the Special Assistant	
Wife:	Margaret G.	
Sources:	BR 1971, 1956 FSL 5/69, 1/64, 6/59, 10/56, 3/56 Paris Diplomatic Lists 6/75, 1/74 Paris Embassy Source	

BERGER, MICHAEL JAY

b. 5 October 1934	New York	
1956	Cornell University BA	
1956-57	Columbia University Graduate School of Business Administration	
1957-58	U.S. Army overseas	
1958-59	private experience manufacturing firm sales management assistant	
1959-60	American University	
1959-60	private experience research office research associate	
1960-62	Department of the Army research analyst	
3/62	Department of State Montevideo, Uruguay (E) Assistant Attache	R-8
6/64	Santo Domingo, Dominican Republic (E) Assistant Attache & political officer	
9/64	Attache & political officer	R-7

1966-69	Department of Defense administrative officer	
11/69	Department of State Dept. foreign affairs officer	GS-13
1970-74	not listed in Department of State records; assignment not known	
as of 11/74	Department of State Paris, France (E) Regional Reports Office	
8/75	Yaoundé, Cameroon (E) political-economic officer	R-4
as of 5/76	First Secretary	
as of 1/78	Dept. (AF)	
Wife:	Ema Garcia	
Sources:	BR 1970, 1966 FSL 8/75, 10/65, 7/64, 7/62 Paris Embassy Source. Yaoundé Diplomatic Lists 10/76, 5/76 Department of State Source	

BERGIN, MARTIN J. Jr.

b. 25 March 1919	New York	
1941	St. Peter's College BA	
1941-46	U.S. Army overseas Captain	
1947-48	private experience law office historical researcher	
1948	Columbia University MIA	
1948-51	Economic Cooperation Administration Paris, France research analyst	
1951-54	Library of Congress research analyst	
6/54	Department of State Tehran, Iran (E) Assistant Attache	S-7
7/57		S-6
as of 1/58	Assistant Attache & political officer	
7/59	Dept.	
10/59		R-5
3/63		R-4

***6/63	Usumbura, Burundi (E) Assistant Attache & political officer	
10/63	Second Secretary, Consul & political officer	
10/65	Dept. (AF)	
4/67	plans & programs officer	GS-14
7/71	Dakar, Senegal (E) international relations officer	R-3
9/73	Abidjan, Ivory Coast (E) political officer	
as of 12/75	Dept. (AF)	
Wife:	Nicole Jachiet	
Sources:	BR 1974, 1961-62 FSL 8/75, 10/73, 10/71, 10/63, 10/59 1/58, 10/54 Department of State Source	

***Usumbura became Bujumbura in 1964.

BERNIER, NORMAN A.

b. not known

7/68	Department of State Santiago, Chile (E) telecoms supervisor	S-6
as of 10/70	telecoms officer	
as of 2/71-7/76	not listed in Department of State records; assignment not known	
as of 8/76	Department of State Athens, Greece (E) probably telecoms	R-6
Sources:	FSL 10/70, 9/68 Athens Embassy Sources Department of State Sources	

BESSETTE, ARTHUR J.

b. not known

4/68	Department of State Kinshasa, Congo (E) telecoms technician	S-6
7/70	Nicosia, Cyprus (E) telecoms technician	
as of 6/72		S-5

as of 2/73-6/75	not listed in Department of State records; assignment not known
7/75	Department of State
	Athens, Greece (E)
	telecoms technician R-6
	(Area Telecommunications Office)
as of 12/77	Dept. (A/OC)
Sources:	FSL 8/75, 10/72, 10/70, 1/69
	Department of State Sources

BIRD, ALBERT O. Jr.

as of 12/75:
Flat 118
15 Portman Square
London W 1
U.K.
486-1001

b.   not known

as of 12/75	Department of State
	London, U.K. (E)
***	SUSLO
Wife:	Betty
Source:	London Embassy Source

***SUSLO is a cover unit for the National Security Agency, not the CIA.

BLACKSHEAR, THOMAS RUSSELL

as of 11/77:
37 Circus Road
St. John's Wood
London NW 8
U.K.
286-1684

b. 11 August 1929	Arkansas
1946-48	U.S. Marine Corps
1952	Claremont Men's College BA
1952	private experience
	newspaper reporter
1952-59	Department of the Army
	economic analyst
1954-56	George Washington University
8/59	Department of State
	Frankfurt, Germany (CG)
	economic officer R-7

10/59	Frankfurt, Germany (CG) Foreign Service Institute German language training	
1/60	economic officer	
9/60	Berlin, Germany (M) consular officer	
11/60	Vice-Consul & consular officer	
12/61	Sofia, Bulgaria (L) economic officer	
3/62	Third Secretary, Vice-Consul & economic officer	
4/62	Second Secretary & Vice-Consul	R-6
4/64		R-5
10/64	Dept.	
7/66	New Delhi, India (E) political officer	
4/67		R-4
7/69	Dept.	
8/69		S-2
as of 1/70	(NEA)	
as of 10/70-9/75	not listed in Department of State records; assignment not known	
as of 10/75- at least 6/78	Department of State London, U.K. (E) Attache & Political Liaison Section	
Wife:	Rosemary P.	
Sources:	BR 1974, 1966, 1960 FSL 5/70, 1/67, 1/65, 7/62, 1/61, 10/59 London Diplomatic Lists 6/78, 10/75 London Embassy Sources	

BLAIR, ROBERT DEW

as of 1/74:
28 Ehinou Street
New Kifissia
Athens
Greece

b. 3 September 1940

4/71	Department of State Ankara, Turkey (E) telecoms officer	R-7

10/73	Athens, Greece (E)	
	telecoms assistant	
	(Regional Relay Facility)	
3/74	telecoms support officer	
as of 5/76	Algiers, Algeria (E)	
	probably telecoms	

Wife: Carol

Sources: BR 1974
                          FSL 8/75, 2/74, 6/71
                          Athens Embassy Source
                          Department of State Source

BLANCHARD, JOHN L.

b.   not known

as of 7/76	Department of State	
	Athens, Greece (E)	
	probably telecoms	R-6

Sources: Athens Embassy Sources
                          Department of State Sources

BLEAM, DENNIS L.

b. 21 March 1939	Pennsylvania	
1955-61	private experience	
	manufacturing company	
	shipping clerk, packer	
1961	Moravian College BS	
1962-64	private experience	
	manufacturing company	
	accountant	
1962-63	U.S. Army	
1965-69	Department of the Army	
	clerk	
3/69	Department of State	
	Nairobi, Kenya (E)	
	political section clerk	S-5
6/71	Kinshasa, Zaire (E)	
	political section clerk	
as of 6/72		S-4
as of 9/74	Dept. (AF)	
as of 10/75	Geneva, Switzerland (M)	
	Attache &	
	SPA	

Wife: Shahnaz Meshkin

Sources:	BR 1974
	FSL 6/74, 9/69
	Geneva Diplomatic Lists 1/76, 10/75
	Geneva Mission Source
	Department of State Source

BLODGET, BENJAMIN B.

b.   not known

2/70	Department of State
	Manila, Philippines (E)
	telecoms officer S-6
11/72	New Delhi, India (E)
	telecoms assistant
as of 11/74	telecoms support officer
as of 8/75	Dept. (NEA)
as of 12/75	Athens, Greece (E)
	probably telecoms
as of 4/78	Guayaquil, Ecuador (CG)
	probably telecoms
Sources:	FSL 8/75, 2/73, 5/70
	Department of State Sources

BOERNER, MARK S.

as of 6/76:
8 Cope Place
London W 8
U.K.
937-8651

b.   not known

as of 12/74	Department of State
	London, U.K. (E)
	Joint Reports & Research Unit &
***	U.S. Liaison Office
	liaison officer
as of 7/76	not listed in Department of State records;
	assignment not known
Sources:	London Embassy Sources

***Boerner was assigned to the British Ministry of Defense as ''liaison officer'' in the ''U.S. Liaison Office''

BOIES, ROBERT E.

b. 21 November 1921	New York
1942	Yale University BA
1942-46	U.S. Marine Corps overseas Captain

1947	Yale University MA
1948	Prague University PhD
1949-59	Department of the Army foreign affairs officer

4/59	Department of State
	    Bombay, India (CG)
	       political officer R-4

5/59	Consul
7/62	Dept.

8/62	Beirut, Lebanon (E)
	    Attache &
	    political officer

9/64	Dept.
4/65	intelligence operations specialist
9/66	S-1
as of 1/67	(NEA)

8/69	Rome, Italy (E)
	    Attache &
	    political officer R-3

as of 11/74- at least 8/75	Dept. (EUR)
Wife:	Donna Stoy
Sources:	BR 1974, 1968 FSL 8/75, 11/74, 1/70, 1/65, 10/62, 7/59 Rome Diplomatic Lists 1/73, 1/70

BONIN, DONALD C.

as of 12/74:
5 Rue de la Ferme
Apt. 323
92 Neuilly
France
722-8844

b.   not known

9/66	Department of State
	    Mexico City, Mexico (E)
	       telecoms specialist S-6

as of 1/70	Dept.
as of 5/70-11/74	not listed in Department of State records; assignment not known

as of 12/74	Department of State
	    Paris, France (E)
	       telecoms

Wife:	Donna A.

Sources:	FSL 1/70, 1/67 Paris Embassy Source	

BONNAFE, LUCIEN R.

as of 3/76:
59 Frient Way
London NW 9
U.K.

b. not known		
5/61	Department of State Manila, Philippines (E) communications specialist	S-8
10/63		S-5
as of 1/64-6/75	not listed in Department of State records; assignment not known	
7/75	Department of State London, U.K. (E) telecoms technician	R-5
as of 12/77	Dept. (A/OC)	
Wife:	Marie	
Sources:	FSL 8/75, 10/63, 7/61 London Embassy Source Department of State Source	

BOVEE, HOWARD W.

as of 12/74:
3 Avenue Franklin Roosevelt
Paris 8
France
359-4363

b. 16 July 1920	Wisconsin	
1942-46	U.S. Army 1st Lieutenant overseas	
1947	University of Wisconsin PhB	
1949	University of Wisconsin LLB	
1949	member of Wisconsin bar	
1949-51	private experience lawyer & research analyst	
1/52	Department of State Karachi, Pakistan (E) Assistant Attache	S-9
8/52	Lahore, Pakistan (CG) Vice-Consul	
1/55	Dept.	

3/55	Saigon, Vietnam (E) Assistant Attache	
8/56		S-8
as of 7/57	Attache & political officer	
1/58	Dept.	
7/59		R-6
9/59	Rabat, Morocco (E) Attache & political officer	
12/59	Second Secretary, Attache & political officer	
4/62		R-5
10/63	Khartoum, Sudan (E) Second Secretary, Attache & political officer	
4/64		R-4
7/64	Dept.	
as of 1/67	(EA)	
3/69	Brussels, Belgium (E) Attache & political officer	
as of 2/73-10/74	not listed in Department of State records; assignment not known	
as of 11/74	Department of State Paris, France (E) American Liaison Section	
Wife:	Yvonne Borg	
Sources:	BR 1966, 1955 FSL 10/72, 5/70, 10/64, 1/64, 3/58, 7/55, 10/52, 4/52 Paris Embassy Source	

BOWMAN, DONALD E.

as of 12/74:
60 Rue Corot
92410 Villa d'Avray
France
945-5286

b.   not known

as of 12/74	Department of State Paris, France (E) Regional Reports Office
Wife:	Janice E.
Source:	Paris Embassy Source

BRADSHAW, BEVERLEY B.

b. 20 November 1940	Virginia
1962-65	U.S. Army overseas
1965-73	Department of the Army electronics engineer
4/73	Department of State Nicosia, Cyprus (E) telecoms technician R-7
6/74	Athens, Greece (E) telecoms technician (Area Telecommunications Office)
as of 8/76	Dept. (A/OC)
Wife:	Thelma Moubray
Sources:	BR 1974 FSL 8/75, 11/74, 6/73 Department of State Source

BRAHAM, A. SPENCER

as of 6/75:
12A Northgate
Prince Albert Road
London NW 8
U.K.
722-4710

b. not known	
as of 6/74	Department of State London, U.K. (E) Political Liaison Section
as of 9/75	not listed in Department of State records; assignment not known
Wife:	Marion W.
Sources:	London Diplomatic Lists 8/75, 6/74 London Embassy Sources

BREAW, ROYCE L.

b. 7 November 1924	
6/62	Department of State Tehran, Iran (E) communications specialist S-8
as of 1/63	S-5
as of 10/64-3/71	not listed in Department of State records; assignment not known
4/71	Department of State Bangkok, Thailand (E) telecoms officer R-5

as of 10/73   Dept. (EA)

7/75   Department of State
                               Athens, Greece (E)
                                    telecoms officer
                                    (Area Telecommunications Office)

Sources: BR 1972
                               FSL 8/75, 10/73, 6/71, 7/64, 10/62

BREHM, VANCE W.

    b. not known

        8/70   Department of State
                               Accra, Ghana (E)   rating
                                    telecoms assistant   not known

        8/71   S-6

        4/74   Prague, Czechoslovakia (E)
                                    telecoms support officer

    as of 8/76   Bern, Switzerland (E)
                                    probably telecoms

    Sources: FSL 8/75, 6/74, 10/71
                               Department of State Sources

BRIGHT, WILLIAM C.

    as of 1/74:
    6 Dryadon Street
    Kokkinara
    Kifissia
    Athens
    Greece
    801-2504

    b. not known

        as of 1/74   Department of Defense
                               Athens, Greece (E)
                                    JUSMAGG

    Wife: Emily

    Source: Athens Embassy Source

BROUTSAS, CONSTANTINE M.

    as of 2/76:
    Buechel Strasse 53B/33
    5300 Bonn-Bad Godesberg
    Germany
    35-61-98

    b. 24 August 1925   Massachusetts

        1944-45   private experience
                                    high school teacher

1945-47	U.S. Army overseas
1949	Middlebury College BA
1949-50	University of Munich
1950	Columbia University
1951-63	Department of the Army political affairs officer
3/63	Department of State Geneva, Switzerland (M) U.S. Mission to the European Office of the United Nations and Other International Organisations economic officer

R-4

8/63	Second Secretary & economic officer
11/65	Dept. (EUR)
as of 10/72-1/75	not listed in Department of State records; assignment not known
as of 2/75- at least 2/76	Department of Defense Bonn, Germany (E) OSD/ISA
Wife:	Jane Bleau
Sources:	BR 1971, 1966, 1964 FSL 6/72, 1/67, 7/63 Bonn Embassy Source

BROWN, CHARLES J.

b. not known	
1/75- at least 8/75	Department of State Bonn, Germany (E) telecoms technician (Regional Communications Office)

S-6

Sources:	FSL 8/75, 4/75 Bonn Embassy Source

BROWN, EDWARD R.

as of 9/77:
Tel. 12718 (Kathmandu, Nepal)

b. 16 February 1927	Montana
1945-46	U.S. Navy overseas
1950	University of Washington BA
1951	Montana State University MA
1951-60	Department of the Army research analyst

4/60	Department of State	
	Tehran, Iran (E)	
	political officer	R-7
3/63		R-6
10/64	Dept.	
5/65		R-5
6/65	Istanbul, Turkey (CG)	
	political officer	
10/65	Consul &	
	political officer	
7/68	Kabul, Afghanistan (CG)	
	political officer	
3/69		R-4
9/70	Dept. (NEA)	
6/72	Karachi, Pakistan (E)	
	economic-commercial officer	
8/73		RU-4
as of 3/74	Consul &	
	economic-commercial officer	
9/75-	Kathmandu, Nepal (E)	
at least 9/77	First Secretary	
2/76		RU-3

Wife:	Reba Jo Guy
Sources:	BR 1974, 1968
	FSL 8/75, 10/72, 10/70, 5/69, 10/65,
	1/65, 7/60
	Islamabad Diplomatic and Consular
	List 3/74
	Kathmandu Diplomatic List 9/77
	Department of State Sources

BROWN, GLENN OTIS

as of 6/75:
Hidalgo de Pinto s/n
Quito
Ecuador
248-201

b. 28 December 1927	Illinois
1949	Southern Illinois University BS
1949-51	University of Illinois
	teaching assistant
1951	University of Illinois MA
1951-53	U.S. Army
1953-54	private experience
	real estate salesman

1954-61	Department of the Army
	    technical writer
	    administrative officer	

1961-65	private experience
	    research society
	        historian, language analyst	

10/65	Department of State
	    Paramaribo, Surinam (CG)
	        political officer
		R-6

12/65	Vice-Consul & political officer	
2/68	Dept.	
5/68		R-5
9/68	Port-au-Prince, Haiti (E) political officer	
9/69	Dept.	
4/70	project officer	GS-14

7/72	Tegucigalpa, Honduras (E)
	    Second Secretary &
	    international relations officer
		R-4

as of 9/74	Dept. (ARA-LA)	
as of 6/75	Quito, Ecuador (E) Attache	

Wife: Maria Vidal-Ribas

Sources: BR 1974, 1966
FSL 6/74, 10/72, 1/70, 9/68, 5/68, 1/67
Tegucigalpa Diplomatic List 1973
Quito Diplomatic List 6/75
Department of State Sources

BROWN, JOHN H.

as of 3/76:
33 Boydell Court
St. John's Wood Park
London NW 8
U.K.
722-3160

b.   not known

as of 12/74-   Department of State
at least 3/76   London, U.K. (E)
                Joint Reports & Research Unit

Wife: Linda

Sources: London Embassy Sources

BROWN, JOHN P.

    as of 4/76:
    24 Forty Lane
    Wembley Park
    Middlesex
    U.K.
    904-3822

b. 27 July 1932	New York
1954-56	U.S. Army
1956-61	Department of the Army administrative assistant

1961-63	Department of State
	    Dept.
	       clerk

1963-69	Department of the Air Force analyst
1967	American University BS

8/69	Department of State
	    Brussels, Belgium (E)
	       political assistant S-4

as of 10/72	Dept. (EUR)
as of 2/73-5/75	not listed in Department of State records; assignment not known

as of 6/75-
at least 4/76
	Department of State
	    London, U.K. (E)
	       Joint Reports & Research Unit

Wife:	Nan
Sources:	BR 1972 FSL 10/72, 1/70 London Embassy Sources

BROYLES, RICHARD G.

b. not known	

2/72	Department of State
	    Rome, Italy (E)
	       telecoms assistant S-7

as of 11/74-10/76	not listed in Department of State records; assignment not known
as of 11/76	Department of State Dept. S-6
Sources:	FSL 6/74, 6/73 Department of State Source

BRUNSON, GERALD L.

    b. not known

7/69	Department of State La Paz, Bolivia (E) telecoms assistant	S-6
1/70	Dept. (A/OC)	
2/70	Vientiane, Laos (E) assistant general services officer	RL-7
as of 6/72-6/74	not listed in State Department records; assignment not known	
7/74	Department of State Yaoundé, Cameroon (E) telecoms officer	R-7
as of 7/77	Rome, Italy (E) probably telecoms	
Sources:	FSL 8/75, 11/74, 2/72, 10/71, 1/70, 9/69 Department of State Sources	

BUCHANAN, GEORGE

b.   not known

8/72	Department of State Brussels, Belgium (E) telecoms assistant	S-7
as of 11/74	Dept. (A/OC)	
as of 4/75	not listed in Department of State records; assignment not known	
Sources:	FSL 11/74, 6/73	

BUCY, HOWARD C.

as of 1/74:
20 Helidonous Street
New Kifissia
Athens
Greece
801-0850

b.   26 October 1939

as of 6/71	Agency for International Development Lusaka, Zambia (E) communications-records supervisor	SL-6
9/72- at least 8/75	Department of State Athens, Greece (E) telecoms officer (Regional Relay Facility)	R-7
Wife:	Judith	
Sources:	BR 1974 FSL 8/75, 2/73, 6/71 Athens Embassy Source	

BULL, RICHARD C.

as of 9/75:
422 Avenue de Tervuren
1150 Brussels
Belgium
770-7360

b. 6 October 1932	Missouri	
1954	Princeton University BA	
1954-57	U.S. Army overseas	
1957-58	Georgetown University	
1958-61	Department of the Army research and reports analyst	

6/61	Department of State
	    Vienna, Austria (E)
	        political officer
		R-7

4/64		R-6
5/66		R-5
11/66	Dept.	
3/68	Cotonou, Dahomey (E) political officer	
3/69		R-4
9/70	Tripoli, Libya (E) economic-commercial officer	
10/72	Dept. (AF)	
as of 10/73-8/75	not listed in Department of State records; assignment not known	

as of 9/75	Department of State
	    Brussels, Belgium (E)
	        cover position not known	

Languages:	French, Thai	
Wife:	Katherine Stark	
Sources:	BR 1973, 1967 FSL 6/73, 2/73, 10/70, 5/68, 1/68, 7/61 Brussels Embassy Source	

BULLOCK, ELEANORE ANNE

as of 6/75:
41 Kynaston Wood
Boxtree Road
Harrow Weald
Middlesex
U.K.
954-6040

b.   not known

as of 12/74	Department of State London, U.K. (E) Joint Reports & Research Unit
as of 9/75	not listed in Department of State records; assignment not known
Husband:	Max E.
Source:	London Embassy Source

BULLOCK, MAX E.

as of 6/75:
41 Kynaston Wood
Boxtree Road
Harrow Weald
Middlesex
U.K.
954-6040

b. not known

as of 12/74	Department of State London, U.K. (E) Joint Reports & Research Unit
as of 9/75	not listed in Department of State sources; assignment not known
Wife:	Eleanore Anne
Source:	London Embassy Source

BUMP, WILLIAM H. III

b. not known

1/75	Department of State Athens, Greece (E) telecoms support officer (Area Telecommunications Office)	S-8
as of 7/77	Tehran, Iran (E) probably telecoms	
Source:	FSL 8/75 Department of State Source	

BURGSTALLER, EUGEN F.

as of 1/76:
47 Avenue Georges Mandel
75016 Paris
France
727-52-93

b. 22 December 1920	Massachusetts
1942	Harvard University BA

1942-46	U.S. Army overseas	
1948	Harvard University MA	
1948	U.S. Post Office Department postal clerk	
1948-55	Department of the Army plans officer	
10/55	Department of State Vienna, Austria (E) political officer	R-4
7/56		R-5
7/57-5/66	Department of the Army foreign affairs officer	
6/66	Department of State Beirut, Lebanon (E) political officer	R-3
as of 2/72-5/74	not listed in Department of State records; assignment not known	

as of 6/74-
at least 1/78
	Department of State
	    Paris, France (E)
	        Office of the Special Assistant
	        (CIA Chief of Station)	

Wife:	Virginia Haskell	
Sources:	BR 1972, 1967, 1956 FSL 10/71, 1/67, 7/57, 1/56 Paris Diplomatic Lists 1/78, 6/74 Paris Embassy Source	

BURK, WILLIAM C.

b. not known		

4/75	Department of State
	Athens, Greece (E)
	    telecoms support officer
	    (Area Telecommunications Office)
		S-7

as of 12/77	Dept. (A/OC)	
Source:	FSL 8/75 Department of State Source	

BURTON, STEWART D.

b. 5 April 1928	Utah	
1947-50	private experience missionary	
1951	Brigham Young University BA	
2/52	Department of State São Paulo Brazil (CG) Vice-Consul	S-11

8/54		S-10
1955	La Salle Extension College LLB	

2/55	Department of State
	  Buenos Aires, Argentina (E)
	    Vice-Consul, Assistant Attache &
	    political officer	

8/56		S-9
6/57	Assistant Attache	
7/57		S-8
7/58	Dept.	
8/59		R-6
1961	George Washington University LLB	
1961	Virginia Bar Association member	

3/62	Department of State
	  Curitiba, Brazil (C)
	    political officer	

4/62		R-5
7/62	Vice-Consul & political officer	

***7/64	Georgetown, British Guiana (CG)
	  Vice-Consul &
	  consular officer	

4/65		R-4
5/66	political officer	
6/67	Rio de Janeiro, Brazil (CG) political officer	
3/69		R-3
5/70	Lima, Peru (E) international relations officer	
as of 10/72	Dept. (ARA-LA)	
as of 6/73-2/74	not listed in Department of State records; assignment not known	

3/74	Department of State
	  Santiago, Chile (E)
	    First Secretary &
	    political officer	

as of 10/76	Brasília Brazil (E) cover position not known	
Wife:	Dorothy Broome	

Sources: BR 1974, 1971, 1967
                                  FSL 8/75, 6/74, 2/73, 10/70, 9/67, 10/64, 7/62,
                                      10/58, 10/56
                                  Santiago Diplomatic Lists 8/75, 12/74
                                  Department of State Sources

***British Guiana achieved independence in May 1966, and its name was changed to
Guyana. Georgetown was elevated to Embassy status.

BUSH, ANNA D.

    as of 6/75:
    6 Chalcot Gardens
    Englands Lane
    London NW 3
    U.K.
    722-9153

    b.   not known

    as of 12/74-   Department of State
    at least 6/75   London, U.K. (E)
                                     Joint Reports & Research Unit

    Source: London Embassy Sources

BUSH, JOHN M.

    as of 3/76:
    76 Windermere Avenue
    Wembley
    Middlesex
    U.K.
    904-7941

    b.   20 November 1929   Maryland

          1946   private experience
                      electronic corporation draftsman

      1946-49   U.S. Coast Guard overseas

      1949-63   unspecified government agency
                      communications officer

         9/63   Department of State
                      Rio de Janeiro, Brazil (E)
                      communications specialist   S-5

      1965-69   not listed in Department of State records;
                      assignment not known

         8/69   Department of State
                      Athens, Greece (E)
                      telecoms officer   S-3

       10/72   Dept. (NEA)

        7/73   London, U.K. (E)
                      telecoms officer   R-4

    as of 8/75   Dept. (A/OC)

Wife:	Mary Leta Dawson
Sources:	BR 1974
	FSL 4/75, 10/73, 9/69, 1/65, 1/64
	London Embassy Sources

BUTLER, RICHARD H.

b. not known

10/66	Department of State	
	Algiers, Algeria (E)	
	telecoms supervisor	S-6
12/67	Salisbury, Rhodesia (CG)	
	telecoms officer	
as of 1/70-8/74	not listed in Department of State records; assignment not known	
9/74- at least 4/75	Department of State Athens, Greece (E) telecoms support officer	
Sources:	FSL 4/75, 11/74, 9/69, 5/68, 1/67	

BUTTERWORTH, DAVID G.

as of 11/75:
28 Portsdown Avenue
London NW 11
U.K.
455-5928

b. not known

as of 12/74- at least 11/75	Department of State London, U.K. (E) Foreign Broadcast Information Service
Wife:	Cynthia
Sources:	London Embassy Sources

CALDWELL, DONNA J.

as of 3/75:
Praça das Aguas Livres 8-6°D. Esq.
Lisbon
Portugal
68-58-11

b. not known

as of 3/75	Department of State Lisbon, Portugal (E) secretary to CIA Chief of Station
Sources:	Lisbon Embassy Source

CAMMARATA, ALFRED J.

 b. not known

11/69- at least 10/72	Department of State Stockholm, Sweden (E) telecoms officer	S-6
as of 2/73	not listed in Department of State records; assignment not known	
Sources:	FSL 10/72, 1/70	

CAMPBELL, NANCY M.

 as of 12/74:
 6 Rue Antoine Bourdelle
 75015 Paris
 France
 544-0919

 b. not known

11/66	Department of State Bucharest, Romania (E) consular assistant	S-6
as of 9/68	Dept. (EUR)	
as of 5/70		S-5
as of 2/71-11/74	not listed in Department of State records; assignment not known	
as of 12/74	Department of State Paris, France (E) Regional Reports Office	
Sources:	FSL 10/70, 5/70, 1/67 Paris Embassy Source	

CAMPBELL, VAN CLEVE

 b. 10 October 1928

4/59	Department of State Manila, Philippines (E) communications assistant	S-9
10/61	Stockholm, Sweden (E) general clerk (Political Section)	
as of 1/63		S-6
3/64	Prague, Czechoslovakia (E) secretary-archivist, administrative specialist	
as of 1/67-5/69	not listed in Department of State records; assignment not known	

6/69	Department of State Hong Kong, U.K. (CG) telecoms supervisor	S-4
as of 10/70	telecoms officer	
as of 10/72-6/75	not listed in Department of State records; assignment not known	
7/75	Department of State Bangkok, Thailand (E) telecoms officer	R-5
as of 10/77	Athens, Greece (E) probably telecoms	
Wife:	Mary Page	
Sources:	BR 1972 FSL 8/75, 10/70, 9/69, 10/65, 7/64, 1/63, 1/62, 10/60 Athens Embassy Sources Department of State Sources	

CANALE, JOSEPH T.

b. not known		
as of 8/76	Department of State Athens, Greece (E) probably telecoms	R-8
Sources:	Athens Embassy Sources Department of State Sources	

CAPELLINI, SUSAN C.

as of 9/74:
18 Viale Della Mura Latine
Rome
Italy
77-53-03

b. not known	
as of 9/74	Department of State Rome, Italy (e) USASEPU
Husband:	Aristide
Source:	Rome Embassy Source

CARLSON, ERIC JOHN

b. 22 March 1943	Pennsylvania
1965	Pennsylvania State University BA
1966	U.S. Army

1966-72	Department of the Army program analyst	
9/72	Department of State Dept. program officer	GS-11
12/72	Foreign Service Institute language and area training	R-6
8/73	Prague, Czechoslovakia (E) consular officer for special services	
as of 7/74	Secretary-archivist, Vice-Consul & consular officer for special services	
2/76		R-5
1/77	Vienna, Austria (E) Second Secretary (Consular Section)	
Wife:	Mary Ann Dore	
Sources:	BR 1974, 1973 ESL 8/75, 10/73, 2/73 Prague Diplomatic List 7/74 Vienna Diplomatic List 6/77	

CARTER, LOY L.

b. not known		
4/72	Department of State Santo Domingo, Dominican Republic (E) telecoms assistant	S-6
8/74- at least 8/75	Athens, Greece (E) telecoms support officer (Area Telecommunications Office)	
Sources:	FSL 8/75, 11/74, 6/72	

CARTER, RUDULPH ELLIS

b. 24 March 1926	Pennsylvania	
1944-45	U.S. Army	
1949	University of Pennsylvania BA	
1949-51	private experience banking company credit officer	
1951-55	Department of the Air Force foreign affairs officer	
12/55	Department of State Stockholm, Sweden (E) Assistant Attache & political officer	R-5
7/56		R-6

9/58	Dept.	
4/59-6/60	Department of the Air Force foreign affairs officer	

7/60	Department of State
	    London, U.K. (E)
	        Attache &
	        political officer
		R-5

12/64	Dept.	
4/67		R-4
as of 5/68	(EUR)	
7/69- at least 11/77	U.S. Mission to the United Nations (USUN) political-security affairs adviser	
1969-70	delegate to U.N. General Assembly	
3/71	political officer	
1971-75	delegate to U.N. General Assembly	
5/75		R-3
as of 11/75	political-security affairs adviser	
as of 11/77	senior adviser for political affairs (CIA Chief of Station)	

Wife: Marife

Sources: BR 1974, 1964, 1956
       FSL 8/75, 9/69, 1/65, 10/60, 4/59, 10/58, 1/56
       List of Delegations to the United Nations
        General Assembly, Thirtieth Session 11/75
       Lists of Permanent Missions to the
        United Nations 8/77, 1/76
       Department of State Sources
       United Nations Source

CARTER, STEPHEN B.

as of 12/75:
42 Norrice Lea
London N 2
U.K.
455-0865

b. not known

as of 12/74- at least 12/75	Department of State London, U.K. (E)	
***	SUSLO	

Wife: Jeanne

Sources: London Embassy Sources

***SUSLO is a cover unit for the National Security Agency, not the CIA.

CARUSO, JOSEPH A.

    b.   not known

4/63	Department of State Asunción, Paraguay (E) probably telecoms	
***9/65	Budapest, Hungary (L) telecoms specialist	S-6
as of 5/68	Dept.	
as of 5/69	(O/OC)	
6/69	El Salvador, San Salvador (E) telecoms officer	
2/70		S-5
as of 5/70	administrative officer	
as of 2/71	telecoms officer	
8/72	Brasília, Brazil (E) telecoms assistant	
12/74- at least 8/75	Athens, Greece (E) telecoms officer (Area Telecommunications Office)	
Sources:	FSL 8/75, 4/75, 11/74, 10/72, 2/71 5/70, 9/69, 5/69, 5/68, 1/67, 10/65	

***Budapest was elevated from Legation to Embassy in 11/66

CASEY, BURKE M.

    b.   not known

as of 2/75	Department of State Bonn, Germany (E) OCA Records Unit	
8/75	Sofia, Bulgaria (E) telecoms support officer	S-5
as of 2/78	Athens, Greece (E) probably telecoms	
Sources:	FSL 8/75 Bonn Embassy Source Department of State Source	

CAVE, GEORGE W.

b. 6 August 1929	New Jersey	
1947-52	U.S. Army	
1955	private experience oil company government relations trainee	

1956	Princeton University BA	
1956-58	International Cooperation Administration international relations officer	

5/58	Department of State
	    Tehran, Iran (E)
	    Attache &
	    political officer
		R-7

2/61		R-6

8/63	Beirut, Lebanon (E)
	    Foreign Service Institute
	    Attache, Arabic language
	    training	

8/64	Attache & political officer	
4/65		R-5
5/68		R-4
9/68	Dept. (NEA)	
6/70	Rawalpindi, Pakistan (E) political officer	
8/73	Tehran, Iran (E) economic-commercial officer	RU-4
4/74		RU-3
as of 1/75	First Secretary & economic-commercial officer	
as of 8/76	Dept. (NEA)	
as of 4/77	Jidda, Saudi Arabia (E) cover position not known	
Wife:	Joan McCarthy	
Sources:	BR 1974, 1961-62 FSL 8/75, 10/73, 10/70, 9/68, 10/64, 10/63, 7/58 Tehran Diplomatic List 1/75 Department of State Sources	

CERRA, RONALD L.

b. 6 March 1943	Massachusetts
1960-63	U.S. Army overseas
1963-67	Department of Defense research analyst
1967	Georgetown University BS
1967-70	Department of Defense linguist

8/70	Department of State	
	Dept.	
	international relations officer	GS-11
3/74	Geneva, Switzerland (M)	
	political officer	R-5
as of 8/75	political officer	
	(executive section)	
as of 10/77	Paris, France (E)	
	Attache	

Wife: Mary Ann Seery

Sources: BR 1974
                          FSL 8/75, 6/74
                          Geneva Diplomatic Lists 1/76, 10/75
                          Paris Diplomatic List 1/78
                          Department of State Sources

CESSNA, LINDA C.

as of 12/74:
6 Rue Chevert
75008 Paris
France
551-6328

b.   not known

as of 12/74	Department of State
	Paris, France (E)
	Regional Administrative Support

Source: Paris Embassy Source

CHALMERS, DUNCAN Y.

b.   not known

1/75	Department of State	
	Athens, Greece (E)	
	(Area Telecommunications Office)	S-7
as of 10/76	Dept. (A/OC)	

Source: FSL 8/75
                          Department of State Source

CHANEY, BRUCE G.

b.   not known

11/70	Department of State	
	Monrovia, Liberia (E)	
	telecoms assistant	S-6
6/73	Bern, Switzerland (E)	
	telecoms officer	
as of 11/74	telecoms support officer	

as of 10/76	New Delhi, India (E) probably telecoms
Sources:	FSL 8/75, 10/73, 2/71 Department of State Source

CHAREST, ELDON E.

b. 6 September 1932	Washington	
1951-55	U.S. Air Force overseas	
1956-57	Department of the Army communications	
3/57	Department of State Nicosia, Cyprus (C) general clerk	S-11
11/58	Jerusalem, Palestine (CG) general clerk	
1959-65	Department of the Army communications	
1965-68	Department of the Air Force communications	
1968-71	Department of the Army communications	
5/71	Department of State London, U.K. (E) telecoms officer	R-5
as of 9/74	Dept. (A/OC)	
as of 7/76	Athens, Greece probably telecoms	
11/77	award for length of service	
Wife:	Susan Gerringer	
Sources:	BR 1974 FSL 11/74, 6/71 Athens Embassy Sources Department of State Sources	

CHELLINO, CATHERINE

as of 9/74:
46 Via Dardanelli
Apt. 10
Rome
Italy
356-9441

b. not known

as of 9/74	Department of State Rome, Italy (E) USASEPU
Source:	Rome Embassy Source

CHIPMAN, HAROLD E.

b. 26 August 1929	Nebraska
1945-50	U.S. Marine Corps
1950-51	U.S. Army
1951	Georgetown University BSFS
1951-62	Department of the Army research analyst

1962-65	private experience
	        unspecified electronics company
	            writer

1965-72	Department of the Army plans officer

8/72	Department of State
	        Hamburg, Germany (CG)
	            political officer

as of 10/74	Dept. (EUR)
Wife:	Lois Ippolito
Sources:	BR 1974 FSL 6/74, 10/72 Department of State Source

R-4

CHOUKALOS, DALE

as of 12/74:
3 Rue Boutard
92200 Neuilly
France
747-8490

b. not known	

as of 12/74	Department of State
	        Paris, France (E)
	            Regional Reports Office

Source:	Paris Embassy Source

CHRITTON, GEORGE A. Jr.

b. 25 February 1933	Illinois
1953	University of Grenoble (France)
1953-54	Robert College (Turkey)
1955	Occidental College BA
1955-56	Princeton University
1957-60	U.S. Air Force 2nd Lieutenant
1960-63	Department of the Air Force

3/63	Department of State	
	Ankara, Turkey (E)	
	Attache &	
	political officer	R-6
9/65	Dept.	
	foreign affairs officer	GS-12
8/67	Kathmandu, Nepal (E)	
	economic officer	R-5
9/69	Dept. (NEA)	
6/72	Valletta, Malta (E)	
	political officer	
5/73		R-4
as of 11/74-	Dept. (EUR)	
at least 8/75		

Wife:	Martha Gilman
Sources:	BR 1974, 1968, 1964
	FSL 8/75, 11/74, 10/72, 1/70, 9/67, 1/67

CIAZZA, ADRIAN B.

as of 9/75:
14 Avenue General de Longueville, Apt. 2
1150 Brussels
Belgium
771-5513

b. 10 December 1932	Alabama	
1953-55	U.S. Army overseas	
1956	no entry in Department of State records;	
	not known	
1957-65	Department of the Army	
	research analyst	
4/65	Department of State	
	Kabul, Afghanistan (E)	
	Assistant Attache &	
	political officer	R-7
10/65	Third Secretary &	
	political officer	
12/65	Third Secretary, Vice-Consul &	
	political officer	
4/67		R-6
as of 9/68	economic officer	
9/69	Dept. (NEA)	
4/70	foreign affairs officer	GS-12
4/71	Colombo, Sri Lanka (E)	
	political-economic officer	

7/73	Dept. (NEA)	
1/74	Tehran, Iran (E) economic-commercial officer	R-5
as of 10/74	Dept. (NEA)	
as of 9/75	Brussels, Belgium (E) cover position not known	

Wife: Susan

Sources: BR 1974, 1968
               FSL 8/75, 11/74, 2/74, 10/73, 6/71,
                  5/70, 9/69, 9/68, 6/65
               Brussels Embassy Sources
               Department of State Source

CIOCI, MARIO L.

as of 9/74:
110 Via Alessandro Fleming
Apt. 14
Rome
Italy
396-6389

b. 14 February 1925	Italy	
1944-46	U.S. Army overseas	
1948	Columbia University BA	
1950	Columbia University MIA	
1951-68	unspecified government experience	
5/68	Department of State Barcelona, Spain (CG) political officer	R-4
9/70	Rome, Italy (E) Attache & political officer	
as of 1/77	Dept. (EUR)	

Wife: Jean Berlanstein

Sources: BR 1974
               FSL 8/75, 10/70, 9/68
               Rome Diplomatic Lists 9/76, 1/73
               Rome Embassy Source
               Department of State Source

CLARK, ROBERT A.

b. 8 October 1937	California
1955-58	U.S. Navy
1959-66	Department of State Dept. telecoms officer

1966-68	Department of the Army communications technician
9/68	Department of State Bogota, Colombia (E) telecoms officer S-6
as of 2/71-11/72	Department of the Army communications technician
12/72	Department of State Kuala Lumpur, Malaysia (E) telecoms officer R-7
8/75	Athens, Greece (E) telecoms officer (Area Telecommunications Office)
as of 8/77	Dept. (A/OC)
Wife:	Betty Burke
Sources:	BR 1974, 1973 FSL 8/75, 2/73, 10/70, 1/69 Department of State Source

CLAYMIER, ROBERT W.

b. not known	
7/75	Department of State Athens, Greece (E) telecoms engineer R-5 (Area Telecommunications Office)
Wife:	Linda
Source:	FSL 8/75

CLAYTON, THOMAS ALLYN

b. 14 February 1927	Washington
1945-47	U.S. Army
1950	San Jose State College BA
1951	San Jose State College MA
1951-56	private experience Spanish teacher & coach
1956-58	Department of the Army research analyst
4/58	Department of State Buenos Aires, Argentina (E) Assistant Attache & political officer R-7
7/60	Lima, Peru (E) Assistant Attache & political officer

4/64		R-6
6/65	Dept.	
6/66		S-4
as of 1/67	(ARA/LA)	
2/68		S-3
5/69		R-5
6/69	Caracas, Venezuela (E) political officer	
4/70		R-4
5/71	La Paz, Bolivia (E) political officer	
8/73	Santo Domingo, Dominican Republic (E) political officer	
4/74		R-3
as of 11/75	Dept. (ARA-LA)	
Wife:	Dawn O'Gara	
Sources:	BR 1974, 1969, 1958 FSL 8/75, 10/73, 6/72, 10/71, 6/71, 9/69, 1/67, 10/65, 10/60, 7/58 Department of State Source	

CLEMENT, CARLOS E.

b. not known		

6/75	Department of State
	Athens, Greece (E)
	    telecoms engineer
	    (Area Telecommunications Office)
		R-4

Wife:	Nancy	
Source:	FSL 8/75 Athens Embassy Source	

CLEVELAND, RICHARD ARTHUR

b. 30 December 1926	Massachusetts
1946-47	U.S. Army
1948	Massachusetts Institute of Technology BS

1948-50	private experience
	    cork company
	        advertising copywriter

1950-52	U.S. Army overseas
summer 1951, 52	School of Advanced International Studies
1952-53	Department of the Army research assistant

1/54	Department of State Jakarta, Indonesia (E) Vice-Consul	S-9
8/56	Dept.	S-8
2/58	Seoul, South Korea (E) economic officer	R-6
4/58	Second Secretary & economic officer	
9/60	Manila, Philippines (e) economic officer	
4/62		R-5
12/62	Dept.	
1/65	Saigon, Vietnam (E) Attache & Second Secretary	
5/66		R-4
11/66	Dept. (EA)	
6/67	foreign affairs officer	GS-14
10/69	Port-au-Prince, Haiti (E) political officer	R-4
12/71	Dept. (ARA-LA)	
5/72	Geneva, Switzerland (M) international economist	
as of 5/75	Dept. (IO)	
Sources:	BR 1974, 1954 FSL 4/75, 6/71, 1/70, 1/67, 6/65, 4/63, 10/60, 4/58, 1/57, 4/54 Geneva Diplomatic List 10/75 Geneva Mission Source Department of State Source	

CLOSE, RAYMOND H.

b. 12 March 1930	New Jersey	
1951	Princeton University BA	
1951-52	Department of Defense research analyst	
11/52	Department of State Beirut, Lebanon (E) political assistant	S-11
8/56		S-10
9/58	Dept.	
5/59		R-7
6/59	Cairo, Egypt (E) Assistant Attache & political officer	

10/59	Third Secretary & political officer	
5/60	Alexandria, Egypt (CG) political officer	
6/60	Vice-Consul	
4/62		R-6
11/62	Dept.	
9/63-7/64	detailed to Princeton University	
4/65		R-5
5/66	Lahore, Pakistan (CG) political officer	
1/68	Rawalpindi, Pakistan (E) political officer	
3/69		R-4
6/70- at least 1977	Jidda, Saudi Arabia (E) Second Secretary & political-economic officer	
5/72		R-3
8/73		RU-3
as of 12/77	private experience Riyadh, Saudi Arabia adviser to the foreign intelligence chief	

Wife: Martha Weir

Sources: BR 1974, 1960
                        FSL 8/75, 10/70, 5/68, 1/67, 1/63, 7/60,
                           10/59, 7/59
                        Jidda Diplomatic List 1973
                        Washington Post—December 20, 1977

COFFEY, JOHN WILLIAM

as of 9/75:
33 Marlborough Hill
London, NW 8
U.K.
586-4104

b. 7 March 1917	Colorado	
1939	Princeton University BA	
1939-42	private experience insurance underwriter	
1942-46	U.S. Army overseas Captain	
1946-50	Department of the Army communications officer	

1948	Georgetown University LLB	
1948	member of Washington, D.C. bar	
10/50	Department of State London, U.K. (E) Attache	S-5
7/52		S-4
11/54-6/63	Department of the Army communications specialist	
7/63	Department of State Dept. Deputy Assistant Secretary of State for Communications	R-1
2/66-9/73	not listed in Department of State records; assignment not known	
as of 10/70-9/73	Department of State London, U.K. (E) Attache & telecoms chief	
as of 10/75	assignment not known; possibly retired	
Wife:	Grahame	
Sources:	BR 1967, 1954 FSL 5/70, 10/65, 10/63, 10/54, 1/51 London Diplomatic Lists 8/75, 12/74, 10/73 London Embassy Sources	

COGAN, CHARLES G.

b. 11 January 1928	Massachusetts	
1949	Harvard University BA	
1949	private experience publications company executive trainee	
1949-51	newspaper reporter	
1951-53	U.S. Army overseas 2nd Lieutenant	
1954	private experience wire service editor	
1954-57	Department of Defense foreign affairs officer	
8/57	Department of State New Delhi, India (E) Assistant Attache & political officer	S-9
4/59		R-7
8/62	Dept.	
3/63	Léopoldville, Congo (E) Attache & political officer	R-6

5/63	Second Secretary, Attache & political officer	
4/64		R-5
9/65	Khartoum, Sudan (E) Second Secretary	
4/67	political officer	R-4
6/68	Dept. (0)	
3/69		R-3
4/69		S-1
as of 9/69	(AF)	
4/70		R-3
7/71	Rabat, Morocco (E) political officer	
as of 8/75	Dept. (NEA)	
Wife:	Susan Yoder	
Sources:	BR 1974, 1967, 1959 FSL 8/75, 10/71, 9/68, 7/63, 10/62, 10/57	

COLBY, MARK T.

b. 16 September 1930	Indiana	
1952	Brown University BA	
1952	U.S. Army	
1952-54	private experience newspaper reporter	
1954-55	news bureau	
11/55	United States Information Service Beirut, Lebanon (E) public affairs trainee	S-10
11/56	Khartoum, Sudan (E) Assistant Attache & information assistant	S-9
4/58	Vientiane, Laos (E) information officer	
6/59	private experience news magazine associate editor	
1960	public relations firm assistant account executive	
***1960-62	Department of the Air Force area analyst	
9/62	Department of State Léopoldville, Congo (E) Assistant Attache & political officer	R-7

9/64	Attache & political officer	R-6
2/65	Blantyre, Malawi (E) political officer	
5/65	Second Secretary & political officer	
8/67	Saigon, Vietnam (E) political officer	
3/69		R-5
7/69	Freetown, Sierra Leone (E) political officer	
10/70	Dept. (AF)	
5/73		R-4
8/73	Casablanca, Morocco (CG) economic-commercial officer	S-2
as of 8/75	Dept. (NEA)	
Wife:	Betty White	
Sources:	BR 1974, 1959 FSL 4/75, 10/73, 2/71, 10/70, 9/67, 6/65, 1/63 7/59, 7/58, 1/57	

***Previously, Colby was probably a bonafide U.S. Information Service employee. With this appointment, he joined the CIA.

COLE, BARBARA R.

as of 12/74:
215 Rue de L'Universite
75007 Paris
France
555-0527

b.   not known

as of 12/74	Department of State Paris, France (E) Office of the Special Assistant
Source:	Paris Embassy Source

COLLINS, JUDITH E.

as of 6/75:
228 Grove End Gardens
18 Abbey Road
London NW 8
U.K.
286-9184

    b.   not known

| as of 6/75 | Department of State London, U.K. (E) telecoms | |
| Source: | London Embassy Source | |

COMBS, WAYNE S.

    b.   not known

| as of 7/76 | Department of State Athens, Greece (E) probably telecoms | R-5 |
| Sources: | Athens Embassy Sources Department of State Sources | |

CONNORS, THOMAS J.

    b.   not known

6/75	Department of State Athens, Greece (E) telecoms support officer (Area Telecommunications Office)	S-8
as of 10/77	Dept. (A/OC)	
Sources:	FSL 8/75 Department of State Source	

CONROY, RICHARD A.

    b.   not known

8/69	Department of State Rio de Janeiro, Brazil (E) telecoms assistant	S-6
7/70	Lisbon, Portugal (E) telecoms officer	
9/73	Monrovia, Liberia (E) probably telecoms	
as of 1/76	Tehran, Iran (E) probably telecoms	
Sources:	FSL 8/75, 10/73, 10/70, 1/70 Department of State Source	

COOK, RICHARD C.

    b.   14 February 1922

| 6/70 | Department of State Athens, Greece (E) telecoms engineer | S-1 |

as of 10/73   not listed in Department of State records;
                                 assignment not known

Sources: BR 1973
                                 FSL 6/73, 10/70

COOPER, KENNETH M.

  b. not known

      11/70   Department of State
                                 Athens, Greece (E)
                                     telecoms assistant   S-7

      7/73   The Hague, Netherlands (E)
                                     telecoms assistant

  as of 6/74   telecoms support officer

  as of 4/77   Abidjan, Ivory Coast (E)
                                     probably telecoms

Sources: FSL 8/75, 10/73, 6/73
                                 Department of State Source

CORRIGAN, JAMES L.

  as of 12/74:
  1 Rue Miquet
  75016 Paris
  France
  288-6195

  b. date not known   Washington, D.C.

  as of 12/74   Department of State
                                 Paris, France (E)
                                     Office of the Special Assistant

      6/77   R-4

      7/77   confirmed as consular officer

  as of 10/77   Yaoundé, Cameroon (E)
                                     cover position not known

Source: Paris Embassy Source
                                 Department of State Sources

CORYDON, JEFF III

  b. 14 March 1929   Illinois

      1950   Northwestern University BS

    1950-52   private experience
                                     university public relations administration

    1952-55   U.S. Air Force 1st Lieutenant

      1953   Northwestern University MS

1955-57	Department of the Air Force political analyst	
5/57	Department of State Saigon, Vietnam (E) Assistant Attache & political officer	S-9
11/59	Dept.	
1/60		R-7
10/61	Rabat, Morocco (E) Foreign Service Institute Arabic language training	
4/62		R-6
7/63	Dept.	
4/65		R-5
8/66	Tunis, Tunisia (E) economic officer	
8/68	Dept. (AF)	
7/73	Yaoundé, Cameroon (E) political-economic officer	
8/73		S-2
as of 12/75	Dept. (AF)	
Language:	Arabic (Moroccan)	
Wife:	Mary James	
Sources:	BR 1974, 1967 FSL 8/75, 10/73, 9/68, 1/67, 10/63, 1/62, 1/60, 7/57 Department of State Source	

COSTANZO, CHRISTOPHER D.

as of 9/74:
31 Via Capo d'Africa
Apt. 20
Rome
Italy
73-47-00

b. 7 October 1941	New York
1962	Harvard University BA
1962	Department of the Navy historian
1963-64	private experience chemical company office manager
1964-66	U.S. Marine Corps overseas

3/66	Department of State Dept.	
	reports officer	GS-7
10/66		GS-9
7/69		GS-11
11/69	Madrid, Spain (E)	
	economic-commercial officer	R-6
as of 6/71	political officer	
2/73	Rome, Italy (E)	
	economic-commercial officer	
5/73		R-5
as of 10/76	Dept. (EUR)	
Wife:	Margaret Lutz	
Sources:	BR 1974, 1971 FSL 8/75, 6/73, 6/71, 1/70 Rome Diplomatic List 7/73 (updated) Rome Embassy Source Department of State Sources	

COVIELLO, JOSEPH LOUIS

as of 12/74:
22 Rue Maurice Berteaux
92130 Sevres
France
626-1709

b. not known

11/69	Department of State Kingston, Jamaica (E)	
	telecoms assistant	S-6
as of 10/70	telecoms officer	
as of 6/71		S-5
as of 2/72	Dept. (ARA-LA)	
as of 6/72-11/74	not listed in Department of State records; assignment not known	
as of 12/74	Department of State Paris, France (E) telecoms	
as of 8/77	Warsaw, Poland (E) probably telecoms	
Wife:	Cheril E.	
Sources:	FSL 2/72, 1/70 Paris Embassy Source Department of State Source	

CRAIGIE, DAVID G.

as of 1/74:
8 Irodou Attikou Street
Maroussi
Athens
Greece
802-8320

b.   not known

10/70	Department of State Phnom Penh, Cambodia (E) telecoms assistant	S-6
2/71	Saigon, Vietnam (E) telecoms assistant	
as of 2/73	Dept. (NEA)	

6/73	Athens, Greece (E)
	    telecoms assistant
	    (Regional Relay Facility)	

as of 11/74	telecoms support officer	
as of 10/75	Dept. (A/OC)	
as of 1/76	Buenos Aires, Argentina (E) telecoms	
as of 11/76	Dept. (A/OC)	
Sources:	FSL 8/75, 2/74, 10/73, 2/73, 6/71, 2/71 Athens Embassy Source Department of State Sources	

CRAM, CLEVELAND C.

b. 21 December 1917	Minnesota	
1938	St. John's University BA	
1938-39	private experience free-lance writer	
1940-41	high-school instructor	
1942-45	U.S. Navy overseas Lieutenant	

1946-48	private experience
	    Harvard University
	    teaching fellow	

1948	Harvard University MA	
1949-53	Department of Defense foreign affairs officer	
1950	Harvard University PhD	

9/53	Department of State
	    London, U.K. (E)
	        Attache
		S-4

1/55		S-3

as of 1/57	Attache & political officer	
as of 10/58-8/72	no entry in Department of State records; assignment not known	

as of 9/72-
at least 6/75
	Department of State
	    Ottawa, Canada (E)
	        Attache
	        (CIA Chief of Station)	

Sources:	BR 1957 FSL 7/58, 1/57, 4/54 Ottawa Diplomatic Lists 6/75, 9/72	

CRAWFORD, SETH TURNER

b. 31 May 1923	Massachusetts	
1943-46	U.S. Army overseas	
1947	Harvard University BA	
1948-49	Harvard Extension Course on Comparative Economies	

8/49	Department of State
	    Paris, France (E)
	        Vice-Consul
		S-11

3/53		S-10
6/57	Dept.	
7/57		S-9

6/58-2/64	private experience
	    Rome, Italy (E)
	        economic consultant to U.S. Embassy	

4/64	Department of State
	    Port-Au-Prince, Haiti (E)
	        Attache &
	        economic officer
		R-4

6/64	Second Secretary & Consul	
10/66	Dept.	
as of 5/68	(EUR) international relations officer	GS-15
as of 9/68-8/75	not found in State Department records; assignment not known	
9/75	Department of State Dept.	R-3

as of 11/75	Luxembourg, Luxembourg (E)
	    First Secretary
	    (CIA Chief of Station)	

Sources:	BR 1972, 1967 FSL 5/68, 1/67, 7/64, 7/58, 1/51 Luxembourg Diplomatic List 1976 Department of State Sources	

CREANE, STEPHEN F.

as of 10/74:
SHI-Sul
QL 3/10
casa 13
Brasília
Brazil
24-9462

b. 31 May 1926	Massachusetts	
1944-46	U.S. Army	
1951	Georgetown University BSFS	
1951-57	Department of the Army area specialist	

1/58	Department of State
	Jakarta, Indonesia (E)
	    Assistant Attache &
	    economic officer
		R-7

9/61	Dept.	
4/62		R-6
2/64	Recife, Brazil (CG) political officer	
4/64		R-5
6/64	Vice-Consul	
3/65	Consul	
7/66	Rio de Janiero, Brazil (E) political officer	
4/67		R-4
1/68		S-2
9/70	Dept. (ARA-LA)	
6/73		R-4
7/73	Rio de Janeiro, Brazil (CG) political officer	
4/74		R-3
8/74	Brasília, Brazil (E) political officer	
as of 10/75	Dept. (ARA-LA)	
Wife:	Katherine	
Sources:	BR 1974, 1966 FSL 8/75, 11/74, 10/73, 10/70, 1/67, 4/64, 1/62, 4/58 Brasília Diplomatic List 10/74 Department of State Sources	

CREE, PAUL G. Jr.

as of 12/75:
6 Dreimarksteingasse, House 4
1190 Vienna
Austria
44-21-68

b. not known

as of 12/75	Department of State
	Vienna, Austria (E)
	Foreign Broadcast Information Service
	chief

| Wife: | Carol Marie |
| Sources: | Vienna Embassy Sources |

CREEDEN, WILLIAM E.

b. 26 December 1931

1/65	Department of State	
	Brussels, Belgium (E)	
	telecoms specialist	S-6
as of 5/67	telecoms supervisor	
10/67	Managua, Nicaragua (E)	
	telecoms supervisor	
as of 1/70	telecoms officer	S-5
3/70	Manila, Philippines (E)	
	telecoms assistant	
as of 10/70	telecoms officer	
5/71		S-4
7/72	Beirut, Lebanon (E)	
	telecoms officer	
8/74-	Athens, Greece (E)	
at least 8/75	telecoms officer	
	(Area Telecommunications Office)	

| Sources: | BR 1974 |
| | FSL 8/75, 11/74, 10/72, 5/70, 1/68, 10/65 |

CROWLING, JOSEPH V.

b. not known

6/75	Department of State	
	Athens, Greece (E)	
	telecoms officer	R-3
	(Area Telecommunications Office)	

Wife:	Beverly
Source:	FSL 8/75
	Athens Embassy Source

CUMBO, ROBERT O.

    b. not known

5/72	Department of State
	  Geneva, Switzerland (M)
	    U.S. Mission to the European
	    Office of the United Nations and Other
	    International Organizations
	      telecoms assistant S-8

as of 6/74	Dept. (A/OC)
as of 11/74- 10/76	not listed in Department of State records; assignment not known

as of 11/76	Department of State
	  Manila, Philippines (E)
	    probably telecoms

Sources:	FSL 6/74, 6/73 Department of State Sources

CUMMINGS, CAROL K.

    as of 9/74:
    38 Via Arno
    Apt. 6
    Rome
    Italy
    845-9303

    b. not known

as of 9/74	Department of State
	  Rome, Italy (E)
	    USASEPU

Source:	Rome Embassy Source

CURTIS, GENE P.

    as of 1/74:
    44 K, Paleologou Street
    Politia
    Kifissia
    Athens
    Greece
    801-6985

b. 13 April 1944	Illinois
1963-66	U.S. Army overseas
1969	Southern Illinois University A.S.

1969-71	private experience
	  electronic business machine manufacturer
	    electronic technician

1972	not given in Department of State records; not known

1/73	Department of State	
	Athens, Greece (E)	
	telecoms technician	R-8
	(Area Telecommunications Office)	

as of 8/76	Dept. (A/OC)
Wife:	Judy Armstrong
Sources:	BR 1974
	FSL 8/75, 10/73, 2/73
	Department of State Sources

CUSICK, CHARLES J.

as of 1/76:
89 Rue de Monceau
Paris 16
75016 Paris
522-10-02

b. 16 March 1923	New York	
1943-46	U.S. Navy overseas Lieutenant	
1947	Queens College BA	
1947	private experience	
	insurance policy rater	
1948	advertising copy writer	
1949-52	unspecified university	
	graduate assistant	
1952	New York University MA	
1952-53	Department of the Army	
	junior analyst	
3/53	Department of State	
	Beirut, Lebanon (E)	
	language training	S-11
7/54	Dept.	
11/55	Dhahran, Saudi Arabia (CG)	
	Vice-Consul &	
	consular assistant	
8/56		S-9
7/57		S-8
12/57	Cairo, U.A.R. (E)	
	Assistant Attache &	
	political officer	
5/59		R-6
9/60	Dept.	
8/62	Tripoli, Libya (Office)	
	Arab language training	

9/62	Attache & political officer	
12/62	Second Secretary, Attache & political officer	
4/64		R-5
1/66	Dept.	
4/67		R-4
6/67	Rabat, Morocco (E) political officer	
3/72	Dept.	
8/73		S-2
6/72	Port Louis, Mauritius (E) consular officer	
as of 11/74- at least 1/76	Paris, France (E) Regional Reports Office	

Wife: Janet Burgess

Sources: BR 1974, 1968
                FSL 6/74, 10/72, 9/67, 1/67, 1/63,
                    4/58, 10/56
                Port Louis Diplomatic Directory 7/74
                Paris Embassy Sources

DAIGLE, DONALD C.

as of 1/74:
25b Kanari Street
Kifissia
Athens
Greece
801-1803

b. 2 February 1936	Vermont	
1956-58	U.S. Army	
1958-73	unspecified government agency electronics technician	

5/73	Department of State
	Athens, Greece (E)
	    telecoms technician
	    (Area Telecommunications Office)
		R-7

as of 10/76	Dept. (A/OC)	

Wife: Mary Stoll

Sources: BR 1974
                FSL 8/75, 6/73
                Athens Embassy Source
                Department of State Source

DALE, CHARLES J.

    b. not known

9/67	Department of State Manila, Philippines (E) telecoms assistant	S-6
8/72	Copenhagen, Denmark (E) telecoms officer	
as of 7/75	Dept. (EUR)	
as of 8/75	Jidda, Saudi Arabia (E) probably telecoms	
as of 6/78	Athens, Greece (E) probably telecoms	
Sources:	FSL 8/75, 11/74, 10/72, 10/70 Department of State Sources	

DAMSCHRODER, LAMONT S.

    b. not known

4/75	Department of State
	Athens, Greece (E)
	    telecoms support officer
	    (Area Telecommunications Office)
		S-8

as of 7/77	Dept. (A/OC)	
as of 11/77	Georgetown, Guyana (E) probably telecoms	
Source:	FSL 8/75 Department of State Sources	

DAVIS, STANLEY W. Jr.

    b. not known

4/67	Department of State Nicosia, Cyprus (E) telecoms technician	S-6
as of 9/69	not listed in Department of State records; assignment not known	

1/75	Department of State
	Athens, Greece (E)
	    telecoms support officer
	    (Area Telecommunications Office)
		R-7

as of 3/77	Dept. (A/OC)	
Wife:	Eulah	
Sources:	FSL 8/75, 5/69, 5/67 Athens Ambassy Sources Department of State Sources	

DEAN, WARREN LaFOREST

b. 1 August 1916	Iowa	
1938	Simpson College BA	
1938-39	private experience accountant	
1940-42	insurance company employee	
1942-43	Department of Justice position not known	
1943	Department of State La Paz, Bolivia (E) Assistant Attache	rating not known
1944	no entry in Department of State records; assignment not known	
1945	Department of State Santiago, Chile (E) position not known	rating not known
1946	no entry in Department of State records; assignment not known	
1947-48	private experience rubber company assistant manager	
5/48	Department of State Buenos Aires, Argentina (E) Attache	S-6
2/50	Dept.	
10/50	London, U.K. (E) Attache	S-5
1/54-7/58	Department of the Army staff planning officer	
8/58	Department of State Mexico City, Mexico (E) political officer	R-3
12/58	First Secretary & political officer	
12/62	Quito, Ecuador (E) Attache & political officer	
4/67		R-2
as of 9/68	Dept. (ARA-LA)	
2/69		S-1
6/69	foreign affairs officer	GS-16
8/70	Oslo, Norway (E) First Secretary & political officer (CIA Chief of Station)	R-2

5/74	Dept. (EUR)
as of 4/75	not listed in Department of State records; assignment not known
Wife:	Robbie Shepherd
Sources:	BR 1974, 1967
	FSL 11/74, 10/70, 9/68, 4/63, 10/58, 7/52, 1/50, 7/48
	Oslo Diplomatic Lists 4/74, 10/70
	Department of State Source

De BLOIS, JEAN P.

b.   8 November 1923

6/70	Department of State	
	London, U.K. (E)	
	telecoms officer	S-2
as of 10/73	not listed in Department of State records; assignment not known	
Sources:	BR1973	
	FSL 6/73, 10/70	

DEGRANDS, DOMINIC J.

b.   not known

11/70	Department of State	
	Rome, Italy (E)	
	telecoms assistant	S-7
as of 2/74	Dept. (EUR)	
as of 11/74	not listed in Department of State records; assignment not known	
Sources:	FSL 6/74, 2/74, 6/73	

DeLONG, SANDRA J.

as of 2/76:
Steubenring 5/1
5300 Bonn-Bad Godesberg
Germany
37-53-51

b.   not known

as of 2/75- at least 2/76	Department of State
	Bonn, Germany (E)
	USAREUR Regional Survey Unit
Husband:	Donald
Source:	Bonn Embassy Source

DENICOURT, RAYMOND F.

b. 30 November 1925	Massachusetts	
1944-45	U.S. Army	
1949	Providence College BS	
1949-50	private experience salesman	
1950-52	U.S. Marine Corps Captain	
1952	private experience chemist	
1952-57	Department of the Army administrative officer	GS-11

11/57	International Cooperation Administration
	   Saigon, Vietnam (E)
	        civil administration advisor
		R-6

6/61-
at least 10/63
	Agency for International Development
	   Vientiane, Laos (E)
	      program analyst	

as of 11/63-8/67	Department of the Army	

9/67	Department of State
	   Asmara, Ethiopia (CG)
	      political officer
		R-4

12/69	Dept.	
4/70	program officer	GS-13
10/70		S-2
as of 2/71	(AF)	
11/72		R-4
12/72	Bamako, Mali (E) economic-commercial officer	
as of 10/74	Dept. (AF)	
Language:	French	
Sources:	BR 1974, 1968, 1961-62 FSL 6/74, 2/73, 2/71, 1/70, 1/68, 10/63, 7/61, 4/58 Department of State Source	

DENNIS, DAVID L.

b. 19 May 1941	Iowa
1959-62	U.S. Army overseas

1962-63	private experience
	   electronics company
	      expediter

1963-64	Department of the Army communications technician

9/64-8/66	Department of State	
	Dept.	rating
	communications assistant	not given

| 9/66-8/72 | Department of the Army | |
| | telecoms specialist | |

9/72-	Department of State	
at least 11/74	Stockholm, Sweden (E)	
	telecoms officer	R-7

| as of 4/75-1/77 | not listed in Department of State records; assignment not known | |

| 2/77 | Department of State | |
| | Dept. | R-6 |

| as of 4/77 | Bujumbura, Burundi (E) | |
| | probably telecoms | |

Sources:	BR 1974	
	FSL 11/74, 2/73	
	Department of State Sources	

DER-VERTANIAN, ANNA

as of 12/74:
45/47 Rue des Vigues
75016 Paris
France
527-9929

b. not known

as of 12/74	Department of State
	Paris, France (E)
	Regional Administration Support
Source:	Paris Embassy Source

DESCOTEAUX, NORMAN M.

b. 15 June 1936	Maine	
1959	University of Maine BA	
1959-61	U.S. Army 1st Lieutenant	
1962-65	Department of the Army	
	political analyst	
7/65	Department of State	
	Guayaquil, Ecuador (CG)	
	political assistant	S-6
6/67	Buenos Aires, Argentina (E)	
	political officer	S-5
4/70		R-5
as of 8/70-6/73	Department of the Army	
	program coordination officer	

7/73	Department of State	
	Guayaquil, Ecuador (CG)	
	political officer	R-4
as of 8/75	Dept. (ARA-LA)	
as of 9/76	Kingston, Jamaica (E)	
	(CIA Chief of Station)	
Wife:	Dolores Corbeil	
Sources:	BR 1974	
	FSL 4/75, 10/73, 5/70, 9/67, 10/65	
	Kingston Embassy Source	
	Department of State Source	

DEVEREUX, ROBERT E.

as of 9/74:
45 Via Luigi Luciana
Bldg. 1
Apt. 8
Rome
Italy
87-84-97

b. 9 December 1922	Wisconsin	
1942	Department of War	
	checker	
1942	University of California (Berkeley) AA	
1942-46	U.S. Army	
1944	Indiana University BA	
1946	National University	
1946-54	Department of the Army	
	research analyst	
1956	George Washington University MA	
1957-63	Department of the Army	
	research analyst	
1961	Johns Hopkins University PhD	
7/63	Department of State	
	Rome, Italy (E)	
	Attache &	
	political officer	R-4
as of 1/67	Dept.	
as of 5/67-9/72	not listed in Department of State records;	
	assignment not known	
10/72-	Department of State	
at least 9/76	Rome, Italy (E)	
	Attache &	
	political officer	

Sources: BR 1966, 1964
                    FSL 1/67, 10/64, 10/63
                    Rome Diplomatic Lists 9/76, 1/73
                    Rome Embassy Source

DIMODICA, JAMES S.

as of 1/74:
11 Constantinou Paleologou Street
Nea Politia
Kifissia
Athens
Greece
801-9749

b.   13 November 1928

5/72	Department of State	
	Athens, Greece (E)	
	telecoms officer	R-7
	(Regional Relay Facility)	
as of 10/74	Dept. (A/OC)	

Wife: Shirley

Sources: BR 1974
                    FSL 6/74, 6/72
                    Athens Embassy Source

DIMSDALE, JOHN H. Jr.

b. 11 July 1925	Kansas	
1943-51	U.S. Army overseas 2nd Lieutenant	
1955	University of Kansas BA	
1957	University of Kansas MA	
1957-68	Department of the Army	
5/68- at least 6/73	Department of State Stockholm, Sweden (E) political officer	R-4

Wife: Virginia Harris

Sources: BR 1973
                    FSL 6/73, 9/68

Di STEFANO, JOSEPH A.

as of 9/74:
11 Via Ermete Novelli
Rome
Italy
87-02-71

b. 25 May 1927	New York	
1945-46	U.S. Marketing Service	
1950	Rutgers University BA	
1951	Johns Hopkins University MA	
1951-55	not given in Department of State records; not known	
1956-61	private experience sales-advertising manager	
1961-66	research associate	
2/66	Department of State Dept. supervisory international relations officer	GS-14
4/67	Caracas, Venezuela (E) political officer	R-4
9/69	Dept. (ARA–LA)	
9/71	Rome, Italy (E) First Secretary & political officer	
5/72		R-3
as of 8/75	Dept. (EUR)	
as of 10/75	Santo Domingo, Dominican Republic (E) Attache	
Wife:	Jane H.	
Sources:	BR 1974, 1969 FSL 4/75, 10/72, 10/71, 5/68, 9/67 Rome Diplomatic Lists 7/73 (updated), 1/73 Rome Embasy Source Santo Domingo Diplomatic List 10/75 Department of State Source	

DOLGE, JAMES J.

b. not known		
6/74	Department of State Dept. (EUR)	R-5
8/74	Berlin, Germany (M) political officer	
as of 10/77	Dept. (EUR)	
Wife:	Emilie	
Sources:	FSL 8/75, 11/74 Berlin Mission Source Department of State Sources	

DOMBROWSKY, DAVID L.

as of 12/75:
29-39 Hartaeckerstrasse, Apt. 8
1190 Vienna
Austria
36-45-12

b.   not known

5/72	Department of State Mogadiscio, Somalia (E) telecoms assistant	S-7
as of 10/74	Dept. (AF)	
10/74	Vienna, Austria (E) telecoms officer	
as of 10/77	Dept. (A/OC)	

Wife: Barbara J.

Sources: FSL 8/75, 11/74, 6/73
                Vienna Embassy Source
                Department of State Sources

DOMINGUEZ, OLGA

as of 9/74:
41 Via Campania
Hotel Victoria
Rome
Italy
48-00-52

b.   not known

as of 9/74   Department of State
                     Rome, Italy (E)
                     USASEPU

Source: Rome Embassy Source

DONOVAN, ANN C.

as of 12/74:
196 Boulevard Pereire
75017 Paris
France
754-4210

b.   not known

as of 12/74   Department of State
                     Paris, France (E)
                     Regional Reports Office

Source: Paris Embassy Source

DOOLEY, BARBARA W.

as of 6/75:
7 Wigmore Street
Apt. A
London W 1
U.K.
580-8209

b.   not known

as of 12/74-   Department of State
at least 6/75   London, U.K. (E)
                                         Joint Reports & Research Unit

Sources: London Embassy Sources

DORVAL, NANCY E.

as of 12/74:
60 Rue Laugier
75017 Paris
France
754-6893

b.   not known

as of 12/74   Department of State
                                    Paris, France (E)
                                         American Liaison Section

Source: Paris Embassy Source

DOWNEY, SALLY MARIE

as of 12/74:
23 Bis Rue de Constantinople
75008 Paris
France
292-2976

b.   not known

as of 12/74   Department of State
                                    Paris, France (E)
                                         Office of the Special Assistant

Source: Paris Embassy Source

DOWNEY, TIMOTHY A.

b.   not known

10/72   Department of State
                                    Kathmandu, Nepal (E)
                                         telecoms assistant   S-7

as of 1/75   Dept. (A/OC)

2/75   Geneva, Switzerland (M)
                                    telecoms support officer

Sources: FSL 8/75, 4/75, 6/73
                         Geneva Mission Source
                         Department of State Source

DUBERMAN, DAVID

as of 12/74:
24 Avenue Charles Floquet
75007 Paris
France
566-7092

b.   not known

as of 12/74   Department of State
                         Paris, France (E)
                             Regional Reports Office

Source: Paris Embassy Source

DUNICAN, THERESA A.

as of 12/75:
228 Grove End Gardens
Abbey Road
London NW 8
U.K.

b. not known

as of 12/75   Department of State
                         London, U.K. (E)
                             telecoms

Source: London Embassy Source

DUNN, EDWARD PAUL

as of 11/77:
23 Abbey Road
St. John's Wood
London NW 8
U.K.
624-0034

b.   26 July 1922   Massachusetts

    1943-46   U.S. Army

    1947   Bates College BA

    1951   Harvard University MA

    1951-56   Department of Defense
                         political affairs officer

    7/56   Department of State
                         Paris, France (E)
                             Assistant Attache &
                             political officer

7/56		R-6
10/58	Dept.	
2/59		R-5
as of 10/59-11/75	not listed in Department of State records; assignment not known	
as of 12/75- at least 11/77	Department of State London, U.K. (E) Political Liaison Section	
Wife:	Claire	
Sources:	BR 1959 FSL 7/59, 1/59, 10/56 London Embassy Sources	

DUNN, JIMMY C.

    b. not known

8/71	Department of State Helsinki, Finland (E) telecoms officer	S-6
as of 11/74-12/76	not listed in Department of State records; assignment not known	
1/77		R-7
as of 2/77	Department of State Yaoundé, Cameroon (E) probably telecoms	
Sources:	FSL 6/74, 10/71 Department of State Sources	

DURKIN, NAOMI C.

    as of 3/76:
    66 Hamilton Terrace
    London NW 8
    U.K.
    286-9237

    b. not known

as of 12/75	Department of State London, U.K. (E) telecoms

EASON, EARL T.

    b. not known

6/66	Department of State Manila, Philippines (E) telecoms assistant	S-7
8/70		S-6

1/72	Rio de Janeiro, Brazil (CG) telecoms assistant
8/74	Accra, Ghana (E) telecoms support officer
as of 10/77	Athens, Greece (E) probably telecoms
as of 10/77	award for length of service
Sources:	FSL 8/75, 4/75, 6/74, 6/72, 10/70 Athens Embassy Sources Department of State Sources

EATON, JOAN C.

as of 12/74:
59 Rue Chauveau
92200 Neuilly
France
637-2029

b. not known

as of 12/74	Department of State Paris, France (E) Regional Reports Office

Paris Embassy Source

EATON, ROBERT FRANCIS

b. 20 April 1935	Oklahoma
1955-58	U.S. Air Force overseas
1961	Howard Payne College BA
1962-63	not given in Department of State records; not known
1964-66	Department of the Air Force
8/66	Department of State Seoul, Korea (E) at Yonsei University language-area trainee
as of 9/67-12/74	not listed in Department of State records; assignment not known
as of 1/75- at least 2/76	Department of State Brussels, Belgium (E) Assistant Attache
Sources:	BR 1967 FSL 5/67, 1/67 Brussels Diplomatic Annual 1975 Brussels Diplomatic List 2/76

R-7

ECKROTE, DONALD G.

b. 16 February 1934	California	
1956	University of California (Los Angeles) BA	
1956-59	U.S. Army overseas	
1960-66	Department of the Army analyst	
1966-67	provincial adviser	
1967-70	programs officer	
6/70	Department of State Helsinki, Finland (E) political officer	R-7
5/71		R-6
as of 10/74	Dept. (EUR)	
Wife:	Virginia O'Brien	
Sources:	BR 1974 FSL 11/74, 10/70	

ECKSTEIN, WILLIAM HERBERT

b. 1 February 1931	Iowa	
1953	State College of Iowa BA	
1953-55	U.S. Army	
1955-57	Department of the Army plans officer	
5/63	Department of State Vienna, Austria (E) Attache & political officer	R-6
1/68	Dept. (0) plans & programs officer	GS-12
7/72	Berlin, Germany (M) political officer	R-5
5/73	economic-commercial officer	
4/74		R-4
as of 11/76	Dept. (EUR)	
Wife:	Sue Barthelmeh	
Sources:	BR 1974 FSL 8/75, 10/72, 1/69, 7/63 Department of State Source	

EDDY, CONDIT N. Jr.

b. 14 October 1927	New York

1945-47	U.S. Army	
1951	Princeton University BA	
1951-53	private experience oil company personnel advisor	
1953-54	Aleppo College (Syria) teacher	
1954-55	private experience high school teacher	
1955-58	Department of the Army analyst	
***1/58-10/60	International Cooperation Administration Amman, Jordan (E) reports officer	R-6
1960-62	Department of the Army foreign affairs officer	
8/62	Department of State Foreign Service Institute language and area training	R-6
9/62	Beirut, Lebanon (E) Foreign Service Institute Field School Attache & language-area trainee	
5/63	Aleppo, Syria (CG) economic officer	
8/63	Vice-Consul	
10/64	Damascus, Syria (E) Attache & political officer	
5/65	Second Secretary & political officer	
4/67		O-5
9/67		R-5
6/68		S-3
7/70	Istanbul, Turkey (CG) political officer	
9/73	Dept. (NEA)	
9/77		R-4
as of 11/77	London, U.K. (E) First Secretary (Political)	
Wife:	Nancy Boardman	
Language:	Arabic	

Sources:	BR 1974, 1968
	FSL 8/75, 10/73, 10/70, 6/65, 7/63, 1/63
	London Diplomatic List 6/78
	Department of State Sources

***ICA was predecessor to the Agency for International Development, established in 1961.

EDMUNDS, BARBARA J.

as of 3/76:
1 Hyde Park Square
London W 2
U.K.
262-0470

b. not known

as of 12/74-	Department of State
at least 3/76	London, U.K. (E)
	Joint Reports & Research Unit

Sources: London Embassy Sources

ELBON, SAM B.

as of 1/74:
19 Romilias Street
Kokkinara
Kifissia
Athens
Greece
801-5062

b.   9 July 1931

5/67	Department of State	
	Vienna, Austria (E)	
	telecoms technician	S-5
as of 9/69-5/72	not listed in Department of State records; assignment not known	
6/72-	Department of State	
at least 8/75	Athens, Greece (E)	
	telecoms technician	R-7
	(Regional Relay Facility)	
as of 10/75	Dept. (A/OC)	

Wife:	Mary
Sources:	BR 1974, 1973
	FSL 8/75, 10/72, 9/67
	Athens Embassy Source
	Department of State Source

ELLAM, KATHERINE T.

    as of 6/77:
    Europastrasse 16
    5300 Bonn-Bad Godesberg
    Germany
    37-42-16

    b.   not known

as of 6/73	Department of State	
	Dept. (IO)	S-7
as of 10/73		S-6
1/74	New York, New York (M)	
	United States Mission to the	
	United Nations	
	reports officer	
	(Political Affairs Section)	
4/74		S-5
as of 4/75	Dept. (IO)	
6/75-	Bonn, Germany (E)	
at least 6/77	economic-commercial officer	
3/77		S-4
Sources:	FSL 8/75, 4/75, 2/74, 6/73	
	Bonn Diplomatic Lists 6/77, 6/76	

ELLIS, HOWARD J.

    as of 9/74:
    5 Piazza Stefano Jacini
    Bldg. 4
    Apt. 16
    Rome
    Italy
    32-13-26

    b.   not known

as of 9/74	Department of State
	Rome, Italy (E)
	USASEPU
as of 1/76	not listed in Department of State records; assignment not known
Wife:	Fay
Source:	Rome Embassy Source

ELMORE, THOMAS P.

    as of 6/75:
    58 South Eaton Place
    London SW 1
    U.K.
    730-3155

b.   not known

as of 12/74   Department of State
                                              London, U.K. (E)
                                                    Joint Reports & Research Unit

as of 1/76   not listed in Department of State records;
                                              assignment not known

Wife: Mary Ellen

Sources: London Embassy Sources

ELMQUEST, KAREN J.

as of 1/74:
61 Anagnostopoulou Street
Athens
Greece
60-55-24

b.   not known

1/72   Department of State
                                    Athens, Greece (E)
                                         secretary in Political Section   S-8

as of 1/74   (secretary to CIA Chief of Station)

as of 11/74   S-7

as of 6/76   Dept. (EUR)

Sources: FSL 8/75, 11/74, 6/73
                                           Athens Embassy Source
                                           Department of State Source

ERACLEOUS, MICHAEL P.

as of 3/76:
15 Burnley Road
Dollis Hill
London NW 10
U.K.
452-3559

b.   not known

as of 10/75-   Department of State
at least 3/76   London, U.K. (E)
                                           Foreign Broadcast Information Service

Source: London Embassy Source

ESCH, PAUL E.

b.   17 August 1929

5/59   Department of State
                                    Manila, Philippines (E)
                                         communications assistant   S-9

as of 10/62-7/71	not listed in Department of State records; assignment not known	
8/71	Department of State London, U.K. (E) telecoms engineer	R-4
as of 8/73	Dept. (A/OC)	
9/73	New Delhi, India (E) telecoms engineer	
as of 10/76	Dept. (A/OC)	
Sources:	BR 1974 FSL 8/75, 10/73, 10/71, 7/62, 7/59 Department of State Source	

ESTES, RONALD EDWARD

as of 1/74:
14 Krinon Street
Philothei
Athens
Greece
671-3980

b. 28 June 1931	Washington, D.C.	
1949-51	private experience book-keeper	
1951-54	U.S. Marine Corps overseas	
1954	private experience trust company note teller	
1957	Virginia Polytechnic Institute BS	
1957-62	Department of the Army	
4/62	Department of State Nicosia, Cyprus (E) communications specialist (Regional Relay Office)	S-8
10/62		S-5
8/64		S-4
8/64	Dept. Foreign Service Institute Czech language training	R-6
5/65	Prague, Czechoslovakia (E) Attache & economic-commercial officer	
10/65	Second Secretary & Vice-Consul	
5/66		R-5
8/67	Dept. (O)	
as of 9/69	(EUR)	

4/70		R-4

7/70   Beirut, Lebanon (E)
                             Second Secretary &
                             economic-commercial officer

as of 1/74   Department of Defense
                             Athens, Greece (E)
                             JUSMAGG

Wife: Ann Lester

Sources: BR 1971, 1967
                             FSL 6/73, 10/70, 9/69, 1/68, 10/65, 10/64, 7/62
                             Beirut Diplomatic List 1973
                             Athens Embassy Source

EVANS, REBECCA T.

　　　as of 9/74:
　　　41 Via Campania
　　　Hotel Victoria
　　　Rome
　　　Italy
　　　48-00-52

　　　b.　not known

　　　as of 9/74   Department of the Army
                             Rome, Italy (E)
                             USASEPU

　　　Source: Rome Embassy Source

EVANS, ROBERT J.

　　　as of 3/76:
　　　89 Highgate West Hill
　　　London N 6
　　　U.K.
　　　340-4407

　　　b.　not known

　　　as of 12/74-   Department of State
　　　at least 3/76   London, U.K. (E)
                                Political Liaison Section

　　　Wife: Heather

　　　Sources: London Embassy Sources

EVANS, WILLIAM J.

　　　as of 1/74:
　　　20 Neapoleos Street
　　　Philothei
　　　Athens
　　　Greece
　　　682-6904

b. 23 November 1929	Pennsylvania
1947-49	U.S. Army
1949-51	Kent State University
1951-52	private experience finance company credit investigator
1952-59	Department of the Army
***4/59	Agency for International Development Jakarta, Indonesia (E) public safety advisor R-6
6/62	Saigon, Vietnam (E) public safety advisor
7/62	R-5
11/62	Hué, Vietnam (CG) public safety advisor
as of 1/65	Saigon, Vietnam (E) public safety advisor
as of 6/65-12/73	not listed in Department of State records; assignment not known
as of 1/74	Department of State Athens, Greece (E) JUSMAGG
Wife:	Sybil
Sources:	BR 1964, 1959 FSL 1/65, 10/64, 7/64, 10/62, 7/59 Athens Embassy Source

***This appointment began with the International Cooperation Administration, the predecessor until 1961 to the Agency for International Development.

EXLER, ELIZABETH

as of 3/76:
Flat 6
Reeves House
Reeves Mews
London W 1
U.K.
493-2492

b. not known

as of 12/74-
at least 3/76
	Department of State
	    London, U.K. (E)
	        Joint Reports & Research Unit

Sources:	London Embassy Sources

FALCON, JACK

as of 2/76:
Büchelstrasse 53B
5300 Bonn-Bad Godesberg
Germany
35-15-00

b.   not known

as of 2/75   Department of State
         Bonn, Germany (E)
            Office of the Coordinator and Advisor

Wife: Virginia

Source: Bonn Embassy Source

FARRELL, KATHLEEN

as of 1/74:
1 Vrassida Street
Athens
Greece
74-62-90

b.   not known

  2/73   Department of State
         Athens, Greece (E)
          telecoms clerk   S-8
          (Area Telecommunications Office)

  4/75   Monrovia, Liberia (E)
         secretary

as of 7/77   Dept. (AF)

Sources: FSL 8/75, 4/75, 6/73
        Athens Embassy Source
        Department of State Source

FARRELL, NANCY A.

as of 12/74:
12 Rue des Marroniers
75816 Paris
France
525-7977

b.   not known

  8/70   Department of State
         Rabat, Morocco (E)
          political assistant   S-6

as of 10/72   Dept. (AF)   S-5

as of 6/73-11/74 not listed in Department of State records;
        assignment not known

as of 12/74	Department of State Paris, France (E) Regional Reports Office
Sources:	FSL 2/73, 10/72, 10/70 Paris Embassy Source Department of State Source

FARRELL, SYLVESTER L.

as of 12/74:
14 Passage du Guesclin
75015 Paris
France
566-9533

b.   5 September 1930

11/68	Department of State Lagos, Nigeria (E) political officer	R-5
3/69	consular officer	
4/71	Dept. (AF)	
as of 6/72-11/74	not listed in Department of State records; assignment not known	
as of 12/74	Department of State Paris, France (E) Regional Reports Office	
Wife:	Elizabeth Springer	
Sources:	BR 1971 FSL 2/72, 5/69 Paris Embassy Source	

FAUGHT, DAVID W.

b.   not known

5/71	Department of State Nicosia, Cyprus (E) telecoms assistant	S-8
10/73	Vientiane, Laos (E) telecoms assistant	
as of 11/74	telecoms support officer	S-7
8/75	Athens, Greece (E) telecoms support officer (Area Telecommunications Office)	
as of 5/78	Dacca, Pakistan (E) probably telecoms	
Sources:	FSL 8/75, 11/74, 2/74, 6/73 Department of State Source	

FEDKIW, CARL P.

    b. not known

6/71	Department of State
	  La Paz, Bolivia (E)
	    telecoms assistant
		S-7

as of 10/73-8/75	not listed in Department of State records; assignment not known	

as of 9/75	Department of State
	  Brussels, Belgium (E)
	    telecoms	

as of 6/78	Rangoon, Burma (E) probably telecoms	
Wife:	Barbara	
Source:	FSL 6/73 Brussels Embassy Source	

FENDIG, PHILIP FRANKLIN

    b. 1 March 1923

b. 1 March 1923	Indiana	
1943-46	U.S. Army overseas 1st Lieutenant	
1947	Kenyon College BA	
1947-50	Department of the Army area specialist	

9/50	Department of State
	  Tokyo, Japan
	  (Office of the U.S. Political Adviser
	  to Supreme Commander for Allied Powers)
	    Vice-Consul
		S-7

7/52		S-6
1953-56	Department of the Army foreign affairs officer	

12/56	Department of State
	  Tokyo, Japan (E)
	    Attache
		R-4

4/57	Second Secretary & political officer	
10/59	Dept.	
3/63		R-3

7/63	London, U.K. (E)
	  Attache &
	  political officer	

12/66		S-1

9/67	Dept. foreign affairs officer	GS-15
6/70	Munich, Germany (CG) political officer	R-3
10/72	Dept. (EUR)	
as of 2/74	not listed in Department of State records; assignment not known	
Wife:	Carlotta Johnston	
Sources:	BR 1973, 1967 FSL 10/73, 2/73, 10/63, 1/60, 1/57, 10/52, 10/50	

FENNER, BILLY A.

b. not known		

8/69	Department of State
	    Copenhagen, Denmark (E)
	        telecoms assistant
		S-6

as of 5/70	Dept. (EUR)	
5/71	Santo Domingo, Dominican Republic (E) telecoms assistant	
11/73	Manila, Philippines (E) telecoms assistant	
as of 6/77	Rome, Italy (E) probably telecoms	
as of 3/78	Dept. (A/OC)	
Wife:	Georgia	
Sources:	FSL 8/75, 2/74, 10/71, 5/70, 1/70 Department of State Sources	

FERENTINOS, JERRY J.

as of 1/74:
15 Herodotou &
Krystali Streets
Kokkinara
Kifissia
Athens
Greece
801-5776

b. 7 February 1929	New York
1952	Syracuse University BA
1952	private experience university business assistant
1952-55	U.S. Army overseas
1955-61	Department of the Army analyst

8/61	Department of State
	    Hong Kong, U.K. (CG)
	        political officer R-6

as of 10/64-12/66	not listed in Department of State records; assignment not known

as of 1/67	Agency for International Development
	    Vientiane, Laos (E)
	        executive assistant R-5

as of 9/68-12/73	not listed in Department of State records; assignment not known

as of 1/74	Department of Defense
	    Athens, Greece (E)
	        JUSMAGG

Wife:	Elizabeth
Sources:	BR 1964 FSL 5/68, 1/67, 7/64, 1/62 Athens Embassy Source

FERNALD, JAMES M.

b. 19 June 1931	New Jersey
1953	Brown University BA
1953-56	U.S. Army overseas
1956-58	private experience petroleum salesman
1959-61	chain store copy writer
1961-62	Department of the Army analyst

11/62	Department of State
	    Beirut, Lebanon (E)
	        Foreign Service Institute
	            Attache &
	            Arabic language-area trainee R-7

11-64	Taiz, Yemen (E)
	    Third Secretary, Vice-Consul &
	    economic officer

12/66	Sana'a, Yemen (Office) economic officer
4/67	R-6
11/67	Amman, Jordan (E) economic-commercial officer
4/70	R-5
9/70	Dept. (NEA)
11/71	Jidda, Saudi Arabia (E) economic-commercial officer

6/72	Abu Dhabi, United Arab Emirates (E)	
	Consular Section	
	economic-commercial officer	
10/72	consular officer	
8/73		RU-5
as of 1/75	Dept. (NEA)	
Wife:	Bera Hickman	
Sources:	BR 1974, 1967, 1966	
	FSL 8/75, 10/72, 10/70, 1/68, 5/67,	
	1/65, 1/63	
	Department of State Source	

FERRIS, RICHARD C.

as of 3/76:
3 Oakhill Way
Hampstead
London NW 3
U.K.
435-4010

b.   not known

7/75-	Department of State	
at least 3/76	London, U.K. (E)	
	telecoms officer	R-4
Wife:	Frances	
Sources:	FSL 8/75	
	London Embassy Source	

FETTEROLF, WALLACE K.

b.   24 June 1924

5/72	Department of State	
	London, U.K. (E)	
	telecoms engineer	R-3
7/72	telecoms officer	
as of 10/74	Dept. (A/OC)	
Sources:	BR 1974	
	FSL 11/74, 6/72	
	Department of State Source	

FISHER, MARGARET V.

as of 12/74:
9 Quai d' Anjou
75004 Paris
France
325-0917

b.   not known

as of 12/74   Department of State
                                        Paris, France (E)
                                            Office of the Special Assistant

Source: Paris Embassy Source

FITZSIMMONS, ZANE R.

b.   not known

5/68   Department of State
                                        Beirut, Lebanon (E)
                                            telecoms officer   S-6

8/70-   Athens, Greece (E)
at least 2/73   telecoms assistant

Sources: FSL 2/73, 10/70

FLING, GRAHAM J. III

as of 12/74:
10 Rue Singer
75016 Paris
France
224-9533

b.   not known

as of 12/74   Department of State
                                        Paris, France (E)
                                            telecoms

as of 1/77   Muscat, Oman (E)
                                        probably telecoms   R-8

Sources: Paris Embassy Source
                                    Department of State Sources

FORD, GEORGE W. II

as of 8/76:
9 Kynance Place
Gloucester Road
London SW 7
U.K.
584-6049

b.   4 September 1929   Ohio

1951   Yale University BS

1951-53   U.S. Army overseas 2nd Lieutenant

1954-60   private experience
                                   methods engineer, foreman

1960-62	Department of Defense analyst	
7/62	Department of State Alexandria, Egypt (CG) consular officer	R-7
9/62	Vice-Consul	
5/65		R-6
7/67	Dept.	
as of 1/69	(NEA)	
3/69		R-5
6/70	Tehran, Iran (E) political officer	
as of 10/72-11/73	not listed in Department of State records; assignment not known	
as of 12/73	Department of State London, U.K. (E) Attache & Political Liaison Section	
as of 6/76	Assistant Political Attache	
Wife:	Eleanore Johnston	
Sources:	BR 1972, 1964 FSL 6/72, 10/70, 1/69, 9/67, 10/62 London Diplomatic Lists 8/76, 12/73 London Embassy Sources	

FORD, NANCY

b. 1 September 1924	New York	
1945	Cornell University BA	
1949	University of Wisconsin MA	
1949-51	no entry in Department of State records; whereabouts not known	
1/52	Department of State Paris, France (E) clerk-typist	S-13
1957-60	Department of Defense clerk-typist	
12/60	Department of State Warsaw, Poland (E) clerk	S-10
10/62		S-7
8/64	Belgrade, Yugoslavia (E) political section general clerk	
12/67	Geneva, Switzerland (M) political assistant	S-6

5/71	political officer	
10/71	Dept. (IO)	
7/72	Geneva, Switzerland (M) political officer & SPA	R-7
3/75		R-6
as of 10/75	Attache	
as of 8/77	New York, New York (M) United States Mission to the United Nations Adviser	
2/78		R-5

Sources: BR 1974
                FSL 4/75, 10/71, 5/68, 10/64
                Geneva Diplomatic Lists 1/76, 10/75
                Geneva Mission Source
                List of Permanent Missions to the United Nations 8/77
                Department of State Sources

FORTNER, LUTHER C.

b. 26 October 1932	Arkansas	
1952-56	U.S. Navy overseas	
1957-59	Department of the Army communications specialist	
6/59	Department of State Nicosia, Cyprus (E) communications assistant	S-12
4/62	Managua, Nicaragua (E) telecoms supervisor	S-7
6/65	Amman, Jordan (E) telecoms officer	S-6
9/67	Bangkok, Thailand (E) telecoms assistant	S-5
as of 11/69-5/71	Department of Defense communications instructor	
6/71	Department of State Addis Ababa, Ethiopia (E) telecoms officer	R-6
4/74		R-5
8/74	Monrovia, Liberia (E) telecoms officer	
as of 9/77	Athens, Greece (E) probably telecoms	

Wife:	Helen Grantz	
Sources:	BR 1974	
	FSL 8/75, 11/74, 10/71, 9/69, 1/68, 10/65	
	Athens Embassy Sources	
	Department of State Sources	

FRANCIS, GEORGE V.

as of 1/74:
16 Elission Street
New Kifissia
Athens
Greece
801-1962

b.   not known

1/71	Department of State	
	Athens, Greece (E)	
	telecoms assistant	S-7
	(Regional Relay Facility)	
as of 3/74	Dept. (A/OC)	
5/74	Rio de Janeiro, Brazil (CG)	
	telecoms support officer	
2/76		S-6
as of 10/76	Dept. (A/OC)	
as of 3/77	Damascus, Syria (E)	
	probably telecoms	
Wife:	Mary Ann	
Sources:	FSL 8/75, 6/74, 6/73	
	Athens Embassy Source	
	Department of State Sources	

FRANK, WARREN E.

as of 6/77:
Martin Luther King Strasse 3/3
5300 Bonn-Bad Godesberg
Germany
37-55-85

b.   4 June 1925

7/70	Department of State	
	Hamburg, Germany (CG)	
	political officer	R-3
9/72	Dept. (EUR)	
7/74-	Bonn, Germany (E)	
at least 6/77	Attache &	
	Office of the Coordinator and Advisor	

as of 6/77   Attache
                                    (CIA Chief of Station)

Wife: Monica

Sources: BR 1973, 1971
                                    FSL 6/74, 2/73, 10/70
                                    Bonn Diplomatic Lists 6/77, 9/74
                                    Bonn Embassy Source

FREY, PHILIP E.

as of 1/74:
23 Avras Street
Kifissia
Athens
Greece
801-2679

b. not known

as of 1/74   Department of State
                                        Athens, Greece (E)   rating
                                        telecoms   not known
                                        (Regional Relay Facility)

as of 8/76   Montevideo, Uruguay (E)
                                        probably telecoms

Wife: Roxanna

Source: Athens Embassy Source
                                    Department of State Source

FRIEND, JULIUS W. Jr.

as of 1/76:
15 Rue Jean-Mermoz
75008 Paris
France
256-0165

b. 3 April 1926   Louisiana

1944   University of Chicago Ph.B.

1944-46   U.S. Army overseas

1949   University of Chicago MA

1949-50   Sorbonne University (France)

1951-66   Department of the Army
                                        political officer

1960   University of Chicago PhD

5/66   Department of State
                                        Rome, Italy (E)
                                        Attache &
                                        political officer   R-4

7/71	political assistant
5/72	political officer
8/72	Dept. (EUR)
as of 10/73-10/74	not listed in Department of State records; assignment not known

as of 11/74- at least 1/76	Department of State
	    Paris, France (E)
	        Office of the Special Assistant

Wife:	Louise Prince
Sources:	BR 1973, 1968, 1966 FSL 6/73, 10/72, 1/67 Rome Diplomatic List 1/72 Paris Embassy Source

FUEHRER, ALLEN

as of 9/75:
62 Avenue Val au Bois
1950 Kraainem
Belgium
731-8265

b. 1 December 1925	Missouri
1944-45	U.S. Army overseas
1949	University of Southern California BFS
1949-50	University of California
1950-66	Department of the Air Force plans officer

6/66	Department of State
	    Bangkok, Thailand (E)
	        Attache &
	        economic-commercial officer R-4

9/69	Dept. (EA)
as of 6/72-8/75	not listed in Department of State records; assignment not known

as of 9/75	Department of State
	    Brussels, Belgium (E)
	        Attache

Wife:	Rosa Marletta
Sources:	BR 1971, 1966 FSL 2/72, 1/70, 1/67 Brussels Diplomatic List 2/76 Brussels Embassy Source

GAFFNEY, RAYMOND C.

as of 1/74:

1 Orpheos Street
Kefalari
Kifissia
Athens
Greece
801-2701

b.   23 June 1927

7/64	Department of State
	    Manila, Philippines (E)
	        telecoms specialist
		S-4

as of 1/68	Dept.	
as of 5/68-4/72	not listed in Department of State records; assignment not known	

5/72	Department of State
	    Athens, Greece (E)
	        telecoms officer
	        (Area Telecommunications Office)
		R-5

as of 8/75	Dept. (A/OC)	
Wife:	Claire	
Sources:	BR 1974 FSL 8/75, 4/75, 6/72, 1/68, 9/67, 10/64 Athens Embassy Source Department of State Sources	

GAGEN, JEANNE M.

as of 3/76:
9 Reeves House
Reeves Mews
London W 1
U.K.
499-3852

b.   not known

as of 12/74
at least 3/76
	Department of State
	    London, U.K. (E)
	        Joint Reports & Research Unit

Sources:	London Embassy Sources

GAHAGEN, ROBERT DALE

as of 11/75:
Daniel Urrabieta, num. 10-3
Madrid
Spain
261-82-43

b. 24 March 1921	Nebraska
1943	Kansas State College BS
1943-46	U.S. Army overseas Captain

1946-47	private experience reporter copy reader	
3/47	Department of State Dept.	S-11
4/47	Guayaquil, Equador (CG) Vice-Consul & political officer	
6/49	Quito, Ecuador (E) Vice-Consul	S-9
8/49	Montevideo, Uraguay (E) Vice-Consul	
3/51	Assistant Attache	S-7
4/53	Dept.	
1953-55	Department of Defense foreign affairs officer	
10/55	Department of State São Paulo, Brazil (CG) political officer	R-4
4/59	Dept.	
3/60		R-3
4/63	Rio de Janeiro, Brazil (E) Attache & political officer	R-2
6/65		S-1
12/66		R-3
3/69		R-2
10/69	Dept. (ARA-LA)	
6/73- at least 5/76	Madrid, Spain (E) Attache, Political Liaison Section (CIA Chief of Station)	
Wife:	Irma Davila	
Sources:	BR 1971, 1967, 1955, 1950 FSL 6/73, 1/70, 7/63, 7/59, 1/56, 4/53, 10/49, 7/49, 7/47 Madrid Diplomatic Lists 5/76, 5/74 Madrid Embassy Source	

GALE, CHARLES R. Jr.

as of 9/74:
170F Vicolo Del Casale Lumbroso
Rome
Italy
690-0377

b. 21 January 1925	New Jersey
1946-50	Post Office Department clerk
1949-50	University of Basel (Switzerland)
1950-52	private experience drug clerk
1951	University of Maryland BA
1952-61	Department of the Army liaison officer

8/61	Department of State
	    Vienna, Austria (E)
	        political officer R-5

4/65	R-4
as of 5/67	assistant general services officer
9/67	Dept. (EUR)
as of 10/70-8/74	not listed in Department of State records; assignment not known

as of 9/74	Department of State
	    Rome, Italy (E)
	        USASEPU

Wife:	Edith
Sources:	BR 1969, 1963 FSL 5/70, 1/68, 5/67, 1/62 Rome Embassy Source

GALLAGHER, JAMES J.

as of 1/74:
16 Rodon Street
New Kifissia
Athens
Greece
801-4607

b. not known	

10/63	Department of State
	    Tehran, Iran (E)
	        communications assistant S-6

2/66	Accra, Ghana (E) telecoms officer
6/68	Guatemala City, Guatemala (E) telecoms officer
as of 5/70	S-5

7/71	Athens, Greece (E)
	    telecoms assistant
	    (Regional Relay Facility)

as of 12/74	Vientiane, Laos (E) probably telecoms
Wife:	Jean
Sources:	FSL 6/74, 10/71, 5/70, 9/68, 1/67, 10/64 Athens Embassy Source Department of State Source

GAMBRELL, BOBBY J.

b. 13 November 1940

6/71	Department of State
	  Manila, Philippines (E)
	    telecoms officer
		R-7

7/73	Dept. (EA)	
6/74	Athens, Greece (E) telecoms support officer	
as of 12/76	Amman, Jordan (E) probably telecoms	
as of 11/77	Dept. (A/OC)	
Sources:	BR 1974 FSL 8/75, 11/74, 10/73, 10/71 Department of State Sources	

GARBLER, PAUL

as of 5/76:
44 Elfviksvägen
181 90 Lidingö
Sweden
765-45-10

b. 4 January 1918	New Jersey	
1939	University of Florida BA	

1939-41	private experience
	  food equipment company
	    sales engineer	

1941-56	U.S. Navy overseas Lieutenant Commander	

4/56	Department of State
	  Stockholm, Sweden (E)
	    Attache
		R-4

6/56	Second Secretary	
9/59	Dept.	
3/60		R-3

8/61	U.S. Navy commander
	  Moscow, U.S.S.R. (E)
	    Assistant Naval Attache
	    Assistant Naval Attache for Air	

as of 10/65-7/68	not listed in Department of State records; assignment not known	

8/68	Department of State
	    Port-of-Spain, Trinidad & Tobago (E)
	        political officer
		R-2

11/72	Dept. (ARA-LA)	

as of 11/73-
at least 5/76
	Stockholm, Sweden (E)
	        Attache
	        (CIA Chief of Station)	

Wife:	Florence Fitzsimmons	
Sources:	BR 1973, 1960 FSL 6/73, 2/73, 9/68, 6/65, 1/62, 10/59, 7/56	

GARRETT, EARL NORBERT III

as of 12/76:
19 Bneid Al-Gar
Kuwait
Kuwait
422-234

b. 25 November 1938	Missouri	
1960	University of Kansas BA	
1960-62	U.S. Navy	
1962-64	Department of the Army economic analyst	
1963-64	George Washington University	

8/64	Department of State
	    Karachi, Pakistan (E)
	        Third Secretary,
	        Assistant Attache &
	        economic officer
		R-7

10/64	Third Secretary & economic officer	
4/66	Lahore, Pakistan (CG) economic-labor officer	
4/67		R-6
1/69	Dept. (NEA)	
8/70	Amman, Jordan (E) economic-commercial officer	
2/72	Cairo, Egypt (E) economic-commercial officer	
6/72		R-5

8/73	Calcutta, India (CG)
	    Consul &
	    political officer
		RU-5

7/75	Kuwait, Kuwait (E) political officer	
2/76		RU-4
as of 12/76	First Secretary	
Wife:	Meredith Osen	
Sources:	BR 1974, 1968 FSL 8/75, 10/73, 6/72, 10/70, 1/70, 1/67, 10/64 Calcutta Diplomatic List 1/75 Kuwait Diplomatic & Consular List 12/76	

GATELY, ROBERT GENE

as of 1/75:
38 Soi Charoenmitr
off Sukhumvit 63
Bangkok
Thailand
913-807

b. 4 July 1931	Texas	
1953	Yale University BA	
1953-55	U.S. Army overseas Lieutenant	
1955-67	private experience international trader journalist	
1/67	Department of State Dept. reports officer	GS-12
3/68	Ōsaka-Kōbe, Japan (CG) political officer	R-5
6/72	Dept. (EA)	
4/73	Bangkok, Thailand (E) Second Secretary & political officer	
4/74		R-4
as of 1/75	First Secretary & political officer	
as of 11/76	Dept. (EA)	
Wife:	Stephanie Bassett	
Sources:	BR 1974 FSL 8/75, 10/73, 10/72, 5/68 Bangkok Diplomatic Lists 1/75, 1/74 Bangkok Embassy Sources Department of State Sources	

GEBHARDT, CARL E.

    b.   8 June 1933

5/72	Department of State Dept. (EUR)	R-5
7/72	Warsaw, Poland (E) political officer	
as of 7/73	Second Secretary & political officer	
as of 11/74	Dept. (EUR)	
3/75		R-4
7/76	Bangkok, Thailand First Secretary	

    Sources: BR 1974
                              FSL 8/75, 11/74, 10/72, 6/72
                              Warsaw Diplomatic List 7/73
                              Bangkok Diplomatic List 7/76
                              Department of State Sources

GEHAN, KENNETH J.

    b.   not known

7/75	Department of State
	   Athens, Greece (E)
	      telecoms officer
	      (Area Telecommunications Office)
		R-6

    Source: FSL 8/75

GELINAS, PAUL R.

    as of 12/74:
    21 Rue Leconte de Lisle
    75016 Paris
    France
    527-8596

    b.   not known

as of 12/74	Department of State
	   Paris, France (E)
	      telecoms

    Wife: Phyllis R.
    Source: Paris Embassy Source

GELWICKS, ORVILLE R.

    b.   not known

2/73	Department of State
	   New Delhi, India (E)
	      telecoms assistant
		S-7

as of 11/74	telecoms support officer	
6/75	Athens, Greece (E) telecoms support officer (Area Telecommunications Office)	
as of 11/77	Dept. (A/OC)	
Sources:	FSL 8/75, 11/74, 6/73 Department of State Source	

GEORGE, CLAIR ELROY

as of 7/76:
24 Rue Ghizi, Psychico
Athens
Greece
671-2831

b. 3 August 1930	Pennsylvania	
1952	Pennsylvania State University BA	
1952-55	U.S. Army overseas	
8/56	Department of State Hong Kong, U.K. (CG) political assistant	S-11
7/58		S-10
1/60	Dept.	
3/60		R-7
4/61	Paris, France (E) political officer	
7/64	Bamako, Mali (E) Attache & economic officer	R-6
8/64	Second Secretary & economic officer	
2/66	Dept.	
4/67		R-5
7/67	New Delhi, India (E) political-economic officer	
1/70	political officer	
4/70		R-4
8/71	Dept. (NEA)	
5/75		R-3
as of 6/75	Beirut, Lebanon (E) cover position not known	
5/76	Athens, Greece (E) First Secretary (CIA Chief of Station)	

as of 10/77	award for length of service

Wife:	Mary Atkinson

Sources:	BR 1973, 1968
	FSL 8/75, 2/73, 10/71, 9/67, 1/67,
	10/64, 1/61, 7/60
	Athens Diplomatic List 7/76
	Department of State Source

GERNER, GEORGE W.

as of 9/74:
5 Piazza Stefano Jacini
Bldg. B, Apt. 25
Rome
Italy
327-4707

b.   not known

as of 9/74	Department of State
	Rome, Italy (E)
	USASEPU

as of 1/76	not listed in Department of State records; assignment not known

Wife:	Margaret

Source:	Rome Embassy Source

GIAMMARINO, JOSEPHINE P.

as of 9/74:
1 Via Del Colli
Apt. 9
Rome
Italy
85-52-22

b.   not known

as of 9/74	Department of State
	Rome, Italy (E)
	USASEPU

Source:	Rome Embassy Source

GIBBS, JOHN H.

b.   not known

5/73-	Department of State
at least 4/75	Bern, Switzerland (E)
	telecoms assistant

as of 11/74	telecoms support officer

S-7

as of 5/78	Kigali, Rwanda (E)
	probably telecoms
Sources:	FSL 4/75, 6/73
	Department of State Source

GIESECKE, FRITZ H.

b. 15 February 1923	Oregon	
1943-46	U.S. Army	
1947	University of Oregon BA	
1948	MA	
1949	JD	
1949	member of District of Columbia, Oregon & U.S. Supreme Court bars	
1949-50	U.S. Army overseas Second Lieutenant	
1950-51	Department of the Army programs analyst	
1/51	Department of State Vienna, Austria (USCOA) (Office of the U.S. High Commissioner for Austria) editorial assistant assistant public affairs officer	S-9
as of 1/52	reports analyst	
as of 10/53-10/69	Department of the Army programs officer	
1963-64	private experience law firm attorney	
11/69	Department of State Dept. program officer	GS-17
5/70	Stockholm, Sweden (E) political officer	R-2
7/73-6/74	Dept. Foreign Service Institute	
as of 11/74	(EUR)	
as of 4/75	not listed in Department of State records; assignment not known	
Wife:	Celeste Olsen	
Sources	BR 1974, 1973 FSL 11/74, 10/73, 10/70, 4/53, 4/51	

GILHOOLY, JOHN F.

as of 1/75:

avenue Moliere 238
1060 Brussels
Belgium
344-71-21

b. 26 September 1926	Connecticut	
1944-46	U.S. Navy overseas	
1951	Colby College BA	

1951-52	private experience
	    manufacturing company
	        junior executive trainee
	        industrial engineer	

1952-56	Department of the Army
	    Taipei, Taiwan
	        foreign affairs officer	

6/56	Department of State
	    Rangoon, Burma (E)
	        political officer
		R-5

7/56		R-6
9/56	Vice-Consul, Second Secretary & political officer	
2/59		R-5
7/59	Dept.	

10/61	Phnom Penh, Cambodia (E)
	    Attache &
	    political officer	

4/64		R-4

10/64	New Delhi, India (E)
	    Attache &
	    political officer	

12/64	Second Secretary & political officer	
4/66	Hong Kong, U.K. (CG) political officer	S-2
12/66		S-1
as of 1/68-6/70	not listed in Department of State records; assignment not known	

7/70	Department of State
	    Bern, Switzerland (E)
	        political officer
		R-4

4/72- at least 2/76	Brussels, Belgium (E) Attache	
Wife:	Suzanne Hall	
Sources:	BR 1971, 1967, 1957 FSL 10/71, 10/70, 1/67, 1/65, 1/62, 10/59, 10/56 Brussels Diplomatic Lists 2/76, 4/74	

Brussels Guide to Ministries 1975-76
Brussels Diplomatic Annual 1975

GILLEN, DAVID J.

as of 1/74:
39 Sokratous Street
Kifissia
Athens
Greece
801-9882

b.   not known

2/68	Department of State
	    Manila, Philippines (E)
	        telecoms assistant
		S-6

8/70	Jidda, Saudi Arabia (E) telecoms officer	

8/72	Athens, Greece (E)
	    telecoms officer
	    (Regional Relay Facility)	

2/76		S-5
as of 10/76	Dept. (A/OC)	
Wife:	Janet	
Sources:	FSL 8/75, 10/72, 10/70, 9/69 Athens Embassy Source	

GILSTRAP, COMER WILEY Jr.

b. 6 August 1926	Alabama	
1945	U.S. Army	
1946	Department of Commerce examiner's assistant	
1949	Department of Justice file clerk	
1950	University of Maryland BA	
1950-55	Department of the Army political analyst	
3/55	Department of State Quito, Ecuador (E) political officer	R-5
7/56		R-6
6/57	Rio de Janeiro, Brazil (E) political officer	
7/58	Pôrto Alegre, Brazil (C)	
8/58	Vice-Consul	
3/60		R-5

3/61	Montevideo, Uruguay (E) Attache & political officer
3/63	R-4
3/64	San Salvador, El Salvador (E) Attache & political officer
2/65	S-2
9/66	Dept. (ARA-LA)
2/68	S-1
3/69	R-4
8/69	Georgetown, Guyana (E) political officer
4/71	San José, Costa Rica (E) Second Secretary & political officer
as of 10/74	Dept. (ARA-LA)
as of 4/75-9/76	not listed in Department of State records; assignment not known
as of 10/76	Department of State Santiago, Chile (E) cover position not known
as of 3/77	confirmed as consular officer
as of 8/77	First Secretary
Wife:	Mary Ann Ellis
Sources:	BR 1974, 1968 FSL 11/74, 6/71, 1/70, 1/67, 7/64 7/61, 10/58, 10/57, 4/55 San Jose Diplomatic List 4/72 Santiago Diplomatic List 8/77 Department of State Sources

GINSBURG, HARVEY H.

b. 25 February 1922	Massachusetts
1943	Yale University BA
1943-45	U.S. Army overseas
1948	Oxford University (U.K.) B. Litt.
1948	Leiden University (Netherlands)
1950	Yale University MA
1950-51	University of Utrecht (Netherlands)
1950-52	private experience Yale University instructor

1952	Yale University PhD	
1952-54	Department of State Dept. analyst	GS-9
1954-55	Department of the Army political officer	
12/55	Department of State The Hague, Netherlands (E) Assistant Attache & political officer	R-5
7/56		R-6
6/58	Attache & political officer	
2/59		R-5
8/60	Dept.	
8/64	London, U.K. (E) cover position not known	
6/68- at least 7/77	Zurich, Switzerland (CG) political officer	R-4
as of 7/77	Consul	
Wife:	Helen Morrey	
Sources:	BR 1974, 1960 FSL 8/75, 9/68, 1/61, 10/60, 10/58, 4/56 Zurich Consular List 7/77	

GLEASON, LYLE K.

b. not known		
as of 6/73	Department of State Lisbon, Portugal (E) telecoms assistant	S-7
as of 10/73-3/74	not listed in Department of State records; assignment not known	
4/74	Department of State Manila, Philippines (E) telecoms officer	S-6
as of 8/76	Lima, Peru (E) probably telecoms	
Sources:	FSL 8/75, 6/74, 6/73 Department of State Source	

GMIRKIN, VASIA C.

as of 12/75:
off Queen Mary Avenue
Floreal

Port Louis
Mauritius
Cpe. 2073

b. 11 February 1926	China
1944	naturalized as U.S. citizen
1944-46	U.S. Navy overseas
1947-48	private experience import-export foreign trader (overseas)
1948	Woodbury College BBA
1948-49	private experience mortgage brokers
1949-50	insurance underwriter
1950-51	manufacturing & sales firm partner
1951-56	Department of Commerce business specialist
1954-55	Claremont Graduate School

4/56	Department of State
	  Dept.
	        conference interpreter (Russian) R-5

7/56	R-6

11/56	Tokyo, Japan (E)
	    Attache &
	    political officer

2/57	Second Secretary, Attache & political officer
9/58	Dept.
as of 10/58-1960	Department of Commerce international economist
1960-6/61	not listed in Department of State records; assignment not known

7/61	Department of State
	  Kathmandu, Nepal (E)
	    Attache &
	    political officer R-5

9/61	Second Secretary & political officer
9/63	Baghdad, Iraq (E) political officer
4/65	R-4
7/67	Dept. (NEA)
3/70	Kinshasa, Zaire (E) political officer
9/71	Dept. (AF)

4/74	Port Louis, Mauritius (E)
	First Secretary & Consul
as of 10/76	Dept. (AF)

Wife:	Mary Nelson
Sources:	BR 1974, 1968, 1958
	FSL 8/75, 6/74, 10/71, 5/70, 9/67,
	1/64, 1/62, 10/58, 1/57, 7/56
	Port Louis Diplomatic Directory 12/75

GOFF, THOMAS L.

as of 1/74:
3 Kalamou Street
Ekali
Athens
Greece
803-1518

b. not known

7/67	Department of State	
	Kaduna, Nigeria (C)	
	telecoms assistant	S-6
10/69	Singapore, Singapore (E)	
	telecoms assistant	
as of 10/70	telecoms support officer	
as of 6/72		S-5
2/73	Athens, Greece (E)	
	telecoms support officer	
	(Regional Relay Facility)	
as of 8/75	Tehran, Iran (E)	
	telecoms officer	R-6
as of 12/77	Monrovia, Liberia (E)	
	probably telecoms	

Wife:	Norma
Sources:	FSL 8/75, 4/75, 6/73, 6/72, 1/69
	Athens Embassy Source
	Department of State Source

GOLDMAN, NORMAN

as of 1/74:
17 Solonos Street
Nea Politia
Kifissia
Athens
Greece
801-9157

b. not known

11/68	Department of State Lahore, Pakistan (CG) economic-commercial officer S-5
as of 2/71	Dept.
as of 10/71-12/73	not listed in Department of State records; assignment not known
as of 1/74	Department of Defense Athens, Greece (E) JUSMAGG
Wife:	Gloria
Sources:	FSL 2/72, 6/71, 10/70, 1/69 Athens Embassy Source

GOMEZ, RUDOLPH EDWARD

b. 27 May 1915	Arizona	
1935-40	Federal Housing Administration auditor	
1940-41	Lend Lease Administration liaison officer	
1941-42	auditor	
1942	War Department censor	
1942-45	Treasury Department customs officer	
1944	University of Miami LLB member of Florida bar	
12/46	Department of State Lisbon, Portugal (E) Attache	S-7
11/48	Dept.	
12/50	Havana, Cuba (E) Attache	S-5
12/52	Buenos Aires, Argentina (E) Attache	
1/55		S-4
8/56		S-3
7/57	Attache & political officer	S-2
10/57	Dept.	
8/59		R-4
10/60	Santiago, Chile (E) Attache & political officer	

4/62		R-3
4/64		R-2
3/65	Dept.	
as of 5/68	(ARA-LA)	

7/69-
at least 6/73
	Lisbon, Portugal (E)
	    economic-commercial officer
	    (CIA Chief of Station)	

as of 1/72	Attache (Political Section)	
as of 11/73	not listed in Department of State records; possibly retired	
Wife:	Elizabeth Bowlby	
Sources:	BR 1973 FSL 6/73, 9/69, 6/65, 1/61, 1/58 4/53, 4/51, 1/49, 7/47 Lisbon Diplomatic Lists 1/73, 11/69 Department of State Source	

GOODMAN, KENNETH R.

b. 15 July 1936	Arizona	

1956-59	private experience
	    Mexico
	        missionary	

1961	University of Arizona BA	
1960-64	unspecified institution teacher, research assistant	
1964	University of Arizona MA	
1964-65	Department of the Army	

8/65	Department of State
	    Caracas, Venezuela (E)
	        political officer
		R-7

5/67	Guayaquil, Ecuador (CG) political officer	
3/69		R-6
7/69	Quito, Ecuador (E) political officer	
4/70		R-5
12/71	Dept. (ARA-LA)	
6/73	San Salvador, El Salvador (E) political officer	
4/74		R-4
7/75		RU-4

as of 11/75- at least 9/76	Guatemala City, Guatemala (E) First Secretary	
as of 10/77	Dept. (ARA-LA)	
Wife:	Carol Downey	
Sources:	BR 1974 FSL 8/75, 10/73, 2/72, 9/69, 9/67, 10/65 San Salvador Diplomatic List 1975 Guatamala City Diplomatic List 9/76 Department of State Sources	

GOODWIN, ROBERT B.

b. 2 April 1940	Massachusetts	
1962	Harvard University BA	
1964	Clark University MA	
1963-64	Department of the Air Force	
2/65	Department of State Calcutta, India (CG) political officer	R-8
5/65	Vice-Consul & political officer	
8/68	New Delhi, India (E) Political-Economic Section economic-commercial officer	
10/68	political-economic officer	
3/69		R-7
1/70	political officer	
4/70		R-6
7/71	Dept. (NEA)	
5/73		R-5
7/73	Istanbul, Turkey (CG) political officer	
2/75		S-3
as of 2/76	Consul (Political Affairs)	
as of 12/77	Dept. (EUR)	
Wife:	Kate Dooley	
Sources:	BR 1974 FSL 8/75, 10/73, 10/71, 9/68, 6/65 Istanbul Diplomatic List 2/76 Department of State Sources	

GORDON, MARION C. Jr.

as of 1/74:
18 Ehinou Street

New Kifissia
Athens
Greece
801-9124

b.   not known

8/72	Department of State	
	Athens, Greece (E)	
	telecoms assistant	S-7
	(Regional Relay Facility)	

| as of 10/73 | | S-6 |

| as of 11/74 | not listed in Department of State records; assignment not known | |

Wife: Donna

Sources: FSL 6/74, 6/73
                Athens Embassy Source

GOSS, BARBARA J.

as of 3/76:
73 Buttermere Court
Boundary Road
London NW 8
U.K.
722-1461

b.   not known

as of 12/74	Department of State
	London, U.K. (E)
	Joint Reports & Research Unit

Sources: London Embassy Sources

GOTCHEF, EDWARD J.

as of 8/75:
Skovridergardsvej 12
2830 Virum
Copenhagen
Denmark
02-85-55-75

b.   2 September 1937

| as of 5/68 | Department of State | |
| | Foreign Service Institute | |

| 8/68 | Budapest, Hungary (E) | |
| | consular officer | R-7 |

| 4/70 | | R-6 |

| 9/71 | Dept. (EUR) | |

| 7/73 | Bombay, India (CG) | |
| | political officer | |

as of 10/74   Dept. (NEA)

as of 8/75-   Copenhagen, Denmark (E)
at least 12/76   Attache

Wife: Tamra Groff

Sources: BR 1974
                                         FSL 11/74, 10/73, 10/71, 1/69, 5/68
                                         Copenhagen Diplomatic Lists 12/76, 8/75
                                         Department of State Source

GOUGH, JOHN S.

b.   not known

6/75   Department of State
                                         Athens, Greece (E)
                                             telecoms support officer   S-6
                                             (Area Telecommunications Office)

as of 6/76   Dept. (A/OC)

Sources: FSL 8/75
                                         Department of State Sources

***GRAHAM, CHARLES O.

b.   not known

6/72   Department of State
                                         Athens, Greece (E)
                                             telecoms assistant   S-7
                                             (Area Telecommunications Office)

as of 11/74   Dept. (A/OC)

Wife: Lillian

Sources: FSL 6/74, 6/73
                                         Athens Embassy Source
                                         Department of State Source

***There is another person in the Foreign Service with exactly the same name, born in 1931 in Arkansas; he is not a CIA employee.

GRAHAM, LILLIAN

b.   not known

as of 1/74   Department of State
                                         Athens, Greece (E)
                                             telecoms
                                             (Regional Relay Facility)

as of 11/74   not listed in Department of State records;
                                         assignment not known

Husband: Charles O.

Source: Athens Embassy Source

GRANT, CHARLES R.

   b.   not known

8/68	Department of State Blantyre, Malawi (E) telecoms assistant	S-6
2/71		S-5
6/71	telecoms officer	
3/72	Monrovia, Liberia (E) telecoms officer	
9/74	Rome, Italy (E) telecoms officer	
as of 7/77	Dept. (A/OC)	
Sources:	FSL 4/75, 6/74, 2/72, 6/71, 1/69 Rome Embassy Source	

GRAVER, WILLIAM J.

   as of 6/76:
Fritz-Erler Strasse 21
5300 Bonn-Bad Godesberg
Germany
22-51-56

b. 25 March 1922	Maryland	
1942	Washington and Jefferson College BA	
1942	private experience college instructor	
1943-44	University of Chicago	
1942-46	U.S. Army overseas	

1946-51	Department of the Army
	    Austria
	        documents analyst-editor	

1952-61	executive officer	
7/61	Department of State Berlin, Germany (M) political officer	R-3
4/64		R-2
10/65	Dept.	
6/66		S-1
as of 5/68	(EUR)	
8/68	Foreign Service Institute Senior Seminar in Foreign Policy	
as of 1/69		R-2
8/69	Vienna, Austria (E) First Secretary & political officer	

9/73-
at least 6/76
	Department of State
	    Bonn, Germany (E)
	        Attache &
	        Office of the Coordinator & Advisor
	        (CIA Chief of Station)

Wife:	Rosemary Smith
Sources:	BR 1973, 1966, 1963 FSL 6/73, 9/69, 1/69, 5/68, 1/67, 1/62 Vienna Diplomatic Lists 11/71, 10/70, 10/69 Bonn Diplomatic Lists 6/76, 12/73 Bonn Embassy Source

GREENE, HARRIS CARL

22 October 1921	Massachusetts	
1942-43	private experience newspaper librarian	
1943	Boston University BS	
1943-46	U.S. Army overseas	

1946-48	Department of the Army
	    Austria
	    (United States Military Government)
	        files and records chief	

1948-49	private experience free-lance writer	
11/49	Department of State Dept.	
12/49	Genoa, Italy (CG) Vice-Consul	S-8
2/50-3/51	Rome, Italy (E) Vice-Consul	
1951-55	Department of the Army area specialist	
1951-52	George Washington University	

1955-60	private experience
	    unspecified motion picture company
	        field representative	

1960-64	Department of the Army operations officer	

5/64	Department of State
	    Athens, Greece (E)
	        Attache &
	        political officer
	        (CIA Deputy Chief of Station)
		R-3

1/69	Dept.	
6/69	Bern, Switzerland (E) political officer	

5/71		R-2
as of 10/73	Dept. (EUR)	
as of 2/74	not listed in Department of State records; assignment not known	
Wife:	Charlotte Wolk	
Sources:	BR 1973, 1967 FSL 10/73, 9/69, 5/69, 7/64, 4/51, 1/50	

GREENFIELD, SAMUEL D.

b. not known

4/74	Department of State
	  Oslo, Norway (E)
	    telecoms support officer
		S-7

as of 8/75	telecoms officer	
Sources:	FSL 8/75, 6/74	

GREGORY, GERALD D.

b. not known

9/66	Department of State
	  Khartoum, Sudan (E)
	    telecoms supervisor
		S-6

as of 9/68	telecoms officer	
6/69	Recife, Brazil (CG) telecoms assistant	S-5
9/71	Nicosia, Cyprus (E) telecoms officer	
as of 6/77	Copenhagen, Denmark (E) probably telecoms	
Sources:	FSL 8/75, 2/72, 9/69, 9/68, 1/67 Department of State Sources	

GRIFFITH, HAROLD W.

as of 4/76:
147 Headstone Lane
North Harrow
Middlesex
U.K.
428-0589

b. not known

as of 12/74-
at least 4/76
	Department of State
	  London, U.K. (E)
	    Joint Reports & Research Unit

Wife:	Caroline
Sources:	London Embassy Sources

GRIMSLEY, WILLIAM C. Jr.

as of 11/77:
Yamamoto Apartments
16-5, Nishi-Azabu 3-chome
Minato-ku
Tokyo
Japan
401-5448

b. 20 April 1927	Florida	
1942-45	Department of the Army clerk	
1945-46	U.S. Navy	
1946-47	Department of the Army warehouse superintendent	
1951	Columbia University BA	
1951-52	Department of the Army Post Exchange assistant manager	
9/52	Department of State Kabul, Afghanistan (E) economic assistant	S-11
1955-56	Department of the Army economic affairs officer	
5/56	Department of State New Delhi, India (E) Assistant Attache	R-6
7/56		R-7
as of 4/57	Assistant Attache & political officer	
10/58	Dept.	
2/59		R-6
4/62		R-5
5/62	New Delhi, India (E) Attache & political officer	
7/62	Second Secretary & political officer	
4/64		R-4
5/66	political-economic officer	S-2
6/67	Kathmandu, Nepal (E) executive assistant to the Ambassador	R-3
as of 5/68	general international relations officer	
5/69	Dept. (NEA)	

5/73		R-2
7/73	New Delhi, India (E) Special Assistant	
as of 11/74	(CIA Chief of Station)	
8/77	Tokyo, Japan (E) Assistant Attache	
Wife:	Madeline Oglesby	
Sources:	BR 1974, 1968, 1957 FSL 8/75, 10/73, 1/70, 9/67, 7/62, 1/59, 7/56 New Delhi Diplomatic List 1/77 Tokyo Diplomatic List 11/77	

GRISWOLD, DONALD M.

b. not known

6/75	Department of State Athens, Greece (E) telecoms support officer (Area Telecommunications Office)	S-7
Source:	FSL 8/75	

GROOMS, CARLTON C.

b. not known

1/73	Department of State Athens, Greece (E) telecoms assistant (Regional Relay Facility)	S-8
as of 10/73		S-7
as of 6/74	telecoms support officer	
as of 5/75	Dept. (EUR)	
as of 8/76	Mogadiscio, Somalia (E) probably telecoms	
as of 3/77	Dept. (A/OC)	
as of 3/78	Lusaka, Zambia (E) probably telecoms	
Wife:	Sandra	
Sources:	FSL 8/75, 4/75, 6/73 Athens Embassy Source Department of State Sources	

GROOMS, SANDRA

b. not known

as of 1/74	Department of State

> Athens, Greece (E)
> telecoms
> (Area Telecommunications Office -
> Logistics section)

***Husband: Carlton C.

Sources: Athens Embassy Source

*** Her husband's transfer in 1976 to Mogadiscio, Somalia would suggest that she is there too. She may or may not have worked in the telecommunications section.

GROSS, JUNE A.

as of 1/74:
15 Ergotimou Street
Pagrati
Athens
Greece
74-33-19

b.   not known

as of 1/74   Department of Defense
                         Athens, Greece (E)
                         JUSMAGG

Source: Athens Embassy Source

GROSSMAN, FREDERICK J.

b.   not known

7/71   Department of State
                         Ankara, Turkey (E)
                              telecoms assistant   S-7

1/73   Athens, Greece (E)
                         telecoms assistant
                         (Regional Relay Facility)

as of 11/74   telecoms support officer

as of 3/76   Dept. (A/OC)

Wife: Janet

Sources: FSL 8/75, 4/75, 11/74, 2/74, 6/73
                        Athens Embassy Source
                        Department of State Source

GROTH, MANFRED

as of 1/78:
49 Mottastrasse
3005 Bern
Switzerland
44-93-53

b.   not known

4/76   Department of State
                         Dept.   R-7

as of 6/76	Vientiane, Laos (E)
as of 7/76	consular officer
as of 5/77	Dept. (EA)
as of 9/77	Bern, Switzerland (E) Third Secretary
2/78	R-6
Wife:	Mary Jane
Sources:	Bern Diplomatic List 1/78 Department of State Sources

GROVE, DEREK A.

as of 12/75:
10 Barwichgasse
2103 Langenzersdorf, N.Oe.
Austria
02244-29763

b.   not known

as of 12/75	Department of State Vienna, Austria (E) Foreign Broadcast Information Service
Source:	Vienna Embassy Source

GRUNER, JAY K.

b. 23 August 1935	Missouri	
1957	University of Southern California BA	
1957-58	Eberhard-Karls Universitaet (Germany)	
1958-59	U.S. Coast Guard Ensign	
1960	private experience high school teacher	
1960-62	Department of the Air Force public information officer	
7/62	Department of State Caracas, Venezuela (E) Assistant Attache & political officer	R-8
4/64		R-7
3/65	Lima, Peru (E) Assistant Attache & political officer	
4/67		R-6
3/69		R-5
9/69	Dept. (ARA-LA)	

6/71	Bucharest, Romania (E) economic-commercial officer	
6/73	commercial officer	
4/74		RU-4
as of 9/74- at least 8/75	Dept. (EUR)	
as of 9/75-6/77	assignment not known	
7/77	Department of State Madrid, Spain (E) Attache	
Language:	Romanian	
Wife:	Marlene	
Sources:	BR 1974, 1968 FSL 8/75, 11/74, 10/71, 1/70, 6/65, 10/62 Bucharest Diplomatic List 1973 Madrid Diplomatic List 11/77 Department of State Sources *Washington Post,* June 13, 1978 *New York Times,* June 13, 1978	

GUDYKA, JOSEPH M.

b. not known		
10/70	Department of State Athens, Greece (E) telecoms assistant	S-7
2/74	Hong Kong, U.K. (CG) telecoms support officer	
as of 5/76	Dept. (A/OC)	
Sources:	FSL 8/75, 6/74, 6/73 Department of State Source	

GUERTIN, WILLIAM J.

b. 30 June 1924	New York
1941-42	University of Toronto
1942-43	private experience apprentice electrician
1943-45	U.S. Navy overseas
1945-47	private experience radio company radio repairman
1951	Milwaukee School of Engineering BS
1951-64	Department of the Army communications specialist

6/64	Department of State
	Manila, Philippines (E)
	communications specialist S-2
as of 1/67	telecoms engineer
as of 9/67-5/71	not listed in Department of State records; assignment not known
6/71	Department of State
	London, U.K. (E)
	telecoms officer R-3
7/72	telecoms engineer
as of 10/74	Dept. (A/OC)
Sources:	BR 1974, 1967
	FSL 11/74, 10/71, 5/67, 7/64
	London Diplomatic Lists 4/74, 10/71
	Department of State Source

GULDSETH, FRANK J.

b.	not known
5/67	Department of State
	Caracas, Venezuela (E)
	(Political Section) S-6
as of 9/69	Dept. (O)
1/70	Addis Ababa, Ethiopia (E)
	political assistant
5/72	Athens, Greece (E)
	administrative officer S-5
	(Area Telecommunications Office)
as of 8/75	Dept. (EUR)
Wife:	Beth
Sources:	FSL 4/75, 10/72, 6/72, 5/70, 9/69, 9/67
	Athens Embassy Source
	Department of State Source

GUNDERSON, LEROY H.

as of 6/75:
113 Shaftsbury Avenue
Harrow
Middlesex
U.K.
907-1204

b. 29 January 1922	Minnesota
1939-42	private experience
	store clerk, farm worker
1942	radio student
1942-43	junior repairman

1943-47	U.S. Army overseas	
1947-49	University of Minnesota	
1949-51	private experience radio station announcer	
1951	assistant chief engineer	
1951-52	chief engineer	
1952-53	Civil Aeronautics Administration communications technician	
8/53	Department of State Bucharest, Romania (L) secretary-archivist	S-10
4/56	Hong Kong, U.K. (CG) communications assistant	
9/58	Ankara, Turkey (E) communications assistant	
7/59		S-9
as of 1/61-10/65	not listed in Department of State records; assignment not known	
11/65	Department of State London, U.K. (E) telecoms specialist	
as of 1/68		S-4
2/68	telecoms officer	
as of 9/68	Dept.	
as of 1/69-11/74	not listed in Department of State records; assignment not known	
as of 12/74	Department of State London, U.K. (E) telecoms	
as of 8/75	not listed in Department of State records; assignment not known	
Wife:	Jane	
Sources:	BR 1967, 1960 FSL 9/68, 1/67, 10/60, 10/59 London Embassy Source	

GUY, RAYMON JAMES

b. not known		
6/74	Department of State Athens, Greece (E) telecoms technician (Area Telecommunications Office)	R-7
as of 11/76	Dept. (A/OC)	

Wife:	Judith Ann	
Sources:	FSL 8/75, 11/74 Athens Embassy Sources Department of State Source	

GYENES, ALFRED

b.   27 August 1925

6/63	Department of State
	    Rio de Janeiro, Brazil (E)
	        communications specialist
		S-5

as of 11/65-9/69	not listed in Department of State records; assignment not known	

10/69	Department of State
	    Manila, Philippines (E)
	        telecoms technician
		S-4

6/71	Bangkok, Thailand (E) telecoms technician	
6/72	Bonn, Germany (E) telecoms technician	
as of 2/73	not listed in Department of State records; assignment not known	
Sources:	BR 1972 FSL 10/72, 10/71, 1/70, 10/65, 10/63	

HAGEN, GERALD E.

as of 1/74:
59 Stratigou Lekka Street
Maroussi
Athens
Greece
802-8047

b. 17 July 1930	Washington	
1951-54	U.S. Army overseas	
1954-62	unspecified government agency communications technician	

10/62	Department of State
	    Brussels, Belgium (E)
	        political assistant
		S-5

4/65	Manila, Philippines (E) telecoms specialist	
7/67	Caracas, Venezuela (E) telecoms specialist	
2/69		S-4
as of 9/69	Dept. (0)	
as of 1/70-6/73	not listed in Department of State records; assignment not known	

7/73	Department of State
	Athens, Greece (E)
	telecoms officer R-6
	(Regional Relay Facility)
as of 11/75	Dept. (A/OC)
Wife:	Joanne White
Sources:	BR 1974, 1969
	FSL 8/75, 10/73, 9/69, 9/67, 6/65, 1/63
	Athens Embassy Source
	Department of State Source

HAM, CAREY ROGER

b.   14 February 1945

7/69	Department of State
***	Kinshasa, Congo (E)
	telecoms technician S-8
as of 10/70-5/74	not listed in Department of State records; assignment not known
6/74	Department of State
	Athens, Greece (E)
	telecoms technician R-7
	(Area Telecommunications Office)
Wife:	Nancy
Sources:	BR 1974
	FSL 8/75, 4/75, 5/70, 9/69

***The Democratic Republic of the Congo became Zaire in 1971.

HANDFORD, JANET MARIE

b.   not known

as of 9/74	Department of State
	Rome, Italy (E)
	Political Section
as of 3/76	Leningrad, U.S.S.R. (CG)
	cover position not known
Source:	Rome Embassy Source
	Department of State Sources

HANSON, DEAN P.

b. 19 April 1928	California
1946-48	U.S. Marine Corps
1951	University of Oregon BS
1951-52	private experience
	sales trainee

1952-54	office manager
1955-56	no entry in Department of State records; not known
1956-61	Department of the Army
1957	University of Southern California MA
10/61	Agency for International Development Phnom Penh, Cambodia (E) public safety officer R-7
1/63	Saigon, Vietnam (E) public safety advisor
3/64	Vientiane, Laos (E) program analyst
11/66	Agency
8/68	Department of State Cochabamba, Bolivia (C) consular officer R-6
1/70	Quito, Ecuador (E) political officer
4/70	R-5
10/72	Dept. (ARA-LA)
as of 2/74-8/74	not listed in Department of State records; assignment not known
as of 9/74	Department of State Rome, Italy (E) USASEPU
as of 1/76-6/77	assignment not known
7/77	Department of State Madrid Spain (E) . Attache
Wife:	Ernestine Lupton
Sources:	BR 1973, 1966 FSL 10/73, 1/69, 1/67, 10/65, 7/64, 7/63, 4/63 Rome Embassy Source Madrid Diplomatic List 11/77

HARBAUGH, LARRY M.

b. 10 December 1940	Iowa
1958-62	U.S. Air Force overseas
1963-64	Department of the Army communications specialist
4/64	Department of State Manila, Philippines (E) telecoms assistant S-8

8/66	Kigali, Rwanda (E) telecoms officer	S-7
1968-8/71	Department of the Army communications technician	
9/71	Department of State Tripoli, Libya (E) telecoms officer	R-7
11/73	Asunción, Paraguay (E) telecoms officer	
1973	received Merit Honor award	
as of 7/76	Geneva, Switzerland (M) probably telecoms	

Wife:	Eva Boisjolie
Sources:	BR 1974 FSL 8/75, 2/74, 10/71 Department of State Sources

HARDCASTLE, LESLIE

as of 6/75:
61 Crown Street
Harrow-on-the-Hill
Middlesex
U.K.
422-8973

b. 25 February 1926	Pennsylvania	
1942-43	private experience manufacturing firm laborer	
1943-44	sheet metal worker	
1944-46	U.S. Army overseas	
1947	not given in Department of State records; not known	
1948-51	private experience radio station technician	
1951-73	unspecified government agency electronic engineer	
6/73	Department of State London, U.K. (E) telecoms engineer	R-5
as of 11/75	Dept. (A/OC)	

Wife:	Nancy Gribben
Sources:	BR 1974 FSL 8/75, 10/73 London Embassy Sources Department of State Source

HARRIS, ALDINE

b. 21 August 1943	Virginia	
1964-68	U.S. Navy	
1968-73	unspecified government agency electronic engineer	
7/73	Department of State New Delhi, India (E) telecoms technician	R-8
as of 1/76	Dept. (A/OC)	
as of 8/76	Athens, Greece (E) probably telecoms	
Wife:	Frances Allen	
Sources:	BR 1974 FSL 8/75, 10/73 Athens Embassy Sources Department of State Sources	

HARRIS, V. DOTT

as of 3/76:
Flat 3
5 Stanhope Place
London W 2
U.K.
723-9191

b. not known

as of 12/74- at least 3/76	Department of State London, U.K. (E) Joint Reports & Research Unit
Sources:	London Embassy Sources

HART, MARY M.

as of 1/74:
6 Neofronos Street
Pagrati
Athens
Greece
74-44-20

b. not known

7/72	Department of State Athens, Greece (E) OSA secretary	S-8
as of 11/74	Dept. (EUR)	
as of 8/75	not listed in Department of State records; assignment not known	
Sources:	FSL 4/75, 6/73 Athens Embassy Sources	

HARWOOD, PAUL VINCENT

as of 2/74:
Las Alcabalas esquina Carlos Darwin
Quito
Ecuador
244-383

b. 4 July 1923	Massachusetts	
1945	University of Michigan BA	
1943-48	U.S. Army overseas	
1948-50	Department of the Army research analyst	
1950	George Washington University	

10/50	Department of State
	    Rangoon, Burma (E)
	    Vice-Consul &
	    political assistant
		S-10

7/52		S-9
1/54	Saigon, Vietnam (E) Assistant Attache	
7/54		S-8
7/56	Dept.	

6/59	Paris, France (E)
	    Attache &
	    political officer
		R-4

8/59	Second Secretary, Attache & political officer	
1/64	Dept.	
5/65		R-3
6/68		S-1
7/69	Mexico City, Mexico (E) political officer	R-3

1/71	Quito, Ecuador (E)
	    First Secretary &
	    political officer	

as of 11/74	Dept. (ARA-LA)	
as of 4/75	not listed in Department of State records; assignment not known	
Wife:	Mary Ellen Considine	
Sources:	BR 1974, 1968 FSL 11/74, 6/71, 10/70, 4/64, 7/59, 10/56 4/54, 4/51 Quito Diplomatic Lists 2/74, 12/72	

HAWKINS, MARTIN C.

b. 20 May 1930	Arkansas	
1950-52	Department of the Army agricultural manager	
1952-54	U.S. Army overseas	
1955	Department of the Army equipment specialist	
1958	University of Arizona BA	
1958-60	Department of the Army analyst	
2/60	Department of State Monterrey, Mexico (CG) political officer	R-7
6/60	Vice-Consul & political officer	
7/62	Managua, Nicaragua (E) Assistant Attache & political officer	
9/64		R-6
11/65	Guatemala City, Guatemala (E) political officer	
5/68		R-5
8/68	Dept. (ARA-LA)	
3/69		S-3
as of 9/69-7/73	Department of the Army program officer	
8/73	Department of State Montivideo, Uruguay (E) political officer	R-4
6/75	Guayaquil, Ecuador (CG) political officer	
as of 8/77	Dept. (ARA-LA)	
Wife:	Peggy Bayless	
Sources:	BR 1974, 1969 FSL 8/75, 10/73, 5/69, 9/68, 1/67, 10/62, 7/60 Department of State Source	

HAYES, EDWARD R.

as of 1/74:
4 Ionias Street
Erithrea
Athens
Greece
801-1827

b.   not known

4/73	Department of State
	   Athens, Greece (E)
	      telecoms assistant S-8
	      (Regional Relay Facility)

as of 11/74	telecoms support officer S-7
as of 8/75	not listed in Department of State records; assignment not known
Wife:	Carol
Sources:	FSL 4/75, 11/74, 6/73 Athens Embassy Source

HEADLEY, ROBERT L. Jr.

b. 10 July 1920	Pennsylvania
1943-45	U.S. Army overseas
1946-51	not given in Department of State records; not known

1952-63	private experience
	   unspecified oil company
	      Arabist
	      government relations representative

1956	Dartmouth College BA
1964-72	unspecified government agency plans & programs officer
7/72	Department of State Dept. (NEA) R-5
11/72	Muscat, Oman (E) consular officer
3/75	R-4
as of 5/77	Dept. (NEA)
Wife:	Caroline Neef
Sources:	BR 1974 FSL 8/75, 2/73, 10/72 Department of State Sources

HEALEY, DONALD J.

b. 11 July 1931	New Jersey
1954-56	U.S. Army
1956-58	private experience telephone company engineer
1958-61	Department of the Army research analyst

1961	Georgetown Universtiy MS
1962-66	private experience industrial surveys associates research analyst
1966-67	Agency for International Development Agency program officer
1/68	Department of State Hong Kong, U.K. (CG) political officer
4/71	Saigon, Vietnam (E) political officer
10/72	Dept. (EA)
as of 11/74	Department of State Paris, France (E) Regional Reports Office
Wife:	Maureen Black
Sources:	BR 1973 FSL 10/73, 6/71, 5/68 Paris Embassy Source

R-5

HEALEY, RICHARD D.

as of 9/74:
5 Piazza Stefano Jacini
Bldg. A
Apt. 26
Rome
Italy
387-8907

b. 24 November 1929	Massachusetts
1951	Boston College BA
1951-68	unspecified government experience
1958	Georgetown University MA
5/68	Department of State Vienna, Austria (E) political officer
8/71	Dept. (EUR)
as of 10/71-8/74	not listed in Department of State records; assignment not known
as of 9/74	Department of State Rome, Italy (E) political officer
as of 1/76	assignment not known
Wife:	Maureen Higgins
Sources:	BR 1972 FSL 6/72, 10/71, 9/68 Rome Embassy Source

R-4

HEINIG, STEWART C. Jr.

    b.   25 October 1932

        3/72   Department of State
                                         Bern, Switzerland (E)
                                            telecoms officer   R-7

    as of 6/74   Dept. (EUR)

    as of 11/74   not listed in Department of State records;
                             assignment not known

    Sources: BR 1973
                             FSL 6/74, 6/72

HEMBREE, EDWARD J.

    b.   not known

    as of 6/72   Agency for International Development
                                           Vientiane, Laos (E)
                                          assistant general services officer   RL-8

    as of 2/74   RL-7

        6/75   Department of State
                                           Athens, Greece (E)
                                          telecoms support officer   S-6

    Sources: FSL 8/75, 11/74, 6/72

HENRY, ALTON L.

    b.   26 September 1928

        6/70   Department of State
                                          Manila, Philippines (E)
                                          telecoms engineer   S-4

      10/74   Athens, Greece (E)
                                            mechanical engineer

    as of 11/76   Dept. (A/OC)

    Sources: BR 1974
                             FSL 8/75, 11/74, 10/70
                           Department of State Sources

HIGHAM, JAMES A.

    b.   24 April 1934   Massachusetts

    1954-57   U.S. Army overseas

      1959   Tufts University BA

    1959-61   private experience
                                          research organization
                                              analyst-translator

    1961-62   Benares Hindu University (India)

1962-63	Osmania University (India)

1963	private experience
	    research organization
	        analyst-translator

11/63	Department of State
	  New Delhi, India (E)
	    Attache &
	    economic officer
		R-6

3/64	Second Secretary & economic officer	
4/67	political-economic officer	R-5
9/68	Dept. (NEA)	
4/70	Lahore, Pakistan (CG) political officer	R-4
2/71	Colombo, Ceylon (E) political officer	
8/73		RU-4
as of 11/74	Dept. (NEA)	
as of 8/76	Tehran, Iran (E) cover position not known	
3/77		RU-3

Wife:	Mary Ryan
Sources:	BR 1974, 1968 FSL 8/75, 11/74, 6/71, 5/70, 5/69, 1/64 Colombo Diplomatic List 1974 Department of State Sources

HILL, FRANCIS A.

b. not known

10/69	Department of State
	  Jakarta, Indonesia (E)
	    telecoms officer
		S-6

6/72	Oslo, Norway (E) telecoms officer	
as of 1/76	Dept. (A/OC)	
Sources:	FSL 8/75, 10/72, 1/70 Department of State Sources	

HILLER, LEMOINE E. Jr.

b. not known

12/71	Department of State
	  Mexico City, Mexico (E)
	    telecoms assistant
		S-6

as of 6/74-6/77	not listed in Department of State records; assignment not known	

as of 7/77   Department of State
                                   Stockholm, Sweden (E)
                                        probably telecoms

Sources: FSL 2/74, 2/72
                              Department of State Sources

HINSON, ARTHUR W.

b.   not known

3/75   Department of State
                                   Athens, Greece (E)
                                        telecoms technician   R-8
                                        (Area Telecommunications Office)

Source: FSL 8/75

HOEPFL, ROBERT F.

as of 8/76:
33 Marlborough Hill
London NW 8
U.K.
586-4104

b.   not known

7/74   Department of State
                                   London, U.K. (E)
                                        Attache &
                                        telecoms officer   R-3

as of 10/75   telecoms chief

as of 6/76   Assistant Communications Attache
                                        & telecoms chief

as of 11/76   Dept. (A/OC)

Wife: Carolyn

Sources: FSL 8/75, 11/74
                              London Diplomatic Lists 8/76, 12/74
                              London Embassy Sources
                              Department of State Source

HOLLIS, ALLAN L.

b.   8 August 1937   Texas

1959-62   U.S. Army

1963-66   Department of the Army
                                   economic analyst

1/66   Department of State
                                   Dept.
                                        foreign affairs officer   GS-9

1966   George Washington University BA

10/67	Department of State São Paulo, Brazil (CG) political officer	R-7
11/69	Dept. (ARA-LA)	
4/70		R-6
6/70	Buenos Aires, Argentina (CG) economic-commercial officer	
as of 1/73	Second Secretary & economic-commercial officer	
4/74		R-5
as of 11/74	Dept. (ARA-LA)	
as of 10/75	Berlin, Germany (M) cover position not known	
as of 10/77	Caracas, Venezuela (E) cover position not known	RU-5

Wife: Caryn Star

Sources: BR 1974
FSL 8/75, 11/74, 10/70, 1/70, 1/68
Buenos Aires Diplomatic List 1/73
Department of State Sources

HOLLOWAY, MASTER SERGEANT BILLY G.

as of 3/76:
17A Carpenders Park
Watford
Hertfordshire
U.K.
428-4078

b.   not known

as of 12/74- at least 3/76 ***	Department of State London, U.K. (E) SUSLO	

Wife: Patsy D.

Sources: London Embassy Sources

***SUSLO is a cover unit for the National Security Agency, not the CIA.

HOLT, PETER G.

b.   not known

7/75- at least 1/77	Department of State Paris, France (E) economic-commercial officer	R-5

Sources: FSL 8/75
Paris Diplomatic List 1/77
Department of State Sources

HONEYCUTT, ARMAND A.

    b. not known

1/69	Department of State Ankara, Turkey (E) telecoms officer	S-7
8/70		S-6
7/71	Manila, Philippines (E) telecoms officer	
10/73	Pretoria, South Africa (E) telecoms officer	
as of 10/76	Dept. (A/OC)	
as of 11/77	Vienna, Austria (E) probably telecoms	
Sources:	FSL 8/75, 2/74, 10/71, 10/70 Department of State Sources	

HORN, MARY JO

    as of 1/74:
21 Pontou Street
Athens
Greece
70-19-21

    b. not known

8/72	Department of State
	Athens, Greece (E)
	    telecoms clerk-typist
	    (Area Telecommunications Office)
		S-8

as of 11/75	Dept. (A/OC)	
Sources:	FSL 8/75, 6/73 Athens Embassy Source Department of State Source	

HOSHEIT, GEORGE W.

    b. not known

as of 6/73	Department of State Nicosia, Cyprus (E) telecoms assistant	S-7

6/74	Athens, Greece (E)
	    telecoms technician
	    (Area Telecommunications Office)	

as of 8/76	Dept. (A/OC)	
Sources:	FSL 8/75, 6/74 Department of State Source	

HOSKINS, JOHN HERBERT

b. 5 June 1927	Massachusetts	
1949	Swarthmore College BA	
1949-53	Department of the Army analyst	
1953-54	U.S. Army 2nd Lieutenant	
1954-56	Department of the Army analyst	
9/56	Department of State Calcutta, India (CG) political officer	R-6
11/56	Vice-Consul	
2/59		R-5
5/61	Dept. foreign affairs officer	
9/63	Tehran, Iran (E) Second Secretary, Attache & political officer	
4/64		R-4
5/66	Attache & political officer	S-2
10/67		R-4
10/68	Dept. (EA) foreign affairs officer	GS-14
4/71	Ankara, Turkey (E) political officer & international relations officer	R-3
as of 9/74	Dept. (NEA)	
as of 8/75	not listed in Department of State records; assignment not known	
Wife:	Martha Peterson	
Sources:	BR 1974, 1968, 1957 FSL 4/75, 10/72, 1/69, 10/63, 7/61, 1/57 Ankara Diplomatic List 4/74 Department of State Source	

HOWARD, ENID M.

as of 1/76:
41 Othonos Street
Kifissia
Athens
Greece
808-0138

b.   not known

as of 1/76	Department of Defense
	Athens, Greece (E)
	JUSMAGG
Source:	Athens Embassy Source

HOWLEY, JAMES M.

b. 4 August 1929	Ohio	
1952	Marquette University BS	
1952-54	U.S. Army	
1954-70	Department of the Army	
	research analyst	
7/70	Department of State	
	Berlin, Germany (M)	
	economic-commercial officer	R-5
10/72-3/73	Department of the Army	
	program analyst	
4/73	Department of State	
	Danang, Vietnam (CG)	
	political officer	S-2
as of 1/75-	Dept. (EA)	
at least 8/75		
Wife:	Lorraine Culhane	
Sources:	BR 1974	
	FSL 8/75, 4/75, 10/73, 10/70	
	Department of State Source	

HUBER, HERBERT GOTTLIEB

as of 12/75:
16 Chimanistrasse, Apt. 2-3
1190 Vienna
Austria
36-32-85

b. 8 January 1931	Maryland	
1951-65	U.S. Air Force overseas	
1963	University of Missouri BA	
1965-72	Department of the Army	
	plans and programs officer	
1971	Boston University MSBA	
6/72	Department of State	
	Dept.	R-6
8/72	Mexico City, Mexico (E)	
	political officer	
as of 11/74-11/75	not listed in Department of State records;	
	assignment not known	

as of 12/75	Department of State
	Vienna, Austria (E)
	Communications Branch

| Wife: | Bernadette Early |

Sources:	BR 1974
	FSL 6/74, 10/72
	Vienna Embassy Source

HUCKEL, FRANK

as of 3/75:
30 Hillside Grove
London NW 7
U.K.
959-7997

b.   not known

as of 12/74	Department of State
	London, U.K. (E)
***	SUSLO

| as of 12/75 | assignment not known |

| Source: | London Embassy Source |

***SUSLO is a cover unit for the National Security Agency, not the CIA.

HUGHES, LESLIE F.

b.   not known

1/67	Department of State	
	San José, Costa Rica (E)	
	telecoms supervisor	S-6
as of 9/68	telecoms officer	
8/70	Kuwait, Kuwait (E)	
	telecoms officer	S-5
6/73	Lisbon, Portugal (E)	
	telecoms officer	
as of 11/75	Dept. (A/OC)	

| Sources: | FSL 8/75, 10/73, 10/70, 5/67 |
| | Department of State Sources |

HULNICK, ARTHUR S.

as of 2/76:
Kennedyallee 127/5
5300 Bonn-Bad Godesberg
Germany
37-81-27

b.   not known

as of 2/75-
at least 2/76
	Department of State
	    Bonn, Germany (E)
	        OCA Research Unit	

Wife:	Eileen	
Source:	Bonn Embassy Source	

HULSE, STACY B. Jr.

as of 6/77:
526 Mariposa Crescent
Rockcliffe Park
Ottawa
Canada
749-0019

b. 25 April 1920	Connecticut	
1941	Harvard University BA	

1941-42	private experience
	    manufacturing company
	        executive trainee	

1942-47	U.S. Army overseas Major	
1947-50	Department of the Army political officer	
1951-52	private experience hotel owner	
1952-55	Department of the Army political officer	

2/55	Department of State
	The Hague, Netherlands (E)
	    Attache &
	    political officer
		R-4

7/56		R-5
6/58	Trieste, Italy (C) Consul	
3/60		R-4

7/62	Rome, Italy (E)
	    Attache &
	    political officer	

10/64	Dept. (EUR)	
2/65		S-2
2/69		S-1
8/71	Foreign Service Institute language training	
5/72		R-3

7/72	Athens, Greece (E) First Secretary & political officer (Executive Section) (CIA Chief of Station)
as of 7/75	Dept. (EUR)
as of 8/75- at least 10/77	Ottawa, Canada (E) Attache (CIA Chief of Station)
Wife:	Lorraine Baken
Sources:	BR 1974, 1955 FSL 4/75, 10/72, 10/71, 1/65, 10/62, 10/58, 4/55 Athens Diplomatic Lists 12/74, 7/73, 7/72 Ottawa Diplomatic & Consular Lists 6/77, 2/76 Department of State Sources

HUNT, DAVID P.

as of 4/76:
2-B Schiotts vei
Oslo
Norway
55-66-31

b. 12 August 1939	New York
1959-61	U.S. Army overseas
1963	Colby College BA
1963-73	Department of the Army plans officer
4/73	Department of State Mogadiscio, Somalia (E) economic-commercial officer
5/73	S-3
as of 10/75	Dept. (AF)
as of 4/76- at least 10/77	Oslo, Norway (E) Attache
Wife:	Randall
Sources:	BR 1974 FSL 8/75, 6/73 Oslo Diplomatic Lists 10/77, 4/76 Department of State Source

HUTCHINS, BRUCE DUANE

as of 5/75:
37 Riddarvägen
181 40 Lidingö
Sweden
767-3366

b. 7 September 1934	Pennsylvania	
1952-57	U.S. Marine Corps overseas	
1962	University of Indiana BA	
1962-64	Department of the Army statistician	

1/65	Department of State
	    Dept.
	        Foreign Service Institute
	        language-area training
		R-7

3/66	Helsinki, Finland (E)
	    Assistant Attache &
	    political officer	

5/68		R-6
9/69	Dept. (EUR)	
5/72		R-5

7/72	Stockholm, Sweden (E)
	    Second Secretary &
	    political officer	

as of 8/75		RU-5
3/76	Dept. (EUR)	
Wife:	LouAnn McDowall	
Sources:	BR 1974, 1971 FSL 8/75, 11/74, 10/72, 1/70, 5/68, 1/68, 1/67, 6/65 Stockholm Diplomatic Lists 5/75, 11/72 Department of State Source	

HUTCHISON, TERRELL WARREN

as of 2/75:
52 Ländlistrasse
Bremgarten
Switzerland
24-17-80

b. 25 February 1924	Alabama
1940-42	Howard College
1943-46	U.S. Navy overseas
1944	Harvard University

1946-47	private experience
	    retail furniture company
	    credit manager

1947-49	head bank teller
1948	George Washington University
1949-52	Federal Deposit Insurance Corporation analyst

1952-56	Department of the Navy	

5/56	Department of State
	    Mexico City, Mexico (E)
	        political officer
		R-6

7/56		R-7
12/58-5/60	Department of the Army administrative officer	

6/60	Department of State
	    Rome, Italy (E)
	        Attache &
	        accounting officer
		R-6

as of 4/63-1/75	not listed in Department of State records; assignment not known	

as of 2/75-
at least 7/76
	Department of State
	    Bern, Switzerland (E)
	        Attache	

Sources:	BR 1963 FSL 1/63, 7/60, 7/56 Bern Diplomatic Lists 7/76 (updated), 2/75	

HYATT, JEFFREY L.

b. not known		

6/75	Department of State
	    Athens, Greece (E)
	        telecoms officer
	        (Area Telecommunications Office)
		R-5

as of 10/77	Dept. (A/OC)	
Wife:	Shirley	
Source:	FSL 8/75 Athens Embassy Sources Department of State Sources	

HYDE, ROGER L.

b. not known		

10/71	Department of State
	    Moscow, U.S.S.R. (E)
	        communications-records assistant
		S-6

7/74	Athens, Greece (E)
	    telecoms support officer
	    (Area Telecommunications Office)	

as of 10/76	Quito, Ecuador (E) probably telecoms	
Sources:	FSL 8/75, 11/74, 10/71 Information Moscow List 8/72 Department of State Sources	

HYNDMAN, JAMES ALBERT

as of 1/74:
5 Drimonos Street
New Kifissia
Athens
Greece
80-19-84

b. 5 March 1937	Georgia	
1954-57	U.S. Army overseas	
1958-61	unspecified government agency communications officer	
4/61	Department of State Asunción, Paraguay (E) general telecoms clerk	S-9
as of 1/63		S-6
7/65	Seoul, South Korea (E) telecoms specialist	S-5
as of 5/68	telecoms officer	S-4
8/68	New Delhi, India (E) telecoms officer	
2/70		S-3
as of 10/70	Dept. (NEA)	
5/73	Athens, Greece (E) telecoms officer (Regional Relay Facility)	R-5
as of 8/76	Dept. (A/OC)	
Wife:	Elizabeth Austin	
Sources:	BR 1974, 1973, 1970 FSL 8/75, 10/73, 10/70, 9/68, 1/67, 10/62 Athens Embassy Sources Department of State Source	

IMBREY, HOWARD

as of 9/74:
154 Via Monserrato
Apt 10
Rome
Italy
65-98-46

b. 10 October 1921	New Jersey
1942-45	U.S. Army overseas
1946	University of North Carolina BA
1946-48	private experience export company assistant to the president

12/48	Department of State Dept.	S-9
12/48	Bombay, India (CG) Vice-Consul	
8/50	Madras, India (CG) Vice-Consul	
9/51	Colombo, Ceylon (E) Assistant Attache	S-7
8/52	Dept.	
***10/52	resigns from Department of State	
1952-55	Department of Commerce economic analyst	
11/55	Department of State Addis Ababa, Ethiopia (E) Assistant Attache	R-5
7/56		R-6
as of 1/58	Assistant Attache & economic officer	
as of 1/59-8/74	not listed in Department of State records; assignment not known	
as of 9/74	Department of State Rome, Italy (E) USASEPU	
as of 1/76	assignment not known	
Wife:	Ina	
Sources:	BR 1958, 1950 FSL 10/58, 1/56, 10/52, 10/51, 1/49 Rome Embassy Source	

***Previously, Imbrey was probably a bona-fide State Department employee. Sometime after this date, he joined the CIA.

INCE, ROBERT W.

as of 9/75:
18 Gobabau Road
Kaduna
Nigeria
42028

b.   3 October 1934

10/68	Department of State Accra, Ghana (E) political officer	R-6
1/71	Dept. (AF)	
6/72- at least 9/75	Kaduna, Nigeria (C) economic-commercial officer	

6/74		R-5
as of 7/75	Dept. (AF)	
Wife:	Jeanne Jourdenais	

Sources: BR 1974
                         FSL 4/75, 10/72, 6/71, 9/68
                         Lagos Diplomatic and Consular List 9/75
                         Department of State Source

IORIO, ARTHUR

b. 22 September 1919	Italy
1942-45	U.S. Army overseas
1943	naturalized as U.S. citizen
1946	Syracuse University BA
1951	Syracuse University MA
1952-55	Department of the Army research analyst

1955-62	private experience
	        unspecified school center
	            vice director

1962-66	Department of the Army political analyst

6/66-
at least 2/73
	Department of State
	        Rome, Italy (E)
	            political officer

Wife:	Ann Gigantelli

Sources: BR 1972, 1967
                         FSL 2/73, 1/67

JACKOLA, ELMER A.

b.   not known

7/65	Department of State
	    . Tehran, Iran (E)
	        telecoms technician
		S-5

as of 9/68-6/76	not listed in Department of State records; assignment not known	

as of 7/76	Department of State
	    Athens, Greece (E)
	        probably telecoms
		R-6

Sources: FSL 5/68, 10/65
                         Athens Embassy Sources
                         Department of State Sources

JACKSON, HENRY F.

    b.   25 January 1924

9/64	Department of State Manila, Philippines (E) telecoms assistant	S-6
9/68	Kuwait, Kuwait (E) telecoms officer	S-5
as of 1/69		S-6
as of 5/70		S-5
6/71	Cairo, Egypt (E) (U.S. Interests Section, Spanish Embassy) telecoms officer	R-7

6/72	Athens, Greece (E)
	   telecoms assistant
	   (Regional Relay Facility)	

as of 6/73	telecoms officer	
10/74	Guatemala City, Guatemala (E) telecoms officer	
as of 6/77	Dacca, Bangladesh (E) ·probably telecoms	

Wife: Phyllis

Sources: BR 1974
                   FSL 8/75, 4/75, 11/74, 10/72, 10/71, 1/69
                      10/65
                 Athens Embassy Source
                 Department of State Source

JACOBSON, IRVIN H.

    as of 3/76:
    16 Boydell Court
    St. Johns Wood Park
    London NW 8
    U.K.
    722-2486

    b.   not known

as of 12/74-
at least 3/76
	Department of State
	   London, U.K. (E)
	      Joint Reports & Research Unit

Wife: Cora

Source: London Embassy Sources

JAMESON, BOBBIE

    as of 1/74:
    8 Dorileou Street

Athens
Greece
642-4097

b.   not known

as of 1/74   Department of Defense
                              Athens, Greece (E)
                                  JUSMAGG

Source: Athens Embassy Source

JAROCKI, JOSEPH P.

   b.   not known

      3/75   Department of State
                              Athens, Greece (E)
                                  telecoms support officer   S-6
                                  (Area Telecommunications Office)

   as of 7/77   Kathmandu, Nepal (E)
                                  probably telecoms

   as of 4/78   Manila, Philippines (E)
                                  probably telecoms

   Sources: FSL 8/75, 4/75
                              Department of State Sources

   Reference: Greece

JEFFERS, EUGENE L. Jr.

   as of 3/75:
   11-86-14 (Addis Ababa, Ethiopia)

   b.   8 May 1926   Ohio

      1944-46   U.S. Navy overseas

      1948-54   private experience
                                  newspaper reporter

      1951   Kent State University BA

      1953   Western Reserve University MA

      1954-60   Department of the Army
                                  plans officer

      10/60   Department of State
      ***   Léopoldville, Congo (E)
                                  Assistant Attache &
                                  political officer   R-6

      2/63   Dept.

      3/63   R-5

      1/66   Lusaka, Zambia (E)
                                  Attache &
                                  political officer

4/67		R-4
6/68	Dept. (O)	
7/69	Vientiane, Laos (E) political officer	
as of 10/71	Dept. (EA)	
as of 10/73-5/74	not listed in Department of State records; assignment not known	
6/74	Department of State Addis Ababa, Ethiopia (E) political officer	R-3
as of 3/75	First Secretary	
as of 11/76	Dept. (AF)	
Wife:	Anne Eberhart	
Sources:	BR 1974, 1971, 1966, 1961-62 FSL 8/75, 6/74, 6/73, 10/71, 9/69, 9/68 1/67, 4/63, 1/61 Addis Ababa Diplomatic List 3/75 Addis Ababa Embassy Source Department of State Sources	

***Léopoldville was renamed Kinshasa in June, 1966.

JENSEN, HANS J.

b. 9 June 1925	California	
1943-47	U.S. Navy overseas Lieutenant	
1949	University of California BA	
1949-52	private experience marketing underwriter	
3/53	Department of State Copenhagen, Denmark (E) consular officer	S-10
1956-59	Department of the Air Force foreign affairs officer	
7/59	Department of State Oslo, Norway (E) political officer	R-6
10/59	Second Secretary & political officer	
4/62		R-5
12/64	Dept.	
3/66		S-3
9/67	Bonn, Germany (E) Attache & economic-commercial officer	R-5

5/68		R-4
3/71	Dusseldorf, Germany (CG)	
5/71	political-economic officer	
as of 6/73	Dept. (EUR)	
as of 10/73	not listed in Department of State records; assignment not known	

Wife: Joyce Freeborn

Sources: BR 1971, 1967
FSL 6/73, 6/71, 1/68, 1/65, 10/59

JENKINS, CYNTHIA A.

as of 2/76:
Kolumbusring 13/9
5300 Bonn-Bad Godesberg
Germany
37-26-48

b. not known

as of 2/75   Department of State
         Bonn, Germany (E)
            OCA Liaison Unit

Source: Bonn Embassy Source

JETON, FRANCIS JOHN

as of 1/76:
Rue Raynouard, 74
75016 Paris
France
527-64-52

b. 1 April 1926	Massachusetts	
1943-46	U.S. Navy overseas	
1947-48	private experience shipping company clerk	
1952	George Washington University BA	
1952-55	Department of the Army analyst	

11/55	Department of State
	    Damascus, Syria (E)
	       consular officer
		R-6

2/56	Vice-Consul	
7/56		R-7
***8/57	Dept.	
11/58	Dakar, Senegal (CG) Vice-Consul	

2/59		R-6
6/60	Vice-Consul & Attache	
10/60	Second Secretary & Vice-Consul	
4/62	Second Secretary, Vice-Consul & Attache	R-5
2/64	Dept.	
12/64		S-3
****6/65	Kinshasa, Congo (E) political officer	
1/66		S-2
2/68		S-1
5/68		R-3
9/68	Tunis, Tunisia (E) political officer	
10/73	Pretoria, South Africa (E) Attache	
as of 1/76- at least 1/78	Paris, France (E) Attache & Office of the Special Assistant	

Wife:	Mary Cowen
Sources:	BR 1971, 1964, 1956
	FSL 6/71, 10/65, 1/59, 1/56
	Pretoria Department of Foreign Affairs List 9/74
	Pretoria Diplomatic List 7/75
	Paris Diplomatic Lists 1/78, 1/76

***Jeton was ordered to leave Syria on August 13, 1957, for alleged participation with two other American diplomats—Howard E. Stone and Col. Robert W. Molloy—in a plot to overthrow the Syrian government. *Keesings Contemporary Archives,* 24–31 August 1957). Cf: Howard E. Stone.

****The Congo was renamed Zaire in 1971.

JOHNS, ROBERT A.

as of 1/74:
19 Eleftherotrias Street
Politia
Kifissia
Athens
Greece
801-6766

b. 24 January 1943	New Jersey
1962	George Washington University BSEE
1965	Michigan State University MSEE
1965-73	Department of the Air Force electronics engineer

4/73- at least 8/75	Department of State Athens, Greece (E) telecoms engineer (Area Telecommunications Office)	R-5

Wife: Carole Herklotz

Sources: BR 1974
                         FSL 8/75, 6/73
                         Athens Embassy Source
                         Department of State Source

JOHNSEN, MARTIN I.

b.   not known

8/75	Department of State Madrid, Spain (E) telecoms officer	S-6

Wife: Dorothy

Source: FSL 8/75
                         Madrid Embassy Sources
                         Department of State Source

JOHNSON, QUENTIN C.

as of 4/76:
20, Thomas Heftyesgate
Oslo 2
Norway
56-54-26

b. 31 January 1922	Iowa	
1939-43	Northwestern University	
1944	University of California BA	
1943-46	U.S. Army overseas	
1946-62	Department of the Army political affairs officer	
11/62	Department of State Copenhagen, Denmark (E) Attache & political officer	R-3
8/66	Dept.	
4/70		R-2
as of 10/73-9/74	not listed in Department of State records; assignment not known	
as of 10/74- at least 10/77	Department of State Oslo, Norway (E) Attache (CIA Chief of Station)	

Wife: Eva Gronneberg

Sources:	BR 1973, 1972, 1963
	FSL 6/73, 1/67, 1/63
	Oslo Diplomatic Lists 10/77, 4/76, 10/74

JONES, FRANK WILLIAMS Jr.

b. 14 June 1921	New York	
1943	U.S. Military Academy BS	
1943-54	U.S. Army overseas Major	
1954-57	private experience evergreen nurseries owner	
***1957-58	International Cooperation Administration Agency international relations officer	
7/58	Department of State Munich, Germany (CG) political officer	R-4
10/58	Consul	
5/59	Warsaw, Poland (E) Attache	
8/59	Second Secretary & political officer	
4/62	First Secretary & political officer	R-3
6/62	Nicosia, Cyprus (E) Attache	
12/62	First Secretary & political officer	
8/65	Dept.	
as of 1/67	(EUR)	
5/67		S-1
5/68	Foreign Service Institute	R-3
6/68	Oslo, Norway (E) political officer	
8/70	Geneva, Switzerland (M) international relations officer general	
5/73	Dept. (EUR)	
8/73	Bern, Switzerland (E) Attache	
as of 7/76	assignment not known	
Language:	Norwegian	
Wife:	Arlene Swift	

Sources: BR 1973, 1967
                                FSL 6/73, 10/70, 9/68, 5/68, 1/67, 10/62, 7/59,
                                    10/58
                                Bern Diplomatic List 2/75

***ICA was the predecessor of the Agency for International Development, established in 1961.

JONES, WILLIAM A. K.

    as of 11/75:
    Basilica, 15
    Madrid
    Spain
    233-18-97

b. 27 October 1921	Spain (of American parents)	
1943-46	U.S. Navy Ensign	
1947	Loyola College BS	
1948	Catholic University	
1950	Georgetown University BSFS	
1950	Department of State typist	
1950-57	Department of the Army analyst	
1953-54	Georgetown University BSFS	

1957-59	private experience
	    police administration school
	    police advisor	

11/59	International Cooperation Administration
	    Saigon, Vietnam (E)
	        public safety officer
		R-4

8/60-2/62	Department of the Army plans officer	

3/62	Department of State
	    Barcelona, Spain (CG)
	        political officer	

5/62	Consul	
as of 1/67	political officer	
9/68	Dept. (EUR)	
9/69	program officer	GS-14

8/71-
at least 11/75
	Madrid, Spain (E)
	    Attache &
	    political officer	

Wife:	Dolores	
Sources:	BR 1971, 1968, 1963 FSL 5/70, 9/68, 7/62, 4/60 Madrid Diplomatic Lists 11/75, 5/72 Madrid Embassy Source	

KABLE, CHARLES H. III

b. not known

8/69	Department of State Georgetown, Guyana (E) clerk (Administrative Section)	S-6
as of 10/70	Quito, Ecuador (E) clerk (Political Section)	
3/73	Santiago, Chile (E) telecoms officer	
as of 6/74		S-5
as of 10/75	Dept. (A/OC)	
as of 6/77	Athens, Greece probably telecoms	R-5
Sources:	FSL 8/75, 6/74, 6/73, 10/70, 1/70 Athens Embassy Sources Department of State Source	

KAHANE, RICHARD A.

as of 9/77:
24 Abercorn Place
London NW 8
U.K.
286-4366

b. 9 August 1938	New York	
1960	Princeton Universtiy BS (education)	
1960-63	U.S. Air Force 1st Lieutenant	
1963-64	Department of Commerce industrial specialist	
7/64 ***	Department of State Léopoldville, Congo (E) Assistant Attache & political officer	R-7
as of 1/65	Third Secretary, Vice-Consul & political officer	
8/66	Algiers, Algeria (E) political officer	
4/67		R-6
12/67	Paris, France (E) political officer	
11/68	Conakry, Guinea (E) consular officer	
3/69		R-5
7/71	Dept.	

8/71	Foreign Service Institute language training	
7/72	Prague, Czechoslovakia (E) Second Secretary & economic-commercial officer	
5/74		RU-5
3/75		RU-4
as of 8/75- at least 6/78	London, U.K. (E) First Secretary & political officer	
as of 12/76	Political Attache	
as of 12/77	First Secretary (Political)	
Languages:	Czech, French	
Wife:	Antonia Sherman	
Sources:	BR 1974 FSL 8/75, 10/72, 1/69, 9/68, 1/67, 10/64 Conakry Diplomatic List 5/71 Prague Diplomatic Lists 7/74, 7/72 London Diplomatic Lists 6/78, 12/75 London Embassy Sources	

***Léopoldville was renamed Kinshasa in June, 1966.

KALARIS, GEORGE T.

b. 4 May 1922	Montana	
1941-45	Athens University (Greece)	
1945-47	U.S. Army	
1949	Montana State University LLB	
1950-51	New York University LLM	
1951	National Labor Relations Board legal assistant	
1951-52	Department of Labor attorney	
1952	Office of Price Stabilization attorney	
1952-58	Department of the Army economic officer	
1/59	Department of State Jakarta, Indonesia (E) economic officer	R-5
3/59	Second Secretary	
8/61	Dept.	

12/62	Vientiane, Laos (E) Second Secretary & economic officer	
4/64		R-4
9/65	Dept. (EA)	
4/67		R-3
3/68	supervisory foreign affairs officer	GS-15
6/70	Manila, Philippines (E) political officer (CIA Chief of Station)	R-2
as of 10/73	First Secretary & political officer (CIA Chief of Station)	
8/74	Brasília, Brazil (E) Attache	
as of 7/75	assignment not known	
Wife:	Ismere Icroutsicos	
Sources:	BR 1974, 1959 FSL 6/74, 10/70, 1/67, 4/63, 1/62, 4/59 Manila Diplomatic List 10/73 (amended to 1/74) Brasília Diplomatic List 10/74	

KAMBA, LAWRENCE F.

as of 9/74:
7 Viale Di Villa Grazioli
Apt. A-2
Rome
Italy
845-0478

b.   not known

3/74	Department of State Rome, Italy (E) telecoms support officer	S-7
as of 8/77	Caracas, Venezuela (E) probably telecoms	
Wife:	Patricia E.	
Sources:	FSL 8/75, 6/74 Rome Embassy Source Department of State Source	

KANE, EDWARD R. M.

as of 2/76:
Villa Sainte-Catherine
Parc-Poirson—El Biar

Algiers
Algeria
78-04-62

b. 15 December 1929	Massachusetts	
1951	Harvard University BA	
1951-52	Istanbul University (Turkey)	
1952-57	Department of the Army area analyst	
1952-54	Ankara University (Turkey)	

11/57	Department of State
	Cairo, Egypt (E)
	    Assistant Attache &
	    political assistant
		S-8

4/59		R-7
8/61	Dept.	
4/62		R-6

5/63	Baghdad, Iraq (E)
	    Attache &
	    political officer	

8/63	Second Secretary & political officer	
4/64		R-5
8/65	Tripoli, Libya (E) political officer	
4/67		R-4
9/68	Dakar, Senegal (E) political officer	
9/71	Dept. (NEA)	
5/73		R-3
6/73	Algiers, Algeria (U.S. Interests Section, Embassy of Switzerland) political officer	
8/73		RU-3
as of 3/75	First Secretary	
as of 8/76	Dept. (NEA)	
Language:	French	
Wife:	Phyllis Jackson	
Sources:	BR 1974, 1967 FSL 8/75, 10/73, 10/71, 9/68, 1/67, 7/63, 1/62, 1/58 Dakar Diplomatic List 1971 Algiers Diplomatic Lists 2/76, 3/75 Department of State Source	

KARPOVICH, SERGE

b. 13 June 1929	New Hampshire	
1950	Harvard University BA	
1951-53	Department of Defense analyst	
1953-54	U.S. Army	

7/55	Department of State
	    Meshed, Iran (C)
	        political assistant
		S-11

8/56		S-9
9/58	Berlin, Germany (M) consular officer	R-7
10/58	Vice-Consul	
10/59	public safety officer	
10/61	Dept.	
4/62		R-6
4/64		R-5
3/65		S-3
1/66		S-2
2/68		S-1
7/69	Vienna, Austria (E) economic-commercial officer	R-3
12/69	political officer	
10/73- at least 8/75	Dept. (EUR)	
Wife:	Margaret Austin	
Sources:	BR 1974, 1967 FSL 8/75, 2/74, 9/69, 1/62, 10/58, 10/56 *New York Times,* December 31, 1976 & June 13, 1978 *Washington Post,* June 13, 1978	

KAULFERS, TERRANCE F.

b. not known		

3/75	Department of State
	    Bamako, Mali (E)
	        telecoms support officer
		S-7

as of 7/77	Athens, Greece (E) probably telecoms	
Sources:	FSL 8/75, 4/75 Athens Embassy Sources Department of State Sources	

KEAR, DONALD L.

    b.   not known

8/71-
at least 10/73
	Department of State
	   Madrid, Spain (E)
	      telecoms officer
		S-7

as of 2/74-5/76	not listed in Department of State records; assignment not known	
6/76		S-6

as of 9/76	Department of State
	   Rome, Italy (E)
	      probably telecoms	

Sources:	FSL 10/73, 6/73 Department of State Source	

KEEFE, JOHN F.

    as of 9/74:
    12 Via Di Parione
    Rome
    Italy
    56-04-84

    b.   not known

as of 9/74	Department of State
	   Rome, Italy (E)
	      USASEPU

Source:	Rome Embassy Source

KEEGAN, MARY T.

    as of 12/75:
    17 Boltzmanngasse, Apt. 98
    1090 Vienna
    Austria
    34-03-88

    b.   not known

3/72	Department of State
	   Geneva, Switzerland (M)
	      Economic-Commercial Section secretary
		S-8

as of 11/74-11/75	not listed in Department of State records; assignment not known	

as of 12/75	Department of State
	   Vienna, Austria (E)
	      secretary to CIA Chief of Station	

Sources:	FSL 6/74, 6/73 Vienna Embassy Source	

KEENAN, THOMAS J.

    as of 2/74:
    1 Acadia Drive
    Kingston 8
    Jamaica
    924-4195

    b. 29 June 1930   Wisconsin

        1953   Marquette University BS

        1953-56   U.S. Navy

        1957-60   Department of the Army

        1/60   Department of State
                                  Mexico City, Mexico (E)
                                      political assistant   S-10

        8/62   S-9

        10/62   S-6

    11/64-1966   Department of the Army

    1966-1967   not listed in Department of State records;
                              assignment not known

        5/67   Department of State
                                  Bogotá, Colombia (E)
                                      political officer   R-6

        4/70   R-5

    as of 5/71   Attache &
                                          political officer

        9/71   Lima, Peru (E)
                                  political officer

        9/73   Kingston, Jamaica (E)
                                  political officer
                                  Second Secretary   R-4

    as of 8/75   Dept. (ARA-LA)

    Language: Spanish

    Wife: Margaret Walsh

    Sources: BR 1974, 1967
                              FSL 4/75, 10/73, 2/72, 9/67, 10/62
                              Bogotá Diplomatic List 5/71
                              Kingston Diplomatic List 2/74
                              Department of State Source

KELLY, DONALD A.

    as of 1/74:
    17 Eleftherotrias Street
    Politia
    Kifissia

Athens
Greece
808-0984

b. 5 October 1937	New York
1955-59	U.S. Air Force
1959-73	Department of the Air Force
	electronics specialist
4/73	Department of State
	Athens, Greece (E)
	telecoms technician R-7
	(Area Telecommunications Office)
as of 8/76	Dept. (A/OC)
Wife:	Carol Baer
Sources:	BR 1974, 1973
	FSL 8/75, 4/75, 6/73
	Athens Embassy Source
	Department of State Source

KELLY, GILES MERRILL

b. 17 July 1921	New York
1942	New York State Marine Academy graduate
1942-46	U.S. Navy
1949	Williams College BA
1951	Princeton University MPA
1951	Department of Defense
	plans officer
1952-57	London, U.K.
	economist, liaison officer
1957-60	economic analyst
6/60	Department of State
	Khartoum, Sudan (E)
	Attache &
	economic-commercial section chief R-3
10/60	First Secretary &
	economic-commercial section chief
12/64	Dept.
	public information specialist
11/66	Speaker Services Division chief
10/67	information officer
7/68	S-1
as of 9/68	U.S. Navy overseas Lieutenant Commander
6/69-2/70	detailed to Department of Defense

3/70	Department of State
	Brussels, Belgium (USNATO)
	information officer
	(NATO International Staff office)

4/74		R-2

as of 11/74	not listed in Department of State records; assignment not known

Wife:	Helen Hackett

Sources:	BR 1974, 1967
	FSL 6/74, 5/70, 5/68, 6/65, 10/60

KELLY, WILLIAM V.

b. 22 January 1924	Tennessee

1942-45	U.S. Army overseas

1946	not given in Department of State records; assignment not known

3/47	Department of State
	Lima, Peru (E)
	clerk	S-11

7/49-9/52	Department of the Army
	chief technician

10/52	Department of State
	Manila, Philippines (E)
	communications assistant	S-10

8/55-4/67	Department of the Army
	electronics engineer

5/67	Department of State
	Athens, Greece (E)
	telecoms engineer	S-4

2/69		S-3

as of 10/70-3/75	not listed in Department of State records; assignment not known

as of 4/75	Department of State
	Geneva, Switzerland (M)
	telecoms

Wife:	Sally Scarborough

Sources:	BR 1970
	FSL 9/69, 9/67
	Geneva Mission Source

KELSALL, ALMA M.

as of 3/76:
229 Grove End Gardens
18 Abbey Road

London NW 8
U.K.
286-3969

b.   not known

as of 12/74-   Department of State
at least 3/76   London, U.K. (E)
                                         Foreign Broadcast Information Service

Sources: London Embassy Sources

KEMERY, RAYMOND F.

as of 1/76:
8 bis Boulevard Maillot
92200 Neuilly
France
624-0104

b.   31 October 1933   Oregon

1954-56   U.S. Army

1958   University of Oregon BA

1958-60   private experience
                                      company research analyst

9/60   Department of State
                                      Vienna, Austria (E)
                                          political officer   S-4

10/66   Dept.
                                      foreign affairs officer

8/67   Foreign Service Institute
                                          language-area training   R-6

7/68   Sofia, Bulgaria (E)
                                      consular officer

4/70   R-5

9/70   Dept. (EUR)

9/73   Foreign Service Institute
                                          language training

6/74-   Paris, France (UNESCO)
at least 1/77   Second Secretary &
                                          political officer

2/76   R-4

Wife: Alva Wells

Sources: BR 1974, 1973
                                FSL 8/75, 11/74, 2/74, 10/70, 9/68, 1/68
                                Paris Diplomatic Lists 1/77, 1/75
                                Paris Embassy Source
                                Department of State Sources

KENNEY, JOHN H.

b.	4 November 1927	Massachusetts	
	5/57	Department of State Singapore, U.K. (CG) political assistant	S-11
	7/58		S-10
	3/60	Dept.	R-7
	4/60	Medan, Indonesia (C) political officer	
	6/60	Vice-Consul	
	9/62	Dept.	
	9/63	Conakry, Guinea (E) Assistant Attache & political officer	
	12/63	Third Secretary	
	4/64	Second Secretary	R-6
	8/65	Zanzibar, Tanzania (C) Vice-Consul & economic officer	
	***4/67	economic officer	O-5
	6/67	Nairobi, Kenya (E) political officer	R-5
	9/68	Dept. (AF)	
	3/69		R-4
	1/72	Paris, France (UNESCO) political officer	
	8/73		RU-4
	8/74	Saigon, Vietnam (E) political officer	
	5/75	Dept. (EA)	
	Wife:	Mary	
	Sources:	BR 1974, 1967 FSL 8/75, 11/74, 6/72, 9/67, 10/65, 1/64, 1/63, 7/60	

***Kenney's 0-5 rating appears to be a mis-print in Department of State records.

KENYON, KYLE G.

b.	not known		
	8/70	Department of State Athens, Greece (E) telecoms technician	S-5

as of 10/73	Dept. (NEA)
as of 2/74	not listed in Department of State records; assignment not known
Sources:	FSL 10/73, 10/70

KETELHUT, DAVID

b.   not known

| 7/71-
at least 10/73 | Department of State
The Hague, Netherlands (E)
telecoms assistant | S-8 |
| Sources: | FSL 10/73, 6/73 |

KIM, JAMES

as of 10/74:
3124 av. de la Caisse d'Epargne & Marinel
Gombe
Zaire
31499

b. 15 March 1921	California	
1941-47	U.S. Army	
1950	Georgetown University BS	
1950-53	U.S. Army overseas Captain	
1953-56	Department of the Army personnel officer	
1956-58	private experience research fellow (Geneva)	
1959-60	travel promoter	
2/61	Department of State Bamako, Mali (E) Vice-Consul consular officer	R-6
5/61	Vice-Consul & Second Secretary	
4/64		R-5
8/64	Dept.	
10/66	Lagos, Nigeria (E) political officer	R-4
3/69		R-3
7/69	Dept. (AF)	
6/70	foreign affairs officer	GS-15
8/71	Kinshasa, Zaire (E) political officer	R-3
as of 10/74	First Secretary	

as of 11/74	Dept. (AF)
as of 4/75	not listed in Department of State records; assignment not known
Wife:	Jane Yang
Sources:	BR 1974, 1964, 1961-62 FSL 11/74, 10/71, 1/70, 1/67, 4/61 Kinshasa Diplomatic List 10/74

***KIMBALL, JOHN W.

b.   23 September 1933

4/66	Department of State New Delhi, India (E) telecoms technician	S-6
as of 5/68-5/71	not listed in Department of State records; assignment not known	
6/71	Department of State Monrovia, Liberia (E) telecoms technician	R-6
as of 9/74	Dept. (AF)	
as of 11/75	Bonn, Germany (E) probably telecoms technician	
Sources:	BR 1974 FSL 11/74, 10/71, 1/68, 1/67 Department of State Sources	

***John Walker Campbell, born in California in 1934, is not a CIA employee.

KINDELL, FLOREND EDWIN

as of 1/74:
3 Efklidou Street
Kifissia
Athens
Greece
801-2520

b.   28 June 1923

5/71	Department of State Athens, Greece (E) telecoms officer (Area Telecommunications Office)	R-2
as of 9/74	Dept. (A/OC)	
Wife:	Betty	
Sources:	BR 1974 FSL 6/74, 10/72, 6/71 Athens Embassy Source Department of State Source	

KINDL, CHARLES L.

    b.   not known

3/69	Department of State Manila, Philippines (E) telecoms assistant	S-5
as of 10/70		S-6
9/71	Kaduna, Nigeria (C) telecoms assistant	

as of 1/75	Department of State
	Bonn, Germany (E)
	    telecoms support officer
	    (Regional Communications Office)	

as of 6/77	Oslo, Norway (E) probably telecoms	
Sources:	FSL 8/75, 4/75, 10/71, 9/69 Bonn Embassy Source Oslo Embassy Source Department of State Sources	

KINGSLEY, ROLFE

b. 24 January 1918	New York	
1939	Yale University BA	

1939-43	private experience
	    advertising firm
	        junior accounts executive	

1943-46	U.S. Marine Corps overseas 1st Lieutenant	
1946-48	Department of War special assistant	

1948-51	Economic Cooperation Administration
	    Agency
	        plans officer	

1951-53	Department of Defense consultant	

6/53	Department of State
	Ankara, Turkey (E)
	    Attache &
	    political officer
		R-2

11/56	First Secretary	
5/57	Copenhagen, Denmark (E) First Secretary	
6/58	Attache	S-1
11/59		R-2
9/60	Ottawa, Canada (E) Attache & Special Assistant to the Ambassador	

5/65		R-1
11/65	Dept. (EUR)	
7/69		S-1
as of 12/70	London, U.K. (E) Attache (CIA Chief of Station)	
as of 10/73	assignment not known; possibly retired	
Wife:	Shirley Roadstrum	
Sources:	BR 1974, 1967 FSL 5/70, 1/67, 10/60, 7/57, 10/53 London Diplomatic Lists 8/73, 12/70	

KIRBY, DAVID A.

b. not known

3/75	Department of State Athens, Greece (E) telecoms technician (Area Telecommunications Office)	R-8
Source:	FSL 8/75	

KIRBY, JOHN THOMAS

as of 9/76:
60 Park Street
London W 1
U.K.
493-1504

b. 9 October 1922	Ohio	
1941-42	private experience news magazine researcher	
1942-45	U.S. Marine Corps overseas	
1945-46	private experience news publications associate editor	
1947	not known	
1948-49	private experience manufacturing firm ad writer	
1949	Kenyon College BA	
1949-53	Department of Defense political analyst	
8/53	Department of State Manila, Philippines (E) Assistant Attache & political officer	S-8
1/55		S-7

5/55	Saigon, Vietnam (E) Assistant Attache	
6/58	Bangkok, Thailand (E) political officer	R-5
8/58	Second Secretary & political officer	
10/60	Paris, France (E)	
10/60	Dept.	
10/63	Dept.	
5/66	Nicosia, Cyprus (E) political officer	R-4
9/68	Dept.	
as of 1/69-5/75	not listed in Department of State records; assignment not known	
as of 6/75- at least 9/76	Department of State London, U.K. (E) political liaison officer	
Wife:	Maryette	
Sources:	BR 1969, 1960, 1955 FSL 5/70, 9/68, 1/67, 7/60, 10/58, 7/55 10/53 London Embassy Sources	

KIYONAGA, JOSEPH YOSHIO

as of 7/76:
SHI-Sul 4/3, casa 19
Brasilia
Brazil
48-0695

b. 31 October 1917	Hawaii	
1935-40	University of Hawaii	
1940-43	private experience secondary school teacher	
1943-45	U.S. Army overseas	
1946-47	University of Michigan Law School	
1947-48	private experience secondary school teacher	
1949	School of Advanced International Studies MA	
1949-60	Department of Army economic analyst	
4/60	Department of State São Paulo, Brazil (CG) Consul & economic officer	R-5

6/60	Consul	
12/63	Dept.	
4/64		R-4
7/66	San Salvador, El Salvador (E) political officer	
4/67		R-3
9/69	Dept.	
4/70		S-1
as of 10/70	(ARA-LA)	
7/71	international relations officer	R-3
8/71	Panama City, Panama (E) general international relations officer	
as of 8/75	Dept. (ARA-LA)	
as of 7/76	Brasília, Brazil (E) Attache	

Wife:	Bina Cady
Sources:	BR 1974, 1960 FSL 4/75, 10/71, 1/70, 1/67, 4/64, 7/60 Brasília Diplomatic List 7/76 Department of State Source

KLEIN, DENNIS

as of 3/76:
34 Boydell Court
St. John's Wood Park
London, NW 8
U.K.
722-3937

b. not known

as of 12/74- at least 3/76	Department of State London, U.K. (E) Joint Reports & Research Unit
Sources:	London Embassy Sources

KLEIN, THEODORE

as of 2/76:
Martin Luther King Strasse 5/1
5300 Bonn-Bad Godesberg
Germany
37-35-79

b. 18 September 1922   Czechoslovakia

1940-45   U.S. Army overseas

1949	Queens College BA
1949-51	Harvard University
1951-65	Department of the Army operations officer

4/65	Department State
	    Vienna, Austria (E)
	        Attache &
	        political officer R-4

9/70	Dept.
as of 2/74	not listed in Department of State records; assignment not known

as of 2/75-
at least 2/76
	Department of State
	    Bonn, Germany (E)
	        Office of the Coordinator & Advisor

Wife:	Barbara Baron
Sources:	BR 1974, 1966 FSL 10/73, 10/70, 6/65 Vienna Diplomatic List 10/69 Bonn Diplomatic List 9/75 Bonn Embassy Source

KLINE, ALBERT HAINES Jr.

as of 1/78:
3, Mannenriedstrasse
3074 Muri
Bern
Switzerland
52-24-37

b. 30 November 1928	Connecticut
1950	Yale University BA
1950-53	U.S. Navy overseas Lieutenant
1954	Sorbonne University (France)
1954-55	private experience teacher
1955-59	Department of the Army area analyst

9/59	Department of State
	    Dept.
	        Foreign Service Institute
	            Romanian language-area trainee R-6

7/60	Munich, Germany (CG) consular officer
10/60	Vice-Consul

9/61	Bucharest, Romania (E)	
	Attache &	
	Vice-Consul	
9/61	Second Secretary &	
	Vice-Consul	
3/63		R-5
3/64	Dept.	
as of 1/67	(EUR)	

as of 9/67-6/75   not listed in Department of State records; assignment not known

7/75-
at least 1/78   Department of State
        Bern, Switzerland (E)
           Attache

Language: Romanian

Sources: BR 1967
           FSL 5/67, 4/64, 1/62, 10/60, 1/60
           Bern Diplomatic Lists 1/78, 7/76 (updated)

KONKLE, CAROLYN L.

as of 6/75:
228 Grove End Gardens
18 Abbey Road
London NW 8
U.K.

b.   not known

as of 6/75   Department of State
        London, U.K. (E)
          telecoms

Source: London Embassy Source

KOPLOWITZ, WILFRED D.

as of 2/76:
368 Avenue Louise
1050 Brussels
Belgium
649-9327

b.   24 June 1925   Connecticut

1943-46   U.S. Marine Corps overseas

1947   Yale University BA

1948   L'Institut des Hautes Etudes Internationales
           certificate

1949	School of Advanced International Studies MA	
1949-51	Department of State economic area trainee	
1951-60	Department of the Army political officer	
10/60	Department of State Paris, France (U.S. Mission to NATO & European Regional Organizations) political officer	R-4
3/63	Dept.	
4/64		R-3
8/66	Foreign Service Institute Senior Seminar in Foreign Policy	
as of 1/68-5/72	not listed in Department of State records; assignment not known	
6/72	Brasília, Brazil (E) political officer	R-2
as of 9/74	Dept. (ARA-LA)	
as of 2/76	Brussels, Belgium (E) Attache (CIA Chief of Station)	
Wife:	Maria	
Sources:	BR 1974, 1967 FSL 4/75, 10/72, 9/67, 4/63, 1/61 Brussels Diplomatic List 2/76 Brussels Embassy Source Department of State Source	

KORN, THOMAS A.

	b. not known		
8/69	Department of State Beirut, Lebanon (E) telecoms assistant	S-6
5/70	Conakry, Guinea (E) telecoms officer	
8/72	The Hague, Netherlands (E) telecoms officer	
as of 12/75	Dept. (A/OC)	
as of 1/76	New Delhi, India (E) telecoms	
Sources:	FSL 8/75, 2/71, 1/70 Department of State Sources	

KOSTIW, MICHAEL V.

as of 9/74:
41 Via Campania
Hotel Victoria
Rome
Italy
48-00-52

b. 13 March 1947	Germany	
1965	naturalized as U.S. citizen	
1969	St. Bonaventure University BA	
1969-71	U.S. Army	
6/72	Department of State Dept. (EUR) assistant foreign affairs officer	GS-9
11/73		R-7
8/74	Rome, Italy (E) political officer	
as of 9/76	Attache	
7/77	confirmed as consular officer	
as of 10/77	Montevideo, Uruguay (E) cover position not known	
Wife:	Carolyn Collins	
Sources:	BR 1974 FSL 8/75, 4/75, 11/74, 2/74 Rome Diplomatic List 9/76 Rome Embassy Source Department of State Sources	

KOWALESKI, FREDERICK J.

b. not known		
as of 6/76	Department of State Athens, Greece (E) probably telecoms	R-6
Sources:	Athens Embassy Sources Department of State Sources	

KOWALEWSKI, STEPHEN J.

b. not known		
as of 1/67	Department of State Kampala, Uganda (E) telecoms	rating not known
5/67	Calcutta, India (CG) telecoms supervisor	S-6

as of 5/68	telecoms officer
8/69- at least 10/72	Brussels, Belgium (E) telecoms officer
Sources:	FSL 10/72, 9/69, 9/67, 1/67

KRAMER, LLOYD L.

b.   2 February 1931

6/72	Department of State Manila, Philippines (E) telecoms officer (Area Telecommunications Office)	R-7
7/75	Athens, Greece (E) telecoms officer (Area Telecommunications Office)	
as of 3/76	Beirut, Lebanon (E) probably telecoms	
as of 5/77	Dept. (A/OC)	
Sources:	BR 1974 FSL 8/75, 10/72 Department of State Sources	

KRIEBEL, NORMAN E. Jr.

as of 6/75:
Coach House
London Court
Lambs Lane
Spencer's Wood
Berkshire
U.K.
0734-88-24-64

b.   not known

as of 12/74- at least 6/75	Department of State London, U.K. (E) Foreign Broadcast Information Service
Wife:	Suzanne
Sources:	London Embassy Sources

KRIESEL, FREDRIC A.

b.   not known

5/74	Department of State Athens, Greece (E) telecoms support officer (Area Telecommunications Office)	S-7

as of 3/76	Beirut, Lebanon (E) probably telecoms	
Sources:	FSL 8/75, 6/74 Department of State Sources	

KRSIEAN, LEROY C.

b. not known

6/72	Department of State Athens, Greece (E) telecoms assistant (Regional Relay Facility)	S-8
8/74	Saigon, Vietnam (E) telecoms support officer	S-7
***as of 4/75	assignment not known	
as of 11/75	Department of State Moscow, U.S.S.R. (E) cover position not known	
Wife:	Carol	
Sources:	FSL 4/75, 11/74, 6/73 Athens Embassy Source Department of State Source	

***The Saigon Embassy closed on April 30, 1975.

KRUMVIEDE, DALE M.

as of 12/75:
116 Weimarer Strasse, Apt. 11
1190 Vienna
Austria
36-56-72

b. 25 July 1935	Minnesota	
1954-57	U.S. Army overseas	
1959	University of Minnesota BA	
1961	University of Minnesota MA	
1961-72	Department of Defense research analyst	
6/72	Department of State Vienna, Austria (E) economic-commercial officer	R-5
2/76		R-4
as of 6/76	First Secretary (Economic and Commercial Section)	
as of 11/76	Dept. (EUR)	
Wife:	Joann Gillie	

Sources: BR 1974
                            FSL 8/75, 10/72
                            Vienna Diplomatic List 6/76
                            Vienna Embassy Source
                            Department of State Sources

KUBLIK, GEORGE

    as of 1/74:
    39 King George II Avenue
    Halandri
    Athens
    Greece
    681-8961

    b. not known
    as of 1/74   Department of Defense
                                    Athens, Greece (E)
                                    JUSMAGG

Wife: Leontine

Sources: Athens Embassy Source

KUNZ, GEORGE J.

    as of 12/75:
    40 Felix Dahn-Strasse
    1190 Vienna
    Austria
    47-33-44

    b. 6 October 1920   Germany

        1934   naturalized as U.S. citizen

    1942-46   U.S. Army

        1946   Office of the Military Government
                            United States (in Germany) (OMGUS)
                                unspecified position

        1947   New York State Teachers College BA

    1947-48   private experience
                                Cornell University
                                    teaching fellow

    1948-49   University of Zurich

    1949-51   Cornell University
                                    teaching fellow

    1951-67   Department of the Army

        4/67   Department of State
                                Geneva, Switzerland (M)
                                    economic officer   R-3

        12/70   international relations officer

8/73- at least 6/77	Vienna, Austria (E) Attache & economic officer
Wife:	Jean Sinclair
Sources:	BR 1973, 1970, 1967 FSL 6/73, 1/68 Vienna Diplomatic Lists 6/77, 6/76, 10/73 Vienna Embassy Source

LAMB, THOMAS WILLIAM

as of 7/77:
2-16 Akasaka
8-chome, Minato-ku
Tokyo
Japan
405-0064

b. 5 May 1924	New York	
1942-48	U.S. Army overseas 1st Lieutenant	
1948-53	Department of the Army plans officer	
1954	University of Maryland BS	
1957	Georgetown University MA	
1956-65	Department of the Army plans officer	
6/65	Department of State Geneva. Switzerland (M) Attache & economic officer	R-5
10/65	Second Secretary & economic officer	
as of 1/67	international organizations officer	
6/68		R-4
11/70	Dept. (IO)	
as of 10/72-2/73	not listed in Department of State records; assignment not known	
3/73	Department of State Bien Hoa, Vietnam (CG) political officer	S-2
as of 9/74	Saigon, Vietnam (E) political officer	
***as of 4/75	Dept. (EA)	
7/75- at least 7/77	Tokyo, Japan (E) Attache	
Wife:	Audrey Prather	

Sources: BR 1974, 1967
                                 FSL 4/75, 10/73, 1/71, 10/65
                                 Tokyo Diplomatic Lists 7/77, 4/76
                                 Department of State Source

***The Saigon Embassy closed on April 30, 1975.

LAMBERT, MORTON A.

as of 3/76:
16 Singers Close
St. Andrew's Road
Henley
Oxon
U.K.
04912-6946

b. not known

as of 12/75   Department of State
                                     London, U.K. (E)
                                         Foreign Broadcast Information Service

Wife: Joel Anne

Source: London Embassy Source

LANDRETH, RODNEY N. II

as of 2/76:
48 Koninginnegracht
The Hague
Netherlands
46-34-37

b.   5 October 1926   Pennsylvania

    1944-46   U.S. Army overseas

      1950   Princeton University BA

    1950-51   Stockholm University

    1950-51   private experience
                                   Swedish State Radio
                                       news editor-broadcaster

    1951-57   Department of the Army
                                   foreign affairs officer

      5/57   Department of State
                                   Port-au-Prince, Haiti
                                       Assistant Attache &
                                       political officer   R-7

      9/59   Dept.

      3/60   R-6

    4/60-12/61   Department of the Air Force
                                   foreign affairs officer

12/61	Department of State
	    Abidjan, Ivory Coast (E)
	        Attache &
	        consular officer
		R-5

3/62	Second Secretary & consular officer	
as of 9/64	Dept.	
1966-69	Paris, France (E) political officer	
8/69	Saigon, Vietnam (E) political officer	R-4
9/73- at least 2/76	The Hague, Netherlands (E) Attache	

Wife:	Marie Steketee
Sources:	BR 1973, 1970, 1964 FSL 6/73, 1/70, 1/65, 1/62, 4/60, 1/60, 7/57 Saigon Diplomatic and Consular List 3/71 The Hague Diplomatic Lists 2/76, 7/75, 9/73

LANE, BERNARD L.

as of 3/76:
15 Moyston Road
Bushey
Hertfordshire
U.K.

b.   not known

as of 12/74-
at least 3/76
	Department of State
	    London, U.K. (E)
	        telecoms

Wife:	Betty
Sources:	London Embassy Sources

LANE, PHILLIP G.

b.   not known

6/69	Department of State
	    Istanbul, Turkey (CG)
	        telecoms officer
		S-6

as of 10/71	Dept. (EA)	
as of 2/72-8/74	not listed in Department of State records; assignment not known	

9/74	Department of State
	    Stockholm, Sweden (E)
	        telecoms officer
		R-7

as of 8/77	Dept. (A/OC)	
as of 11/77	award for length of service	

Wife:	Gloria
Sources:	FSL 8/75, 11/74, 10/71, 9/69
	Stockholm Embassy Sources
	Department of State Sources

LANHAM, CHARLES E.

b.   not known

5/71	Department of State	
	Athens, Greece (E)	
	telecoms assistant	S-8
10/73	Jakarta, Indonesia (E)	
	telecoms assistant	
as of 11/74		S-7
Sources:	FSL 11/74, 2/74, 10/73	

LANNON, JOHN M.

b.   not known

11/72	Department of State	
	Kuala Lumpur, Malaysia (E)	
	telecoms assistant	S-6
as of 11/74	telecoms support officer	
4/75	Copenhagen, Denmark (E)	
	telecoms officer	
Sources:	FSL 8/75, 11/74, 2/73	

LARSON, ROBERT H.

as of 6/76:
6, Andreas Avraamides Street
Dassoupolis
Nicosia
Cyprus
23776

b. 31 March 1933	Minnesota	
1955	University of Minnesota BA	
1955-58	U.S. Air Force 1st Lieutenant	
1961	Harvard University LLB	
1961-63	Department of the Air Force	
	legal assistant	
9/63	Department of State	
	Bombay, India (CG)	
	consular officer	R-7
5/65		R-6
1/66	Dept. (NEA)	

1/68	Foreign Service Institute
7/68	Nicosia, Cyprus (E) political officer
3/69	R-5
as of 2/72	Dept. (NEA)

6/74	Athens, Greece (E)
	    Attache &
	    political officer R-4

3/75	Nicosia, Cyprus (E) political officer
as of 6/76	First Secretary
as of 11/76	Dept. (NEA)
Wife:	Anne Rice
Sources:	BR 1974, 1972 FSL 8/75, 4/75, 6/74, 2/72, 9/68, 1/67, 1/64 Athens Diplomatic List 12/74 (updated) Nicosia Diplomatic List 6/76 Athens Embassy Source Department of State Sources

LATRASH, FREDERICK WALDO

b. 29 November 1925	New York
1942-46	U.S. Navy overseas Ensign
1947	University of Southern California BA
1947-48	Walker School of Foreign Service
1948-49	Department of the Navy administrative assistant

2/49	Department of State
	    Calcutta, India (CG)
	        Vice-Consul S-11

1/51	New Delhi, India (E) Vice-Consul
1951-54	Department of the Navy political analyst
1953	Georgetown School of Foreign Service

1954-56	private experience
	    research organization
	        research director

9/56	Department of State
	    Amman, Jordan (E)
	        Second Secretary, Vice-Consul &
	        political officer R-6

2/59	Dept.
3/60	R-5

6/60	Agency for International Development Cairo, U.A.R. (E) operations officer	
as of 10/60		R-4
as of 4/61		R-5
9/61-4/63	not listed in Department of State records; assignment not known	

5/63	Department of State
	Caracas, Venezuela (E)
	    Attache &
	    political officer
		R-4

4/65	Panama City, Panama (E) cover position not known	
6/67	Accra, Ghana (E) political officer	R-3
10/70	Dept. (AF)	
5/71	Santiago, Chile (E) political officer	
6/73	La Paz, Bolivia (E) political officer	
as of 10/75- at least 1/77	Montevideo, Uruguay (E) First Secretary	
Wife:	Flor Teresa Padron	
Sources:	BR 1974, 1968, 1964, 1950 FSL 8/75, 10/73, 10/71, 9/67, 7/63, 4/61, 10/60, 1/57, 4/51, 1/50 Montevideo Diplomatic List 1/77 Department of State Sources	

LATTA, MERRON L. Jr.

b. 2 May 1929	Ohio	
1951	Ohio State University BA	
1951-53	U.S. Army overseas	
1953-55	private experience optician	
1955-57	Refugee Relief Program prosecuting officer	
1957-58	unspecified federal agency administrative officer	

10/58	Department of State
	Dept.
	    Foreign Service Institute
	        Polish language-area trainee
		R-7

3/59	Warsaw, Poland (E)
	    Attache &
	    visa officer	

5/59	Vice-Consul, Attache & visa officer	
2/61		R-6
7/61	Frankfurt, Germany (CG) political officer	
3/63		R-5
6/63	Hamburg, Germany (CG) political officer	
8/63	Consul	
4/66	Dept. foreign affairs officer	GS-12
as of 5/66-5/72	not listed in Department of State records; assignment not known	
6/72	Department of State Dept.	R-4
8/72	Berlin, Germany (M) Consul	
as of 8/75	Dept. (EUR)	
Wife:	Ames Auburn	
Sources:	BR 1974, 1964, 1959 FSL 8/75, 10/72, 10/65, 10/63, 1/62, 1/59 (West) Berlin Official List of Military Missions and Consular Officers 6/75 Department of State Sources	

LAWLER, JAMES N.

as of 1/76:
Avenida do Brasil 28
Cascais
Portugal
286-5300

b. 23 November 1930	Minnesota
1948	University of Mexico
1953	Georgetown University BSFS
1953-55	U.S. Navy
1955	University of Minnesota
1955	private experience tour guide
1955-56	manufacturing company international division trainee
1956-57	salesman
1958	Harvard University MA
1958	private experience tour guide (Europe)

1958-59	jr. highschool teacher	
10/60	Department of State Rio de Janeiro, Brazil (E) political assistant	S-11
10/61	political officer	R-8
3/63	Dept.	

8/63	Santiago, Chile (E)
	   Assistant Attache &
	   political officer	

4/64		R-7
12/65	Dept.	
5/66		R-6
7/66	Caracas, Venezuela (E) political officer	
7/68	Dept.	
6/70	Brasília, Brazil (Office) political officer	R-4
as of 10/71	Rio de Janeiro, Brazil (CG) political officer	
9/72	São Paulo, Brazil (CG) political officer	
5/73	Dept.	
as of 6/73	Rio de Janeiro, Brazil (CG) political officer	

as of 3/75-
at least 1/76
	Lisbon, Portugal (E)
	   Attache &
	   political officer	

Wife:	Sara	
Sources:	BR 1974, 1966 FSL 8/75, 4/75, 6/73, 10/70, 9/68, 1/67, 10/63, 1/62 Lisbon Diplomatic List 1/76 Lisbon Embassy Source	

LAWRENCE, JOHN S.

   as of 3/76:
   Flat 38
   20 Harley Street
   London W 1
   U.K.
   636-3108

   b.   not known

as of 12/74- at least 3/76	Department of State London, U.K. (E)
***	SUSLO

Wife:	Ruth M.
Sources:	London Embassy Sources

***SUSLO is a cover unit for the National Security Agency, not the CIA.

LAX, MORRIS H.

as of 9/74:
94 Via U. De Carolis
Apt. 20
Rome
Italy
349-8544

b. 1 June 1923	Michigan	
1941-49	U.S. Navy Lieutenant	
1944	U.S. Naval Academy BS	
1949-50	University of Grenoble (France)	
1950-51	University of Paris	
1951	Middlebury College MA	
1951-52	University of Michigan instructor	
1952-54	Department of Defense political analyst	
1955-57	private experience aviation company translator (France)	
1957-59	Department of Defense political analyst	
3/59	Department of State Karachi, Pakistan (CG) political officer	R-5
5/59	Second Secretary & political officer	
2/62	Bombay, India (CG) political officer	
4/62	Consul	
8/64	Dept.	
5/65		R-4
3/66	Paris, France (E) Second Secretary & political officer	
as of 5/68	political-military officer	
as of 9/69	Dept. (EUR)	
as of 1/70-8/74	not listed in Department of State records; assignment not known	

as of 9/74   Department of State
                                        Rome, Italy (E)
                                            political officer

as of 1/76   not listed in Department of State records;
                                    assignment not known

Language: French

Wife: Patricia

Sources: BR 1969, 1960
                                    FSL 9/69, 1/67, 10/64, 7/62, 7/59
                                    Rome Embassy Source

LEE, RONALD L.

as of 1/74:
21 Dryadon Street
Politia
Kifissia
Athens
Greece
801-8177

b.   not known

as of 6/73   Department of State
                                        Athens, Greece (E)
                                            telecoms assistant   S-7
                                            (Regional Relay Facility)

as of 2/74   not listed in Department of State records;
                                    assignment not known

Wife: Anne Marie

Sources: FSL 10/73, 6/73
                                    Athens Embassy Source

LEINER, CHARLES P.

as of 6/75:
Flat 31
60 Park Lane
London W 1
U.K.
491-2951

b.   not known

as of 12/74   Department of State
                                        London, U.K. (E)
        ***   SUSLO

as of 8/75   not listed in Department of State records;
                                    assignment not known

Sources: London Embassy Sources

***SUSLO is a cover unit for the National Security Agency, not the CIA.

LEVEN, CHARLES H.

as of 10/77:
26 Sophie-Charlotte-Strasse
Berlin 37
Germany
813-61-00

b.   not known

as of 6/75-
at least 10/77
	Department of State
	   Berlin, Germany (M)
	      Vice-Consul (Visa)

R-7

Sources: (West) Berlin Official List of Military
                 Missions and Consular Offices 10/77
              Berlin Mission Sources
              Department of State Sources

LEVINE, DIANE H.

as of 6/75:
11 Reeves House
Reeves Mews
London W 1
U.K.
629-5197

b.   not known

as of 12/74-   Department of State
at least 6/75   London, U.K. (E)
                        Joint Reports & Research Unit

Sources: London Embassy Sources

LEWIS, WHITNEY N.

as of 2/76:
Plieninger Strasse 215
6000 Frankfurt/Main
Germany
98-55-48-53

b.   not known

2/73-   Department of State
at least 2/76   Bonn, Germany (E)
                       telecoms technician
                       (Regional Communications Office)

S-6

Wife: Marjorie

Sources: FSL 4/75, 2/73
                 Bonn Embassy Source

LEWIS, WILLIAM M.

as of 1/74:
66 Harilaou Tricoupi Street
Kifissia
Athens
Greece
801-2163

b.   not known

6/61	Department of State
	Bogotá, Colombia (E)
	    political section
	        general clerk
		S-6

1/66	Ankara, Turkey (E) telecoms supervisor	S-5
1/68	telecoms officer	
as of 9/69-7/72	not listed in Department of State records; assignment not known	

8/72	Department of State
	Athens, Greece (E)
	    telecoms assistant
	    (Regional Relay Facility)
		S-6

as of 11/74	Dept. (EUR)	
as of 4/75	not listed in Department of State records; assignment not known	
Wife:	Jeanne	
Sources:	FSL 11/74, 6/74, 6/73, 10/72, 5/69, 1/67 10/63 Athens Embassy Source	

LEWON, LEROY C.

b.   13 December 1946

2/72	Department of State Belgrade, Yugoslavia (E) communications-records officer	R-8

7/74	Athens, Greece (E)
	    telecoms support officer
	    (Area Telecommunications Office)	

as of 1/77	Dept. (A/OC)	
as of 5/77	Nicosia, Cyprus (E) probably telecoms	
12/77	award for length of service	
2/78		R-7
Sources:	BR 1974 FSL 8/75, 11/74, 6/72 Department of State Sources	

LICHTY, DONIVAN D.

    b.   not known

9/63	Department of State
	  New Delhi, India (E)
	    telecoms
		grade
		not listed

as of 11/65-1/70	not listed in Department of State records; assignment not known	

2/70	Department of State
	  Kuala Lumpur, Malaysia (E)
	    telecoms officer
		S-6

as of 6/73-7/75	not listed in Department of State records; assignment not known	

8/75	Department of State
	  Athens, Greece (E)
	    telecoms officer
	    (Area Telecommunications Office)
		R-7

Sources:	FSL 8/75, 2/73, 5/70, 10/65	

LIESER, WILLIAM D.

    b.   13 April 1939

	California	
1960-61	private experience mechanical manufacturing company	
1963	University of California BA	
1963-67	Department of the Army analyst	

10/67	Department of State
	  Oslo, Norway (E)
	    political officer
		R-7

3/69		R-6
8/72	Dept. (EUR)	
8/73	Foreign Service Institute language training	
3/74	Leningrad, U.S.S.R. (CG) consular officer	
3/75		R-5
9/76- at least 6/77	Vienna, Austria (E) Second Secretary (Political Section)	
Wife:	Mary Keffer	
Sources:	BR 1974 FSL 8/75, 6/74, 10/73, 2/73, 1/68 Vienna Diplomatic List 6/77 Department of State Sources	

LINDAMOOD, DOUGLAS W.

    b. not known

4/75	Department of State	
	Caracas, Venezuela (E)	
	telecoms support officer	S-6
as of 10/77	Athens, Greece (E)	
	probably telecoms	
as of 3/78	Dept. (A/OC)	
Sources:	FSL 8/75, 4/75	
	Athens Embassy Sources	
	Department of State Sources	

LINDSAY, GERALD G.

    b. not known

6/70	Department of State	
	Brussels, Belgium (E)	
	telecoms officer	S-7
11/73	Bamako, Mali (E)	
	telecoms support officer	
8/74		S-6
as of 4/77	Buenos Aires, Argentina (E)	
	probably telecoms	
Sources:	FSL 8/75, 2/74, 6/73	
	Department of State Sources	

LIPSCOMB, SUZANNE

    as of 2/76:
    Kolumbusring 9/1
    5300 Bonn-Bad Godesberg
    Germany
    37-81-09

    b. not known

9/71	Department of State	
	Lima, Peru (E)	
	Political Section secretary	S-8
as of 3/74-1/76	not listed in Department of State records;	
	assignment not known	
as of 2/76	Department of State	
	Bonn, Germany (E)	
	Office of the Coordinator and Advisor	
Sources:	FSL 10/73, 6/73	
	Bonn Embassy Source	

LITTLE, GEORGE R.

    b. not known

8/67	Department of State
	  Manila, Philippines (E)
	    telecoms technician
		S-6

9/69	Bonn, Germany (E) telecoms technician	
6/73	Dept. (EUR)	
as of 10/73	not listed in Department of State records; assignment not known	
Sources:	FSL 6/73, 1/70, 1/68	

LIVINGSTON, JAMES A.

    b. not known

7/76-
at least 6/77
	Department of State
	  Vienna, Austria (E)
	    Second Secretary
	    (Economic and Commercial Section)
		R-5

Sources:	Vienna Diplomatic List 6/77 Department of State Sources	

LOFGREN, WILLIAM S.

    as of 7/76:
    3 Rue Kalvou
    Psychico
    Athens
    Greece
    671-3980

b. 27 December 1936	Colorado	
1962	University of Colorado MA	
1967	University of Indiana PhD	
9/67	Department of State Dept.	R-7
3/69		R-6
as of 5/69	(EUR)	
6/69	New Delhi, India (E) political-economic officer	
1/70	economic-commercial officer	
8/71	Dept. (NEA)	

10/71	Beirut, Lebanon (E)
	  Second Secretary &
	  political officer	

5/73		R-5

9/73	Dept. (NEA)

10/73	Nicosia, Cyprus (E)
	political officer

1/75-	Athens, Greece (E)
at least 2/77	Second Secretary,
	Political Section

2/76		R-4

as of 10/77	Copenhagen, Denmark (E)
	Attache

Wife: Joan Muller

Sources: BR 1974, 1971
FSL 4/75, 10/73, 2/72, 10/71, 9/69, 1/68
Athens Diplomatic Lists 2/77, 7/76, 12/74 (updated)
Copenhagen Diplomatic List 10/77

LOFTIN, DANNY M.

  b. 8 March 1943

1966	Wake Forest University BA

1967	University of Kentucky MA

1968-72	unspecified government agency
	research analyst

5/72	Department of State
	Dept. (IO)
	international economist R-6

as of 10/72	U.S. Mission to the United Nations (USUN)
	cover position not known

as of 6/73	Dept (IO)

10/73	Leningrad, U.S.S.R. (CG)
	general services officer

as of 7/76	Geneva, Switzerland (M)
	cover position not known

Sources: BR 1974
FSL 8/75, 2/74, 6/72
Department of State Source

LONAM, WILLIAM B.

  as of 3/75:
  Via V. Monti
  20123 Milan
  Italy
  482-442

b. 2 January 1926	Nebraska

1944-46	U.S. Navy overseas

1950	Georgetown University BS

1951-54	Department of the Army junior analyst (overseas)	
1954-58	senior analyst	
1958-65	plans officer	
6/65	Department of State Rome, Italy (E) supervisory consular officer	R-4
8/70	Dept. (EUR)	
10/70	projects officer	
as of 2/71-4/73	not listed in Department of State records; assignment not known	
5/73	Department of State Milan, Italy (CG) Consul & visa officer	
as of 8/76	Dept. (EUR)	
Wife:	Mary Helldorfer	
Sources:	BR 1974 FSL 8/75, 6/73, 10/70, 10/65 Milan Consular Lists 3/75, 3/74 Rome Embassy Source Department of State Source	

LONG, RICHARD MAXWELL

b. 19 September 1922	Oklahoma	
1940-45	U.S. Army overseas	
1946-47	U.S. Air Force assistant base personnel officer	
1950	Phillips University BS	
1950-51	private experience radio station administrative officer	
2/51	Department of State Frankfurt, Germany (HICOG) space examiner	S-8
1951	chief information control officer (Office of Intelligence)	S-7
1951-58	Department of the Army foreign affairs analyst	
6/59	Department of State Pretoria, South Africa (E) Attache & political officer	R-5
10/59	Second Secretary & political officer	

6/61	Johannesburg, South Africa (CG) economic officer
8/61	Consul
9/62	Dept.
11/63	Agency for International Development Addis Ababa, Ethiopia (E) public safety adviser R-4
7/66	Department of State Dept. foreign affairs officer GS-14
12/69	Tripoli, Libya (E) political officer R-3
11/70	Hamburg, Germany (CG) consular officer
as of 10/73	not listed in Department of State records; assignment not known
Wife:	Elizabeth Hogan
Sources:	BR 1973, 1960 FSL 6/73, 2/71, 1/70, 1/64, 1/63, 7/61, 10/59, 2/52, 7/51

LOURIE, ALAN E.

b. 4 January 1940	New Jersey
1959-62	U.S. Air Force overseas
1962-63	private experience telegraph company telegrapher
1963-68	unspecified government agency telecommunications specialist
9/68	Department of State Dacca, Pakistan (CG) telecoms assistant S-6
as of 10/70	telecoms officer
as of 2/71-5/73	not listed in Department of State records; assignment not known
6/73	Department of State Geneva, Switzerland (M) telecoms officer R-8
as of 10/76	Dept. (A/OC)
Wife:	Alice Jewell
Sources:	BR 1974 FSL 8/75, 10/73, 10/70 Geneva Mission Source Department of State Source

LOWELL, FRANK W.

    as of 3/75:
    Praça das Aguas Livres 8-8° C Esq.
    Lisbon 2
    Portugal
    68-30-13

    b. not known

5/73	Department of State	
	Lisbon, Portugal (E)	
	telecoms assistant	S-8
as of 8/75	Dept. (EUR)	
as of 1/76	Beirut, Lebanon (E)	
	probably telecoms	
as of 4/76	Addis Ababa, Ethiopia (E)	
	probably telecoms	
Sources:	FSL 8/75, 4/75, 6/74, 5/73	
	Lisbon Embassy Source	
	Department of State Sources	

LUIZ, ROBERT C.

    b. not known

2/68	Department of State	
	Athens, Greece (E)	
	telecoms assistant	S-6
as of 10/71	Dept. (NEA)	
as of 2/72-1/78	not listed in Department of State records; assignment not known	
as of 2/78	Department of State	
	Geneva, Switzerland (M)	
	probably telecoms	
Sources:	FSL 10/71, 9/69	
	Department of State Source	

LUKE, DOROTHY P.

    as of 3/76:
    69 Buttermere Court
    Boundary Road
    London NW 8
    U.K.
    722-0913

    b. not known

as of 12/74-
at least 3/76
	Department of State
	   London, U.K. (E)
	      Joint Reports & Research Unit

LUTHER, RICHARD M.

as of 6/75:
41 Carlton Hill
London NW 8
U.K.
328-2283

b. 4 October 1929	Wisconsin	
1951	University of Wisconsin BS	
1951	unspecified government experience	

1952-57	Department of the Army
	    Germany
	        analyst	

1957-59	location unknown analyst	
1959-68	Greece liaison officer	
1968-69	location unknown plans officer	
8/69	Department of State Dept.	R-4
as of 1/70	Foreign Service Institute language training	
7/70	Warsaw, Poland (E) political officer	

9/72	London, U.K. (E)
	    Second Secretary &
	    political officer	

4/74		R-3
as of 10/74	First Secretary & political officer	
as of 10/75	Dept. (EUR)	
Wife:	Jean Gikas	
Sources:	BR 1974 FSL 8/75, 2/73, 10/70, 1/70 London Diplomatic Lists 8/75, 10/74, 12/72 London Embassy Sources Department of State Source	

LUTHY, WALTER P.

b. 24 July 1918	
5/63	Department of State Nicosia, Cyprus (E)

	communications specialist (Regional Relay Office)	S-3
3/64	Athens, Greece (E) communications specialist	
as of 1/67-4/70	not listed in Department of State records; assignment not known	
5/70- at least 6/73	Department of State Athens, Greece (E) telecoms officer	S-2
as of 10/73	not listed in Department of State records; assignment not known	
Sources:	BR 1973 FSL 6/73, 5/70, 10/65, 7/64, 10/63	

LYON, KEITH W.

as of 4/76:
32 Prestwood Avenue
Kenton
Harrow
Middlesex
U.K.
907-3398

b. 14 December 1938	Oregon	
1957-59	U.S. Navy overseas	
1963	Oregon State University BSEE	
1963-74	unspecified government agency electronics engineer	
5/74	Department of State London, U.K. (E) telecoms engineer	R-4
as of 11/77	Dept. (A/OC)	
Wife:	Susan Jamieson	
Sources:	BR 1974 FSL 8/75, 6/74 London Embassy Sources Department of State Sources	

LYONS, RODDY G.

b. not known		
5/75	Department of State Athens, Greece (E) telecoms support officer (Area Telecommunications Office)	S-8
Source:	FSL 8/75	

MAAS, ERNST S.

as of 2/76:
Martin Luther King Strasse 3/5
5300 Bonn-Bad Godesberg
Germany
37-94-03

b.   not known

as of 2/75- at least 2/76	Department of State Bonn, Germany (E) OCA Liaison Unit
Wife:	Jeanette
Source:	Bonn Embassy Source

MacDONALD, CHARLES R.

as of 2/76:
Hansa Allee 137/4
600 Frankfurt/Main
Germany
59-30-97

b.   not known

3/67 ***	Department of State Kinshasa, Congo (E) telecoms technician	S-6
as of 5/69	Dept.	
7/70	Saigon, Vietnam (E) telecoms technician	S-5
7/72- at least 2/76	Bonn, Germany (E) telecoms technician (Regional Communications Office)	
Sources:	FSL 8/75, 10/72, 10/70, 5/69, 5/67 Bonn Embassy Source Department of State Source	

***The Congo became Zaire in 1971.

MALOY, KEVIN A.

b. 7 May 1936	New York	
1958	Princeton University BA	
1958-61	U.S. Marine Corps overseas	
1962-72	Department of the Army research analyst	
10/72	Department of State Dept. international relations officer	GS-13

5/73	Geneva, Switzerland (M)	
	Office of the Special Assistant	R-5
as of 9/76	Nicosia, Cyprus (E)	
	Second Secretary	
2/78		R-4

Wife: Joan St. Peter

Sources: BR 1974
FSL 8/75, 6/73
Geneva Diplomatic Lists 7/76, 10/75
Geneva Mission Source
Nicosia Diplomatic List 6/77
Department of State Sources

MALTON, CHARLES TROFFORD Jr.

as of 12/75:
Unterer Schreiberweg 26
Vienna
Austria
32-13-47

b. 22 October 1927	Massachusetts	
1945-47	U.S. Army	
1950	Harvard University BA	
1951-66	Department of the Army	
	plans officer	
1/67	Department of State	
	Dept.	R-5
3/69	(EUR)	R-4
4/70		R-3
8/70	Vienna, Austria (E)	
	Attache &	
	political officer	
	Peripheral Reporting Section	
as of 10/76	Dept. (EUR)	

Wife: Barbara

Sources: BR 1974
FSL 8/75, 10/70, 5/67
Vienna Diplomatic Lists 6/76, 12/73, 10/70
Vienna Embassy Source
Department of State Sources

MALZAHN, RICHARD L.

as of 2/76:
Europa Strasse 3/2
5300 Bonn-Bad Godesberg
Germany
37-49-03

b. 17 May 1934	Wisconsin	
1956	Yale University BA	
1956	Department of the Army research analyst	
1956-59	U.S. Air Force 1st Lieutenant	
1959-60	Department of the Army research analyst	

5/60	Department of State
	    The Hague, Netherlands (E)
	        political officer
		R-8

4/64		R-7
1/65	Dept.	
5/65		R-6
5/68		R-5
2/69	international relations officer	GS-13
as of 5/69-1/75	not listed in Department of State records; assignment not known	

as of 2/75-
at least 2/76
	Department of State
	    Bonn, Germany (E)
	        Office of the Coordinator & Advisor	

Wife:	Mildred McCormick	
Sources:	BR 1974 FSL 1/69, 6/65, 7/60 Bonn Embassy Source	

MAPOTHER, JOHN RUBEL

as of 2/76:
Martin Luther King Strasse 9/1
5300 Bonn-Bad Godesberg
Germany
37-28-49

b. 13 November 1922	Kentucky	
1944-46	U.S. Army	
1947	University of Louisville BME	
1947-49	Department of the Army political analyst	

10/49	Department of State
	    Frankfurt, Germany (CG)
	        Office of the U.S. High
	        Commissioner for Germany—
	        Land Commissioner for
	        Bavaria
	            political analyst
		S-7

as of 10/50		S-6

as of 7/51	political reporting officer	
as of 7/52-9/55	Department of the Army political officer	
10/55	Department of State Vienna, Austria (E) political officer	R-4
7/56		R-5
9/58	Dept.	
2/59		R-4
as of 10/60-1/75	not listed in Department of State records; assignment not known	
as of 2/75- at least 2/76	Department of State Bonn, Germany (E) OCA Research Unit	
Wife:	Margaret	
Sources:	BR 1960, 1957 FSL 7/60, 10/58, 1/56, 7/51, 10/50, 4/50 Bonn Embassy Source	

MARQUES, JOSEPH J.

as of 1/77:
"Casa Refugio"
Charneca, Cascais
Lisbon
Portugal
285-03-91

b.   8 August 1940

5/72	Department of State Rio de Janeiro, Brazil (CG) political officer	R-7
10/74	Brasília, Brazil (E) Assistant Attache & political officer	
as of 1/76- at least 1/77	Lisbon, Portugal (E) Third Secretary	
2/76		R-6
Sources:	BR 1974 FSL 8/75, 11/74, 10/72, 6/72 Brasília Diplomatic List 7/75 Lisbon Diplomatic Lists 1/77, 1/76 Department of State Source	

MARX, JOHN P.

as of 7/75:

67 van Zaeckstraat
The Hague
The Netherlands
24-79-00

b.   not known

4/68	Department of State Rome, Italy (E) political assistant	S-5
as of 10/70-5/74	not listed in Department of State records; assignment not known
as of 6/74- at least 7/75	Department of State The Hague, Netherlands (E) Attache
as of 2/76	assignment not known
Sources:	FSL 5/70, 5/68 The Hague Diplomatic Lists 7/75, 6/74

MASTERSON, RICHARD B.

b.   not known

11/72	Department of State Manila, Philippines (E) telecoms assistant	S-8
as of 11/74	telecoms support officer	
as of 12/74	Nicosia, Cyprus (E) telecoms support officer	S-7
as of 7/77	Copenhagen, Denmark (E) probably telecoms	
as of 10/77	award for length of service	
Sources:	FSL 8/75, 4/75, 2/74, 6/73 Department of State Sources	

McAVOY, CLYDE RICHARD

b. 27 March 1926	New York
1944-46	U.S. Marine Corps
1951	Bucknell University BA
1951-52	U.S. Marine Corps overseas Captain
1952-53	private experience newspaper reporter
1953-57	Department of the Army analyst
1954	American University

7/57	Department of State Bangkok, Thailand (E) political officer	
		R-6
9/57	Second Secretary & political officer	
12/59	Dept.	
3/60		
		R-5
8/60	Foreign Service Institute Indonesian language training	
7/61	Jakarta, Indonesia (E) Second Secretary & economic officer	
as of 10/62	Second Secretary & political officer	
4/64		
		R-4
5/66	Dept. (EA)	
4/67		
		R-3
7/67		
		S-1
1/68	Vientiane, Laos (E) political officer	
11/68		
		R-3
8/71	Rangoon, Burma (E) First Secretary & political officer	
as of 9/74	Dept. Foreign Service Institute	
as of 8/75	(EA)	
Language:	Indonesian	
Wife:	Lola Mae Gulymer	
Sources:	BR 1974, 1967 FSL 8/75, 11/74, 10/71, 5/68, 1/67, 1/62, 10/60, 4/60, 10/57 Rangoon Diplomatic List 1/72	

McBRIDE, MICHAEL G.

as of 12/74:
9 Avenue Daniel Lesueur
75007 Paris
France
306-4971

b.   not known

as of 12/74	Department of State Paris, France (E) Regional Reports Office

Sources: Paris Embassy Source

McCABE, WALTER CASSATT

   b.   20 August 1928   Canada

       1946-49   U.S. Army overseas

         1952   Georgetown University BSFS

       1953-59   Department of the Army
                        Berlin, Germany
                            political officer

       1959-64   private experience
                        unspecified oil company
                            assistant to president

       1964-69   Department of State
                        London, U.K. (E)
                            political officer   R-5

         7/69   New Delhi, India (E)
                            political officer   R-3

         8/71   Dept. (NEA)

    as of 10/73   Ottawa, Canada (E)
                        Attache

   as of 10/76-   Stockholm, Sweden (E)
  at least 10/77   First Secretary
                        (CIA Chief of Station)

    Wife: Dorothy Baetty

    Sources: BR 1972
                       FSL 6/73, 10/71, 9/69
                       Ottawa Diplomatic Lists 2/76, 10/73
                       Stockholm Diplomatic Lists 10/77, 10/76

McCARTHY, JOHN F. III

as of 3/77:
Pawa Mansion Third Floor
71-1 Yamamotodori, 2-chome
Ikata-ku, Kobe-shi
Ōsaka-Kōbe
Japan
(078)240-3455

   b.   5 September 1941   Washington, D.C.

       1959-62   U.S. Army overseas

         1966   George Washington University BA

         1967   George Washington University MA

       1967-69   no entry in Department of State records;
                       not known

         8/69   Department of State
                        Dept.   S-4

as of 1/70	Foreign Service Institute	
2/70	area specialist	R-6
2/70	Saigon, Vietnam (E) political officer	
8/72	Phnom Penh, Khmer Republic (E) consular officer	
***as of 4/75	assignment not known	
as of 11/75	Department of State Dept. (EA)	
as of 4/76	Foreign Service Institute language training	
7/76- at least 9/77	Ōsaka-Kōbe, Japan (CG) Consul	
Sources:	BR 1974 FSL 4/75, 10/72, 5/70, 1/70 Phnom Penh Diplomatic List 11/73 Tokyo Consular Lists 9/77, 3/77 Department of State Source	

***The Phnom Penh Embassy closed on April 12, 1975.

McCLUNG, DONALD C.

b. not known		
7/75	Department of State Montevideo, Uruguay (E) telecoms officer	R-6
as of 10/77	Athens, Greece (E) probably telecoms	
Sources:	FSL 8/75 Athens Embassy Sources Department of State Sources	

McCULLOUGH, JOHN P.

as of 9/75:
50 Avenue Tir aux Pigeons
1150 Brussels
Belgium
770-2870

b. 4 June 1927	New York
1945-47	U.S. Army overseas
1949-50	private experience Yale University research assistant
1950	BA

1950	Columbia University	
1950-52	Department of the Army research analyst	
1951	Georgetown University	

12/52	Department of State
	    Brussels, Belgium (E)
	        Vice-Consul &
	        consular officer
		S-9

as of 7/56		S-8

8/56-1959	private experience
	    unspecified educational foundation
	        research associate	

8/60	Department of State
	    Brazzaville, Congo (E)
	        economic officer
		R-6

10/60	Second Secretary, Vice-Consul & economic officer	

10/63	Dakar, Senegal (E)
	    Second Secretary, Vice-Consul &
	    consular officer	

5/65		R-5
11/65	Dept. (AF)	
6/67	programs officer	GS-13
as of 9/67-8/75	not listed in Department of State records; assignment not known	

as of 9/75	Department of State
	    Brussels, Belgium (E)
	        cover position not known	

Wife:	Caroline Maphis	
Sources:	BR 1972, 1966 FSL 5/67, 1/67, 1/64, 10/60, 10/56 Brussels Embassy Source	

McDERMOTT, JOHN E.

b. not known		

10/70
***
	Department of State
	    Dacca, Pakistan (CG)
	        telecoms officer
		S-6

6/71	New Delhi, India (E) telecoms assistant	
as of 7/73	Dept. (NEA)	
9/73	Brussels, Belgium (E) telecoms officer	

as of 2/76   Athens, Greece (E)
                                    probably telecoms

Sources: FSL 8/75, 2/74, 10/73, 10/71, 10/70
                                    Department of State Sources

***Dacca, East Pakistan became Dacca, Bangladesh in May, 1972.

McGEE, JOSEPH V.

   as of 3/76:
   20-A Clareville Street
   London SW 7
   U.K.
   373-1883

b. 10 January 1928	New York	
1946-53	U.S. Air Force overseas	
1952-53	Hofstra College	
1953-59	Department of the Army communications specialist	
1954-56	University of Maryland	
1956-58	George Washington University	

11/59	Department of State
	   Nicosia, Cyprus (E)
	   communications specialist
		S-8

12/60-7/63	Department of the Army communications specialist	

8/63	Department of State
	   Accra, Ghana (E)
	   communications specialist
		S-4

11/65	Dept.	
as of 1/67	(O/OC)	
as of 5/68-4/74	not listed in Department of State records; assignment not known	

5/74	Department of State
	   London, U.K. (E)
	   telecoms officer
		R-4

as of 12/76	Dept. (A/OC)	
Sources:	BR 1974, 1967 FSL 8/75, 6/74, 1/68, 1/67, 10/60, 1/60 London Embassy Sources Department of State Source	

McGHEE, WILLIAM MORROW

   as of 9/77:
   11 Chester Square
   London SW 1

U.K.
730-5641

b. 8 July 1922	South Carolina	
1942-46	U.S. Army overseas	
1943-44	University of California	
1946	Department of the Army area specialist	
1947	George Washington University BA	
1947-48	George Washington University Law School	
1948-53	Department of the Army assistant to the chief	

1/53	Department of State
	    Manila, Philippines (E)
	    Attache &
	    political officer
		S-5

1/55		S-4
3/55-4/58	Department of the Army foreign affairs officer	

5/58	Department of State
	    Addis Ababa, Ethiopia (E)
	    economic officer
		R-5

8/58	Second Secretary & economic officer	
2/61		R-4
12/61	Dept.	
8/65	Hong Kong, U.K. (CG) political officer	
10/65	Consul & political officer	
5/68	Singapore, Singapore (E) political officer	
4/70		R-3
as of 10/71	Dept. (NEA)	
as of 2/72-11/74	not listed in Department of State records; assignment not known	

as of 12/74-
at least 6/78
	Department of State
	    London, U.K. (E)
	    Attache &
	    political liaison officer	

Wife:	Nancy Mersh	
Sources:	BR 1971, 1966, 1953 FSL 10/71, 9/68, 7/62, 7/58, 4/55, 4/53 Singapore Diplomatic and Consular List 1/71 London Diplomatic Lists 6/78, 8/76, 12/74 London Embassy Sources	

McGILVRAY, JAMES J.

b. 20 May 1937	Massachusetts	
1955-58	U.S. Navy overseas	
1959	no entry in Department of State records; not known	
1960-67	unspecified government agency communications officer	
6/67	Department of State Amman, Jordan (E) telecoms officer	S-6
10/69	Athens, Greece (E) telecoms assistant	
as of 1/70	Amman, Jordan (E) telecoms	
as of 10/70	Athens, Greece (E) telecoms officer	
as of 10/72-3/74	not listed in Department of State records; assignment not known	
4/74	Department of State Nairobi, Kenya (E) telecoms officer	R-6
as of 10/76	Athens, Greece (E) probably telecoms	
Wife:	Barbara Doherty	
Sources:	BR 1974 FSL 8/75, 6/74, 6/72, 10/70, 1/70, 9/69, 9/68 Athens Embassy Sources Department of State Sources	

McINTYRE, JOHN T.

as of 1/74:
3 Tyrteon Street
Kifissia
Athens
Greece
801-3182

b. not known		
8/72	Department of State Athens, Greece (E) telecoms assistant (Regional Relay Facility)	S-7
as of 11/74	telecoms support officer	
as of 7/75	Dept. (A/OC)	
as of 1/76	Caracas, Venezuela (E) probably telecoms	

as of 10/77	Dept. (A/OC)
Wife:	Edythe
Sources:	FSL 4/75, 11/74, 6/73
	Athens Embassy Source
	Department of State Source

McKEON, TIMOTHY J.

as of 1/74:
28 Irodotou Street
Nea Politia
Kifissia
Athens
Greece
801-3717

b.   not known

5/71	Department of State	
	Bern, Switzerland (E)	
	telecoms assistant	S-7
7/73- at least 8/75	Athens, Greece (E) telecoms assistant (Area Telecommunications Office)	
as of 11/74	telecoms support officer	
as of 10/75	Dept. (A/OC)	
Wife:	Barbara	
Sources:	FSL 8/75, 4/75, 11/74, 10/73, 6/73 Athens Embassy Source Department of State Source	

McMANUS, GERALD R.

b.   15 December 1942

10/70	Department of State Athens, Greece (E) telecoms assistant (Regional Relay Facility)	R-7
8/73	San'a, Yemen Arab Republic (E) telecoms assistant	
3/74	telecoms support officer	
6/75	Georgetown, Guyana (E) telecoms support officer	
as of 12/77	Jerusalem, Jerusalem (CG) probably telecoms	
Wife:	Carolyn	

Sources:	BR 1974	
	FSL 8/75, 4/75, 10/73, 6/73	
	Athens Embassy Source	
	Department of State Source	

McWILLIAMS, JAMES W.

b. not known

9/69	Department of State	
	Bombay, India (CG)	
	economic-commercial officer	S-5
as of 11/69	Dept. (NEA)	
4/72	Calcutta, India (CG)	
	consular officer	
as of 6/74	Dept. (NEA)	
5/75		R-6
6/75-	Athens, Greece (E)	
at least 3/78	Attache &	
	political officer	
as of 2/77	Second Secretary	
2/78		R-5
Sources:	FSL 8/75, 4/75, 11/74, 6/74, 6/72, 1/70	
	Athens Diplomatic Lists 3/78, 7/76,	
	12/74 (updated)	
	Athens Embassy Source	
	Department of State Sources	

MEINBRESSE, JERRY D.

b. 30 December 1933

as of 1/67-	Department of State	
at least 5/67	Bucharest, Romania (E)	rating
	probably telecoms	not listed
as of 9/67-11/69	not listed in Department of State records;	
	assignment not known	
12/69	Department of State	
	Athens, Greece (E)	
	telecoms officer	S-5
2/71		S-4
as of 2/73	Dept. (NEA)	
as of 6/73-4/76	not listed in Department of State records;	
	assignment not known	
5/76	Department of State	
	Dept.	R-5
as of 7/76	Monrovia, Liberia (E)	
	probably telecoms	

Sources:	BR 1972
	FSL 2/73, 1/70, 5/67, 1/67
	Department of State Sources

MELI, ARTHUR S.

as of 3/76:
Howe Farmhouse
Hambleden
Henley
Oxon
U.K.
0491-66-411

b.   not known

as of 11/75-	Department of State
at least 3/76	London, U.K. (E)
	Foreign Broadcast Information Service

Wife:	Marcelle
Source:	London Embassy Sources

MELTON, MARILYN ELAINE

as of 5/76:
6 Buttermere Court
Boundary Road
London NW 8
U.K.
722-3605

b.   not known

as of 12/74-	Department of State
at least 5/76	London, U.K. (E)
	Political Liaison Section
	(secretary to CIA Chief of Station)

Sources:	London Embassy Sources

MERIKOSKI, JUHA OLIVA

as of 2/76:
Puolaharju 26 B
00930 Helsinki 93
Finland
33-16-67

b. 7 March 1942	Finland
1964	Wayne State University BA
1969	Wayne State University MA
1970-73	not listed in Department of State records; not known

1/74	Department of State Dept. (EUR)	R-7
8/74- at least 1/78	Helsinki, Finland (E) Third Secretary & political officer	
3/77		R-6
Wife:	Mary Ann Drummy	
Sources:	BR 1974 FSL 8/75, 6/74 Helsinki Diplomatic Lists 1/78, 8/75 Department of State Sources	

METHVEN, STUART E.

b. 3 September 1927	Netherlands	
1945-47	U.S. Army overseas	
1951	Amherst College BA	
1951-52	private experience manufacturing company production foreman	
1952-59	Department of the Army administrative assistant	
***5/59	International Cooperation Administration Vientiane, Laos (E) executive assistant	R-5
7/62-6/69	not listed in Department of State records; assignment not known	
7/69	Department of State Jakarta, Indonesia (E) political officer	R-4
4/70		R-3
as of 11/73	Dept. (EA)	
as of 6/74	(AF)	
as of 1/75	Kinshasa, Zaire (E) Political Section (CIA Chief of Station)	
Sources:	BR 1973, 1961-62 FSL 6/74, 5/70, 1/62, 7/59 Kinshasa Embassy Source	

***Predecessor of the Agency for International Development, established in 1961.

MEYER, CORD Jr.

as of 8/76:
24 South Eaton Place

London SW 1
U.K.

b. 10 November 1920	Washington D.C.
1942	Yale University BA (summa cum laude)
1942-45	U.S. Marine Corps overseas Lieutenant
1945	private experience aide to Harold Stassen at drafting of United Nations Charter
1947-49	United World Federalists president
1950	not known
1951	Central Intelligence Agency
1954-72	chief of International Organizations Division
as of 1/73	Assistant Deputy Director of Plans

as of 10/73-9/76	Department of State
	    London, U.K. (E)
	        Attache &
	        Political Liaison Section chief
	        (CIA Chief of Station)

as of 6/76	Political Attache &
	        Political Liaison Section chief
	        (CIA Chief of Station)

1977	Central Intelligence Agency Assistant Deputy Director of Plans
12/77	resigns from Central Intelligence Agency

3/78	private experience
	    Field Newspaper Syndicate
	        weekly newspaper columnist

Wife:	Starke P.
Sources:	London Diplomatic Lists 8/76, 10/73 London Embassy Sources *New York Times*, March 30, 1967 *New York Times Magazine*, January 7, 1973 *International Bulletin*, December 19, 1977 *Washington Post*, February 7, 1978 *Washington Post*, March 17, 1978

MILANOVICH, JOANNE

as of 3/76:
300 Grove End Gardens
London NW 8
U.K.
286-4475

b.   not known

as of 12/74-
at least 3/76
	Department of State
	    London, U.K. (E)
	        Joint Reports & Research Unit

Sources: London Embassy Sources

MILLER, JUDITH A.

as of 12/74:
103 Rue de Miromesnil
75008 Paris
France
522-5950

b.   not known

as of 12/74   Department of State
                              Paris, France (E)
                                  Office of the Special Assistant

Source: Paris Embassy Source

MILLER, RAYMOND E.

b.   not known

1/75   Department of State
                          Abu Dhabi, United Arab Emirates (E)
                              telecoms support officer   S-7

as of 8/75   Dept. (NEA)

as of 12/75   Lisbon, Portugal (E)
                              probably telecoms

Sources: FSL 8/75, 4/75
                          Department of State Sources

MILLER, WILLIAM B.

as of 7/75:
Jakob Leisler Strasse 8/4
6000 Frankfurt/Main
Germany
98-55-77-10

b.   11 December 1935   Washington, D.C.

1954-58   U.S. Navy

1958-59   private experience
                          loan company adjuster

1959   electrician

1959   insurance company
                          computer operator

1959-65   unspecified government agency
                          electronics specialist

8/65   Department of State
                          Athens, Greece (E)
                              telecoms technician   S-6

as of 1/68-6/73   unspecified government agency
                          electronics specialist

7/73- at least 10/75	Department of State Bonn, Germany (E) telecoms technician (Regional Communications Office)	R-6
as of 11/75	Dept. (A/OC)	
Wife:	Patricia Morat	
Sources:	BR 1974 FSL 8/75, 10/73, 9/67, 10/65 Bonn Embassy Source Department of State Source	

MILLS, ROBERT H.

b. 3 November 1937		
10/67	Agency for International Development Bangkok, Thailand (E) public safety program assistant	R-6
as of 10/70	public safety advisor	RL-6
6/72	Department of State Surabaya, Indonesia (C) political officer	R-6
4/74		R-5
as of 11/74	Dept. (EA)	
as of 10/75	Foreign Service Institute language training	
as of 12/76	Kiev, U.S.S.R. (C) cover position not known	
Wife:	Eugenia	
Sources:	BR 1974 FSL 8/75, 11/74, 10/72, 10/71, 9/68 Department of State Sources	

MILLS, THOMAS JOHN Jr.

b. 25 July 1930	Michigan	
1951-55	U.S. Air Force overseas	
1956	University of Michigan BA	
1956	University of Michigan MA	
1957-66	Department of the Army plans officer	
10/66	Department of State Dept. (EUR) foreign affairs officer	R-5

as of 1/68	Foreign Service Institute language training	
6/68	Belgrade, Yugoslavia (E) economic-commercial officer	
9/70	Berlin, Germany (M) political officer	
as of 10/71	Eastern Affairs Section political officer	
5/72		R-4
as of 10/75	Dept. (EUR)	
Language:	Serbo-Croatian	
Wife:	Joan Kinsel	
Sources:	BR 1974, 1969, 1967 FSL 8/75, 10/71, 2/71, 9/68, 1/68, 1/67 Department of State Source	

MINIER, FREDERICK

b.   21 October 1923

6/63	Department of State Amman, Jordan (E) probably telecoms	rating not known
8/65	Tehran, Iran (E) telecoms assistant	rating not known
as of 1/67		S-6
11/67	Athens, Greece (E) telecoms assistant	
as of 5/70-5/74	not listed in Department of State records; assignment not known	
6/74	Department of State Athens, Greece (E) telecoms officer (Area Telecommunications Office)	R-6
as of 8/75	Dept. (EUR)	
Sources:	BR 1974 FSL 8/75, 11/74, 1/70, 1/68, 1/67, 10/65	

MINOR, WILLIAM B.

b.   not known

4/72	Department of State Beirut, Lebanon (E) telecoms assistant	S-8
as of 10/73		S-7

8/74	Brussels, Belgium (E) telecoms support officer
as of 2/77	Belgrade, Yugoslavia (E) probably telecoms
Sources:	FSL 8/75, 10/74, 6/73 Department of State Source

MITCHELL, JAMES C.

b. not known		
1/75	Department of State Bern, Switzerland (E) telecoms support officer	S-6
Sources:	FSL 8/75, 4/75	

MITCHELL, JAMES W.

b. 14 May 1938	California	
1959	University of Santa Clara BA	
1959-68	U.S. Army overseas Major	
2/69	Department of State Mexico City, Mexico (E) political officer	R-6
6/70	Buenos Aires, Argentina (E) consular officer	S-4
as of 11/74	Dept. (ARA-LA)	
as of 3/76	Barcelona, Spain (CG) Vice-Consul	S-3
Wife:	Star Hellman	
Sources:	BR 1974 FSL 8/75, 11/74, 10/70, 5/69 Madrid Consular List 3/76 Department of State Source	

MOERGELI, RICHARD N.

as of 1/74:
36 Othonos Street
Kifissia
Athens
Greece
801-1393

b.

5/73	Department of State
	Athens, Greece (E)
	        telecoms assistant
	        (Regional Relay Facility)
		S-7

as of 6/74	telecoms support officer	

as of 6/76	Dept. (A/OC)
Sources:	FSL 8/75, 6/74, 6/73
	Department of State Source

MONTGOMERY, HUGH

as of 1/76:
Sant' Alberto Magno 9
Rome
Italy

b. 29 November 1923	Massachusetts	
1942-45	U.S. Army overseas	
1947	Harvard University BA	
1948	Harvard University MA	
1952	Harvard University PhD	
1953-61	Department of the Army executive officer	

2/61	Department of State
	    Athens, Greece (E)
	        Attache
		R-4

2/62	Moscow, U.S.S.R. (E) Attache	
6/63	Dept. (O)	

1/65	Rome, Italy (E)
	        Attache &
	        supervisory political officer	

4/65		R-3
5/69	Paris, France (E) political officer	
8/73	Vienna, Austria (E) Attache	

11/75-
at least 3/78
	Rome, Italy (E)
	        Attache &
	        political officer
	        (CIA Chief of Station)	

Wife:	Annemarie Janak	
Sources:	BR 1973, 1964 FSL 6/73, 9/69, 6/65, 10/63, 7/62 Paris Diplomatic List 6/73 Vienna Diplomatic Lists 6/75, 12/73 Rome Diplomatic Lists 3/78, 9/76 Rome Embassy Sources	

MONTGOMERY, JAMES D.

as of 7/77:

Rue Abdul Malek Ben Marwan
Imm. malas
Damascus
Syria
55-78-69

b. 1 January 1928	Florida	
1948-49	U.S. Navy	
1954	Yale University BA	
1957-61	Department of the Air Force research analyst	
9/61	Department of State Algiers, Algeria (CG) economic officer	R-7
3/62	Vice-Consul & economic officer	
9/62	Oran, Algeria (C) Vice-Consul	
4/64		R-6
2/65	Algiers, Algeria (E) Attache & political officer	
5/65	Second Secretary & political officer	
5/66		R-5
12/66	Dept.	
7/67	Brussels, Belgium (E) political officer	
10/69	Yaoundé, Cameroon (E) political-economic officer	
4/70		R-4
1/71	Dept.	
8/73	Port-au-Prince, Haiti (E) political officer	
8/75	Damascus, Syria (E) First Secretary (Political Affairs)	
as of 12/77	Dept. (NEA)	
Language:	French	
Wife:	Jeanette Noland	
Sources:	BR 1974, 1964 FSL 8/75, 10/73, 1/70, 9/67, 1/67, 6/65, 1/63, 10/62, 1/62 Damascus Diplomatic List 7/77 Department of State Sources	

MOODY, JACK B.

    b. not known

11/71	Department of State Jakarta, Indonesia (E) telecoms assistant	S-7
5/74	Beirut, Lebanon (E) telecoms support officer	
as of 3/76	Athens, Greece (E) probably telecoms	
Sources:	FSL 8/75, 6/74, 6/73 Athens Embassy Sources Department of State Sources	

MOORE, CHERYL A.

    as of 3/76:
    46 Gainsborough Gardens
    London NW 11
    U.K.
    455-1013

    b. not known

as of 12/75	Department of State London, U.K. (E) telecoms
Husband:	William R.
Source:	London Embassy Source

MOORE, FELIX E.

    b. not known

9/66	Department of State Manila, Philippines (E) telecoms supervisor	S-6
as of 5/69	Dept.	
9/69	Athens, Greece (E) telecoms assistant	
6/73	San José, Costa Rica (E) telecoms assistant	
as of 11/74	telecoms support officer	
as of 11/75	Karachi, Pakistan (CG) probably telecoms	
Sources:	FSL 4/75, 10/73, 1/70, 5/69, 1/67 Department of State Sources	

MOORE, WILLIAM R.

    as of 3/76:

46 Gainsborough Gardens
London NW 11
U.K.
455-1013

b.   not known

7/75	Department of State London, U.K. (E) telecoms engineer	R-4
as of 10/77	Dept. (A/OC)	
Wife:	Cheryl A.	
Sources:	FSL 8/75 London Embassy Source	

MORAN, ALFRED C.

b.   not known

1/63	Department of State Accra, Ghana (E) unspecified post	rating not known
11/66	Monrovia, Liberia (E) administrative assistant	S-6
as of 5/67	Dept.	
as of 9/67	(O)	
as of 5/69-4/75	not listed in Department of State records; assignment not known	

5/75	Department of State
	Athens, Greece (E)
	    administrative officer
	    (Area Telecommunications Office)
		S-4

as of 10/77	Dept. (A/OC)	
Wife:	Carole F.	
Sources:	FSL 8/75, 1/69, 1/67, 10/65 Athens Embassy Source Department of State Sources	

MORAVEK, JOSEPH

as of 6/75:
Flat 2
1 Hemstal Road
London NW 6
U.K.
624-7471

b.   not known

as of 12/74- at least 6/75	Department of State London, U.K. (E) Joint Reports & Research Unit
Sources:	London Embassy Sources

MORDEN, JAMES P.

    as of 1/76:
    12 Rotherwick Road
    London NW 11
    U.K.
    455-0115

    b. 5 October 1931

6/68	Department of State
	  New Delhi, India (E)
	    telecoms officer
		S-4

2/71		S-3
9/73	Dept. (NEA)	
6/74	London, U.K. (E) telecoms officer	
as of 10/77	Bangkok, Thailand (E) probably telecoms	

Wife: Karren Fife

Sources: BR 1974
                FSL 8/75, 11/74, 11/73, 9/68
                London Embassy Sources
                Department of State Sources

MORGAN, BRUCE A.

    as of 1/74:
    16 Frinis Street
    Politia
    Kifissia
    Athens
    Greece
    801-0317

    b. 4 September 1920

7/72-
at least 6/74
	Department of State
	  Athens, Greece (E)
	    telecoms officer
	    (Regional Relay Facility)
		R-7

as of 11/74	not listed in Department of State records; assignment not known	

Wife: Pauline

Sources: BR 1974, 1973
                FSL 6/74, 10/73, 10/72
                Athens Embassy Source

MORGAN, DONNIE E.

    b. not known

| 4/61 | Department of State
San Salvador, El Salvador (E)
political assistant | S-6 |

as of 10/64-5/70   not listed in Department of State records; assignment not known

| 6/70 | Department of State
Rome, Italy (E)
telecoms officer | S-5 |

as of 2/74-6/77   not listed in Department of State records; assignment not known

as of 7/77   Department of State
Monrovia, Liberia (E)
probably telecoms

Sources: FSL 10/73, 10/70, 7/64, 10/63
Department of State Source

MORGAN, JOHN STINARD

b.   17 December 1923   New York

1942   private experience
summer resort recreation director

1943-46   U.S. Army overseas

1946-49   private experience
Syracuse University
assistant to the dean

1948   National University of Mexico

1949   Syracuse University BA

1950   School of Advanced
International Studies MA

1950-52   private experience
research organization
analyst

10/52	Department of State Mexico City, Mexico (E) Assistant Attache & political officer	S-9
8/56		S-7
6/57	Buenos Aires, Argentina (E) Attache & political officer	
7/57		S-6
5/59		R-6
10/60	Dept.	
3/63		R-5
4/65		R-4

8/66	São Paulo, Brazil (CG) political officer	
4/67		R-3
2/69	Quito, Ecuador (E) political officer	
12/70	Montevideo, Uruguay (E) international relations officer	
as of 6/73	Dept. (ARA-LA)	
as of 1/74	Lisbon, Portugal (E) Attache & political officer (CIA Chief of Station)	

Wife: Rosemary Luke

Sources: BR 1972, 1967
               FSL 6/73, 2/71, 5/69, 1/67, 1/61, 7/57, 4/53
               Lisbon Diplomatic List 1/74
               Lisbon Embassy Source

MORGAN, JUNE S.

    b. not known

11/71	Department of State
	Athens, Greece (E)
	   telecoms administrative assistant
	   (Area Telecommunications Office)
		S-6

as of 1/76	Dept. (EUR)	

Source: FSL 8/75, 4/75, 10/71
               Athens Embassy Source
               Department of State Source

MORRILL, ALAN G. Jr.

    as of 11/75:
    Arenal, 7
    Madrid
    Spain
    222-20-85

b. 1 February 1930	Oregon
1951	Oregon State University BA
1952-59	Department of the Army analyst
1960-62	private experience self-employed
1962-63	teacher
1963-64	commercial consultants representative

1964-66	economic consultant for unspecified foreign government
10/66	Department of State Caracas, Venezuela (E) economic officer
11/66	political officer
5/71	economic-commercial officer
as of 10/71	Dept. (ARA-LA)
7/73- at least 5/76	Madrid, Spain (E) Attache & political liaison officer

Corresponding R-codes:
- 10/66 economic officer — R-5
- 5/71 economic-commercial officer — R-4

Language: Spanish

Wife: Mabel Isebrands

Sources: BR 1971, 1967
                 FSL 6/73, 10/71, 1/67
                 Madrid Diplomatic Lists 5/76, 10/74
                 Madrid Embassy Sources

MORRISON, CHARLES R.

as of 1/74:
78 Nikolau Plastira Street
Nea Erithrea
Athens
Greece
801-0040

b.   not known

6/71- at least 6/74	Department of State Athens, Greece (E) telecoms assistant S-7 (Regional Relay Facility)
as of 11/74-4/77	not listed in Department of State records; assignment not known
5/77	R-7

Wife: Joan

Sources: FSL 6/74, 6/73
                 Athens Embassy Source

MOSEBEY, WILLIAM L. Jr.

as of 3/75:
N'Garagba
Route de Odango
Bangui
Central African Republic
30-11

b. 23 March 1938	Pennsylvania	
1959	Pennsylvania State University BA	
1960-61	U.S. Army	
1960-65	Department of the Army training officer	

12/65	Department of State
	    Khartoum, Sudan (E)
	        political officer
		R-8

5/68		R-7
11/68	Dept. staff management officer	
3/69		R-6
as of 5/69	Dept.	
3/70	Addis Ababa, Ethiopia (E) economic-commercial officer	
4/70		R-5
7/72	Dept. (AF)	
5/73		R-4
***6/73	Bangui, Central African Republic (C) political officer	
as of 3/75	Second Secretary & political officer	
as of 10/75	Dept. (AF)	
Wife:	Carolyn Culbertson	
Sources:	BR 1974 FSL 8/75, 10/73, 10/71, 5/70, 5/69, 1/67 Bangui Diplomatic List 3/75 Department of State Source	

***Became the Central African Empire in December, 1976.

MUNCY, LARRY M.

b. not known		

as of 6/76	Department of State
	    Athens, Greece (E)
	        probably telecoms
		R-8

Sources:	Athens Embassy Sources Department of State Sources	

MUNSON, JERALD H.

    b.   not known

4/73	Department of State	
	Athens, Greece (E)	
	telecoms assistant	S-7
	(Regional Relay Facility)	
as of 11/74	telecoms support officer	
5/75	Managua, Nicaragua (E)	
	telecoms officer	
2/76		S-6
Wife:	Pamela	
Sources:	FSL 8/75, 11/74, 4/75, 6/73	
	Athens Embassy Source	
	Department of State Source	

MURPHY, CHARLES M.

b. not known		
10/69	Department of State	
	Tripoli, Libya (E)	
	telecoms officer	S-6
4/72	Managua, Nicaragua (E)	
	telecoms officer	S-5
6/73	New Delhi, India (E)	
	telecoms support officer	
as of 10/75	Dept. (A/OC)	
as of 11/75	Madrid, Spain (E)	
	probably telecoms	
Wife:	Claire	
Sources:	FSL 8/75, 10/73, 6/72, 1/70	
	Madrid Embassy Sources	
	Department of State Sources	

MURPHY, DAVID E.

b. 23 June 1921	New York	
1942	Cortland State Teachers College BS	
1942-46	U.S. Army overseas	
1946-48	Department of the Army	
	language officer	
1948-61	foreign affairs officer	
1961-68	Department of Defense	
	consultant	
3/68	Department of State	
	Paris, France (E)	
	special assistant	
	to the Ambassador	R-1
	(CIA Chief of Station)	

| as of 11/74 | Dept. (EUR) |
| as of 4/75 | not listed in Department of State records; assignment not known |

Wife:	Marian Escovy
Sources:	BR 1974
	FSL 11/74, 5/68
	Paris Diplomatic Lists 6/73, 2/69

MURPHY, JAMES G.

as of 12/74:
Hotel Union Etoile
44 Rue Hamelin
75016 Paris
France
553-1495

b.   not known

as of 12/74	Department of State
	Paris, France (E)
	telecoms

| Wife: | Patricia |
| Source: | Paris Embassy Source |

MURPHY, JAMES M.

as of 12/74:
170 Rue de l'Universite
75007 Paris
France

b.   not known

as of 12/74	Department of State
	Paris, France (E)
	Office of the Special Assistant

| Wife: | Edna M. |
| Source: | Paris Embassy Source |

MURPHY, PATRICIA A.

b.   not known

8/72	Department of State
	Quito, Ecuador (E)
	political section secretary

S-7

as of 1/74	Department of Defense
	Athens, Greece (E)
	JUSMAGG

12/74	Department of State
	Rome, Italy (E)
	secretary

as of 4/77	Seoul, South Korea (E)	
	cover position not known	
Sources:	FSL 8/75, 11/74, 6/73	
	Department of State Source	

MURRAY, DELMAR E.
b.   21 May 1935

8/67	Department of State	
	Karachi, Pakistan (CG)	
	telecoms supervisor	S-6
as of 5/68	telecoms officer	
as of 5/69-5/71	not listed in Department of State records;	
	assignment not known	
6/71	Department of State	
	Athens, Greece (E)	
	telecoms officer	R-7
8/72-	telecoms assistant	
at least 6/73		
Sources:	BR 1973	
	FSL 6/73, 10/71, 1/69, 1/68	

MURRAY, JAMES T.
b.   not known

9/67	Department of State	
	Chiengmai, Thailand (C)	
	telecoms assistant	S-6
as of 1/70-6/74	not listed in Department of State records;	
	assignment not known	
7/74-	Department of State	
at least 8/75	Athens, Greece (E)	
	telecoms support officer	
	(Area Telecommunications Office)	
Sources:	FSL 8/75, 11/74, 9/69, 1/68	

MURRAY, JOSEPH A. Jr.
b.   22 May 1934

1954-57	U.S. Army
1960	Boston College BA
1961-62	Department of the Army
1962-63	private experience
	methods analyst
1963-67	Department of the Army
	management analyst

8/67	Department of State
	Taipei, Taiwan (E)
	    Foreign Service Institute
	    Taichung Language School
	      language training
		R-6

9/68	Dept.	
11/69	Singapore, Singapore (E) university training	
3/70	Dept. (NEA)	
8/70		S-4
9/70	Kathmandu, Nepal (E) economic-commercial officer	
as of 7/73	Attache & Vice-Consul	
4/74		S-3
as of 9/74	Dept. (NEA)	
8/77		R-4
as of 11/77	confirmed as consular officer	

Wife: Linda Mittermaier

Sources: BR 1974, 1971
           FSL 6/74, 2/71, 5/70, 1/70, 1/68
           Kathmandu Diplomatic List 7/73
           Department of State Source

MUSSER, VICTORIA

as of 9/75:
84 Avenue de l'Atlantique
1150 Brussels
Belgium
770-8187

b.   not known

as of 9/75	Department of State Brussels, Belgium (E) Political Section

Source: Brussels Embassy Source

MYERS, JOHN H.

b.   28 August 1930

6/70- at least 6/73	Department of State Athens, Greece (E) telecoms officer	S-1
as of 10/73	not listed in Department of State records; assignment not known	

Sources: BR 1973
           FSL 6/73, 10/70

NATIRBOFF, MURAT

> as of 3/76:
> 30 Karura Avenue
> Nairobi
> Kenya
> 65029

b. 4 February 1921	Soviet Union
1943	naturalized as U.S. citizen
1943	Pratt Institute BCE
1944-45	U.S. Marine Corps

1946-47	private experience
	  contracting company
	    office manager

1947-49	manufacturing company project engineer
1949-50	University of Texas
1950-51	Columbia University
1952-60	Department of the Army training officer

***11/60	International Cooperation Administration
	  New Delhi, India (E)
	    assistant training officer R-4

8/61	Agency for International Development
	  Jakarta, Indonesia (E)
	    assistant training officer

as of 4/64-4/72	not listed in Department of State records; assignment not known

5/72	Department of State
	  Khartoum, Sudan (E)
	    First Secretary &
	    political officer R-3

as of 2/75	Dept. (AF)
as of 3/76	Nairobi, Kenya (E) First Secretary (Political)
Wife:	Marian
Sources:	BR 1974, 1964 FSL 8/75, 10/72, 1/64, 1/62, 4/61 Khartoum Diplomatic List 1/75 Nairobi Diplomatic List 3/76 Department of State Source

***The International Cooperation Administration became the Agency for International Development in 1961.

NELSON, CATHERINE L.

> b.   not known

as of 9/74	Department of State
	    Rome, Italy (E)
	        Office of the Special Assistant	

as of 1/76	not listed in Department of State records; assignment not known	
Source:	Rome Embassy Source	

NELSON, GLENN WALTER

as of 2/75:
Martin Luther King Strasse 23/2
5300 Bonn-Bad Godesberg
Germany
37-58-27

b. 10 July 1921	Wyoming	
1938-39	Civilian Conservation Corps assistant educational adviser	
1941-42	private experience aircraft company supervisor	
1943-47	U.S. Marine Corps overseas 1st Lieutenant	
1947	University of Nebraska BS	
8/47	Department of State Dept.	S-9

10/47	Tokyo, Japan (Office)
	        Office of the U.S. Political
	        Adviser to the Supreme Commander
	        for Allied Powers
	            Assistant Attache	

11/50	Dept.	
as of 4/53-1/75	not listed in Department of State records; assignment not known	

as of 2/75	Department of State
	    Bonn, Germany (E)
	        OCA Liaison Unit	

Wife:	Donna B.	
Sources:	BR 1950 FSL 10/52, 1/51, 1/48 Bonn Embassy Source Department of State Source	

NELSON, MELVIN W.

b. not known		
4/71	Department of State Dept.	S-6
5/71	Chiengmai, Thailand (C) telecoms assistant	

4/74	Belgrade, Yugoslavia (E) telecoms officer
as of 9/77	Athens, Greece (E) probably telecoms
Sources:	FSL 8/75, 2/73, 6/71 Athens Embassy Sources Department of State Sources

NESS, RUDOLPH WALTER

as of 1/74:
4 Ippokratous Street
Nea Politia
Kifissia
Athens
Greece
801-0596

b. 30 July 1921	Germany
1936	naturalized as U.S. citizen
1939-42	private experience bank clerk
1942-43	college instructor
1943-46	U.S. Army overseas
1946-56	Department of the Army communications specialist
1955	George Washington University BEE
1/56	Department of State Manila, Philippines (E) communications officer R-5
7/56	R-6
as of 10/58-4/73	Department of the Army communications specialist
5/73	Department of State Athens, Greece (E) telecoms officer R-3 (Area Telecommunications Office)
as of 8/75	not listed in Department of State records; assignment not known
Wife:	Edna Trantham
Sources:	BR 1974, 1973, 1958, 1957, 1956 FSL 4/75, 6/73, 7/58, 10/57, 4/56 Athens Embassy Source

NIBLEY, LLOYD E.

b.   16 January 1939

8/69	Department of State	
	Saigon, Vietnam (E)	
	telecoms technician	S-6
as of 10/70	Dept. (EA)	
as of 2/71-3/72	not listed in Department of State records; assignment not known	
4/72	Department of State	
	Saigon, Vietnam (E)	
	telecoms technician	R-7
6/75	Bonn, Germany (E)	
	telecoms technician	
as of 10/77	Athens, Greece (E)	
	probably telecoms	
Sources:	BR 1974	
	FSL 8/75, 6/72, 10/70, 1/70	
	Department of State Sources	

NICKERSON, DAVID

b. 1 January 1933	Hawaii	
1955	Harvard University BA	
1956-59	U.S. Air Force overseas Captain	
1959-61	not listed in Department of State records; not known	
1961-63	Department of the Air Force	
	analyst	
8/63	Department of State	
	Reykjavik, Iceland (E)	
	political assistant	S-6
3/66	Dept.	
	projects officer	GS-12
1/70	Paris, France (Office)	
	UNESCO	
	political officer	R-5
4/72	Dept. (EUR)	
as of 8/75-3/77	assignment not known	
as of 4/77	Department of State	
	Stockholm, Sweden (E)	
	First Secretary	
Wife:	Kristin Helgadottir	
Sources:	BR 1974	
	FSL 4/75, 11/74, 2/73, 6/72, 5/70, 10/65	
	Stockholm Diplomatic List 7/77	
	Department of State Sources	

NINER, ARTHUR M. Jr.

as of 5/77:
Sh. Amnar Ben Yasser
Tripoli
Libya
35844

b.   14 September 1935   Washington D.C.

7/61	Department of State Dept. Foreign Service Institute language training	R-8
8/61	Beirut, Lebanon (E) FSI Field School Arabic language trainee	
5/62	Baghdad, Iraq (E) Vice-Consul, Third Secretary & Attache	
4/64		R-7
5/65	Taiz, Yemen (E) Vice-Consul & Third Secretary	
12/66	consular officer	
4/67	San'a, Yemen (E) consular officer	R-6
7/67	Aden, Southern Yemen (E) political officer	R-6
9/68	Dept. (NEA)	
4/70		R-5
7/72	Cairo, Egypt (E) political officer	
5/73		R-4
8/73		RU-4
as of 10/74	Alexandria, Egypt (CG) political officer	
as of 8/75	Dept. (NEA)	
as of 10/76	Tripoli, Libya (E) cover position not known	
as of 5/77	First Secretary	

Language: Arabic

Wife: Ursula Hinsch

Sources: BR 1974, 1967
                       FSL 8/75, 11/74, 10/72, 5/69, 1/68
                          10/65, 7/62, 1/62
                       Tripoli Diplomatic List 5/77
                       Department of State Sources

NOLAN, EDMUND J.

    as of 1/74:
    2 Themidos
    Ekali
    Athens
    Greece
    803-1638

    b. 25 April 1918   New Jersey

        1942-43   U.S. Navy

        1943-45   U.S. Army

        1946-53   private experience
                                 engineering equipment company president

        1953-73   unspecified government agency
                                 supply officer

         5/73-   Department of State
    at least 8/75   Athens, Greece (E)
                                     procurement-supply officer   R-6
                                     (Area Telecommunications Office -
                                     Logistics section)

    Wife: Barbara Miller

    Sources: BR 1974
                             FSL 8/75, 6/73
                             Athens Embassy Source

NOONAN, JOHN H.

    as of 3/76:
    Flat 3
    30 Clarges Street
    London W 1
    U.K.
    493-3778

    b. not known

    as of 12/74-   Department of State
    at least 3/76   London, U.K. (E)
         ***   SUSLO

    Wife: Sally

    Sources: London Embassy Sources

***SUSLO is a cover unit for the National Security Agency, not the CIA.

NORDEEN, RONALD O.

    as of 1/74:
    3 Sirinon Street
    New Kifissia
    Athens
    Greece
    801-6141

b.   21 December 1922   Maryland

10/62   Department of State
                           New Delhi, India (E)
                              political assistant   S-6

2/64   Madras, India (CG)
                                  Vice-Consul

8/64   S-5

as of 5/67   Dept.   S-4

as of 9/67-4/68   not listed in Department of State records;
                           assignment not known

as of 5/68   Department of State
                           Dept.

as of 10/70-12/73   not listed in Department of State records;
                           assignment not known

as of 1/74   Department of Defense
                           Athens, Greece (E)
                              JUSMAGG

Wife: Thelma

Sources: BR 1967, 1966
                           FSL 5/70, 5/68, 5/67, 4/64, 1/63
                           Athens Embassy Source

NORWOOD, THOMAS L. Jr.

b.   27 September 1939   Florida

1957   U.S. Army

1960-61   U.S. Army

1963   University of Florida BS

1964-72   Department of the Army
                              economic analyst

11/72   Department of State
                           Dept.
                              economic-commercial officer   R-5

11/72   Medan, Indonesia (C)
                                  economic-commercial officer

as of 10/76   Dept. (EA)

Wife: Tracey Windham

Sources: BR 1974
                           FSL 8/75, 2/73
                           Department of State Source

NUNNO, LEONARD J.

as of 3/76:

12 Mertoun Terrace
Seymour Place
London W1
U.K.
724-0616

b.   not known

as of 12/75	Department of State
***	London, U.K.
	SUSLO
Wife:	Barbara
Source:	London Embassy Source

*** SUSLO is a cover unit for the National Security Agency, not the CIA.

NYFELER, EDWARD KEITH

b.   not known

9/63	Department of State	
	New Delhi, India (E)	
	communications specialist	S-6
as of 1/67-9/70	not listed in Department of State records; assignment not known	
as of 10/70	Department of State	
	Manila, Philippines (E)	
	telecoms technician	S-5
as of 2/73-5/75	not listed in Department of State records; assignment not known	
6/75	Department of State	
	Athens, Greece (E)	
	telecoms technician	R-5
	(Area Telecommunications Office)	
Sources:	FSL 8/75, 10/72, 10/70, 10/65, 1/64	

NYHUS, PAUL GRAHAM

as of 1/76:
94 Avenue de Suffren
75007 Paris
France
783-50-02

b. 6 June 1938	Canada (American parents)	
1960	Yale University BE	
1960-63	U.S. Air Force 1st Lieutenant	
1963-64	Department of the Air Force	
8/64	Department of State	
	Port-au-Prince, Haiti (E)	
	Assistant Attache &	
	political officer	R-8

10/64	Third Secretary & political officer	
1/67	Dept.	
5/68		R-7
6/68	Rio de Janeiro, Brazil (E) political officer	
3/69		R-6
4/70		R-5
10/71	Dept. (ARA-LA)	
3/72	Guatemala City, Guatemala (E) political officer	
as of 9/74	Santiago, Chile (E) cover position not known	
as of 11/74- at least 1/76	Paris, France (E) Office of the Special Assistant	
7/77		R-4
as of 9/77	Brasília, Brazil (E)	
10/77	confirmed as consular officer	

Wife: Elinor Rolger

Sources: BR 1974, 1967
                         FSL 6/74, 6/72, 9/68, 1/67, 10/64
                         Paris Embassy Source
                         Department of State Sources

OGINO, JACK S.

as of 1/78:
24, Maitland Crescent
Colombo 7
Sri Lanka
94675

b. 9 October 1935	California	
1953-56	U.S. Army	
1960	University of Utah BS	
1960-62	University of Utah	
1963	not given in Department of State records; not known	
1964-65	Department of the Army	

6/65
***
	Department of State
	  Cairo, U.A.R.
	    Assistant Attache &
	    political officer
		R-7

4/67		R-6

8/67	Dept. (NEA)	
9/69	Kathmandu, Nepal (E) political officer	
4/70		R-5
6/72	Madras, India (CG) political officer	
4/74		R-4
as of 9/74	Dept. (NEA)	
as of 8/75		S-2
7/76		R-4
8/76- at least 1/78	Colombo, Sri Lanka (E) First Secretary (Economic- Commercial Affairs)	
Wife:	Georgia Oliver	
Sources:	BR 1974, 1967 FSL 8/75, 11/74, 10/72, 1/70, 9/67, 10/65 Colombo Diplomatic List 1/78 Department of State Sources	

*** The United Arab Republic became the Arab Republic of Egypt in 1971.

OLNHAUSEN, CHARLES B.

as of 3/76:
53 Boydell Court
St. John's Wood Park
London NW 8
U.K.
722-0036

b. not known

as of 12/75	Department of State London, U.K. (E) Joint Reports & Research Unit	
Sources:	London Embassy Sources	

OLSON, ROBERT WILLIAM

b. not known

8/63	Department of State Manila, Philippines (E) communications assistant	S-6
as of 1/67-11/74	not listed in Department of State records; assignment not known	
12/74	Department of State Dept.	S-5

as of 1/75-   Athens, Greece (E)
at least 8/75   telecoms support officer
                                              (Area Telecommunications Office)

Sources: FSL 8/75, 4/75, 10/65, 10/63
                                       Athens Embassy Source
                                       Department of State Source

OLSON, RUTH

    b.   not known

as of 1/74   Department of Defense
                                           Athens, Greece (E)
                                               JUSMAGG

Source: Athens Embassy Source

OLSON, WILLIAM L.

    b.   not known

6/70-   Department of State
at least 10/73   Athens, Greece (E)
                                               telecoms technician   S-6

as of 6/72   S-5

as of 2/74   not listed in Department of State records;
                                       assignment not known

Sources: FSL 10/73, 10/70

O'MALLEY, MICHAEL P.

    b.   9 September 1937

5/72   Department of State
                                           Manila, Philippines (E)
                                               telecoms engineer   R-5

as of 8/75   Dept. (A/OC)

4/77   R-4

as of 6/77   London, U.K. (E)
                                           probably telecoms

Sources: BR 1974
                                       FSL 8/75, 6/72
                                       Department of State Sources

O'NEAL, EVERETT C.

as of 1/75:
route Gouvernementale 45
1150 Brussels
Belgium
731-11-51

b. 1 February 1921	Indiana	
1943	Ohio State University BA	
1943-47	U.S. Army overseas Captain	
1947-50	Department of the Army plans officer	

4/50	Department of State
	    Vienna, Austria (E, USCOA)
	        Assistant Attache
		S-7

7/51	Attache & economic officer	S-6
as of 7/52-5/58	Department of the Army liaison officer	

6/58	Department of State
	    Athens, Greece (E)
	        Attache &
	        political officer
		R-3

7/60	New Delhi, India (E)
	        Attache &
	        political officer	

10/60	First Secretary & political officer	

6/62	Beirut, Lebanon (E)
	        First Secretary &
	        political officer	

4/65		R-2
8/66	Dept. (NEA)	
6/68		S-1
as of 5/69	(EA)	
as of 5/70-7/72	not listed in Department of State records; assignment not known	

8/72-
at least 1/75
	Department of State
	    Brussels, Belgium (E)
	        Attache
	        (CIA Chief of Station)	

Sources:	BR 1969, 1967, 1959 FSL 1/70, 5/69, 1/67, 10/62, 10/60, 10/58, 4/52, 7/50 Brussels Diplomatic Lists 1/75, 4/74 Brussels Guides to Ministries 1975-76, 1974-75	

ONEIL, FRANCIS E.

b. not known		

9/72	Department of State
	    Manila, Philippines (E)
	        telecoms assistant
		S-7

11/74-   Bonn, Germany (E)
at least 8/75   telecoms support officer
                                            (Regional Communications Office)

Sources: FSL 8/75, 4/75, 6/73
                                         Bonn Embassy Source

ONIMUS, DAVID R.

    as of 1/74:
    10 Thrakis Street
    Maroussi
    Athens
    Greece
    802-3654

    b. not known

        5/72   Department of State
                                            Athens, Greece (E)
                                               telecoms assistant   S-7
                                               (Area Telecommunications Office)

    as of 11/74   not listed in Department of State records;
                                         assignment not known

    Wife: Jane

    Sources: FSL 6/74, 6/73
                                         Athens Embassy Source

OWEN, MARY J.

    as of 12/75:
    142 Gersthofer Strasse
    House 4, Apt. 27
    1180 Vienna
    Austria
    472-8164

    b. not known

    as of 12/75   Department of State
                                            Vienna, Austria (E)
                                               Foreign Broadcast Information Service

    Source: Vienna Embassy Source

PACENTA, CAROLYN D.

    as of 6/75:
    75 Buttermere Court
    Boundary Road
    London NW 8
    U.K.
    722-1693

    b. not known

as of 12/74- at least 6/75	Department of State London, U.K. (E) telecoms
Sources:	London Embassy Sources

PAGANO, LOUIS J.

as of 1/74:
Fyllidos Street
Kokkinara
Kifissia
Athens
Greece
801-8461

b.   not known

as of 1/74	Department of Defense Athens, Greece (E) JUSMAGG
Wife:	Adele
Source:	Athens Embassy Source

PALEVICH, JOHN EDWARD

as of 1/74:
3 Arthanassiou Diakou Street
Nea Erithrea
Athens
Greece
801-7696

b. 21 August 1932	Pennsylvania	
1953-56	U.S. Army overseas	
1958	Pennsylvania State University BA	
1958-61	Department of the Army research analyst	
8/61	Department of State Berlin, Germany (M) foreign service officer general	R-7
3/62	Vice-Consul	
4/63	Warsaw, Poland (E) Attache & Vice-Consul	R-6
8/63	Vice-Consul, Third Secretary & visa officer	
4/64	Vice-Consul, Second Secretary & visa officer	
5/66		R-5
8/66	Vientiane, Laos (E) political officer	

9/67	Dept. (O)
as of 10/70	(EA)
as of 10/72-12/73	not listed in Department of State records; assignment not listed
as of 1/74	Department of Defense Athens, Greece (E) JUSMAGG
Wife:	Bonnie Jones
Sources:	BR 1972, 1967, 1964 FSL 6/72, 5/70, 1/69, 1/68, 1/67, 7/63, 1/62 Athens Embassy Source

PALMERI, STEPHEN A. Jr.

b. not known

6/69	Department of State Sofia, Bulgaria (E) telecoms officer	S-6
as of 10/71-6/74	not listed in Department of State records; assignment not known	
7/74	Department of State Helsinki, Finland (E) telecoms officer	R-7
as of 10/77	Rangoon, Burma (E) probably telecoms	
Sources:	FSL 8/75, 11/74, 6/71, 1/70 Department of State Sources	

PARKE, MARGARET

as of 12/74:
32 Rue du Ranelagh
75016 Paris
France
527-8389

b. not known

as of 12/74	Department of State Paris, France (E) Regional Reports Office
Source:	Paris Embassy Source

PARSONS, CARL R.

b. 27 October 1927	Iowa
1947	unspecified government experience
1948-68	Department of the Army communications officer

7/68	Department of State Manila, Philippines (E) telecoms specialist	S-2
as of 10/70	telecoms officer	
as of 10/71-6/74	not listed in Department of State records; assignment not known	
7/74	Athens, Greece (E) telecoms officer (Area Telecommunications Office)	R-3
as of 10/77	Dept. (A/OC)	
Wife:	Beatrice Davis	
Sources:	BR 1971, 1969 FSL 8/75, 11/74, 6/71, 1/69 Department of State Source	

PARSONS, JOHN P.

b. not known

10/68	Department of State Karachi, Pakistan (CG) telecoms officer	S-7
8/69		S-6
9/71	Monrovia, Liberia (E) telecoms assistant	
7/74- at least 8/75	Athens, Greece (E) telecoms support officer (Area Telecommunications Officer)	
Sources:	FSL 8/75, 11/74, 10/71, 9/69	

PARSONS, RONALD C.

b. not known

5/72	Department of State Stockholm, Sweden (E) telecoms assistant	S-8
as of 10/74	Dept. (A/OC)	
Sources:	FSL 6/74, 6/73 Department of State Source	

PAVITT, JAMES L.

b. not known

5/76- at least 6/77	Department of State Vienna, Austria (E) cover position not known	R-8
as of 7/76	appointed as consular officer	

3/77		R-7
as of 4/78	Berlin, Germany (M)	
	cover position not known	
Sources:	Vienna Diplomatic List 6/77	
	Department of State Sources	

PAYNE, MASON C.

b. not known		
6/69	Department of State	
	Saigon, Vietnam (E)	
	telecoms assistant	S-6
as of 10/71	not listed in Department of State records;	
	assignment not known	
1/74-	Department of State	
at least 8/75	Athens, Greece (E)	
	telecoms assistant	S-5
	(Area Telecommunications Office)	
as of 11/74	telecoms support officer	
Sources:	FSL 8/75, 2/74, 6/71, 10/70	

PEARSON, FRANCIS J.

b. not known		
6/70-	Department of State	
at least 10/73	Athens, Greece (E)	
	telecoms assistant	S-8
as of 2/74	not listed in Department of State records;	
	assignment not known	
Sources:	FSL 10/73, 6/73	

PECHOUS, EDWIN J.

b. 18 January 1935	Illinois	
1956	University of Illinois BA, MA	
1956-59	U.S. Army overseas	
1959-61	University of Illinois	
1962-63	Department of the Army	
	research officer	
3/63	Department of State	
	Calcutta, India (CG)	
	political officer	R-7
8/63	Vice-Consul	
5/65		R-6

8/65	New Delhi, India (E)
	    Assistant Attache &
	    economic officer

as of 1/67	Assistant Attache & political-economic officer
9/67	Dept.
3/69	
as of 5/69	(NEA)
6/70	Karachi, Pakistan (CG) economic-commercial officer
as of 10/72- at least 2/73	Dept. (NEA)
as of 6/73-6/76	not listed in Department of State records; assignment not known

7/76-
at least 6/77
	Department of State
	    Vienna, Austria (E)
	        Attache

Wife:	Martha Orfanos
Sources:	BR 1972, 1967 FSL 2/73, 10/72, 10/70, 5/69, 1/67, 7/63 Vienna Diplomatic List 6/77

R-5

PEIFFER, LYNDA L.

as of 6/75:	
31 Haveden Road London NW 2 U.K. 452-1691	
b. not known	

as of 12/74-
at least 6/75
	Department of State
	    London, U.K. (E)
	        telecoms

Sources:	London Embassy Sources

PENA, PAUL A.

b. not known	

7/73	Department of State
	    Accra, Ghana (E)
	        telecoms support officer

as of 1/76	Athens, Greece (E) probably telecoms
as of 3/78	Ankara, Turkey (E) probably telecoms

S-7

Sources: FSL 8/75, 10/73
                            Athens Embassy Sources
                            Department of State Sources

PEREIRA, JOHN F.

    as of 5/76:
    3 Wilton Street
    London SW 1
    U.K.
    235-9751

    b. not known

    as of 12/75-   Department of State
    at least 5/76   London, U.K. (E)
                           Political Liaison Section

    Wife: Abigail

    Sources: London Embassy Sources

PERKINS, LILIAN

    as of 12/75:
    19 Hameaustrasse, Apt. 3
    1190 Vienna
    Austria
    441-9382

    b. not known

    as of 12/75   Department of State
                          Vienna, Austria (E)
                          Foreign Broadcast Information Service

    Husband: Clinton C.

    Source: Vienna Embassy Source

PESHOFF, ROY G.

    b. not known

    9/71   Department of State
                          Kingston, Jamaica (E)
                          telecoms assistant   S-8

    as of 10/73   S-7

    3/74-   Athens, Greece (E)
    at least 8/75   telecoms support officer
                          (Area Telecommunications Office)

    Sources: FSL 8/75, 6/74, 10/73, 6/73

PETERS, WAYNE E.

    as of 1/74:

7 Vernadaki Street
Nea Lesvos
Maroussi
Athens
Greece

b.   not known

5/71	Department of State	
	Buenos Aires, Argentina (E)	
	telecoms assistant	S-7
11/73	Athens, Greece (E)	
	telecoms assistant	
	(Regional Relay Facility)	
as of 11/74	telecoms support officer	
as of 11/75	Dept. (A/OC)	
1/77		R-7

Wife: Donna

Sources: FSL 8/75, 2/74, 6/73
                    Athens Embassy Source
                    Department of State Sources

PETERSEN, W. GARY

as of 1/74:
10 Pallinis Street
New Kifissia
Athens
Greece
801-0806

b.   17 July 1940

6/71	Department of State	
	Athens, Greece (E)	
	telecoms technician	R-8
	(Regional Relay Facility)	
as of 9/74	Dept. (A/OC)	
as of 12/77	London, U.K. (E)	
	probably telecoms	
2/78		R-7

Wife: Bonnie

Sources   BR 1974, 1973
                    FSL 8/75, 11/74, 10/71
                    Athens Embassy Source
                    Department of State Sources

PETTY, PAUL R.

b.   not known

as of 7/76-
at least 6/77
	Department of State
	    Vienna, Austria (E)
	        Second Secretary (Political Section) R-5

Sources:	Vienna Diplomatic List 6/77 Department of State Sources

PIANTOSI, ROBERT

as of 6/75: 34 Boydell Court St. John's Wood Park London NW 8 U.K. 722-3937	
b. not known	

6/67	Department of State
	    Bern, Switzerland (E)
	        telecoms assistant S-6

as of 9/69	Dept.
as of 1/70-11/74	not listed in Department of State records; assignment not known

as of 12/74-
at least 6/75
	Department of State
	    London, U.K. (E)
	        Joint Reports & Research Unit

Wife:	Greta
Sources:	FSL 9/69, 5/69, 1/68 London Embassy Sources

PICCOLO, JOSEPH Jr.

b. 8 December 1935	Florida
1953-55	Department of Justice clerk
1956	private experience union claims adjustor
1957-63	Department of the Air Force
1961-62	U.S. Air Force
1963	Georgetown University BS
1963-65	not given in Department of State records; not known

8/65	Department of State
	    Mexico City, Mexico (E)
	        political officer R-7

3/68	Dept. (O)

4/68	Managua, Nicaragua (E) political officer	
5/68		R-6
12/68	Dept. (ARA-LA)	
4/70		R-5
***6/70	Rio de Janeiro, Brazil (E) political officer	
9/73	Managua, Nicaragua (E) political officer	
4/74		R-4
as of 8/75	Dept. (ARA-LA)	
Wife:	Norma Wyatt	
Sources·	BR 1974, 1967 FSL 8/75, 10/73, 5/69, 9/68, 10/65	

***Rio de Janiero became a Consulate General in 1971, when Brasília was upgraded to Embassy status

PINEAU, JOHN A.

b.   not known

8/69	Department of State Kuching, Malaysia (C) telecoms assistant	S-6
as of 10/70	Dept. (EA)	
5/71	Moscow, U.S.S.R. (E) communications & records assistant	
10/71	Nicosia, Cyprus (E) telecoms assistant	
3/74	Freetown, Sierra Leone (E) telecoms support officer	
as of 7/77	Helsinki, Finland (E) probably telecoms	
Sources:	FSL 8/75, 6/74, 2/72, 10/71, 2/71, 1/70 Department of State Sources	

PLATT, JOHN C. III

as of 12/74:
32 Avenue Foch
92420 Vaucresson
France
970-1774

b.   18 February 1936

8/66	Department of State	
	Vienna, Austria (E)	
	economic assistant	S-6
as of 5/68		S-5
as of 10/71	Dept. (EUR)	
9/72	Vientiane, Laos (E)	
	clerk (Economic Section)	
5/73		S-4
as of 10/74	Dept. (EA)	
as of 11/74	Paris, France (E)	
	Office of the Special Assistant	
Wife:	Paige G.	
Sources:	BR 1974	
	FSL 11/74, 10/72, 10/71, 1/67	
	Paris Embassy Source	
	Department of State Source	

PLAYER, ADGER EMERSON

as of 2/76:
Europa Strasse 17/4
5300 Bonn-Bad Godesberg
Germany

b. 6 May 1932	Colorado	
1954	University of Colorado BA	
1954-55	Universitaet Erlangen (Germany)	
1956-59	U.S. Army	
1960	University of Colorado MA	
1960-62	Department of Defense	
	area specialist	
7/62	Department of State	
	Accra, Ghana (E)	
	Assistant Attache &	
	political officer	R-7
9/64	Attache &	
	political officer	R-6
***1/65	Léopoldville, Congo (E)	
	Second Secretary &	
	political officer	
5/67	Dept. (AF)	
3/68	Taichung, Taiwan	
	Foreign Service Institute	
	Regional Language School	
	language student	R-5

8/70	Vientiane, Laos (E)
	political officer &
	economic-commercial officer
as of 10/72	Dept. (EA)
as of 2/73-1/75	not listed in Department of State records;
	assignment not known
as of 2/75-	Department of State
at least 2/76	Bonn, Germany (E)
	USAREUR Regional Survey Unit
Language:	Chinese (Mandarin)
Wife:	Barbara Brown
Sources:	BR 1972, 1967
	FSL 10/72, 1/70, 5/68, 5/67, 6/65, 10/62
	Bonn Embassy Source

***Léopoldville was renamed Kinshasa in June, 1966.

POLGAR, THOMAS

as of 7/76:
Alcazar de Toledo 445 (Lomas)
Mexico City
Mexico
596-27-19

b. 24 July 1922	Hungary
1943	naturalized as U.S. citizen
1943-44	Yale University
	foreign area studies
1943-46	U.S. Army overseas 2nd Lieutenant
1946-51	Department of the Army
	liaison officer
1951-54	Department of State
	Berlin, Germany (HICOG)
	Office of the
	U.S. High Commissioner
	for Germany
	executive officer
1954-57	Department of the Army
	area specialist
8/57	Department of State
	Hamburg, Germany (CG)
	liaison officer	R-4
9/57	Consul
3/60		R-3
9/61	Vienna, Austria (E)
	Attache &
	political officer

12/62	First Secretary	
4/64		R-2
10/65	Dept. (ARA-LA)	
4/66		S-1
5/69		R-2
6/69	Buenos Aires, Argentina (E) political officer (CIA Chief of Station)	
1971	award for valor	
1/72	Saigon, Vietnam (E) political officer (CIA Chief of Station)	
***as of 4/75	Dept. (EA)	R-1
as of 9/75-6/76	assignment not known	
as of 7/76	Department of State Mexico City, Mexico (E) Attache (CIA Chief of Station)	
Wife:	Patricia Williams	
Sources:	BR 1974, 1966, 1958 FSL 8/75, 6/72, 9/69, 1/67, 1/62, 10/57 Mexico City Diplomatic List 7/76 Department of State Source	

***The Saigon Embassy was closed on April 30, 1975.

POLLOCK, BERNARD CHARLES

as of 4/76:
Fernsicht 5
Hamburg
Germany

b. 22 May 1931	Rhode Island
1954	Fitchburg College BS
1954-57	U.S. Army overseas
1957-59	private experience public school teacher
1960-61	not given in Department of State records; not known
1962-74	Department of the Army analyst

5/74	Department of State
	  Hamburg, Germany (CG)
	    political officer
		R-4

as of 4/76	Consul	
as of 11/76	Dept. (EUR)	
as of 10/77	Istanbul, Turkey (CG) cover position not known	
Wife:	Hedwig Horn	
Sources:	BR 1974 FSL 8/75, 6/74 Hamburg Diplomatic List 4/76 Department of State Sources	

POLTAR, ROBERT S.

as of 12/74:
5 Rue de la Ferme
Apt. 122
92200 Neuilly
France
624-8527

b. 28 March 1939

6/70	Department of State
	  Tripoli, Libya (E)
	    telecoms assistant
		S-6

4/71	Port-au-Prince, Haiti (E) telecoms technician	R-7
as of 2/74-11/74	not listed in Department of State records; assignment not known	

as of 12/74	Department of State
	  Paris, France (E)
	    Regional Administrative
	    Support section
	      telecoms	

Wife:	Constance	
Sources:	BR 1973 FSL 10/73, 6/71, 10/70 Paris Embassy Source	

PONSART, CHARLES M.

b. 7 August 1930	Ohio
1948-51	unspecified private experience
1951-53	U.S. Marine Corps overseas
1953-56	unspecified private experience
1956-67	Department of the Army

8/67-	Department of State	
at least 10/72	Vienna, Austria (E)	
	political officer	R-5
Wife:	Shirley Rindfleisch	
Sources:	BR 1972	
	FSL 10/72, 1/68	

POTEAT, S. EUGENE

b. not known

as of 12/74	Department of State	
	London, U.K. (E)	
	Joint Reports & Research Unit	
as of 8/75-9/77	assignment not known	
as of 10/77	Department of State	
	Oslo, Norway (E)	
	Attache	
Wife:	Martha	
Sources:	London Embassy Sources	
	Oslo Diplomatic List 10/77	

POTTS, JAMES M.

b. 9 September 1921	Louisiana	
1942	Yale University BE	
1942-45	no entry in Department of State records;	
	not known	
1946-47	private experience	
	CARE	
	Prague, Czechoslovakia	
	mission director	
1947-48	Sofia, Bulgaria	
1948-49	executive	
1951	Columbia University MA	
1951-60	Department of the Army	
	analyst	
	plans officer	
11/60	Department of State	
	Athens, Greece (E)	
	Attache &	
	political officer	R-3
	(CIA Deputy Chief of Station)	
10/64	Dept.	
9/67		S-1

2/68	Athens, Greece (E) Attache & political officer (CIA Chief of Station)	
10/68		R-3
5/71		R-2
8/72	Dept. (NEA)	
as of 2/74	not listed in Department of State records; assignment not known	
Wife:	Mary Lister	
Sources:	BR 1973 FSL 10/73, 10/72, 5/68, 1/65, 1/61 Athens Diplomatic Lists 7/72, 6/69	

POTTS, ROBERT D.

b. not known

8/67	Department of State Kabul, Afghanistan (E) telecoms supervisor	S-6
as of 9/68- at least 1/69	Dept. (A/OC)	
as of 5/69-7/70	not listed in Department of State records; assignment not known	
8/70	Department of State Copenhagen, Denmark (E) telecoms officer	
as of 6/73-4/76	not listed in Department of State records; assignment not known	
5/76	Department of State Dept.	R-6
as of 7/76	New Delhi, India (E) probably telecoms	
Sources:	FSL 2/73, 10/70, 1/69, 9/68, 1/68 Department of State Source	

PREGANO, VIRGINIA C.

as of 9/74:
101 Via Salaria
Apt. 15
Rome
Italy
86-83-95

as of 9/74	Department of State Rome, Italy (E) Political Section

Source: Rome Embassy Source

PREHN, JERRY G.

as of 3/76:
7 Alma Square
London NW 8
U.K.
286-4086

b.   20 July 1931

9/62	United States Information Agency Agency	R-6

12/62	Moscow, U.S.S.R. (E)
	        Attache &
	        assistant cultural affairs officer	

. 1/64		R-5
12/65	Vienna, Austria (E) assistant information officer	
3/67		R-4
as of 5/67	information office liaison	
8/67	Agency	
***7/68	Department of State Dept.	
as of 10/70-11/74	not listed in Department of State records; assignment not known	

as of 12/74-
at least 3/76
	Department of State
	        London, U.K. (E)
	            political liaison officer	

Language: Russian

Wife: Shirley Ann

Sources: BR 1971, 1966, 1964
                                 FSL 5/70, 1/69, 1/67, 4/63, 10/62
                                 London Embassy Source

***Previously, Prehn may have been a bonafide U.S. Information Agency employee. Sometime
after this date, he joined the CIA.

PRICE, BENJAMIN J.

as of 8/75:
Flat 5
35 Bryanston Square
London W 1
U.K.
262-9379

b.   not known

as of 10/72-
at least 8/75
 	
***
	Department of State
	   London, U.K. (E)
	     Attache &
	     SUSLO chief

Wife:	Florence I.
Sources:	London Diplomatic Lists 8/75, 12/74, 10/72 London Embassy Sources

***SUSLO is a cover unit for the National Security Agency, not the CIA.

PRICE, RICHARD J.

as of 1/74:
4 Efklidou Street
Kifissia
Athens
Greece
801-6495

b. not known

10/72	Department of State
	   Athens, Greece (E)
	     telecoms assistant
	     (Regional Relay Facility)
		S-7

4/75	Singapore, Singapore (E) telecoms officer	
2/76		S-6
Wife:	Dorothy	
Sources:	FSL 8/75, 4/75, 6/73 Athens Embassy Source	

PROCTOR, EDWARD WILLIAM

b. 30 December 1920	Rhode Island
1942	Brown University BA
1943-44	not known
1945-47	Brown University Teaching Fellow
1947	Brown University MA
1947-50	Harvard University Teaching Fellow
***1951	Harvard University PhD Graduate School of Arts and Sciences
1950-53	Pennsylvania State University Assistant Professor
1953-70	Central Intelligence Agency economist
1971-76	Deputy Director for Intelligence

as of 10/76- at least 6/78	Department of State London, U.K. (E) Political Attache & Political Liaison Section chief (CIA Chief of Station)
Sources:	London Diplomatic Lists 6/78, 12/76 London Embassy Sources Harvard University Alumni Directories 1974, 1970, 1965 1960, 1951 Pennsylvania State University Alumni Directory 1955 American Economic Association Handbooks 1974, 1964

***The subject of his Doctoral dissertation: "Antitrust Policy and the Industrial Explosives Industry"

RACKHAM, JOHN SCOTT

as of 12/74: 64 Rue Emeriau 75015 Paris France	
b. not known	
as of 12/74	Department of State Paris, France (E) Regional Reports Office
Wife:	Jeanne E.
Source:	Paris Embassy Source

RADER, OWEN R.

b. not known	
8/69	Department of State Surabaya, Indonesia (C) telecoms assistant
3/71	Manila, Philippines (E) telecoms officer
6/73	Rome, Italy (E) telecoms officer
as of 11/74	Dept. (EUR)
Sources:	FSL 11/74, 10/73, 6/71, 1/70

S-7

RANDOLPH, CHARLES LEROY

b. 27 September 1932	Washington D.C.
1951-55	U.S. Air Force overseas
1957-65	Department of the Army clerk analyst

1960	District of Columbia Teachers College BS	
1960	Howard University	
12/65	Department of State Lagos, Nigeria (E) Assistant Attache & political officer	R-7
5/68		R-6
2/69	Dept. (AF)	
4/70		R-5
5/72	Dakar, Senegal (E) economic-commercial officer	
as of 11/74	Dept. (AF)	
as of 8/75	not listed in Department of State records; assignment not known	
Wife:	Arthuree Reeves	
Sources:	BR 1974, 1966 FSL 4/75, 11/74, 6/72, 5/69, 1/67	

RAUDENBUSH, PETER VROOM

b. 13 August 1935	Minnesota	
1957	Harvard College BA (magna cum laude)	
1957-61	U.S. Navy Lieutenant	
1962-73	Department of the Army analyst	
2/73	Department of State Dept. (AF)	R-5
3/73	Conakry, Guinea (E) consular officer	
4/75	Dept. (AF)	
Wife:	Helen Carey	
Sources:	BR 1974 FSL 8/75, 10/73, 6/73 Harvard Alumni Directory 1965	

RAYLE, ROBERT F.

as of 1/74:
1 Athranassiou Diakou Street
Nea Erithrea
Athens
Greece
801-7696

b. 4 August 1929	South Carolina
1950	Clemson Agricultural & Mining College
1950-51	Duke University
1951-58	U.S. Army overseas Captain

1958-61	private experience
	    manufacturing company
	        sales engineer

1961-62	marketing consultant
1963-65	research organization researcher

7/65	Department of State
	    New Delhi, India (E)
	        Attache,
	        political officer &
	        political-economic officer R-4

10/65	Second Secretary & political-economic officer
as of 5/68	Dept.
as of 9/68	(O/MA)
as of 5/69	(NEA)
as of 10/70-12/73	not listed in Department of State records; assignment not known

as of 1/74	Department of Defense
	    Athens, Greece (E)
	        JUSMAGG

Wife:	Ramona
Sources:	BR 1971, 1966 FSL 5/70, 5/68, 10/65, 1/65 Athens Embassy Source

REDMOND, PAUL J. Jr.

b. 8 February 1941	Massachusetts
1963	Harvard University BA
1963-64	not given in Department of State records; not known
1965-67	Department of the Army plans officer

5/68	Department of State
	    Kuala Lumpur, Malaysia (E)
	        political-economic officer R-7

3/69	R-6

as of 10/70	political officer	
10/71	Dept. (EA)	
8/72	Foreign Service Institute language training	
8/73	Zagreb, Yugoslavia (CG) consular officer	
as of 11/75	Beirut, Lebanon (E) cover position not known	
6/77		R-5
as of 10/77	Athens, Greece (E) cover position not known	
10/77	confirmed as consular officer	
Language:	Serbo-Croation	
Wife:	Katherine Record	
Sources:	BR 1974, 1969 FSL 8/75, 10/73, 2/72, 10/70, 9/68 Department of State Sources	

REINHARDT, ARTHUR F.

b. 31 October 1925	New York	
1943-46	U.S. Army overseas	
2/46	Department of State Tehran, Iran (E) clerk	rating not listed
2/47	Lima, Peru position not given	
7/48-9/52	Department of Defense communications officer	
1948-50	George Washington University	
10/52	Department of State Manila, Philippines (E) Assistant Attache & communications officer	S-8
11/55-5/62	Department of the Army communications specialist	
5/62	Department of State Nicosia, Cyprus (E) communications specialist	S-3
10/62		S-2
10/64	Attache & communications specialist	
9/65	Dept. (A/OC)	

4/70	London, U.K. (E)
	telecoms officer R-3
5/72	R-2
as of 10/73	Dept. (EUR)
as of 2/74	not listed in Department of State records; assignment not known
Wife:	Mildred
Sources:	BR 1973, 1966
	FSL 10/73, 5/70, 1/67, 7/62, 10/55, 4/53

REUTER, RONALD E.

as of 1/74:
6 Agravlis Street
New Kifissia
Athens
Greece
801-6190

b.   not known

4/71	Department of State
	Athens, Greece (E)
	telecoms assistant S-7
	(Regional Relay Facility)
as of 6/74	Dept. (NEA)
as of 11/74	not listed in Department of State records; assignment not known
Wife:	Marilyn
Sources:	FSL 6/74, 6/73
	Athens Embassy Source

RICE, ARTHUR G.

as of 1/74:
Rodon & Helidonous Streets
New Kifissia
Athens
Greece
801-7569

b.   18 June 1924

9/70	Department of State
	Athens, Greece (E) S-5
	mechanical engineer
	(Regional Relay Facility)
3/72	S-4
as of 9/74	Dept. (NEA)

as of 8/75	not listed in Department of State records; assignment not known
Wife:	Agnes
Sources:	BR 1974
	FSL 4/75, 11/74, 10/70
	Athens Embassy Source

RICHARDSON, JARREL H.

as of 1/76:
1 Amilcar Cabral Road
Accra
Ghana
75234

b. 5 August 1940	Oregon	
1962	University of Oregon BA	
1964	University of Oregon MA	
1965-66	private experience college instructor	
1966-68	Department of the Army analyst	

3/68	Department of State
	    Dept.
	        Foreign Service Institute
	            language training
		S-5

1/69	Addis Ababa, Ethiopia (E) economic-commercial officer	R-7
5/70		R-6
8/71	Dept. (AF)	
5/73		R-5
8/73	Pretoria, South Africa (E) economic-commercial officer	

6/75	Accra, Ghana (E)
	    Second Secretary (Political) &
	    political officer	

as of 10/77	Dept. (AF)	
Wife:	Virginia Holady	
Sources:	BR 1974	
	FSL 8/75, 10/73, 2/72, 5/69, 5/68	
	Pretoria Diplomatic Lists 1/75, 7/74	
	Accra Diplomatic List 1/76	
	Department of State Sources	

RICKARD, SAMUEL HARMER III

b. 10 July 1924	New Jersey

1943-46	U.S. Army overseas 2nd Lieutenant	
1949	Bucknell University BA	
1949	University of Edinburgh (U.K.)	
1950	Georgetown University BSFS	
10/51	Department of State Rangoon, Burma (E) Vice-Consul	S-11
8/54		S-10
3/55	Dept.	
8/56		S-9
2/57	New Delhi, India (E) Attache & political officer	R-6
4/57	Second Secretary & political officer	
7/59	Jerusalem, Palestine (CG) political officer	
8/59	Vice-Consul & political officer	
2/61		R-5
11/62	Dept.	
12/63	Lahore, Pakistan (CG) political officer	
3/64	Consul	
4/65		R-4
9/66	Dept.	
2/67	supervisory foreign affairs officer	GS-14
6/72- at least 8/75	Kabul, Afghanistan (E) political officer	R-3
Wife:	Dorothy Lornquest	
Sources:	BR 1974, 1966 FSL 8/75, 10/72, 4/64, 1/63, 10/59, 4/57	

RIEBHOFF, DONALD R.

b. not known		
4/71	Department of State Saigon, Vietnam (E) telecoms assistant	S-7
9/74	Phnom Penh, Khmer Republic (E) telecoms support officer	

7/75	Lisbon, Portugal (E) telecoms officer
as of 10/77	Dept. (A/OC)
Sources:	FSL 8/75, 11/74, 6/73 Department of State Source

RIEFE, ROBERT H.

as of 3/75:
309 Church Street
Georgetown
Guyana
63162

b. 15 April 1922	Connecticut	
1944	Colby College BA	
1946-48	private experience salesman	
1948	Boston University MA	
1950-52	private experience teaching fellow	
1952	Boston University PhD	
1952-64	Department of the Army junior analyst, political officer	
1956-57	Harvard University	
8/64	Department of State Montevideo, Uruguay (E) Attache & political officer	R-4
10/68	Dept. (O) foreign affairs officer	GS-14
6/71	Bogotá, Colombia (E) Attache & political officer	R-3
8/73	Georgetown, Guyana (E) First Secretary (Political) & political officer	
as of 12/75	Dept. (ARA-LA)	
Wife:	Miriam Dawson	
Sources:	BR 1974, 1966 FSL 8/75, 10/73, 10/71, 1/69, 10/64 Bogotá Diplomatic List 5/73 Georgetown Diplomatic List 3/75 Department of State Source	

RILEY, BYRON B.

> as of 6/75:
> 34 Bengeworth Road
> Harrow
> Middlesex
> U.K.
> 904-8559

> b.   not known

5/63	Department of State Rome, Italy (E) accounting clerk	S-6
as of 11/65-11/74	not listed in Department of State records; assignment not known	
as of 12/74	Department of State London, U.K. (E) Joint Reports & Research Unit	
as of 8/75	not listed in Department of State records; assignment not known	
Wife:	Betty	
Sources:	FSL 10/65, 10/64 London Embassy Sources	

ROBERTS, JAMES W. Jr.

b. 11 July 1924	Tennessee	
1942-43	Department of War	
1943-46	U.S. Army	
1946-49	National Archives	
1949-65	Department of the Army position not listed	
1951	George Washington University BS	
7/65	Department of State Rome, Italy (E) political officer	R-4
as of 1/68	Dept.	
Sources:	BR 1974 FSL 5/68, 10/65 Rome Diplomatic Lists 1/67, 1/66	

ROBERTS, ROWLAND E. Jr.

b. 8 May 1928	Pennsylvania
1950	Princeton University BA
1951-53	U.S. Navy Lieutenant

1953-54	private experience machine manufacturing company	
1954-61	Department of the Army plans officer	
11/61	Department of State Copenhagen, Denmark (E) Attache & political officer	R-5
9/66	Dept. (EUR)	
12/67		S-3
11/69		R-5
4/70		R-4
8/70	Antwerp, Belgium (CG) economic-commercial officer	
as of 1/75- at least 8/75	Dept. (EUR)	
Wife:	Jane Hoy	
Sources:	BR 1974 FSL 8/75, 4/75, 6/74, 10/70, 1/67, 1/62	

ROGERS, JERRY L.

b. not known		
6/71	Department of State Oslo, Norway (E) telecoms assistant	S-7
as of 9/74	Dept. (A/OC)	
as of 11/74	not listed in Department of State records; assignment not known	
Sources:	FSL 6/74, 6/73 Department of State Source	

ROGERS, WAYNE M.

b. not known		
5/71	Department of State Athens, Greece (E) telecoms assistant	S-8
9/73- at least 8/75	Madrid, Spain (E) telecoms officer	
as of 11/74		S-7
as of 12/75	Dept. (A/OC)	

Sources: FSL 8/75, 11/74, 2/74, 6/73
                                  Madrid Embassy Source
                                  Department of State Sources

ROLLINS, NORA M.

as of 5/76:
69 Buttermere Court
London NW 8
U.K.
722-1387

b. not known

as of 12/74-   Department of State
at least 5/76   London, U.K. (E)
                                          Joint Reports & Research Unit

Sources: London Embassy Sources

ROSE, JOHN A. Jr.

b. not known

4/74   Department of State
                                      Geneva, Switzerland (M)
                                          telecoms support officer   S-7

as of 11/77   San'a, Yemen Arab Republic (E)
                                          probably telecoms

Sources: FSL 8/75, 6/74
                                  Geneva Mission Source
                                  Department of State Source

ROSENBERG, NATHAN A.

as of 12/75:
5-9 Bindergasse, Apt. 22
1090 Vienna
Austria
340-0225

b. not known

as of 12/75   Department of State
                                      Vienna, Austria (E)
                                          Foreign Broadcast Information Service

Source: Vienna Embassy Source

ROSS, SHARON L.

as of 3/76:
Flat 2
11 Upper Berkeley Street
London W 1
U.K.
723-4300

b.   not known

as of 12/74- at least 3/76	Department of State London, U.K. (E)
***	SUSLO

Sources: London Embassy Sources

***SUSLO is a cover unit for the National Security Agency, not the CIA.

ROSSALL, MICHAEL F.

as of 6/75:
36 Vincent Close
Hainault, Essex
U.K.

b.   not known

as of 6/75	Department of State London, U.K. (E)
***	SUSLO

Source: London Embassy Sources

***SUSLO is a cover unit for the National Security Agency, not the CIA.

ROTH, ROBERT HUGH

as of 2/76:
21 Avenue Alphonse XIII
1180 Brussels
Belgium
374-1525

b. 8 May 1927	New York	
1948	Yale University BA	
1948-55	Department of the Army	
10/55	Department of State Vienna, Austria (E) political officer	R-5
7/56		R-6
2/59		R-5
7/59	Dept.	
5/60-7/66	Department of the Army area analyst	
8/66	Department of State Foreign Service Institute Czech language & area training	R-4
6/67	Prague, Czechoslovakia (E) Second Secretary & economic officer	

10/69	Dept.
6/73	Beirut, Lebanon (E) political officer
as of 2/76	Brussels, Belgium (E) Attache

Language:	Czech
Wife:	Irene
Sources:	BR 1974, 1968, 1959 FSL 8/75, 10/73, 10/70, 9/67, 1/67, 4/60, 10/59, 1/56 Prague Diplomatic List 7/74 Brussels Diplomatic List 2/76 Brussels Embassy Source

ROUNDS, ROBERT R.

b. not known

11/71	Department of State
	    San José, Costa Rica (E)
	        telecoms assistant
		S-7

5/74	Rio de Janeiro, Brazil (CG) telecoms support officer	
as of 4/76	Athens, Greece (E) telecoms	
as of 1/77	Dept. (A/OC)	
Sources:	FSL 8/75, 6/74, 6/73 Department of State Sources	

RUCKMAN, JAMES R.

as of 1/74:
23 Vassileos Pyrrou Street
Politia
Kifissia
Athens
Greece
80-15-99

b. not known

3/68	Department of State
	    Monrovia, Liberia (E)
	        telecoms officer
		S-4

8/69	Nicosia, Cyprus (E) telecoms officer	S-5

7/72	Athens, Greece (E)
	    telecoms officer
	    (Regional Relay Facility)	

as of 11/74	telecoms support officer	

as of 11/75 Manila, Philippines (E)
                  telecoms

Wife: Joan

Sources: FSL 8/75, 10/72, 1/70, 9/68
             Athens Embassy Source
             Department of State Sources

RUDIN, JOHN A.

 b. not known

 9/74 Department of State
             Athens, Greece (E)
                  telecoms technician   S-6
                  (Area Telecommunications Office)

as of 7/76 Dept. (A/OC)

Sources: FSL 8/75, 11/74
             Department of State Source

RUSSELL, ARTHUR F.

 as of 1/74:
 14 Kokkinara Street
 Kifissia
 Athens
 Greece
 801-1283

 b. not known

 7/73 Department of State
             Athens, Greece (E)
                  telecoms assistant   S-6
                  (Area Telecommunications Office)

as of 11/74 telecoms support officer

 as of 8/76 Dept. (A/OC)

Wife: Patricia

Sources: FSL 8/75, 6/73
             Athens Embassy Source
             Department of State Source

SABIN, FREDERIC H. III

 as of 3/75:
 Mutanabi Street
 Jamal Amman
 4th Circle
 Amman
 Jordan
 41633

 b. 20 January 1934 Minnesota

1956	Williams College BA	
1957-61	U.S. Marine Corps overseas	
1961-62	private experience private school teacher	
1962-63	Department of the Air Force administrative assistant	

10/63	Department of State
	  Dept.
	      Foreign Service Institute
	      language trainee
		R-8

3/64	Beirut, Lebanon (E)
	  Attache &
	  Foreign Service Institute
	  Arabic language training	

3/65		R-7

9/65	Baghdad, Iraq (E)
	  Assistant Attache &
	  consular officer	

10/65	Vice-Consul & Third Secretary	
4/67		R-6
11/67	Dept. (O)	
***1/69	Cairo, U.A.R. (U.S. Interests Section, Spanish Embassy) consular officer	
4/70		R-5
1/72	Dept. (NEA)	
2/72	foreign affairs officer	GS-12
5/74	Amman, Jordan (E) political officer	R-5
as of 3/75	Second Secretary	
as of 8/76	Dept. (NEA)	
Wife:	Mary Ould	
Sources:	BR 1974, 1966 FSL 8/75, 6/74, 6/72, 5/69, 1/68, 1/67, 7/64, 1/64 Amman Diplomatic List 3/75 Department of State Source	

***The United Arab Republic was renamed the Arab Republic of Egypt in 1971.

SABOE, DONALD L.
    as of 12/74:
    33 Rue Croulebarbe
    75013 Paris
    France
    331-5589

    b. not known

as of 12/74	Department of State Paris, France (E) telecoms	rating not known
2/77		R-7
as of 4/77	Manila, Philippines (E) probably telecoms	
Wife:	Pricilla	
Sources:	Paris Embassy Source Department of State Sources	

SALA, LAWRENCE B.
    b. not known

8/69	Department of State Rangoon, Burma (E) telecoms assistant	S-6
10/70	Mexico City, Mexico (E) telecoms assistant	
11/72	New Delhi, India (E) telecoms assistant	
as of 11/74	telecoms support officer	
7/75	The Hague, Netherlands (E) telecoms officer	
as of 10/77	Dept. (A/OC)	
Sources:	FSL 8/75, 4/75, 2/73, 10/70, 1/70 Department of State Sources	

SALTSMAN, JOSEPH IRL
    as of 6/75:
    11 bis Avenue de Suffern
    75007 Paris
    France
    567-1323

b. 16 October 1924	Ohio
1943-45	U.S. Army overseas
1948	Montana State University BSF
1948-50	U.S. Forest Service forester

1950-53	private experience lumber company assistant logging superintendent	
1952-53	Montana State University	
1953-57	Department of the Army research analyst	
5/57	Department of State Isfahan, Iran (C) political officer	R-7
7/57	Vice-Consul	
11/59	Dept.	
1961	American University MA	
10/61-5/70	Department of Defense research analyst	
6/70	Department of State Paris, France (E) economic-commercial officer	R-4
as of 11/75	Dept. (EUR)	
Languages:	French, Persian	
Wife:	Marion Malloy	
Sources:	BR 1974, 1972, 1960 FSL 8/75, 10/70, 4/61, 1/60, 7/57 Paris Diplomatic Lists 6/75, 10/71 Paris Embassy Sources Department of State Sources	

SAMSON, DAVID TORREY

b. 2 May 1943	Florida	
1965	University of California (Berkeley) BA	
1966	University of California (Los Angeles) MA	
1966-73	Department of the Air Force program analyst	
9/73	Department of State Dept.	R-5
10/73	Singapore, Singapore (E) Second Secretary & political officer	
as of 3/76	Dept. (EA)	
as of 1/78	Ankara, Turkey (E) cover position not known	
Wife:	Colleen Marie Murphy	

Sources:
BR 1974
FSL 8/75, 2/74
Singapore Diplomatic List 1/75
Department of State Sources

SANCHEZ, NESTOR D.

b. 28 July 1927	New Mexico	
1945-46	U.S. Army	
1948-50	private experience college instructor	
1950	New Mexico Military Institute BA	
1951	Georgetown University MA	
1951-52	U.S. Army overseas 1st Lieutenant	
1953-55	Department of the Army political officer	
3/55	Department of State Casablanca, Morocco (CG) Vice-Consul & economic officer	R-5
7/56		R-6
2/59		R-5
8/59	Consul	
2/60	Dept.	
4/62		R-4
6/64		S-2
2/65	Caracas, Venezuela (E) Attache & political officer	
8/65		R-4
8/67	Guatemala City, Guatemala (E) First Secretary & supervisory political officer	
9/68		R-3
7/71	Dept. (ARA-LA)	
7/72	Bogotá, Colombia (E) First Secretary, Consul & political officer	
as of 11/74	Dept. (ARA-LA)	
as of 8/75-7/76	not listed in Department of State records; assignment not known	

8/76- at least 11/77	Department of State Madrid, Spain (E) First Secretary & Consul (CIA Chief of Station)	

Wife: Joan Russell

Sources: BR 1974, 1955
                     FSL 4/75, 11/74, 6/74, 10/72, 10/71,
                         9/67, 1/67, 6/65, 4/60, 4/55
                     Guatemala City Diplomatic List 1971
                     Bogotá Diplomatic List 5/73
                     Madrid Diplomatic Lists 11/77, 11/76
                     Department of State Sources

SANDEL, LEO

b. 30 December 1923	Germany	
1943-46	U.S. Army overseas	
1944	naturalized as U.S. citizen	
1946-47	Department of War	
1950	Kent State University BA	
1950-51	George Washington Law School	
1951-60	Department of the Army area analyst	
10/60	Department of State Copenhagen, Denmark (E) Attache & political officer	R-5
5/63	Dept.	
5/64	Rome, Italy (E) Attache & political officer	R-4
6/70	Geneva, Switzerland (M) international relations officer	R-3
as of 10/75	First Secretary	
as of 8/76	Dept. (IO)	
Sources:	BR 1974, 1964 FSL 8/75, 10/70, 10/65, 4/64, 1/61 Geneva Diplomatic Lists 1/76, 10/75 Geneva Mission Source Department of State Source	

SAROFF, PHIL

as of 1/74:
18 Argolidos Street
Ambelokipi

Greece
646-9945

b.   not known

as of 1/74	Department of Defense Athens, Greece (E) JUSMAGG
Source:	Athens Embassy Source

SCARLATA, LAWRENCE J. Jr.

b.   26 February 1938

12/66	Department of State New Delhi, India (E) telecoms technician	S-6
as of 5/69		R-7
as of 9/69-4/72	not listed in Department of State records; assignment not known	
5/72	Department of State Athens, Greece (E) telecoms engineering technician	
4/74	telecoms technician	R-6
as of 10/75	Dept. (A/OC)	
5/77		R-5
as of 7/77	Bonn, Germany (E) probably telecoms	
Wife:	Lisa	
Sources:	BR 1974, 1973 FSL 8/75, 6/74, 6/72, 5/69, 5/67 Athens Embassy Source Department of State Source	

SCHULDASKI, ERNEST A.

b.   not known

9/58	Department of State Montevideo, Uruguay (E) political assistant	S-9
as of 4/61-6/66	not listed in Department of State records; assignment not known	
7/66	Department of State Manila, Philippines (E) telecoms supervisor	S-6
as of 5/70	telecoms officer	S-5

9/70- at least 10/72	Athens, Greece (E) telecoms officer
Sources:	FSL 10/72, 10/70, 1/67, 1/61, 10/60

SCHNEIDER, PHILLIP M.

as of 12/75:
165A Sieveringerstrasse
1190 Vienna
Austria
441-5465

b. not known

as of 12/75	Department of State Vienna, Austria (E) Foreign Broadcast Information Service deputy chief
Wife:	Chris
Sources:	Vienna Embassy Sources

SCHNEIDER, ROBERT W.

b. not known

3/71	Department of State Saigon, Vietnam (E) telecoms assistant	S-6
as of 2/73-8/74	not listed in Department of State records; assignment not known	
as of 9/74	Vientiane, Laos (E) probably telecoms	R-7
11/74	Amman, Jordan (E) telecoms support officer	
as of 3/77	Bonn, Germany (E) probably telecoms	
Sources:	FSL 8/75, 11/74, 10/72, 6/71 Department of State Sources	

SCHOLPP, GEORGE E.

as of 1/74:
47 Avras Street
Kifissia
Athens
Greece
801-2925

b. not known

8/67	Department of State Tehran, Iran (E) telecoms technician	S-6

8/70	Athens, Greece (E) telecoms technician (Regional Relay Facility)
as of 6/72	S-5
as of 2/73-12/73	not listed in Department of State records; assignment not known
as of 1/74	Department of State Athens, Greece (E) telecoms technician (Regional Relay Facility)
Wife:	Margaret
Sources:	FSL 10/72, 6/72, 10/70, 1/68 Athens Embassy Source

SCHWARTZ, STEVEN A.

b. not known

7/71	Department of State Athens, Greece (E) telecoms assistant S-7 (Regional Relay Facility)
5/74	Montevideo, Uruguay (E) telecoms support officer
as of 11/76	Dept. (A/OC)
Wife:	Catherine
Sources:	FSL 8/75, 6/74, 6/73 Athens Embassy Source Department of State Source

SEDNAOUI, MICHAEL C.

as of 9/74:
140 Via Alberto Cadlolo
Rome
Italy
349-6555

b. 6 November 1925	Egypt
1943-44	American University (Beirut)
1945-46	Columbia University
1946-55	U.S. Army overseas Captain
1949	naturalized as U.S. citizen
1956	Department of the Army political affairs officer
6/56	Department of State Rabat, Morocco (E) political officer R-5

7/56		R-6
8/56	Vice-Consul, Second Secretary & political officer	
2/59		R-5
8/59	Consul, Second Secretary & political officer	
9/61	Dept.	
3/63		R-4
1/65	Rabat, Morocco (E) Attache & political officer	R-3
3/65	First Secretary & political officer	
8/68	Dept. (AF)	
6/70	foreign affairs officer	GS-14
as of 10/70-8/74	not listed in Department of State records; assignment not known	
as of 9/74	Department of State Rome, Italy (E) USASEPU chief (CIA Deputy Chief of Station)	
Wife:	Anne Russell	
Sources:	BR 1971, 1966, 1957 FSL 5/70, 9/68, 6/65, 1/62, 10/56 Rome Embassy Source	

SEIDEL, JOHN J. Jr.

b. 21 August 1925	Maryland	
1943-46	U.S. Navy overseas	
1947	Princeton University BA	
1947-52	private experience finance company branch manager	
1953-55	U.S. Navy Lieutenant	
1955-59	Department of the Army foreign affairs officer	
1956-58	Georgetown University	
5/60	Department of State Cairo, U.A.R. (E) Attache & political officer	R-5

12/64	Karachi, Pakistan (E) Attache	
5/65	Second Secretary	R-4
7/66	Rawalpindi, Pakistan (Office) economic officer	
2/68	Dept. (O)	
5/68		S-2
5/69	(NEA)	
7/71	Beirut, Lebanon (E) political officer	R-3
as of 10/75	Dept. (NEA)	
Wife:	Annette Lewis	
Sources:	BR 1974, 1966, 1961-62 FSL 8/75, 10/71, 5/68, 1/67, 7/60 Beirut Diplomatic List 1975 Department of State Source	

SELSKY, OLEG N.

as of 1/76:
31 bis Boulevard Suchet
75016 Paris
France
647-4885

b. 17 June 1927

6/69	Department of State Santiago, Chile (E) political officer	R-4
10/71	Dept. (ARA-LA) program officer	GS-14
as of 6/72-10/74	not listed in Department of State records; assignment not known	
as of 11/74- at least 1/76	Department of State Paris, France (E) Office of the Special Assistant	rating not known
Sources:	BR 1972 FSL 2/72, 9/69 Paris Embassy Source	

SEPTON, ARTHUR B. Jr.

as of 4/76:
5 Jl. Kiai Maja (U)
Kebayoran

Jakarta
Indonesia
71515

b. not known

12/68	Department of State	
	Manila, Philippines (E)	
	telecoms assistant	S-6

9/72   Athens, Greece (E)
                             telecoms assistant
                             (Regional Relay Facility)

as of 11/74   telecoms support officer

9/75   Jakarta, Indonesia (E)
                             Attache

as of 12/76   Dept. (A/OC)

Wife: Naomi

Sources: FSL 8/75, 11/74, 10/72, 10/71
                         Athens Embassy Source
                         Jakarta Diplomatic & Consular List 4/76
                         Department of State Source

SEPTON, NAOMI

as of 4/76:
5 Jl. Kiai Maja (U)
Kebayoran
Jakarta
Indonesia
71515

b. not known

as of 1/74   Department of State
                         Athens, Greece (E)
                             telecoms
                             (Area Telecommunications Office)

Husband: Arthur B.

Sources: Athens Embassy Source
        ***   Jakarta Diplomatic & Consular List 4/76

***The transfer of her husband to Jakarta, Indonesia in September, 1975 indicates her presence
also. She might or might not have worked within the telecoms office there.

SEVIER, LEWIS V.

as of 12/74:
22 Rue Marbeau
75016 Paris
France
553-5406

b. 14 March 1918   Colorado

1937-39	l'Ecole Libre des Sciences Politiques	
1940-41	not given in Department of State records; not known	
1942-45	U.S. Army overseas 1st Lieutenant	
1945-47	private experience manufacturing company salesman	
1947-59	Department of the Army program analysis officer	
***10/59	Agency for International Development Cairo, U.A.R. (E) assistant program officer	R-5
3/60	operations officer	
8/60	Karachi, Pakistan (E) program analyst	
4/64		R-4
6/66	Department of State Beirut, Lebanon (E) political officer	S-2
2/69		S-1
7/72	Marseille, France (CG) consular officer	
8/73	Paris, France (E) consular officer	
as of 8/77	Dept. (EUR)	
Wife:	Doris Wrigley	
Sources:	BR 1974, 1963 FSL 8/75, 10/73, 10/72, 1/67, 1/61, 1/60 Paris Embassy Source Department of State Sources	

***Appointment began under AID's predecessor agency until 1961, the International Cooperation Administration.

SHAFFER, RONALD D.

as of 1/74:
7 Pallinis Street
New Kiffisia
Athens
Greece
801-4441

b.   not known

8/67	Department of State Oslo, Norway (E) telecoms supervisor	S-6
as of 1/70-5/71	not listed in Department of State records; assignment not known	

6/71	Department of State
	Athens, Greece (E)
	    telecoms assistant
	    (Regional Relay Facility)
		S-7

as of 9/74	Dept. (A/OC)	
Wife:	Gladys	
Sources:	FSL 6/74, 6/73, 9/69, 9/67 Athens Embassy Source	

SHEA, JOHN J.

as of 1/74:
24 Voriou Ipirou Street
Philothei
Athens
Greece
682-2200

b. 13 November 1924	New York	
1942-46	Cathedral College of the Immaculate Conception (graduated)	
1947-48	private experience theater usher	
1948-49	bank cashier	
1949-50	U.S. Army	
11/50	Department of State Dept.	O-6

1/51	Rome, Italy (E)
	    Vice-Consul &
	    Third Secretary	

5/54	Baghdad, Iraq (E) political officer	
9/54	Vice-Consul & Second Secretary	O-5
1/56	Dept. Foreign Service Institute Arabic language-area training	
7/56		O-6
9/56	Dept.	
***9/57	resigns as foreign service officer	
10/57	Department of State Rome, Italy (E) political officer	R-6
12/57	Second Secretary & political officer	
2/61		R-5

5/65		R-4
8/65	Dept.	
5/67		S-2
as of 5/68	Foreign Service Institute	
7/68	Paris, France (E) First Secretary & political officer	R-3
6/70	Rome, Italy (E) political officer	
as of 10/72	Dept. Foreign Service Institute	
6/73- at least 3/76	Athens, Greece (E) Attache & Office of the Special Assistant	

Language:	French
Wife:	Mary
Sources:	BR 1972, 1966, 1957 FSL 6/73, 2/73, 10/72, 2/71, 10/70, 1/69, 5/68, 10/65, 1/58, 4/56, 10/54, 4/51, 1/51 Athens Diplomatic List 12/74 (updated) Athens Embassy Source

*** Shea resigned from the State Department in September 1957, at which time he joined the CIA.

SHEKMER, MICHAEL E.

b. not known

8/68	Department of State Jidda, Saudi Arabia (E) telecoms officer	S-6
8/73	Athens, Greece (E) telecoms assistant (Regional Relay Facility)	
as of 11/74	telecoms support officer	
as of 12/75	Dept. (A/OC)	

Wife:	Rhea
Sources:	FSL 8/75, 10/73, 5/70, 1/69 Athens Embassy Source Department of State Source

SHERMAN, JOSEPH PETER

as of 6/75:
75 Ossulton Way
London NW 2
U.K.
883-5612

b. 4 November 1925	Michigan
1944-46	U.S. Army
1948	Michigan State University BA
1948-49	private experience secondary school teacher
1950	Michigan State University MA
1951	private experience secondary school teacher
1951-55	U.S. Army overseas 1st Lieutenant
1955-56	unspecified university graduate teaching assistant
1956-60	Department of the Army analyst

6/59	Department of State
	    Munich, Germany (CG)
	        political officer R-6

10/59	Vice-Consul & political officer
9/61	Frankfurt, Germany (CG) political officer
4/62	R-5

***6/62	Budapest, Hungary (L)
	    Attache &
	    political officer

7/62	Second Secretary
12/62	Second Secretary, Consul & political officer
10/64	Dept.
5/66	R-4
7/67	Moscow, U.S.S.R. (E) political officer
8/69	Bangkok, Thailand (E) economic officer
as of 10/70	economic-commercial officer
11/71	Dept. (EA)

as of 10/73-
at least 8/75
	London, U.K. (E)
	    Attache &
	    political liaison officer

Languages:	German, Hungarian
Wife:	Barbara Quayle

Sources: BR 1973, 1966, 1960
       FSL 6/73, 2/72, 10/70, 9/69, 9/67,
         1/65, 1/63, 1/62, 10/59
       London Diplomatic Lists 8/75, 10/73
       London Embassy Sources

***Budapest was elevated from Legation to Embassy status in November, 1966.

SHERMAN, VAUGHN A.

b. 1 October 1927	Washington	
1945-46	U.S. Navy	
1947-50	Department of the Interior management biologist	
1951	University of Washington BA	
1951-52	private experience unspecified State government aquatic biologist	
1952-57	Department of the Army reports officer, research analyst	
10/57	Department of State Stockholm, Sweden (E) Attache & political officer	R-7
3/60		R-6
8/62	Dept.	
5/64	Madrid, Spain (E) Attache & political officer	R-5
5/68		R-4
7/69	Copenhagen, Denmark (E) Attache & political officer	
as of 8/73	Dept. (EUR)	
Wife:	Eunice Iverson	
Sources:	BR 1973, 1966, 1959, FSL 6/73, 9/69, 7/64, 4/62, 1/58 Department of State Source	

SHERRY, FRANCIS S. III

as of 11/75:
Raimundo Fernández Villaverde, 61
Madrid
Spain
254-74-87

b. 7 May 1927	France (of American parents)	
1947-48	U.S. Army overseas	
1951	Harvard University BA	
1952-53	Department of the Army junior analyst	
1953-60	Department of State Saigon, Vietnam (E) Liaison Mission	rating not known
7/60	Antwerp, Belgium (CG) economic officer	R-6
10/60	Vice-Consul	
3/63		R-5
8/63	Consul	
as of 9/64		R-4
10/64	Dept.	
8/66	Mexico City, Mexico (E) consular officer	
as of 1/70-4/73	not listed in Department of State records; assignment not known	
as of 5/73- at least 5/77	Department of State Madrid, Spain (E) Attache & political liaison officer	
Wife:	Margaret	
Sources:	BR 1969, 1966 FSL 9/69, 1/67, 1/65, 10/60 Madrid Diplomatic Lists 5/77, 11/75, 5/73 Madrid Embassy Source	

SHERRY, JOHN

b. 13 March 1925	New York	
1943-46	U.S. Army overseas	
1947	Yale University BA	
1947-48	Department of the Army research assistant	
8/48	Department of State Canton, China (CG) Vice-Consul	S-9
10/49	Hong Kong, U.K. (CG) Vice-Consul	

as of 7/51-11/57	Department of the Army political officer	
12/57	Department of State Saigon, Vietnam (E) political officer	R-5
2/58	Second Secretary & political officer	
9/60	Dept.	
3/62	Tokyo, Japan (E) Attache & economic officer	
3/63		R-4
6/64	Phnom Penh, Cambodia (E) Second Secretary & political officer	
6/65	Bangkok, Thailand (E) political officer	
9/66	Dept. (EA)	
3/67	foreign affairs officer	GS-14
as of 9/67-6/76	not listed in Department of State records; assignment not known	
as of 7/76	Department of State Geneva, Switzerland (M) cover position not known	R-3
Sources:	BR 1967, 1966, 1961-62 FSL 5/67, 10/65, 7/64, 7/62, 1/61, 1/58, 4/51, 1/50, 10/48 Department of State Sources	

SHUMAN, A. DELL

b. not known

as of 10/74	Department of State London, U.K. (E) Joint Reports & Research Unit
as of 8/75-4/76	not listed in Department of State records; assignment not known
as of 5/76	Department of State Yaounde, Cameroon (E) cover position not known
Source:	London Embassy Source Department of State Source

SHUMWAY, JEDDY K.

b. not known

3/71	Department of State
	Monrovia, Liberia (E)
	telecoms assistant	S-8

| 8/73 | Montevideo, Uruguay (E) |
| | telecoms support officer | S-7 |

| as of 12/76 | The Hague, Netherlands (E) |
| | probably telecoms |

Sources: FSL 8/75, 6/73
Department of State Sources

SIEMIENKIEWICZ, GERALD

as of 1/74:
16 Aeginis Street
Kifissia
Athens
Greece
801-4507

b. 28 September 1937

8/67	Department of State
	Manila, Philippines (E)
	telecoms technician	S-6

| as of 5/70 | | S-5 |

| 7/72 | Athens, Greece (E) |
| | telecoms technician | R-6 |

| as of 11/76 | Dept. (A/OC) |

Sources: BR 1974, 1973
FSL 8/75, 10/72, 5/70, 1/68
Athens Embassy Source
Department of State Sources

SILVER, ARNOLD M.

as of 2/76:
Heer Strasse 13
5309 Meckenheim
Germany
02225-25-37

| b. 4 December 1919 | Massachusetts |

| 1941 | Tufts College BA |

| 1942 | Harvard University MA |

| 1942-46 | U.S. Army overseas |

1946-48	Department of the Army
	Germany
	Office of the U.S. Military
	Government (OMGUS)
	analyst

1948-57	area specialist	
7/57	Department of State Dept.	R-4
10/57	Luxembourg, Luxembourg (E) political officer	
12/57	Second Secretary & political officer	
6/60	Dept.	
2/61		R-3
as of 10/62-1/76	no entry in Department of State records; assignment not known	
as of 2/76	Department of Defense Bonn, Germany (E) OSD/ISA	
Wife:	Annemarie	
Sources:	BR 1961-62 FSL 7/62, 10/60, 1/58, 10/57 Bonn Embassy Source	

SIMENSON, WILLIAM CHARLES

as of 8/76:
Grasantie 14
02160 Espoo 16
Helsinki
Finland
42-52-32

***b. 3 June 1925	Wisconsin	
1943-46	U.S. Army overseas	
1948	University of Oslo	
1949	University of Wisconsin BS	
1949-50	University of Oslo	
1951	University of Wisconsin MA	
1952-55	Department of Defense political analyst	
2/55	Department of State Reykjavik, Iceland (E) Assistant Attache & political officer	R-6
7/56		R-7
3/57	Oslo, Norway (E) Third Secretary	
2/59	Second Secretary	

9/60-7/62	Department of the Army political analyst	

8/62	Department of State
	  Dept.
	    Foreign Service Institute
	    Finnish language-area training
		R-5

2/64	Helsinki, Finland (E)
	    Attache &
	    political officer	

3/64	Second Secretary	
4/65		R-4
7/70	Dept. (EUR)	
8/71-4/74	Department of the Army plans and programs officer	

5/74-
at least 1/78
	Department of State
	  Helsinki, Finland (E)
	    First Secretary &
	    political officer
	    (CIA Chief of Station)
		R-3

Wife:	Katherine Gimmler	
Sources:	BR 1974, 1966, 1955 FSL 8/75, 6/74, 6/71, 10/70, 4/64, 10/62, 7/57, 4/55 Helsinki Diplomatic Lists 1/78, 8/75, 1/66	

***Simenson's year of birth is given as 1927 in the 1974 *Biographic Register,* but all earlier sources show the year to be 1925.

SIMON, JOSEPH J.

b. 14 November 1928	Minnesota	
1946-47	U.S. Navy	
1951	Tulane University BA	
1951-54	U.S. Navy overseas Lieutenant	
1956	Yale University MA	
1956-58	no entry in Department of State records; not known	

1959-69	Central Intelligence Agency
	    Foreign Broadcast Information Service
	    research analyst	

1970-71	Saigon, Vietnam (E) bureau chief	

5/71-
at least 8/75
	Department of State
	  Hong Kong, U.K. (CG)
	    political officer
		R-3

3/75		R-2

Wife:	Elizabeth Brandau
Sources:	BR 1974, 1973
	FSL 8/75, 6/71
	Department of State Source

SIMPSON, GRANT F.

b. 12 December 1939

7/71- at least 6/73	Department of State Athens, Greece (E) telecoms officer	R-7
10/73	Dept. (NEA)	
as of 2/74	not listed in Department of State records; assignment not known	
Sources:	BR 1973 FSL 10/73, 10/71	

SIMPSON, ROBERT K.

b. 2 December 1940	Rhode Island	
1962	Dartmouth College BA	
1962-66	U.S. Marine Corps overseas Lieutenant	
1966-71	not listed in Department of State records; not known	
8/71	Department of State Helsinki, Finland (E) Second Secretary & political officer	R-6
2/76		R-5
8/76- at least 11/77	Madrid, Spain (E) Second Secretary	
Wife:	Margaret Philip	
Sources:	BR 1974 FSL 8/75, 10/71 Helsinki Diplomatic List 8/75 Madrid Diplomatic Lists 11/77, 11/76 Department of State Sources	

SIMS, WILLIAM P.

as of 1/74:
6 Trias Street
Erithrea
Athens
Greece
801-4092

b. not known

12/69	Department of State
	Jerusalem, Jerusalem (CG)
	visa officer S-6
5/72	Athens, Greece (E)
	telecoms assistant
	(Regional Relay Facility)
as of 10/74	Dept. (A/OC)
Wife:	Joy
Sources:	FSL 6/74, 6/72, 5/70, 1/70
	Athens Embassy Source
	Department of State Source

SINCLAIR, ROBERT

as of 3/76:
36 Chalcot Crescent
London NW 1
U.K.
722-5536

b.   not known

as of 12/74-	Department of State
at least 3/76	London, U.K. (E)
	Joint Reports & Research Unit
Sources:	London Embassy Sources

SINGLETON, STEPHEN E.

as of 9/74:
47 Via Massimi
Apt.1
Bldg. 2
Rome
Italy
345-3757

7/71	Department of State
	Ankara, Turkey (E)
	telecoms assistant S-6
1/72	Manila, Philippines (E)
	telecoms assistant
6/74	Rome, Italy (E)
	telecoms support officer
as of 10/77	Dept. (A/OC)
Wife:	Joetta F.
Sources:	FSL 8/75, 11/74, 2/72, 10/71
	Athens Embassy Source
	Department of State Sources

SIRIANO, HAROLD J.

as of 1/74:
21 Herakleous &
Sirinon Streets
New Kifissia
Athens
Greece
801-7809

b. 19 March 1931	New York	
1951-55	U.S. Navy overseas	
1956-73	unspecified government agency communications officer	
7/73	Department of State Athens, Greece (E) telecoms officer (Area Telecommunications Office)	R-5
as of 10/76	Dept. (A/OC)	
Wife:	Jessica Pincombe	
Sources:	BR 1974 FSL 8/75, 10/73 Athens Embassy Source Department of State Source	

SISTERMAN, JOHN B.

b. not known		
9/73	Department of State Karachi, Pakistan (CG) telecoms assistant	S-7
as of 4/76	Vienna, Austria (E) probably telecoms	
Sources:	FSL 8/75, 10/73 Department of State Sources	

SKOVE, JAMES R.

as of 5/75:
37 Constantiavägen
181 31 Lidingö
Sweden
767-45-24

b. not known	
as of 11/74- at least 5/75	Department of State Stockholm, Sweden (E) Attache
Wife:	Florence
Sources:	Stockholm Diplomatic Lists 5/75, 11/74

SLACK, GEORGE LEE

b. 29 September 1940	Ohio	
1959-62	U.S. Air Force	
1966	University of Dayton BSEE	
1966-73	Department of the Army electronic engineer	
1971	George Washington University BEA ***	
4/73	Department of State Nicosia, Cyprus (E) telecoms engineer	R-7

5/74	Athens, Greece (E)
	          telecoms engineer
	          (Area Telecommunications Office)	

as of 8/76	Dept. (A/OC)	
Wife:	Paula Kerrigan	
Sources:	BR 1974 FSL 8/75, 6/74, 6/73 Department of State Source	

*** Master's Degree in Electronic Analysis

SLIFER, HARRY SEGER Jr.

b. 22 February 1929	Michigan	
1951-55	U.S. Air Force overseas	
1956	University of Michigan BA, MA	
1956-57	Department of the Army political analyst	

11/57	Department of State
	Phnom Penh, Cambodia (E)
	          Assistant Attache &
	          political officer
		S-9

4/59		R-7

3/61	Saigon, Vietnam (E)
	          Assistant Attache,
	          economic officer &
	          labor-political officer	

4/62		R-6
5/63	Dept. political-military analyst	
9/65	Paris, France (E) foreign affairs analyst	

10/69	Tokyo, Japan (E)
	          political-military
	          affairs officer
		R-4

9/70	Phnom Penh, Cambodia (E) economic-commercial officer
7/71	Dar-es-Salaam, Tanzania (E) economic-commercial officer
4/74	R-3
as of 11/74	Dept. (AF)
as of 12/77	Jakarta, Indonesia (E) cover position not known
Wife:	Tonia Carvalho
Sources:	BR 1974, 1964 FSL 8/75, 11/74, 10/71, 1/70 10/63, 7/61, 1/58 Dar-es-Salaam Diplomatic & Consular List 1/73 Department of State Source

SMITH, CHARLES S.

as of 11/75:
Basilica, 17
Madrid
Spain
254-00-34

b. 22 November 1936	Missouri
1959	Yale University BA
1960-63	U.S. Army overseas
1963-64	private experience insurance agent
1964-66	Department of the Army program analyst
7/66	Agency for International Development Vientiane, Laos (E) assistant program officer R-7
2/67	community analyst
as of 5/69-7/74	not listed in Department of State records; assignment not known
8/74- at least 5/76	Department of State Madrid, Spain (E) Attache & political liaison officer
Wife:	Phyllis
Sources:	BR 1968 FSL 1/69, 1/67 Madrid Diplomatic Lists 5/76, 5/75

SMITH, JAMES

    as of 5/76:
    Lingard House
    Chiswick Mall
    London W4
    U.K.
    995-0707

b. 6 December 1920	Ohio	
1939-46	U.S. Marine Corps overseas	

1946-51	private experience
	    business services
	        engineer	

1952-65	Department of the Army communications specialist	

5/65	Department of State
	    Manila, Philippines (E)
	        area telecoms officer
		S-2

2/68	telecoms engineer	S-1
8/68	Dept.	
as of 5/69-6/75	not listed in Department of State records; assignment not known	

as of 7/75-
at least 6/78
	Department of State
	    London, U.K. (E)
	        Attache &
	        telecoms officer	

as of 12/76	Administrative Attache	
Wife:	Dorothy	
Sources:	BR 1971 FSL 8/75, 1/69, 9/68, 10/65 London Diplomatic Lists 6/78, 4/76, 10/75 London Embassy Sources Department of State Sources	

SNELL, PHILLIP W.

    as of 3/75:
    Rua da Beira 6
    Carcavelos
    Portugal
    247-04-84

b. not known	
1960-64	U.S. Navy
1964-65	private experience
5/65-1/66	Department of the Army

2/66	Department of State San Salvador, El Salvador (E) cover position not known
12/68-1970	private experience
1971-72	University of Denver
4/73-8/74	Department of the Army
9/74	Department of State Lisbon, Portugal (E) political officer R-7
as of 2/76	Dept. (EUR)
Wife:	Zulema
Sources:	FSL 8/75, 11/74 Lisbon Diplomatic List 1/76 Lisbon Embassy Source Department of State Sources

SOHLER, RONALD B.

b. not known

5/74	Department of State Athens, Greece (E) telecoms support officer S-7 (Area Telecommunications Office)
as of 1/77	Dept. (A/OC)
Sources:	FSL 8/75, 6/74 Department of State Source

SORRELL, ALLEN R.

b. not known

as of 7/76	Department of State Athens, Greece (E) probably telecoms R-7
Sources:	Athens Embassy Sources Department of State Sources

SPANGLER, RODNEY L.

as of 3/76:
61 Crown Court
Harrow-on-the-Hill
Middlesex
U.K.
422-8973

b. not known

10/65	Department of State Bucharest, Romania (E) telecoms specialist	S-6
3/68	Nairobi, Kenya (E) telecoms officer	
as of 2/71	Dept. (AF)	
as of 6/71		S-5
as of 2/72-3/75	not listed in Department of State records; assignment not known	
4/75- at least 3/76	Department of State London, U.K. (E) telecoms officer	R-5
Wife:	Jeanne	
Sources:	FSL 8/75, 10/71, 5/68, 1/67 London Embassy Sources	

SPINELLI, ROBERT L. Jr.

b. not known	New Jersey	
1962	William and Mary College BA	
1962-63	private experience junior draftsman	
1963-65	U.S. Army overseas	
1966-67	unspecified government experience	
8/68	Department of State Rome, Italy (E) Third Secretary & political officer	R-7
11/70	Dept. (EUR)	
as of 10/72-6/74	not listed in Department of State records; assignment not known	
7/74	Department of State Dept.	R-6
8/74	Milan, Italy (CG) Vice-Consul & economic-commercial officer	
as of 10/77	Buenos Aires, Argentina (E) cover position not known	
2/78		R-5
Wife:	Bruna	
Sources:	BR 1972 FSL 8/75, 9/74, 6/72, 2/71, 9/68 Rome Diplomatic List 7/70 Milan Consular List 3/75 Department of State Sources	

SPINNEY, NORMAN J.

    b. not known

        9/74   Department of State
                            Vientiane, Laos (E)
                                telecoms officer   R-7

  as of 11/75   Madrid, Spain (E)
                            probably telecoms

  Sources: FSL 8/75
                        Madrid Embassy Source
                        Department of State Sources

STARR, GAIL A.

  as of 12/74:
  10 Avenue E. Zola
  75015 Paris
  France
  577-7200

    b. not known

  as of 12/74   Department of State
                            Paris, France (E)
                                Office of the Special Assistant

  as of 10/77   Guatemala City, Guatemala (E)
                              cover position not known

  Sources: Paris Embassy Source
                        Department of State Source

STAUBER, PHILIP L.

  as of 9/74:
  6 Via Salandra
  Apt. 35
  Rome
  Italy
  48-10-61

    b. not known

      10/72   Department of State
                            Rome, Italy (E)
                                Attache &
                                political officer

  as of 1/76   not listed in Department of State records;
                        assignment not known

  Wife: Barbara E.

  Sources: Rome Diplomatic Lists 7/73 (updated), 1/73
                      Rome Embassy Source

STENGER, JEROME JOSEPH Jr.

as of 8/75:
Smedsintie 11
02700 Kauniainen
Helsinki
Finland
50-30-44

b. 5 December 1924	France	
1943-46	U.S. Army overseas 1st Lieutenant	
1948	Georgetown University BS	
1948-51	not given in Department of State records; not known	

3/51	Department of State
	    Stockholm, Sweden (E)
	        Vice-Consul
		S-11

10/54-5/66	Department of the Army plans officer	

6/66	Department of State
	    Tokyo, Japan (E)
	        political officer
		R-4

8/68	Bangkok, Thailand (E) political officer	
12/70	Dept. (EA)	
5/72- at least 1/78	Helsinki, Finland (E) political officer	
as of 8/75	First Secretary & political officer	
6/76		RU-4
as of 9/77	award for length of service	
2/78		RU-3
Languages:	French, Swedish	
Wife:	Gladys Collins	
Sources:	BR 1974, 1967 FSL 8/75, 6/72, 2/71, 1/69, 1/67, 7/51, 4/51 Helsinki Diplomatic Lists 1/78, 8/75 Department of State Sources	

STEWART, EDWIN

as of 1/74:
17 Paradissou Street
New Kifissia
Athens
Greece
801-0399

b.	24 March 1937	
6/72	Department of State	
	Athens, Greece (E)	
	telecoms officer	R-7
	(Area Telecommunications Office)	

as of 8/75   Dept. (EUR)

Wife: Edna

Sources: BR 1974
                    FSL 8/75, 4/75, 10/72
                    Athens Embassy Source

STILKE, RICHARD F.

as of 9/75:
15 Winkelstraat
3078 Everberg
Brussels
Belgium
759-9321

b.   not known

6/69	Department of State	
	Kingston, Jamaica (E)	
	telecoms assistant	S-6

as of 10/71   Dept. (ARA-LA)

as of 2/72-2/74   not listed in Department of State records;
                    assignment not known

3/74   Department of State
                    Jidda, Saudi Arabia (E)
                       telecoms support officer

as of 6/76   Dept. (A/OC)

as of 9/75   Brussels, Belgium (E)
                     probably telecoms

Wife: Sharon R.

Sources: FSL 8/75, 6/74, 10/71, 10/70
                    Brussels Embassy Source
                    Department of State Sources

STOLZ, RICHARD F. Jr.

b.	27 November 1925	Ohio
	1943-46	U.S. Army overseas
	1949	Amherst College BA
	1949-50	private experience
		with private corporation
	1950-59	Department of the Army
		political affairs officer

1956-57	Monterrey, California Army Language School	
7/59	Department of State Frankfurt, Germany (CG) political officer	R-5
1/60	Sofia, Bulgaria (L) Second Secretary & political officer	
3/62	Dept. (INR)	
4/62		R-4
2/64	intelligence operations specialist	
4/64		R-3
7/64	Moscow, U.S.S.R. (E) First Secretary & political officer	
2/65	Dept. international relations officer	
3/65	supervisory international economist	
7/66	Rome, Italy (E) political officer	
9/69	Dept.	
6/70	foreign affairs officer	GS-15
2/72		R-3
8/72	Foreign Service Institute language training	
6/73	Belgrade, Yugoslavia (E) political officer	
as of 9/74	Dept. (EUR)	

Language:	Serbo-Croatian
Wife:	Betty Elder

Sources:	BR 1974, 1966, 1960
	FSL 8/75, 11/74, 10/73, 10/72, 9/69,
	  1/67, 6/65, 10/64, 7/62, 4/60,
	  10/59
	Rome Diplomatic List 1/69
	Department of State Sources

STONE, HOWARD EDWARD

as of 9/74:
94 Via di Torre Rossa
Rome

Italy
622-3156

b. 3 March 1925	Ohio	
1939-43	private experience dairy bar manager	
1943-44	U.S. Army	
1945-46	private experience jewelry company co-owner	
1946-47	indemnity company claims adjustor	
1947	National University of Mexico	
1947-49	University of Southern California teaching assistant	
1949	University of Southern California BA	
1949-50	School of Advanced International Studies	
1951	not given in Department of State records; not known	
2/52	Department of State Tehran, Iran (E) Assistant Attache & political officer	S-9
as of 7/54-8/55	Library of Congress analyst	
9/55	Department of State Khartoum, Sudan (E) assistant liaison officer	R-5
7/56		R-6
4/57	Damascus, Syria (E) political officer	
6/57	Second Secretary & political officer	
***8/57		
12/57	Dept.	
2/59		R-5
3/59	Karachi, Pakistan (CG) Second Secretary & political officer	
8/62	Kathmandu, Nepal (E) Second Secretary & political officer	
3/63		R-4
5/65	First Secretary & political officer	R-3
8/65	Attache	S-1

2/66	Saigon, Vietnam (E) Attache & political officer
12/67	Dept.
as of 5/68	(O)
as of 5/69	(EA)
6/71	Rome, Italy (E) Special Assistant R-2 (CIA Chief of Station)
as of 11/75	assignment not known
Wife:	Alice Mueller
Sources:	BR 1974, 1966, 1954 FSL 8/75, 10/71, 10/70, 5/69, 1/67, 6/65, 10/62, 4/59, 1/58, 7/57, 1/56, 4/54, 4/52 Rome Diplomatic Lists 7/73 (updated), 1/73 Rome Embassy Sources

***Stone was ordered to leave Syria for alleged participation with two others from the American Embassy in a *coup* against the Syrian government. (*Keesings Contemporary Archives,* 24–31 August 1957.) In the ranks of the CIA, Stone is known by his nickname, "Rocky," with a reputation as one of the Agency's best *coup* engineers. Cf.: Francis John Jeton.

STONE, HUNTER L. Jr.

as of 6/75:
30 Hillside Grove
London NW 7
U.K.
959-7997

b.   not known

as of 12/74- at least 6/75 ***	Department of State London, U.K. (E) SUSLO
Wife:	Barbara
Sources:	London Embassy Sources

***SUSLO is a cover unit for the National Security Agency, not the CIA.

STRATHERN, CLIFTON R.

b. 15 January 1928	New Hampshire
1945-48	U.S. Navy
1950	Boston University BA
1951	Boston University MA
1951-55	Department of the Navy analyst

1/56	Department of State
	Dept.
	    Foreign Service Institute
	    Chinese language-area trainee
		R-5

7/56		R-6
11/56	Surabaya, Indonesia (CG) economic officer	
1/57	Vice-Consul	
2/59		R-5
8/59	Dept.	
11/59	Vientiane, Laos (E) political officer	
12/59	Second Secretary & political officer	
2/62	Dept. foreign affairs officer	GS-13
as of 7/62-6/72	not listed in Department of State records; assignment not known	

7/72	Department of State
	Jakarta, Indonesia (E)
	    Attache &
	    political officer
		R-2

as of 6/73	Attache & Special Assistant (CIA Chief of Station)	
as of 7/75	Dept. (Deputy Under Secretary for Management office)	
Wife:	Annemarie Billings	

Sources:	BR 1974, 1970, 1961-62, 1956
	FSL 8/75, 6/73, 10/72, 1/62, 1/60, 10/59,
	    1/57, 4/56
	Jakarta Diplomatic and
	    Consular Lists 6/74, 1/73
	Department of State Source	

STUCKNER, KENNETH E.

b. 19 June 1930	New Jersey
1948-52	U.S. Air Force overseas
1952-53	private experience manufacturing firm wireman
1953-64	unspecified government agency telecoms specialist

9/64 ***	Department of State Léopoldville, Congo (E) communications assistant	S-6
as of 1/67	telecoms supervisor	
as of 1/68	Dept. (O)	
as of 5/68-6/73	unspecified government agency telecoms specialist	
7/73	Department of State Madrid, Spain (E) telecoms officer	R-8
as of 8/75	Dept. (EUR)	
Wife:	Rosemary Martin	
Sources:	BR 1974 FSL 8/75, 4/75, 10/73, 1/68, 1/67, 10/64	

***Léopoldville became Kinshasa in June, 1966.

SUITER, CHRISTOPHER A.

as of 3/76:
8 Heronsforde
London W 13
U.K.
997-6537

b.   not known

3/67	Department of State Singapore, Singapore (E) political assistant	S-6
7/69	Amman, Jordan (E) political assistant	S-5
as of 10/70	political officer	
as of 2/71-11/74	not listed in Department of State records; assignment not known	
as of 12/74- at least 3/76	Department of State London, U.K. (E) telecoms	
Wife:	Carol	
Sources:	FSL 10/70, 9/69, 5/67 London Embassy Sources	

SULIK, MICHAEL J.

as of 1/74:
14 Aristidou Street
Kifissia
Athens

Greece
801-8405

b.   4 September 1945

4/71	Department of State Athens, Greece (E) telecoms technician (Area Telecommunications Office)	R-8
as of 11/74	Dept. (EUR)	
as of 4/75	not listed in Department of State records; assignment not known	
Wife:	Carol	
Sources:	BR 1974 FSL 11/74, 10/73, 6/71 Athens Embassy Sources	

SUSAN, EDWARD R.

b.   11 April 1940

6/71	Department of State Bonn, Germany (E) telecoms technician	R-7
as of 10/73	Dept. (EUR)	
as of 2/74-7/75	not listed in Department of State records; assignment not known	
8/75	Department of State Athens, Greece (E) telecoms technician (Area Telecommunications Office)	
Sources:	BR 1973 FSL 8/75, 10/73, 10/71	

SWERDLIN, GEORGE D.

as of 5/76:
2 Hagstigen
181 42 Lidingö
Sweden

b. 15 October 1923	Germany	
1943	naturalized as U.S. citizen	
1943-65	U.S. Army overseas Major	
1960	University of Maryland BS	
8/66	Department of State Geneva, Switzerland (M) economic officer	R-4
as of 5/68	international economist	

7/69	Dept.
5/73	Stockholm, Sweden (E) First Secretary & political officer
2/76	S-1
as of 10/76	Dept. (EUR)
Wife:	Camile Zaccaro
Sources:	BR 1974 FSL 8/75, 10/73, 9/69, 5/68, 1/67 Stockholm Diplomatic Lists 5/76, 11/73 Department of State Sources

TACCONELLI, DOMINIC J.

as of 12/74:
88 Rue de la Fédération
75015 Paris
France
273-0421

b.   24 February 1918

4/64 ***	Department of State Léopoldville, Congo (E) political assistant	S-6
6/67	Mexico City, Mexico (E) administrative assistant	S-5
as of 5/68		S-4
2/70		S-3
10/70	Dept. administrative assistant	GS-13
as of 2/71-10/74	not listed in Department of State records; assignment not known	
as of 11/74	Department of State Paris, France (E) Regional Administrative Support	
Sources:	BR 1972 FSL 10/70, 9/67, 7/64 Paris Embassy Source	

***Léopoldville was renamed Kinshasa in June, 1966.

TANES, MICHAEL

b. 8 July 1924	Albania
1927	naturalized as U.S. citizen
1943-46	U.S. Army overseas
1950	Middlebury College BA

1950	private experience high school football coach	
1950-55	Department of the Army political officer	
1/56	Department of State Salonika, Greece (CG) political officer	R-5
2/56	Vice-Consul	
7/56		R-6
9/57	Athens, Greece (E) Attache & political officer	
2/59		R-5
1/60	Karachi, Pakistan (CG) Attache & political officer	
2/61		R-4
11/62	Dept.	
9/64	Buenos Aires, Argentina (E) Attache & political officer	
10/64	Second Secretary & political officer	
1/66		S-2
2/67	Dept.	
as of 5/69	(ARA-LA)	
6/71	Rome, Italy (E) political officer	
9/73- at least 8/75	Dept. (EUR)	
Wife:	Barbara Barker	
Sources:	BR 1974, 1966 FSL 8/75, 6/74, 10/73, 10/71, 5/67, 1/65, 1/63, 4/60, 10/57, 4/56	

TAYLOR, RICHARD L.

b. not known		
4/74- at least 8/75	Department of State Helsinki, Finland (E) telecoms support officer	S-7
as of 2/78	Moscow, U.S.S.R. (E) probably telecoms	
Sources:	FSL 8/75, 6/74 Department of State Sources	

TAYLOR, ROBERT L. Jr.

    b. not known

7/74	Department of State
	Athens, Greece (E)
	    telecoms officer
	    (Area Telecommunications Office)
		R-5

as of 11/76	Dept. (A/OC)	
Wife:	Martha	
Sources:	FSL 8/75, 11/74 Athens Embassy Source Department of State Source	

TAYLOR, ROGER F.

    b. 23 April 1926

9/63	Department of State Manila, Philippines (E) communications assistant	S-6
as of 5/67	Dept. (O)	
as of 9/67-6/70	not listed in Department of State records; assignment not known	
7/70- at least 2/73	Department of State Athens, Greece (E) telecoms officer	S-4
as of 6/73	not listed in Department of State records; assignment not known	
Sources:	BR 1972 FSL 2/73, 10/70, 5/67, 1/64	

TEDESCHI, JOHN J.

    b. not known

5/73	Department of State Manila, Philippines telecoms assistant	S-8
as of 9/74	Dept. (A/OC)	
as of 3/75	Athens, Greece (E) telecoms	
as of 8/75	Dept. (A/OC)	
Sources:	FSL 4/75, 6/73 Department of State Sources	

TERRELL, EDWIN McCLELLAN

    b. 22 May 1915   Kansas

1935-42	Department of Agriculture clerk	
1937-41	George Washington University business school	
1942	War Production Board junior industrial analyst	
5/42	U.S. Navy	
9/42-10/49	War Department assistant divisional chief	
1947-49	George Washington University unspecified capacity	
10/49	Department of State Dept.	S-5
12/49	Havana, Cuba (E) Assistant Attache & political officer	
5/52	private experience real estate business	
9/52	Department of State Havana, Cuba (E) Attache	S-4
6/54	San Salvador, El Salvador Attache & political officer	
1/55		S-3
4/55	Bogotá, Colombia (E) Attache & political officer	
11/58	Dept.	
7/59		R-4
11/61	La Paz, Bolivia (E) Attache & political officer	
2/63	Santo Domingo, Dominican Republic (E) Attache & political officer (CIA Chief of Station)	
3/63		R-3
8/65	Dept. (ARA-LA)	
4/68		S-1
5/69		R-3
7/69	Panama City, Panama (E) administrative officer (CIA Chief of Station)	

5/71		R-2
8/71	Guatemala City, Guatemala (E) political officer (CIA Chief of Station)	
6/74	Dept. (ARA-LA)	
as of 8/75	not listed in Department of State records; possibly retired	

Wife: Betty Caswell

Sources: BR 1974, 1966, 1956, 1950
FSL 4/75, 6/74, 10/71, 1/70, 1/67,
7/63, 1/62, 1/59, 7/55, 10/54,
10/52, 1/50

THEN, JOSEPH LEE

as of 9/77:
39 Montague Square
London W1
U.K.
262-3573

b. 20 November 1927	Illinois	
1945-46	U.S. Navy overseas	
1949	Latin American Institute BS	
1949	private experience newspaper proof-reader	
1949-50	banking firm foreign teller	
1950	George Washington University unspecified capacity	
1950-55	Department of the Army political officer	
11/55	Department of State Montevideo, Uruguay (E) Assistant Attache & political officer	R-5
7/56		R-6
7/59	Dept.	
6/61	Bogotá, Colombia (E) Assistant Attache & political officer	
4/62		R-5
4/64	Attache & political officer	R-4
12/64	Dept. (ARA-LA)	
2/65		S-2

6/67	Tegucigalpa, Honduras (E) political officer	R-4
as of 5/69-11/73	not listed in Department of State records; assignment not known	

as of 12/73-
at least 9/77
	Department of State
	    London, U.K. (E)
	        Attache &
	        political liaison officer	

as of 6/76	Assistant Political Attache & political liaison officer	
Wife:	Nancy Ann	
Sources:	BR 1967, 1957 FSL 1/69, 9/67, 1/65, 1/62, 10/59, 1/56 London Diplomatic Lists 9/77, 8/76, 12/73 London Embassy Sources	

THOMAS, JON R.

as of 11/75:
Av. Generalísimo 38
num. 38
Madrid
Spain
250-03-55

b. 7 January 1946	Minnesota	
1966-69	U.S. Army overseas	
1971	University of Minnesota BA	
1971-73	Department of the Army analyst	

1/73	Department of State
	    Madrid, Spain (E)
	    political officer
		R-7

as of 11/75	Third Secretary, Vice-Consul & political officer	
as of 5/77	Second Secretary & Vice-Consul	
as of 8/77	Geneva, Switzerland (M) cover position not known	
Wife:	Susan	
Sources:	BR 1974 FSL 8/75, 2/73 Madrid Diplomatic Lists 5/77, 11/75, 10/74 Madrid Embassy Source Department of State Sources	

THOMAS, RICHARD LEE

as of 1/74:

6 Skiathou Street
Kifissia
Athens
Greece
801-4445

b. 7 November 1929	Kentucky
1950-54	U.S. Air Force overseas
1955	no entry in Department of State records; not known
1956-57	U.S. Naval Research Laboratory electronics technician
1958-61	private experience electronics research firm electronics technician
1961-73	Department of the Army electronics specialist
6/73	Department of State Athens, Greece (E) telecoms technician (Regional Relay Facility)

R-7

as of 11/75	Dept. (A/OC)
Wife:	Nancy Hutchinson
Sources:	BR 1974 FSL 8/75, 4/75, 10/73 Athens Embassy Source Department of State Source

THOMAS, WADE ELBERT

b. 14 May 1922	South Carolina
1942-43	Army Corps of Engineers engineering aide
1943-45	U.S. Navy overseas
1948	University of Havana
1949	University of South Carolina BA
1951	Georgetown University BSFS
1951	private experience news release service reviewer
1951-55	Department of the Army political analyst
5/55	Department of State La Paz, Bolivia (E) political officer

R-6

7/56	

R-7

9/57	Guatemala City, Guatemala (E) Assistant Attache & political officer	
2/59		R-6
4/61	Dept.	
3/63		R-5
5/63	Mexico City, Mexico (E) political officer	
4/65		S-3
9/66		R-5
9/68	Dept. (ARA-LA)	R-4
8/71	Caracas, Venezuela (E) political officer (CIA Chief of Station)	
6/72	international relations officer	
4/74		R-3
6/74	Guatemala City, Guatemala (E) First Secretary & political officer (CIA Chief of Station)	
as of 10/77	Dept. (ARA-LA)	
Wife:	Miriam Blostine Hicks	
Sources:	BR 1974, 1969, 1967, 1964 FSL 8/75, 11/74, 10/71, 9/68, 10/63, 7/61, 1/58, 7/55 Guatemala City Diplomatic List 9/76 Department of State Sources	

THOMPSON, FRANCIS A. II

as of 1/74:
Halkidos & Agravlis Street
New Kifissia
Athens
Greece
801-5884

b. 30 January 1939	Indiana	
1964	University of Denver BA	
1964-65	not given in Department of State records; not known	

2/66	Department of State
	  Dept.
	    telecoms specialist
		S-7

1968-72	Department of the Army telecoms specialist-supervisor	

| 12/72 | Department of State
  Athens, Greece (E)
    telecoms officer
    (Regional Relay Facility) | R-7 |

| as of 8/75 | Dept. (EUR) | |

| Wife: | Karen Graff | |

| Sources: | BR 1974, 1973
FSL 8/75, 4/75, 2/73
Athens Embassy Source | |

THOMPSON, KATHERINE A.

as of 6/75:
14 Sloane Gardens
London SW 1
U.K.
730-4922

b.   not known

| as of 12/74-
at least 6/75 | Department of State
  London, U.K. (E)
    Joint Reports & Research Unit | |

| Sources: | London Embassy Sources | |

THOMPSON, MICHAEL S.

| b.   20 February 1928 | England (American parents) | |

| 1949 | Harvard University BA | |

| 1949-52 | private experience
  free-lance writing & newspaper work | |

| 1950 | Columbia University | |

| 1952-53 | University of Paris | |

| 1953-56 | U.S. Army 1st Lieutenant | |

| 1956-58 | Department of the Army
  foreign affairs officer | |

| 6/58 | Department of State
  Rabat, Morocco (E)
    Attache &
    political officer | R-7 |

| 10/58 | Third Secretary &
    political officer | |

| 4/62 | Second Secretary &
    political officer | R-6 |

| ***12/62 | Léopoldville, Congo (E)
    Second Secretary &
    political officer | |

| 4/64 | | R-5 |

5/65	Dept.	
8/66		S-3
as of 1/67	(AF)	
3/67	foreign affairs officer	GS-14
5/68	Algiers, Algeria (E) political officer	R-4
8/71	Brussels, Belgium (E) First Secretary & political officer	
5/72		R-3
9/75- at least 3/78	Rome, Italy (E) Attache	
Wife:	Beverley Long	
Sources:	BR 1974, 1966 FSL 8/75, 10/71, 9/68, 6/65, 4/63, 10/58 Brussels Diplomatic List 4/74 Brussels Guides to Ministries 1975-76, 1974-75 Brussels Diplomatic Annual 1975 Rome Diplomatic Lists 3/78, 9/76 Department of State Source	

***Léopoldville was renamed Kinshasa in 6/66.

THOMSON, RICHARD C. Jr.

b. not known

10/71	Department of State Vientiane, Laos (E) telecoms assistant	S-8
6/74	Athens, Greece (E) telecoms support officer (Area Telecommunications Office)	
as of 10/76	Rangoon, Burma (E) probably telecoms	
Sources:	FSL 8/75, 6/74, 6/73 Department of State Source	

THORNBURGH, CHARLES T.

as of 1/74:
29 Kapodistriou Street
Kifissia
Athens
Greece
801-0479

b. not known

9/70	Department of State
	Athens, Greece (E)
	telecoms assistant S-7
	(Regional Relay Facility)
6/74	Manila, Philippines (E)
	telecoms support officer
as of 12/77	Kinshasa, Zaire (E)
	probably telecoms
Wife:	Lois
Sources:	FSL 8/75, 4/75, 6/73
	Athens Embassy Source
	Department of State Source

THORNE, RICHARD LEVERE

as of 6/75:
14 Gilbert Road
Pinner
Middlesex
U.K.
868-9908

b. 13 June 1927	New York
1944	private experience
	manufacturing assembler
1944-46	U.S. Navy overseas
1947-50	no entry in Department of State records;
	not known
1951	private experience
	electronic designer
1951-66	Department of the Army
	communications officer
9/66	Department of State
	Monrovia, Liberia (E)
	telecoms assistant S-3
as of 5/68	telecoms officer
as of 5/69	Dept. (O)
as of 9/69-4/73	Department of the Army
	communications officer
5/73	Department of State
	London, U.K. (E)
	telecoms officer R-4
as of 8/75	Dept. (A/OC)
Wife:	Dorothea Darstein
Sources:	BR 1974, 1968
	FSL 4/75, 6/73, 5/69, 1/67
	London Embassy Sources
	Department of State Source

THUN, LEONARD L.

    b. not known

6/75	Department of State
	Athens, Greece (E)
	   telecoms support officer
	   (Area Telecommunications Office)
		S-8

as of 12/77	Dept. (A/OC)	
Sources:	FSL 8/75 Department of State Source	

TICKNOR, JOEL D.

b. 27 September 1939	New York	
1960	Union College BA	
1960-62	Columbia University	
2/62	Department of State Dept.	R-8
4/62	Foreign Service Institute French language training	
5/62		0-8

***9/62	Usumbura, Burundi (E)
	   Vice-Consul &
	   Third Secretary	

9/63		0-7
***1/65	Dept. Foreign Service Institute	

6/66	Kinshasa, Congo (E)
	   Assistant Attache &
	   political officer
		R-7

4/67		R-6
9/67	Dept.	
8/68	foreign affairs officer	GS-12
12/71		GS-13
5/73	Accra, Ghana (E) political officer	R-5
as of 8/75	Dept. (AF)	
Wife:	Elizabeth Marten	
Sources:	BR 1974, 1966 FSL 4/75, 6/73, 1/68, 1/67, 1/65, 1/63, 7/62 Department of State Source	

***Usumbura was renamed Bujumbura in 1964.

****Previously, Ticknor was a bonafide State Department employee. Sometime between this date and the posting to Kinshasa, he joined the CIA.

TYREE, DAVID L.

    as of 1/74:
    28 Korai Street
    Kifissia
    Athens
    Greece
    801-4427

    b. not known

8/67	Department of State	
	Abidjan, Ivory Coast (E)	
	telecoms supervisor	S-6
as of 5/68	telecoms officer	
10/69	Bangkok, Thailand (E)	
	telecoms assistant	
as of 6/71		S-5
5/72	Athens, Greece (E)	
	telecoms officer	
	(Regional Relay Facility)	
as of 9/74	Dept. (A/OC)	
Wife:	Shirley	
Sources:	FSL 6/74, 6/72, 6/71, 1/70, 5/68, 1/68	
	Athens Embassy Source	

URQUHART, EDWARD

    b. not known

9/71	Department of State	
	Madrid, Spain (E)	
	telecoms officer	S-7
1/74	Rabat, Morocco (E)	
	telecoms officer	
as of 8/75		S-6
as of 5/76	Dept. (A/OC)	
Sources:	FSL 8/75, 2/74, 6/73	
	Department of State Source	

USTASKI, WALTER

    b. not known

2/71	Department of State	
	Belgrade, Yugoslavia (E)	
	telecoms officer	S-6
5/73	La Paz, Bolivia (E)	
	telecoms assistant	
11/74	Peking, China (U.S. Liaison Office)	
	communications & records officer	

5/75	Athens, Greece (E) telecoms support officer (Area Telecommunications Office)
as of 7/77	Dept. (A/OC)
Sources:	FSL 8/75, 11/74, 6/73, 10/71 Department of State Sources

VAGO, RICHARD L.

b.   not known

as of 10/71	Department of State San José, Costa Rica (E) telecoms assistant	S-7
as of 2/72	Dept. (ARA-LA)	
5/72	Helsinki, Finland (E) telecoms assistant	
as of 9/74	Dept. (A/OC)	
as of 11/74-4/77	not listed in Department of State records; assignment not known	
5/77	Department of State Dept.	R-7
as of 6/77	Islamabad, Pakistan (E) probably telecoms	
Sources:	FSL 6/74, 10/72, 10/71 Department of State Sources	

VAN DER RHOER, JAMES PHILIP

as of 7/77:
64 C Brunnadernstrasse
3006 Bern
Switzerland
44-46-13

b.   not known

6/75	Department of State Dept. (EUR)	R-7
8/75	Bern, Switzerland (E) Third Secretary	
as of 9/77	Bonn, Germany (E) cover position not known	
2/78		R-6
Wife:	Nancy	
Sources:	FSL 8/75 Bern Diplomatic List 7/77 Bonn Embassy Source Department of State Sources	

VAN MARX, PAUL ERNEST ALEXANDER

as of 2/75:
3 Mannenriedstrasse
Bern
Switzerland
52-24-37

b. 24 January 1926	Netherlands	
1944	naturalized as U.S. citizen	
1944-46	U.S. Army overseas 2nd Lieutenant	
1946-49	Yale University	
1949-51	Columbia University School of Law	
1951-57	Department of the Army foreign affairs officer	

1/58	Department of State
	        Zurich, Switzerland (CG)
	            economic officer
		R-6

4/58	Vice-Consul	
2/61		R-5
8/61	Consul	
8/63	Dept.	
4/64		R-4
12/64		S-2
8/65	Bogotá, Colombia (E) political officer	
1/66		R-4
as of 6/66-6/73	not listed in Department of State records; assignment not known	

as of 7/73-
at least 2/75
	Department of State
	        Bern, Switzerland (E)
	            Attache	

Sources:	BR 1967, 1966, 1959 FSL 5/70, 10/65, 1/64, 4/58 Bern Diplomatic List 2/75	

VAN TWISK, TONY M.

b. 30 August 1931		

1/72	Department of State
	        Monrovia, Liberia (E)
	            telecoms officer
		R-7

8/75	Lisbon, Portugal (E) telecoms officer	
Sources:	BR 1974 FSL 8/75, 2/72	

VAN WINKLE, RICHARD D.

b. 1 November 1926	New Jersey	
1945-46	U.S. Marine Corps overseas	
1950	Georgetown University BSFS	
1951-55	Department of Defense area specialist	

1955-57	private experience
	    Nicaragua
	        adviser to Nicaraguan government	

1957	Department of Defense analyst	

8/57	Department of State
	    São Paulo, Brazil (E)
	        political officer
		R-7

2/58	Vice-Consul	

12/59	Buenos Aires, Argentina (E)
	    Assistant Attache &
	    political officer	

3/60		R-6
5/62	Dept.	

7/63	Agency for International Development
	    Rio de Janeiro, Brazil (E)
	        public safety adviser
		R-5

as of 1/64	Recife, Brazil (CG) public safety adviser	
as of 10/64	São Paulo, Brazil (CG) public safety adivser	
7/68	Guatemala City, Guatemala (E) public safety adviser	R-4
as of 10/70-6/71	not listed in Department of State records; assignment not known	

7/71	Department of State
	    Madrid, Spain (E)
	        political officer	

as of 8/73	Dept. (EUR)	
as of 2/74	not listed in Department of State records; assignment not known	

Sources:	BR 1973, 1964
	FSL 10/73, 10/71, 5/70, 9/68, 10/65,
	    10/64, 1/64, 10/63, 7/62, 1/60,
	    10/57
	Department of State Source	

VELTE, ROBERT

    as of 2/76:
    Martin Luther King Strasse 25/3
    5300 Bonn-Bad Godesberg
    Germany
    37-22-59

    b. not known

as of 2/75
at least 2/76
	Department of State
	    Bonn, Germany (E)
	        OCA Liaison Unit

Wife:	Grita
Source:	Bonn Embassy Source

VIDAL, EVALENA S.

    as of 12/74:
    14 Rue Petrarque
    75016 Paris
    France
    553-9641

    b. not known

| as of 12/74 | Department of State
    Paris, France (E)
        Regional Reports Office |
| Source: | Paris Embassy Source |

VISELLI, THOMAS L. Jr.

b. 4 January 1942	New York
1960-64	U.S. Air Force
1965-73	unspecified government experience

3/73	Department of State
	    Athens, Greece (E)
	        telecoms officer
	        (Regional Relay Facility)

as of 8/75	Dept. (A/OC)
Wife:	Linda Gillespie
Sources:	BR 1974, 1973 FSL 4/75, 6/73 Athens Embassy Source Department of State Source

R-8

VOGEL, DONALD FREDERIC

| b. 4 July 1930 | New York |
| 1951 | Williams College BA |

1951-55	U.S. Navy Lieutenant	
1955-62	Department of the Army	
1963-64	private experience consultant for unspecified foreign government	
1/65	Department of State Dept.	

2/65	Buenos Aires, Argentina (E)
	    Attache &
	    political officer
		R-5

8/65	Dept. (EUR)	
4/67		R-4
6/67	Mexico City, Mexico (E) political officer	
5/70	Dept. (ARA-LA)	
10/70	foreign affairs officer	GS-14

4/74	Islamabad, Pakistan (E)
	    First Secretary &
	    political officer
		R-3

as of 10/77	Dept. (NEA)	
Wife:	Joan Fiery	
Sources:	BR 1974, 1973 FSL 8/75, 6/74, 10/70, 9/67, 5/67, 10/65, 6/65 Islamabad Diplomatic & Consular List 3/77 Department of State Sources	

VON SASSENSCHEID, BERTRAM E.

as of 1/74:
15 Kifissou Street
New Kifissia
Athens
Greece
801-4164

b.   not known

6/73	Department of State
	    Athens, Greece (E)
	        telecoms general services assistant
	        (Area Telecommunications Office-
	        Logistics section)
		S-7

as of 11/75	Dept. (EUR)	
Wife:	Ellen Louise	
Sources:	FSL 8/75, 4/75, 10/73 Athens Embassy Source Department of State Source	

VREELAND, FREDERICK DALZIEL

as of 1/76:
2 Rue Fabert
75007 Paris
France
551-11-59

b. 24 June 1927	Connecticut
1945-47	U.S. Merchant Marine overseas

1948	private experience
	    newspaper reporter
	    assistant editor

1951	Yale University BA
1951-52	Department of Defense administrative assistant
not known	University of Geneva

8/52	Department of State
	    Geneva, Switzerland (CG)
	        Vice-Consul &
	        economic assistant

S-11

1954-57	U.S. Delegation to the
	United Nations European Office &
	United Nations Conferences
	    member &
	    assistant economic officer

8/56		S-9
7/57	Berlin, Germany (M) economic officer	S-7
10/58		R-5

10/59	Bonn, Germany (E)
	    Attache &
	    political officer	

12/59	Second Secretary & political officer	
2/61		R-4

***4/63	Dar-es-Salaam, Tanganyika (E)
	    Second Secretary &
	    economic officer	

9/63	Rabat, Morocco (E)
	    Second Secretary &
	    economic officer	

8/67	Dept.
	    U.S. Mission to the United Nations (USUN)
	        political-security affairs adviser	

5/68		R-3

1967-70	U.S. Delegation to the United Nations General Assembly member
3/71	political officer
8/71- at least 1/77	Paris, France (E) First Secretary & political officer
Wife:	Elizabeth Breslauer
Sources:	BR 1974, 1966, 1957 FSL 8/75, 10/71, 1/68, 1/64, 7/63, 1/60, 10/57, 10/56 Paris Diplomatic Lists 1/77, 10/71 Paris Embassy Source

***Tanganyika became Tanzania in October 1964.

WAGNER, BRIAN A.

as of 3/76:
11 New Road
Harrow
Middlesex
U.K.
864-1469

b.   not known

as of 12/74- at least 3/76 ***	Department of State London, U.K. (E) SUSLO
Wife:	Linda
Source:	London Embassy Sources

***SUSLO is a cover unit for the National Security Agency, not the CIA.

WALKER, EDWARD LEE

b.   not known

9/73	Department of State New Delhi, India (E) telecoms assistant
as of 11/74	telecoms support officer
as of 5/76	Athens, Greece (E) probably telecoms
Sources:	FSL 8/75, 10/73 Athens Embassy Sources Department of State Sources

S-8

WALKER, RICHARD T.

b.   not known

8/70	Department of State
	   Tehran, Iran (E)
	      telecoms assistant S-6

3/73	Vienna, Austria (E) telecoms assistant
as of 11/74	telecoms support officer
as of 8/76	Dhahran, Saudi Arabia (CG) probably telecoms

Wife: Janet

Sources: FSL 8/75, 6/73, 10/70
                         Vienna Embassy Source
                         Department of State Source

WALSH, GEORGE T.

as of 11/75:
14 Cowley Street
London SW 1
U.K.
222-7149

b. 9 July 1925	Massachusetts
1943-46	U.S. Army overseas
1948	Sorbonne University (France)
1949	Harvard University BA
1949-50	Harvard University unspecified post
1950-51	Department of Defense research analyst

1951-52	private experience
	   unspecified cultural foundation
	      public relations manager

1953-54	unspecified airlines public relations adviser
1954-55	George Washington University Law School

1955-57	private experience
	   unspecified motion picture company
	      foreign representative

1957-58	unspecified travel publications company public relations adviser

11/58	Department of State
	   Colombo, Ceylon (E)
	      Attache &
	      political officer R-6

4/61	Dept.
4/62	R-5

6/63	Rawalpindi/Murree, Pakistan (Office) Attache & economic officer	
9/63	Second Secretary & economic officer	
5/66		R-4
***8/66	Cairo, U.A.R. (E) political officer	
10/67	consular officer	
7/69	Dept. (NEA)	
11/69	coordination officer	GS-15
6/72	Dacca, Bangladesh (E) economic-commercial officer	R-4
as of 11/74	Dept. (NEA)	
as of 12/74	London, U.K. (E) Foreign Service Institute (at Royal College of Defence Studies)	
as of 3/76	Dept. (EUR/NEA)	
Wife:	Eloise Rathbun	
Sources:	BR 1974, 1966, 1959 FSL 8/75, 11/74, 10/72, 1/67, 10/63, 7/61, 1/59 London Embassy Sources Department of State Source	

***The United Arab Republic was renamed the Arab Republic of Egypt in 1971.

WALSH, MICHAEL JOHN

as of 6/76:
Flachsgraben 13
Bonn-Bad Godesberg
Germany
36-28-15

b. 2 July 1934	Missouri
1952	U.S. Geological Survey topographic aide
1953	Department of the Air Force cartographic aide
1956	St. Louis University BS
1956-60	private experience aircraft manufacturing company design engineering
1957	U.S. Army
1960-63	Department of the Army analyst

1961	St. Louis University MA	
7/63	Department of State Dept.	R-7
8/63	Frankfurt, Germany (CG) visa officer	
12/63	Vice-Consul	
7/64	Berlin, Germany (M) Vice-Consul	
5/66		R-6
9/66	political officer	
10/68	Dept. (EUR)	
3/69		R-5
as of 10/70-8/74	not listed in Department of State records; assignment not known	
9/74	Department of State Bonn, Germany (E) economic-commerical officer	R-4
as of 9/75	First Secretary & economic-commerical officer	
as of 10/77	Geneva, Switzerland (M) cover position not known	
Wife:	Betty Ruthmeyer	
Sources:	BR 1970 FSL 8/75, 11/74, 5/70, 10/64, 1/64, 10/63 Bonn Diplomatic Lists 6/77, 9/75 Department of State Sources	

WALSON, ROBERT C.

b.   not known

9/74	Department of State Addis Ababa, Ethiopia (E) political officer	R-6
as of 11/77	Geneva, Switzerland (M) cover position not known	
2/78		R-5
Sources:	FSL 8/75, 11/74 Geneva Mission Source Department of State Sources	

WARREN, EVERETT G.

b.   not known

| 4/72 | Department of State
Copenhagen, Denmark (E)
telecoms assistant | S-7 |

8/74	Manila, Philippines (E) telecoms officer	
as of 11/76	Dept. (A/OC)	
Sources:	FSL 8/75, 11/74, 6/73 Department of State Source	

WASZKIEWICZ, JOHN H.

b. not known

7/74	Department of State Athens, Greece (E) telecoms support officer (Area Telecommunications Office)	S-8
as of 1/77	Cairo, Egypt (E) probably telecoms	
Sources:	FSL 8/75, 11/74 Department of State Source	

WATTS, LUELL A.

as of 1/74:
3 Papaflessa & Konitsis Streets
Kastri
Athens
Greece
801-3511

b. not known

5/69	Department of State New Delhi, India (E) telecoms technician	S-5
6/70- at least 1/74	Athens, Greece (E) telecoms officer (Area Telecommunications Office)	
as of 6/72		S-4
Wife:	Alice	
Sources:	FSL 10/72, 6/72, 10/70, 9/69 Athens Embassy Source	

WEBB, BRENDA J.

as of 1/74:
117 Michalakopoulou Street
Athens
Greece
70-62-42

b. not known

10/73	Department of State Athens, Greece (E) telecoms clerk (Area Telecommunications Office)	S-10
as of 11/74		S-9
as of 12/76	Dept. (A/OC)	
Sources:	FSL 8/75, 10/73 Athens Embassy Source Department of State Source	

WEBB, JOHN FREDERICK

b. 28 August 1935	New Hampshire	
1957	Tulane University BA	
1957-60	U.S. Marine Corps 1st Lieutenant	
1960-67	Department of Commerce international investment specialist	
6/67	Department of State San José, Costa Rica (E) economic-commercial officer	R-6
3/69		R-5
8/73	Buenos Aires, Argentina (E) economic-commercial officer	
as of 1/73	Second Secretary & economic-commerical officer	
8/73	Tegucigalpa, Honduras (E) political officer	
as of 7/76	Dept. (ARA-LA)	
8/76-	Madrid, Spain (E) Attache	
Wife:	Jane Haile	
Sources:	BR 1974 FSL 8/75, 10/73, 10/70 Buenos Aires Diplomatic List 1/73 Madrid Diplomatic Lists 11/77, 11/76 Department of State Sources	

WEBER, RONALD L.

b. not known		
8/70	Department of State Geneva, Switzerland (M) U.S. Mission to the European Office of the United Nations and Other International Organizations telecoms officer	S-6

1/74	Dhahran, Saudi Arabia (CG)
	telecoms officer
as of 10/76	Monrovia, Liberia (E)
	probably telecoms

Sources: FSL 8/75, 2/74
Department of State Sources

WEBSTER, DANIEL K.

as of 1/74:
101 Leoforos Metaxa
Kifissia
Athens
Greece
801-3241

b. 22 July 1941	Texas	
1963	American University BA	
1963	U.S. Army	
1963-65	Department of the Army	
	editorial assistant	
7/65	Department of State	
	Dept.	
	Foreign Service Institute	
	language-area trainee	R-8
3/66	Beirut, Lebanon (E)	
	Attache &	
	Arabic language-area trainee	
6/67	Tripoli, Libya (E)	
	political officer	
5/68		R-7
12/68	Dept. (AF)	
	personnel assistant	
3/69		R-6
6/70	program officer	GS-12
8/71	Athens, Greece (E)	
	political officer	R-5
as of 8/75	Dept. (EUR)	

Languages: Arabic, Greek

Wife: Michel Ann Critchfield

Sources: BR 1974, 1966
FSL 8/75, 4/75, 10/71,1/70, 5/69,
9/67, 1/67, 10/65
Athens Diplomatic Lists 12/74 (updated), 7/73
Athens Embassy Source

WEISZ, GEORGE

> as of 12/75:
> 18 Wolfsgrubergasse
> 1190 Vienna
> Austria
> 32-35-74

b. 27 August 1918	Hungary (American parent)	
1937-41	New York University	
1941-46	U.S. Army overseas Captain	

1946-48	Department of the Army
	    Office of the Military Government
	    United States (in Germany) (OMGUS)
	        executive officer,
	        chief of branch	

1948-49	chief of section	

10/49	Department of State
	    Frankfurt, Germany (HICOG)
	        Office of Political Affairs
	            dislodged German advisor
		S-3

2/50		S-2
as of 10/50	displaced populations adviser	
12/50		S-1
1951-62	Department of the Army foreign affairs officer	
1953	New York University BA	
1955	George Washington University MA	

7/62	Department of State
	    Frankfurt, Germany (CG)
	        political officer
		R-3

4/64		R-2

10/64	Bonn, Germany (E)
	    Attache &
	    political officer	

as of 1/68	Dept. (O)	
2/68	Saigon, Vietnam (E) cover position not known	GS-16
2/69	Dept. foreign affairs officer	GS-17

6-8/70	Columbia University
	    senior executive
	    management course	

9/70-3/71	not listed in Department of State records; assignment not known	

4/71	Department of State
	    Berlin, Germany (M)
	        political officer
		R-2

as of 11/74	Dept. (EUR)	

10/75-
at least 6/77
	Vienna, Austria (E)
	    Attache &
	    political officer
	    Peripheral Reporting Section chief
	    (CIA Chief of Station)	

Wife: Etta McAndree

Sources: BR 1974, 1971, 1964, 1950
                FSL 8/75, 11/74, 6/71, 1/68, 1/65,
                    10/62, 1/51, 10/50, 4/50
                Vienna Diplomatic Lists 6/77, 6/76
                Vienna Embassy Source

WELCH, RICHARD SKEFFINGTON

as of 12/75:
5 Rue Vassillissis Friderikis
Psychico
Athens
Greece
671-2933

b. 14 December 1929	Connecticut	
1951	Harvard University BA	
1951-60	Department of the Army economic analyst	

5/60	Department of State
	    Nicosia, Cyprus (CG)
	        economic officer
		R-6

8/60	Attache, Vice-Consul & economic officer	
3/63		R-5
12/64	Dept.	

5/66	Guatemala City, Guatemala (E)
	    political officer
	    (CIA Deputy Chief of Station)	

3/67	Georgetown, Guyana (E) political officer	
4/67		R-4
3/69		R-3
9/69	Dept.	
as of 6/71	(ARA-LA)	

6/72	Lima, Peru (E)
	    general international
	    relations officer	

8/73		RU-3
as of 6/74	First Secretary	

7/75	Athens, Greece (E) First Secretary, political officer & Special Assistant (CIA Chief of Station)
Wife:	Maria Cristina Hartleben Topke
Sources:	BR 1974, 1961-62 FSL 4/75, 10/72, 6/71, 1/70, 5/67, 1/67, 6/65, 7/60 Lima Diplomatic List 6/74 Athens Diplomatic List 12/74 (updated)

WHEELER, HENRY P.

b.   not known

6/70	Department of State Athens, Greece (E) telecoms assistant	S-8
9/73- at least 8/75	Manila, Philippines (E) telecoms assistant	
as of 11/74	telecoms support officer	
Sources:	FSL 8/75, 10/73, 6/73	

WHIPPLE, DAVID D.

as of 1/77:
Avenida Portugal 7
Estoril
Portugal
26-11-68

b. 26 December 1923	Ohio	
1943-46	U.S. Army overseas	
1948	University of Southampton (England)	
1949	Dartmouth College BA	
1950	School of Advanced International Studies MA	
***11/50	Department of State Hanoi, Vietnam (C) Vice-Consul & economic officer	S-11
12/53	Rangoon, Burma (E) political officer	
8/54		S-9
8/56		S-8
11/56	Dept.	
6/58		R-6

****8/58	International Cooperation Administration Bangkok, Thailand (E) police advisor	
2/61 *****	Department of State Elizabethville, Congo (C) political officer	R-5
5/61	Vice Consul	
7/63	Dept.	
4/64		R-4
8/66	National War College	
6/67	London, U.K. (E) Attache	
·8/70	Dept. foreign affairs officer	GS-15
4/71- at least 6/74	Helsinki, Finland (E) political officer	R-3
7/74	Dept. (EUR)	
as of 11/74-12/75	not listed in Department of State records; assignment not known	
as of 1/76- at least 1/77	Department of State Lisbon, Portugal (E) Attache (CIA Chief of Station)	
Wife:	Carolyn Decker	
Sources:	BR 1973, 1971, 1966, 1955 FSL 6/74, 6/71, 5/67, 10/63, 4/61, 1/59, 1/57, 10/56, 1/55, 10/54, 7/51, 4/51 London Diplomatic Lists 8/70, 8/67 Lisbon Diplomatic Lists 1/77, 1/76 Department of State Source	

***According to the 1973 *Biographic Register*, Whipple was actually in Saigon from 11/50 to 1/51, and in Hanoi from 1/51.

****The International Cooperation Administration became the Agency for International Development in 1961.

*****Elizabethville was renamed Lubumbashi in June, 1966.

WHITACRE, GORDON C.

as of 1/74:
14 Akakias Street
Ekali
Athens
Greece
803-2466

b. not known

6/72	Department of State
	Athens, Greece (E)
	general services assistant &
	telecoms S-7
	(Area Telecommunications Office-Logistics section)
as of 9/74	Dept. (A/OC)
Wife:	Joan
Sources:	FSL 6/74, 6/73
	Athens Embassy Source
	Department of State Source

WHITE, JOSEPH E.

b.   not known

11/71	Department of State
	Karachi, Pakistan (CG)
	telecoms assistant S-8
3/74	Bern, Switzerland (E)
	telecoms officer
as of 7/77	Helsinki, Finland (E) S-7
	probably telecoms
Sources:	FSL 8/75, 6/74, 6/73
	Department of State Source

WHITFIELD, GEORGE P.

b.   not known

12/72	Department of State
	Jakarta, Indonesia (E)
	telecoms assistant S-7
as of 11/74	telecoms support officer
2/75	Athens, Greece (E)
	telecoms support officer
	(Area Telecommunications Office)
as of 5/77	Dept. (A/OC)
Sources:	FSL 8/75, 11/74, 6/73
	Department of State Source

WICHTERMAN, ALVIN R.

b.   10 October 1926

5/70	Department of State
	Athens, Greece (E)
	telecoms technician S-4
3/72	S-3

as of 10/73	Dept. (NEA)
as of 2/74	not listed in Department of State records; assignment not known
Sources:	BR 1973
	FSL 10/73, 10/70

WILDER, THROOP M. Jr.

b. 16 November 1928 New York

1947	private experience manufacturing company apprentice	
1951	Harvard University BA	
1951-55	U.S. Army overseas	
1955-56	Department of Defense foreign affairs officer	
9/56	Department of State Zagreb, Yugoslavia (C) consular officer	R-6
12/56	Vice-Consul	
9/59	Vienna, Austria (E) political officer	
3/60		R-5
6/61	Salzburg, Austria (CG) Vice-Consul & political officer	
9/61	Consul	
as of 10/63	Dept. (EUR)	
10/63	Vienna, Austria (E) Attache, Consul & consular officer	
12/63	Second Secretary & Consul	
4/64		R-4
10/65	Dept.	
7/66		S-2
as of 1/67	(EUR)	
9/68		R-4
8/70	Geneva, Switzerland (M) political officer	
4/74		R-3
as of 11/76	Dept. (EUR)	

Wife: Katrinka Kip

Sources: BR 1974, 1966
                               FSL 8/75, 1/67, 1/64, 1/62, 1/60, 1/57
                               Geneva Diplomatic Lists 1/76, 10/75
                               Geneva Mission Source
                               Department of State Source

WILHELM, JOHN J. Jr.

   as of 1/74:
   3 Alkeou Street
   Ekali
   Athens
   Greece
   803-3220

   b. not known

      8/69   Department of State
                                 Zanzibar, Tanzania (C)
                                   telecoms officer   S-6

      5/71   Lima, Peru (E)
                                   telecoms assistant

  as of 6/72   telecoms officer

      8/73   Athens, Greece (E)
                                   telecoms officer
                                   (Regional Relay Facility)

  as of 11/76   Dept. (A/OC)

Wife: Norma Jean

Sources: FSL 8/75, 4/75, 10/73, 6/72, 10/71, 1/70
                               Athens Embassy Source
                               Department of State Sources

WILLCOX, JOHN M.

   as of 12/74:
   23 Rue de Constantine
   75007 Paris
   France
   551-3595

   b. not known

  as of 12/74   Department of State
                                 Paris, France (E)
                                   Regional Reports Office

Wife: Maria

Source: Paris Embassy Source

WILLIAMS, GARY M.

   as of 12/74:

11 Rue Vaneau
75007 Paris
France
555-0474

b. not known

as of 12/74   Department of State
                        Paris, France (E)
                            Regional Reports Office

Wife: Robin Ann

Source: Paris Embassy Source

WILLIAMS, JIMMIE C.

as of 1/74:
8 Olympias Street
Kifissia
Athens
Greece
801-0508

b. not known

4/71   Department of State
                        Jidda, Saudi Arabia (E)
                            telecoms assistant   S-8

8/73-   Athens, Greece (E)
at least 8/75   telecoms assistant
                            (Regional Relay Facility)

as of 11/74   telecoms support officer   S-7

as of 11/75   Dept. (A/OC)

Wife: Margaret

Sources: FSL 8/75, 10/73, 6/73
                    Athens Embassy Source
                    Department of State Source

WILSON, EDWARD

as of 9/74:
7 Viale Di Villa Grazioli
Apt. B-13
Rome
Italy
845-0586

b. not known

5/73   Department of State
                        Rome, Italy (E)
                            telecoms assistant   S-7

as of 11/74   telecoms support officer

as of 8/76   Dept. (A/OC)

as of 5/78   Kabul, Afghanistan (E)
                                    probably telecoms

Wife: Wendy A.

Sources: FSL 8/75, 6/73
                                Rome Embassy Source
                                Department of State Source

WILT, EDWARD JAMES II

as of 9/74:
290 Via Flaminia Nuova
Bldg. 6
Rome
Italy
327-8470

b. 26 December 1930	Florida	
1950-51	private experience hospital psychiatric aide	
1951-54	U.S. Army	
1954	University of Michigan BA	
1954-55	private experience hospital psychiatric aide	
1955	University of Michigan MA	
1955-56	Department of the Army area specialist	
3/57	Department of State Tehran, Iran (E) political officer	S-9
5/59	Attache & political officer	R-7
11/61	Dept.	
3/63		R-6
3/64	coordinating officer	GS-13
as of 7/64-8/74	not listed in Department of State records; assignment not known	
as of 9/74	Department of State Rome, Italy (E) USASEPU	
Language:	Persian	
Wife:	Mary Smith	
Sources:	BR 1973, 1966 FSL 4/64, 1/62, 7/57 Rome Embassy Source	

WINSKY, STEPHEN

> as of 6/77:
> 31 Amberwood Crescent
> Ottawa
> Canada
> 825-4689

b. 1 January 1930	Pennsylvania	
1952	Temple University BS	
1953-56	U.S. Navy overseas	
1956-60	Department of the Army analyst	
1960	American University MA	

4/61	Department of State
	   Helsinki, Finland (E)
	      consular officer
		R-7

8/61	Vice-Consul & Third Secretary	
4/64	Consul & Second Secretary	R-6
5/66		R-5
9/66	Dept. (EUR)	
2/71	plans and programs officer	GS-13
as of 6/71-12/73	not listed in Department of State records; assignment not known	

as of 1/74	Department of Defense
	   Athens, Greece (E)
	      JUSMAGG	

as of 10/76-
at least 6/77
	Department of State
	   Ottawa, Canada (E)
	      Attache	

Language:	Greek	
Wife:	Anne	
Sources:	BR 1974, 1966 FSL 2/71, 1/67, 7/64, 7/61 Ottawa Diplomatic & Consular Lists 6/77, 10/76	

WITECKI, THOMAS A.

> as of 12/75:
> 116 Weimarer Strasse, Apt. 7
> 1190 Vienna
> Austria
> 36-56-21

b. 30 August 1940	
1961	University of Michigan BA
1963	MA

1963-65	U.S. Air Force	
1965-67	Department of the Army programs officer	
7/71	Department of State Vienna, Austria (E) Attache & economic-commercial officer	R-6
8/72	political officer	
2/76		R-5
as of 6/76	Second Secretary (Political Section) & political officer	
as of 10/76	Dept. (EUR)	
Wife:	Mary Louise Nashar	
Sources:	BR 1974 FSL 8/75, 10/71 Vienna Diplomatic Lists 6/76, 11/72 Department of State Sources Vienna Embassy Source	

WOLFE, LARRY L.

    b.   14 March 1938

5/72	Department of State London, U.K. (E) telecoms officer	R-6
as of 9/74	Dept. (A/OC)	
Sources:	BR 1974 FSL 6/74, 6/72 Department of State Source	

WRIGHT, ORRIN M.

    b.   not known

11/70- at least 6/73	Department of State Rome, Italy (E) telecoms assistant	S-7
as of 10/73	not listed in Department of State records; assignment not known	
Source:	FSL 6/73	

WRIGHT, STEPHEN E.

    as of 1/74:
    44 Constantinou Paleologou Street
    Politia
    Kifissia
    Athens
    Greece
    801-8428

   b.   not known

7/72	Department of State
	   Athens, Greece (E)
	      telecoms assistant
	      (Area Telecommunications Office)
		S-8

as of 11/74	telecoms support officer	
as of 11/75	New Delhi, India (E) telecoms	
Wife:	Sharon Anne	
Sources:	FSL 8/75, 6/73 Athens Embassy Source Department of State Source	

WUJICK, JOHN T. Jr.

   b.   12 January 1940

5/71	Department of State
	   Bern, Switzerland (E)
	      telecoms officer
		R-7

as of 8/73	Dept. (A/OC)	
Sources:	BR 1973 FSL 10/72, 10/71 Department of State Source	

WYATT, FELTON MARK

b. 23 May 1920	California	
1938-39	Alliance Française (Paris)	

1939-42	private experience
	   food packing company
	      canning inspector,
	      fruit grader	

1943	University of California BA	
1941-46	U.S. Navy overseas Lieutenant	

1946	private experience
	   U.S. Capitol
	      position not known	

1947-48	secretary to U.S. Senator	
1948	George Washington University MA	
9/49	Department of State Dept.	S-10
10/49	Rome, Italy (E) Vice-Consul	
8/52	Genoa, Italy (CG) Vice-Consul	S-9

1/55		S-8
7/57		S-7
3/58	Dept.	
***1959-70	Department of the Army political analyst	
1970-73	Department of Commerce industry-trade specialist	
5/73	Department of State Luxembourg, Luxembourg (E) political officer	R-4
as of 12/75	Dept. (EUR)	
Wife:	Ann Storrow	
Sources:	BR 1974, 1959, 1950 FSL 8/75, 6/73, 10/59, 4/58, 10/52, 1/50 Department of State Source	

***From 1949-58, Wyatt was apparently a bona-fide State Department employee, and joined the CIA in 1959.

YORK, GEORGE S.

    b. not known

7/70	Department of State Athens, Greece (E) telecoms technician	S-5
as of 10/73	Dept. (NEA)	
as of 2/74-5/78	not listed in Department of State records; assignment not known	
as of 6/78	Department of State New Delhi, India (E) probably telecoms	
Sources:	FSL 10/73, 10/70	

ZANIN, JOSEPH D.

    as of 1/74:
4 Eleftherotrias Street
Politia
Kifissia
Athens
Greece
801-8571

    b. 24 December 1935

5/72	Department of State Athens, Greece (E) telecoms engineer (Area Telecommunications Office)	R-5
as of 10/75	Dept. (A/OC)	

Wife:	Tonia
Sources:	BR 1974
	FSL 8/75, 10/72
	Athens Embassy Source
	Department of State Source

ZAPOLI, GERALD E.

b.   not known

***as   of   5/75

(ETA)	Department of State
	Lisbon, Portugal (E)
	telecoms

| 5/75 | Mogadiscio, Somalia (E) | |
| | telecoms officer | S-6 |

| as of 12/77 | Dept. (A/OC) |

Sources:	FSL 8/75
	Lisbon Embassy Source
	Department of State Sources

***Originally scheduled to serve in Portugal, Zapoli apparently never actually went there but was sent to Somalia, possibly as a result of being identified in Agee's "Letter to the Portuguese People".

ZASLOW, MILTON S.

as of 12/77:
Flat 5
35 Bryanston Square
London W 1
U.K.
262-9379

b.   not known

as of 10/75-	Department of State
at least 6/78	London, U.K. (E)
***	SUSLO chief

| as of 6/76 | Political Attache & |
| | SUSLO chief |

Wife:	Elinor
Sources:	London Diplomatic Lists 6/78, 8/76, 10/75
	London Embassy Source

***SUSLO is a cover unit for the National Security Agency, not the CIA.

ZIEMER, SUZANNE E.

as of 2/76:
Robert-Koch Strasse 48
5300 Bonn-Bad Godesberg

Germany
33-09-15

b. not known

as of 2/75-   Department of State
at least 2/76   Bonn, Germany (E)
                                       Office of the Coordinator & Advisor

8/77   Dept.
                                   Foreign Service Institute   R-6

10/77   confirmed as consular officer

Sources: Bonn Embassy Source
                               Department of State Sources

ZSCHACK, HARRY M.

b. not known

6/75-   Department of State
at least 10/77   Oslo, Norway (E)
                                       telecoms support officer   S-7

Sources: FSL 8/75
                               Oslo Embassy Source
                               Department of State Source

III. Who's Where

The following listing of the nations of Western Europe include each person listed in the Biographies who was at any time posted in each country. For some countries, additional information about the U.S. intelligence activities there is given, as are additional sources beyond articles published in this book. Because of their appearance in articles, some persons who did not serve in Western Europe are also to be found in the Biographies. These persons are listed at the end of this section, with the country of most recent known posting given. Full details for each person in this section may be found by referring to the biographical listing.

Austria

AMERICAN EMBASSY
IX Boltzmanngasse 16
A-1091 Vienna
34-66-11, 34-75-11

The CIA Station in Vienna has for many years been one of the most vital to the Agency in all Europe. It is what is known in intelligence circles as a "listening post" for Eastern Europe, and serves as the base for vital planning and tactical support for ongoing covert operations in the region. It is therefore no coincidence that, both currently and over most of the post-war era, many veterans in the Clandestine Service served time under cover in Vienna.

ALLNER, FREDERICK A. Jr.
BAKKE, ALFRED C.
BERG, JOHN W.
BULL, RICHARD C.
BURGSTALLER, EUGEN F.
CARLSON, ERIC JOHN
CREE, PAUL G. Jr.
DOMBROWSKY, DAVID L.
ECKSTEIN, WILLIAM HERBERT
ELBON, SAM B.
GALE, CHARLES R. Jr.
GIESECKE, FRITZ H.
GRAVER, WILLIAM J.
GREENE, HARRIS CARL
GROVE, DEREK A.
HEALEY, RICHARD D.
HONEYCUTT, ARMAND A.
KARPOVICH, SERGE
KEEGAN, MARY T.
KEMERY, RAYMOND F.
KLEIN, THEODORE
KRUMVIEDE, DALE M.
KUNZ, GEORGE J.

LIESER, WILLIAM D.
LIVINGSTON, JAMES A.
MALTON, CHARLES TROFFORD Jr.
MAPOTHER, JOHN RUBEL
MONTGOMERY, HUGH
O'NEAL, EVERETT C.
OWEN, MARY J.
PAVITT, JAMES L.
PECHOUS, EDWIN J.
PERKINS, LILIAN
PETTY, PAUL R.
PLATT, JOHN C. III
POLGAR, THOMAS
PONSART, CHARLES M.
ROSENBERG, NATHAN A.
ROTH, ROBERT HUGH
SCHNEIDER, PHILLIP M.
SISTERMAN, JOHN B.
WALKER, RICHARD T.
WEISZ, GEORGE
WILDER, THROOP M. Jr.
WITECKI, THOMAS A.

Belgium

AMERICAN EMBASSY
27 Boulevard du Regent
Brussels
513-3830

As the home of a number of international institutions of great importance to the CIA and to overall U.S. foreign policy (such as NATO, the European Common Market, and the International Confederation of Free Trade Unions), Brussels is one of the more significant European stations within the CIA's priorities.

BOVEE, HOWARD W.
BROWN JOHN P.
BUCHANAN, GEORGE
BULL, RICHARD C.
CIAZZA, ADRIAN B.
CREEDEN, WILLIAM E.
EATON, ROBERT FRANCIS
FEDKIW, CARL P.
FUEHRER, ALLEN
GILHOOLY, JOHN F.
HAGEN, GERALD E.
HUBER, HERBERT GOTTLIEB
KEEGAN, MARY T.
KELLY, GILES MERRILL

KOPLOWITZ, WILFRED D.
KOWALEWSKI, STEPHEN J.
LINDSAY, GERALD G.
McCULLOUGH, JOHN P.
McDERMOTT, JOHN E.
MINOR, WILLIAM B.
MONTGOMERY, JAMES D.
MUSSER, VICTORIA
O'NEAL, EVERETT C.
ROBERTS, ROWLAND E. Jr.
ROTH, ROBERT HUGH
SHERRY, FRANCIS S. III
STILKE, RICHARD F.
THOMPSON, MICHAEL S.

Cyprus

AMERICAN EMBASSY
Therissos St. & Dositheos St.
Nicosia
65151/5

BATSON, CHARLES C.
BEHRENS, JAMES E.
BESSETTE, ARTHUR J.
BRADSHAW, BEVERLEY B.
CHAREST, ELDON E.
DAVIS, STANLEY W. Jr.
ESTES, RONALD EDWARD
FAUGHT, DAVID W.
FORTNER, LUTHER C.
GREGORY, GERALD D.
HOSHEIT, GEORGE W.
JONES, FRANK WILLIAMS, Jr.

KIRBY, JOHN THOMAS
LARSON, ROBERT H.
LOFGREN, WILLIAM S.
LUTHY, WALTER P.
MALOY, KEVIN A.
MASTERSON, RICHARD B.
McGEE, JOSEPH V.
PINEAU, JOHN A.
REINHARDT, ARTHUR F.
RUCKMAN, JAMES R.
SLACK, GEORGE LEE
WELCH, RICHARD SKEFFINGTON

Denmark

AMERICAN EMBASSY
Dag Hammarskjolds Alle 24
Copenhagen
(01) 12-31-44, 12-77-91

The Copenhagen CIA Station was first revealed in the newspaper *Information.*

Source: *Information,* "CIA, Diplomat-Agenter i Danmark," 12-13 July 1975

BENEDICT, GARY D.
DALE, CHARLES J.
FENNER, BILLY A.
GOTCHEF, EDWARD J.
GREGORY, GERALD D.
JENSEN, HANS J.
JOHNSON, QUENTIN C.
KINGSLEY, ROLFE

LANNON, JOHN M.
LOFGREN, WILLIAM S.
MASTERSON, RICHARD B.
POTTS, ROBERT D.
ROBERTS, ROWLAND E. Jr.
SANDEL, LEO
SHERMAN, VAUGHN A.
WARREN, EVERETT G.

Finland

AMERICAN EMBASSY
Italinen Puisotie 14
SF-00140 Helsinki 14
11931

The Helsinki CIA Station was first revealed by a British journalist living in Sweden, George Lennox.

Source: *Dagens Nyheter,* Tor Hognas, "Vi stoppade inte Lennox-intervjun," 8 November 1975

DUNN, JIMMY C.
ECKROTE, DONALD G.
HUTCHINS, BRUCE DUANE
MERIKOSKI, JUHA OLIVA
PALMERI, STEPHEN A. Jr.
PINEAU, JOHN A.
SIMENSON, WILLIAM CHARLES

SIMPSON, ROBERT K.
STENGER, JEROME JOSEPH Jr.
TAYLOR, RICHARD L.
VAGO, RICHARD L.
WHIPPLE, DAVID D.
WINSKY, STEPHEN

France

AMERICAN EMBASSY
2 Avenue Gabriel
75008 Paris
265-7460

Sources: *Liberation,* "32 Agents de la CIA a Paris Identifiés," "La CIA a Paris: Deuxieme Liste," & "Les 3 Jours de la CIA," 13-15 January 1976.
Le Nouvel Observateur, Rene Backmann, Franz-Olivier Giesbert and Oliver Todd, "Ce Que Cherchent les Agents de la CIA en France".

One of the larger CIA complements in Europe, the Paris Station has been headed by a Special Assistant to the Ambassador, the veteran Eugen F. Burgstaller. Besides Burgstaller's office, the Station also includes three other well-defined units—the Regional Reports Office, Regional Administrative Support, and the American Liaison Section—as well as a small telecommunications group.

The names first appeared in *Liberation,* an independent left-wing daily in Paris, which gives prominent coverage to the activities of the CIA throughout the world.

ACON, WILLIAM J.
AMIANO, SUZANNE K.
BAIRD, DOROTHY H.
BERG, JOHN W.
BERGER, MICHAEL JAY
BONIN, DONALD C.
BOVEE, HOWARD W.
BOWMAN, DONALD E.
BURGSTALLER, EUGEN F.
CAMPBELL, NANCY M.
CERRA, RONALD L.
CESSNA, LINDA C.
CHOUKALOS, DALE
COLE, BARBARA R.
CORRIGAN, JAMES L.
COVIELLO, JOSEPH LOUIS
CRAWFORD, SETH T.
CUSICK, CHARLES J.
DER-VERTANIAN, ANNA
DONOVAN, ANN C.
DORVAL, NANCY E.
DOWNEY, SALLY MARIE
DUBERMAN, DAVID
DUNN, EDWARD PAUL
EATON, JOAN C.
FARRELL, NANCY A.
FARRELL, SYLVESTER L.
FISHER, MARGARET V.
FLING, GRAHAM J. III

FORD, NANCY
FRIEND, JULIUS W. Jr.
GELINAS, PAUL R.
GEORGE, CLAIR ELROY
HARWOOD, PAUL VINCENT
HEALEY, DONALD J.
HOLT, PETER G.
JETON, FRANCIS JOHN
KAHANE, RICHARD A.
KEMERY, RAYMOND F.
KENNEY, JOHN H.
KIRBY, JOHN THOMAS
KOPLOWITZ, WILFRED D.
LANDRETH, RODNEY N. II
LAX, MORRIS H.
McBRIDE, MICHAEL G.
MILLER, JUDITH A.
MONTGOMERY, HUGH
MURPHY, DAVID E.
MURPHY, JAMES G.
MURPHY, JAMES M.
NICKERSON, DAVID
NYHUS, PAUL GRAHAM
PARKE, MARGARET
PLATT, JOHN C. III
POLTAR, ROBERT S.
RACKHAM, JOHN SCOTT
SABOE, DONALD L.
SALTSMAN, JOSEPH IRL

SELSKY, OLEG N.
SEVIER, LEWIS V.
SHEA, JOHN J.
SLIFER, HARRY SEGER Jr.
STARR, GAIL A.

TACCONELLI, DOMINIC J.
VIDAL, EVALENA S.
VREELAND, FREDERICK DALZIEL
WILLCOX, JOHN M.
WILLIAMS, GARY M.

Germany

AMERICAN EMBASSY
Mehlemer Avenue
5300 Bonn-Bad Goldesberg
(02221) 89-55

Source: *Informations-Dienst,* 31 January 1976

With over 1000 people, the Bonn Embassy is believed to be the biggest in the world. Even larger than the Paris operation, the CIA Station in Bonn has until recently been headed by William J. Graver, who held the nominal post of Coordinator and Advisor (OCA), under cover of the Department of State. The new Chief at this vital Station is reported to be Warren E. Frank. His office contains separate Research, Records, and Liaison offices, and there are also CIA personnel under the Office of the Secretary of Defense for International Security Affairs (OSD/ISA) and the United States Army Europe (USAREUR), Regional Survey Unit.

Prior to publication, the Editors contacted seven different offices at the Department of State and the Pentagon which deal with German affairs, in an effort to get an accurate and official clarification regarding the formal link of these offices. The sole clarification came from the Department of the Army intelligence people, who said through a press spokesperson: "We can not confirm or deny that we own the two units" (OCA and USAREUR). Therefore, the Editors have decided to designate these two CIA offices as formally under cover of the Department of State.

Other CIA offices appear under State Department cover in regular Embassy sections, and there is also a telecommunications unit at the Rhein-Main Air Base in Frankfurt.

The names of the CIA people first appeared in the alternative news service *Informations-Dienst*.

ALBRIGHT, JOY
ALLNER, FREDERICK A. Jr.
ARNST, WILLIAM F.
BARNES, EDWARD O.
BENNETT, WILLIAM E.
BLACKSHEAR, THOMAS RUSSELL
BROUTSAS, CONSTANTINE M.
BROWN, CHARLES J.
CASEY, BURKE M.
CHIPMAN, HAROLD E.
DeLONG, SANDRA J.
DOLGE, JAMES J.
ECKSTEIN, WILLIAM HERBERT
ELLAM, KATHERINE T.
FALCON, JACK
FENDIG, PHILIP FRANKLIN
FRANK, WARREN E.
GRAVER, WILLIAM J.
GYENES, ALFRED
HOLLIS, ALLAN L.
HOWLEY, JAMES M.
HULNICK, ARTHUR S.
JENSEN, HANS J.
JENKINS, CYNTHIA A.
JONES, FRANK WILLIAMS JONES Jr.
KARPOVICH, SERGE
KIMBALL, JOHN W.
KLEIN, THEODORE
KLINE, ALBERT HAINES Jr.
LANHAM, CHARLES E.
LATTA, MERRON L.
LEVEN, CHARLES H.

LEWIS, WHITNEY N.
LIPSCOMB, SUZANNE
LITTLE, GEORGE R.
LONG, RICHARD MAXWELL
LUTHER, RICHARD M.
MAAS, ERNST S.
McCABE, WALTER CASSATT
MacDONALD, CHARLES R.
MALZAHN, RICHARD L.
MAPOTHER, JOHN RUBEL
MILLER, WILLIAM B.
MILLS, THOMAS JOHN Jr.
NELSON, GLENN WALTER
NIBLEY, LLOYD E.
ONEIL, FRANCES E.
PALEVICH, JOHN EDWARD
PLAYER, ADGER EMERSON
POLGAR, THOMAS
POLLOCK, BERNARD CHARLES
SCARLATA, LAWRENCE J. Jr.
SCHNEIDER, ROBERT W.
SHERMAN, JOSEPH PETER
SILVER, ARNOLD M.
STOLZ, RICHARD F. Jr.
SUSAN, EDWARD R.
VAN DER RHOER, JAMES PHILIP
VELTE, ROBERT
VREELAND, FREDERICK DALZIEL
WALSH, MICHAEL JOHN
WEISZ, GEORGE
ZIEMER, SUZANNE E.

Greece

AMERICAN EMBASSY
91 Vassilissis Sophia's Boulevard
Athens
71-29-51, 71-84-01

Probably the largest CIA operation anywhere in Europe, the Athens CIA Station includes a massive telecommunications complex—the Regional Relay Facility and supporting units—which transmits top-secret coded messages between the CIA Headquarters in Langley, Virginia, and CIA Stations beyond Greece. The Athens Station also has its own ample telecommunications group, while the operations officers are divided among the Office of the Special Assistant, the Embassy Political Section, and the Joint U.S. Military Assistance Group—Greece (JUSMAGG).

The first exposé of CIA identities in Greece, which carried the name of the later-assassinated Station Chief Richard Skeffington Welch, appeared in the English-language *Athens News*. Other articles are also reprinted in this book.

Sources: *Athens News*, "Letter of the Committee of Greeks and Greek-Americans," 25 November 1975

Athens News, News Stories (see p. 85)

Liberation, "Communique of the November 17 Revolutionary Organization"

Philip Agee, "The American Factor in Greece: Old and New," *Anti*, May 1977.

ALDRIDGE, MILTON
ALLEN, THOMAS M.
BAFFA, FRANCIS R. Jr.
BAKER, JESSE L.
BAKER, ROBERT J.
BAKOS, DENNIS M.
BALDWIN, JAMES DONALD
BARRETT, JOHN W.
BARTLEBAUGH, RICHARD T.
BATCH, JAMES E.
BATSON, CHARLES C.
BECKETT, DONALD F.
BEGLEY, JOSEPH M.
BEHRENS, JAMES E.
BENDER, JACOB E. Jr.
BENDER, PAT
BERNIER, NORMAN A.
BESSETTE, ARTHUR J.
BLAIR, ROBERT DEW
BLANCHARD, JOHN L.
BLODGET, BENJAMIN G.
BRADSHAW, BEVERLEY B.
BREAW, ROYCE L.
BRIGHT, WILLIAM C.
BUCY, HOWARD C.
BUMP, WILLIAM H. III
BURK, WILLIAM C.
BUSH, JOHN M.
BUTLER, RICHARD H.
CAMPBELL, VAN CLEVE
CANALE, JOSEPH T.
CARTER, LOY L.
CARUSO, JOSEPH A.
CASEY, BURKE M.
CHALMERS, DUNCAN Y.
CHAREST, ELDON E.
CLARK, ROBERT A.
CLAYMIER, ROBERT W.
CLEMENT, CARLOS E.
COMBS, WAYNE S.

CONNORS, THOMAS J.
COOK, RICHARD C.
COOPER, KENNETH M.
CRAIGIE, DAVID G.
CREEDEN, WILLIAM E.
CROWLING, JOSEPH V.
CURTIS, GENE P.
DAIGLE, DONALD C.
DAMSCHRODER, LAMONT S.
DAVIS, STANLEY W. Jr.
DIMODICA, JAMES S.
EASON, EARL T.
ELBON, SAM B.
ELMQUEST, KAREN J.
ESTES, RONALD EDWARD
EVANS, WILLIAM J.
FARRELL, KATHLEEN
FAUGHT, DAVID W.
FERENTINOS, JERRY J.
FITZSIMMONS, ZANE R.
FORTNER, LUTHER C.
FRANCIS, GEORGE V.
FREY, PHILIP E.
GAFFNEY, RAYMOND C.
GALLAGHER, JAMES J.
GAMBRELL, BOBBY J.
GEHAN, KENNETH J.
GELWICKS, ORVILLE R.
GEORGE, CLAIR ELROY
GILLEN, DAVID J.
GOFF, THOMAS L.
GOLDMAN, NORMAN
GORDON, MARION C. Jr.
GOUGH, JOHN S.
GRAHAM, CHARLES O.
GRAHAM, LILLIAN
GREENE, HARRIS CARL
GRISWOLD, DONALD M.
GROOMS, CARLTON C.
GROOMS, SANDRA

GROSS, JUNE A.
GROSSMAN, FREDERICK J.
GUDYKA, JOSEPH M.
GULDSETH, FRANK J.
GUY, RAYMON JAMES
HAGEN, GERALD E.
HAM, CAREY ROGER
HARRIS, ALDINE
HART, MARY M.
HAYES, EDWARD R.
HEMBREE, EDWARD J.
HENRY, ALTON L.
HINSON, ARTHUR W.
HORN, MARY JO
HOSHEIT, GEORGE W.
HOWARD, ENID M.
HULSE, STACY B. Jr.
HYATT, JEFFREY L.
HYDE, ROGER L.
HYNDMAN, JAMES ALBERT
JACKOLA, ELMER A.
JACKSON, HENRY F.
JAMESON, BOBBIE
JAROCKI, JOSEPH P.
JOHNS, ROBERT A.
KABLE, CHARLES H. III
KAULFERS, TERRANCE F.
KELLY, DONALD A.
KELLY, WILLIAM V.
KENYON, KYLE G.
KINDELL, FLOREND EDWIN
KINDL, CHARLES L.
KIRBY, DAVID A.
KOWALESKI, FREDERICK J.
KRAMER, LLOYD L.
KRIESEL, FREDERIC A.
KRSIEAN, LEROY C.
KUBLIK, GEORGE
LARSON, ROBERT H.
LEE, RONALD L.
LEWIS, WILLIAM M.
LEWON, LEROY C.
LICHTY, DONIVAN D.
LINDAMOOD, DOUGLAS W.
LOFGREN, WILLIAM S.
LUTHER, RICHARD M.
LUTHY, WALTER P.
LYONS, RODDY G.
McCLUNG, DONALD C.
McDERMOTT, JOHN E.
McGILVRAY, JAMES J.
McINTYRE, JOHN T.
McKEON, TIMOTHY J.
McMANUS, GERALD R.
McWILLIAMS, JAMES W.
MEINBRESSE, JERRY D.
MILLER, WILLIAM B.

MINIER, FREDERICK
MOERGELI, RICHARD N.
MOODY, JACK B.
MOORE, FELIX E.
MORAN, ALFRED C.
MORGAN, BRUCE A.
MORGAN, JUNE S.
MORRISON, CHARLES R.
MUNCY, LARRY M.
MUNSON, JERALD H.
MURPHY, PATRICIA A.
MURRAY, DELMAR E.
MURRAY, JAMES T.
MYERS, JOHN H.
NELSON, MELVIN W.
NESS, RUDOLPH WALTER
NIBLEY, LLOYD E.
NOLAN, EDMUND J.
NORDEEN, RONALD O.
NYFELER, EDWARD KEITH
OLSON, ROBERT WILLIAM
OLSON, RUTH
OLSON, WILLIAM L.
O'NEAL, EVERETT C.
ONIMUS, DAVID R.
PAGANO, LOUIS J.
PALEVICH, JOHN EDWARD
PARSONS, CARL R.
PARSONS, JOHN P.
PAYNE, MASON C.
PEARSON, FRANCIS J.
PENA, PAUL A.
PESHOFF, ROY G.
PETERS, WAYNE E.
PETERSEN, W. GARY
POTTS, JAMES M.
PRICE, RICHARD J.
RAYLE, ROBERT F.
REUTER, RONALD E.
RICE, ARTHUR G.
ROGERS, WAYNE M.
ROUNDS, ROBERT R.
RUCKMAN, JAMES R.
RUDIN, JOHN A.
RUSSELL, ARTHUR F.
SAROFF, PHIL
SCARLATA, LAWRENCE J. Jr.
SCHOLPP, GEORGE E.
SCHULDASKI, ERNEST A.
SCHWARTZ, STEVEN A.
SEPTON, ARTHUR B. Jr.
SEPTON, NAOMI
SHAFFER, RONALD D.
SHEA, JOHN J.
SHEKMER, MICHAEL E.
SIEMIENKIEWICZ, GERALD
SIMPSON, GRANT F.

SIRIANO, HAROLD J.
SIMS, WILLIAM P.
SLACK, GEORGE LEE
SOHLER, RONALD B.
SORRELL, ALLEN R.
STEWART, EDWIN
SULIK, MICHAEL J.
SUSAN, EDWARD R.
TANES, MICHAEL
TAYLOR, ROGER F.
TAYLOR, ROBERT L. Jr.
TEDESCHI, JOHN J.
THOMAS, RICHARD LEE
THOMPSON, FRANCIS A. II
THOMSON, RICHARD C. Jr.
THORNBURGH, CHARLES T.
THUN, LEONARD L.
TYREE, DAVID L.
USTASKI, WALTER

VISELLI, THOMAS L. Jr.
VON SASSENSCHEID, BERTRAM E.
WALKER, EDWARD LEE
WASZKIEWICZ, JOHN H.
WATTS, LUELL A.
WEBB, BRENDA J.
WEBSTER, DANIEL K.
WELCH, RICHARD SKEFFINGTON
WHEELER, HENRY P.
WHITACRE, GORDON C.
WHITFIELD, GEORGE P.
WICHTERMAN, ALVIN R.
WILHELM, JOHN J. Jr.
WILLIAMS, JIMMIE C.
WINSKY, STEPHEN
WRIGHT, STEPHEN E.
YORK, GEORGE S.
ZANIN, JOSEPH D.

Iceland

Laufasvegur 21
Reykjavik
29100

NICKERSON, DAVID   SIMENSON, WILLIAM CHARLES

Italy

AMERICAN EMBASSY
Via V. Veneto, 119/A
00187 Rome
(06) 4674

Sources: *La Repubblica,* Steve Weissman, "Ecco La CIA in Italia," 15 January 1976.

L'Espresso, Mario Scialoja, "Quelli della CIA" & "En Ecco Che Ci Ha Dato I Nomi,"
25 January 1976.

The most vulnerable of the CIA operations in Europe, the CIA Station
in Rome has received widespread publicity for its ongoing intervention
into Italian politics, as revealed in the report of the Pike committee of
the U.S. House of Representatives. The Station itself is largely divided
between an office under cover of the Embassy Political Section and a
United States Army Europe Southern European Projects Unit
(USASEPU) also located in the Embassy. There is a CIA telecommunications group, and various other CIA officers have been found in
different sections of the Embassy.

As in the case of Germany, the Editors contacted both the Department of State and the Pentagon for some official comment about the formal affiliation of the USASEPU organization. No one, including the State Department's Italy desk officers, knew a thing about it. Once again, the Editors have designated it as a functional unit under cover of the Department of State.

The first articles naming recent CIA officers in Italy appeared in the Rome daily *La Repubblica* and the weekly magazine *L'Espresso*.

ACON, WILLIAM J.
AFRICH, ROSE F.
ALHIMOOK, DANIEL
ATKINS, EDWIN FRANKLIN
BERG, JOHN W.
BOIES, ROBERT E.
BROYLES, RICHARD G.
BRUNSON, GERALD L.
CAPELLINI, SUSAN C.
CHELLINO, CATHERINE
CIOCI, MARIO L.
COSTANZO, CHRISTOPHER D.
CRAWFORD, SETH TURNER
CUMMINGS, CAROL K.
DEVEREUX, ROBERT E.
DEGRANDS DOMINIC J.
Di STEFANO, JOSEPH A.
DOMINGUEZ, OLGA
ELLIS, HOWARD J.
EVANS, REBECCA T.
FENNER, BILLY A.
FRIEND, JULIUS W. Jr.
GALE, CHARLES R. Jr.
GERNER, GEORGE W.
GIAMMARINO, JOSEPHINE P.
GRANT, CHARLES R.
GREENE, HARRIS CARL
HANDFORD, JANET MARIE
HANSON, DEAN P.
HEALEY, RICHARD D.
HULSE, STACY B. Jr.
HUTCHISON, TERRELL WARREN

IMBREY, HOWARD
IORIO, ARTHUR
KAMBA, LAWRENCE F.
KEAR, DONALD L.
KEEFE, JOHN F.
KOSTIW, MICHAEL V.
LAX, MORRIS H.
LONAM, WILLIAM B.
MARX, JOHN P.
MONTGOMERY, HUGH
MORGAN, DONNIE E.
MURPHY, PATRICIA A.
NELSON, CATHERINE L.
PREGANO, VIRGINIA C.
RADER, OWEN R.
RILEY, BYRON B.
ROBERTS, JAMES W. Jr.
SANDEL, LEO
SEDNAOUI, MICHAEL C.
SHEA, JOHN J.
SINGLETON, STEPHEN E.
SPINELLI, ROBERT L. Jr.
STAUBER, PHILIP L.
STOLZ, RICHARD F. Jr.
STONE, HOWARD EDWARD
TANES, MICHAEL
THOMPSON, MICHAEL S.
WILSON, EDWARD
WILT, EDWARD JAMES II
WRIGHT, ORRIN M.
WYATT, FELTON MARK

Luxembourg

22 Boulevard Emmanuel Servais
Brussels
40123/7

CRAWFORD, SETH TURNER
SILVER, ARNOLD M.

WYATT, FELTON MARK

Netherlands,

AMERICAN EMBASSY
102 Lange Voorhout
The Hague
62-49-11

One of the smaller units, the CIA Station in The Hague was first revealed by the Dutch weekly *Vrij Nederland*.

Source: *Vrij Nederland,* Rudi Van Meurs, "De Firma-Nogmaals: de CIA in Nederland,"
31 January 1976.

ALHIMOOK, DANIEL
BANE, HOWARD T.
COOPER, KENNETH M.
GINSBURG, HARVEY H.
HULSE, STACY B. Jr.
KETELHUT, DAVID

KORN, THOMAS A.
LANDRETH, RODNEY N. II
MALZAHN, RICHARD L.
MARX, JOHN P.
SALA, LAWRENCE B.
SHUMWAY, JEDDY K.

Norway

AMERICAN EMBASSY
Drammensveien 18
Oslo 1
56-68-80

DEAN, WARREN LaFOREST
GREENFIELD, SAMUEL D.
HILL, FRANCIS A.
HUNT, DAVID P.
JENSEN, HANS J.
JOHNSON, QUENTIN C.
JONES, FRANK WILLIAMS Jr.

KINDL, CHARLES L.
LIESER, WILLIAM D.
POTEAT, S. EUGENE
ROGERS, JERRY L.
SHAFFER, RONALD D.
SIMENSON, WILLIAM CHARLES
ZSCHACK, HARRY M.

The CIA Station in Oslo was first revealed in the newspaper *Ny Tid*.*

Portugal

AMERICAN EMBASSY
Avenida Duque De Loule 39
Lisbon
57-01-02

First revealed by former CIA officer Philip Agee in his "Letter to the Portuguese People," the Lisbon CIA Station has maintained an extremely low profile through Portugal's time of troubles.

***Ny Tid,* "Fagbevegelsen viktig mal for CIA-agenter med diplomatstatus," 24 November 1977.

Sources: Philip Agee, "A Letter to the Portuguese People," August, 1975.

Philip Agee, "Changes in the CIA in Portugal," July, 1976.

ANDERSON, GARY I.
CALDWELL, DONNA J.
CONROY, RICHARD A.
GLEASON, LYLE K.
GOMEZ, RUDOLPH EDWARD
HUGHES, LESLIE F.
LAWLER, JAMES N.
LOWELL, FRANK W.

MARQUES, JOSEPH J.
MILLER, RAYMOND E.
MORGAN, JOHN STINARD
RIEBHOFF, DONALD R.
SNELL, PHILLIP W.
VAN TWISK, TONY M.
WHIPPLE, DAVID D.
ZAPOLI, GERALD E.

Spain

AMERICAN EMBASSY
Serrano, 75
Madrid
276-3400, 276-3600

A small number of CIA people have been identified in Spain, though the total is known to be larger. The names first appeared in Spain's largest weekly news magazine, *Cambio 16*.

Source: *Cambio 16,* "La CIA, Aqui, Ahora," 12-18 January 1976.

ALMY, DEAN J.
CIOCI, MARIO L.
COSTANZO, CHRISTOPHER D.
GAHAGEN, ROBERT DALE
GRUNER, JAY K.
HANSON, DEAN P.
JOHNSEN, MARTIN I.
JONES, WILLIAM A. K.
KEAR, DONALD L.
MITCHELL, JAMES W.
MORRILL, ALAN G. Jr.
MURPHY, CHARLES M.

ROGERS, WAYNE M.
SANCHEZ, NESTOR D.
SHERMAN, VAUGHN A.
SHERRY, FRANCIS S. III
SIMPSON, ROBERT K.
SMITH, CHARLES S.
SPINNEY, NORMAN J.
STUCKNER, KENNETH E.
THOMAS, JON R.
URQUHART, EDWARD
VAN WINKLE, RICHARD D.
WEBB, JOHN FREDERICK

Sweden

AMERICAN EMBASSY
Strandvagen 101
Stockholm
63-05-20

Like the list of CIA in Finland, the identities of the Stockholm CIA Station were first revealed by the freelance journalist George Lennox, following a trip to Sweden by Philip Agee.

The activities of the CIA in Sweden were exposed and examined in depth, after a year-long examination, by the Stockholm bi-weekly magazine *Folket-i-Bild: Kulturfront*.

Sources: *Expressen*, "Sa arbetar USA: 5 agenter i Sverige," 21 October 1975.

   Folket-i-Bild: Kulturfront, Jan Guillou and Roger Wallis, "CIA i Sverige," 4-17 March 1976.

ALTMAN, DAVID R.
CAMMARATA, ALFRED J.   KARPOVICH, SERGE
CAMPBELL, VAN CLEVE   LANE, PHILLIP G.
CARTER, RUDULPH ELLIS   McCABE, WALTER CASSATT
DENNIS, DAVID L.   NICKERSON, DAVID
DIMSDALE, JOHN H. Jr.   PARSONS, RONALD C.
GARBLER, PAUL   SHERMAN, VAUGHN A.
GIESECKE, FRITZ H.   SKOVE, JAMES R.
HUTCHINS, BRUCE DUANE   SWERDLIN, GEORGE D.

Switzerland

JUBILAEUMSTRASSE 93
3005 Bern
(031) 43-00-11

CIA personnel have been identified operating under cover in the Embassy in Bern, as well as in the U.S. Mission to the European Office of the United Nations in Geneva and the Consulate General in Zurich.

Switzerland is one of the CIA's most important operational centers because of the many international organizations based in Geneva. Not only does the Agency collect a great deal of information about Third World countries there, but it also has a continual program aimed at recruitment of diplomats to work for the CIA upon returning home.

In addition, the Agency makes use of liberal Swiss banking practices to provide cover for many of its ongoing international financial operations.

ALLNER, FREDERICK A. Jr.   CHANEY, BRUCE G.
BARBIER, CLARENCE E.   CLEVELAND, RICHARD ARTHUR
BEARMAN, SIDNEY   CUMBO, ROBERT O.
BEMUS, HERMAN H.   DOWNEY, TIMOTHY A.
BLEAM, DENNIS L.   FORD, NANCY
BREHM, VANCE W.   GIBBS, JOHN H.
BROUTSAS, CONSTANTINE M.   GILHOOLY, JOHN F.
CASEY, BURKE M.   GINSBURG, HARVEY H.
CERRA, RONALD L.   GREENE, HARRIS CARL

GILHOOLY, JOHN F.
GINSBURG, HARVEY H.
GROTH, MANFRED
HARBAUGH, LARRY M.
HEINIG, STEWART C. Jr.
HUTCHISON, TERRELL WARREN
JONES, FRANK WILLIAMS Jr.
KARPOVICH, SERGE
KELLY, WILLIAM V.
KLINE, ALBERT HAINES Jr.
KUNZ, GEORGE J.
LAMB, THOMAS WILLIAM
LOFTIN, DANNY M.
LOURIE, ALAN E.
LUIZ, ROBERT C.

MALOY, KEVIN A.
McKEON, TIMOTHY J.
MITCHELL, JAMES C.
PIANTOSI, ROBERT
ROSE, JOHN A. Jr.
SANDEL, LEO
SHERRY, JOHN
SWERDLIN, GEORGE D.
VAN DER RHOER, JAMES PHILIP
VAN MARX, PAUL ERNEST ALEXANDER
VREELAND, FREDERICK DALZIEL
WEBER, RONALD L.
WHITE, JOSEPH E.
WILDER, THROOP M. Jr.
WUJICK, JOHN T. Jr.

Turkey

AMERICAN EMBASSY
110 Ataturk Boulevard
Ankara
26-54-70

BROWN, EDWARD R.
CHRITTON, GEORGE A. Jr.
EDDY, CONDIT N. Jr.
GOODWIN, ROBERT B.
GROSSMAN, FREDERICK J.
GUNDERSON, LEROY H.

HONEYCUTT, ARMAND A.
HOSKINS, JOHN HERBERT
KINGSLEY, ROLFE
LANE, PHILLIP G.
LEWIS, WILLIAM M.
SINGLETON, STEPHEN E.

United Kingdom

AMERICAN EMBASSY
24-31 Grosvenor Square
London W1
499-9000

One of the largest CIA units in Europe, the London Station was headed from October 1973 until the summer of 1976 by Cord Meyer, Jr., who previously ran the Agency's International Organizations Division, the division which secretly subsidized labor, student and cultural groups throughout the world. Meyer's official cover in London was as chief of the so-called Political Liaison Section, which shares offices with another CIA unit called the Joint Reports and Research Unit (JRRU). A separate CIA office, the Foreign Broadcast Information Service (FBIS) is also located in the Embassy. A separate operation, also officially under cover of the Department of State—the Office of the

Special U.S. Liaison Officer (SUSLO)— appears to be a cover unit for the National Security Agency, rather than for the CIA.

Late in the summer of 1976, Meyer was replaced as Chief of Station by Edward W. Proctor.

Over 100 CIA and NSA employees have so far been identified in London, with as many as 60 to 70 serving at any one time. The major exposés have appeared in the London weekly magazine *Time Out* and the newspaper of the International Marxist Group, *Red Weekly*.

Sources,   *Time Out,* Mark Hosenball and Phil Kelly, "Spotting Spooks in Grosvenor Square," 18-24 April 1975

"Who's Who in the CIA," 9-15 May 1975

"Naming Names," 23-29 January 1976.

Red Weekly, Mick Gosling, "We Name the CIA in Britain," 4 March 1976.

ANDRESS, ROSEMARIE
BAILEY, MALCOLM B.
BAKER, ROBERT J.
BATSON, CHARLES C.
BAXTER, MORRIS V.
BEARMAN, SIDNEY
BENEDICT, JULIA L.
BENISH, ALBERT
BENISH, ROSALIE
BIRD, ALBERT O. Jr.
BLACKSHEAR, THOMAS RUSSELL
BOERNER, MARK S.
BONNAFE, LUCIEN R.
BRAHAM, A. SPENCER
BROWN, JOHN H.
BROWN, JOHN P.
BULLOCK, ELEANORE ANNE
BULLOCK, MAX E.
BUSH, ANNA D.
BUSH, JOHN M.
BUTTERWORTH, DAVID G.
CARTER, RUDULPH ELLIS
CARTER, STEPHEN B.
CHAREST, ELDON E.
COFFEY, JOHN WILLIAM
COLLINS, JUDITH E.
CRAM, CLEVELAND C.
DE BLOIS, JEAN. P.
DOOLEY, BARBARA W.
DUNICAN, THERESA A.
DUNN, EDWARD PAUL
DURKIN, NAOMI C.
EDDY, CONDIT N. Jr.
EDMUNDS, BARBARA J.
ELMORE, THOMAS P.
ERACLEOUS, MICHAEL P.
ESCH, PAUL E.

EVANS, ROBERT J.
EXLER, ELIZABETH
FENDIG, PHILIP FRANKLIN
FERRIS, RICHARD C.
FETTEROLF, WALLACE K.
FORD, GEORGE W. II
GAGEN, JEANNE M.
GINSBURG, HARVEY H.
GOSS, BARBARA J.
GRIFFITH, HAROLD W.
GUERTIN, WILLIAM J.
GUNDERSON, LEROY H.
HARDCASTLE, LESLIE
HARRIS, V. DOTT
HOEPFL, ROBERT F.
HOLLOWAY, MASTER SERGEANT BILLY G.
HUCKEL, JOHN FRANK
JACOBSON, IRVIN H.
KAHANE, RICHARD A.
KELLY, GILES MERRILL
KELSALL, ALMA M.
KINGSLEY, ROLFE
KIRBY, JOHN THOMAS
KLEIN, DENNIS
KONKLE, CAROLYN L.
KRIEBEL, NORMAN E. Jr.
LAMBERT, MORTON A.
LANE, BERNARD L.
LAWRENCE, JOHN S.
LEINER, CHARLES P.
LEVINE, DIANE H.
LUKE, DOROTHY P.
LUTHER, RICHARD M.
LYON, KEITH W.
McCABE, WALTER CASSATT
McGEE, JOSEPH V.
McGHEE, WILLIAM MORROW

MELI, ARTHUR S.
MELTON, MARILYN ELAINE
MEYER, CORD Jr.
MILANOVICH, JOANNE
MOORE, WILLIAM R.
MORAVEK, JOSEPH
MORDEN, JAMES P.
NOONAN, JOHN H.
NUNNO, LEONARD J.
OLNHAUSEN, CHARLES B.
O'MALLEY, MICHAEL P.
PACENTA, CAROLYN D.
PEIFFER, LYNDA L.
PEREIRA, JOHN F.
PETERSEN, W. GARY
PIANTOSI, ROBERT
POTEAT, S. EUGENE
PREHN, JERRY G.
PRICE, BENJAMIN J.
PROCTOR, EDWARD WILLIAM

REINHARDT, ARTHUR F.
RILEY, BYRON B.
ROLLINS, NORA M.
ROSS, SHARON L.
ROSSALL, MICHAEL F.
SHERMAN, JOSEPH PETER
SHUMAN, A. DELL
SINCLAIR, ROBERT
SMITH, JAMES
SPANGLER, RODNEY L.
STONE, HUNTER L. Jr.
SUITER, CHRISTOPHER A.
THEN, JOSEPH LEE
THOMPSON, KATHERINE A.
THORNE, RICHARD LEVERE
WAGNER, BRIAN A.
WALSH, GEORGE T.
WHIPPLE, DAVID D.
WOLFE, LARRY L.
ZASLOW, MILTON S.

OTHERS NAMED IN THIS BOOK
(latest country known posted)

AMES, ROBERT C.—Kuwait
BARRETT, THOMAS JOSEPH Jr.—Brazil
BEAM, JOHN C.—Algeria
BERGIN, MARTIN J. Jr.—Ivory Coast
BROWN, GLENN OTIS—Ecuador
BURTON, STEWART D.—Brazil
CAVE, GEORGE W. —Saudi Arabia
CLAYTON, THOMAS ALLYN—Dominican Republic
CLOSE, RAYMOND H.—Saudi Arabia
COGAN, CHARLES G.—Morocco
COLBY, MARK T.—Morocco
CORYDON, JEFF III—Cameroon
CREANE, STEPHEN F.—Brazil
DENICOURT, RAYMOND F.—Mali
DESCOTEAUX, NORMAN M.—Jamaica
FERNALD, JAMES M.—United Arab Emirates
GARRETT, EARL NORBERT III—Kuwait
GATELY, ROBERT GENE—Thailand
GEBHARDT, CARL E.—Thailand
GILSTRAP, COMER WILEY Jr.—Chile
GMIRKIN, VASIA C.—Mauritius
GOODMAN, KENNETH R.—Guatemala
GRIMSLEY, WILLIAM C. Jr.—Japan
GRUNER, JAY K.—Romania
HAWKINS, MARTIN C.—Ecuador
HEADLEY, ROBERT L. Jr.—Oman
HIGHAM, JAMES A.—Iran
INCE, ROBERT W.—Nigeria
JEFFERS, EUGENE L. Jr.—Ethiopia

KALARIS, GEORGE T.—Brazil
KANE, EDWARD R. M.—Algeria
KEENAN, THOMAS J.—Jamaica
KIM, JAMES—Zaire
KIYONAGA, JOSEPH YOSHIO—Brazil
LATRASH, FREDERICK WALDO—Uruguay
McAVOY, CLYDE RICHARD—Burma
McCARTHY, JOHN F. III—Japan
METHVEN, STUART E.—Zaire
MILLS, ROBERT H.—U.S.S.R.
MOSEBEY, WILLIAM L. Jr.—Central African Empire
MURRAY, JOSEPH A. Jr.—Nepal
NATIRBOFF, MURAT—Kenya
NINER, ARTHUR M. Jr.—Libya
NORWOOD, THOMAS L. Jr.—Indonesia
OGINO, JACK S.—Sri Lanka
PICCOLO, JOSEPH Jr.—Nicaragua
RANDOLPH, CHARLES LEROY—Senegal
RAUDENBUSH, PETER VROOM—Guinea
REDMOND, PAUL J. Jr.—Lebanon
RICHARDSON, JARREL H.—Ghana
RICKARD, SAMUEL HARMER III—Afghanistan
RIEFE, ROBERT H.—Guyana
SABIN, FREDERICK H. II—Jordan
SAMSON, DAVID TORREY—Singapore
SEIDEL, JOHN J. Jr.—Lebanon
SIMON, JOSEPH J.—Hong Kong
STRATHERN, CLIFTON R.—Indonesia
TERRELL, EDWIN McCLELLAN—Guatemala
TICKNOR, JOEL D.—Ghana
VOGEL, DONALD FREDERIC—Pakistan